PENGUIN REFERENCE BOOKS

# THE PENGUIN DICTIONARY OF
# INTERNATIONAL RELATIONS

Graham Evans was educated at Jesus College, Oxford, and at the University of Wales, Swansea, where he is currently Senior Lecturer in International Relations. He has held visiting posts at the universities of Cape Town, Natal (Pietermaritzburg) and Zimbabwe-Rhodesia, and senior research fellowships at the South African Institute of International Affairs, Johannesburg, and the Centre for Southern African Studies at the University of the Western Cape. He has published extensively on international affairs and has also worked for the United Nations and the Organization for Security and Cooperation in Europe as electoral supervisor in South Africa, Mozambique and Bosnia. He is a member of the Southern Africa Study Group at the Royal Institute of International Affairs, Chatham House.

Jeffrey Newnham was educated at University College, London, and lectures on American foreign policy at the University of Wales, Swansea. He co-authored (with Graham Evans) the *Dictionary of World Politics* (1989, 1992). His research interests include security studies and global economic relations.

# THE PENGUIN DICTIONARY OF
# INTERNATIONAL
# RELATIONS

*Graham Evans*
*and Jeffrey Newnham*

PENGUIN BOOKS

PENGUIN BOOKS

Published by the Penguin Group
Penguin Books Ltd, 80 Strand, London WC2R 0RL, England
Penguin Putnam Inc., 375 Hudson Street, New York, New York 10014, USA
Penguin Books Australia Ltd, Ringwood, Victoria, Australia
Penguin Books Canada Ltd, 10 Alcorn Avenue, Toronto, Ontario, Canada M4V 3B2
Penguin Books India (P) Ltd, 11 Community Centre, Panchsheel Park, New Delhi – 110 017, India
Penguin Books (NZ) Ltd, Cnr Rosedale and Airborne Roads, Albany, Auckland, New Zealand
Penguin Books (South Africa) (Pty) Ltd, 24 Sturdee Avenue, Rosebank 2196 South Africa

Penguin Books Ltd, Registered Offices: 80 Strand, London WC2R 0RL, England

www.penguin.com

First published in Penguin Books 1998

7

Copyright © Graham Evans and Jeffrey Newnham, 1998
All rights reserved

The moral right of the authors has been asserted

Set in 9/10.5pt Monotype Bembo
Typeset by Rowland Phototypesetting Ltd,
Bury St Edmunds, Suffolk
Printed in England by Clays Ltd, St Ives plc

Except in the United States of America, this book is sold subject
to the condition that it shall not, by way of trade or otherwise, be lent,
re-sold, hired out, or otherwise circulated without the publisher's
prior consent in any form of binding or cover other than that in
which it is published and without a similar condition including this
condition being imposed on the subsequent purchaser

*A fo ben, bid bont*

He who would be a leader, let him be a bridge
(Old Welsh proverb)

# PREFACE

The end of the Cold War proved traumatic for practitioners and theorists of International Relations (IR) alike. For over forty-five years after the end of World War II, the East–West conflict was regarded as the central factor in international affairs. Few areas of the world escaped its baleful influence in terms of either their domestic dispositions or their diplomatic orientations. Certainly in the dominant Anglo-American tradition of thinking and acting in foreign affairs, everything else seemed subordinate to it. That the Cold War lens afforded an extremely myopic and distorted view of international relations is now being gradually (though sometimes grudgingly) acknowledged: both by academic specialists in IR for whom the discipline has in an important sense been liberated and by foreign policy elites for whom this confrontational behavioural paradigm had achieved the status of an unquestioned 'grundnorm' from which virtually all policies and perspectives logically flowed. In the early 1990s this deceptively simplistic policy and ideational framework disappeared resulting in widespread uncertainty on the campus and in the chancellery about foreign policy agendas and the ranking of priorities and interests within them. Thus, not only did the end of the Cold War highlight serious shortcomings in the discipline of IR itself, it also robbed it of much of its empirical rationale since the main actors and problems it identified were located within the discourse of the Cold War standoff and its implications for the workings of the global system.

With hindsight it is easy to see that the events of the last quarter of 1989 in eastern Europe brought about a revolution in international relations comparable in scope to those of 1815, 1848, 1918 and 1945. That the 'New World Order' so confidently predicted by US President George Bush in the wake of the Persian Gulf War did not materialize and was followed instead by a spate of virulent, ethnically based conflicts and the disintegration of established orders, is beside the point: 1989 really did signal a fundamental change in both the scope and domain of world politics. *The Penguin Dictionary of International Relations* was conceived in part as an attempt to capture, record and evaluate the thinking that surrounds these developments and their uncertain aftermath. In this sense it represents a substantial revision of an earlier work (*The Dictionary of World Politics*, Harvester Wheatsheaf, 1989 and 1992). While the format remains the same, the entries and explanations offered are designed to reflect the dramatic changes that have taken place over the past decade both in the academic discipline of IR and in actual foreign policy formulation and conduct. As with the previous volume, my colleague Jeffrey Newnham was invited to join the project: the idea being that a collaborative approach, particularly in the contested sub-fields of strategic/security studies and international political economy, would greatly strengthen the revisioning and rewriting process. The overall division of responsibility was roughly 60 per cent (GE) and 40 per cent (JDN).

Selection of entries was governed by three main considerations: first, those ideas, theories, concepts and events which we considered essential to any sophisticated understanding of IR (e.g. Diplomacy, International Law, National Interest); second, those which are only likely to be encountered in specialized texts or journals (Unit Veto, Agent-structure, Neorealism) and third, those which indicate developments and shifts of understanding which have greatly affected the subject since the end of the Cold War (Nineteen eighty-nine, Critical theory, Ethnic cleansing). *The Dictionary* has a cross-reference facility. The items preceded by an arrowhead symbol are those which might usefully be followed up to gain a most extensive explanation, or to indicate the family of ideas to which the particular entry belongs. For example, the entry on Realism contains references to ➤Thucydides, ➤Hobbesian, the ➤state, ➤state-system, ➤power, ➤balance of power, ➤self-help, ➤sovereignty, ➤national interest, ➤international law, ➤international organizations, ➤equality, ➤high politics, ➤great powers, ➤anarchy and ➤neorealism – all of which, singly or together, should provide the reader with a comprehensive overview of the item in question. At the end of the book a select bibliography is included to acknowledge and follow up sources cited in the text and to aid further study.

*Graham Evans*
*Swansea, September 1997*
(Email: G.Evans@swansea.ac.uk)

# ACKNOWLEDGEMENTS

The authors particularly wish to thank the following for their assistance, encouragement and advice during the production of this volume:

Val Davies, Kirsty Dagnall, Jennifer Dineen, Karen McCullough, Ann Burton-Davies, Christine Roberts, Katrina Ferguson, Ros Bryer, David Ryall and Peter Vale. In addition, the Library Staff at the University of Wales, Swansea, were unfailingly helpful and courteous at all times, as indeed was Stefan McGrath, Commissioning Editor at Penguin Books.

Graham Evans would also like to acknowledge a special intellectual debt owed to members of the Southern African Study Group at the Royal Institute of International Affairs, Chatham House, London.

# A

**ABC Weapons** ➤weapons of mass destruction

**ABM** Anti-ballistic missile. This is a system of interceptor missiles and accompanying ➤radar which would seek to defend designated targets against incoming offensive missiles. Until the ➤Strategic Defence Initiative of the 1980s, it was always assumed that an ABM system could most effectively be deployed as a 'point' defence of 'hard' targets (e.g. missile silos). However, the systems first mooted in the 1960s were susceptible to various countermeasures, in particular pre-emptive attacks on their radars. Furthermore, the development of multiple independently targeted re-entry vehicles (MIRVs) meant that any system could potentially be saturated by incoming missiles and confused by decoys all carried on one 'bus'. The originally envisaged ABM systems would have intercepted incoming missiles relatively late in their midcourse phase, thus creating the paradox that high-altitude defensive detonations would severely degrade the environment of the defender.

The shortcomings of these earlier systems led to the ABM Treaty of 1972. This limited ABM deployment to two sites: one to protect the capital, the other an intercontinental ballistic missile (ICBM) site. In 1974 a further ➤protocol was agreed, limiting ABM deployment to one site. The US system was dismantled in 1975 although the former Soviet Union continued to deploy the Galosh system around Moscow.

The ➤technology of space-based defence, developed during the 1980s, implies that some offensive missiles could be destroyed before re-entry into the earth's atmosphere. The significance of the type of system discussed above would therefore be reduced.

Although the ABM Treaty continues to be the cornerstone of the Russian and American nuclear relationship (President Clinton in effect reaffirmed this in 1993 when he killed off President Reagan's SDI programme) the debate concerning strategic vulnerability in the post-➤Cold War nuclear age is unresolved. Whereas the Strategic Defence Initiative envisaged astrodome defences of orbiting weapons that could protect entire countries from attack, developments in the 1990s are now much more specific. The US decision to acquire Theatre Missile Defenses (TMDs) – designed to protect troop concentrations, airfields, ports and so on against slower, shorter-range missile strikes – is a good example. For many ➤hawks inside and outside the US Administration the 1972 ABM Treaty was 'violative of the US national interest' (Casper Weinberger,

1994) and there is now an urgent need to develop a new long-range multi-site defence system to act as a shield against ballistic missile attacks by ➤pariah/ rogue states armed with nuclear, chemical or biological weapons capability. How long the ABM Treaty will survive in its present form is clearly a function of threat-perception differences within the American defence establishment.

**Accidental war** The term may appropriately be used in two senses. First, where ➤war occurs literally by 'accident'; thus through some technical malfunction an act of violence occurs which nobody intended. A variation of this might be where, through insubordination or incompetence, an individual or group commits an act of violence, against the intentions of the political ➤leadership, which leads to war.

Second, accidental war may occur because one or a number of parties in conflict misread the situation and initiate violence. 'Accident' in this second sense may be seen as a function of ➤misperception rather than technical failure or failure in the chain of command. This misperception is particularly likely in periods of ➤crisis where time pressure is a situational factor which often accounts for considerable psychological stress among political leaders and their senior advisers. Historians and political scientists have identified the European crisis of the summer of 1914 as exemplifying many of the characteristics of accidental war in both senses used here.

The advent of ➤nuclear weapons has greatly increased concern about preventing accidental war. ➤Arms control theories and measures have been directed to reduce the incentives to attack and to seek to reassure adversaries, particularly in times of crisis, that they can manage the situation without recourse to war. Attention has also concentrated upon the ➤proliferation of all ➤weapons of mass destruction and the likelihood that this will increase the dangers of accidental war. ➤➤Crisis management; pre-emption

**Accommodation** Term much beloved of ➤crisis management theorists and practitioners of negotiational ➤diplomacy. It refers to the process whereby ➤actors in ➤conflict agree to recognize some of the others' claims while not sacrificing their basic interests. The source of conflict is not removed but the ➤aggression it often generates is presumed to be. It assumes that international conflict is not ➤zero-sum, where the gain of one party is automatically the loss of the other. It also assumes that total ➤harmony of interests does not prevail. Thus, it can be described as a halfway house (place of 'accommodation') between confrontation and harmony. The term is normally used in association with 'interests' and as such is not without sophistry.

**ACP** The African/Caribbean and Pacific states. ACP is ➤European Union shorthand for those states in the ➤Third World, some of whom are also members of the ➤Commonwealth, that have negotiated a special ➤aid and ➤trade regime with the EU. These arrangements have a long history going back to 1963

when eighteen states, known as Associated African States and Madagascar (AASM), signed the ➤Yaoundé Convention with the original six members of the European Economic Community (➤European Community). The Yaoundé Convention was supplanted by the Lomé Convention in 1975 following the accession of the UK to the community. Lomé has been renewed on a regular basis since its inception and is currently in its fourth revision. Membership has expanded from the founding eighteen to seventy states at the same time. The ACP system has its own institutions which mirror those of the Union: a Council of Ministers, Committee of ➤Ambassadors and Joint Assembly. The existence of a directly elected European Parliament since 1979 has potentially enhanced the democratization of Community aid and trade policy under Lomé.

The ACP/Lomé regime was designed for an era when the conventional wisdom about development was attuned to the compensatory version of ➤economic liberalism. The Lomé states' share of the European market has been reduced substantially since 1975; moreover, the ACP countries are in the unenviable position of needing Europe more than Europe needs them. The end of the ➤Cold War and the collapse of ➤communism as a viable developmental ➤paradigm has removed much of the political impetus behind such aid/trade schemes. The whole idea of the Third World has fractured beyond repair and out of that collectivity a group of actual and potential 'First World' economies has emerged. The recent reaction to the South African bid for accession to Lomé is instructive. Africa has the largest contingent of states in ACP/Lomé so on these grounds South African exclusion looks somewhat discriminatory. In point of fact South Africa competes with a number of Mediterranean members of the EU and is arguably not the paradigm Third-World economy that the regime was designed to accommodate. It may well be that, in future, regional groupings such as ➤ASEAN will provide more viable vehicles for ➤negotiation between Europe and the Third World.

**Act of war** Literally, any act which is incompatible with a state of ➤peace. Under customary ➤international law states had the right to resort to ➤war whenever they deemed it necessary. The principal restraint upon this behaviour was thus the laws of warfare. Distinction must immediately be made between the laws covering the conduct of war – ➤*jus in bello* – and the laws governing the resort to conflict – ➤*jus ad bellum*. The idea of an act of war, therefore, properly comes under *jus ad bellum*.

Before the establishment of universal international institutions in the twentieth century, there was a good deal of auto-interpretation attached to this concept. In practice states could decide for themselves what constituted an act of war. Once war had been declared between the parties then notice was served upon the whole state system that relations had changed from peace to war. A complicating factor in this was the ➤alliance. States entering alliances took upon themselves obligations to fight each other's wars. If the alliance was to function properly the parties needed to know what constituted an act of war against themselves whereby the alliance would become operational. This is referred to as the *casus foederis*.

The current century has seen important changes in the laws of war, both *ad bellum* and *in bello*. Treaty law, such as that set out in the ►United Nations Charter, now draws a clear distinction between the legal and illegal use of ►force. The presumption is now made that force can only be used in ►self-defence. In the absence of more effective means of ►conflict resolution, states still resort to force. The twentieth century has required its statesmen to be more imaginative in seeking justification for doing so than in the past. At the same time use of less direct modes of ►aggression, such as ►guerrilla warfare, have made it more difficult to apply the laws of war. External ►intervention in civil wars has become widespread in the twentieth century. Some of the most intractable regional conflicts – such as the ►Arab–Israeli conflict – originated as communal differences. In sum, just as international lawyers have attempted to establish new criteria for the use of force, other developments have increased uncertainties. ►belligerency

**Action—reaction** The term which describes a relationship where two ►actors are stimulated to respond to what the other is doing in an immediate reactive way. The term has been widely applied to ►conflict analysis, particularly by ►game theorists and scholars influenced by behavioural psychology. Students of ►arms races, such as Lewis Fry Richardson, have applied action—reaction ideas to this phenomenon. According to the Richardson process, therefore, State A reacts to State B's increase in military ►capability by increasing its own expenditure. State B perceives this as justifying its own initiative but, at the same time feeling that A's reaction has reduced its margin of safety, B further increases its own arms budget. Richardson's work on action—reaction in arms races is set out in *Arms and Insecurity* (1960). Like many models, the Richardson processes represent highly simplified versions of the real world and few would want to attempt to support the proposition that arms races cause ►wars. Nonetheless, arms races frequently precede hostilities and may, in themselves, contribute to the tension and hostility associated with violent conflict.

Action—reaction ideas have also been applied to ►decision-making. The influence here has been particularly felt from behavioural psychology. Sometimes the term input—output is used rather than action—reaction. In this approach decision-making is conducted by a system. The system reacts to its environment, which includes other decision-making systems. Thus an action—reaction pattern can be again stipulated. The application of action—reaction models to decision-making in ►international relations was widely established in the third quarter of the twentieth century as a productive and plausible way of conceiving the activity.

**Actor** Any entity which plays an identifiable role in ►international relations may be termed an actor. The Pope, the ➤Secretary-General of the UN, British Petroleum, Botswana and the IMF are thus all actors. The term is now widely used by both scholars and practitioners in international relations as it is a way of avoiding the obvious limitations of the word ➤state. Although it lacks precision it does possess scope and flexibility. Its use also conveys the variety of personalities, organizations and institutions that play a role at present. Some authors have argued that, in effect, the system can be conceived of as a ➤mixed actor model because the relative significance of the state has been reduced. More precise distinctions between actors can be made by introducing additional criteria. Such criteria might include the tasks performed by actors and the constituency affected by this task performance. Some commentators suggest that actors should be judged according to their degree of ➤autonomy rather than the legalistic concept of ➤sovereignty. ➤➤pluralism

**Adjudication** A method of settling disputes by referring them to an established court; as such, it ought not to be confused with ➤arbitration. The basis of adjudication is that the adjudicator applies ➤international law to settle the dispute. The creation of the World Court in the present century has meant that the means for international adjudication now exist on a permanent basis. In 1920 the ➤Permanent Court of International Justice (PCIJ) was established by the ➤League of Nations and between 1922 and 1940 it made thirty-three judgments and gave twenty-seven advisory opinions. In 1945 the ➤International Court of Justice (ICJ) was established as its successor. The main difficulties both courts have experienced are the limitations upon their jurisdiction. Parties can only submit a case for adjudication by express consent, although there is an optional clause in the statute of the ICJ (see Article 36). Moreover, only ➤states may be party to cases before the Court (Article 34). This has had the effect that important non-state ➤actors, including individuals, cannot directly initiate litigation.

It must be recognized that many disputes are simply not justiciable. International actors find that other modes of ➤conflict settlement allow greater flexibility for bargaining and compromise and do not imply the same loss of control over the outcome that is inherent in adjudication. Also, international law tends to have a ➤status quo orientation. ➤Revisionist states thus tend to find that the use of adjudication does not allow sufficient scope for peaceful change. This must be said notwithstanding the ability of the World Court to apply principles ➤*ex aequo et bono* if the parties agree (see Article 38).

Although the World Court represents the most significant attempt yet to apply the rule of law in international disputes instead of the more traditional modes of settlement (➤war, diplomacy, arbitration), it is severely hampered in its operation by the absence of the principle of compulsory jurisdiction. International adjudication is always dependent on the consent of states, and this is rarely given on matters of vital importance. The doctrine of ➤sovereignty is therefore seen by many as an insuperable barrier to the development of the international judicial system. Compulsory jurisdiction is not on the horizon and the international judicial process has played no significant part in the major issues of world politics since 1946 (e.g. the ➤Cold War, the anti-colonial revolution, the ➤North–South division, or the regulation of ➤nuclear weapons).

**Administered territory** Refers to the 'Mandates system' established in Article XXII of the Covenant of the ➤League of Nations usually credited to Jan Smuts but actually first proposed by G. L. Beer, a member of Woodrow Wilson's staff at Paris in 1919. It involved control and administration, though not ➤sovereignty, over former ➤colonial possessions of Germany (in Africa and the Pacific) and Turkey (in the Near and Middle East) and was largely a US-inspired attempt to avoid the traditional ➤imperial relationship. Administration of these territories was ceded to certain 'responsible' ➤states in 'sacred trust' to the League. Thus South Africa, by mandate in 1920, was given administrative responsibility for the former German South West Africa (now Namibia). The principles of trusteeship, tutelage, guardianship and ultimately international supervision and control were envisaged but the international supervisionary dimension, as instanced by the case of Namibia, has proved a particularly difficult matter to enforce. The system was clearly a compromise between outright ➤annexation of these territories and direct international administration. The struggle between the old realist and the newer ➤idealist approaches can be seen in the language of the Article dealing in this matter: it was designed to foster and develop territories 'which are inhabited by people not yet able to stand by themselves under the strenuous conditions of the modern world' (Article XXII). The term 'stand by themselves' is clearly a reference to the principle of ➤self-determination, the intention being that the mandatory state held administrative authority until such time (to be determined by the League) that these territories and their populations became sufficiently sophisticated to manage self-rule and achieve full legal title. To this end three classes of mandate were introduced depending on the degree of development attained and a Permanent Mandates Commission was established to oversee the process. With the creation of the UN the mandates system and administered territory was transmuted into the system. Most of the former territories have now achieved full ➤independence (including Israel, Jordan, Lebanon, Syria, Iraq and Namibia).

Despite its obvious faults and despite what today might appear to be its paternalistic overtones it should be noted that the mandates system was 'the world's first experiment in the international control of dependent territories' (F. S. Northedge, *The League of Nations*, 1976). In this way, it contributed much to the downfall of the ➤colonial system that had hitherto dominated ➤international relations.

**Afghanistan** The large-scale military ➤intervention by forces of the former Soviet Union in Afghanistan in late December 1979 was one of the defining moments in the ➤Cold War relationship between Soviet Russia and the United States of America. As with other Soviet interventions of the period (for instance, the 1968 case of Czechoslovakia), the move could be seen as primarily a defensive reaction by the Communist ➤leadership fearing that domestic instabilities and uncertainties within the target state would produce political and social changes which would profoundly damage Soviet interests. The motivation behind the Afghan initiative was particularly controversial since the 'defensive' analysis of Soviet intentions was broadly rejected by American ➤elites in favour of more offensive/confrontational interpretations. The consequential American reaction produced dissension in the ➤Atlantic Alliance as leading European states refused to subscribe to the American policy of selective ➤economic sanctions against the USSR. Implicit in this secondary intra-mural dispute within ➤NATO was the ➤issue area of ➤*détente*. For the American leaders the 'invasion' of Afghanistan signalled that *détente* should finally be abandoned. France and West Germany in particular refused to subscribe to this ➤definition of the situation.

In the nineteenth century Afghanistan had been seen as a buffer state between the British and Tsarist Empires. Following the Russian ➤revolution and the conclusion of the First World War the two states agreed to abrogate any special interests in Afghanistan and to recognize its ➤independence. The gradual decline in British influence in the Indian sub-continent meant that perforce the Afghans came increasingly under Soviet influence. The immediate reality of the Cold War added to the ➤geopolitical significance of Afghanistan in Soviet ➤perceptions. American partiality towards Pakistan further ➤polarized the area.

In the spring of 1978 a group of radical Army officers staged a successful ➤*coup d'état*. A loose power sharing Revolutionary Council was formed comprising the military and the ➤Marxist People Democratic Party of Afghanistan (PDPA) which had been formed in 1965. The subsequent attempt by the new leadership to introduce reforms and to ➤modernize Afghan society met with stiff resistance from traditional leaders. As a result an ➤Islamic fundamentalist ➤insurgency began to take hold in a country which had a strong tradition of tribal and provincial ➤subsidiarity in any event. By the winter of 1978–9 most of the provinces of Afghanistan were experiencing some degree of civil strife and organized anti-centric resistance. In a ➤scenario which was redolent of American policy in Vietnam during the Kennedy years, the Soviet Union became inexorably involved in Afghan domestic politics at a time when that system was evincing great instability and uncertainty. At the end of 1978 the two governments concluded a ➤Treaty of Friendship, Good Neighbourliness and Cooperation. The treaty included a military dimension in a number of articles and specifically talked of the need for an 'effective security system in Asia' in its 8th article.

Faced with a deteriorating security situation throughout the state, pressure upon the Soviet leadership to intervene more directly began to mount throughout the summer and autumn of 1979. An internecine power struggle within the Afghan Communist leadership developed in the autumn and purges within the ruling clique failed to stabilize the situation. Garthoff (1994a) has argued that at the Politburo meeting of 12 December 1979 the decision was taken to intervene with force in Afghanistan to replace the leadership in Kabul. Thereafter military preparations were put in hand and the intervention began over Christmas 1979. By the end of the year a more compliant clique was installed and by the end of January 1980 some 80,000 Soviet troops were in Afghanistan. Technically the logistical side of the intervention was efficiently and rapidly effected. Soviet air-lift capabilities were impressively demonstrated and resistance from sections of the Communist party identified as anti-Soviet was suppressed.

Various rationalizations and justifications were offered by the Soviet leadership for the intervention. Ostensibly the intervention was by invitation and could be justified by the Friendship Treaty and the ►Brezhnev Doctrine. As *ex post facto* pretexts these may be adequate. As substantial analyses of motivations and perceptions they are not. Clearly the situation in Afghanistan in the winter of 1979 was ripe for intervention. The existing Communist party faction was seen by the Soviets as unstable and unreliable. The country was sliding into internal chaos and civil strife. Externally Pakistan and China were opposed to the regime. The incipient Islamic rebellion raised the possibility of such contagion spreading to non-Russian Muslim republics in the USSR. In the USA the Carter presidency seemed preoccupied with the Iranian hostage issue. Failure by the Soviet Union to intervene might have looked like a failure of nerve and damaged their ►credibility, particularly in Eastern Europe. Valenta (1984) has analysed the decision on Afghanistan in the light of a modified ►bureaucratic politics model, suggesting that the Politburo gradually came to the decision to intervene by the late autumn because of an absence of attractive alternatives.

Opinion in the USA was much more ready to see the intervention as expansionist and offensive rather than in the defensive framework suggested above. Fundamentally by taking such coercive action outside the ►scope and ►domain of the ►Warsaw Pact, Soviet Russia was held to have infringed the tacit rules of the Cold War confrontation which had delimited spheres of influence which Afghanistan seemed to contest. Western observers speculated that the move was inspired by traditional Russian expansionism involving access to the Persian Gulf oilfields and a warm water port. The fact that Afghanistan was ►landlocked weighed lightly in this analysis. Subsequently the invasion was condemned in the ►United Nations and by ►non-aligned states. Within the USA it produced a reappraisal of policy towards the Soviet Union and it led directly to the promulgation of the ►Carter Doctrine and to significant American rearmament. US military ►aid to the ►partisans (mujaheddin) was initiated under Carter and expanded under his successor Ronald Reagan. Electorally Afghanistan seemed to suggest to many Americans that President Carter had been naïve before the event and confrontational afterwards. The charge of inconsistency was hard to avoid. As with the ➤Cuban missile crisis, the Soviets seemed to misread American intentions and reactions in their planning.

The ➤war that ensued between the Soviet forces, their putative allies in the central government and the partisan Islamic forces proved very costly and fundamentally inconclusive. The Afghan war caused a major displacement of peoples into Pakistan and Iran as a result of the fighting. The territory was flooded with weapons by both ➤superpowers and it is probable that some were diverted into other uses and other hands than those intended by the donors. Vast tracts of the territory were made uninhabitable as a result of the indiscriminate sowing of anti-personnel mines. The failure of the Soviet Union to achieve any of their goals in Afghanistan was recognized by the Gorbachev leadership after 1985. Deciding that its prosecution should not interfere with the objective of a new *détente* with the USA, Gorbachev demoted Afghanistan to a ➤regional conflict which allowed United Nations ➤good offices to broker an agreement at Geneva in 1988. The parameters of the agreement were:

1  withdrawal of Soviet forces
2  non-interference in internal affairs of states
3  right of return for ➤refugees
4  USA and the Soviet Union to become co-guarantors of the accord.

Whilst the Soviet withdrawal was generally welcomed by the international community which saw it as evidence of Gorbachev's 'new thinking' on Soviet ➤foreign policy, the net costs to Afghanistan, as shown above, were profound. The cessation of outside intervention did not produce the stable coalition government and the commitment to power sharing that it implied. The Afghan episode showed once again the perils and pitfalls for parties intervening in situations of civil strife and communal violence. It confirmed the finding that military power is not particularly ➤fungible and it demonstrated how readily policy makers can misperceive others' intentions and responses in their definition of the situation.

**Agent−structure**  Associated with the ➤level of analysis problem, the agent−structure issue refers to the question of how best to conceptualize the relationship between ➤state ➤actors and the ➤international system. The problematic nature of this issue was imported from social theory and introduced to IR by Alexander Wendt (1987). It revolves around two basic truisms: '(i) human beings and their organizations are purposive actors whose actions help reproduce or transform the society in which they live and (ii) society is made up of social relationships which structure the interactions between these purposeful actions.' The 'problem' is how agency (i) relates to structure (ii) and vice versa. The properties of agents and structures are both relevant to accounts of social behaviour, but the central question, as Smith and Hollis (1991) point out, is how to combine them in a single explanation of international behaviour. This philosophical-cum-methodological debate is located primarily in critiques of ►neorealism, especially K. N. Waltz's influential *Theory of International Politics* (1979). In this work, Waltz argued that it was the 'structure' of the international system which limits the potential for cooperation between states and which therefore generates the ►security dilemma, arms races, and ►war. Because of this, 'reductionist' studies of 'agents' (i.e. individual statesmen, or the character of states) can never be satisfactory and must always be secondary to theories of the international system (unipolar, bipolar or multipolar) since it is this structure which conditions state behaviour. The issue of how to conceptualize agents and structure and how to conceive of their interrelationship in order to construct a 'complete theory' of world politics is now at the heart of the debate between conventional and ►critical international theorists.

**Aggression** This word has a number of distinct meanings. It is used in ►international law and ►international organizations as a concept and a form of proscribed behaviour. It has been widely studied by social scientists, in particular by psychologists and social psychologists. It is a term used in political discourse and debate, usually in a pejorative and condemnatory way. Consideration of the term will largely concentrate upon the first two contexts suggested above.

First, in law, the term aggression has been used to distinguish between ►just and unjust ►wars and between legal and illegal ►force.

Broadly it refers to an illegal, unjustified, improper or immoral attack or ►intervention by one ►state, or its agents, upon another. As such, it is 'offensive' rather than 'defensive', although the notion of a pre-emptive strike can blur even this broad distinction. It is usual to distinguish between 'direct' aggression (e.g. Japan's attack on ►Pearl Harbor in 1941) and 'indirect' aggression (e.g. the American U2 spy-flights over the Soviet Union between 1955 and 1960). Again, in common international usage it may not be limited to overt or covert military acts as in the examples above, but may take the form of economic measures employed by states against others (e.g. ►blockade or ►boycott).

The difficulty of definition and the manifest lack of a common international standard has not inhibited its employment as a central concept in theories of peaceful change. In so far as international law has attempted to regulate the behaviour of states and establish universally agreed methods of promoting ►national interests, efforts have been made from the beginning of the ►state-system to label and consequently forbid 'aggression'. Medieval theories of the ►just war can be seen as faltering though oblique steps in this direction. In a sense, international law has always concerned itself with this issue, but it was in the aftermath of the First World War that more self-conscious efforts were made by the international community to pinpoint and thus eliminate its occurrence. The Covenant of the ►League of Nations, with its emphasis on the doctrine of ►collective security, was premised on the belief that (a) aggression could be easily identified and (b) the rest of the international community could, in concert, rise up against its perpetrators. Neither assumption held and it is commonly argued that the League floundered, at least in part, because of its inability to deal with this problem. The omission of a definition of aggression from the Charter of the UN, and the allocation of the task of determining its occurrence to the ➤Security Council, was a tacit recognition by the framers of the need for political ➤realism in the new organization. 'Acts of aggression' were what the Security Council decided them to be; thus the invasion of South Korea by the North in June 1950 was, in the absence of the Soviet representative, deemed to fall into this category.

Apart from these international institutions, the most thorough attempt at definition was made in 1933 by Litvinov, the Soviet foreign minister in the Convention for the Definition of Aggression. In this view, the phenomenon occurs when any of the following take place: (a) a declaration of ➤war is made against another state; (b) an armed invasion of another's territory, without a declaration of war; (c) an attack without a declaration of war, on the territory, naval vessels or aircraft of another state; (d) a naval blockade of the ports or coast of another state; (e) aid to invading armed bands within another state and a refusal to take all possible measures on its own territory to deprive the armed bands of aid and protection. There has been no definition as specific as this since 1933. It became more obscure during the ➤Cold War from 1946 onwards, when the term itself was caught up in the ideological rivalry between the United States and the Soviet Union.

Thus apart from its general legal definition (a resort to war or measures or armed coercion undertaken in violations of ➤treaty obligations), the term defies stricter delineation. Indeed, the term and the phenomena it describes are endemic in the anarchical system, the main feature of which is a jealously guarded and permissive interpretation of the doctrine of ➤sovereignty. Attempts to define and hence limit its occurrence are inevitably bound up with the degree of cohesion the international community achieves.

Second, the ➤social science approach to aggression may be divided, in broad terms, into those who favour an instinct theory of aggression and those who favour a learning theory of aggression. Instinct theory argues that man is innately aggressive, whereas learning theory argues that aggression is a response to various situations that individuals encounter from early childhood. All the social sciences and applied studies, such as criminology, have taken an interest in the concept, its definition, causes and manifestations. Social science, moreover, would distinguish between aggression as an attitude, or predisposition, and aggression as overt behaviour. Thus someone feeling aggressive might not express it overtly, or might displace or project that aggression into a substitute object.

At the turn of the century Freud argued for a drive towards death – *thanatos* – as an intrinsic part of human nature. Consequentially, aggression was an instinct. This powerful, but probably erroneous, idea took hold of popular thinking about aggression thereafter. Apart from the need to treat the concept of an instinct with great caution, most social scientists reject neo-Freudian approaches to aggression. Important research published in the 1930s in the United States suggested that aggression might be regarded as a function of the amount of frustration experienced by an individual. The rather dogmatic position of the early social scientists on frustration – aggression has been modified now with researchers preferring to regard frustration as an instigator of aggression. More recently, social scientists have built upon these ideas to suggest that much aggression is learned as a result of socialization. Aggression is thus seen as instrumental rather than instinctive. Most social systems tend to encourage assertive and competitive behaviour while ritualized forms of aggression – for example in competitive sports – are rewarded both in material wealth and social status.

It is difficult to extrapolate from the individual behaviour motivations to the types of violence within and between societies that can broadly be called social ➤conflict. Moreover, studies of combat soldiers have suggested that obedience to authority and/or feelings of solidarity with fellow soldiers are stronger motives than aggression in explaining why people are willing to kill on the battlefield. Modern ➤technology has made killing more efficient and more remote; it has also separated the political decision to go to war from the battlefield decision to kill and be killed. Moreover, the study of ➤decision-making in ➤international relations would tend to suggest that the actual decision to go to war cannot be properly explained via aggression theories. Other psychological states of mind may be equally significant and important cultural, social and environmental factors cannot be ignored.

**AICs** Advanced Industrial Countries. UN abbreviation for North America, Western Europe, Japan and Australasia. These ➤states are often referred to simply as the ➤North in documents such as the ➤Brandt Report 1980.

**Aid** The transfer of goods and services between international ➤actors on a concessionary basis. Aid is an extremely generalized term. It covers both grants and loans, both ➤bilateral and ➤multilateral, both governmental and private. It excludes, specifically, commercial transactions where the donor makes no concessions. Aid may be given without strings or it may be tied in some way by the donor so that the recipient is restricted in the way the aid is utilized. Aid may be given for humanitarian reasons or it may have the most overt political connotations. Aid may be given to alleviate some short-term problem or it may be part of a long-term strategy for development or redevelopment.

Aid relationships, in all the contexts discussed above, have been a growing feature of IR in the twentieth century. Notwithstanding the developing impact of non-➤state actors the greatest amounts of aid are still disbursed on a government-to-government basis. The United States, the most powerful economic state actor in the post-1945 system, has also been the largest donor. The first major aid programme was the European Recovery Programme (ERP). The obvious success of the ERP, or ➤Marshall Plan, encouraged the United States to attempt the same policies *vis-à-vis* the ➤Third World. The magnitude and scope of the problems facing any donor are totally different as between Western Europe and the Third World. State-to-state aid reached its peak in the early 1960s and has declined since. There are a number of factors behind this decline. Politically, donor states have found that aid is an expensive and inefficient instrument of ➤foreign policy. A sudden change of ➤regime in a recipient state may mean the loss of political influence and, with it, of economic resources. Economically, aid has simply not achieved the self-sustained growth in the recipient countries originally anticipated. Political leaders and ➤attentive publics now tend to argue that regime change is required if the Third World is to avoid a series of major economic ➤crises before the end of the century. ➤➤Donor fatigue; foreign aid

**AIDS** Acquired Immune Deficiency Syndrome. This was first clinically diagnosed in the USA in 1981 among homosexual men. Within two years researchers in France and the USA had established the finding that AIDS was caused by the Human Immunodeficiency Virus (HIV). This was later named HIV-1 when a second strain, appropriately termed HIV-2, was identified in West Africa. The HIV is transmitted by unprotected sexual contacts, by infected blood and blood products, and by perinatal contact between mother and child. In almost all populations where AIDS has been identified, the most common epidemiological factors in its occurrence have been sexual activity and drug abuse. In short, the AIDS pandemic is as much a behavioural problem as a biological one.

The ➤World Health Organization (WHO) estimates that about 10 million people are now infected with HIV, and forecasts that this will reach 20 million by the year 2000. While a large proportion of reported cases are presently located in the ➤Third World (especially Eastern and Central Africa), much of the projected increase is likely to occur in the developed world. The pandemic is thus truly a global threat to health. Moreover, the death rate from AIDS, once it has developed from HIV infection, is known to be very high. It would appear that the pandemic has two infection patterns: in the AICs the virus is found predominantly among homosexual males and users of intravenous drugs; in the third world (at present Africa and South America) the method of transmission is heterosexual activity, hence perinatal contact is more prevalent in these regions.

It is now recognized that the AIDS pandemic is a pressing and immediate problem for the international community and one that cannot be addressed from a ➤state-centric perspective. The WHO has initiated a Global Programme on AIDS (1986). This programme has three objectives: to prevent the spread of HIV; to provide a caring environment for those already infected and in particular to protect them from discrimination; thirdly, to coordinate national and international research, treatment and prevention. This pandemic reinforces the notion that the state-centric bias of ►international relations must, as a matter of urgency, give way to a ►world society perspective.

**Air power** One of the most important developments in the twentieth century has been that of heavier-than-air flight. Its potential was made apparent early in the century by wars such as the 1914–18 First World War, where manned aircraft were used for surveillance, interception and bombing. During the inter-war years strategists such as Giulo Douhet and William Mitchell began to argue for the primacy of air power in future warfare. Douhet in particular argued that in coming wars 'command of the air' should be sought and could be achieved by offensive bombing of enemy targets from the outset. Douhet also suggested that civilian morale would be quickly destroyed by such a strategy. In the event, the experience of the Second World War showed mixed results. Strategic bombing was seen to be highly inaccurate, very costly and often controversial in terms of what later became known as ►collateral damage. The main changes wrought by the Second World War were scientific and ►technological, in particular ►nuclear weapons and ballistic missiles. It was these changes which appeared to vindicate Douhet and the cult of the offensive.

The mid-century conflicts in ►Korea and ►Vietnam employed similar technologies to those used in the 1940s. Again the results were equivocal. The ►Persian Gulf War of 1991 seemed to suggest to the proponents of air power that a ►paradigm shift was occurring. Using a number of innovative technologies, in particular Stealth, Smart and Situation Awareness, the United States Air Force was able to achieve Douhet's dream-command of the air. A ►Revolution in Military Affairs (RMA) is now being heralded as the plausible future in which air power will play a central role.

**Alien** A person usually resident in one ►state but owing allegiance to another. In ►international law it is inseparable from the concept of sovereign territorial jurisdiction, the assumption being that people legally belong to particular states (i.e. nationals). Some ►idealist writers, wishing to break down national boundaries and reduce the authority of the sovereign state, regard the idea of aliens as atavistic and reactionary, preferring internationalism as the focus for loyalty and allegiance (►Kant's *Perpetual Peace*).

Protection of aliens is a controversial issue in international law and it illustrates the divergent approaches to ►international relations by developed and developing states. ►Developed (usually Western, capitalist) states argue that foreign nationals are protected by an 'international minimum standard' which must be upheld regardless of how the host state treats its own nationals. Developing states maintain, on the other hand, that the 'national treatment standard' is sufficient. The issue is political rather than legal in the sense that developing states, resenting economic penetration and ➤dependency, lay stress on absolute ➤sovereignty and complete ➤independence, whereas the developed states, wishing to protect their investment and property, argue for a more expansive interpretation of these concepts. The most glaring and dramatic breach of the 'international minimum standard' in recent times was Uganda's expulsion of Asians in 1972. ➤➤Asylum; immigration; migration; refugee

**Alliance** A formal agreement between two or more ➤actors – usually ➤states – to collaborate together on ➤perceived mutual ➤security issues. By allying themselves together it is anticipated that security will be increased in one, some or all of the following dimensions: by joining an alliance a system of ➤deterrence will be established or strengthened, by joining an alliance a ➤defence pact will operate in the event of a war, by joining an alliance some or all of the actors will be precluded from joining other alliances. Allies will stipulate in ➤treaty form the conditions under which a military response will be required. At a minimum this collaboration will cover mutual obligations upon the outbreak of hostilities, but collaboration often extends beyond this. Joint military exercises, staff training and weapons procurement may all be regarded as proper activities under the rubric of 'being allies'. Allies may feel the need to support each other diplomatically in the conduct of their ➤foreign policies. As with any ➤diplomacy, alliances may be secret or open, ➤bilateral or ➤multilateral. It is not difficult to see why, under traditional concepts of ➤state-centrism, alliance diplomacy was regarded as paradigm ➤high politics.

The alliance was a key variable in the ➤balance of power system. States were assumed to 'balance' against a revisionist state or coalition to maintain stability. In this context alliances were contingent, issue-orientated. Waltz (1979) has suggested that an equally plausible dynamic in the balance of power would be for states to 'bandwagon' behind a putative victor rather than balance against it. In a ➤bipolar system, ➤bloc leaders and ➤superpowers will engage in ally-seeking in order to counter perceived threats at the margin or periphery. Since military ➤capabilities are unevenly distributed in bipolar alliances serious conflicts can occur within the blocs over the ➤scope and ➤domain of bloc leadership and followership. This tendency is often referred to as ➤polycentrism.

In a ➤multipolar system, alliance dynamics are intrinsically more fluid and there may be greater uncertainty and less predictability about foreign policies and alliance dynamics. As Christensen and Snyder (1990) have suggested, under conditions of multipolarity states may either 'chain gang' (rush headlong into hostilities in support of their allies) or 'buck pass' (stand off from hostilities in the expectation or hope that others will not do so). This dilemma is built into multipolarity and – as the authors suggest – non-systemic, perceptual agent-centred considerations may ultimately decide the dilemma.

The twentieth century has seen ally-seeking and alliance-construction as typical repertoires of state behaviour. The examples of 1914 and 1939 have been widely studied to extrapolate and validate theories about alliances and occurrence of war. The findings seem to be ambivalent as to whether alliances inhibit or encourage states to go to war. The outbreak of the ➤Cold War confirmed many of the bipolar dynamics already referred to. Both the United States and the former Soviet Union found that bloc leadership could not presume bloc followership. Many saw ➤nuclear weapons as exacerbating these tendencies to centrifugalism. ➤Gaullism was perhaps the most explicit statement of these views. The end of the Cold War and the demise of the Soviet Union has left the system with 'morning after the night before' remnants of the old bipolar structure. Whilst the ➤Warsaw Pact has now gone, NATO continues to re-invent itself although whether it is still an 'alliance' remains a moot point.

**Alternative world futures** The study of what the world system, including the world political system, may look like in the future. Despite the implication of prophecy in the nomenclature there is a methodology. It consists of extrapolating certain trends, identified at present, into the future on the basis of certain working assumptions. The term ➤futurology is often used to describe the methodology and the area of study.

The study has grown apace in the last quarter of the twentieth century. This is a reflection of growing concern about a number of global issues such as ➤population growth, environmental degradation, consumption of non-renewable resources and so on. This concern was originally expressed in the 1970s when private institutions such as the Club of Rome began to publish pessimistic projections about the future. The most distinguished of these documents was *The Limits to Growth* (1972). Other groups such as the Hudson Institute were more optimistic. In 1980 the US government published its *Global 2000 Report*. This suggested that a major shift in ➤policy-making was required if the pessimists were to be confounded.

Growing interest in Alternative World Futures has formed part of the ➤pluralist perspective on ➤international relations. This views the problems for the planet as only amenable to solutions which escape from the straitjacket of traditional ➤state-centred politics.

**Ambassador** A diplomatic representative or agent of one sovereign ➤state usually resident in another. As ➤international relations implies a system of communications between states, the idea of an ambassador came to be its principal enabling vehicle. Although the practice is usually associated with the development of the European ➤state-system, references to it can be found in ancient China and India where Kautilya's *Arthashastra* is a striking example of early articulated diplomatic practice and statecraft. However, in neither of these ancient state-systems is there evidence of an ambassadorial system involving permanent embassies, missions or legations. The prevailing practice, as elsewhere in the ancient world, was the use of heralds or envoys (really, messengers) or else temporary plenipotentiaries (agents who were authorized to work out agreements).

The modern practice of resident ambassadors began to appear in Europe in the fourteenth and fifteenth centuries, probably first in Venice and Milan. The idea of ►diplomatic immunity was inseparable from residency and formed the basis of modern ►international law. The inviolability of the ambassador's person (and later that of his staff) was a necessary feature of this system and immunity is still regarded as the bedrock of diplomatic practice. Even its dramatic violation in Teheran (1979) when American Embassy staff were held hostage by government forces does not disprove the universal acceptance of the notion of immunity. Iran was, almost without exception in the international community, strongly condemned for this clear breach of the basic rules of diplomatic communication. However, whether the principle of immunity can be extended to cover aspects other than personal safety and private diplomatic affairs (e.g. parking offences or drug trafficking) is less widely accepted and subject to much current debate.

The development of the resident ambassadorial system became fully self-conscious at the Congress of Vienna (1815) which, as well as recognizing the existence of a *corps diplomatique*, strictly defined categories of representation and issued a ►protocol determining the functions and order of precedence of diplomatic missions. This protocol is still in use today: it underlines the importance of immunity and establishes that the doyen or spokesperson of the *corps diplomatique* is either the papal representative or, more usually, the longest accredited serving ambassador regardless of the status or ►power of the country he (or she) represents. Vienna thus established the ambassadorial system as a vital institution in international relations, and one that has continued largely unchanged to the present day. In 1961 the Vienna Convention on Diplomatic Relations underlined and endorsed the achievement of the Congress.

Some writers on ►diplomacy have questioned the continued need for an ambassadorial system. The argument is that modern technology, especially in the field of communications, as well as the decline of the traditional ►nation-state, has destroyed the very foundation of the institution. However, although many governments are concerned to prune the resources available to the diplomatic service and direct its functions more towards ►trade and commerce rather than traditional matters of ►high policy, it is extremely unlikely that so useful a system will disappear. The old ►bilateral diplomatic pattern may well be undergoing significant change, especially with the increasing collectivization of international life, but the need for diplomatic machinery and representation, whether this be bilateral or ►multilateral, will remain for as long as the international state-system lasts. One is bound up with the other. ►►Diplomacy; diplomatic immunities and privileges

**Amnesty** Refers to a decision to set aside prosecution or punishment for certain types of offenders (usually political). It is similar to a pardon but without the connotations of forgiveness that this usually carries. Amnesties can be general or specific, complete or partial. The term is widely used in relation to ➤prisoners of war and prisoners of conscience. ➤Amnesty International is a non-government organization devoted to overseeing, on a world-wide basis, cases where individuals or groups are punished for their political or religious views.

**Amnesty International** An INGO working in the ➤issue area of ➤human rights. Amnesty began as a protest movement but quickly took on an organizational structure commensurate with its goals and tasks. The original conception for an international campaign in support of those detained throughout the world for political or religious beliefs was that of Peter Benenson. Benenson's article in the British Sunday *Observer* in May 1961, entitled 'The Forgotten Prisoners', caught the imagination of ➤world public opinion. Within a year over 200 cases had been taken up and representations on behalf of prisoners of conscience had been made.

Amnesty pursues three broad policy goals: the release of all prisoners of conscience; an end to all forms of torture (including the death penalty); and fair and prompt trials for all political prisoners. Amnesty is essentially a monitoring organization and it critically depends upon a well-developed responsiveness from ➤attentive publics throughout the system. In addition its reputation for impartiality and reliability makes it an important information source which is widely used by political ➤elites across the world.

At the time of writing Amnesty has over one million members and supporters in over 150 ➤states and territories. It is governed by a nine-member Executive Committee and a ➤Secretary-General who implements policy decisions and heads the Secretariat. Its headquarters are based in London, UK. It is represented at the ➤United Nations and in 1978 was awarded the UN human rights prize in recognition of its work in this area. Amnesty is officially recognized by the ➤European Union, the ➤Council of Europe, the organization of American states and the ➤Organization of African Unity. It was awarded the Nobel peace prize in 1977.

**Anarchy** A crucial but highly contentious concept in ➤international relations. Its literal meaning is 'absence of government' but it is often used as a synonym for disorder, disarray, confusion or chaos. In its formal sense, it designates the lack of a central authority. As such it is manifestly a feature of the international system and it defines the socio/political framework in which international relations occur. In this sense it has neither positive nor negative connotations. It is descriptive rather than prescriptive, a general condition rather than a distinct structure. In this way, it is considered to be 'the starting point' of thinking about international relations. For some though, anarchy implies the absence of any authoritative institutions, rules or norms above the sovereign state. This view leads to the quite erroneous assumption that international relations is permanently in 'the state of nature' which is itself 'a state of war of all against all.' This vision of inter-state relations which supposedly derives from the work of Thomas Hobbes (1588–1679) is highly questionable and not warranted by any careful reading of the literature – especially of Hobbes himself.

Discarding this negative portrayal, anarchy remains an essentially contested concept in IR and a plausible, if somewhat oversimplified, account of the history of thought in international relations can be given in terms of it. Thus, in traditional or classical texts, international theory is often presented as a dialogue or a debate between those who accept the condition of anarchy but argue that this does not necessarily preclude order, society or community beyond the nation-state, (►realists) and those who argue that anarchy is incompatible with these goals and their realization is only possible once anarchy is replaced by governance of one sort or another, (►idealists or ►liberals). For the former, the ►domestic analogy – the argument that the conditions of an orderly social life are the same among states as within them – is invalid. The lack of a common government or universal authority is thus what distinguishes the international from the domestic realm of politics and law. For realists, decentralization is the defining characteristic of relations between sovereign states. In contrast, the latter maintain that the domestic analogy is crucial and argue that the conditional prerequisites of a peaceful and orderly world are that governmental institutions be replicated above and between states. Only if anarchy is overcome would it be possible to speak of a genuine ►international society or community. Political philosophers most closely identified with these theoretical positions are Hobbes (see Chapter 13 of *Leviathan*) and Kant (*Perpetual Peace*), with the international lawyer Grotius occupying a place somewhere in between.

While most contemporary theorists regard this debate as somewhat sterile and unproductive, the essential differences concerning the meaning and implications of anarchy remain in the ongoing tension between the state-centric ►neorealists and the more pluralistic ►neoliberals. ►Critical theorists and ►postmodernists, however, dismiss both schools precisely because both are rooted in the 'anarchy problématique'; the first seeking to work within its structural constraints, the second seeking to ameliorate it (Ashley, 1984). In mainstream Anglo-American international theory anarchy remains the fundamental assumption of international politics and as such it poses the key research questions in the discipline. Under what conditions do self-regarding states cooperate with each other? Are there limits to this cooperation? Can the ►security dilemma created by anarchy be overcome? What distribution of ►power is most conducive to ►peace and/or stability? To what extent is independence compatible with ►interdependence? If the state ►actor really is declining in significance, what replaces it? Can the distinction between ►high and ►low politics be sustained in the face of the disutility of military force? How is change effected and who is most vulnerable to changes in the international system? Do differences in domestic political arrangements affect international behaviour and outcomes? Is relative gain more important than absolute gain? All of these 'puzzles' of contemporary international theory are directly related to assumptions about 'international anarchy' (the phrase was first used by G. Lowes Dickinson in 1916), and its implications for agency, process and structure. They all revolve around the key question of what in anarchy is immutable, and what is amenable to change.

On the face of it, the logic of anarchy is compelling: states are the main actors existing in a ➤self-help environment in which the security dilemma is always pressing. States are presumed to act rationally in terms of perceptions of the ➤national interest, but they are not entirely unconcerned with rules and norms. So, conflict and cooperation can and do co-exist within the same social milieu. This is the common terrain occupied (though, of course, disputed) by the heirs of the realist and idealist traditions. Recent dissenters from this discourse (sometimes referred to as 'reflectionists') argue that there is no inherent 'logic' of anarchy. The concepts that appear to follow from it – self-help, power politics, sovereignty – are really socially constructed institutions rather than essential features of anarchy. Anarchy, in fact, is 'what states make of it' (Wendt, 1992). In this way, new thinking in IR has begun to question the epistemological (knowledge) and ontological (being) status of conventional theory and argues that the presumption of anarchy is myopic, ahistorical and inherently self-serving. In particular it privileges states rather than people or individuals and by persisting with anarchy's binary distinctions – public/private, inside/outside, self/other etc. – it distorts reality through marginalization, exclusion and silencing. It omits from its purview large sections of social life which ought to be of concern to students of IR. In sum, the tendency to view anarchy as the basic condition of international relations underestimates its inherent ambiguity and overestimates its explanatory powers.

**ANC** African National Congress, founded in 1912 with the aims of improving the political, social and economic conditions of blacks in South Africa. Originally an organization committed to non-violence and redressing grievances through constitutional means, believing that the key to progress was the gaining of full equality initially for the black middle classes. Its gradualist opposition to segregationism received an irreversible setback in 1948 with the election of the Nationalist Party to power. From 1948 to 1960, the ANC shifted its policy from a reformist stance to a revolutionary one. The names associated with this major change in political strategy are Anton Lembede, Walter Sisulu, Albert Luthuli, Oliver Tambo and Nelson Mandela, who became the main spokesman for the ANC in this crucial period of confrontation. After the Sharpeville affair of 21 March 1960 (where sixty-nine Africans were killed by police) the ANC was outlawed, and it subsequently went underground. Nelson Mandela (born 1918) was arrested and sentenced to life imprisonment in 1964. In his absence,

Oliver Tambo assumed the leadership of the ANC from exile in Lusaka and London. The ANC was committed to an armed struggle against ►apartheid, from within and from without.

The organization has undergone a number of developmental phases: from 1912 to 1948 it was reformist in character, from 1948 to 1960 it became radical and revolutionary and from the early 1960s to the early 1990s the aim was the violent and complete overthrow of the South African state. As Mandela eloquently put it at his trial defending the use of force, '. . . the hard facts were that fifty years of non-violence had brought the African people nothing but more and more repressive legislation, and fewer and fewer rights.'

It is not just in this third phase that the organization has had an international dimension – as early as 1913 a delegation was sent to London and in 1919 the ANC was present at ►Versailles. But it is since being outlawed in South Africa in the early 1960s that it figured predominantly in the diplomatic councils of the ►front-line states and others opposed to the continued existence of apartheid in South Africa.

During 1989 a fourth evolutionary phase began to emerge, the negotiational. The election to the presidency of F. W. de Klerk and the legalization of the ANC ahead of the release of the world's most famous political prisoner, Nelson Mandela, in 1990 opened up the possibility of a negotiated settlement between the ANC Alliance and the Nationalist government. This ►rapprochement, however, did not halt the communal violence within South Africa between supporters of the ANC and right-wing white groups, supporters of the Zulu-based Inkatha Freedom party and black radical organizations such as the Pan-Africanist Congress who rejected the ANC's apparent collaborationist stance. During the 1990–94 period the ANC Alliance moved from being an exiled irritant on the fringes of South African life to an almost universally recognized government-in-waiting. The power-sharing arrangements with the Nationalist government were institutionalized in the Transitional Executive Council which was effectively the ruling body of South Africa until the first non-racial, multiparty elections of April 1994. A major task of the ANC's International Department headed by Thabo Mbeki during this period was to persuade the international community to keep its principal coercive instrument, ►economic sanctions, in place and to continue to isolate South Africa until majority rule had been established. The ANC was unsuccessful in this quest as Western states in particular eagerly sought to engage with the 'new' South Africa.

The elections of April 1994 represented the ANC's 'rite of passage'; the moment when hegemony and control passed from a white minority regime which for over 300 years had assumed and exercised power unilaterally, to a majoritarian, pluralist order based (temporarily) on a concept of power sharing within the framework of a negotiated democratic constitution. Although the ANC Alliance did not achieve the two-thirds majority necessary to be solely responsible for governing and writing the new constitution (and many UN

Observers believed that this was a deliberately designed outcome), it did achieve an overwhelming electoral victory, winning 252 seats in the new National Assembly and gaining overall control in seven out of the nine newly created provinces.

A fifth developmental stage emerged with the ANC-led Government of National Unity (GNU) headed by President Mandela in May 1994. In May 1996 the National Party officially left the GNU giving the ANC Alliance virtually sole control over South Africa's government. The second general election is due in 1999 and will witness the end of any power-sharing arrangements still in place. Attention is now focused on divisions within the ANC Alliance, particularly between the ANC, the South African Communist party and the trades union organization, COSATU. The ANC has hitherto been a complicated ideological package united by the common aim of opposing white dominance and devoted to establishing a majoritarian system in a unitary state. There have always been divisions within the movement, especially concerning the nature of the 'armed struggle' and the social, economic and political character of the post-apartheid state. Up until the early 1990s these differences did not fragment the alliance and the objective remained the practical, ➤realpolitik, one of forcing the whites to negotiate and share power. In foreign policy terms, the ANC-led government appeared to be split between the 'pragmatists' (those who advocated full integration into the Western-led international system) and the 'solidarists' (those who advocated a more heroic, human rights and ideologically based foreign policy). The tensions between the two approaches were highlighted by the refusal of Nigeria to respond to President Mandela's policy of ➤constructive engagement by executing the writer Ken Saro-Wiwa and eight other civil rights activists in November 1995. Other examples of the ANC's ambivalence in foreign policy during the 1994–6 period relate to the conflict between needing Western foreign investments, and rewarding informal alliances forged with states such as Cuba and Libya during the apartheid period. The tension generated by these conflicting needs has not been resolved. Foreign policy is still contested ground in South African politics: the contest now though is not over the legitimacy of the state but its general orientation in world politics. Thus, South Africa is now, more or less, a 'normal' state in international relations.

**Annexation** A mode of acquiring territory which belonged to another ➤state, or to no one. It is usually a ➤unilateral act, but the acquiescence of the former possessor is presumed. It involves the extension of full ➤sovereignty by the new owner and the exercise of exclusive jurisdiction and control in the area. It differs from military occupation though annexation may arise from this. The ➤Anschluss of 1938 when Austria became part of the German Reich is an example of annexation.

**Anschluss** Literally means union. It specifically refers to the unification of

Germany and Austria in 1938 (which was expressly forbidden by the Treaty of ►Versailles which concluded the First World War). As a consequence, Austria became a province of the German Third Reich from 1938 to 1945.

**Antarctica Treaty** ►Treaty concluded in 1959 among twelve states – seven territorial claimants (Argentina, Australia, Chile, France, New Zealand, Norway and the United Kingdom), two ►superpowers (the USA and the Soviet Union), and three others (Belgium, Japan and South Africa). All of these operated Antarctic research stations in the territory during the International Geophysical Year 1957–8. The treaty came into force in 1961 and is subject to periodic review. It has since been supplemented by a number of conventions and ►protocols relating to ►ecological/environmental concerns and now constitutes an important international ►regime covering a number of resource, military and environmental ►issue areas. This regime involves five communal norms or principles: acknowledgement of an 'Antarctic community' for the use and management of the area, non-militarization, scientific cooperation, environment protection and holding territorial claims in abeyance for the duration of the treaty. The treaty was significant in 1959 in that it was the first ►disarmament agreement involving the USA and the former Soviet Union, and it effectively rendered the Antarctic a ►nuclear-free zone. The regime has subsequently been joined by fourteen other states with declared interests and substantial scientific research interests in the area. Brazil, China and India, three of the most powerful states of the ►South, have accordingly widened membership though some argue that expansion is at the cost of regime coherence. The Antarctica Treaty operates outside the ►United Nations framework and this has led to calls from non-signatory states (led by Malaysia) to relocate the treaty within the ►domain of the ►Common Heritage of Mankind principle. There have also been calls, mainly from environmental non-governmental organizations (NGOs), for the Antarctica to be declared a 'world wilderness reserve,' thereby denying the right to resource exploitation by signatory states. This would bring the treaty into the broad remit of of ►global governance proposals.

**ANZUS** Security ►treaty concluded between Australia, New Zealand and the United States at San Francisco on 1 September 1951. Under the terms of the treaty each signatory recognized that an armed attack on one of the others in 'the Pacific area' would be 'dangerous to its own peace and safety'. The conclusion of this pact marked a significant turning point in the defence postures of Australia, New Zealand and the United Kingdom (which is not a signatory and was excluded from participation). Australia and New Zealand redefined their security priorities and turned to the United States as the protecting power, which in fact had assumed this role since the fall of Singapore (1942). Under the terms of the pact, an Australia-New Zealand Army Corps (ANZAC) fought in ►Vietnam. Between 1965 and 1973 469 were killed. Recently, serious tensions have appeared in the ►alliance due to the New Zealand government's commitment to a nuclear-free Pacific ocean and as a consequence its future as a genuine ►trilateral pact must now be in doubt.

New Zealand did not intend that the prohibition of visits by nuclear powered US warships should signal the end of its participation in the treaty. However, the US viewed this action as non-fulfilment of treaty obligations and declared that the security guarantee ANZUS gave to New Zealand was rendered inoperative. New Zealand's status is now that of 'friendly country' rather than partner in a tripartite alliance.

**Apartheid** Afrikaans word meaning 'aparthood' or 'separateness'. It refers particularly to policies of racial segregation practised by the Republic of South Africa since the accession to power of the National Party in 1948. The population was officially divided into four main racial groups: white (European), black (African), coloured (Mixed) and Asian (mostly Indian). In 1990 the ►World Bank estimated the total population figure as *c.*34 million, the racial make-up being as follows: white 13.6%, black 75.2%, Asian 2.6% and coloured 8.6%. The question of population statistics was a thorny one in South Africa and was bound up with the issue of apartheid. Accurate, verifiable figures were impossible to obtain but most South Africa-watchers estimated that by 1994 the total population was about 40 million with a rise of 2 – 2.6% annually, mainly amongst the black segment. The policy pillars of the apartheid system involved legislation dealing with virtually every aspect of life in the social, political and economic fields including places of residence, work, property rights, marriage, movement, social and recreational amenities, schools, universities, rights of association and of course, the franchise. Apartheid granted a virtual monopoly of ►power to the minority white group (which sometimes rather defensively referred to itself as 'the white tribe of Africa'). The constitution was amended in 1984 to give some political representation to the coloured and Asian population groups. Africans, though, were excluded from political participation in South Africa on the grounds that, under the distorted logic of 'grand apartheid', they were citizens of their own separate 'homelands'. (Transkei 1976, Bophuthatswana 1977, Venda 1979 and Ciskei 1981 – Chief Buthelezi of Kwazulu/Natal refused 'independence' for the Zulus). These homelands, which the Pretoria government alleged were separate sovereign states, were in fact puppet regimes and were not accorded international ►recognition.

Other Afrikaans words and concepts frequently associated with apartheid and inseparable from it in the political context were 'baaskap' (boss-rule), 'verligte' (enlightened or reformist, especially in relation to so-called 'petty apartheid') and 'verkrampte' (rigid, conservative adherence to policies of complete separate development on ethnic/racial lines). During the critical period in South Africa's history in the mid 1980s when the state appeared to be on the brink of collapse, white politics was characterized by a tension or interplay between the forces of 'verligte', epitomized later by F. W. de Klerk, and of 'verkrampte', embodied in the person of 'the old crocodile', P. W. Botha. Up until 1989, the latter appeared to be the dominant element especially with regard to issues of ➤security, law and order which clearly took precedence over reformist tendencies.

Apartheid was unique to South Africa. Since the transformation of Rhodesia into Zimbabwe (1980), the Republic during the 1980s was the one glaring example of a political system dedicated to White dominance in a continent which had all but completely shaken off the vestiges of European ➤colonial rule. The black ➤revolution which had characterized African politics in the second half of the twentieth century could not be seen as complete by the majority of Africans until the racial domination by the whites in South Africa ended. South Africa therefore was in theory, if not in practice, a besieged ➤state. It was besieged from within and from without. Before 1948 the South African political system was unexceptional and did not have any significant implications for its general position in ➤world politics. Traditionally its importance to the outside world lay in its geographical position on the shortest route from Europe to Asia. This was the reason first for Dutch colonization (1652) and then for British (1795). Subsequent discoveries of gold, gems and diamonds as well as andalusite, chrome ore, vanadium, platinum, coal, iron ore and uranium, all in significant and recoverable quantities, made South Africa a powerful, developing industrial state existing prominently and self-consciously in a very poorly developed continent. South Africa was and is, without doubt, the ➤superpower of the region. Until 1948, South Africa was not singled out for special consideration by the international community. Indeed, South Africa had in 1939 entered the ➤war against Nazi Germany and in the immediate post-war years it was widely assumed that with its vast mineral wealth and its prime strategic location straddling the South Atlantic and the Indian Oceans, it would be a valuable and valued member of the Western, non-➤communist grouping in the international system. The election of the Afrikaner Nationalist Party and the rigid application of its policy of apartheid in 1948 radically changed South Africa's place in world affairs. The policy of apartheid and the perpetuation of white dominance which it involved was universally recognized as morally repugnant and indefensible. The question that dominated most political analyses of South Africa in the late 1980s was: how long could South Africa and apartheid survive?

Since 1948 various forms of coercion ranging from partial economic, diplomatic and sporting ➤boycotts to full-scale expulsions from ➤international organizations, were the standard responses of the majority of states in the international community (a community, incidentally, which is well known for its tolerance of deviant behaviour). The UN in particular played a prominent part in the general outlawry of South Africa. Almost annually since 1948, the ➤General Assembly of the UN passed resolutions condemning and criticizing the policy of apartheid and the government of South Africa (both of which were seen to be synonymous). In 1962 the UN asked member states to break off diplomatic and economic relations with South Africa and created a permanent Special Committee on Apartheid to review racial developments within the Republic. In 1973 the General Assembly formed an International Convention on the Suppression and Punishment of the Crime of Apartheid and declared it to be 'a crime against humanity', and by 1980 fifty-eight states had agreed to be bound by the terms of this convention. Indeed, it could be argued that a constant theme of UN General Assembly politics and of ➤Third World rhetoric was the continuous condemnation of apartheid. It became one of the moral absolutes of the age, indeed virtually the only one to straddle the ideological divide between East and West in world politics. The high-water mark of this movement occurred in 1977 when the ➤Security Council of the UN, which because of the ➤veto power enjoyed by its permanent members had previously confined itself to condemnatory statements, implemented a mandatory arms embargo on South Africa. This was an historic step, not just in relation to the general ➤Great Powers' disapproval of the Pretoria government's policies, but also because it was the first time that the Security Council had undertaken such action against a member state under Chapter 7 of the ➤UN Charter.

Apart from the UN, international reaction to apartheid, and hence South Africa, could until 1990 be summarized as follows:

(a) The West (especially the United Kingdom and the United States): publicly to endorse opposition to apartheid, privately to engage in constructive efforts to encourage *verligte* and to preserve economic investments, always mindful of the strategic importance of the Cape and of South Africa's mineral wealth. The American policy of ➤constructive engagement was designed to preserve regional stability, to encourage reform and to maintain Western influence.

(b) The East (especially the Soviet Union and China): to encourage national ➤liberation movements, to ➤destabilize the region, to play upon the ambiguities of Western policies so as to embarrass the West, and eventually to dislodge and replace its influence in the region.

(c) The Black Neighbours or ➤front-line states (primarily Zimbabwe, Mozambique, Zambia, Angola, Tanzania): to complete the anti-colonial, anti-white revolution, while not sacrificing domestic economic development and growth. South Africa is the economic giant of the region, and all its black neighbours to some extent are economically dependent on it. Lesotho, Swaziland and Botswana have near total dependence, while Zimbabwe, Mozambique, Tanzania and Zambia have varying but significant degrees of ➤dependence. The formation of SADCC in 1980 was the culmination of this process.

(d) The ➤Commonwealth: although South Africa withdrew from the Commonwealth when the Republic was inaugurated on 31 May 1961, it had always been prominent in the world campaign against apartheid. In 1985, at their summit at Nassau in the Bahamas, it appointed the Commonwealth Group of Eminent Persons to investigate conditions inside South Africa and to seek ways of establishing there a genuine non-racial democracy. Their report of 1986 recommended among other initiatives that South Africa's major trading partners should apply economic pressures on a continuing and incremental basis in order to bring about reform. The intransigence of the UK government seriously damaged the collective impact of the Commonwealth's recommendations.

In sum, apartheid and efforts to implement and maintain it profoundly affected world politics on a number of levels in the twentieth century. The resistance to it, especially though by no means exclusively by the African National Congress (➤ANC), formed the framework of domestic and regional politics from 1948 onwards. It also affected the ➤foreign policy of South Africa both in terms of its external projection (the overall objective of successive Nationalist administrations was to ensure the states' security, status and legitimacy within the international community), and in terms of the reaction of outside states, especially neighbouring ones. From 1948 to 1989, South Africa was effectively shielded from active external ➤intervention by aligning itself with the West within the framework of ➤Cold War politics. Its shrewd manipulation of the Afrikaner adage that the 'swart gevaar' (black danger) equalled the 'rooi gevaar (red danger) plus the fact that black liberation movements were undoubtedly backed and bankrolled by Eastern bloc states, meant that conservative governments in the West, especially in Europe and the USA, regarded Pretoria as a bulwark against communist influence in southern Africa. The end of the Cold War, and the 'de-ideologization' of foreign policy that accompanied the collapse of the Soviet Empire, presented a window of opportunity to South Africa. From 1989 onwards the de Klerk administration set about the twin tasks of normalizing the Republic's relations with the outside world and seeking a mode of ➤accommodation with the ANC. During the 1989–94 period most of the offensive apartheid legislation disappeared from the statute books and by April 1994, when the first multiracial elections were held, South Africa entered its post-apartheid phase. The legacy of the apartheid years, both internally and externally, will however continue to frustrate President Mandela's Government of National Unity, particularly with regard to nation-building, domestic reconstruction and regional cooperation.

**Appeasement** Commonly used to describe the Munich settlement (1938) which effected the dismemberment of Czechoslovakia and gave Germany virtual command of Eastern Europe. The term has acquired derogatory overtones both in common parlance and historical scholarship as it supposedly symbolizes the sacrifice of principle (the sovereign ➤independence of a ➤small state) for expedience (placating a dictator and buying time). In the post-war period such was the opprobrium associated with it, especially in the United Kingdom and the United States, that it became synonymous with weakness and cowardice. It was therefore used to justify policies of uncompromising firmness and rigidity in, for example, Korea (1951), Suez (1956) and ➤Vietnam (1954–75).

However, this contemporary connotation is not reflected in traditional theories of ➤international relations, especially those associated with the realist school, where appeasement, properly conducted, is regarded as an integral part of the ➤balance of power process, the purpose of which is to maintain order and reduce the incidence of great ➤power conflict. In this connection it is akin to ➤accommodation where quarter is given to facilitate peaceful change. Even so, it is largely a matter between ➤great powers and may often involve a total disregard for the vital interests of smaller states.

**Arab–Israeli conflict** One of the most intractable conflicts in twentieth-century ➤macropolitics. The issue originated as a ➤communal conflict which then escalated to take in neighbouring ➤states and four of the permanent members of the UN ➤Security Council. The location of the dispute is the territory historically known as Palestine. The land is the focus of sanctification for the three monotheistic religions: Judaism, Christianity and ➤Islam. Politically it was loosely controlled as a part of the Ottoman Empire until the end of the First World War when a ➤League of Nations Mandate was granted to Britain to administer the territory. Under the aegis of this and in line with the Balfour Declaration of 1917, Jewish immigration into Palestine began on a scale and with a self-conscious determination never seen before. These Jews were emboldened by a nationalist, socialist ➤ideology known as ➤Zionism and they soon created communal tensions with the majority population, who were Arab peoples. Arab ➤nationalism which was of its own volition undergoing an awakening at the time came to take on an increasingly confrontational edge as the implications of Jewish immigration became clear. Early indications of Arab opposition to the idea of the Jewish state were voiced to the US funded King–Crane Commission in the 1920s. By the end of that decade the Mandate Authority was finding that the ➤implementation of the Balfour promises was increasingly plunging the territory into communal strife and disorder. At the end of the 1930s a British Royal Commission proposed that the territory be partitioned between the two communities and bifurcation in one form or another has been the basis of settlement proposals ever since.

A necessary consequence of the mandate system was that the issue of Palestine became an international one. This characteristic has continued, and indeed increased, since 1945. On the Zionist side, the United States has proved a most generous and significant supporter of the principle of a Jewish home and the actuality of a Jewish State. Although it only comprises a small minority of the American electorate, American Jewry has exercised an influence over post-1945 American foreign policy in the Middle East out of all proportion to its numbers. Working under an umbrella organization, the American–Israel Public Affairs

Committee (AIPAC), American Jewry has succeeded in establishing and maintaining a supportive framework within the American polity for pro-Israeli policies.

On the Palestinian Arab side, neighbouring Arab states, individually and collectively through the ➤Arab League has provided assistance of all types. In the process the conflict became ➤regional as well as a communal dispute. Indeed it has been noted that opposition to the Jewish state was seen as a touchstone of Arab nationalism for leaders and peoples within the area. During the Cold War years the Soviet Union maintained close diplomatic and ➤aid links with the PLO, and a number of Arab states perceived as being 'radical' (at least in the context of the conflict and in their opposition to Western influence in the region). The UN, as successor to the League, has continued to assist the internationalization tendency. The Organization has on occasions taken important policy initiatives on the issue. In 1947 a partition plan for Palestine was proposed by a UN special commission. In 1956 an emergency ➤peacekeeping force was sent to Egypt by the Organization. In 1967 and again in 1973 important declaratory resolutions were passed by the ➤security council. Resolutions 242 and 338 have been widely seen as establishing the broad parameters for ➤conflict resolution in that they have established certain principles which are ineluctable. The UN has consistently favoured a policy of establishing an international ➤regime for Jerusalem owing its spiritual significance for the three Faiths.

➤*De facto* partition of Palestine took place in 1948 with the establishment of the State of Israel. The majority of the old mandate territory came under the control of the new State; however, the state of Transjordan made significant gains on the West Bank of the river. With these developments a new dimension was added to the problem when the majority of the Arab inhabitants of Palestine became ➤refugees. The cause of the refugee problem has become one of the issues of conflict since 1948. Certainly, the invasion of the Arab League armies, immediately independence was declared, served to exacerbate a deteriorating communal situation. Conversely, the protagonists who served to benefit from an Arab exodus, at least territorially, were the Zionist forces. The Arab refugees from Palestine were settled in the neighbouring Arab states. In many instances little attempt was made to integrate them with the indigenous population. As a result, the Palestinians became susceptible to two political consequences in the years after 1948. First, there was a natural carry-over of the inter-War nationalism into the post-1948 situation. This led in time to the establishment of a number of nationalist organizations which collectively came under the umbrella of the PLO. Second, the politicization of the refugee question and the presence of large numbers of these people in other Arab lands spilled over into the domestic politics of the host states. This was very apparent during the Lebanese civil war which commenced in the mid-1970s.

Violence between the State of Israel and its neighbours has fitted into two types. First, short, highly intense outbreaks of ➤conventional warfare usually characterized by mobility and rapidly changing fortunes. The wars of 1956, 1967 and 1973 fit into this pattern; second, the War of Independence in 1948, the War of Attrition 1970–73 and the Israeli ➤interventions in the Lebanese ➤civil war since 1978. Here the characteristics of the warfare have been more protracted and in the case of the Lebanon costly, controversial and indecisive. Moreover, the effect of this cycle of violence has left Israel currently in possession of Arab territories on the West Bank and the Golan Heights. Israel has also incorporated the city of Jerusalem into its state structure notwithstanding UN policy to the contrary.

Given the nature and intensity of the conflict, third party mediation attempts have been regularly made. Probably the first concentrated attempt at settlement was made during the mandate period when the British set up the Peel Royal Commission. With the establishment of the Israeli state, and the circle of violence referred to above, mediation has often taken the form of short-term palliatives – cease-fire agreements, ➤truce supervision, exchange of prisoners and so on. A long-term solution has been more difficult to find. Two principal mediators have been the UN and the United States. The former was initially favoured for its impartiality and ability to reflect a more global perceptive. Some would argue that the developments of late in the Organization have shown it to be partial to the Arab position. Conversely the United States, as Israel's staunchest ally, is seen as being able to exert leverage on that state.

The most intractable problem remains the ➤issue area of Palestinian Arabism. The acceptance by the PLO in 1988 of the 'two-state' solution dramatically moved the dispute towards putative resolution because it signalled the abandonment of a unitary state, power-sharing approach which had been its favoured position since the Peel Commission days. Israeli leaders and public have evinced great difficulty in accepting the full implications of Palestinian statehood as an appropriate ➤goal throughout the period. This scepticism continues at the time of writing. Israeli politics has moved towards the right in the last twenty years and the Likud leadership which has consequentially enjoyed long periods in the office is probably more ➤ideologically inhibited than Labour about accepting the principle of a Palestinian state.

Developments in the global system during the decade of the 1990s have profoundly influenced the framework in which this conflict can be seen to operate. The ➤Persian Gulf War proved to be a diplomatic disaster for the PLO. The unequivocal support for Saddam's Iraq placed them in a near ➤pariah status amongst the more conservative Arab regimes. Palestinians working in the Gulf states have been persecuted, whilst Arab states have withdrawn or restricted financial support for the PLO. The end of the Cold War and the collapse of the Soviet Union has left the radical Arabs bereft of the kind of international support they had previously enjoyed. The growth of Islamic fundamentalism threatens to insert into any putative peace process a wild card of unknown complexity. Operating ➤transnationally, factions such as Hamas and Islamic Jihad are by definition autonomous actors.

The seismic movements in the system referred to above enabled the USA to emerge centre stage as the pre-eminent broker of a new round of negotiations. Beginning with the convening of the Madrid Conference in 1991, a momentum has been established towards substantive negotiations which continues up to this writing. The regaining of power by Labour in June 1992 in the Israeli election and the initiation of secret negotiations in Norway in January 1993 can, in retrospect, be seen as landmark developments. Following in effect a two-track approach public and private diplomacy between Israel, and various Palestinian groups, Jordan and Syria have been taking place on a continuous basis since the end of the Persian Gulf War. In September 1993 the State of Israel and the PLO signed a Declaration of Principles in Washington which was, notwithstanding the ➤propaganda effort of the world's media, an agreement to mutually recognize each other and to begin substantive discussions.

As of this writing there are four substantive issues between the State of Israel and the PLO which require resolution: agreement must be reached on the territorial scope of the territory to be regarded as Palestinian, agreement must be reached on the degree of autonomy for this territory, agreement must be reached on the status of Jerusalem, agreement must be reached on the rights of the Palestinian Diaspora and their status in the future. Concurrently a time frame for the ➤implementation of any or all of these understandings must be established.

Whether 1993 proves to be a landmark year remains to be seen. It is prudent to suppose that as the parties approach the kernel of this most intractable of disputes both will see the stakes increasing. The Arab–Israeli conflict is crucially balanced between amity and enmity. Whether the window of opportunity presented by the developments in the early 1990s will be entered is still not certain. ➤➤Arab League; Camp David accords; Islam

**Arab League** Properly known as the League of Arab States. This is a regional ➤international governmental organization (IGO). As the name implies, it is confined to the Arab states of North Africa and the Middle East. The formation of the League was announced at a meeting of foreign ministers at Alexandria in September 1944. Formal agreement was reached in March 1945 between Egypt, Iraq, Transjordan (now Jordan), Lebanon, Saudi Arabia, Syria and Yemen. At the time of writing there are twenty-one member states of the League. In addition to the founders the following states are fully represented: Algeria, Bahrain, Djibouti, Kuwait, Libya, Mauritania, Morocco, Oman, Palestine, Qatar, Somalia, Sudan, Tunisia, United Arab Emirates. The conclusion of the ➤Camp David accords in 1979 and the signing of a separate peace ➤treaty with Israel led to the suspension of Egyptian membership. The ➤status quo ante was restored in May 1989 and the headquarters were moved back from Tunis to Cairo.

The League is a consultative body with no pretensions towards ➤supranationalism, notwithstanding the ideological influences of Arab ➤nationalism which helped its foundation. Each member state is represented on the Council, while day-to-day business is handled by a secretariat headed by a ➤Secretary-General. Although the League is a multi-purpose organization, it is best known as the instrument for collaboration and coordination of policy on the ➤Arab–Israeli conflict. Opposition to the idea of the state of Israel was often held to be the touchstone of Arabism. However, mainstream Arab sentiment is somewhat more permissive on Israel's right to exist, providing the ➤issue area of the Palestinians is addressed at the same time.

The ➤Gulf War badly divided the Arab states between one another and in some cases divided ➤leaderships from mass ➤public opinion. The intrusion of the United States of America into what was seen by some as an inter-Arab ➤conflict has without doubt damaged self-confidence and regional susceptibilities. Support for the American-led coalition was strongest in Saudi Arabia, Egypt and Syria and it seems likely that, in the short term at least, these three countries – the wealthiest, the most populated and the most nationalistic of Arab states – will attempt a triumvirate of ➤influence in the area.

**Arbitration** A method of ➤conflict settlement involving third-party ➤intervention. Arbitration is a favoured method of settlement in domestic labour-management conflicts, at least in the advanced industrial countries (➤AICs). The basis of an arbitration award is that the parties to the conflict agree to submit their differences to the third party to make a binding decision to settle the dispute. The arbitrator may apply known rules, precedents and laws in seeking a settlement and the arbitration award may be reinforced by sanctions to secure compliance. It is possible, and desirable, for the parties to agree to these rules, at least implicitly, in advance. This means that existing rules and practices can be abandoned in favour of any agreed-upon set of principles. Thus arbitration is more flexible than ➤adjudication because the latter process tends to rigorously eschew innovation and to reflect a ➤status quo frame of reference.

In ➤international relations arbitration as a form of settlement has always had powerful advocates but, apart from a short period in the late nineteenth and early twentieth centuries, it has been little used. Anglo-American ➤diplomacy provides the best examples in the modern world. The Jay ➤Treaty of 1794 inaugurated arbitration as a method of settlement between the two ➤states. The most famous case is that of the Alabama Arbitration of 1872. Scholars are generally agreed that this settlement in favour of the United States was prompted by the desire of both parties to improve their relations rather than by any philosophical commitment to the arbitration process.

Many ➤idealists regarded the development of arbitration as essential if ➤war was to be eradicated from international relations. The two ➤Hague Peace

Conferences (1899 and 1907) failed to achieve agreement on compulsory arbitration but succeeded in creating the Permanent Court of Arbitration. This was, in point of fact, neither permanent nor a court. It was a list of persons from which the parties to a conflict could select a name.

Arbitration has not had the success or impact that the nineteenth and twentieth century idealist believed. Essentially the consensus that is required to make arbitration work has been absent. Moreover, although it is marginally more flexible than adjudication, arbitration appears not to be favoured in the present system as a means of settlement. The growth of international regional institutions in the contemporary system must be accounted a major force in reducing the potential for arbitration as a third party mode.

**Armistice** The cessation or suspension of hostilities pending a ➤peace settlement. It is not a peace ➤treaty and as such does not legally terminate the state of ➤war, but clearly affords an opportunity to do so. It is ➤bilateral, not ➤unilateral, and can be distinguished from a ➤truce by the fact that the latter usually refers to a temporary and specific declaration by belligerents with or without confirmation by the highest authorities. Sometimes, when a peace treaty proves impossible because of the intractable nature of the conflict, an armistice becomes ➤*de facto* the ➤status quo. This was the case with the 1949 armistice agreements between Israel and the Arabs until the ➤Camp David accords.

**Arms control** The exercise of restraint in the acquisition, deployment and use of military ➤capabilities. Furthermore, the term also covers any measure that enables ➤actors to conduct themselves in a more restrained way, for example by developing techniques of ➤crisis management. One of the most important underlying assumptions of arms control is that weapons are a continuing and persistent feature of ➤international relations and that ➤deterrence policies are a valuable and positive means of coercive ➤diplomacy. Thus ideologically the arms control theorists differ, in principle, from the advocates of ➤disarmament. While the latter may eventually look to a world without weapons, or at least a world where weapons and the threat of the use of force are substantially removed, the arms controller is quite willing to work with the existing structure. Both approaches are agreed, however, that an uncontrolled ➤arms race will upset the system to the detriment of all.

During the ➤Cold War era in world politics, arms control was essentially seen as a policy instrument which would enhance the stability of the ➤bipolar relationship between the ➤superpowers. In the post-Cold War world the priorities of restraint remain as before but the ➤actors in need of restraint and the ➤issue areas wherein this takes place have changed. At the top of most arms control agendas is the question of ➤non-proliferation and the consequential issue of regime creation and maintenance for the so-called ABC ➤weapons. With the demise of the Soviet Union, the United States is in a position of great ➤structural power in this ➤security regime.

**Arms race** Literally a competitive building-up of armaments by at least two
►actors in ►conflict. The basic process in the arms race is the ►action–reaction
pattern. In ►cybernetics the arms race is an example of positive ►feedback.
Such races have often preceded wars and outbreaks of violence. The outbreak
of the First World War was preceded by a naval race between the United
Kingdom and Imperial Germany. Sometimes, in persistent, chronic periods of
►crises an arms race will be a more or less continuous feature. The ►Arab–Israeli
conflict is an example of this.

Arms races can appear to generate a dynamic of their own, particularly in a
system experiencing rapid technological innovation. The race between the
►superpowers since 1945 has had a tendency to create this kind of dynamic.
When this happens other tendencies take over and the dynamic is no longer
simply the arms levels of the perceived opponents. Vested interests, in particular
the military and industrial establishments, find that the continuation of a high
level of arms expenditure and the prerequisite research is to their advantage.
In such circumstances the pure model of the arms race must be modified to
take account of these other factors.

The relationship between the pure type of arms race and war is tentative.
An arms race is neither a necessary nor sufficient condition for the outbreak of
war. Moreover theories which borrow heavily from ideas about ►deterrence
usually assume that a certain level of arms is necessary to prevent war. In these
formulations it is the balance between the two sides that is crucial rather than
the absolute level of arms. According to this view it is imbalance in the arms
race that is more likely to cause a breakdown of the system into war. This
process is closely related to the concept of the ►balance of power.

It should be noted that two separate arms races can interact, as, for example,
the Arab-Israeli conflict and the superpowers referred to above.

**Arms sales/trade** The ability of man as a tool-maker has been recognized
by students of the past, including the primeval past. This ability has, similarly,
been used to make weapons. Once an economic system evinces a division of
labour, specialist manufacture becomes possible. In this way production of
weapons, their sale and the system known as trade has developed. The development of industrialized modes of production, first in Europe, has meant that
much more is at stake in the creation, maintenance and growth of the arms
►trade. The market for arms is an important source of wealth creation for a
small number of states. In the contemporary system the major inputs into the
arms trade have come from the USA, Russia (and the former Soviet Union)
China, France and the UK – the ►P5 members of the ►Security Council.
There is some evidence that this picture is currently undergoing change. A
number of ►Third World states can be identified as emerging arms traders and
the oligarchy that controlled the trade is now under threat. All regions of the
Third World show evidence of burgeoning arms manufacture: Argentina and

Brazil, South Africa, Israel, and India are perhaps the principal exemplars.

The ➤Persian Gulf War brought to the fore this whole issue area. During the decade of the 1980s the Iraqi regime engaged in an orgy of arms acquisition as Timmerman (1991) has shown. Although attention has been directed at the Iraqi ➤CBW and ➤nuclear weapons proclivities, at the level of ➤conventional weapons the build-up was inexorable and far more operationally significant. In the wake of the conclusion of the war the P5 ➤states sought through the London Guidelines of October 1991 to cap and control the flow of arms into countries and regions. Specifically agreement was reached to avoid sales into areas of ongoing violence and to avoid sales which might significantly upset an existing regional ➤power balance (SIPRI 1992). Subsequently the parties were unable to ➤implement this putative code of conduct and all of the P5 – particularly the United States – continue to sell some of their most sophisticated equipment into areas of great political instability.

A major problem in effecting more control over these transfers is the issue of visibility or 'transparency' of sales. The ➤League of Nations attempted to publicize transfers by compiling a register of statistics. In December 1991 the ➤General Assembly of the United Nations also voted to establish a register. The ➤peace movement and ➤peace research INGOs like SIPRI have a distinguished record of support for transparency through their own work. The fact remains that there are strong incentives amongst the major suppliers to choke off and obfuscate publicity. Arms sales can be an important source of income for particular industries/localities amongst the supplier states and political ➤elites may be reluctant to sacrifice these interests on the altar of greater international cooperation.

**ASEAN** Association of South East Asian Nations. This was formed in 1967 following the Bangkok Declaration of 8 August by the foreign ministers of Indonesia, Malaysia, Philippines, Singapore and Thailand. Brunei joined in 1984 and Vietnam in 1995. Papua New Guinea has observer status. The original agreements were strengthened and extended at the Bali summit of February 1976. A secretariat was established and agreement was reached on the outline of a ➤trade ➤bloc. Internally, ASEAN covers a spectrum of economies which have one thing in common – actual and potential economic dynamism. The whole ➤Pacific Basin has witnessed the most impressive economic growth rates globally over the last two decades, within this ➤region South East Asia has shown the greatest self-awareness of the need for cooperation and coordination of policy in both the military-security and wealth-welfare contexts. Structurally China and Japan threaten to dominate the sub-region in both these key ➤issue areas. The ASEAN states have sought to balance against this putative domination by involving the entire Pacific basin and outside parties such as the ➤European Union and the United States in regional diplomacy. The ending of the ➤Cold War, the demise of the Soviet Union and what many see as the hesitancy within the USA to exercise ➤leadership might be seen as exacerbating these needs. 1993 witnessed two key developments that were headed by ASEAN: the formation of the ASEAN Regional Forum, which linked the ASEAN states with eleven Pacific Basin countries plus the EU, and the institutionalization of Asia–Pacific Economic Cooperation (often referred to as APEC) with the establishment of a Secretariat in Singapore.

Politically and diplomatically ASEAN began to develop a distinctive regional role with the ending of the Vietnam War in 1975. This coordination and cooperation has continued apace. The need for balancer and facilitator at both the sub-regional and regional levels has been argued above. ASEAN sits astride one of the growth triangles in that area: Malaysia-Indonesia-Singapore. It also sits astride one of the key strategic choke points: the South China Sea. Its membership could well be expanded in the medium term by the admission of further Indo-Chinese states and Myanmar. ASEAN is redolent of the growing importance of Regional actors in the present and future structure and processes of ➤international relations.

**Asian Tigers** A colloquialism for a group of Asian economies which have experienced dynamic economic growth patterns in their recent past and have come to be regarded as standard bearers for ➤economic liberalism and market economics. Five economies are normally understood to be in this categorization: Hong Kong, Japan, South Korea, Singapore and Taiwan. Putative Tigers – popularly called 'cubs' – are thought to include Indonesia, Malaysia and Thailand. China – which after 1997 will include Hong Kong – might be described figuratively as the 'Asian Dragon'. ➤Big emerging markets (BEMs); East Asian crisis; NICs

**Association** General meaning is the formation of a society of sorts, and is often used in IR to distinguish between the (loose) ties between ➤states and the (firm) ties between individuals within the state. The phrase 'association of states' is sufficiently anaemic to enable the writer to avoid complications inherent in the phrase ➤international society. More specifically, in world politics the term has carried ➤imperial or ➤colonial overtones, especially in France. The principle of association was devised by colonial administrators and theorists in Paris (1910) to meet the practical problems created by the paradox of French imperialism existing side by side with French democratic republicanism. The French, unlike the more pragmatic British, have always felt uneasy about colonial possessions. As Europe's foremost democratic republic created out of a passion for universal liberty, equality and fraternity, it was clearly morally wrong to regard colonies as subordinate entities. Logically, overseas possessions, if they exist at all, must be fully assimilated into metropolitan France. As a practical expedient, though, assimilation gave way to association (which in effect meant subordinate status) and this attempted compromise became the orthodoxy practised by and preached to French colonial administration in the *école coloniale* in Paris until the Second World War.

In the United Kingdom, the concept of 'associated status' was used in 1967 specifically to cater for former colonies which desired limited ➤independence from the United Kingdom but were economically unable or unwilling to stand alone. ➤➤*Francophonie*

**Assured destruction** A term used in nuclear strategy. It has two meanings. As a ➤capability it refers to the technical potential to launch attacks against an adversary which lead to large-scale destruction of people and property. Before the advent of ➤air power and ➤nuclear weapons such destruction was only possible via a land invasion. Such constraints no longer operate. The capability required to achieve assured destruction is normally referred to as a ➤second strike capability.

As a policy it is an example of what is termed counter-city targeting. It is particularly associated with the conduct of US defence policy in the 1960s and with the former Secretary of Defense Robert McNamara. The United States has moved steadily away from assured destruction as a policy since the 1970s, preferring to look for allegedly greater flexibility under various ➤counterforce options. ➤➤MAD

**Asylum** Literally a sanctuary or place of refuge. It refers to a quasi-legal process where one ➤state grants protection to a national or nationals of another. In ➤international law it can be challenged by request for ➤extradition. Indeed, it is sometimes said that asylum ends where extradition begins, but in the absence of a specific ➤treaty there is no legal duty to extradite. Rights of asylum belong to states not to individuals, although Article 14 of the Universal Declaration of ➤Human Rights (1948) does give individuals a right of political asylum. But as the Declaration took the form of a resolution of the ➤General Assembly, it is not legally (though it may be morally) binding on states.

**Atlantic Alliance** ➤NATO

**Atlantic Charter** Often regarded as the genesis of the ➤UN. In fact it was a ➤bilateral declaration of ➤war aims issued in 1941 by F. D. Roosevelt and Winston Churchill on board a warship in mid-Atlantic. The keynote of the Charter was the notion of 'The Four Freedoms' (freedom from fear and want, freedom of speech and religion) which to them was the basis of the Allied cause. Other principles associated with it are: ➤self-determination, freely elected government, economic collaboration, freedom of the seas, renunciation of the use of ➤force in disputes and the post-war establishment of a permanent system of global security. These, of course, were in direct contrast to the ➤ideology of the ➤Axis powers.

**Atom bomb** Using a process known as fission it is possible to produce

37

explosive devices which have much greater power than ►conventional methods. Uranium 235, a natural mineral, is highly unstable and it is possible to produce a chain reaction using this mineral whereby all the fissionable material is affected at once. It is this chain reaction which generates the explosive power of the uranium bomb. Uranium 235 is also used to produce ►plutonium 239. Both these substances can be used to produce bombs.

The ability to produce explosive devices using a controlled chain reaction was known to physicists before the outbreak of the Second World War. The outbreak of the ►war and the knowledge that Nazi Germany could develop a bomb added a new dimension to research. In 1941 the United States began work on the ►Manhattan Project to build, test and if necessary use an atomic bomb in the context of the war. No weapons were produced in time for use or demonstration against Germany but, controversially, two bombs were dropped on Japanese cities. Uranium was used in the bomb dropped upon ►Hiroshima and plutonium in the bomb dropped on ►Nagasaki.

The fission process is also used for civilian purposes in the generation of electricity. Here, of course, the process is slowed down and controlled. The spread of nuclear reactors and the production thereby of plutonium has meant that ►proliferation of ►nuclear weapons is technically hard to control. In 1974 India tested an atomic bomb produced by material diverted from a civilian energy programme.

**Attentive public** A concept used in ►public opinion analysis. It refers to that proportion of the people in mass society who hold articulate, informed and coherent attitudes about public policy issues. It excludes, at the top, those who actually make, or participate in making, policy. On the other hand, it excludes those at the bottom, the mass public, who do not hold consistent and coherent views about policy. The concept lacks precision. However, a rough and ready idea can be obtained of the size of the attentive public in advanced industrial countries (►AICs) by quantifying the readership of what is known as the 'quality' press (e.g. the London *Times*, the *New York Times*, *Die Welt*, *Le Monde*, etc). This is only approximate because sales and readership do not necessarily coincide. The size of the attentive public also varies as between domestic and ►foreign policy issues. In general, on the latter membership is smaller.

The idea of the attentive public is particularly crucial to the ►pluralist approach to ►international relations. Writers in this mode argue that interest groups and political parties have an important influence upon ►policy-making. Although these organizations do not actually or formally take the decisions they do contribute to the milieu in which ►decision-making occurs. They also serve as reservoirs from which the political leadership is recruited. It is through these channels that the mass public is often mobilized and made more aware of international issues. The attentive public plays an important linkage function in this pyramid.

**Attrition** Literally means 'wearing out'. It usually refers to the strategy adopted by the Allies in the First World➤War who turned from an initial policy of annihilation (utter and rapid destruction of the enemy's forces) to one of attrition. Wars of attrition are usually long-drawn-out affairs, and place the entire range of the ➤state's resources at the disposal of the military. The most recent example of a war of attrition is the Iran–Iraq war of 1980–89, which displayed all the features referred to above almost to the point of total exhaustion on both sides.

**Autarky** Not to be confused with 'autarchy' (self-rule), autarky is the absence of ➤trade and therefore self-sufficiency. The term is most often used in international economics. However, because of the close relationship between economics and politics in the world system, it has relevance to both. Complete autarky is impossible. From the earliest times human communities have exchanged goods and services. As social systems have become more complex, and in particular as economic systems have experienced industrialization, the costs of autarky have become more manifest. Classical nineteenth-century economic ➤liberalism, heavily influenced by the theories of Ricardo, rejected autarky as inefficient and argued for the absolute and comparative advantages of international trade. As these theories became accepted a ➤regime based on these ideas became established. International payments were handled through a ➤gold standard while London became the commercial conduit for the system. Scholars would now describe this nineteenth-century system as one of ➤interdependence. The events of the early decades of the twentieth century, in particular the First World War and the rise of ➤fascism and ➤communism destroyed this system. The United Kingdom was no longer able to function as the pivot of the system. In Europe political ➤leaderships came to ➤power determined to use economic relations as an instrument of policy. As a result a new drive to increase autarky was evident in Germany and the Soviet Union. In Asia, Japan rejected autarky for a policy known as co-prosperity. The attempts by Anglo–American diplomats to restore a form of ➤liberalism at ➤Bretton Woods checked the drift away from free trade liberalism for a time. Recently developments in the world system have suggested moves back towards greater self-sufficiency where possible. The ➤EU has instituted an agricultural policy which has created a largely self-sufficient market within its member ➤states. As suggested above, pure autarky is an ideal type against which the policies of international ➤actors can be measured. ➤➤Mercantilism

**Authority** Person or institution which legitimizes acts or commands; as such it must be differentiated from ➤power which indicates capacity rather than right. It is the lack of a common and accepted authority which is said to distinguish international from domestic politics and law. Consequently, some writers argue that because of its absence ➤international law is not law properly so-called, and ➤international politics is politics only by courtesy of name. ➤idealists in international thought frequently argue, pursuing the ➤domestic analogy, that the solution to continuing and continual international conflict is the creation of a universal authority to regulate relations, establish a properly constituted legal order and to settle disputes. The ➤League of Nations and the UN are sometimes (though wrongly) seen as early prototypes. Other theorists argue that the absence of universal authority, particularly since the decline of the Holy Roman Empire, is a source of strength, not weakness, in ➤international relations since it reinforces the arguments for the ➤sovereignty, liberty and ➤independence of the ➤state.

**Autonomy** Literal meaning is self-government. As such the term is associated with the idea of sovereignty and ➤independence. In traditional international relations all states were assumed to be autonomous, that is, not subject to external authority whether this was spiritual (e.g.: the Church) or temporal (e.g: the Holy Roman Empire). The Treaties of Westphalia, 1648, are supposed to mark the beginning of the autonomy of the state and hence the anarchic nature of the international system.

Recent scholarship has used the concept of autonomy to cast doubt on the traditional linkage between autonomy and the state. Autonomy is now regarded, particularly by ➤pluralist writers, as a matter of degree rather than an absolute. Thus it is now no longer used as a substitute for sovereignty but as an alternative criterion. ➤Actors in ➤world politics are now held to exercise relative autonomy and state and non-state actors can be compared on this basis. Pluralism fully expects these comparisons to show that on occasions the state does not come out very well.

Writers on ➤ethnic nationalism and ➤communal conflict have also taken up the concept of autonomy of late. The argument begins with the observation that few if any states are autonomous in the true sense, rather all display centrifugal tendencies, majority/minority dichotomies (sometimes indeed minority/minority/minority . . . tendencies). These groups within states are held to be pursuing autonomy as a ➤goal and in the process they are eroding the unity of the state. The end result of this process may clearly be the creation of more states as demands for autonomy succeed in breaking up existing ones. In this sense the classical view of autonomy is to some extent salvaged from the wreck of the state structure.

**Axis** Refers specifically to the German–Italian pact of 1936 in which both ➤states pledged to oppose republicanism in Spain and ➤communism in general. It was underlined by the mutual defence ➤treaty signed in 1939 ('Pact of Steel') and later extended to include Japan (1940). It has ➤geopolitical and strategic overtones (the Berlin–Rome–Tokyo axis) and its use rather than the more conventional word ➤alliance was intended to signify a pivotal centre in ➤world politics around which other states might cluster. It was first used in this connection by Mussolini to illustrate the common Nazi–➤fascist approach to ➤international politics.

# B

**Bacteriological weapons** ►chemical and biological warfare (CBW)

**Balance of payments** A term used in international economics. It is used to refer to balance of all economic transactions between a ►state and the rest of the system. The main elements are visible ►trade, investment and transactions between the monetary authorities within the state and those in the rest of the system, for example the ►IMF. Equilibrium in the balance of payments literally means that credits plus debits are at zero. This is a normative rather than an empirical statement and thus states may find themselves in the short-term in disequilibrium. Long-term or fundamental disequilibrium is much more serious. States with a continual balance of payments surplus, such as Japan, and those in constant deficit, such as many ►Third World non-oil producers will come under pressure from other ►actors to take remedial measures. The rise in oil prices in the 1970s placed many states in fundamental disequilibrium and this issue was discussed in such publications as the ►Brandt Reports. The United States of America's balance of payments crisis of the 1980s inspired speculation about ►declinism in the US ►leadership position in world politics. There is clearly a significant overlap area between politics and economics in the ►international system and the repercussions of the balance of payments position of many states is regarded as crucial for the continued working of a viable system of trade and payments.

**Balance of power** A pervasive and indispensable concept which is part of the stock-in-trade of both students and practitioners of ►diplomacy. Indeed, it is regarded by some scholars as the nearest thing we have to a political theory of ►international relations. However, its meaning is by no means clear and it is open to a number of different interpretations. Martin Wight, for example, distinguishes nine different meanings of the term:

1  An even distribution of ►power.
2  The principle that power should be evenly distributed.
3  The existing distribution of power. Hence, any possible distribution of power.
4  The principle of equal aggrandizement of the ►great powers at the expense of the weak.
5  The principle that one side ought to have a margin of strength in order to avert the danger of power becoming unevenly distributed.

6 (When governed by the verb 'to hold') A special role in maintaining an even distribution of power.
7 (When governed by the verb 'to hold') A special advantage in the existing distribution of power.
8 Predominance.
9 An inherent tendency of ➤international politics to produce an even distribution of power.

Given this wide variety of meaning, it is helpful to distinguish between balance of power as a policy (a deliberate attempt to prevent predominance) and as a system of international politics (where the pattern of interaction between ➤states tends to limit or curb the quest for ➤hegemony and results in general equilibrium). British ➤foreign policy in relation to Europe from the sixteenth century to the early twentieth century is an example of the former, while the European ➤state-system itself, from 1648 to 1789 and from 1815 to 1914, is an example of the latter. The break in this chronological sequence is the period of the rise of French radicalism and its refusal to be bound by notions of balance. In 1815 France, after a period of Napoleonic expansion, was restored to her former territorial limits and the balancing system was institutionalized. The Congress of Vienna and the ➤Concert system it spawned throughout the nineteenth century represents the most articulate and self-conscious expression of balance in international history. Thus the most widely accepted meaning of the term is where it refers to the process whereby no one state, or group of states, gains predominance so that in Vattel's words 'it can lay down the law to others'. It is associated particularly with ➤independence, its main function being to preserve intact the multiplicity of states and to oppose empire in particular, and change in general. Order and stability are prized values rather than considerations of justice or fair play.

*History*
The idea of balance is inseparable from the mechanics of international politics and the practice was familiar to the ancient Greeks. ➤Thucydides' *History of the Peloponnesian War*, although not specifically acknowledging the concept, is widely regarded as a classic account of its occurrence, albeit in ➤bipolar form, revolving around the relationship between Athens and Sparta in the fifth century BC. However, although the process undoubtedly occurred in the ancient world (in Europe, in China and in India) it was not until the Renaissance that it was self-consciously recognized as one of the basic formulas of political life. The Italian ➤city-state system of the fourteenth and fifteenth centuries, which besides being fairly self-contained had a number of distinct and independent locations of power (Florence, Milan, Naples, Venice and the Vatican), was a lively arena of diplomatic forces where the principle was able to develop. Surprisingly, it was not ➤Machiavelli who first elaborated the idea (despite his obsessive concern with ➤power politics), but his contemporary, Guicciardini, in *History of Italy*

(1537). This is generally regarded as the first systematic analytical treatment of the theme. The first explicit reference to it in ►treaty form was in the Treaty of Utrecht (1713), where the idea of maintaining the balance of power was regarded as essential for the peace of Europe.

Balance of power both as policy and system is inseparable from the diplomatic history of the modern world and a plausible account of international politics up until 1914 can be given in terms of it. The ►League of Nations was a specific attempt to replace it: the principle of ►collective security which was at the heart of the organization was designed to obviate the need for balance. Many realists argue that its absence in the inter-war period resulted directly in the Second World War. Since 1945 the international political system is not so readily explained in terms of the concept and notions of bipolarity and ►multi-polarity have replaced it. However, echoes of it are still common in the language of diplomacy, especially ►balance of terror. Most scholars would agree that changes in the character of the basic ►actors in ►world politics (especially the growth of non-state actors) has led to a general disregard of the concept as an explanatory device. It is now more often used as a journalistic metaphor rather than as a theory of international behaviour.

### Theoretical implications

Balance of power, according to Hedley Bull, has fulfilled three positive functions in the modern ►state-system:

1 It has prevented the system from being transformed by conquest into a universal empire.
2 Local balances of power have served to protect the ►independence of states in particular areas from absorption by a preponderant power.
3 It has provided the conditions in which other institutions on which the international order depends might develop, e.g. diplomacy, ►war, ►international law, ►great power management.

Bull's analysis is perceptive but it should be noted that in relation to the first function, empire and balance have existed side by side in state policy and although the whole system was not transformed into a universal empire, parts of it were. Thus European ►imperialism took place during the same period that balance of power was the orthodox power management technique. In relation to the second function, some states have lost their independence as a result of it, e.g. the partition of Poland in the eighteenth century and Czecho-slovakia in 1939. With regard to the third function, although it has provided the conditions for mitigating general ►anarchy, war is a central feature of the system, its function being either to restore the balance or to rearrange it. Thus ►action–reaction, challenge–response, ►revisionist/►status quo, dissatisfied/satisfied, are key ideas associated with the operation of the system. It clearly presupposes some shared beliefs among the participants, especially concerning the nature, role and ►legitimacy of the state, yet the system is inherently unstable. A simple balance involving two states (a bipolar system) is likely to be more unstable than a complex balance (a multipolar system). This is because a sudden technological change which dramatically increases the power of one of the poles (e.g. the success of the Soviet Sputnik in 1957 and its perception in the United States) can, unless immediately corrected, destroy the equilibrium. Multipolar systems, because of the possibility of shifting combinations, can more readily cope with these occurrences. Indeed, flexibility of alignment and diplomatic ►mobility are important characteristics; under such a system states must be able to change sides regardless of ideological affinity (the Nazi-Soviet pact of 1939 is a classic example). The corollary is also true; states must be willing to abandon an erstwhile ally when conditions change. A further point to note is that the system, because it involves constant calculation of power and interest, is likely to produce an international hierarchy where states are categorized into at least three divisions: ►great powers, ►middle powers and ►small powers. ►Equality therefore exists only in a formal legal sense. All states are equal, but some are more equal than others. The balance of power era has been described as the golden age of diplomacy and it is not difficult to see why. Although war is essential to it, the wars that did occur tended to be fought with limited means for limited ends. The delinquent state which had upset the balance was allowed to re-enter the system and replay the game (e.g. France after defeat in the Napoleonic Wars, 1815). It was premised on a recognition of common interests and it permitted the development of international law on the basis of ►reciprocity – one of its most important ground-rules being non-interference in the domestic affairs of other states. Obviously, it was bound up with the conditions that created it, and in the second half of the twentieth century (despite attempts by neo-realists to prove otherwise) these conditions have all but disappeared. But whatever else might be said of it, balance of power as a method of ►conflict management was the first, and some would say, the most sophisticated, attempt to provide a practical political solution to the problem of coexistence in a decentralized international system, so much so that it became synonymous with the very idea of international relations. ►►Collective security; realism

**Balance of terror** The term refers to a situation where two ►actors can credibly threaten each other with destruction. This ►capability need not be total but should certainly be unacceptable to the parties concerned. Moreover, for the balance to be stable neither side should be able to avoid the consequences of destruction by, for example, striking first and without warning. The situation described as a balance of terror would normally be understood to operate between states and during the ►Cold War period it was taken to refer specifically to the relationship of nuclear ►deterrence between the United States and the former Soviet Union. However to the extent that terror is a state of mind, any punishment threat can induce such an outcome. Thus in principle a balance of terror might be held to exist between non-state actors such as ►terrorist groups. Schelling has argued that the balance of terror is simply a modern version of an old idea, 'the exchange of hostages'. In terms of its etymology the balance of terror is clearly derived from the balance of power.

**Balkanization** Term used by historians and diplomats to describe the deliberate fragmentation of a ►region into a number of independent or quasi-independent, mutually hostile centres of ►power; the purpose being the prevention of a unified, concentrated threat to the imposer. In this sense, a variant of the old 'divide and rule' ►colonial maxim. Originally used to describe late nineteenth-century Russian policy towards the Balkan peninsula states – Albania, Bulgaria, Greece, Romania and Yugoslavia (and its successor states). These states were once part of the Ottoman Empire and the term 'Balkan' is derived from the Turkish word for 'forested mountain'. After the break-up of ►Yugoslavia between 1992 and 1996, the term has taken on more sinister connotations. In particular, it is now linked in the public mind with ►genocide and ►ethnic cleansing.

**Bandung Conference** Held at Bandung (Indonesia) in April 1955. This conference is generally regarded as the first demonstration of the growing diplomatic significance of the ►Third World. The conference grew out of the Columbo Conference of 1954. The majority of the twenty-nine participants at Bandung were Asian states. Bandung provided a platform for leaders such as Nehru (India) and Sukarno (Indonesia) to give voice to the new ►diplomacy of positive ►neutralism or ►non-alignment. It also enabled the new revolutionary leaders in states such as China and Egypt to associate themselves with these ideas. The Bandung states were particularly reacting against the perception that the United States was following a policy of extending the ►Cold War ►alliances into the area, the establishment of the South East Asia Treaty Organization (SEATO) in 1954 being the best example.

The Bandung Conference restated the five principles of peaceful coexistence first set out in the Sino-Indian agreement on Tibet in 1954. These principles were (a) mutual respect for each other's territorial integrity and ►sovereignty; (b) non-aggression; (c) non-interference in each other's internal affairs; (d) ►equality and mutual benefits and (e) peaceful coexistence.

The spirit of cooperation among these non-aligned states developed rapidly throughout the rest of the decade. With the growing independence of the African continent and the emergence of Tito's Yugoslavia as a new influence, the movement became more genuinely global. By the time of the Belgrade conference the non-aligned movement had become a significant trend in ►world politics.

**Bank for International Settlements** This institution is the central bankers' bank. It functions to assist the financial institutions of its member ➤states to iron out short-term fluctuations in their currency positions. These operations are conducted through the central banks of the member states. Members are also enabled to resist speculative attacks upon their currencies. The BIS has its central office in Switzerland and its members include most European states plus the USA, Canada, Japan, Australia and South Africa.

The bank originated in the 1930s in the wake of the Young Plan on German ➤reparations. It was then hoped that it might help to assist in the development of international ➤trade within Europe in order to generate wealth to fund reparations. With the rapid revival of the European economies in the aftermath of the ➤Marshall Plan, the bank staged an impressive resuscitation. The bank now plays a key role in the management and supervision of global financial institutions within a ➤transnational financial ➤regime.

**Banking system** There is no centralized banking system in international affairs that is isomorphic with banking systems in the advanced industrial countries (➤AICs). On a number of occasions such an initiative has been proposed; for example, after 1945 the UK economist J. M. Keynes proposed the establishment of a world clearing bank. Instead the system that has been established under the IMF has some of the characteristics of a banking system. Private commercial banks operate in world politics and can be regarded as ➤transnational ➤actors. Since the early 1970s these private banks have recycled funds into the system by making loans to ➤states to assist their development or their external balances. The resulting ➤debt crisis highlighted the problems of finanical management in an increasingly complex global system.

**Bases** Traditionally these refer to points of military supply and troop concentration and are located at strategic points dictated by a number of factors including: the current state of military ➤technology, the nature of ➤alliance commitments and the ➤perception of likely external threat. Clearly bases are only likely to become ➤issue areas in ➤international relations if they are located outside home territories (including territorial waters). During the ➤Cold War era both of the ➤superpowers located bases on the territory of allies, associates and friends (friendship ➤treaties were a particular feature of Soviet ➤diplomacy). Undoubtedly one of the most valued results of the ➤special relationship between the USA and UK during these years was the ability it afforded the former to locate basing facilities in the latter. As the history of the end of ➤colonialism and the ➤Vietnam and ➤Afghanistan traumas all show, a base set down in hostile territory can become a liability rather than an asset.

**Bay of Pigs** An ill-fated venture by the Kennedy administration in April 1961 to land a force of Cuban exiles, trained by the Central Intelligence Agency (CIA) at an outlet in Southern Cuba (Cochinos Bay). The purpose of the invasion was to encourage a general anti-Castro rising and thus restore Cuba to the orbit of American influence and to remove a bastion of ➤communist influence from the Caribbean. Within forty-eight hours of landing, the invaders had all been killed or captured by Cuban forces. President Kennedy was forced to admit responsibility and the captives were subsequently ransomed by the American government with $10 million in medical supplies as the payment to Cuba. Kennedy was reported after the event as being concerned that the fiasco would encourage the Soviet leader Khrushchev to doubt the American President's resolve. In a classic ➤misperception it now seems from the record that the Soviet leader reasoned that Kennedy would seek revenge for the Bay of Pigs and that a second invasion of Cuba – possibly with overt American support – would be staged. It is certainly the case that the Kennedy brothers became obsessed by the Castro regime and that there was an active policy of ➤destabilization – known as Operation Mongoose – vented on Cuba after the Bay of Pigs.

The Bay of Pigs has been studied by ➤foreign policy analysts as a 'perfect failure'. Janis (1972) includes it as one of his examples of 'groupthink'. It seems to confirm the argument of the ➤bureaucratic politics approach that foreign policy making cannot be viewed as the product of unified groups making decisions on the basis of perfect information. In the case of the Bay of Pigs it would seem that too much weight was given to untested assumptions by CIA officials and that 'expert' opinion was shown to be reckless.

**Behaviouralism** ➤social science approach

**Belligerency** A term in ➤international law which indicates when an armed dispute reaches the point at which the participants are accorded the status of belligerents. Recognition of such a condition and status involves certain legal consequences. It means, for example, that the participants are bound by the international legal rules of ➤war, so that provisions such as those relating to ➤neutrality and ➤prisoners of war become operative. ➤Recognition itself is a political matter rather than a legal one and not surprisingly international law lacks precision and clarity on some issues associated with it. Sometimes, for example, the status of belligerency is distinguished from that of ➤insurgency, the latter referring to a mid-way stage between mere law-breaking and full belligerency. But since the issues involved are political rather than strictly legal, modern behavioural practice tends to obliterate this distinction. Insurgency is more properly regarded as a provisional or intermediate classification pending a more definite recognition of status, which in turn may depend on the outcome of the conflict.

**Benelux** A ➤customs union between Belgium, Luxembourg and the Netherlands which was established on 1 January 1948. A fuller economic union of the same three participants came into operation on 1 November 1960, since by this time the parties were members of the ➤European Economic Community;

the Treaty of Rome explicitly provided for the Benelux union within the wider community. Benelux is widely seen as being the historical precursor of the later Western European initiatives. Support for ➤supranationalism remains high amongst political ➤elites, ➤attentive and mass publics in all three Benelux states and some of the leading proponents of European ➤integration have been drawn from the union. In all respects Benelux is a paragon for all that is best in the supranationalist ideal.

**Berlin crises** This former capital of Weimar Germany was the setting for two major ➤crises of the ➤Cold War era. The first occurred in 1948–9 and is often referred to as the 'Berlin Airlift', because of the use made of air power by the United States and the United Kingdom to fly supplies into the city in defiance of a ➤blockade instituted by the Soviet Union. The second crisis ran from 1958 to 1962. The proximate cause was the Soviet proposal to sign a separate peace treaty with East Germany (DDR). This culminated in the construction of the Berlin Wall in 1961 which provoked a crisis within a crisis as a result.

Berlin, like Germany itself, was divided into occupation zones as a result of the defeat of the ➤Axis powers in the Second World War. Physically, Berlin was located deep in the Soviet zone after 1945. The Western allies maintained access rights into Berlin after the German ➤surrender but these facilities were crucially dependent upon the continuation of inter-allied cooperation. When the relationship between the Soviet Union and the Western side began to deteriorate and degenerate into the post-war confrontation, the Berlin arrangements began to look very fragile. Indeed the whole German question became an ➤issue area between the protagonists. In particular the US and UK began to take steps to establish a greater degree of ➤autonomy for their zones (which were unified in the so-called 'Bizone' in July 1946). The impression was certainly created thereby that a long-term ➤goal for Anglo-American policy at this time was an independent West German state. In early 1948 France, ➤Benelux, the UK and the US decided to encourage political activity in West Germany and to make ➤Marshall Plan ➤aid available to the nascent state.

The proximate cause of the subsequent first Berlin crisis was the series of decisions reached at the London Conference. The Soviet view was that such decisions violated the principle that policy on the future of Germany should be decided by Four-Power agreement. On April 1 1948 the Soviets began to impose restrictions on the movement of military supplies through their zone into Berlin. In June 1948 the three Western states announced a currency reform for their zones – but not for Berlin – and the Soviet response was to institute further restrictions on movements into Berlin. When these currency reforms were extended to the Western sectors of Berlin later in June 1948 the Soviet authorities responded with a full blockade of all land-based access routes into the former capital of Germany. In a move which Leffler (1992) describes as 'defensive but provocative' the Soviets had escalated the dispute to the maximum point of confrontation.

The response from the West to these moves was to institute an airlift of supplies into Berlin. This can be regarded as a paradigm example of ►brinkmanship since, while it physically avoided the blockade, the Anglo-American initiative left the next move to the adversary. In retrospect the Soviets – with little experience of this kind of airlift ►capability – miscalculated badly. The airlift was never challenged militarily and the blockade was called off in May 1949. As a 'trial of strength' Berlin was less ►coercive than ►Cuba. The original airlift response had been a compromise between doing nothing to help Berlin, which would have meant in effect abandoning the Western position in the city, and forcing an armed convoy through the blockade. Because the crisis was terminated without formal negotiations, the possibility was left open that the issue could emerge again in the future.

Structurally, the first Berlin crisis produced a hardening of the divisions in Europe after 1945. By 1949 a separate West German state had been established and ►NATO had been founded with full US participation. In the autumn of 1949 the German Democratic Republic was established in the Soviet zone and the post-war division of Germany – which was only ended following the events of 1989 (►nineteen eighty-nine) – had become a formality. Unlike the Cuban missile crisis – which initiated a period of ►*détente* – Berlin led to an increase in tension and hostility between the parties to the Cold War.

Berlin again became a crisis point in ►superpower relations in November 1958, when the Soviet leader Khrushchev announced against a six-month time limit that the Soviet Union wanted to negotiate a more permanent settlement to the German question. These proposals were based upon the concept of 'two Germanies'. These states would be internationally recognized as ►neutrals and their territories would become part of a ►nuclear-free zone. Berlin would be internationalized. The six-month time limit stipulated that, failing agreement, the Soviet Union would sign a separate peace with DDR (as the US had done with Japan). This escalation would involve the Western powers in ►*de facto* relations with the DDR in order to maintain access into Berlin. The United States countered by proposing limited disengagement and free elections in both parts of Germany prior to ►unification. At the same time the economic system in the DDR was being constantly undermined by the open border with West Berlin. With the approval of the Soviet Union and the other ►Warsaw Pact states the DDR closed the border between the two Berlins in August 1961.

Western reaction to the closing of the crossing routes was initially very restrained. Only when it became clear that a potentially damaging loss of confidence was occurring among the population of West Berlin did the new Kennedy Administration in Washington take the steps to increase the size of its garrison in the city. Indeed the United States used the crisis to attempt to advance plans for changes in NATO strategy towards more flexibility and balance between ➤conventional and nuclear forces. Notwithstanding, the crisis emphasized potential differences in the strategy and tactics between the US and its European allies. Many West German ➤leaders drew ➤Gaullist conclusions from the 1961 crisis. It undoubtedly helped to encourage Franco-German cooperation at all levels in the years that followed.

The issue area of Berlin was eventually resolved by the 1971 Quadripartite Agreement which guaranteed Western access into the city and gave West Berlin limited ties with the Federal Republic in exchange for *de facto* recognition of DDR control over East Berlin. This agreement would not have been possible without the significant improvement in relations occasioned by Ostopolitik and the Nixon/Kissinger policy of *détente*. The collapse of the Berlin Wall, the DDR and the unification of the two Germanies closed this chapter in European ➤geopolitics.

**Big emerging markets (BEMs)** These are ten states identified by the US Department of Commerce in 1994 as potential growth points within the International Economy. The ten are: China, Indonesia, India, South Korea, Mexico, Argentina, Brazil, South Africa, Poland and Turkey. The stipulation of these BEMs has a number of repercussions at both the ➤international system and the ➤foreign policy levels. It further weakens the value of such catch-all terms as ➤South and ➤Third World. Like the term ➤NIC and the colloquial ➤Asian Tigers, it shows that a group of states previously thought of as being in the Third World (or even the Second World in the case of Poland) have now been promoted into some higher division. It also reinforces the pervasive influence of➤economic liberalism as arguably a dominant ➤paradigm in ➤international relations since these states are without question following market orientated paths to development. At the ➤foreign policy level it shows how with the end of the ➤Cold War, the USA is no longer pursuing its foreign policy interests in a ➤bipolar framework.

**Bilateral** Literally refers to matters affecting two parties, in contrast to unilateral (one party) and multilateral (many parties). It is normally used in international affairs to indicate joint policies adopted by ➤states, especially but not exclusively in matters of ➤trade, ➤defence and ➤diplomacy.

Economic or trade bilateralism is employed to facilitate easier commerce as well as to establish closer political relations between the parties. The former Soviet Union, in particular, favoured this pattern of activity both with its Eastern European allies and with respect to foreign ➤aid. The Western world, in contrast, has tended to view bilateralism as divisive and discriminatory. The General Agreement on Tariffs and Trade (➤GATT) was signed in 1947 to expand multilateralism and to mitigate the effects of narrow bilateralism in international commerce.

In defence matters, bilateralism usually refers to a ➤treaty, or agreement between two states involving degrees of military support in event of an attack or threat from a third state. In this sense, pacts can be specific and active or general and consultative. In either case, bilateralism serves to guarantee the ➤status quo. Most major states in the ➤international system have defence postures which combine bilateral and multilateral security pacts. The United States since the inception of the ➤Truman Doctrine and the quest for ➤containment in 1947 is a good example.

Bilateral diplomacy refers to traditional modes of dialogue between two states in contrast to the more modern practice of multilateral or collective diplomacy. Diplomacy based on bilateralism has been widely criticized. In particular, many commentators have felt it to be inadequate because it failed to prevent two world ➤wars. The ➤League of Nations and the UN were seen as specific attempts to create multilateral collective diplomatic institutions to supplement the existing bilateral system.

**Billiard ball model** ➤state-centrism

**Biological weapons** ➤chemical and biological warfare (CBW)

**Bipartisanship** Refers to traditions of cooperation or collaboration between different political parties, ➤leadership and institutions in the making of ➤foreign policy. In principle, any two-party or multi-party system can evince trends towards bipartisanship, particularly if there is a common ➤perception of great external threat. However, the term is more often used in the specific context of American foreign policy where the constitutional separation of powers actually implies a sharing of powers in certain ➤issue areas: notably ➤war power and ➤treaty making. Bipartisanship is therefore a response to the concern felt by many commentators on domestic politics (de Toqueville, 1835, being foremost among them) that the price for extensive discussion and participation in domestic matters could be paralysis or sterility in external affairs. In this sense it is a practical political variation on the old adage that 'politics stops at the water's edge'.

It is generally agreed that the 'golden age' of bipartisanship in America coincided with the first three 'modern Presidents': Roosevelt, Truman and Eisenhower. Roosevelt appointed bipartisan delegations to such conferences as ➤Bretton Woods and ➤Dumbarton Oaks. Truman worked closely with Arthur Vandenburg, the Republican senator and chair of the Senate Foreign Relations Committee over the ➤Marshall Plan and the foundations of NATO. From the outset, the incoming Republicans signalled in 1952 that they would seek to work with Congress ona bipartisan basis. The ➤Vietnam trauma and the Watergate débâcle eroded the level of trust between the Presidency and the Congress, which was, in reality, the unstated assumption behind bipartisanship. In retrospect, 1968 seems to have been a turning point. During the Reagan years the level of partisan diffrence was sufficiently serious for the President to appoint two special commissions of inquiry into contentious policies in an attempt to rebuild bipartisanship: the Scowcroft Commission on Strategic Forces and the Kissinger Commission on Central America. The end of the ►Cold War has removed the 'clear and present danger' that was a defining reality for most Americans. It is hard to envisage the return of bipartisanship to earlier levels accordingly.

**Bipolar** A concept associated particularly with the ►Cold War period when the structure of the international political system was imagined to revolve around two poles – the Soviet Union and the United States. The system was said to be organized in terms of ►power, ►regimes and ►ideologies which coalesced around two huge blocs, each of which was dominated by the interests and perceptions of the two ►superpowers. The model includes a crude notion of balance (really equilibrium), though it is a mistake to confuse bipolarity with the system of ►balance of power, which some theorists have tended to do. The simplicity of the model (which may or may not have corresponded with the real world it purported to describe) was often alleviated by characterizing it as either rigid or loose. Bipolarity existed in contrast to ►multipolarity or ►polycentrism where the system is dominated by a number of ►power centres, independent loci of ►decision-making and interests which are not directly or even necessarily related to superpower equilibrium. Thus, it is often argued that ►international relations were bipolar in the 1950s and that this gave way in the 1960s to multipolarity and polycentrism. This shift is said to have occurred in accordance with the degree of cohesion/fragmentation among and within the power blocs.

Bipolarity is associated with ►zero-sum perceptions of policy revolving around the military balance (i.e. my gain is your loss), whereas multipolar models focus attention on patterns of interaction where the outcome is not so dramatic or one-dimensional and goes well beyond traditionally defined security concerns. One way of highlighting this may be to say that bipolarity is concerned almost exclusively with East/West issues as the basis for ►international order, whereas multipolar approaches see a much wider and richer range of issues including the ►North–South debate, as critical points of reference on the map of international relations.

**Blitzkrieg** German strategic term evolved during the inter-►war years, denoting a series of short, rapid engagements against isolated targets. These 'lightning wars' were carried out by aerial assaults from dive-bombers combined with mass formations of tanks to give maximum mobility and surprise. The strategy was adopted by Hitler and his general staff to avoid a long-drawn-out war of ►attrition against Russia and the British Empire, which Germany was bound to lose given the likelihood of eventual American entry into the fray. Swift, highly mechanized thrusts by the German forces directed specifically at isolated enemies would, it was hoped, permit rapid victory without alerting the international community to any grand design.

Blitzkrieg had diplomatic, economic and psychological dimensions as well as the purely military ones. In ➤diplomacy it required Germany to discourage the formation of military ➤alliances in Europe, and in particular to prevent a Franco-Russian combination. The Nazi-Soviet pact of 1939 was the culmination of this quest. On the economic level, blitzkrieg avoided the need for total mobilization of the domestic German economy and if successful would bring access to new sources of raw materials. In psychological terms, its purpose was to bludgeon or stun the enemy into ➤surrender or submission before any real or protracted resistance could be offered. The brilliant success of these tactics against Poland in 1939 persuaded Hitler to bring forward his planned offensive against France and the Low Countries in 1940. Ironically, the outstanding successes of blitzkrieg in its initial operations may have contributed to the eventual downfall of the Third Reich. In the post-war world the Israelis used blitzkrieg tactics in their campaigns of 1956, 1967 and 1973, but the term is normally associated with the German tradition of attempting to avoid a European war on two ➤fronts.

**Bloc** French word originally used in the domestic context to describe combinations or groupings of parties in support of, and later in opposition to, government. Now in common use in IR describing a combination of ➤states supporting particular military, economic or political interests, e.g. the Western bloc, the sterling bloc, the ➤communist bloc. It is used extensively in studies of voting behaviour in the ➤General Assembly of the UN where collective and recurring patterns have been identified, e.g. the ➤Third World bloc and the African bloc. The term is often used synonymously with coalition and ➤alliance though in the case of the latter it does not have the same legal standing since it does not require a ➤treaty commitment or a common and specific declaration of policy.

**Blockade** Action designed to prevent access to, or egress from, enemy territory. It usually takes the form of a land blockade or a naval blockade but air forces could also be involved. Commonly, it is employed during a state of ➤belligerency where its aim is to deny resources and food to enemy forces and/or civilian populations. It can also be employed in peacetime ('pacific blockade') where it falls short of an act of ➤war and is a ➤reprisal for the commission of an illegal act. In both, ➤international law confers rights and duties to imposer, target and neutrals. For example, in wartime blockade ➤neutrals must be given advance warning and a reasonable time in which to comply with the conditions imposed. Pacific blockades are now generally seen as an aspect of reprisals and may be instituted by the UN ➤Security Council but are forbidden to individual ➤states. In this context, the legality of the ➤quarantine imposed by the United States on Cuba in 1962 to prevent Soviet missiles reaching the island is questionable. Similarly 'paper blockades' are forbidden by international law, which requires that sufficient force is used to make a blockade effective. In this case, neutrals are not required to respect the wishes of the imposer. To 'run a blockade' is to attempt to evade it and if unsuccessful is likely to result in seizure or confiscation of goods or cargoes.

Blockade has always played a part in inter-state conflict, especially so in modern times because of the high degree of economic ➤interdependence. To be effective blockades ought to involve overwhelming local ➤force superiority plus an identifiable degree of ➤vulnerability on the part of the target. Thus Britain, for whom naval forces and strategy were an essential part of ➤foreign policy, frequently favoured this technique. It was employed, for example, during the Napoleonic Wars against France, and in the twentieth-century wars against Germany. An example, albeit unsuccessful, of a land blockade is the Soviet attempt to seal off ➤Berlin in 1948–9.

**BMD** An abbreviation of Ballistic Missile Defence. This is an umbrella term that covers a number of ➤capabilities, deployments and strategies. Thus a BMD can be either endoatmospheric or exoatmospheric. A BMD can be either a point defence or an area defence. Interest in BMD increased with the publicly declared commitment towards a space-based system known in the United States as the Strategic Defense Initiative (SDI). Earlier attempts by the ➤superpowers to develop a BMD in the 1960s led to the Anti-Ballistic Missile (➤ABM) ➤treaty. Following the end of the ➤Cold War, interest in BMD has focused in the ➤issue area of ➤proliferation of ➤missile ➤technology to ➤pariah/rogue states and the perceived need for an antidote to these offensive ➤capabilities.

**Bosnia** ➤Yugoslavia

**Boundary** This term is used in a number of contexts in ➤international relations. In its legal usage a boundary represents an absolute change of legal status. Thus a legal boundary may be regarded as a demarcation line between one legal competence and another. In this sense the term is consonant with the sovereign ➤state-system. A boundary is a limit upon the territorial jurisdiction of states. Within the boundary the ➤state is sovereign, outside it is not. In practice this dichotomy has always been hard to sustain. The exercise of effective control requires the ability and willingness to do so. Dominant states in a system would often effect boundary changes in their favour through a policy of ➤annexation. Boundary changes and adjustments were regarded as appropriate means for expressing the policies of leading states in the ➤balance of power. Through the principle of ➤recognition states would either indicate their assent or opposition to boundary changes. While non-recognition does not prevent a state from exercising effective control, it does indicate that the control is *➤de facto*, not *➤de jure*.

➤Geopolitical usage has identified a number of categories of boundary. The best known is probably the 'natural' boundary. What geographers have in mind here are significant physical features such as a mountain chain, a river system or a waterway. Excessive determinism should certainly be avoided in this usage. A river may divide or unite. A mountain chain may locate natural resources which require cooperative relations for purposes of exploitation. Geographers have also delimited 'natural' boundaries where the limits are based upon ethnic identity. 'Contractual' boundaries are based upon legal norms while 'geometric' boundaries reflect lines of longitude and latitude. Finally, 'power-political' boundaries reflect the roles of dominant states and may be seen as akin to the balance of power usage.

The ►behavioural approach, and in particular ►systems theorists, have taken a transactions approach to the question of boundaries. Thus Burton has argued for a conceptualization of the subject 'without reference to political boundaries, and indeed, without reference to any physical boundaries.' Likewise, Deutsch has argued that boundaries mark 'relative discontinuities' in human relations. Recent scholarship on the concept of ►regimes has also tended to argue against the legal and geographical concept of boundary. Regimes operate under transnational criteria and therefore transcend the more traditional view of the boundary. Whatever the theoretical and heuristic merits of this approach, there can be no doubt that the idea of boundary, as traditionally understood, is still a potent force in world politics. The politics of Africa, for example, would be impossible to comprehend without an appreciation of the power-political boundary-making of European ►imperialism which established the contours of the present state-system in that continent. ►►Frontier

**Boycott** Originally practised in Ireland in 1880 and named after its first target, it involves a systematic refusal to enter into social, economic, political or military relations with a particular ►state or group of states in order to punish or bring about compliant behaviour. It is most commonly used in international economic relations, where goods and services produced by a particular target would be boycotted. It can be primary, where the imposer adopts policies directly aimed at the target, or secondary, where the imposer penalizes those maintaining contact or patronage with the target. In addition it can be general, a wholescale boycott of goods and services, or specific, confined to one particular item or class of goods. It is increasingly used in IR in all the above senses by states and non-state ►actors alike although it appears to have no specific ►recognition in ►international law besides the strictures covering embargoes or economic sanctions. The targets with the highest profile in recent international history has been the Republic of South Africa during the ►apartheid years, and Iraq after the ►Persian Gulf War.

**Brandt Reports** The Independent Commission on International Development Issues met for two years from December 1977 to December 1979 under the chairmanship of the former West German Chancellor, Willy Brandt. Its terms of reference were to consider the past, present and future for economic development as an ►issue area in IR. Their report entitled *North–South: A*

*Programme for Survival* was published in 1980. Three years later the Commission produced an update, *Common Crisis*, because it was felt that in the interim many of the problems identified in the first report had worsened.

The two Brandt Reports are striking testimony to the view that crucial areas of problem-solving in world politics can be tackled by a greater commitment to cooperation and the acceptance that ►interdependence holds the key to the future. At the same time the Reports are essentially a restatement of arguments and attitudes that had been prominent for decades in the development literature. As such the Reports are an urgent manifesto to governments, particularly in the advanced industrial countries (►AICs) and to ►attentive publics in those areas. Ideologically, the Brandt approach can be regarded as an example of ►economic liberalism, although in this particular instance the liberalism is tempered to take account of the differential needs of the ►Third World states. This modified liberalism has been termed 'compensatory' or 'International Keynesianism' by writers on this subject area.

**Bretton Woods** A series of multilateral agreements on international economic relations were reached at Bretton Woods (United States) in July 1944 under the aegis of the embryo UN. Forty-four ►states agreed to a Final Act establishing an ►IMF and an International Bank for Reconstruction and Development (►IBRD). The proposals that were discussed at Bretton Woods were the outcome of a series of ►bilateral ►negotiations conducted between the United States and the United Kingdom over the previous two years. The IBRD was described by the London *Economist* in 1945 as a 'much simpler project which has attracted neither much discussion nor much hostility . . .'. The IMF, on the other hand, was from its inception more controversial. The two ►states concerned with these preliminaries, the United States and the United Kingdom, had rather divergent ideas about the future monetary ►regime. These differences were made public in, respectively, the White Plan, originating in the US Treasury, and the Keynes Plan, originating in the UK Treasury. White envisaged a Stabilization Fund made up entirely of contributions from member states; Keynes envisaged a Clearing Union based on the overdraft principle and employing a new unit of account – the 'bancor'. Whereas the total available liquidity remained constant under White – so that drawing rights equalled liabilities – in the Keynes scheme additional liquidity could be pumped into the system to enable debtor states to overdraw. Conversely, creditor states would provide the main collateral in this arrangement.

The Anglo-American differences over the putative IMF are sometimes presented as the conservative versus the radical views of the future. It should be noted, however, that both schemes tended to reflect the perceived ►national interests of the parties advocating them. In the event, the US bargaining position was more credible and the Bretton Woods conference produced a fund which bore a close family resemblance to the White Plan.

The term 'Bretton Woods system' is often used to refer to these two institutions and to the regimes thereby established. Both have changed considerably since their inception. Accordingly, the reference to 'Bretton Woods' is of historical, rather than contemporary, validity.

**Brezhnev Doctrine** In the aftermath of the Soviet bloc's ►intervention in Czechoslovakia in 1968 following the pluralistic tendencies of the 'Prague Spring' *an ex post facto* justification was offered in *Pravda* in September which spoke of the 'limited ►sovereignty' of individual socialist states that existed within a 'socialist commonwealth'. In November 1968 it was given the endorsement of the Soviet leader Leonid Brezhnev in a speech to the Fifth Congress of the Polish ►communist party which asserted that the 'socialist commonwealth as a whole' had a right of intervention in the territory of any one of its members whenever forces hostile to socialism threatened its ideological alignment. What became known thereafter as the Brezhnev Doctrine because of the November imprimatur was in effect a considered statement by the Soviet ►leadership which asserted that the unity of the communist bloc took precedence over such principles as ►domestic jurisdiction and ►equality of states.

The doctrine had unsettling effects on the process of ►*détente* with the West, on the other Eastern bloc states and particularly on China and the Sino-Soviet conflict. It was used to justify the Soviet intervention in ►Afghanistan in December 1979. Thus the new Afghan leader, Karmal, spoke of Soviet policy as 'proletarian internationalism in action'.

It would be simplistic to regard the Brezhnev Doctrine as either a complete sham or a blank cheque to justify intervention in all circumstances. It is clear from the analysis of Soviet writings over a long period that leading members of the Communist Party were willing to make fundamental distinctions between the Socialist Commonwealth and the world outside and to argue that ►international relations within these two systems might be organized differently. Similarly the two historical examples of intervention referred to above were clearly seen as significant – if rather different – challenges to Soviet ►hegemony. It is clear from the ►bureaucratic politics of both decisions that intervention was only settled upon after lengthy debate within an essentially collective leadership.

**Brinkmanship** Brinkmanship is a strategy adopted during a ►crisis to coerce one's adversary into making a conciliatory move. The essence of the strategy is to manipulate the shared risks of violence – which it is assumed that neither party wants – to get the other to 'back down'. Thomas Schelling (1966) discusses brinkmanship in some detail and more recently Richard Ned Lebow (1981) has added impressively to the literature on the subject in his book on the international crisis.

Diplomatically, the US Secretary of State J. F. Dulles popularized the idea during the Eisenhower Administration of the 1950s. The most famous example of the use of this idiom, certainly by American statesmen, came during the ➤Cuban missile crisis of 1962 when the J. F. Kennedy Administration succeeded in their commitment to the removal of perceived offensive missiles from the island of Cuba.

Brinkmanship is clearly a high-risk strategy which depends for its successful outcome on the mutual recognition of parties that ➤war would be clearly the worst outcome. ➤Game theorists claim a certain isomorphism with the mixed motive game of 'Chicken', wherein similar manipulative strategies are involved.

**Buffer state** A ➤geopolitical term most often associated with ➤balance of power. It refers to small or weak ➤states which exist on the borders of powerful states and which, from the security standpoint of the latter, serve as intermediate 'cushions' or 'crush zones'. Before the advent of ➤air power buffer states were seen as an insurance against direct and, more importantly, surprise hostilities between ➤great powers. The continued ➤independent existence of these states thus precariously depended on the current state of play regarding both the local and general balance of power. While not satellite states their freedom of action was a direct function of the security needs of their powerful neighbours. For example, the states of central Europe, and especially Poland, were widely regarded during the inter-war years as buffers between Germany and the Soviet Union. In the same way, ➤Afghanistan and Thailand were the crush zones that could absorb and delay Russian and French penetration into British India in the late nineteenth century.

**Bureaucratic politics** A model of foreign policy making developed from the seminal work *Essence of Decision* (Allison 1971). In the 1971 volume Allison actually refers to it as Governmental (Bureaucratic) Politics. By 1972 in collaboration with Halperin (Tanter & Ullman) the term Bureaucratic Politics Model was settled upon and Halperin (1974) also used this designation. The basic assumptions behind this approach to the subject matter are: that the state-centric premise that states are unified ➤actors is dropped. Governments are made up of individuals who may be pursuing widely differing ➤goals, indeed conflicting goals. Furthermore it is assumed that decisions are made under conditions of uncertainty. Uncertainty may be situational – that is to say one may be uncertain about what has occurred – or uncertainty may be motivational – that is to say one may be uncertain about why something has occurred. Thus in the case of the ➤Cuban missile crisis (which was the referent for *Essence of Decision*) uncertainty may surround the operational status of the missiles, the position of the US Navy or the loss of a surveillance aircraft. Additionally, uncertainty may surround the reasons why the Soviet ➤leadership decided to send missiles to Cuba in the first instance. Lastly the Bureaucratic Politics model drops assumptions about rationality in policy making. 'Imperfect rationality' is substituted for 'perfect rationality' in this view. 'Bounded rationality' in terms of organizational theory is the key to understanding this approach. Policy makers will frequently 'muddle through' looking for outcomes that are the best available in the circumstances. Not infrequently outcomes will be the result of 'bargains' struck within the decision system and players may seek to defend individual or organizational positions accordingly. 'Where you stand depends on where you sit' was the aphorism which summed up the influence of position upon preference.

Allison has not been without his critics since the publication of *Essence*. Art (1973) was an early critic writing from a broadly ➤neorealist perspective whilst more recently Bendor and Hammond (1993) have systematically re-examined all the models offered up in *Essence*. It may well be that – as some critics have noted – the bureaucratic politics approach is particularly effective in explaining policy implementation. Certainly Allison's original empirical referent of Cuba was well chosen. Recent analyses, for example by Lebow and Stein (1994), seem to confirm that on both the American and the Soviet side crucial policy decisions were made by Kennedy and Khrushchev in disregard of or without reference to other members of their respective groups. Although some of the historical interpretations made by Allison are now in dispute (for example the status of the so-called Turkish missiles) in other respects the work retains considerable relevance for foreign policy analysis today.

# C

**C⁴I** This refers to command, control, communications, computer, and ►intelligence. It is a term used in military/►security policy-making and analysis. It refers to the ►capability to monitor factors confronting ►decision-makers in a ►war situation or in a situation where war threatens. During the ►Cold War era when the threat of ►nuclear war was a significant variable in political calculations it was the inviolability of command and control systems to a ►first strike that was thought to be particularly significant. This threat was referred to in the jargon of ►strategic studies as 'Nuclear decapitation'. Post Cold War ►interventions such as the ►Persian Gulf War and speculation about a ►revolution in military affairs (RMA) have changed the agenda somewhat as far as C⁴I issues are concerned. Intruding into an enemy (or putative enemy) C⁴I facility to 'read the mind of the opponent' may be more important than decapitation it seems.

**Calvo Doctrine** Carlos Calvo, an Argentinian jurist, challenged, in 1868, the accepted doctrine of the ►legitimacy of state-►intervention in another ►state's internal affairs to protect the rights of ►aliens. The Calvo Clause (which is a common feature of public contracts between Latin American governments and aliens) asserts that aliens have no claim to preferential treatment and that in this regard all sovereign states must be treated as equals. The ►Monroe Doctrine, while denying interventionist rights to Europeans, tacitly reserved them for the United States. The Calvo Doctrine, along with that advanced by fellow Argentinian Luis Drago in 1903, was an attempt to limit the scope of Monroe and to reassert the rights of absolute ►sovereignty. It was subsequently embodied in a section of Article 1 of the second Hague Convention of 1907.

**Camp David Accords** Historic agreement reached between Israel and Egypt in 1978 through the ►good offices of the United States and named after the presidential mountain retreat in Maryland. The accords were published as two documents – the 'Framework for Peace in the Middle East' and the 'Framework for Conclusion of a Peace Treaty Between Egypt and Israel'. The first document, as its title implies, was a general statement of agreed principles relating mainly to self-government for the Palestinians, the second referred specifically to Israeli occupation of Sinai. This dual approach was deliberate and was designed to link a ►bilateral Israeli–Egyptian agreement to a broader ►Arab–Israeli settlement and thus avoid the accusation that Egypt was selling out the Palestinians in order to achieve a separate peace. In all, five major agreements were reached and under the terms of them Israel was to withdraw from the territory conquered in the 1967 ➤war in a series of timed and monitored stages. The essence of the deal was an exchange of land for the promise of peace. Israel promised to evacuate settlements in Sinai, while Egypt recognized the Jewish state. In addition, Israel was committed to negotiate on the issue of Palestinian ➤autonomy, but pending a final settlement, still retained the Gaza Strip.

The process became known as 'step-by-step' ➤diplomacy whereby the overall settlement was divided into discrete segments, each of which had to be satisfactorily resolved before the next phase was activated. This approach was regarded as preferable to a more comprehensive settlement of all the outstanding issues in the Arab–Israeli conflict, not least because the latter would require a single summit conference that would have inevitably involved the Soviet Union. None of the parties involved, not least the United States, wanted to enhance the Soviet role in the Middle East, nor did they wish to widen the Arab participation which such a conference would necessarily invoke.

Although at the time Camp David was hailed as a dramatic breakthrough in Middle Eastern politics and as a triumph of US mediatory diplomacy, the net results were disappointing. Egypt, in particular, became isolated in the Arab world and led by Syria (and backed by the Soviet Union) a 'rejectionist' front soon surfaced. In addition, Egypt briefly lost its status as host to the ➤Arab League headquarters. Carter's diplomatic ➤*démarche*, like his enhanced reputation, was destined to be short lived.

**Capability** A term used in the analysis of ➤power. It refers to an attribute or possession of ➤actors. Traditionally capability analysis concentrated upon observable factors such as military or economic possessions rather than intangibles. This has been modified of late and both tangible and intangible attributes (such as morale, diplomatic skill) are recognized as relevant. Capability analysis has also been traditionally thought of in relative rather than absolute terms. One actor was held to possess more attributes than others and therefore to be potentially more powerful. Although such analyses frequently ignored the problem of converting capability into power relationships, they were instructive and heuristic. Stratification systems based upon identifying 'great', 'super' or 'small' actors were the product of such speculation.

Capability is a necessary condition for power relationships to exist. The link between the two is mediated by the factors of ➤domain and ➤scope. It is now generally agreed that discussions on the capabilities of actors, without specifying the domain and scope within which such attributes are exercised, is meaningless. Converting capability into power relations thus constitutes an empirical test, however rudimentary, of the utility of the attribute.

**Carter Doctrine** Refers to President Carter's January 1980 State of the Union Address where he declared that 'any attempt by an outside force to gain control of the Persian Gulf region will be regarded as an assault on the vital interests of the United States of America and such an assault will be repelled by any means necessary, including military force.' The statement was in direct response to developments in Iran in 1979 (the fall of the Shah and his replacement by the Ayatollah Khomeini) and the Soviet invasion of ➤Afghanistan in the same year. These two events were perceived to threaten US vital interests in the Gulf region – access to oil and strategic advantage being the key motivations. Under the Carter doctrine the United States publicly declared its resolve to defend the Gulf and in so doing removed any doubt about its intentions following the ambiguity of the ➤Nixon Doctrine and the mood of ➤non-interventionism following the débâcle in ➤Vietnam. The major policy initiative generated by the doctrine was the creation of a Rapid Deployment Joint Task Force geared for instant dispatch to the area in case of attack. It also involved renewed US efforts at securing ➤bases or basing rights from which such a task force could be deployed. President Carter and his national security adviser, Zbigniew Brzezinski, regarded the Soviet invasion in particular as a grave threat to regional security. Afghanistan was perceived to be a stepping-stone to Soviet hegemony in the Gulf. The twin advantages of access to warm water ports and control over a major portion of the world's oil supplies were seen as historic impulses of Soviet ➤foreign policy, which the Soviets were determined to realize. The language of the Carter doctrine is redolent of the ➤Monroe Doctrine while its content, with its implicit belief in the ➤domino theory, is clearly a variant of President Truman's policy of ➤containment. Its overall significance was that despite President Carter's projection of his administration's determination to restore a moral dimension to US foreign policy (especially concerning ➤human rights), the underlying ➤realpolitik of American globalism remained undiminished. ➤Rapid deployment force; Persian Gulf War

**Chargé d'affaires** ➤Diplomatic term meaning the head of a diplomatic mission (*Chargé d'affaires en titre*) attached to a Minister for foreign affairs. As an interim appointment, or in the absence of the head of mission, a state *Chargé d'affaires ad interim* would be appointed.

**Charter of Paris** The Charter of Paris for a New Europe was signed in November 1990 by the states that were participating members in the ➤CSCE (Conference on Security and Cooperation in Europe). The Charter is significant for two reasons: it is widely regarded as ending the ➤Cold War and it formalized the conversion of the CSCE into a permanent ➤IGO. This agreement would not have been possible without the initiatives taken under the rubric of the ➤Gorbachev Doctrine in the second half of the 1980s. Gorbachev had floated the idea of a 'common European home' for some time and in 1990 the French President Mitterrand had responded with proposals for a European ➤confederation. The unintended consequence of the Gorbachev initiative was the collapse of the Eastern bloc after the events of 1989 and the demise of the

Soviet Union. This is surely a salutary reminder of how human agency can unwittingly influence structural consequences.

**Chemical and biological warfare (CBW)** Chemical weapons fall into three broad categories: poison gases, incapacitants and anti-plant agents. Similarly, biological weapons are of three types: viruses, rickettsiae and bacteria. Both classes of esoteric weapons have been the subject of significant attempts to establish an international legal ➤regime. The Chemical Weapons Convention was opened for signature in Paris in January 1993 and sufficient ratifications have now been effected to ➤implement it. The 1972 Biological Weapons Convention is weaker than the CWC in respect of verification procedures. The salutary lessons of the ➤Persian Gulf War in respect of Iraq's attempts to circumvent ➤proliferation controls on its ➤nuclear weapons programme have been reflected in the CWC's ➤inspection capabilities.

Chemical and biological agents are now grouped together with fission/fusion weapons under the broad rubric of ➤weapons of mass destruction. In all three respects the rules of the game are similar: under the ➤leadership of the United States and with the sometimes qualified support of the other P5 states, these weapons are to be controlled in respect of the following ➤goals: their acquisition, development, sales/transfers and use.

**Chemical Weapons Treaty** This is the most ambitious, most complicated and most intrusive international ➤arms control agreement ever signed. Unlike its predecessor, the Geneva Protocol of 1925, the Chemical Weapons Convention (CWT) of 1993 bans all use of chemical weapons not just first use. Furthermore, it also prohibits their development, production, stockpiling, and transfer. In effect it eliminates an entire class of weapons from national arsenals. Because of the dual-use nature of chemicals and chemical equipment the CWC has interventionist consequences for domestic commercial activities which will be monitored by the newly created Organization for Prohibition of Chemical Weapons, which will become the repository of information on chemical industrial sites world-wide, including about 3000 plants in the USA. This inspection regime began work in 1996. The CWC is an unprecedented multilateral effort to eradicate a category of catastrophic weapons which most states either possess or have the capacity to develop. The impetus for the CWC was provided by the public opprobrium generated through global TV coverage of Saddam Hussein's use of chemical weapons in a genocidal attempt to eradicate the Kurds in 1989.

**Choke points** Strategic and ➤geopolitical term used in naval ➤diplomacy referring to international straits or narrows, control of which could hamper warship or commercial transit. In 1982 the UN Convention on the Law of the Sea recognized the right of transit passage through 116 specified international straits, although some strait ➤states (e.g. Spain and Morocco in relation to the

Strait of Gibraltar) attempted to restrict the rights of movement upon, over and under these waterways to the legal ➤regime covering ➤innocent passage. This would have given these contiguous states discretionary control over traffic flow. ➤➤Law of the Sea

**City-state** An independent unit of political organization which flourished in three periods of international history: in the ancient Near East, in classical Greece and in medieval and Renaissance Europe. In ➤international relations it is particularly associated with ancient Greece from the Dark Ages to the Hellenistic period, and with medieval Italy. The Greek city-state, or *polis*, was equivalent to a small ➤state or civic republic centred around an urban development but also drawing in the surrounding rural areas.

Indications as to size vary, but scholars have estimated that the population of Athens at the height of its glory was between 40,000 and 140,000. Territorial extent also varied; Athens covered approximately one thousand square miles while at the other extreme the island of Ceos covered ten by six miles and was itself divided into four city-states. Citizens of these states generally knew each other personally, were acquainted with their leaders and identified with the *polis* itself rather than with Greece or Italy as a whole. The city-state was virtually self-contained and conducted its own foreign and defence policies. They often formed leagues. ➤Alliances and federations for mutual advantage and bilateral ➤treaties were also quite common. Greeks, for example, formed such collective groupings after 499 BC to resist the advancing Persians. Policies could also be ➤imperialistic and because of their size, these empires were usually sea-based. The most famous conflict between city-states in the ancient world was that between Athens and Sparta, the Peloponnesian Wars (432–404 BC). Indeed, its principal chronicler, ➤Thucydides, is still regarded as an important point of departure in the classical study of international relations. The city-states of medieval and Renaissance Italy – Milan, Venice, Genoa and Florence – were similar in outlook and organization and their external relations are often cited as sinister case-studies in the more cynical dimensions of the politics of ➤realism (see, for example: Machiavelli's *The Prince* and *The Discourses*). Apart from the ➤Vatican the most successful example of a contemporary city-state is Singapore which became independent from Malaysia in 1965. It is a republic of *circa* 3 million and occupies an island territory of 619 square kilometres. Economically, it is one of the most buoyant ➤Asian Tigers or ➤NICS. Formally ➤non-aligned in its ➤foreign policy orientation Singapore is a member of ASEAN although it does have close ties with the West, particularly the USA. ➤➤Vatican City-state

**Civil war** Civil war is protracted internal violence aimed at securing control of the political and legal apparatus of a ➤state. Because it is protracted, it is possible to distinguish a civil ➤war from a ➤*coup d'état*. Because it is internal it is possible to distinguish a civil war from external ➤intervention. Because it involves protracted violence it is possible to distinguish civil war from a communal ➤conflict.

In the analysis of civil wars it is generally possible to distinguish two sides: incumbents and ➤insurgents. In such circumstances other members of the society will find that they have to define their attitude to the conflict. If they become drawn into supporting one side or the other then the war would be said to have 'polarized' the whole society. Degrees of participation in the war will obviously differ between individuals and groups in the society. For some, participation may be restricted to passive support for one side or the other. For others, the war may draw them into political and military activities.

The stipulation of civil war above may be regarded as the norm from which a number of deviations are possible. Three may particularly be noted. Civil wars that arise as a result of attempts being made to end ➤colonialism; civil wars that result from the desire by part of a state to break away; civil wars that result from the desire of states that have been separated to achieve reunion.

The desire by colonial peoples and territories for ➤independence is one of the most significant trends in the nineteenth and twentieth centuries. Colonial wars can become civil wars whenever a significant body of opinion within the polity wants to continue with the existing colonial ➤regime. This would most obviously be the case where large numbers of settlers had arrived in the territory during colonial control. These people may perceive that they had a vested interest in the maintenance of the ➤status quo, fearing that the anti-colonial insurgents might adversely alter political, legal and economic arrangements. This instance is a departure from the norm because these colonial civil wars have three parties – incumbents, insurgents and the settlers – rather than the usual two.

Civil wars that arise from ➤secessionist tendencies and civil wars that arise from ➤irredentist tendencies may usefully be regarded as being opposite sides of the same coin. Seccessionist civil wars are particularly associated with ➤ethnic nationalism and the desire of ethnically homogeneous peoples for greater self-determination. Civil wars that are prompted by the desire for reunion are, again, nationalistic in character, although in this instance the ethnic factor may not be so evident.

The role of third parties, external to the territory of the state, can be crucial in determining the outcome of civil wars. Most obviously third parties can provide assistance to incumbents or insurgents in a variety of ways. Diplomatic assistance – for example, by allowing insurgents to establish a government in exile – is both practical and symbolic. Economic assistance can help parties to finance the war. Finally, military assistance can provide the ➤capability required to prosecute the violence. Such assistance is clearly a form of intervention, but this behaviour pattern can be taken much further if the third party actively engages its own forces in the war. Such interventions can be decisive, as the case of the Indian intervention in the Pakistan-Bangladesh civil war in 1971 shows.

There are a number of structural factors in the contemporary world political system which serve to exacerbate the incidence and severity of civil wars. First, the state membership of the system has increased substantially since 1945. This simply gives more opportunities for civil wars to occur than in the past. Second, many states, particularly those located in the ➤Third World, are inherently unstable. Third, the differential possession of capability, as between the states at the top of the ➤hierarchy and those at the bottom, increases the proclivities for intervention. Clearly a civil war is not a necessary condition for intervention but it may be a sufficient one. Fourth, notwithstanding its charter, provisions in favour of the territorial integrity of states (see in particular Article 2: 4) the UN has failed to develop sufficient efficacy in its own instruments to prevent intervention in civil wars by third parties. Finally, the growth of transnational ➤terrorism has increased the extent to which private armies can feed off a civil war situation to further their own interests.

**Clash of civilizations** Concept associated in particular with the prominent American political scientist and ➤foreign policy advisor, Samuel Huntington. In a highly controversial essay in the influential journal *Foreign Affairs* (1993) Huntington warned that the end of the ➤Cold War had created the conditions for the rise of a new and particularly dangerous form of international conflict – that associated with parochial and cultural identities based on ethnic and religious allegiances. He asserted that:

It is my hypothesis that the fundamental source of conflict in this new world will not be primarily ideological or primarily economic. The great divisions among humankind and the dominating source of conflict will be cultural. National states will remain the most powerful actors in world affairs, but the principal conflicts of global politics will occur between nations and groups of different civilizations. The clash of civilizations will be the battle lines of the future. (p. 22)

Although he identified a number of possible clash scenarios, he went on to assert that there is little doubt that 'a central focus of conflict for the immediate future will be between the West and several Islamic-Confucian states.' Huntington subsequently denied that his hypothesis was anything other than an alternative disciplinary ➤paradigm for the study of world affairs but most commentators argue that his essay constituted a warning of the dangers posed by the politicization of ➤Islam and the rise of Islamic fundamentalism, to the Western attempt to establish an international order constituted by democratic states, liberal values and a belief in the free market. The coming challenge to the legitimacy of the dominant liberal international order has led some to characterize the conflict as one between 'The West and The Rest'.

Huntington's thesis, notwithstanding its intrinsic contradictions and imprecision, sparked off a debate about the Islamic threat, in particular the perceived aim of establishing a 'pax Islamica' among the world's 1.1 billion Muslims

(Hippler and Lueg 1995). The Muslim world is centred on the Middle East and South East Asia (although Saudi Arabia is its spiritual home the most populous Muslim country is Indonesia), but there are large communities spread throughout Europe, Africa and Asia as well as sizeable segments in the Americas, China and India. Regarding geographical spread, Huntington identified an anti-Western front constituted by 'a crescent-shaped Islamic bloc of nations from the bulge of Africa to Central Asia' (p. 31). This geopolitical fault-line between the Western and Islamic civilizations has generated conflict for at least 1,300 years, culminating in the 1990–91 ►Persian Gulf War, and the continuing violence between Muslims on the one hand, and Orthodox Serbs in the Balkans, Jews in Israel, Hindus in India, Buddhists in Burma and Catholics in the Philippines. He concludes grimly that 'Islam has bloody borders' (pp. 34–5). Huntington has been accused by critics of exaggerating the Muslim threat, of misunderstanding the nature of political and fundamentalist Islam, of advocating the 're-ideologization' of foreign policy and of encouraging the reassertion of the ►self-fulfilling prophecy syndrome in foreign affairs (Halliday 1995). However, given his position as an eminent member of the US foreign policy establishment it is not surprising that the political geography of Islam is now receiving widespread attention by conservative sections of the strategic establishments in the West for whom the 'Green Peril' has now replaced the 'Red Peril' as the major obstacle to the ►globalization and ►good governance project.

**Clausewitzian doctrine** Karl von Clausewitz (1780–1831) was a Prussian officer who is widely regarded, even in the nuclear age, as the greatest ever writer on military theory and ►war. He is best known for propagating the thesis that the political and social circumstances out of which conflicts arise should also determine their conduct. This is popularly, but inaccurately, rendered in the aphorism 'war is the continuation of policy by other means'; that is, that war is indistinguishable from political and social structures and should therefore be conceived in terms of them. The essence of the Clausewitzian doctrine is contained in this passage from *On War* (1968, p. 89):

As a total phenomenon its dominant tendencies always make war a remarkable trinity – composed of primordial violence, hatred and enmity, which are to be regarded as a blind natural force; of the play of chance and probability, within which the creative spirit is free to roam; and of its element of subordination, as an instrument of policy, which makes it subject to reason alone. The first of these aspects mainly concerns the people; the second, the commander and his army; the third, the government. . . . A theory that ignores any one of them or seeks to fix an arbitrary relationship between them would conflict with reality to such an extent that for this reason alone it would be totally useless.

This insight, despite the bourgeois, militarist background from which it came, was taken up by Marx, Engels, Lenin and Trotsky and subsequently influenced the military thinking of an entire generation of Soviet leaders. In the West, however, Clausewitzian doctrines were regarded as excessively militaristic, typically Teutonic and casually cynical. Following the outbreak of the ➤Cold War and particularly with the growth of ➤strategic studies in the USA, there was a reappraisal of his contribution. Clausewitz's appreciation of the essential socio-political character of warfare and the early distinction he made between ➤limited and ➤total warfare endeared him to the new civilian strategists who flourished in the so-called 'Golden Age' of strategic thought.

**Clinton Doctrine** As the first genuinely post-➤Cold War and post-➤containment US President, Bill Clinton was anxious from the outset of his first administration (1993–7) to establish his own specific ➤foreign policy doctrine, i.e. a body of beliefs, principles or guidelines to inform policy formulation and conduct. However, although the broad outlines of such a doctrine were articulated in the 1994 National Security document entitled *A Strategy for Engagement and Enlargement*, international events and developments inherited from the Bush–Reagan administrations (especially the problems of ex-➤Yugoslavia, North Korea and relations with post-Tiananmen Square China) effectively scuppered progress on fresh foreign policy initiatives. It is therefore to his second administration (1997–2001) that we should look for evidence of a new American doctrine in international affairs. According to the 1994 National Security document which remains the clearest articulation of US foreign policy imperatives into the millennium, US National Security strategy will rest on three 'pillars': the retention of global military predominance, the quest for continued economic prosperity and the promotion of free market democracy abroad. So unlike the Cold War base-line of containment and its fellow traveller, ➤deterrence, this new policy directive does not involve an open-ended commitment to military ➤intervention. It does not envisage a Kennedy-like pledge to 'bear any burden, pay any costs.' On the contrary, since this new definition of interests is driven by concerns about the economic foundations of national security and the inevitability of the spread of free market democracy, the key policy planning task will be to prioritize and select.

The disappearance of the Soviet Union as the second ➤superpower, the sudden collapse of the command economies and the global rise of free markets in the early 1990s is viewed as a new window of opportunity for active American penetration. This is regarded by the Clinton team as an opening for the US to revise the ➤declinist/imperial overstretch, syndrome that troubled the American public mind during the late 1980s. Therefore on this view, military pactomania, one of the hallmarks of containment and overstretch, should now give way to 'trade pactomania', particularly with the emerging democracies in Central and Eastern Europe, South America and the Asia–Pacific regions.

This is the essence of the Clinton Doctrine. Its aim is the retention of global hegemony; its objective is to prise open markets, tear down tariff walls and open doors to American enterprise, expertise and money. Whereas the economic implications of containment revolved around Dollar Diplomacy – massive government-directed foreign aid programmes often with the sole purpose of shoring up reactionary regimes – this new doctrine carries no such financial or human rights costs. All that Bill Clinton's 'Big Mac Diplomacy' requires is a commitment to the promotion of US exports and a firm adherence to enforcing the principle of global free trade. The market does the rest. As long as military predominance is maintained (this is characterized operationally as the ability to fight and win two regional wars simultaneously) then the fifty-year abnormal American detour away from the primacy of commerce in foreign affairs is over. As in the past, the return to normalcy means that America's business is, once again, business and geoeconomics rather than geopolitics returns to drive policy considerations.

Intellectually, the Clinton doctrine rests on a very simple, (but disputable) proposition. This is the Kantian thesis that democracies do not go to war with one another – or as one analyst wryly interpreted: 'no two countries that both have a McDonald's have ever fought a war against each other'. Today, this classical ►liberal/democratic peace theory is an article of faith amongst US policy intellectuals and it clearly forms the philosophical discourse that underpins En-En. It is the logic behind the enlargement of ►NATO, the Partnership for Peace and other cooperative arrangements with Russia. The extension of the American military guarantee eastward converts 'out of area' into 'in-house' and encourages the maturation of select semi-democracies into eventual full membership of the pacific union. Linkage of US security with the spread of democracy is not new. Its most famous advocate was President Woodrow Wilson, in many respects Bill Clinton's intellectual (though of course, not moral) mentor. The main difference between old style Wilsonianism and new style Clintonianism lies not in the degree of commitment to the liberal peace ideas, but rather in the manner of its supposed implementation. For Wilson, as he indicated in his ►fourteen points, this required an undifferentiated and, if necessary, unilateral strategy of global activism; in effect a commitment to fight wars to make the world safe for democracy. For Clinton it means 'assertive' but selective multilateralism: encouraging the spread of the democratic ►zone of peace through constructive engagement and crucially, burden-sharing. Clinton's identification of US interests with the success of democracy does not necessarily involve a crusade against the 'the troublemakers'. However, the right to confront them is clearly reserved. What it does involve though, is the belief that absolute security can only be achieved with the total victory of democracy. Thus, Clinton's neo-Wilsonianism must also be seen as a prescription for intervention. But in this instance, when, where and how is to be decided on a case-by-case basis in accordance with a prudential calculus of interest and power. American policy in the non-democratic ►zone of turbulence is therefore highly differentiated. Rogue states (Iran, Syria, Lybia) would be firmly opposed, potential power rivals (Russia, Ukraine, China) would be engaged and accommodated while peripherals and laggards (Sub-Saharan Africa) largely ignored, at least until concrete signs of renaissance emerge.

Whilst 'Engagement and Enlargement' is undoubtedly Wilsonian in spirit, in practice it also carries a distinctive Churchillian stamp. In geopolitical terms, it is a variant of the 'Three Circles' idea regarding post-World War II British foreign policy. In this case, the Clinton doctrine sees the USA as 'the indispensable country' at the intersection of three overlapping circles of world power – Europe, Asia-Pacific and the Western Hemisphere. Within these zones of democratic peace, collective security arrangements are based on undisputed US leadership and burden sharing. Constitutionally, the US is 'primus inter pares' in a new and expanding multipolar system of governance. It extends its security guarantee to all members but where feasible encourages the principle of ➤subsidiarity. Local players are expected to resolve local problems within the context of an overall American guarantee (e.g. Bosnia). For President Clinton the role is that of nightwatchman rather than global policeman. (Evans, G., 1997)

**Coercion** Coercion is a form of ➤power relationship. Like all such relationships it depends first upon the possession of a ➤capability that can be converted into policy instruments for making threats. When considering coercive behaviour in the abstract most people think first of military capabilities and the making of punitive threats, Coercion is thus related to ideas about ➤deterrence. However, economic instruments of policy can also be highly coercive. ➤Economic sanctions, particularly since they seek to deprive a target ➤actor of scarce goods and services, should be properly included in the repertoire of coercive strategies.

Since costs are involved, both in making threats and in carrying them out, an actor seeking to impose its will upon a recalcitrant target will often hope that the mere threat of coercion is enough to secure compliance. If this proves not to be the case, the imposer has to face the difficult decision of making up its mind whether to carry through with the threat or not. Such decisions will often hinge upon considerations of ➤credibility and reputation.

**Cold War** A term coined by the American journalist H. B. Swope and popularized by Walter Lippman which is used to describe the state of 'neither ➤war nor ➤peace' between the Western (non-communist) and Eastern (➤communist) ➤blocs after the Second World War. Traditional ➤great power rivalries stopped short of actual armed engagements although both bloc leaders, the United States of America and the former Soviet Union came close during a number of acute ➤crises – notably the ➤Cuban missile confrontation in 1962 and in 1973 during the ➤Arab–Israeli violence. In other respects the Cold War confrontation years evince typical adversarial ➤diplomacy: ➤arms racing, alley-seeking, ➤brinkmanship, ideological antagonism, assertive ➤interventionism. However it would be wrong to conceive of the Cold War as a relationship of unrelieved hostility, rivalry and tension since it is possible to stipulate periods of ▸*détente* of gradually increasing ▸scope and ▸domain. Four such time frames were: the period following the death of Stalin in 1953, the period following the conclusion of the Cuban missile crisis in 1962, the period associated with the ▸Nixon Doctrine and the period known as the ▸Gorbachev Doctrine. Indeed during the Gorbachev years (1985–91) a negotiated ending of the Cold War was effected via a series of summit conference with the United States of America.

In terms of a more overtly ideological framework it is possible to see the Bolshevik revolution of November 1917 as a challenge to the basic tenets of American exceptionalism and to this extent the presence of two members of the ▸state-system with such different assumptions about society would constitute a necessary – if not sufficient – cause for ▸conflict. Revolutionary challenges of the Bolshevik type – or for that matter of the Mexican pattern – were inimical to the ▸Wilson Doctrine. American intervention in the subsequent civil strife in the former Russian Empire against the Bolsheviks was accompanied by the first 'red scare' of 1919–20 in America. In 1919 also Lenin seemed to imply that the new Soviet state would not be able to co-exist with 'bourgeois' states for any appreciable length of time. The early indications of the possibility of peaceful coexistence between the two systems seemed chimerical.

The Second World War served to propel the United States and the Soviet Union into the very front rank of international significance to such an extent that the term ▸superpower was coined to identify this status. Active collaboration in the pursuit of victory over the ▸Axis meant that each was involved in diplomatic efforts to establish a post-war system that would be commensurate with their war aims and core values. At a series of summit conferences during the war the leaders of the two states – plus the United Kingdom – sought to reach agreements and understandings (sometimes very tacit) about their preferred global system. As ever, American thoughts were expressed through a resuscitated ▸multilateralism which was given the strongest ▸implementation in the raft of ▸IGOs associated with the ▸Bretton Woods conference. Soviet war aims were more geostrategically confined to Europe and within that context towards German dismemberment and a Soviet ▸sphere of influence in Central and Eastern Europe. The Soviet implementation of these ▸goals and differing ▸perceptions of the principle of ▸self-determination led to mutual suspicion and hostility. Moreover some of the earlier more ideologically motivated antagonisms of 1917–20 began to surface as ▸worst-case thinking impacted upon by political ▸leaderships on both sides of the ▸Iron Curtain. The extent of Stalin's arbitrary rule was revealed by Khrushchev in the 1950s, the use of labour camps and mass deportations was subsequently well established. In America anti-communism became an effective political weapon that was used (and abused) by politicians from both parties. The election of an 80th Congress in 1946 with a Republican majority in both Houses seemed to signify a move to the Right which culminated in the instigation of a form of political inquisition under the rubric of 'McCarthyism'.

As Kennedy (1988) has noted, the end of hostilities in 1945 left the USA with an impressive military and economic ➤capability which was topped-off by the possession of ➤nuclear weapons. The use of the first generation against Japanese targets in 1945 left America with a free hand to settle a ➤peace ➤treaty with Japan that was wholly congruent with the principles of American exceptionalism. In Europe Soviet ➤conventional military capabilities seemed to threaten Western European states with a putative hostage status unless and until American military capability could be reintroduced to redress the balance. The extent of Western Europe's exhaustion rapidly dawned upon American leaders in the winter of 1946–7 and the resultant ➤Marshall Plan was designed to reconstruct the economic basis of Europe. Its rejection by the Soviets (which probably ensured its passage through the US Congress) meant that in implementation it hardened the Cold War divisions in Europe. The Marshall initiative had been preceded in the spring of 1947 by the ➤Truman Doctrine which is generally agreed to have been presented to the American people in terms which depicted the burgeoning Cold War in Manichean formulations. Within Europe the division in Germany between West and East and the incorporation of the larger Western part into the non-communist camp precipitated the first ➤Berlin crisis and agreement in principle that America should make some tangible ➤security guarantees to ➤deter Soviet coercion. This resulted in the signing of the North Atlantic Treaty in 1949 and its conversion into an IGO following the outbreak of the ➤Korean War in 1950. By this time the United States was fully engaged in the extension of its Cold War policy of ➤containment to Asia. The ➤conflict settlement of the Chinese ➤civil war in favour of Mao Tse-Tung's forces had thoroughly alarmed the American leadership. The Communist victory in China initiated a series of introspective investigations into how China was 'lost'. The subsequent intervention of China in the Korean War exacerbated the situation and poisoned relations with the People's Republic for two decades. The ➤domino theory seemed to provide the rationalization for these events.

Structurally the Cold War system had given a distinct ➤bipolar configuration to world politics. As if to give these configurations a further twist the United States seemed determined to extend the European alliance construction into a global trend during the 1950s. Often referred to disparagingly as 'pactomania' the United States signed ➤bilateral agreements with Japan, South Korea, the Philippines and Taiwan during the years 1951–4, whilst multilateral treaties included ➤ANZUS and SEATO. In Europe the Soviet Union responded to the inclusion of West German forces in ➤NATO with the formation of the ➤Warsaw Pact (WTO). Following the death of Stalin in 1953 the first *détente* period was initiated with the successful ➤neutralization of Austria, ➤summit diplomacy and recognition of the need for peaceful coexistence.

By the mid-1950s it was clear that the first *détente* period was ending. Both superpowers intervened within their respective spheres of influence – the United States in Guatemala, the Soviet Union in Hungary – to prevent changes that were seen to damage Cold War interests. Indeed the American repertoire of interventionist instruments was extended during these years as the Central Intelligence Agency (CIA) was 'unleashed' to destabilize states seen to have regimes that were anti-American (and therefore by definition anti-Western). The successful destabilization of Iran was to return to haunt the United States leadership during the Carter years, of course. In ➤Vietnam, America actively encouraged the creation of a non-communist regime in the South after 1954 using the same instruments of policy.

The establishment of the ➤European Communities in the 1950s presaged a trend towards a more diffuse picture of the Cold War structure in terms of political economy. The subsequent economic revival of Western Europe (and in Asia–Pacific of Japan) was to produce a more ➤tripolar arrangement between these three actors as the Soviet bloc increasingly slipped out of contention as a putative rival to the West in economic terms. Although there was a short flirtation with the idea of a 'Communist model' of economic development in the late 1950s and early 1960s this ➤paradigm was more evident in the imagination of academics and 'Cold Warriors' than in reality. As Spero and Hart (1997) note, the structural characteristics of the Cold War in economic terms were always different from the military–security dimension.

During the 1950s the ➤Third World became a major ➤issue area in the Cold War. Both the US and the SU confronted each other and the Third World states with a baggage of ideologically-driven incentives to incline in their direction. The response from the first generation of such leaders in Africa, Middle East and Asia was to embrace various theories of neutralism and ➤non-alignment. The perception that ➤wars of national liberation in the Third World were a threat to Western interests led to the search for an appropriate ➤counter-insurgency response. The Kennedy Administration invested heavily in the efficacy of these measures, seeing the growing security situation in South Vietnam as a testing ground for these theories.

The Cuban missile crisis was a defining moment in the Cold War. It provoked a change of leadership in the SU. It provoked the Chinese to launch anew their complaints against the Soviet leadership of the communist states. It provoked a significant increase in defence expenditure in the SU as the ➤military–industrial complex used the crisis to obtain a commitment to achieve ➤parity with the US. The ➤NATO Alliance fractured as the crisis showed how hollow consultation could become in extremis. ➤Gaullism now struck out as the Western European version of ➤polycentrism. Despite this litany, Cuba also encouraged a second round of détente-related initiatives of which the ➤partial test ban was the most public. The death of Kennedy and the demise of Khrushchev removed the two leading 'players' in the crisis making it more difficult to sustain the momentum towards cooperation and collaboration. America's increasing preoccupation with the Vietnam War under the Johnson Administration did not help either.

The domestication of the Vietnam War in the second half of the 1960s, combined with the Nixon Administration's penchant for state-sponsored retribution against domestic and international opponents led to a national crisis of confidence in the US about their institutions of government – crucially about the 'Imperial Presidency'. The effective collapse of the American position in Vietnam following the Tet offensive – disguised by Nixon in the 1968 election as 'peace with honor' – produced a reappraisal of policy in Asia and eventually globally. This was the background to the ➤Nixon Doctrine which was without doubt the most imaginative and intellectually challenging of the several doctrinal messages handed down by Truman's successors. The Doctrine's impact was to shift the definition of the Cold War onto a more tripolar emphasis. The Administration's return to *détente* was more thoroughgoing and principled than earlier instances.

Although the decade of the 1970s came to be called by some American conservatives 'the decade of neglect' a more balanced judgement would recognize that significant changes in world politics were reflected back onto the Cold War. The collapse of the Bretton Woods system and the questioning of American ➤hegemony in the field of political economy produced the first stirrings of the ➤declinist thesis. Rosecrance's (1976) *America as an Ordinary Country* is typical of this introspection. In Europe, Ostopolitik, the ➤Helsinki accords and the settlement over ➤Berlin pointed towards significant tension reduction. The Middle East crisis of 1973 over the Arab–Israeli conflict produced the OAPEC initiative to use the 'oil weapon' and the 'Alert Crisis' between the US and SU. Lebow and Stein (1994) see this crisis as the beginning of the end of superpower *détente*. The Soviet incursion into ➤Afghanistan and the collapse of the ➤SALT process were two end-of-decade outcomes which pointed towards the 1980s and the 'Second' Cold War.

Ronald Reagan rode into the White House in 1981 with a perception of the Cold War which was perhaps the most ideologically driven of any incumbent. The term 'Second Cold War' is accepted usage for the approach taken during Reagan's first term. Historically it is marked off by the Afghanistan crisis and the collapse of the SALT process as start points and the ➤Gorbachev Doctrine (and the Reagan response) as endings. Historically the Second Cold War was relatively short lived and it was certainly less comprehensive than the 1940s version. The Second Cold War was aimed at Soviet power rather than the Communist bloc. Nixon's opening to China and Carter's ➤recognition were regarded as inviolate. Domestically the Second Cold War was popular with Americans but it was not accompanied by anything like the McCarthyism of the late 1950s. In the 1980s it was American fears of subversion in the Third World not in America itself which were crucial. In Europe the idea of a Second

Cold War had at best a mixed press. The Thatcher government in Britain was supportive but other European leaders were more detached seeing too much at stake in terms of Ostpolitik and investment possibilities to want to follow America into a more confrontational position. For many Europeans the Reagan rhetoric was too harsh and too dogmatic. Probably no American President had a greater 'two-audience' problem as between America and Europe than Ronald Reagan. Reagan's policies encouraged the growth of the ►peace movement in Europe after 1980 and even at the formal governmental level it did little to improve the Atlantic partnership idea. The unfolding of the Gorbachev doctrine into a wholesale redefinition of the US/SU relationship was the lasting legacy of that initiative. Once the ►scope and ►domain of these changes were understood the Reagan response was positive. Domestically Reagan was by 1986 under pressure to address the growing problem of the American economy. The ►Declinist attack was in full cry and the 'Irangate' revelations threatened to tarnish the Reagan record. If not beleaguered, Reagan certainly looked bereft of ideas and responding to the Gorbachev initiatives was likely to ensure the President a more exalted place in history.

The ►Charter of Paris is now the preferred point of reference for the end of the Cold War. ►Nineteen eighty-nine remains the watershed year when changes assumed their own dynamic. The collapse of Communism and the implosion of the Soviet Union make an assessment of the Cold War more difficult. Terms like 'Long Peace' are Eurocentric since violent conflict as a global occurrence was widespread and highly destructive during the Cold War years. It may be asserted that in seeking the causes of systemic conflict after 1945 the Cold War is not itself a principal causal factor. It is arguable however that the Cold War exacerbated many conflicts by encouraging contending parties to seek allies from amongst the Cold War protagonists. The domestic political, economic and cultural consequences of the Cold War for the protagonists were again mixed. Particularly in the US, pursuit of the policy of anti-communism and confrontation with Soviet power led to the creation of a national security apparatus which impinged upon democratic norms by limiting participation in policy making and information on policy outcomes. The Cold War shaped the lives of all who experienced it. Its shadow is still cast over the last years of the century which are appropriately referred to as the 'post-Cold War period'.

**The Cold War and the discipline of IR** Apart from substantive accounts of events and developments during the period covered by the Cold War, academic analyses revolve around two broad questions: why did it arise and why did it end? Regarding causes, earlier commentaries tended to assign responsibility to the USSR and international communism's long term and often expressed commitment to world ►revolution. Thus, within the orthodox ►action–reaction dynamic of conventional IR theory, this Soviet strategic objective occasioned the Western response of ►containment. This was the intellectual frame of reference within which most Western academics and policy-makers located the conflict. It was viewed as a particular representation of the ►security dilemma, no different in essence from that described by ►Thucydides in the fifth century BC regarding the cause of the Pelopennesian War: 'What made war inevitable was the growth in Athenian power and the fear that this caused in Sparta' (Thucydides, 1982 ed.). Reacting to this realist view, radical or 'revisionist' accounts began to appear in the late 1960s and early 1970s, which while accepting the ideational framework of the orthodox reading, assigned blame not to the Soviets but to Western ►imperialism and in particular, the capitalist quest for global economic dominance. In the 1980s a 'post-revisionist' school completed the historiographical triangle by allotting blame to both camps, often citing ►misperception as the proximate cause (Jervis, 1976, Lebow and Stein, 1994).

Regarding the demise of the Cold War, there is a consensus that the single most important factor was ►Gorbachev's 'new thinking' and his pursuit of 'glasnost' (openness), 'perestroika' (restructuring) and ►democracy in the USSR from 1985 onwards. The wide ranging concessions that these initiatives engendered (accelerated or complemented by the ►Reagan Doctrine), effectively brought the Cold War to an end. That this involved the disintegration of the Soviet Union itself, is generally viewed as an unintended, unforeseen consequence. In addition to acknowledging the crucial role played by Gorbachev, many of the more ideological Western accounts have also concluded that the end of the Cold War in fact represented the 'triumph' of the West and its conceptions of politics and economics. Thus, Francis Fukuyama, in a celebrated essay published in 1989, wrote that: 'What we are witnessing is not just the end of the Cold War, or the passing of a particular period of post war history, but the end of history as such: that is, the endpoint of mankind's ideological evolution and the universalization of Western liberal democracy as the final form of human government' (p. 4). Although the unabashed triumphalism of Fukuyama may have abated somewhat, the Wilsonian idea that liberal democracy is the solution to international conflict has now become a pervasive one in post-Cold War Anglo-American scholarship.

Universally welcomed as it was, the end of the Cold War occasioned something of a crisis in conventional IR theory. Neither of the two main paradigms, ►neorealism and ►neolibralism had predicted systemic change of this order of magnitude. That none of the major theories of world politics anticipated the end of the Cold War led one prominent specialist to conclude that this was damning evidence against IR scholarship and that the field had proved to be 'bankrupt' (Gaddis, 1992 p. 44). This is an extreme view but few would doubt that the events of ►nineteen eighty-nine constitute a 'complex failure' for the discipline as a whole (i.e. a failure to interpret properly the information at hand). IR scholars, and to a lesser extent their Soviet Studies counterparts, were collectively misled by their attachment to untested deterministic assumptions about ➤great power behaviour and the role of ideas, belief systems and ➤leaderships in effecting outcomes. As a consequence, the research agenda of mainstream IR was obsessed with questions relating to maintaining ➤superpower stability ('the long peace') rather than questions relating to change or transformation. (A notable exception to this was Gilpin, 1981.) Accordingly, the post-Cold War period has witnessed not just a return to ➤normative theory, but also a renewed interest in cooperation under conditions of anarchy and the exploration of alternative modes of explanation and alternative political, social and economic orders, (Lebow and Risse-Kappen, 1995). ➤➤Critical theory/postmodernism

**Collateral damage** A term used in strategic analysis. It refers to the devastation of persons and property adjacent to a target. The issue of intentionality will often divide attacker and victim. Evidence that collateral damage has been deliberately caused may be used for ➤propaganda purposes or to support allegations of ➤war crimes. Recent developments in ➤international law have set out clear distinctions between legitimate targets. The 1977 Geneva Protocol to the 1949 Convention has thus identified civilian populations and civilian objects as illegitimate in this context. Intent and negligence will loom large in substantiating such charges against an attacker.

Recent developments in ➤technology heralded as the ➤revolution in military affairs means that it is now possible to attack targets with ➤conventional precision guided weapons of great accuracy. The term collateral damage was widely used during the ➤Persian Gulf War and it has accordingly passed into the lexicon of media analysis.

**Collective security** Like the ➤League of Nations with which it is most closely identified, the concept of collective security is an important innovation of twentieth-century ➤international relations. It asserts that the ➤security dilemma of ➤states can best be overcome not through national ➤self-help and the ➤balance of power, but through the institution of communal commitments whereby each state undertakes to join in common actions against those which threaten the territorial integrity or political ➤independence of others. Its major premise is the musketeer oath of 'all for one and one for all'. The idea of a common ➤defence is not a new one; it is a familiar theme in international history from at least the ancient Greeks onwards, and elements of it feature prominently in the writings of reformers and radicals such as Pierre Dubois (1306), the duc de Sully (1638), Kant (1795) and Bentham (1789). But it was not until the First World War, and the collapse of the notion that international ➤anarchy was tolerable, that the collective security ideal gained momentum.

Accordingly, the idea of a universal, permanent and collective commitment to oppose ➤aggression and to guarantee security was enshrined in the Covenant of the League of Nations (Article 10), and reappeared in a modified form in the ➤United Nations Charter (Chapter VII). Its efficacy depended on each

77

state, regardless of its particular or immediate interests, being prepared to pledge to act against law breakers, the assumption being that in this way it would always be possible to organize a preponderant coalition of like-minded states against an indeterminate aggressor. Thus ➤deterrence, as well as punishment and restoration of order, was part of its rationale. The abject failure of the League to provide communal security (Manchuria 1931, Ethiopia 1935, the Rhineland 1936, Austria 1938, Czechoslovakia 1939 and Finland 1940) is a reminder of the perverse persistence of individual rather than common perspectives in the formulation and conduct of ➤foreign policy.

Given this poor track record it may seem surprising to find that the ➤United Nations followed in the footsteps of the League at its Charter Conference in 1945. The five ➤veto powers were given special status – and commensurate responsibility – under the UN system and Chapter 7 provides a full repertoire of coercive measures for the ➤IGO to use in the event of a threatened or actual breach of the peace. These powers have been activated on two occasions since 1945: in the case of the ➤Korean War of 1950 and in the ➤Persian Gulf War of 1990. In the first instance the enabling resolutions were 'fluked' through the Council in the absence of the former USSR and with the People's Republic excluded from the Chinese seat. The ➤Cold War was then at its height and the Truman Administration was intent upon extending its ➤perception of ➤containment into the Asian context. This controversial exercise compromised the neutrality of the UN and fatally damaged the standing of the incumbent ➤Secretary-General with important sections of the organization.

The dramatic deployment of military power by a coalition of 28 states against Iraq in 1990 was regarded by many as evidence that collective security had come of age in international relations and that in the post-Cold War period the obstacles that had prevented the UN from achieving its objectives in the field of peace and security had been removed. The widespread solidarity of the condemnation of Iraq's annexation of Kuwait and the speed with which the UN Security Council responded was after all, precisely the kind of scenario envisaged by the founding fathers in 1945. However, this early optimism about the UN and collective security proved premature, since many of the conflicts it subsequently was called upon to address were conflicts within state borders, rather than across them. The Persian Gulf War was unique in post-war international politics in the sense that it was the only case of a UN member state having its territory completely occupied by another state. Further, there are legitimate doubts as to whether this operation really was an example of UN action. The war was not actually conducted under UN aegis; it was primarily an American-led and American inspired operation. Throughout, the chain of command led to the Oval Office in Washington, and not to the UN in New York. The conditions which contributed to the success of this operation are extremely unlikely to be replicated in the future.

Analytically, the two cases cited above amount to ➤compellence rather than

➤deterrence versions of the use of force, although it is impossible to tell how many would-be recalcitrants are deterred by such resolute measures. The danger inherent in the ➤implementation of collective security is likewise clear: that, in a system that lacks cohesion and cultural unity, collective security will take on the appearance and character of those states most committed to its application in a particular instance. The assumption that all states are pursuing the same ➤goals and that they are willing to wage ➤war to achieve them is probably not warranted. Conversely, if this assumption cannot be made, then collective security can become fatally identified with the policy preferences of the leading actors rather than UN membership as a whole. It can thus become a device for maintaining the ➤status quo. In the post-Cold War period, analysts have begun to speak of 'cooperative security' rather than collective security. This, too, is based on the idea that peace is indivisible. It's a more nuanced version of collective security in the sense that it does not rely on spontaneous power balancing techniques, which are only likely to occur when vital interests are at stake. Cooperative security thus envisages collective action through regional institutions. The expansion of ➤NATO eastwards, is predicated on this idea.

**Colonialism** This is a variety of ➤imperialism. It involves the settlement of foreign territories, the maintenance of rule over a subordinate population and the separation of the ruling group from the subject population. The relationship between the 'mother country' and the colony is usually exploitive. The earliest colonies (e.g. ancient Greek settlements in the Mediterranean or British settlement in North America) involved emigration into what were considered to be politically empty spaces and were not thought to be overtly racist, but the more modern variety usually entails this dimension. Characteristic features thus involve political and legal domination by an ➤alien minority, economic exploitation and ➤dependency and racial and cultural inequality. Unlike imperialism, which can involve complete assimilation, colonialism involves more or less strict separation from the metropolitan centre, the reason being that colonies exist to serve the needs of the colonizing power and as such occupy a subordinate and servile role. Historically, the phenomenon is associated with Europe and the major colonial powers from the fifteenth to the nineteenth centuries were Portugal, Spain, Holland, Britain and France. These were joined in the late nineteenth and early twentieth century by Belgium, Germany, Italy, the United States, Japan and Russia. The unwilling targets for these competing penetrative drives were the Americas, Africa, Asia and Australasia.

Colonialism, and its antithesis anti-colonialism, have been major forces in shaping the political and economic character of the modern world. Until the nineteenth century, the practice was so common in international affairs that it generated little opposition. It was seen to be an inevitable consequence of ➤great power politics. With the rise of ➤liberalism, ➤nationalism and especially with the ➤Marxist/Leninist critique of conventional social economic and political mores, the concept and the practices associated with it increasingly came to be regarded as illegitimate. Indeed, the very success of the anti-colonial movement was directly dependent on doctrines and ➤ideologies developed by the colonial powers themselves.

The incorporation of the ideas of ➤self-determination, ➤sovereignty, ➤independence and formal ➤equality into the major institutions of the international community has ensured the demise of the colonial ideal. In the ➤League of Nations the ➤administered territory and mandates system reflected the general disquiet about the practice although it did not outlaw it completely. The ➤UN, on the other hand, has always been at the forefront of the anti-colonial movement and the ➤General Assembly in particular has been the single most important ➤actor in effecting its near universal rejection. It is a moot point whether the colonization process had beneficial effects on the targeted areas, but such is the opprobrium associated with it now that it finds few contemporary supporters. An important legacy of colonization, especially in Africa, is the contentious ➤boundary issue which frequently bedevils African politics. The boundaries established by the colonial powers rarely, if ever, reflected indigenous racial, tribal and cultural patterns.

Clearly, the concept is not a precise one but its essence involves unequal rights, separation and deliberate exploitation. These themes are echoed in the term 'neo-colonialism' which refers to the continued domination of post-colonial independent ➤states by the ➤developed world. Reliance on foreign investment capital, technical skills and training, manufactured goods and markets are viewed by many developing states as deliberately engineered by-products of colonialism. Thus, ➤aid is in no sense humanitarian or altruistic. It is either belated repayment for past exploitation or else is a partially concealed attempt by the donor at obtaining political concessions. In either case, uneven development persists. Another variant is the term ➤'internal colonialism' which refers to cases where an economically dominant segment of a state treats a peripheral ➤region as a subordinate and dependent entity. The Asian peoples of the former Soviet Union, for example, were commonly regarded as victims of this practice. Again, the South African state under ➤apartheid (1948–94) displayed many of the features associated with the concept and its political/social system was often referred to as 'colonialism of a special type'.

**Comecon/CMEA** Council of Mutual Economic Assistance was established by the Soviet Union in 1949 to integrate the economies of Eastern Europe. Along with the ➤Warsaw Pact this regional organisation represented the infrastructure for the Soviet ➤bloc in terms of military/security and wealth/welfare ➤issue areas. The founder members of the CMEA were: Bulgaria, Czechoslovakia, Hungary, Poland, Romania and the Soviet Union. Albania was a member from 1949 to 1961, the German Democratic Republic joined in 1950. Non-European members were Mongolia (1962), Cuba (1972) and Vietnam (1978).

As the membership listing shows Comecon functioned as an instrument for Soviet ➤economic statecraft firstly in Eastern Europe and then later in the ➤Third World. Although Comecon – like any IGO – had a permanent institutional structure headed by a Council and staffed by a secretariat, in reality it operated as a ➤supranational planning agency for the Soviet Union. The economic objectives were politically directed from Moscow and involved specialization of production in member countries. Growing ➤polycentrism led some states, particularly Romania and Bulgaria to question the roles assigned to them by central planning.

The events following 1989 in Eastern Europe, in particular the demise of ➤communism and the collapse of the Soviet Union led to the termination of the Comecon system. The economy of Eastern Germany is now fully integrated into the ➤European Union (EU) via their ➤unification with West Germany. Other former Comecon members have sought and ratified special association agreements with the EU known as 'Europe Agreements'. These basically expand the original idea of the association agreement (which guaranteed ➤free trade) to include political and individual liberties. It is likely that the long-term ➤goal of many of these former Comecon member states will be full membership of the EU. Comecon was formally dissolved in the autumn of 1991.

**Common Heritage of Mankind (CHM)** A quasi-legal concept associated with the ➤South, especially least developed countries, which asserts that resources not yet covered by a legal ➤regime, belong to mankind as a whole and not to particular states, or groups of states. Part of a general claim for distributive justice, the common heritage principle has been applied to a number of contemporary North/South ➤issue areas, in particular relating to the Antarctica Treaty, Moon Treaty, Outer-Space Treaty and the Seabed Treaty. In relation to Unclos III, this idea appealed especially to non-coastal or ➤landlocked states which under traditional ➤international law, are denied legal rights concerning the natural resources of the sea. The old rule relating to international resource allocation beyond coastal jurisdiction had been a variant of the adage 'finders keepers, losers weepers'. This clearly favours the great maritime states and those with the technological ability to exploit off-shore, non-living resources.

At Unclos III, this viewpoint was well expressed by the Singapore delegate and broadly represented views of the geographically disadvantaged states:

Every state, whether coastal or landlocked, should be entitled to a fair share of the resources of the sea in accordance with the principle of the common heritage of mankind. If that principle was to have any meaning, as great an area as possible of the continental margin and the seabed should be reserved for the international regime.

The CHM principle, especially as it relates to the status of the deep seabed, has not yet achieved the status of customary law and continues to be a bone of contention between the North and the South in world politics.

However, most commentators believe that the CHM represents a positive advance in the democratization of international law, the ➤globalization of resources and the general advance of considerations of distributive justice in international affairs.

**Common market**  The common market is a form of interstate ➤integration. The key to the market is the ➤customs union. It is also the building block, because the theory of the common market is that, once the customs union is successfully implemented, it will create needs for further integration. In particular, the free movement of two factors of production, labour and capital, are prerequisites for the common market if it is to expand dynamically upon this basis. As a result a free common market for goods and services will be established. Rules governing competition within the market will be required and a common fiscal system would be progressively instituted. In particular, harmonization of sales taxes are essential in a common market. In order to facilitate the free movement of labour, ➤harmonization of social welfare policies would be required.

In the continuum of economic integration, the common market is the median position between the customs union and full economic union. The ➤trade implications of the common market are exactly the same as the customs union, so the tendency of supervisory institutions such as the General Agreement on Tariffs and Trade (➤GATT) has been to concentrate their attention upon the latter. Common markets are more the concern of integration theorists and in particular of the functionalist approach (➤functionalism). Historically, common markets have been a feature of ➤state building. Thus in nineteenth-century Europe the development of a common market in Germany followed upon the establishment of the *zollverein*. The economic history of the United States is also a good example of the positive gains from the formation of a common market. In both these nineteenth-century instances protective ➤tariffs were used to shelter the nascent market.

The ➤European Community (EC) has as one of its stated objectives in the Treaty of Rome the establishment of a common market. The term 'common market' was often used colloquially to refer to the EC. Developments during the 1980s culminating in the Single European Act (SEA) of 1986 and the ➤Maastricht Treaty of 1992 have revised the terminology. ➤Single market rather than common market is the broadly accepted usage now.

**Commonwealth**  A voluntary ➤association of 53 ➤states, most of whom were former parts of the British Empire. The term 'commonwealth' originated in the fifteenth century as an English equivalent of the Latin ➤*res publica*, meaning the public good, or 'common weal'. In this sense, the word has been used to describe many kinds of political systems. The component units of the former Soviet Union for example, referred to themselves after 1992 as the ➤Commonwealth of Independent States. Generally however, in world politics the term is associated with British imperial history and was specifically employed at the end of the nineteenth century to refer to those territories (the 'Dominions') which although formally part of the Empire, had full internal self-government and significant degrees of latitude in ➤foreign policy. In this sense, the term signified a looser, less subordinate relationship than that implied by 'colony' or 'empire'.

The Commonwealth is a voluntary, unstructured group of states with no formal commitments or charter, although it does have a secretariat. The British monarch is nominally Head of the Commonwealth although this carries no necessary constitutional implications for members. Most members (e.g. India) are republics and no longer accept the monarchical principle. Where this principle is still accepted (e.g. Canada) the sovereign is formally Head of State and is represented by a Governor General whose appointment is a matter for the host state alone. This office is the last vestige of British imperial authority. The origins of the Commonwealth can be traced back to 1867 when Canada was given Dominion status, followed by Australia in 1900 and New Zealand in 1907. British imperial authority was further relaxed at the imperial conference of 1926 when the UK and the Dominions were defined as autonomous entities. In 1931 the Statute of Westminster reinforced the principle of ➤autonomy and the term 'British Empire' was replaced in official usage by the 'British Commonwealth of Nations'. By 1948 the terms 'British' and 'Dominion' were dropped and the modern Commonwealth with its emphasis on voluntarism and equality emerged. The official title of the British foreign ministry is now the Foreign and Commonwealth Office.

The Commonwealth is still developing and membership is not static. In 1949 the Irish Republic withdrew followed by South Africa (1961–94) and Pakistan (1972–89). Fiji's membership lapsed in 1987 and Nigeria was suspended in 1985. Burma (Myanmar) is the only former British colony not to have joined after independence. It is highly unlikely that Hong Kong will join after re-incorporation with China in 1997. The only ➤region not represented in the Commonwealth at present is the Middle East. It is thus virtually a universal organization and new eligibility criteria may soon make this a reality. Non-British colonies that have recently been admitted are: Namibia (1990), Cameroon (1995) and Mozambique (1995). In addition, Angola, Yemen, Eritrea, Rwanda and the Palestinian Authority have also expressed an interest in joining. At present, over twenty-five per cent of the world's states are members with a total population of around 1.56bn making it the second largest international organization after the ➤United Nations.

The following states are now Commonwealth members (dates of independence in brackets):

AFRICA: Botswana (1966), Cameroon (1995), Gambia (1965), Ghana (1957), Kenya (1963), Lesotho (1966), Malawi (1964), Mauritius (1968), Mozambique (1995), Namibia (1990), Seychelles (1976), Sierra Leone (1961) South Africa (1910), Swaziland (1968), Tanzania (1961), Uganda (1962), Zambia (1964), Zimbabwe (1980).

ASIA: Bangladesh (1972), Brunei (1984), India (1947), Malaysia (1957), Maldives (1965), Pakistan (1947), Singapore (1965), Sri Lanka (1948).

CARIBBEAN and AMERICAS: Antigua (1981), Bahamas (1973), Barbados (1966), Belize (1981), Canada (1867), Dominica (1978), Granada (1974), Guyana (1966), Jamaica (1962), St Christopher and Nevis (1963), St Lucia (1979), St Vincent (1979), Trinidad (1962).

EUROPE: United Kingdom, Cyprus (1961), Malta (1964).

AUSTRALASIA/OCEANIA: Australia (1900), Kiribati (1979), Nauru (1968), New Zealand (1907), Papua New Guinea (1975), Solomons (1978), Tonga (1970), Tuvalu (1978), Vanatu (198), Western Samoa (1962).

Membership requires the unanimous agreement of all participating states and although no formal law-making body exists, Heads of Government meetings are held bi-annually and decisions are taken by consensus. Given the absence of any clear overall common ethnic, cultural, political, social or economic bonds, it is hardly surprising that consensus is very difficult to achieve, except on the broadest of issues. Issues which have threatened Commonwealth unity in recent years are ➤apartheid in South Africa, British membership of the then ➤European Community and the ➤North–South divide. Although it has no identifiable political or economic rationale and no effective coercive ➤power, supporters argue that it serves as one of the few global arenas in which dominant systemic values can be articulated (e.g. promotion of ➤human rights and ➤good governance) as well as a communications conduit between disparate and often conflicting sectors of the international community. It is clearly not a power ➤bloc in the usual sense and given its minimalist institutional structure and modest resources it will never play a major role in world affairs. Notwithstanding this, it remains an important channel for cooperation between widely different states with little in common except perhaps a desire to remain together. In this sense, it is a much more coherent international grouping than its French-dominated counterpart, ➤*Francophonie.*

**Commonwealth of Independent States** An international organization of twelve former republics of the Soviet Union. Formed in 1991 it is often referred to as Russia's 'near abroad' and consists of Armenia, Azerbaijan, Belarus, Georgia, Kazakstan, Kyrgyzstan, Moldova, Russia, Tajikstan, Turkmenistan, Ukraine and Uzbekistan. The agreement stipulated a unified command over the former Soviet Union's military forces, a commitment to develop a common Eurasian market, recognition of borders and acknowledgement of cultural and political rights for all citizens. Headquarters are in Minsk, capital of Belarus. A succession of crises has dogged the organization since its founding. The most serious are the following: the war between Armenia and Azerbaijan over the disputed territory of Nagorno-Karabakh, responsibility for paying Soviet debt obligations the Russian-Ukraine quarrel over the Black Sea fleet and Russia's claim to the Crimea. Virtually the only thing the twelve states share is their (dubious) common experience of being members of the former Soviet Union. The impending enlargement of ➤NATO could pose serious problems for this fragile organization, particularly if Ukraine sought membership, since Russia regards the CIS as being firmly within its own ➤sphere of influence. The CIS has clearly failed as a military union, as an economic union and as a currency union and its ability to survive as a meaningful ➤IGO is seriously in doubt. However, its continued existence gives extra credence to the idea that Russia is a ➤great power in regional as well as global terms.

**Communal conflict** Conflicts within communities – ➤states, ➤nations, ethnic groups – are commonplace in ➤international relations. However, if a communal conflict becomes chronic and persistent its dynamic can lead to ➤civil war and even external ➤intervention. Empirical evidence seems to suggest that certain changes take place within the conflict process which leads to these developments. The conflict changes from being about interests to being about values. That is to say, rather than disagreeing about what they want, the parties disagree about what they stand for. As a result new, more ideologically defined issues come to the forefront. These issues will be presented in a biased, one-sided context and, as a result, the ➤conflict will become more violent and antagonistic. Once a cycle of violence and counter-violence has begun a communal conflict is close to becoming chronic and persistent. Individual acts of heroism or terrorism become mythologized into the folk history of the conflict. The process of ➤polarization has now set in and clear physical lines of demarcation become evident between the communities. Often the physical movement of peoples will spontaneously occur as separate communities attempt to draw ➤boundaries between each other. A new style of ➤leadership will emerge to symbolize the polarization that is now evident to all. The new leadership will, moreover, have an investment in the continuation of the conflict. Communication will break down between the now separate communities and, if the conflict persists over several generations, a form of 'autistic hostility' will become evident. Stereotypes of the other group will be reinforced behind the communications barrier and individuals will be socialized into a culture of group hostility and suspicion.

Some of the most intractable and violent conflicts in contemporary world politics began as communal conflicts which then escalated horizontally as outside parties were drawn in as allies and protectors. The ➤Arab–Israeli conflict is a paradigm example of this process, as indeed is the continuing conflict in Yugoslavia. ➤➤Ethnic cleansing

85

**Communism** A political ➤ideology aimed at the common ownership of land and capital and the elimination of the coercive ➤power of the ➤state. According to its principal exponent, Karl Marx, it must be distinguished from socialism, which is characterized as a transitional stage between capitalism and full communism when the state has 'withered away'. In this categorization, communist states are properly socialist states, since the apparatus of the state are still in place. In ➤international relations the significance of the ideology from a theoretical perspective is the prominent place it assigns to ➤imperialism as the fundamental cause of persistent international conflict. Indeed, the equation, capitalism = imperialism = ➤war could be seen to constitute the communist theory of IR.

In practice international communism has been a major force in world politics since the Bolshevik ➤revolution in the Soviet Union in 1917, yet ever since the publication of the *Communist Manifesto* in 1848 by Marx and Engels its ideals have had a profound impact on international affairs. The central aim has been the creation of a unified international workers' movement ('proletarian internationalism') to overcome and defeat the capitalist world market. Revolution has always been central to its thesis. The creation of the 'internationals' in the late nineteenth and early twentieth century was an attempt at its practical realization. The first International was the International Working Men's Association and this lasted from 1864–76, the Second (or Socialist) International, or Comitern, lasted from 1919 to 1943. The aim of these 'internationals' was the creation of a global network of communist parties united by the ideal of overthrowing the existing capitalist ➤international system. After 1919, under Lenin and later Stalin, the movement was dominated by Moscow and was regarded as a global extension of Soviet domestic and ➤foreign policy. The Second World War and its aftermath wrought significant changes in perspectives; in particular, the focus began to move away from Western Europe to Eastern Europe, Asia and Africa. By 1948 those countries within the Allied-recognized Soviet ➤sphere of influence – Poland, Hungary, Romania, Bulgaria, Czechoslovakia, East Germany, Yugoslavia and Albania – had all formally become communist. By 1949, China and North Korea brought Asia into the communist orbit. Increasingly, during the post-war period efforts were directed at creating communist or pro-communist ➤regimes in other parts of the under-developed world, especially in Africa and Latin America. Hopes that international communism would develop into a coherent unified alternative world system, however, were dashed by increasing ➤polycentrism (represented by the defection of Albania and Yugoslavia in Europe and by the Sino-Soviet split in Asia), and by the persistence of radical ➤nationalism in Africa and Latin America. During the 1950s a shift occurred in Soviet strategy. Khrushchev publicly declared that war between capitalist and communist states was not inevitable, and that there could be 'different roads to socialism'. The dominant position was still held by Moscow, but the idea of a union of Moscow-led communist states was replaced by the concept of a world socialist system which could be and indeed was, ►pluralist in character. Since then, and particularly under Gorbachev, the communist ►bloc developed into a looser ►association where the aim was coexistence and not domination or the overthrow of the existing world ►state-system. In the post-war world the main ►international organizations associated with international communism have been the ►Warsaw Treaty Organization and ►Comecon/CMEA (Council of Mutual Economic Assistance), which was established in 1949 to integrate the economies of Eastern Europe under Soviet direction and control. Both these organizations were formed in direct response to American military and economic initiatives in Western Europe (►NATO and the ►Marshall Plan).

In the communist view of ►international relations the primary units of analysis are class and the relations of production, therefore the notion of ►state and the state-system are strictly speaking expendable. However, international communism showed a remarkable degree of flexibility in this regard and communist states, after theoretical ►revisionism of original doctrines, indicated a willingness to operate within, rather than against the traditional institutions of the post-►Westphalian world.

During the 1989–91 period communism all but ceased to exist as a political force in international relations as result of the transformation in political thinking produced by the ►Gorbachev Doctrine. This set in motion pressures which led to the collapse of the USSR and the international sub-system that it created (►nineteen eighty-nine). Communism is now a spent force in world politics and even in China the events following the Tiananmen Square Massacre (1989) demonstrate that the new freedom set in motion by the ideas of *glasnost* (openness) and *perestroika* (restructuring) are difficult to contain within the traditional theoretical mould. There is now near-universal acceptance that economic prosperity and political freedom are intimately linked. ►►Good governance; Marxism/Leninism

**Compellence** A sub-field of ►deterrence theory developed by Schelling (1966) largely on the basis of the ►Cuban missile crisis of 1962. Schelling argues that 'deterring' an ►actor from a behaviour pattern that it might wish to follow is sufficiently different from 'compelling' it to do something different (including undoing what it has already done) as to justify an analytical distinction. In the Cuban case, Schelling argues that the Kennedy administration's handling of the ►crisis enabled the ►leadership in the United States to manipulate the risks of ►escalation to ►nuclear war to 'compel' the Soviet leaders to agreee to withdraw the offending ►ballistic missiles from the island. Paradoxically this risk manipulation makes compellence a dangerous strategy to pursue. Its elegant – if somewhat complex – logic depends upon adherence to views of ►rationality amongst ►decision-makers which might break down when they are most needed. Recent work by Lebow and Stein (1994) suggests that the compellence

►paradigm only partly fits the decision calculus in Cuba. Both leaderships seem to have overestimated the other's propensity for risk taking and in this sense Cuba might be better seen as an instance of mutual compellence. There is some evidence to suggest that in approaching the ►Persian Gulf War of 1991 the Bush administration sought to 'compel' the Iraqi withdrawal from Kuwait via the Desert Shield build-up. In any event, compellence remains a highly contingent and very dangerous ►crisis management behaviour repertoire.

**Complex emergencies**  Sometimes called 'political' or 'permanent' emergencies, this term emerged in the discourse on ►humanitarian intervention in the late 1980s in response to the protracted famines in the Horn of Africa and the Sudan. It signifies a new approach to famine and humanitarian relief. Instead of viewing these emergencies in economistic or natural terms (ie that they are the result of economic failure or natural disasters) this approach highlights their underlying political character. It argues that famine is a complex socio–political phenomenon which cannot be addressed simply through the provision of relief or ►aid. Indeed, technical interventions of this kind often exacerbate the problem since they can reinforce the policies and programmes that contributed to, or produced the crisis in the first place, resulting in a structure of 'permanent' emergency. On this view, humanitarian intervention becomes part of the problem of famine rather than its solution.

**Complex interdependence**  A term used by Keohane and Nye in their 1977 book. Unlike the concept of ►interdependence, complex interdependence was clearly intended as an ideal type. In particular, the two authors sought to compare and contrast this model with ►realism as a competing paradigm of IR. Three central assumptions of realism are challenged simultaneously: ►states are not necessarily coherent units nor are they always the dominant ►actors, ►force itself may now be an ineffective instrument of policy and the traditional ►hierarchy of issue where military/security matters take precedence over economic and social ones is now largely anachronistic. 'Complex interdependence' is the term used to reflect this new portrayal of reality. As an explanatory model of IR it assumes multiple channels of contact between societies, an absence of hierarchy among issues and the disutility of military power or at best, a minor role for the use of force. Thus it gives rise to 'distinctive political processes, which translate powers sources into power as control of outcomes' – among which are ►linkage strategies, agenda control and coalition building.

The pioneering work of Keohane and Nye has been of crucial importance in the development of alternative, ►pluralistic perspectives to that of power and security. By focusing attention on interdependence and ►transnational relations, they have presented a vision of world politics in which actors, environments, structures, processes and outcomes are far less certain and more complex that the rather unitary and static insights offered by traditional realism.

However, as the authors are at pains to point out, this approach does not make claim to exclusivity – it is a *competing* ➤paradigm and does not altogether dispense with the earlier orthodoxy.

**Comprehensive test-ban treaty (CTB)** Moves to ban the testing of ➤nuclear weapons, particularly ➤hydrogen weapons, date from the early 1950s. For many years it was felt that a ban on testing in all environments, which is what a CTB involves, was impossible without a significant amount of on-site ➤inspection. The burden of scientific opinion now appears to reject this necessity. Problems with the realization of a CTB accordingly appear to be political and strategic rather than scientific and technical. These can be reduced to two propositions: first, that periodic testing of nuclear warheads is required in order to maintain confidence in their utility – this is the so-called 'shelf-life' argument. Second, some testing of new warheads is bound to be required whenever one of the nuclear weapon states wishes to introduce new delivery systems into their arsenals.

A CTB has been advocated by those individuals and interests within the existing nuclear states wanting to see the nuclear proliferation ➤regime strengthened. In particular those sections of the Treaty on the Non-Proliferation of Nuclear Weapons (➤NPT) which require the existing nuclear states to pursue meaningful arms control regarding ➤vertical proliferation would be enhanced by a CTB ➤treaty. In the long run the goal of a workable CTB agreement is likely to be a matter of politics rather than seismology.

**Compromise** A form of ➤conflict settlement involving mutual – although not necessarily balanced – concessions by parties who are engaged in ➤negotiations. Before a compromise settlement can be reached the parties must agree in principle that they will settle their differences in this manner. Having made this commitment they can then commence the substantive bargaining aimed at achieving a sufficient modification of the other's position to make a settlement possible. Each party will normally have a clear perception of how far they are willing to go to make concessions and this may be termed the maximum concession point.

If a conflict is lengthy or persistent, parties may change their maximum concession points as they feel their overall position has strengthened or weakened. Sometimes parties will reject a particular compromise at the start of a conflict which they will be happy to accept at a later stage when they see how costly the conflict has become. Again the bargaining process may of itself alter the perceptions that parties have of their maximum concession points.

Third-party ➤mediation is often necessary to effect a compromise. The mediator may suggest a settlement within the maximum concession points of the parties. The mediator may offer to supervise the implementation of the settlement. Mediation is likely to be more successful between parties pursuing 'mixed motive' strategies, that is to say, by parties willing to see their relations with each other in cooperative terms. Provided that the parties can trust each other to keep their commitments, compromise settlements can produce positive ►feedback and lead to a general improvement in relations. Parties will then come to expect that future conflicts will be settled by compromise rather than by confrontation.

**Concert system** The Concert system arose out of the deliberations at the Congress of Vienna in 1815. It refers to the *ad hoc* system of conferences held by the major powers to regulate diplomatic ►crises in Europe between 1815 and 1854. Although it had no formal institutional structure its purpose was overtly managerial – to control, through mutual consultation, the ►balance of power in post-Napoleonic Europe. The settlement at Vienna and the concept of ►conference diplomacy which it inaugurated, remained the basis for international conduct throughout the nineteenth century, even though the Concert system as such was ended by the Crimean War. In this sense, it was the world's first deliberately contrived ►security regime. The second and third attempts at recreating and managing the ►international order, in 1919–20 and again in 1945–6, owed much to the pioneering efforts of the group of 1815. The Concert met sporadically throughout the nineteenth century with the specific purpose of settling contentious issues that threatened European ►great power stability. The unity of purpose it achieved was impressive and some commentators have called it a 'revolution in diplomatic history'. A number of factors contributed to its 'successful' operation (in the sense that there were no wars between the great powers for forty years):

1  There was a reasonably even distribution of ►power at the end of the Napoleonic War. Members of this great power club (Britain, Russia, Austria, Prussia, France, later joined by Italy and Turkey) were perceived to be roughly equal in military ►capability and diplomatic importance.

2  There was a common realization that the politics of untutored balance of power led to great power confrontation, therefore concerted action was needed to avert the danger.

3  Great power collaboration in bringing down Napoleonic France had the ►spillover effect of maintaining a unified ►front after the period of conflict was over. Emphasis on great power unity reinforced the conception of the European great powers as a special group with special responsibilities and privileges.

4  Meetings were confined to the great powers themselves. Sometimes lesser states were consulted, but never on the basis of ►equality. (This practice of according special status to the great powers was to reappear in both the ►League of Nations and the ►UN.)

5  It did not challenge the ultimate ►sovereignty of ►states. The unanimity rule was preferred, so that if vital ►national interests were affected the system remained inactive.

6 It was not a vehicle for reform; its purpose was to manage and maintain the
➤status quo.

7 It did not seek to eradicate conflict, simply to manage it.

8 Despite great ideological differences between the powers – the three Eastern
powers were conservative and counter-revolutionary, and the Western states
were more liberal in outlook – they all shared assumptions about the need
to keep 'the public law of Europe' and to establish a responsible code of
international behaviour.

For all these reasons, the Concert system was an innovation in diplomatic
relations. The balance of power was now tutored, guided and controlled and
it was generally understood that the great powers had the right and the
responsibility to impose their collective will on the European ➤state-system.
However, it was not an unqualified success and in this connection it is important
to distinguish the 'Congress era' from the Concert system. The Congress era
was characterized by an attempt by the more conservative states (in particular
the ➤Holy Alliance between Prussia and Austria) to intervene, by force of arms
if necessary, in the internal affairs of states to prevent a resurgence of radicalism,
➤nationalism and ➤liberalism. This interventionist stance led to bitter disputes
among the powers and Britain formally withdrew from it in 1820 following
demands for active Congress ➤intervention in Greece and Spain. British Foreign
Secretary George Canning did not come to view the Congress (or indeed the
Concert) system in this way. He said it was '. . . never intended as a union . . .
for the superintendence of the internal affairs of other states.' With the death
of the Tsar in 1825 the Congress system of management through consultation
survived. The Concert system succeeded because it was a loose ➤Association
of states sharing the same general purpose, whereas the Congress system collapsed
because it was much more specific and ideological in orientation.

**Conciliation** A form of third party ➤intervention in ➤conflict situations. In
the case of conciliation, the third party activity is non-partisan, neutral and
mediatory. The primary aim of conciliation is to restore communication
between the parties and to assist them to reach a better understanding of each
other's position. In theory, the parties may decide that this greater clarity
confirms their original hostility and suspicion and, accordingly, continue to
oppose each other's interests and values. If a conflict has a long history of
mistrust, conciliation may begin with the two parties refusing to discuss their
➤definition of the situation in the presence of the other. A stage of 'talking out'
the conflict may be required before conciliation can even attempt resolution.

Any solution to the conflict which emerges from these procedures will have
to be self-supporting. That is to say, the parties will come to see that a solution
to their differences is available to them via the conciliation process without
feeling that in any way the solution has been imposed. In this respect conciliation
is one of the least intrusive modes of ➤conflict resolution.

**Concordat** A diplomatic term which refers in general to an agreement between church and ➤state and in particular to agreements between states and the Holy See at the ➤Vatican.

**Condominium** Sovereign control over a dependent territory by two or more outside ➤states. In this sense it is a form of joint ➤imperialism where jurisdiction within the territory resides in arrangements made between the external states. It resembles co-ownership in municipal law and existed in the Sudan (between the United Kingdom and France) and in the New Hebrides islands in the Pacific (again the United Kingdom and France). It is a comparatively rare form of political and legal control and it should be distinguished from military occupation. Thus, the joint control undertaken by the Allied states over post-Second World War Germany would not properly be called a condominium. The term has also been used to describe ➤alternative world futures where the dominant ➤superpowers jointly, and by agreement, preside over the ➤international system itself. However, this usage is as fanciful as the situation it purports to describe.

**Confederalism** Confederalism, like all theories of ➤integration, is both a process and an end state. As a process it is often referred to as ➤intergovernmentalism. Certainly this is the case at present in the ➤European Union where the Intergovernmental Conference (IGC) structure has been a crucial factor in the 'relaunching' of the integrative process in the last two decades of the twentieth century. As an end state the confederal union is arguably the most centrifugal form of union that is commensurate with using the term confidently. Confederal unions recognize ➤state-centrism as a fact of life and do not seek to go 'beyond the ➤nation-state' in the manner of ➤federalism and ➤functionalism/neo-functionalism.

In the modern era confederal unions have enjoyed little support as appropriate state structures, the failure of the confederal experiments in the United States in the eighteenth and nineteenth centuries being cases in point. The semi-detached characteristic of the constituent parts in the confederal whole, which is seen as an inherent weakness of confederal unions, is a positive virtue in the context of inter-state integration. Confederalism – which may be regarded as the ➤ideology in this respect – saves the state from the sacrificial altar of federalism. It cannot save it from the invasive influences of ➤interdependence and ➤globalization. Indeed confederalism does not even try. Instead it seeks to meet the needs created by these influences through collaboration and cooperation. Empirically it is clear that these activities can substantially redefine the relationship between the constituent parts and the confederal whole if they proceed beyond a certain degree of complexity. In the EU at present, the ➤single market is a case in point.

**Conference diplomacy** A characteristic feature of twentieth-century ➤international relations, mainly as a result of the creation of permanent ➤international organizations, has been the extraordinary growth of ➤multilateral diplomacy, especially in the guise of large-scale international conferences. Although not unknown in the past (the ➤treaties of Westphalia in 1648 and the Congress of Vienna in 1815 being good examples), diplomacy by conference, whether permanent or *ad hoc*, is now standard practice. Indeed, the UN can be regarded as a permanent standing international diplomatic conference, and there are also regional varieties, such as the ➤European Union or the Nordic Union. A phenomenon associated with it is what some refer to as 'parliamentary diplomacy' (a term associated with the US statesman Dean Rusk), which refers to the creation of regional or interest groupings on matter which do not adversely affect the ➤national interest. These voting groups are formed according to a variety of criteria – political and cultural affinity, stage of economic development, geographic location, ideological like-mindedness and treaty links. Among the more prominent are the African group and the former ➤frontline states, the EU, the Arab states, the Group of '77, the Socialist group and the Western group. All these seek to construct more or less permanent majorities within the conferences so that particular policies are adopted or particular officers sympathetic to their interests are elected to the constituent committees and agencies. (The withdrawal of US participation in Unesco was on the grounds that this organization had been 'captured' by groups hostile to American interests.) Conference diplomacy has been regarded by ➤idealists from Woodrow Wilson onwards as part of the general solution to the problem of international ➤anarchy, whereas some realists believe that it may actually exacerbate it.

**Conflict** Conflict is a social condition that arises when two or more ➤actors pursue mutually exclusive or mutually incompatible goals. In ➤international relations conflict behaviour can be observed as ➤war – both as a threatened outcome and as an existential reality – and bargaining behaviour short of the violent idiom. Hostile attitudes are evinced by ➤elites, ➤attentive and mass publics through such psychological dispositions as ➤aggression and suspicion. Conflict can serve positive functions, however. In particular it can consolidate group cohesion and enhance the position of a ➤leadership. It is certainly chimerical to think that conflict can be eliminated. Strategies of ➤deterrence and ➤power balancing are traditional forms of ➤conflict management, whilst ➤conflict settlement initiatives may be associative or dissociative. If conflict is to be resolved or settled then third-party ➤intervention will often be required to facilitate these processes. The profile of the ➤paradigm third party is controversial with a clear dichotomy between those who see such third parties as power-brokers and those who see them as persuaders. According to some points of view, the putative third party requires 'leverage' to make her/his presence felt among the parties. At the other end of the continuum, problem-solving workshops seek resolution through facilitation and non-➤coercive methods. Successful mediation is often a matter of timing and Zartman's work (1985) is pre-eminent in this respect. ➤➤Arms race; civil war; *coup d'état*; game theory; insurgency; pacifism; revolution; terrorism

**Conflict management** A term used to describe any situation where a ➤conflict continues but where its worst excesses are avoided or mitigated. Conflict management would, in particular, seek to avoid or terminate violence between parties. Conflict management is normally achieved by strategies of mutual, general ➤deterrence. Traditionally conceived, the ➤balance of power was a system of conflict management based upon these ideas. A situation of neither ➤war nor ➤peace under a ➤regime of mutual and general deterrence can continue for relatively long period of time. Normally relations between the putative adversaries will show signs of improving or deteriorating as the case may be. If deterioration spills over into violence then management can be restored through palliatives such as cease-fire and ➤truce agreements. peace-making should properly be regarded as the function of ➤conflict settlement and ➤conflict resolution rather than management.

**Conflict research** This is a field of academic inquiry within ➤international relations. Its most basic premise is that ➤conflict is a systemic process which is common to all behavioural systems. It is therefore possible to borrow insights, ideas and research methods from other disciplines and apply them to the field of study. Its theories, concepts and approaches have been applied at every ➤level of analysis and in this sense conflict research is endemically eclectic. Unlike either ➤strategic studies or ➤peace research, conflict research seeks to avoid making basic a priori, philosophical commitments either in favour of or against ➤war and other forms of violence. Structurally it tends to take a mixed-actor, ➤pluralist viewpoint avoiding the ➤state-centric bias of strategic studies. In this respect at least its affinities are closer to peace research. Indeed it is sometimes empirically difficult to see where peace research ends and conflict research begins. Thus Burton's recent work (1990) is currently cited under the rubric of conflict research (Mitchell in Groom & Light, 1994). Others might see in this kind of work a tendency to import values into the study thus making it closer to peace research.

**Conflict resolution** A highly challenging approach to the analysis of the causes and solutions to conflict situations. In order to achieve resolution it is thought necessary for the parties to redefine their relationships in such a way as to ➤perceive either that they can realize their ➤goals without conflict or that they can redefine their relationship so that their goals no longer conflict. Unlike ➤conflict settlement techniques, resolution tends to rely heavily upon academic, rather than diplomatic, techniques (although no doubt the academics would say that they are also being 'good diplomats' in what they seek). Resolution techniques have used in particular small group experimental studies ('problem-solving workshops') borrowed from social psychology. Burton has dubbed these workshops 'controlled communication' exercises. Experimental studies have particularly concentrated upon ➤communal conflict situations where strong inhibitions prevent face-to-face communication and where it is held these techniques can be particularly effective. Although highly imaginative and provocative, conflict resolution is probably destined to remain an ideal type in the lexicon of conflict termination against which actual diplomatic outcomes can be judged.

**Conflict settlement** A portmanteau term for the ending or termination of ➤conflict situations. A conflict may be settled by one side prevailing over the other. Winning as a form of conflict settlement implies conquest, defeat and submission. Historically, this has been a significant form of settlement. Another is to change the political ➤leadership in one or several of the key parties to the conflict. A new leadership may be willing to settle for an arrangement which the outgoing office-holders found unacceptable. Settlement of this latter type implies a willingness by parties to ➤compromise. Zartman's work (1989) although termed 'ripe for resolution' is closer to the idea of settlement as defined here. In the same way Fisher's concept of 'yesability' (1981 and 1988) is about settlement of conflicts through bargaining. In a small number of cases ➤adjudication and ➤arbitration may be used as techniques for settling differences.

**Constructive engagement** Term used to describe US policy towards Southern Africa from 1980 onwards. The term was coined by Chester Crocker, assistant secretary of state for African affairs, and refers to US attempts to reform the South African system by working within it and honouring its rules. A form of 'quiet' ➤diplomacy which sought to encourage White-led change in the region, focusing especially on Namibia and the withdrawal of Cuban troops from Angola. Although Southern Africa was high on its ➤foreign policy agenda the United States in reality never had much political leverage in the region and ➤unilateral efforts without the active assistance of the Soviet Union were always likely to fail. The contradictions implicit in US policy (wanting an end to ➤apartheid while simultaneously maintaining a pro-Western ➤regime) which were evident in the very selective sanctions imposed against South Africa by the Anti-Apartheid Act of 1986, meant that the United States was not seen as an honest broker by all parties involved. In 1988–9, as a result of Gorbachev's new Soviet initiatives in Southern Africa, agreement was reached on ➤linkage of the Namibian ➤independence issue with the phased withdrawal of Cuban troops. Namibia achieved independence in 1990 and was regarded in some quarters as a vindication of the constructive engagement policy. This term is often used synonymously with 'critical dialogue'.

**Containment** An ambiguous concept, supposedly the guiding principle of post-war ➤US foreign policy. Originally advocated by diplomat George Kennan (➤X) when he declared in 1947 that the basis of US foreign policy should involve 'long-term, patient but firm and vigilant containment of Russian expansionist tendencies'. Implicit in Kennan's argument was the notion that Soviet foreign policy was motivated by ➤Marxist/Leninist assumptions concerning world ➤revolution and the destruction of capitalism, and necessitated therefore a carefully constructed policy of ➤counterforce at its perimeters. The underlying aim of such a policy was to keep the Soviet Union within the lines of military demarcation established at the end of the Second World War. As such, containment could be seen as accommodationist rather than overtly aggressive, as some revisionist ➤Cold War analysts have suggested. Instrumentally, containment merged with the ➤Truman Doctrine and the ➤Marshall Plan and its main ingredients were the creation of military ➤alliances (in Western Europe, Latin America, the Middle East and the Far East), economic ➤aid and covert forms of political and economic warfare both within and without the Soviet ➤sphere of influence. As interpreted by the Truman and Eisenhower administrations containment also involved counter-revolutionary notions of liberation of those areas under communist control or threat. Thus, the ➤Korean War and Vietnamese War are often presented in terms of this framework. However, Kennan in his *Memoirs* (1967) has objected to this orthodox interpretation of the doctrine associated with his name and in particular argued that his early formulation of containment did not imply either the militarization of US foreign policy or the globalist dimensions it so quickly assumed. In a somewhat belated rearguard defence, Kennan argued that his original intention was to suggest the 'political containment of a political threat' and not active containment of the Soviet Union by military means. He also objected to the apparently unlimited capacity of US power which it assumed, to the extension of US vital interests beyond Western Europe and the Western Hemisphere and especially to the distorted image it carried about the nature of the communist threat:

If I was the author in 1947 of a 'doctrine' of containment, it was a doctrine which lost much of its rationale with the death of Stalin and with the development of the Soviet-Chinese conflict. I emphatically deny any efforts to involve that doctrine today in situations to which it has, and can have, no proper relevance. (1967)

Although some commentators argue that containment (albeit in a looser form) was still the bottom line of US foreign policy up to 1989, most analysts agree that ➤*détente*, ➤polycentrism, the Sino-Soviet split, the US ➤rapprochement with China, the settlement in South East Asia as well as the various ➤arms control agreements, had watered it down to such an extent that the term was no longer particularly helpful in understanding the philosophical or ideological framework out of which US foreign policy emerged. None can doubt, though, the near pathological commitment to the doctrine by US ➤decision-makers in the early post-war period. Whether this was the cause of the ➤Cold War or the result of it is now a matter of historical rather than political dispute. ➤Clinton Doctrine

**Contraband** Categories of ➤war materials which, under ➤international law, may be seized by one ➤belligerent when supplied by a neutral to another. However, the exact definition of 'war materials' has always been a contentious matter and interpretations have tended to be expansive. Thus, the category of 'conditional contraband' refers to seized material which may have been destined for innocent peacetime use but which has been deemed by a belligerent as useful to the war effort. In the age of ➤total warfare, the distinction between permissible and non-permissible goods has further collapsed with the result that during the two twentieth-century world wars relations between belligerents and neutrals were often strained. Lack of clear unequivocal legal guidance has inevitably resulted in a good deal of auto-interpretation on this issue.

**Conventional** An adjective meaning 'normal' or 'traditional', its application to the analysis of ➤international relations and ➤foreign policy is appropriate wherever the analyst wishes to draw a distinction between what has happened in the past and what is happening in the present or is envisaged for the future. The adjective is particularly apposite in circumstances where change has occurred and some point of comparison with the past is required.

Thus, conventional weapon is a distinction frequently used in strategic analysis to differentiate between ➤weapons of mass destruction and the traditional or 'conventional' weapons used for centuries in warfare. The advent of nuclear weapons has certainly not reduced the scope for conventional weapons. Indeed, the reverse may well be true, namely that the drawbacks and difficulties of actually using nuclear weapons has enhanced the importance of the 'threshold' between nuclear and conventional. The US desire that ➤NATO should move towards ➤flexible response after 1962 was in part prompted by these perceptions.

Similarly a distinction can be made between conventional and unconventional warfare. The latter is often thought of as ➤guerrilla warfare which is regarded as 'unconventional' because of the types of forces and tactics employed rather than the types of weapons.

**Conventions on the rules of warfare** Rules relating to conduct during armed ➤conflict were, until the mid-nineteenth century, part of customary ➤international law. Since then there have been a number of attempts to codify the rules of warfare in a succession of ➤multilateral international conventions. These are commonly referred to as 'the law of Geneva' and the 'law of the Hague'. The law of Geneva dealt mainly with the rights and protection of those who took no direct part in the fighting and the law of the Hague was concerned with the rights and duties of the actual ➤belligerents. The Geneva conventions took place as follows: 1864 and 1907 (humane treatment of the wounded and sick in battle), 1929 (wounded and sick plus treatment of ►prisoners of war), 1949 (wounded, sick and shipwrecked, prisoners of war and protection of civilians in wartime); 1977 (additional ►protocols dealing with more extensive non-combatant protection and with problems arising from internal wars). By 1986 there were over 160 parties to these Geneva Conventions (including non-state ►actors such as the Palestine Liberation Organization (►PLO), the Pan African Congress and the South West Africa People's Organization (SWAPO)). As well as these codified rules, which of course lack effective sanctions, belligerents, whether or not they are party to the conventions, are bound by customary international humanitarian law which forbids unnecessary cruelty or wanton behaviour. From 1864 onwards, these conventions have been associated with the activities of the ►International Red Cross movement (initially known as the International Committee for aid to wounded soldiers) which was founded in Switzerland in 1863, and which in 1949 formally extended its brief to protect civilians caught up in armed conflict.

**Convergence theory** The idea that the logic of industrial and ►technological growth in advanced ►states leads to convergent patterns of political, economic and social structures regardless of formal ideological or historical differences. Propagated by prominent theorists such as Raymond Aron and J. K. Galbraith, the theory holds that the imperatives of technological growth and the technical and managerial requirements of the post-industrial state compel societies to adopt common or core practices with regard especially to the economic sector. Critics have pointed out that, despite being at similar stages of technological and economic growth, there is no absolute necessity for convergence. Different types of political system can, and do, coexist at similar stages of economic development, without evolving common forms of social organization. In ►international relations the idea could be seen as a variant of the traditional realist view that despite formal ideological differences, ►great powers are likely to behave in much the same way regarding the problems of national security and the protection of interests.

**Council of Europe** The Statute of the Council signed in May 1949 by Belgium, Denmark, France, Ireland, Italy, Luxemburg, The Netherlands, Norway, Sweden and the United Kingdom was dedicated in its preamble to a 'closer unity between all like-minded countries of Europe.' Notwithstanding such references to 'unity' the Council is an ►international organization with no pretensions or ambitions towards ►supranationalism. Indeed, later in the same preamble the document refers only to a 'closer association' between its member ►states. Article I of the Statute explicitly precludes the Council from considering matters relating to national ►defence. There were two reasons for this very explicit exclusion at the time: the recently signed North Atlantic Treaty meant that what was to become the ►NATO ►Alliance would deal with these matters and the presence of ➤neutral states such as Ireland and Sweden in the Council precluded any reference to military issues.

Membership is open under Article II to all states accepting the principles of the rule of law, fundamental freedoms and ➤human rights. A subsequent ➤protocol to the ➤treaty of London pledged the signatories to the holding of free elections at reasonable intervals by secret ballot. The strong inclination of the Council towards the human rights agenda was reinforced in November 1950 when the members concluded the European Convention for the Protection of Human Rights and Fundamental Freedoms. The Convention created a Commission and a Court of Human Rights. The work of this Court has made a substantial contribution to the development of general principles of ➤international law on this ➤issue area since that time. In addition to this work the main activity of the Council throughout the ➤Cold War period was to act as a communication channel for European states – particularly between the members of the ➤EC/EU and the rest – and to act as a touchstone for the principles of representative and responsible government within the continent. Thus the Council suspended the membership of both Greece and Turkey during periods of military rule and it validated the democratization of Portugal and Spain in the 1970s.

The events following 1989 have created an expanded role for the Council as a validator of democratic credentials. The collapse of the Soviet Union has created a waiting-room of Central and Eastern European states wishing to join the full panoply of regional organizations. Membership of the Council is thus seen as both a confirmation of their change of status as democracies and a foot in the door for the future. Membership has now grown to 38 states with a further 6 in the special category of 'guests'. The principal organs of the Council are the Committee of Ministers and the Parliamentary Assembly (formerly the Consultative Assembly). There is also a Congress for Regional and Local Assemblies and a European Commission for Democracy through Law.

**Counter-insurgency** A type of irregular warfare which seeks to demoralize and defeat insurgencies by employing the same tactics in reverse to neutralize the planning of the insurgents. In particular counter-insurgency seeks to separate ➤guerrilla bands from the local population by winning the latter away from the former. This is sometimes referred to in the US idiom as 'hearts and minds' campaigns. Working out from secure ➤base areas, the counter-insurgents then attempt to extend their security zones into disputed and ➤insurgent territories. This 'pacification' programme is essential if an acceptable level of civil order is to be secured. Counter-insurgency requires recognition that certain political, economic and social reforms need to be effected to remove popular grievances. This last prerequisite is often the hardest to achieve, as the US experience in attempting to build up an autonomous South Vietnam during their ➤intervention in the Vietnam War shows. Notwithstanding this experience, successful counter-insurgency wars were fought in the Philippines and Malaya after 1945.

**Counterforce** A term in strategic analysis. It has two distinct usages. Broadly used, it refers to the deliberate decision to target a potential enemy's forces in advance of hositilities and to carry through a series of disarming attacks once ➤war had commenced. In this sense, counterforce has been seen as providing the traditional rationale for the possession and use of military forces by an ➤actor. Although counterforce strategies can be employed at any stage during the violence, their use at an early stage has often been held to increase the efficacy of such moves.

During the➤Cold War era in ➤international relations, the word was often used in a narrower sense to refer to a particular ➤capability. Strategists of ➤nuclear war in particular would refer to a 'counterforce capability' meaning the possession of weapons of such accuracy as to enable the putative attacker to significantly disarm another before the latter could attack with its own forces. Recent developments in weapons technology variously identified as producing 'smart' or 'brilliant' systems under the aegis of the ➤revolution in military affairs (RMA) has allegedly enhanced the counterforce capabilities of the states deploying these technologies. Claims that such weapons may significantly minimize the likelihood of ➤collateral damage may need to be treated with caution.

*Coup d'état* Literally, this refers to a sudden and decisive stroke of government policy. Popular usage now associates the term with sudden and unconstitutional change of government or regime. As such the coup is part of the repertoire of radical and revolutionary movements, although it is not only the revolutionary who stages or attempts coups. Conversely it is not necessary to stage a coup to have a ➤revolution. The link between the coup as an instrument and the revolution as a means of change is neither necessary nor sufficient.

As an instrument of change the coup may most clearly be contrasted with the mass uprising. In the former situation the perpetrators will be a small group of conspirators who will seize their opportunity to remove the incumbents by moving with great dispatch and determination to apprehend the ➤leadership, restrict their movements and take control of the main arteries of state ➤power. They may use great violence to effect these changes or they may be achieved in a 'bloodless' fashion. A crucial determinant of these outcomes will be the extent to which the incumbent leadership is defended. For this reason the military institutions of the ➤state will play an important role in deciding the level of violence required to achieve a successful coup. If the military themselves stage the coup this will usually settle the issue, at least in the short term, because their ability to provide sufficient coercive power will carry the day. If the coup leaders cannot be assured of the support or assistance of the military they may have to face their opposition afterwards. In this situation a coup attempt that is resisted by some or all of the armed forces can lead to ➤civil war. The civil strife in Indonesia in 1965 followed an abortive coup attempt that was opposed by the army and the Biafra civil war followed hard upon two coups in Nigeria in 1966. Trotsky's dictum that a coup can succeed without the ➤army but that it cannot succeed against the army seems instructive here.

A high propensity to use the coup instrument as a means of political change is currently demonstrated in the ➤Third World. All the constituent continents – Latin America, Africa and Asia – have shown this propensity. Almost without exception such coups have been openly staged or supported by the military institutions in these states. Indeed, sometimes lengthy periods of military rule follow these ➤interventions. Sometimes the military reverts to barracks fairly quickly but not before purging the political leadership.

Under the legal principle of ➤recognition other states have to face the decision to grant or withhold this facility. Given the unconstitutional nature of the change, withholding immediate recognition might seem the more appropriate course of action. On the other hand, if the new leadership is clearly in effective control there may be little point in prevarication. Often these decisions will be influenced by political and diplomatic considerations as much as by legal ones.

**Credibility** A noun meaning literally that a statement or an action shows the true intentions of the ➤actor. Such inferences are by the nature subjective. Credibility is likely to be contingent upon the reputation of the actor and upon the circumstances in which the action takes place. Given these conditions, it is argued that certain actions or statements are inherently credible and that the others are not. Moreover, it is generally agreed that there is a grey area of uncertainty where credibility is equivalent to dubiety. This dilemma, at the very heart of the concept, has been of particular concern to the theorists of ➤deterrence. The advent of weapons of mass destruction has greatly increased the cost of calculations that arise when statesmen and others make deterrent threats that cover these contingencies. Deterrence is, moreover, not a one-way street and, accordingly, threats are met with counter-threats. Credibility is not immune from this ➤action–reaction dynamic. Credibility now becomes a relative concept. What might appear credible to threaten an unarmed opponent with, looks very dubious against an adversary equally as capable as oneself.

Credibility has, thus, become a benchmark against which deterrent policies are evaluated. ➤Massive retaliation was criticized for lacking credibility. Many see the issue of credibility as central to the idea of extended deterrence. The uncertainty dilemma referred to above has divided strategic analysis. Some see uncertainty as reinforcing deterrence because the adversary will not know exactly when, where or how the deterrer will act. Others argue that such uncertainties will cause deterrence theory to break down at the margin and this may be the situation where it is most needed. In statistical language, credibility is a matter of probability not proof.

**Crisis** A crisis is a perceived turning point in relationships between ➤actors or between actors and their environment. Thus the ➤Cuban missile crisis was a potential turning point in strategic relations between the United States and the Soviet Union. The placement of 'offensive' missiles in Cuba threatened to change both the global strategic balance and the local strategic balance against the interests of the United States. One of the unanticipated consequences of the crisis was that the relations between the ➤superpowers moved into a ➤*détente* phase for a brief period afterwards. The ➤debt crisis was perceived as a turning point in relations between Latin American states and their creditors in the ➤First World. Again unanticipated consequences of the moves to buy time for the debtors may lead to further turning points in relations. Issues arising from the deterioration of the global ➤ecological system may be perceived as crises in the sense suggested above. The ongoing destruction of the earth's ozone layer is clearly a turning point in man's relationship with his environment.

Contemporary literature on crises in ➤international relations and ➤foreign policy has shown a burgeoning output of late. Two broad approaches may be discerned and distinguished. The first approaches the subject from the ➤decision-making perspective. Clearly, there are good intuitive reasons for concentration here. In an acute international crisis, if the decision-makers get it wrong then events may rapidly escalate out of control and lead to violence, or lead to the exacerbation of violence that has already started. The second approach to crises takes a situational/structural perspective looking at crises as interaction sequences between international actors. A good deal of formal modelling – derived from ➤game theory – has been productively applied here. This approach also sensitizes the study of crises to the environmental constraints and opportunities that different system structures might have for the occurrence and duration of the phenomena.

Decision-making approaches to crisis begin with the insight that the ➤policy-makers perceive that the consequence of their actions – even if they do nothing – will involve them in significant risk taking. Crisis decision-making is thus conceptually separate from 'normal' decision-making, where perceptions that high risks are part of the ➤definition of the situation are absent. Because of the high risk factor, crisis decision-making is recognized as being highly stressful. As stress increases in a crisis other factors may be consequentially affected. Decision-makers may experience pressure to act quickly, they may feel that their search for alternatives is limited. Physiologically, stress may produce exhaustion, emotionalism and poor performance. There is general agreement that while a certain amount of stress is likely to increase efficiency in the decision-making system, too much will lead to a degeneration in performance and the other physiological effects already noted.

During a crisis situation the size of the decision-making group will usually narrow. Group solidarity and cohesion may increase and while this may be conducive to better performance, it can lead to ➤groupthink. The group *qua* group will have to cope with a substantial increase in the amount of information coming into the system from the environment. Information processing via these communication channels will intensify and in order to relieve this overload, and to save time, *ad hoc* channels may be used. During the Cuban missile crisis, message flows between the US and the Soviet leaderships increased substantially during the days after the announcement of the ➤quarantine.

Hermann (1969), who has probably contributed more than any other analyst to the decision-making approach to crises, argues for three defining characteristics. First, the crisis situation threatens core values in the decision-making system. Second, the decision situation is highly time dependent. Third, the occurrence of the crisis comes as a surprise to the decision system. The first two traits have been covered in the discussion above. Surprise as a trait is perhaps more controversial. Diplomatic and strategic surprise bear a close family resemblance to crisis, but to require surprise as a necessary definition of crisis precludes the possibility that at least one party to the crisis will knowingly initiate the situation in order to force concessions from the other. Since perception of high risk has already been stipulated as a defining characteristic of crisis, it is a small step for one party to manipulate this risk to achieve its own ends. This is normally thought of as ➤brinkmanship. As Lebow (1981) has argued following an empirical examination of twenty-six crises, 'more than half can be described as brinkmanship'. Brinkmanship aims to force concessions from the other side, or at a minimum, a ➤trade-off between the adversaries. It seems fairly clear that the first ➤Berlin crisis was, from the Soviet perception, an instance of brinkmanship, with the looked for trade-offs being some significant retreat by the West from its initiative to establish a separate West German state.

Unlike the decision-making approach, the situational/structural perspective rests its analysis upon the basic assumption that ➤conflict is a systemic process and that, as a result, crises will occur almost naturally. One of the most influential recent texts on crises defines the phenomenon as arising 'in severe conflict, short of war, but involving the perception of a dangerously high probability of war' (Snyder and Deising, 1977). Some writers, indeed, following Schelling's (1966) argument that most ➤wars are a form of bargaining behaviour, would want to argue that 'short of war' is too restrictive. Crises are then seen as generically linked to coercive bargaining between putative adversaries. Linkage between the mainstream decision-making literature and this bargaining view of crises is provided by the literature on ➤crisis management.

Situational/structural approaches to crises include also the holistic type of analysis of the system into ➤bipolar or multipolar configurations. Waltz (1964), the leading modern advocate of bipolarity, argues that crises are a symptom that the system is working. Conflict is endemic, so too is change, therefore crises cannot be avoided. Given this line of reasoning, Waltz concludes that the 'absence of crises is more worrisome than their recurrence'. In the bipolar system the assumption is that the leading states will show interventionist tendencies in all crisis situations. This ➤intervention need not always be competitive, but when it is a crisis may result. Thus in 1973 during the Yom Kippur War in the ➤Arab–Israeli conflict competitive intervention by the ➤superpowers produced the 'alert' crisis.

Advocates of the multipolar structure also see conflict, and therefore crises, as endemic. Here the existence of more leading ➤state actors in the system means that even if two of them conflict, a number of third party roles are still available to the other powers. Indeed in a crises situation in a multipolar system between two of the leading states, the behaviour of the remaining polar actors may be crucial. If they commit themselves to one side or the other then third party mediation may be impossible and if this happens then, as July 1914, the system collapses into a bipolar confrontation.

The advent of ➤nuclear weapons as a systemic variable has affected the occurrence and outcome of crises at this ➤level of analysis. Since it was clear from the outset that high risk was a situational characteristic of crises, it would seem to follow that nuclear weapons have served to exacerbate the perception of risk even more. This is particularly pertinent for those states actually possessing them. Again ➤proliferation, at least in ➤horizontal directions, will further increase risks during crises. In game theory analysis the nuclear crisis is analogous to the Chicken game where the costs of both parties choosing to reject cooperation are very high indeed.

**Crisis management** Crisis management is the attempt to control events during a ➤crisis to prevent significant and systematic violence from occurring. The decision problem facing the would-be 'crisis manager' is to find a balance between being tough and being tender, between using ➤coercion and offering concessions, between ➤aggression and ➤accommodation. Too much coercion can lead to violence which may get out of control and take on a dynamic of its own. Too much accommodation can lead to ➤surrender and to 'peace at any price'. For the ➤diplomat the essence of crisis management is to know when to give ground and when to stand firm.

The balance between coercion and accommodation will differ over time. A typical crisis pattern is for coercion to mark the early stages so that a rapid and marked escalation occurs. Accommodation becomes more evident as the dangers of uncontrolled violence increase. Concessions may be made on a more or less reciprocal basis or, more usually, one side or the other will clearly and unambiguously make the first conciliatory gesture. Accommodation may spill over into the post-crisis phase so that the former adversaries, recognizing the tensions in their relationship, move towards a more cooperative mode thereafter.

During the coercive stage, the aim of using this strategy is to manipulate the risk of war – which from a rational ➤actor perspective, it is assumed neither side wants – to force concessions and get the opponent to give ground. Snyder (Hermann, 1972) has suggested that the key risk to avoid is miscalculation. This may occur for a variety of reasons: poor communication, ➤misperception, overestimating one's own ➤capabilities or underestimating those of the adversary. For whatever cause, violence that nobody wants or expects can occur if key ➤decision-makers miscalculate during this coercive stage. The concept of ➤groupthink is perhaps the most relevant exposition for the situation where a group of decision-makers apparently suspend rationality and become swept along in a group dynamic which proves to have disastrous consequences.

Again, manipulation of risk can go wrong because subordinates further down the chain of command act in an independent and unauthorized fashion. It is inevitable that during a crisis situation it will be necessary to issue rules of engagement to military leaders. Equally diplomats and envoys may find themselves operating at the edge of, or even outside, their instructions. In such situations individual decision-making 'on the spot' can be crucial to a particular outcome. It is against this potential scenario that efforts to improve ➤C⁴I facilities have assumed so much significance.

Following on from the works published by Schelling in the 1960s, effective coercion of one's opponents is held to involve the commitment strategy. Commitment is convincing your opponent that you mean what you say; in short, that your intentions are credible. One favoured method is to make a commitment to stand firm, leaving the next move to the adversary. The Soviet move to blockade ➤Berlin during the 1948–9 crisis and the US ➤blockade (or ➤quarantine) of Cuba in the 1962 crisis would both be instances here of the commitment strategy. Again a commitment may be verbal. For example, it may take the form of a ➤treaty of guarantee or collective ➤self-defence, or it may be a vague and generalized statement to the effect that 'we will not stand idly by . . .' or 'we will not hesitate to make difficult decisions . . .' Often the most effective form of coercive commitment will be to combine the physical and the verbal.

The dilemma with the act of commitment is inherent in its strength. It 'burns one's bridges'. It reduces flexibility. As a result of an over-enthusiastic pursuit of victory at all costs, the chances of reaching a compromise will be lost. Since the defining characteristic of crisis management is to balance coercion and accommodation, then victory at all costs is not really sought. For this reason it has been suggested that a commitment that leaves some flexibility is to be preferred. It might be better to issue warnings rather than to make specific threats but herein the risk of having one's bluff called may have to be faced.

Escalation is a probable outcome of the strategy of commitment. The term escalation often implies beginning with fairly modest commitments and increasing the risks thereafter in order to slowly coerce the adversary into compromise, for fear that the alternative will take the parties higher up the escalation ladder. Thus in escalation the commitment strategy is double-edged. There is an explicit commitment to a particular option and an implicit commitment to further, more risky, options if the initial options do not work. Thus, in the case of the Cuban missiles it could be argued that the quarantine implied an air strike or invasion as the next significant move if the quarantine itself failed to work.

Accommodation is the antithesis of much of the above discussion. Accommodation is a way of settling the crisis – so management implies settlement – without totally capitulating to the wishes and aims of the other parties. The immediate difficulty with offering concessions is that it may be perceived as a sign of weakness which will encourage the opponent to stand out for more. The dynamic in accommodation is therefore de-escalation. If concessions become mutual it may be possible for the adversaries to reciprocate concessions. Thus a significant improvement in their relationships may result from crisis management.

Most crises are settled by one side making a differentially greater concession than the other. Sometimes, as in Cuba, the winner will make a face-saving gesture to the adversary in order to make it easier to accept the outcome or to make it easier to sell the outcome to others (but see Lebow and Stein, 1994).

Crisis management, then, involves finding a balance between coercion and accommodation. This is a common problem in ►diplomacy. Should one be a ►hawk or a ►dove on a particular ►issue area? In this sense crisis management is rightly seen as a form of diplomacy. It is diplomacy in a ►coercive mode, certainly it is not routine diplomacy, but rather it is the ►high politics of the formal office holders.

**Critical Theory/Postmodernism**   These terms are often used synonymously in IR literature. Though not altogether correct, this is understandable since many critical theorists are also postmodernists (or as some prefer 'late modernists'). The confusion is confounded by a fetish in contemporary theorizing for linguistic paradoxes, dialectics and niche labelling as well as an inherent ambiguity in the terms themselves. There is clearly a sense in which all theory is 'critical' as well as a sense in which everything which succeeds 'modern' is, *ipso facto*, 'postmodern'. As a consequence, precise meanings and definitions are sources of contention and dispute, even amongst self-proclaimed adherents to these schools of thought (Brown, 1994 and Devetak, 1996). A common distinguishing feature of both positions is that they represent a sustained challenge to existing theoretical traditions and moreover they reject IR as a discrete field of inquiry and seek to situate it in the wider intellectual context of social, political, cultural, philosophical and literary studies.

Critical Theory (CT) is associated with a body of thought generally known as the Frankfurt School, and in particular with the work of the German social theorist, Jurgen Habermas. For Habermas, CT entails questioning the very epistemological (source of knowledge) and ontological (nature of being) foundations of an existing social order; the central claim being that all knowledge is historically and politically based. In IR this mode of analysis appeared in the 1980s as a reaction to the dominance of the ►neorealist/neoliberal orthodoxy.

It claims that in spite of their differences and apparent opposition, both are premised on 'the Enlightenment project'; that is a belief in the liberation of humanity through reason and the judicious application of scientific knowledge. This, in essence, is 'modernity'. The 'critique' of modernity involves revealing its self-serving, particularist and privileged nature. The 'crisis' of modernity is that belief that the dominant trends of progressivist nineteenth- and twentieth-century political thought (in this case liberalism, Marxism and social democracy) has led not to emancipation and liberation as promised, but to new modes of enslavement and dehumanization, reaching its apogee in Nazi Germany and Stalinist Russia. The intellectual origins of these approaches are found in the works of Kant, Hegel, Marx and especially for the postmodernists, Friedrich Nietzsche, for whom the triumph of rationality portends disaster. The differences between critical theorists and postmodernists lie in their respective reactions to the supposed 'failure' of the Enlightenment project; the latter work towards its complete demise whilst the former strive for its deconstruction and eventual recasting. In IR both subscribe to the Marxist view that the basic task is not to interpret the world, but rather to change it. Thus both involve radical assaults on conventional theory which remains stubbornly rooted in the '➤anarchy problématique'; neorealism seeking to work within its structural constraints and neoliberalism attempting to ameliorate its worst effects. The driving belief is that through the deconstruction of orthodox theory, 'thinking spaces' are opened up (thus circumventing discourse 'closure') and new possibilities for social and political transformations are made available. The belief that 'theory is always for someone or something' (i.e. that theories are always embedded in social and political life) is the starting point in the quest for emancipation and empowerment. In IR the villain of the piece is the ➤Westphalian system and its privileging of the sovereign ➤nation-state within a behavioral framework of an anarchical social order. Feminist and ➤gender scholarship originates within this discourse and is a powerful exemplar of its central thesis since women in particular are 'silenced' or 'excluded' in the meta-text/narrative.

A major point of difference between the new scholarship and the old, in the words of a leading exponent of CT, is that traditional (or 'problem-solving') theory 'takes the world as it finds it with the prevailing social and power relationships and institutions into which they are organized, as the given framework for action' (Cox, 1981). Working within this order neorealism and neoliberalism serve to preserve it thereby perpetrating existing inequalities of ➤power and wealth. Orthodox theory is therefore inherently conservative and ➤status quo orientated. In contrast, through the exposure of the social basis of knowledge, power and values, the new scholarship 'liberates' international theory to the extent that injustices and inequalities built in to the prevailing order can be addressed. This challenge to orthodoxy is regarded by some as the 'Third Great Debate' in the subject. It supposedly pits the guardians or gatekeepers of the old order (represented by scholars such as K. N. Waltz and

R. O. Keohane in the USA and by the ➤English school in the UK) against the vanguard or Young Turks of the profession, many of whom, despite the essentially iconoclastic nature of their challenge, now occupy senior positions within a discipline which in their categorization does not formally exist.

It is difficult at this stage to assess the overall contribution made by CT and Postmodernism. There is no doubt that at least in terms of language, concepts and method, they have transformed, probably for ever, the nature and scope of the subject. It is now much more self-consciously inter-disciplinary. But whether or not its central focus has been relocated into the realm of normative social theory is a moot point. The main contribution of new thinking has been to expose the essentially static, exclusive and insular nature of traditional international theory and to render genuine political and social change at least a theoretical possibility. However, like the ➤behaviouralists of the Second Great Debate, they have not so far produced the goods. Deconstruction has not yet given way to reconstruction or to emancipation. As such, the research and teaching programme in IR remains essentially contested territory.

**Cruise missile** A cruise missile is, in effect, a small pilotless aircraft. The original ➤technology was developed during the Second World War when Germany produced the V-1 'flying bomb'. Significant improvements were made to this technology in two respects during the years following 1945. First, it became possible to produce small, very economical jet engines, using either the turbo-jet or the turbo-fan principle. Second, significant developments in missile guidance techniques made it possible to 'read' the terrain over which the missile was flying and compare this information with that stored on computer. This guidance facility is particularly crucial if the cruise missile is intended for strategic purposes because, given a flight time of up to six hours, course corrections will be essential.

Cruise missiles can carry either nuclear or ➤conventional warheads. It is, moreover, not possible to distinguish the type of warhead from the external appearance of the missile. This has potentially daunting implications for ➤arms control because counting missiles is of little value in establishing their nuclear/conventional status. This facility is referred to as 'dual ➤capability'.

Cruise missile development has proceeded apace since these new technologies became available. This has been particularly evident in the USA. Production and deployment has taken place in respect of air, ground and sea-launch systems. It is plausible to argue that these developments rival the advances in multiple warheads in their significance.

**CSCE/OSCE** Conference on Security and Cooperation in Europe. This formed part of the ➤Helsinki process and its Final Act was signed on 1 August 1975 by 35 states – comprising all the European countries, except Albania, together with the USA and Canada. (Albania was subsequently admitted as a participating state in June 1991.) The Final Act was not a binding ➤treaty but rather a declaratory statement of political intent and commitment. It contained three main sections or 'baskets' relating to ►security, economic cooperation and ►human rights. These ►issue areas reflected the main interests of the two ►blocs: the West's concern for human rights and the Eastern bloc's concern for closer economic cooperation. The two sides came together in a shared concern for the military/security issue area. Within this basket the signatories undertook to abide by 'guiding principles' in their ►international relations: respect for sovereign equality, renunciation of force, inviolability of frontiers, ►non-intervention in internal affairs and respect for human rights. Agreement was also reached at Helsinki on a document on confidence-building, security and disarmament. In particular it was envisaged that for the future large-scale military exercises conducted by either ►NATO or the ►Warsaw Pact would be notified to the other ►alliance in advance.

The Conference and its outcome represented a significant advance for the policy of ►*détente* and a coming together of the European strand of that initiative – seen in ostopolitik – and the ►superpower version launched by the ►Nixon Doctrine. The Soviet Union had to give more ground on the issue area of human rights and the free movement of peoples than perhaps they would have liked but they did ►perceive that in return the status quo in Europe at the time seemed to have been validated. In the West in general, and in the USA in particular, the CSCE produced a growth in 'monitoring' activity – particularly in the US Congress – to ensure that the human rights provisions were being observed by the Soviets.

Following the agreement on the ►Charter of Paris in November 1990 the CSCE process endorsed the principles of democracy, human rights and free market economics. At the same time the ad hoc conference structure was superseded and made permanent. Structurally it has now become the Organization for Security and Cooperation in Europe (OSCE). A Council of Foreign Ministers now heads up the organization supported by a secretariat based in Vienna. The Conflict Prevention Centre is also in Vienna whilst the Office for Democratic Institutions and Human Rights is based in Warsaw and a High Commissioner on National Minorities is located in the Hague. The OSCE also has a Parliamentary Assembly which held its initial meeting in Budapest in July 1992. In 1992 the OSCE declared itself to be a regional organization within the meaning of Chapter VIII of the ►United Nations Charter. Thus it will intervene only with the consent of the belligerents and after the establishment of a cease fire. Although the CSCE/OSCE has contributed significantly to the ending of the ►Cold War and its aftermath in Europe, it is handicapped by the lack of effective instruments for settling disputes (e.g. Bosnia) and it has no military forces of its own.

The CSCE/OSCE is a paradigm case of the kind of organizational task expansion that ►IGOs can undergo in contemporary international relations. In terms of the kinds of ►functionalist logic that has been a significant strand in

➤integration theory this task expansion can be anticipated and expected. What is of note is that it has taken effect in the issue area of military/security relations rather than the wealth/welfare field beloved of classical functionalism. The fact that it is, as yet, the only European security organization in which Russia has full membership gives it an advantage over other organizations such as NATO and the WEU currently located in the European security architecture. The monitoring role played in the implementation of the Dayton peace agreement in Bosnia (1996) and its efforts to set up a peace-keeping force in Nagorno-Karabakh is testimony to its ➤crisis management and ➤preventive diplomatic potential, particularly in Central and Eastern Europe. ➤➤Helsinki Accords

**Cuban missile crisis** The proximate cause of the Cuban missile crisis of October 1962 was the placement on that island, less than one hundred miles off the coast of Florida, of medium and intermediate range ballistic missiles, capable of carrying ➤nuclear weapons, by the Soviet Union. The discovery of these placements by the United States' ➤intelligence services led to an acute ➤crisis situation between the two ➤superpowers as the Kennedy Administration took prompt and ➤coercive counter-measures. In point of fact there had been a time-lag between the introduction of the weapons and their discovery by the intelligence services. Until their ➤definition of the situation changed in October, the United States was acting upon the assumption that the Soviet ➤leadership would not introduce such weapons into the hemisphere. This was only one of several ➤misperceptions that subsequent study of the crisis has brought to light.

The realization after 14 October that the United States had failed to ➤deter the Soviets from such precipitate action came as a salutary shock to the Kennedy team. Once the intelligence picture was revealed, the Executive Committee of the National Security Council (Excom) met in secret session to consider Soviet motivations and American responses. At the time American inclinations were to see the Soviet move in the context of their superpower relationship and therefore as an attempt to steal a march on themselves in the nuclear confrontation. It now seems clear that – although the Soviets did perceive themselves to be in an inferior position in the ➤arms race – equally significant in their decision-making was the desire to deter a further American incursion against Cuba following on from the abortive ➤Bay of Pigs episode. The American policy of active ➤destabilization of the ➤communist regime in Cuba had convinced the Soviet leadership that their bastion in the Caribbean was ripe for further ➤intervention. In this respect the Cuban crisis takes on a more tripolar configuration than many ➤strategic studies analyses have suggested since 1962. Cuba/American and Cuba/Soviet Union were important factors in the Soviet perception. The placement of their missiles in Cuba served a number of Soviet ➤goals in one fell swoop (a not uncommon occurrence in policy-making).

After some deliberation – and considerable dissension – the Excom settled on a naval ►blockade of Cuba as the preferred response. Owing to the legal dubiety of this move the blockade was termed a ►quarantine, a policy response which had echoes of Roosevelt. Although the quarantine was an apt demonstration of American resolve it did nothing to secure the removal of missiles that had already reached Cuba. The crisis escalated to a high level of tension as the United States implied that direct action would be taken against Cuba. At the same time secret 'back channel' communications were opened with the Soviet leadership. Via these facilities Kennedy was able to signal a much more conciliatory stance – even to the extent of contemplating a trade-off with missiles in Turkey. The American public opinion was left with the impression that in the 'eyeball to eyeball' confrontation the Soviets had been forced to blink. Lebow and Stein (1994) have suggested that, in point of fact, the American President was willing to do the same. At the end of the second week of the crisis the Soviets agreed to remove their missiles in exchange for an American pledge not to invade Cuba. To his chagrin, the Cuban leader was not consulted about these conciliatory moves.

The Cuban missile crisis produced a good deal of triumphalist analyses of ►crisis management which purported to show that Cuba was the antithesis to ►groupthink. The end of the ►Cold War and the availability of former Soviet documents and players to analysis and examination show that – as suggested earlier – the crisis was tripolar rather than strictly ►bipolar. There is evidence of substantial misperception on both sides and a picture of a much more placatory Kennedy emerges. In the aftermath of the crisis relations between the two protagonists improved substantially and a period of ►*détente* ensued. The assassination of Kennedy and the demotion of Khrushchev removed the two leaders who had the most to learn from this confrontation.

**Customs union** The customs union is a form of interstate ►integration. In this arrangement state ►actors agree to abolish ►tariffs between themselves while they maintain a tariff ►regime against third parties. The establishment of the common external tariff (cet) against the rest of the system gives the customs union a discriminatory characteristic. Conversely, the establishment of the union between the member states gives it a ►free trade characteristic. Customs union arrangements are normally phased in over a number of agreed stages. This process is known as ►harmonization.

Economic opinion is rather divided about the efficacy of customs unions. On one hand, by encouraging free trade, they reward efficiency. On the other hand, by encouraging ►protectionism, they reward inefficiency, particularly at the margin. The move towards internal free trade within the arrangement also creates a larger domestic market for goods and services behind the tariff wall. Again, this can lead to greater efficiency if, but only if, the economies of the constituent parts of the union are highly competitive. In these circumstances production will become located in the most efficient units. This balance sheet analysis of the customs union is often referred to as the balance between trade creation and trade diversion.

The ➤Treaty of Rome, which established the ➤European Economic Community (EEC) in January 1958, is a paradigm example of the customs union in reality. In this case the economic arguments for the move were somewhat subsumed by the political justifications for integration. Certainly both tendencies pointed in the same direction but it would probably be valid to conclude that in the case of the ➤European Community (EC) idea politics dictated economic decisions rather than vice versa.

# D

**Damage limitation** A term used in ►strategic studies. Its use appears in two contexts: as a principle and as a posture. In the first sense, damage limitation is shorthand for the maxim that the main function of the military ►capability of the ►state is to deny the forces of the enemy their opportunities to cause destruction by relentlessly seeking them out and destroying them. In a more passive sense, damage limitation refers to the range of measures taken by a state to deny the enemy his gains. A whole range of active and passive ►defence measures are regarded as appropriate under this latter heading.

**Debt crisis** Problems arising from the foreign indebtedness of ►states have been persistent features of the ►state-system since its inception. In this respect the ►crisis of the 1980s was not peculiar, although its causes were contingent upon certain factors in the political economy of the system. Clearly indebtedness in states – as in individuals – is only critical if the debtor cannot generate enough income to service the payments. This was precisely the problem that confronted a number of states, including most Latin American countries, in the early years of the 1980s. The ratio of debt to ►export earnings moved against the debtors to such an extent that a crisis was provoked in the international credit system.

Financial flows to states in the form of grants and loans may be funded on a public or private basis. Private funding by the banks located in the ►AICs became an increasingly significant factor during the 1970s. The steep rise in oil prices following the first ►oil shock of 1973–4 meant that significant amounts of capital moved into the coffers of the ►OPEC states. The decision to allow these petrodollars to be recycled through the ►First World's banking system meant that significant sums became available for lending on to would-be borrowers. Private corporations often ask fewer questions than governments and they certainly make fewer demands – particularly of a political nature – than are made in government-to-government dealings. Borrowing by middle income countries on a significant scale began in the mid 1970s. Private lending was the significant source of the credit. Interest charges were higher than would be expected in state-to-state dealings.

Borrowing on the scale referred to above requires a 'virtuous circle' of earnings/debt servicing repayments to sustain it. This circle was broken when the ►terms of trade moved against the debtors, when the second oil shock increased energy costs and when interest rates in America were raised. The crisis came to a head when Mexico announced in 1982 that is was unable to meet its foreign debt payments. Solutions proposed included the cautiously conservative idea of debt rescheduling to the more radical idea of debt forgiveness (cancelling the debts altogether). Substantially leverage was given to the donor states and ➤IGOs like the ➤IMF by the debt crisis. Given their approach to the issue of conditionality in IMF lending, it was expected that the Fund would require debtor states to adjust their economic activity towards greater privatization and market-orientation. Debtor states are not powerless to bargain with their creditors. In particular, the idea of a coordinated default was floated on more than one occasion.

The debt crisis has not been resolved but it has been managed. Additionally in some cases it has become obsolete as a number of ➤big emerging market economies have broken from the ranks of 1980s debtors. It is salutary to remember that the greatest debtor in the 1980s was the United States itself. Although the US enjoys the special privileges of a hard currency this does not gainsay the point that debt *per se* is not a problem. Confidence in the creditor/debtor relationship is the problem.

**Decision-makers** Those who make decisions on behalf of international ➤actors. Despite the circularity of the definition, identifying who are actually the decision-makers in particular instances is often a difficult task. In the limiting case where the actor is an individual – for instance, the ➤Secretary-General of the ➤United Nations – then the distinction is collapsed. In those many more frequent situations where the actor is a collectivity, a plausible starting point would be the documentation setting out the original purposes and functions of the actor – such as the constitution or custom of the ➤state. This may be described as identifying the formal office holders as the decision-makers.

Growing awareness of the significance of groups in decision-making leads to a different and more complicated ➤recognition. In pluralist systems the role of political parties and interest groups cannot be discounted. In some systems the military may play a key role. In those systems where decision-making is bureaucratized it may be necessary to look at particular departments of state. In the final analysis, the answer to the question, 'Who are the decision-makers?' will vary according to context and content of policy.

**Declinism** One side in the persistent 'debate' about the future ➤domain and ➤scope of American ➤power and ➤influence, the declinists – as the name signifies – believe that the relative power position of the United States is waning. The standard text on declinism is Paul Kennedy's (1988) work which spoke of the corroding effects of 'imperial overstretch' upon the ➤Pax Americana. At the height of its pre-eminence America undertook commitments and responsibilities which proved too onerous to sustain but which America was too tardy to withdraw from before debilitation ensued. Kennedy's work sets the USA within the tradition of ➤great powers which have experienced the same – or similar – gaps between commitments and power. Comparisons with the British experience in particular are extensively used in the Kennedy text. Indeed his critics, notably Nye (1990) have deemed many of these comparisons to be inappropriate. In a seminal review article the Sprouts (1968) had themselves suggested that the 'dilemma' of balancing rising demands with available power resources was virtually endemic in any political community. In the Kennedy treatment too, imperial overstretch is seen to be inevitable and therefore deterministic. The task of political ►leadership is thus to take the long view and to seek to adapt to changing circumstances rather than to buck these trends.

Behind the idea of imperial overstretch lurked the familiar trade-off between economic growth and defence expenditure. High military expenditure over a long period produces a shadow on the lung of the economy which results in relatively sluggish economic growth. Because America's main economic competitors were her military allies, during the ►Cold War period these states – particularly Japan – could free-ride under the American security umbrella. In the Kennedy volume therefore the costs of the Pax Americana in the form of relatively high and continuing levels of defence expenditure are causally related to poor economic performance. The coincidence of the publication of the book in 1988 with the burgeoning American deficit during Reagan's second term merely served to ensure that the work had best seller status.

The roots of the declinist case can be traced back to the early years of the 1970s when the collapse of the ►Bretton Woods system of finance and payments and the withdrawal from the Vietnamese war seemed to presage an end of an era. Rosecrance's (1976) edition suggesting that America was now an 'ordinary' great power recognized the limits of American power. The Nixon/Ford/Kissinger diplomacy of ►*détente* was predicated on a system of power sharing in an increasingly ►multipolar world. The events in Vietnam undermined the Cold War consensus in the United States which had created a permissive environment for the policy of ►globalism after the ►Truman Doctrine and the President's election victory in 1948.

The ending of the Cold War, the collapse of the Communist regimes in Europe and the ►Persian Gulf War seemed to drive declinism underground. Reports of America's demise now seemed premature and ►renewalism gained centre stage. The declinist implication that in some senses both the ►superpowers had lost the Cold War was submerged in renewalist triumphalism. Declinism is now the stable-mate of ►neo-isolationist and ►neo-mercantilist analyses of post-Cold War foreign policy options for America.

**Decolonization** The process whereby European control of overseas territories and peoples was ended. This culminated in the movement towards ►independence within these areas. A substantial increase in the number of ►states within the ►international system resulted and terms such as the ►Third World became increasingly used as collective expressions for these new ►actors. It should be noted that the correlation between being a former colony and being a Third World state is not perfect.

The principal states involved in the process of decolonization were located in Europe. Two merit special identification: the United Kingdom and France. In the case of the former, decolonization led to the creation of the ➤Commonwealth, which in its early years was significantly underpinned by economic ties, in particular the preferential ➤tariff system of Imperial Preference and the Sterling Area. The French decolonization experience was more traumatic than that of the United Kingdom, particularly in Algeria and ➤Vietnam. Unlike their near neighbours, the French were briefly attracted to the idea of assimilation rather than independence, and it was only when the Fourth Republic collapsed in 1958 that the issue was finally settled in favour of decolonization.

It should not be thought that policies of ➤intervention in the affairs of overseas territories and peoples ended with decolonization. While formal political control may have ceased, more informal methods of intervention and penetration have proliferated. It should be noted that the last vestiges of colonial control created significant ➤foreign policy ➤issue areas for the United Kingdom in respect of the ➤Falklands, Gibraltar and Hong Kong.

**De facto/de jure**  Terms used in ➤international law and ➤diplomacy usually in association with ➤recognition. *De facto* normally refers to provisional recognition that a particular government exercises factual ➤sovereignty, whereas *de jure* implies recognition of both factual and legal sovereignty. The *de facto* variety thus implies doubt either about the long term viability of a ➤regime or else of its ➤legitimacy; *de jure* implies complete diplomatic acceptance of the new ➤state or government. For example, the United Kingdom recognized the Soviet government *de facto* in 1921 and *de jure* in 1924. Clearly, political calculations play a major part in distinguishing the two categories, but it should be noted that *de facto* usually applies to governments rather than states – a state may for all practical purposes be *de jure* while its government for political reasons may be considered *de facto*. The guiding principle is usually whether or not a government exercises effective control over the territory of the state in question, but ideological issues can, and do, intrude. During the ➤Cold War, for example, selective use or non-use of these recognition categories became important discretionary instruments for registering approval or disapproval. Thus, from 1949 to 1979 the United States refused *de jure* recognition of ➤communist China.

*De facto* recognition is not necessarily a pre-condition of *de jure* recognition although in practice this has tended to be the case as it was in the Sino-American example above. The differences between them are not just a matter of degree or of political preference since *de jure* recognition entails the establishment of normal diplomatic relations whereas *de facto* does not of itself include the exchange of diplomatic relations. In addition, *de jure* can be 'express' (involving the immediate exchange of diplomatic notes) or 'tacit' (involving the declared intention at some future date to do so). Neither categories are final, although withdrawal of *de facto* recognition is easier than *de jure*.

**Defence** A means of protecting scarce values from attack. There is a strong tradition within ➤international relations thinking which conceives of defence ➤issue areas in terms of military-➤security questions. Accordingly defence is seen primarily as a matter for ➤states and ➤alliances to resist physical assault from without by raising the costs to the attacker so that the initiative will fail. In the limiting case a putative attacker will be so impressed by the ability and the resolve of the would-be defender that the attack will not be launched. In these circumstances defence is coterminous with ➤deterrence. In other usages the two terms can be envisaged as alternatives as Snyder (1961) first suggested.

In international relations the need for ➤actors to defend themselves has often been positively correlated with the idea that the system was one of ➤anarchy. The greater the anarchy, the greater the need for defence. The emergence of the state as the dominant actor in ➤IR from the seventeenth century onwards increased the significance of defence as a ➤goal of state policy. Defending the territoriality of the state was held to be the first requirement. Thereafter certain assets, symbolic as well as instrumental – such as the state capital – might assume more importance than others. Because defence capabilities are not distributed evenly between state actors, some states were better able to defend themselves than others. The latter would be forced to seek alliances and guarantee treaties if they were to avoid the unenviable fate of being 'pawns' in the system. Occasionally such states could seek sanctuary in the ➤orientation of ➤neutrality. More often they would 'bandwagon' behind an alliance leader.

An important parameter in the defence of any ➤actor is likely to be the available ➤technology. The balance of advantage between the defender and the attacker will be affected by this technological variable. In the twentieth century history of warfare most students are agreed that whereas in the 1914 ➤war the balance favoured the defence, by 1939 the balance favoured the offence. Moreover as Buzan (1987) has noted the balance in 1914 was ➤misperceived with costly results. The balance between defence/offence has recently been held to be a crucial variable in ➤multipolarity in deciding whether allies will commit themselves to support one another in the event of hostilities or seek to 'free-ride' in the hope that someone else will do the fighting.

In the contemporary system the development of ➤air power and ➤nuclear weapons have made the task of defence almost insuperable and the consequences of war almost impossible to imagine. Nuclear strategy – particularly in European hands – almost completely uncoupled military security from defence at least in terms of high intensity violence. The ultimate version of this decoupling was the theory of mutual assured destruction (➤MAD) which made a virtue out of the need to leave population centres undefended.

As an issue area in a state's foreign policy, defence questions will be correlated with the extent to which conflict, and in particular the expectation that it will turn into destructive violence, is high on the list of priorities for the leaders and the ➤attentive publics. At the time of writing defence is an immediate and pressing issue for the government and people of Israel to an extent not evident for the government and people of Ireland. Even for the Israelis there still has to be a trade-off between the costs and benefits of defence. It is a commonplace assertion – which is none the less valid – that sums devoted to defence are sums denied to other causes. Moreover as the ➤superpowers discovered during the ➤Cold War continuing high levels of defence expenditure can create a ➤military–industrial complex with a vested interest in its continuation. The end of the Cold War has removed some of the immediacy of the defence-security dilemma from political considerations. Although the hoped for 'peace dividend' might not have proved as large as once expected, there has been a significant redefinition of defence needs as security threats are seen in non-traditional ways. Deutsch (1957) in his studies of ➤integration has suggested that whole groups of states can now be identified in the system where regional relationships are not fundamentally and constantly being defined in terms of the most stringent and pressing defence-security contexts. If this is an important trend for the future then defence matters assume a relatively reduced profile in the foreign policy concerns of some groups of states. For others the defence question will remain of crucial importance in their ➤definition of the situation. ➤➤Non-offensive defence

**Definition of the situation** A term that has been originally attributed to the US sociologist Thomas (1958), and widely applied since by both sociologists and social psychologists. It refers to the processes of social ➤perception whereby individuals and groups 'construct' their reality in all its manifestations. This view, that individuals and groups respond and react to situations as they perceive them, and not as they really are, has led policy analysts to speak of a psychological environment in which policy is made. This approach is encapsulated in the phrase – again from Thomas – that 'if men define situations as real, they are real in their consequences'.

Since the processes of perception involve selecting certain cues and ignoring others, policy analysts have suggested that this insight may help others to understand how apparent 'mistakes' can be made in ➤policy-making. What might be seen objectively as an 'error' becomes more understandable if the definition of the situation that produced the policy is first investigated. Some of the most critical and costly 'errors', such as the US failure to anticipate the attack on ➤Pearl Harbor in 1941, notwithstanding their access to Japanese ➤intelligence, are susceptible to this explanation.

The concept of the definition of the situation is equally applicable to the analysis of mass public perceptions as to those of the ➤leadership. Indeed, any analysis that seeks to describe and explain how people view world events must take a position that is congruent with the definition of the situation idea. It remains an empirical question as to the content of that definition, of course.

**Démarche** A ➤diplomatic term referring to a fresh initiative adopted by one side following an impasse in ➤bilateral ➤negotiation. A *démarche* does not usually involve any significant alteration to the ➤national interest and it may have been part of the overall diplomatic strategy in the first place. It has the advantage of indicating a willingness on the part of one side to find an acceptable solution to the problem.

**Demilitarization** A policy whereby military forces are prohibited from an area. The prohibition will normally be absolute. If any forces remain they would be expected to confine themselves to non-provocative ➤defence measures, typically associated with ➤UN ➤peacekeeping. Demilitarization may follow upon a withdrawal of forces or it might apply to an area where military ➤force has not been introduced. Demilitarization might occur as part of a peace ➤treaty or ➤truce agreement and, therefore, some ➤verification and observation of the situation would be built into the arrangement. Finally, if the demilitarization agreement was coterminous with the territory of a ➤state, it would be expected that the ➤foreign policy of that state would be of a neutral or ➤non-aligned orientation thereafter. ➤➤Disengagement

**Democracy and foreign affairs** Two broad propositions about democracies have now become part of conventional IR wisdom. First, that democracies are deficient in the formulation and conduct of ➤foreign policy – the de Toqueville thesis. Second, that democracies are more ➤peace-loving than other kinds of political systems and seldom, if ever, go to war against one another – the Kantian or 'democratic peace' thesis.

The issue of the incompatibility of democracy and foreign policy was first enunciated by Alexis de Toqueville in *Democracy in America* (1835). Referring specifically to the USA he said that, 'Foreign politics demand scarcely any of those qualities which are peculiar to a democracy; they require on the contrary, the perfect use of almost all those in which it is deficient.' Furthermore, 'a democracy can only with great difficulty regulate the details of an important undertaking, persevere in a fixed design and work out its execution in spite of serious obstacles.' His central theme was that democracies are 'decidedly inferior' to more centralized political systems since they are 'prone to impulse rather than prudence'. Therefore they can be slow responding to crises and when it comes, the response is likely to be extreme. In addition 'there are two things that a democratic people will always find difficult, to start a war and to end it.' The reason for this state of affairs, according to de Toqueville, is the 'intrusion' of domestic politics into foreign policy making and the constant need to respond to ➤public opinion. In contrast, authoritarian regimes are advantaged because closed political systems facilitate ➤decision-making that is quick, consistent and not handicapped by the need to refer to a potentially critical public. Therefore, the concentration of ➤power and the denial of public scrutiny and debate gives centralized political systems decisive advantages in foreign affairs. This thesis has been an important theme in the debate between ➤realism and ➤idealism in international theory and throughout the twentieth century, but particularly during the ➤Cold War, democratic societies and their ➤leaderships were acutely conscious of these apparent policy shortcomings. In fact though, in most Western democracies including the US and UK, constitutional arrangements virtually always allocate the balance of advantage in foreign policy conduct to the executive over other branches of government precisely because of an awareness of the de Toqueville problem. Thus, in the USA the Presidency is almost always 'imperial' and in the UK, Parliament plays a decidedly inferior role to the Cabinet and the Foreign and Commonwealth Office.

The issue of regime-type and its impact on international affairs is also a key concern in international theory. The Kantian proposition that democracies do not go to war with one another (*Perpetual Peace* 1795) is for some 'the closest thing we have to an empirical law in the study of international relations.' (J. S. Levy in J. M. Owen, 1994). This thesis is now an essential pillar of ➤liberal and ➤neoliberal theories. The special characteristics that democracies supposedly possess are usually categorized in terms of institutional constraints and ➤normative or cultural ones. (M. Doyle, 1986). Institutionally, democracies are designed to respond to the views of their electorates. Since people generally prefer peace to war and since it is the people that suffer in war, democratic governments are sensitized to the costs of conflict. They are therefore more likely to pursue war-avoidance strategies. Regarding norms and culture, democracies assume that other democracies similarly subscribe to the idea of the pacific settlement of disputes and the use of force as a last resort. This mutually reinforcing perception of policy preferences thus leads to ➤accommodation rather than confrontation. Relations between democracies leads on a systemic level to the creation of ➤zones of peace and ➤security communities where the expectation of violent conflict between the units is virtually nil.

Not surprisingly, ➤neorealists dispute these claims and argue that the empirical evidence is not compelling. The dispute is partly definitional (what is a democracy and what counts as war?) but it is also a function of the realist belief that the structure of the ➤international system overrides regime-type in producing foreign policy behaviour. Therefore a universal awareness of ➤anarchy and the ➤security dilemma it entails, means that democracies respond no differently to their predicament than non-democratic states. In the absence of a rule-making and enforcing authority, international politics remains a competitive ➤self-help system in which ➤power and self-interest predominates. For realists systemic structure is the primary determinant of unit behaviour, therefore the issue of unit type is a decidedly secondary variable. (C. Layne, 1994). Notwithstanding these objections, the democratic peace theory has now become an orthodoxy in Western policy making circles and it forms the rationale for the ➤Clinton Doctrine and the expansion of ➤NATO.

**Demontage** Diplomatic term used in connection with ➤war reparations. It refers to the dismantling of factories, industrial plant and other installations connected to the war potential of the offending ➤state and their subsequent transfer to the state or states receiving reparations. It is sometimes demanded simply as a war prize by the victors but more usually it is regarded as a necessary precautionary measure against possible future hostile action by the defeated state. Thus, at the Potsdam conference of 1945 the Allies demanded the demontage or destruction of post-war Germany's war potential in all four zones of occupation.

**Dependence** Dependence is the opposite of ➤independence. It refers to a lack of ➤autonomy and control over outcomes. Dependence stems from the simple yet crucial factor of reliance. It can be demonstrated hypothetically by saying that if ➤actor 'A' relies upon Actor 'B' for the provision of some goods and services then 'A' may be said to be dependent upon 'B'. Reliance of this type is a commonplace in international relations and where it is clearly *mutual* – so that in our example 'B' also relies upon 'A' for goods and services – it is possible to speak of ➤interdependence rather than dependence. Interdependence may therefore be seen as a median position between independence on the one hand and dependence on the other. Thus the same developments in world politics that can be identified as leading to greater interdependence can also lead to greater dependence, since both are moves away from the same starting point: independence and autonomy.

Dependence can be identified in the following contexts: military, economic and technological. Military dependence is perhaps the oldest form of reliance in international politics and is still one of the most pervasive. The establishment of ➤alliances and the provision of military ➤aid are the key attributes of dependence here. Economic dependence is in the contemporary system, the most pervasive but also the most ambiguous. This ambiguity has led some writers to the view that economically dependent relationships currently constitute a ➤power structure called ➤dependency. Others have resisted this line of argument preferring to adapt ➤free trade ideas to contemporary circumstances and to suggest that economic dependence is a welcome and necessary feature of an expanding world economy. Technological dependence is the least unequivocal and the most obvious. Unlike military and economic dependence it is also readily susceptible to quantitative ➤verification, a simple but effective indicator of this type of dependence being the holdings of internationally registered patents. These clearly show that ➤technology, particularly 'state of the art', is very unevenly distributed around the system, a small number of ➤developed states and multinational corporations (MNCs) being crucial suppliers of technology.

**Dependency** Sometimes rendered as 'dependencia', the term seeks to identify and analyse a ➤power structure of complex dependence between international ➤actors. This genre is particularly associated with the study of ➤international political economy (IPE) and it was the dominant ➤paradigm amongst Latin American scholars in the second half of the twentieth century. In this field the writings of Fernando Cardoso (1979) and Peter Evans (1979) are representative. Implicitly – and sometimes explicitly – this school rejected ideas about ➤modernization and 'partners in development' assumptions that were the conventional wisdoms advanced by ➤economic liberalism, by most ➤IGOs and by political ➤elites in the ➤North. Instead the 'dependencistas' antitheses presented a conflictful and exploitive version of relations – particularly within the Americas – between ➤states. As Packenham (1992) has suggested the dependency 'movement' stormed the citadel of American development studies thereafter. It also provided ➤liberation theology with a version of the past which seemed more commensurate with the realities of the present. Institutionally, it provided the intellectual framework behind calls for a ➤New International Economic Order in the last quarter of the twentieth century.

Dependency theories are about asymmetries in power relations, in particular in economic ➤capability. Albert Hirschman (1945) analysed the economic offensive of Nazi Germany into South East Europe in the 1930s in terms of the operation of these economic asymmetries. Economic interests in the dominant economy are able to determine the parameters of the economic relations between the dominant and the dominated – or in the preferred terms of most dependencistas, the 'core' and the 'periphery' – and in this way a relationship of structural inequality is established. Vested interests in both the 'centre' and the 'periphery' thereafter seek to maintain and extend these power structures, promoting and prolonging dependency *inter alia*. These distortions may seriously hamper and impair economic development. Dependent states may find themselves importing costly and inappropriate ➤technologies, whilst dependency can have implications in the military-security context with respect to ➤ally-seeking and ➤alliance construction. ➤➤Marxism/Leninism, structuralism, structural power

**Dependent state** Originally, a dependent state was a synonym for a protectorate, that is to say, a ➤state which has surrendered significant areas of its jurisdiction to an external ➤actor in return for protection. A common division of responsibility under this arrangement would be for ➤defence and external affairs to be handled by the protecting state, and for domestic matters to remain under the control of the dependent state. Third parties would assent to this through the mechanism of ➤recognition.

The term now has an entirely different meaning. A dependent state is one that is identified as being in a ➤dependence relationship with another actor or actors. The sort of legal approval implied by the mechanism of recognition no longer applies in the contemporary usage.

**Dependent territory** The term by which colonial states now refer to their remaining colonies. The twentieth century has witnessed the almost total elimination of colonial rule, and the residual holdings are normally referred to by this form of words. Sometimes, as in the case of the ➤Falklands/Malvinas, the dependent territory can be the subject of considerable ➤conflict between ➤states. In principle, colonial states stand ready to grant ➤independence to these territories, if such a demand is expressed. The perverse outcome of a territory opting to remain under colonial control is not unknown, notwithstanding the prevailing climate of opinion in institutions such as the UN that ending ➤colonialism is now *de rigueur*.

**Deportation** The enforced removal of an ➤alien from one ➤state to another usually as a consequence of a perceived offence to the host state. However, in ➤international law no reasons for deportation have to be given. Thus, in the United Kingdom the Aliens Order of 1953 empowers the Home Secretary to deport an alien if he 'deems it to be conducive to the public good' (Article 20, 2, b). Given the principle of ➤reciprocity this means that a decision to deport is all but uncontestable. M. Akenhurst (1970) quotes the case of a UK woman lecturer being deported from Malawi in 1969 for wearing a miniskirt at a party. At the airport, having prudently changed into an ankle-length dress, she told reporters that she was 'simply delighted' to be leaving! In fact, most challenges do not focus on the decision to deport, but on the conditions under which the deportee has been held. Extended periods in prison, torture, humiliation and ridicule are not unusual preliminaries to deportation.

Under the rules of ➤nationality, when a national of one state is deported from another the 'home' state is obliged to receive him, unless he is willing to go to another state which accepts him. Since states have such wide powers in relation to deportation, it is often used as a substitute for ➤extradition, especially in cases where no formal ➤bilateral extradition treaty exists. Sometimes the term is used in relation to the enforced expulsion of ➤diplomats, but here the process is different. The receiving state, usually on the advice of its Foreign Ministry, simply declares the offending diplomat ➤*persona non grata*. Tit-for-tat expulsions of this kind were an integral part of ➤Cold War politics.

**Destabilization** In ➤foreign policy analysis this refers to ➤hegemonial attempts to promote fundamental change in a target ➤state's policies without resort to overt armed ➤intervention by the hegemon. As such it involves a combination of military, ➤diplomatic, economic, social and ➤ideological instruments. The primary objective though is a political one. This may involve attempting to secure structural movements in an opponent's stance even to the extent of aiming for ➤regime change. The intention to destabilize is not, as is commonly thought, to cause fringe irritation or discomfort; rather it is designed to bring about major changes in the diplomatic behaviour or ➤perception of the target, if necessary by promoting a change of ➤leadership, faction or ruling group. It commonly takes a covert form and is sometimes mediated through a third party or proxy. It characteristically involves targeting vulnerable sectors in the population, transport, infrastructure, energy supply, ➤food production and distribution and dissident groups in the society. The policy ➤goal of destabilization is aimed at securing a more compliant regime and leadership. Successful destabilization may thus produce a ➤*coup d'état* or ➤civil war outcome in the target.

Destabilization was a familiar policy instrument during the ➤Cold War when both of the ➤superpowers, the United States and the Soviet Union, attempted covert interference aimed at destabilizing a number of target states. Thus American policy towards Cuba following the 1959 ➤revolution sought to destabilize the Castro regime using the CIA (Central Intelligence Agency). This programme culminated in the abortive ➤Bay of Pigs operation in 1961. The Cuban campaign was planned on lines similar to the 1954 destabilization of Guatemala which had been judged a success by the Eisenhower Administration of the day. In the former Soviet Union the ➤transnational links available through the ➤communist party gave Soviet leaders a facility at hand for destabilization. In the former ➤Yugoslavia Stalin attempted to destabilize the Tito leadership of the communist party in the spring of 1948. Like the Cuban case, this attempt ended in failure and ultimately in the growth of ➤polycentrism in the Soviet ➤bloc.

Perhaps one of the most successful examples of destabilization was the use of this technique under the aegis of the ➤Reagan Doctrine. In both ➤Afghanistan and in Nicaragua (with the so-called Contras) the Reagan Administration sought to provide military ➤aid and assistance to factions and groups perceived to be anti-Communist ('freedom fighters' in the rhetoric of the Great Communicator). In both instances, particularly the Afghan case, American destabilization was assisted by the active participation of other states from the ➤region.

The term was also used in connection with the policies of the South African government during the ➤apartheid period. Pretoria targeted a group of states in the region including: Angola, Botswana, Lesotho, Mozambique, Swaziland, Zambia and Zimbabwe. The object was to keep these states economically ➤dependent upon the Republic, thereby severely limiting their freedom of action in making ➤foreign policy. Destabilization was an integral part of South Africa's 'Total Strategy' and although successful in regional terms, it had damaging international repercussions. As Booth and Vale have noted (1995) South African destabilization was dependent upon a particular ➤definition of the situation regarding the idea of ➤security which in turn produced a militarization of policy-making. In all three cases cited the Cold War had a profound ➤influence upon the decision to initiate destabilization instruments of policy. The risk of the rebound effect makes the option of destabilization a matter of extremely delicate political calculation.

**D'Estaing Doctrine** Term which refers to a ➤foreign policy initiative expressed by French President Giscard D'Estaing in December 1974 when he stated that the main principles upon which France's world posture rested were *mondialisme et conciliation* (➤globalism and reconciliation). The general philosophy was that France would move away from the narrow ➤nationalism that had sometimes seemed to characterize its foreign policy (especially under De Gaulle) and would capitalize on its independent stance to offer itself as a mediator in major international disputes. Thus, through the ➤good offices of France, diplomatic dialogue between the North Vietnamese and the United States began in Paris in 1970. ➤➤*Francophonie*; Gaullism

**Détente** A diplomatic term meaning a relaxation or a slackening of tension in the previously strained relations between ➤states. In diplomatic history the term is particularly associated with the ➤concert system established in post-1815 Europe. Again, the period following the Locarno ➤treaties of 1925 and resulting in the ➤Kellogg–Briand pact of Paris in 1928 (which sought to outlaw ➤war between states) is often described in these terms. However, the term is now most often used in connection with a perceived easing of relations between the United States and the Soviet Union which began, from most accounts, in the early 1960s. In this way it is sometimes used, not altogether correctly, as a synonym for ➤rapprochement and peaceful coexistence. *Détente* is sometimes referred to as the antithesis of the ➤Cold War, but may also be viewed as just a stage in its development – a shift from the doctrinaire confrontational policies of the 1950s to the more flexible ➤diplomacy of the 1960s and 1970s. At any rate it is useful to distinguish between *détente* as a policy a state may pursue (eg the Nixon/Kissinger initiatives of 1972 and 1973) and *détente* as a condition or a process (e.g. post-1962 East-West relations). It should also be noted that *détente* is not restricted to ➤great power ➤multilateral relationships alone. ➤Bilateral *détentes* between lesser states are also a significant feature of contemporary international relations. West Germany's policy of ostpolitik and UK efforts in the early 1960s to play the part of 'honest broker' can be viewed in this context.

Although no formal treaty established the recent period of *détente*, commentators usually cite the ➤Cuban missile crisis of 1962 as the beginning of the process and the Soviet invasion of ➤Afghanistan in 1979 as its most fragile point. Indeed, for many the events of 1979–80 (Afghanistan and the election of President Reagan) signalled the end of *détente* and the beginning of the 'Second Cold War'. Looking at it as a historical process, though, many analysts disagree as to exactly when it began and when and if it ended. Some scholars date it from as early as the Eisenhower administration and the death of Stalin (1953), others give Kennedy and Khrushchev the honour of its inauguration and yet others fix its inception with the Nixon/Kissinger overtures to China in 1972. However, most agree that it refers to a structural change in post-war ➤superpower relations and that it set in train a number of significant points of dialogue between them, including the ►Helsinki Accords (1975) and the Strategic Arms Limitation Talks (►SALT).

*Détente* does not mean that conflicts have been resolved or that either side accepts the ideological principles of the other. Rather it should be seen as a response to changed perceptions of the ►international system – an awareness of the possibility of mutual destruction, the emergence of new clusters of ►power and perhaps the promptings of domestic economic priorities – all of these played their parts in fostering improved public relations between the superpowers. Critics of *détente*, especially in the Reagan administration, have argued that far from being a mutually understood halfway point between extreme hostility and overt amicability (►entente), *détente* is little short of ►appeasement, which served to strengthen the East at the expense of the West. This, however, is a distortion of the term.

**Deterrence** Deterrence is a conditional commitment to retaliate, or to exact retribution if another party fails to behave in a desired, compliant manner. Deterrence is thus about relationships between individuals and groups. Indeed, it can be said to cover an extremely broad set of social relations from child-rearing through penal systems to international affairs. It is possible to identify this relationship in its simplest two-person version by speaking of an Imposer and a Target. Hence the Imposer seeks to deter the Target from behaving in an unacceptable fashion by threatening punishment.

Deterrence concentrates exclusively on negative sanctions, or threats, and upon preventing undesirable behaviour. It is therefore more usual to find that deterrence is mostly prevalent and significant in relationships of antipathy rather than in relationships of harmony. Imposers are more likely to make threats in situations which they find uncongenial and *vis-à-vis* Targets whose behaviour, and even presence, they wish to oppose. In this way deterrence is a special instance of the ►power relationship – those situations of social opposition characterized by the use of sanctions. Moreover, deterrence is unequivocally about negative sanctions.

Since deterrence is based upon ideas about threat systems and conditional commitments to carry out punishment it has proved particularly congenial to the ►strategic studies fraternity within the realist tradition. The advent of ►nuclear weapons after 1945 provided a new challenge to these scholars because it seemed to many that making and potentially activating nuclear threats, had special problems both for the analyst and for the ►policy-maker. The inherent difficulty with this class of threats is that they lack ►credibility. Faced with the knowledge that the opponent possesses nuclear weapons the nuclear threat is a conditional commitment that the Imposer has no incentive to carry out, rationally, since he will gain nothing from its activation. If the Imposer is placed in the position of actually having to fulfil the threat then its purpose is lost and carrying it out is valueless. Paradoxically, this need not be the case if the Target can be persuaded that the threat is not idle, that the Imposer will not hesitate to activate it. In short, the more certain the contingent fulfilment, the less likely the actual fulfilment will need to be activated.

As suggested above the problem of making this contingent threat sufficiently powerful is referred to as the problem of credibility. Credibility is the process whereby threats are made operational. First, operationalizing the threat requires that it be communicated – as unambiguously as possible. Second, the threat must actually deprive the Target of scarce values which they would otherwise wish to retain. The Target must value that which will be sacrificed, if they disobey, higher than any values that will be forgone if they comply. This is why it is difficult to coerce a Target who feels that they have nothing to lose. In these situations deterrence may break down and the Imposer will be faced with the prospect of activating the threat in order to retain their credibility – and not to be seen to be bluffing. This problem is referred to in the literature as the ➤*ex post ex ante* situation, namely, that a threat may look quite plausible before it is carried out, yet may look totally implausible afterwards. Opponents of mutual assured destruction (➤MAD) hold that this strategy looks much less credible in the light of this distinction.

The *ex post ex ante* issue is approached in a somewhat different way by Schelling in his 1966 volume. Using the distinction between deterrence and ➤compellence, he seeks to separate situations where the Imposer is seeking to prevent a behaviour sequence (deterrence) from situations where the Imposer is seeking to redress a situation afterwards (compellence). Schelling argues that achieving a relationship of effective compellence may be more difficult because the behaviour sequence is already under way and the Imposer is, in effect, seeking to 'put the clock back' by requiring the Target to change what he is already doing.

Credibility, requires the Imposer to possess the requisite military ➤capability to make and carry out threats. Glenn Snyder (1961) distinguishes two types of deterrence situations that are dependent upon different capabilities and therefore different intentions. Snyder's distinction is between deterrence by denial and deterrence by punishment. Denial deterrence works by contesting the control of territory and populations traditionally associated with any territorial ➤defence. Prior to the development of ➤nuclear weapons both denial and punishment functions would have been fulfilled with the same capability. However, the development of long-range ➤air power, ➤ballistic missiles and fission and fusion weapons has meant that any ➤state possessing this capability may be able to inflict great punishment upon an adversary without having the capability of denying the opponent any significant gains. In this argument deterrence and defence become alternatives, if not opposites.

With MAD the uncoupling of deterrence from defence was completed. MAD could not threaten to deny the enemy his would-be gains, so instead it threatens punishment in the form of ➤genocide. One result of the uncoupling of deterrence and defence has been that confusion has arisen about the role of different weapons systems. From the viewpoint of defence an anti-ballistic missile (➤ABM) can be justified if it allows the possessor to thereby limit damage to his territory. From the viewpoint of deterrence an ABM system may seem to be destabilizing because it reduces ➤vulnerability, which is a prerequisite for MAD.

Deterrence theory raises acute questions about the circumstances in which threats can be an effective means of controlling behaviour and, conversely, conditions when they may be self-defeating. There is considerable evidence for a very qualified view of deterrence assumptions. First, a threat is often perceived by a Target as motivated by the desire to injure rather than by the needs of ➤self-defence. Second, a threat may be seen as an attempt to restrain legitimate behaviour which the Target feels entitled to engage in. Third, the threat may not deter aggressive behaviour but rather deflect it on to substitute objects. Fourth, a threat by creating stress within a ➤decision-making group may vitiate the rational behaviour pattern that is such a necessary prerequisite for deterrence to work. Behaviour particularly under stress, may be counter-productive as far as deterrence is concerned. Accurate communication may be made more difficult. Stress can greatly increase the likelihood that certain values will be misperceived and that issues may be seen as matters of principle about which no concessions can be made. Jervis's (1976) discussion of the spiral theory in his work on ➤perception and ➤misperception suggests that hostility can be self-defeating in certain circumstances and reinforces the queries raised above about this influential, but flawed, theory of social control.

**Developed state** A ➤state which has achieved self-sustained economic growth over a sufficient period of time to show development in primary, secondary and tertiary sectors of industry and to have achieved thereby a consistent improvement in living standards for the population as a whole. The advanced industrial countries (➤AICs) are generally held to be the paradigm developed states.

It is the case that the kinds of changes associated with developed status have only been available to peoples and states over the last two hundred years. As a result of a series of initiatives taken originally in Western Europe it became possible through the processes of industrialization and mechanization to create wealth in a relatively benign fashion. This process is often referred to as the 'industrial revolution'. Originally, the leading example of a developed state was Great Britain but this position was lost to the United States towards the end of the last century. There is some reason to suppose that the United States is similarly losing its status as the leading developed state and that Japan is currently the most dynamic example of the genre. ➤➤First World; yen power

**Diplomacy** The word is often used, incorrectly, as a synonym for ➤foreign policy. Whereas the latter can be described as the substance, aims and attitudes of a ➤state's relations with others, diplomacy is one of the instruments employed to put these into effect. It is concerned with dialogue and ➤negotiation and in this sense is not merely an instrument of state, it is also an institution of the ➤state-system itself. Since the emergence of the state-system in Europe in the fifteenth century an organized and fairly coherent system of permanent relations has developed among the ➤actors and, even when these relations have been interrupted by armed conflict, diplomacy has still been the principal means of communication. Indeed, although it is common to separate the diplomatic and the military means at a state's disposal, actual practice has tended to blur the distinction. As Frederick the Great once remarked, 'diplomacy without force is like music without instruments'. So diplomacy as an instrument and as an institution is an essential part of the whole rationale of ➤international relations.

The main function of diplomacy is negotiation – which broadly means discussions designed to identify common interests and areas of ➤conflict between the parties. To establish the conditions under which negotiations can take place a number of other tasks are undertaken. The first is representation. The emissary, or ➤ambassador, is one of the earliest political roles established in human society, but it was not until the fifteenth century in the Italian ➤city-states that the concept of a permanent representative mission (or legation) was formalized. During the Renaissance period a systematic and largely professional diplomatic service was established with the purpose of obtaining information, interpreting policies and trends, safeguarding military and political interests and promoting commerce and ➤trade links. Certainly the promotion of trade has always been a central part of the activity of diplomacy and is not, as some allege, a comparatively recent innovation. The Venetian diplomatic service was initially a commercial venture and there is much evidence that the spur to organized diplomacy on a permanent and spatially static basis was just as much economic as political or military. A second function of diplomacy besides representation of a state's interests is to formulate and identify these ➤goals and objectives. Preparing policy guidelines and initiatives for their political masters to accept or reject is usually the task of a Foreign Ministry, rather than an ambassador on location, although their views will obviously be influential. Another function, in the larger sense, is the overall management of orderly relations as well as being the means whereby change is effected. Finally, diplomacy is concerned with establishing and renewing the rules and procedures which regulate the ➤international system. In this last sense, diplomacy is the enabling vehicle for the operation of ➤international law and ➤international organizations.

The rules which established a common and coherent diplomatic system were developed in piecemeal fashion from the fifteenth to the twentieth centuries. The ➤extraterritoriality rule was established during the period of Louis XIV, the notion of the *corps diplomatique* emerged in the eighteenth century, and the Congress of Vienna in 1815 can be credited with laying down the procedures for precedence and with promoting the doctrine of the formal ➤equality of states. In the twentieth century the Vienna conventions of 1961, 1963 and 1969 have codified international law relating to Diplomatic Relations, Consular Relations and the Law of Treaties, thus tightening up and giving new impetus to past and future practice. Most states now recognize and implement these developments. The near universal acceptance of diplomacy and its trappings has not, however, had as smooth a ride as the foregoing might suggest. It has come under attack from all aspects of the ideological spectrum in recent times. The Soviet Union rejected it in 1917 as did China from 1949 to the early 1970s, the United States, especially under Woodrow Wilson, expressed qualms about it, the new states established during the 1950s and 1960s as a result of the anti-colonial ►revolution were very uneasy about it and of course Iran and ►Islamic fundamentalism is its most bitter contemporary opponent. Nevertheless, after an initial period of formal ideological rejection most states, including all of the above, have been drawn into the system, mainly because there exist no alternatives to it. Changes have occurred both in the conduct of diplomacy and in the personnel associated with it. Most commentators point to the following developments which occurred as a result of the increasing complexity of inter-state relations: the intrusion of ideological conflict and the opening up of diplomatic dialogue; the change of emphasis from ►bilateral to ►multilateral dealings; the decline in the ►decision-making power of the ambassador; the advent of personal diplomacy; the increased use of experts and specialists; the involvement of ministries not normally associated with foreign affairs; the increased number of ►treaties; the growth in importance of the media and the expansion of the international community and of non-state actors. This enhancement and enlargement of the ►scope of modern diplomacy and the widening of its agenda has resulted in a change of emphasis (more on economic issues than on traditional ►high politics), rather than on any major change in function. This remains in essence the same as it has always been; namely, to manage and conduct orderly relations in a multi-state, politically fragmented international system. ►►Conference diplomacy; diplomatic immunities and privileges; dollar diplomacy; summit diplomacy

**Diplomatic immunities and privileges** The reciprocal granting of certain immunities and privileges to diplomatic agents is grounded in the concept of ►sovereignty and mutual respect for the political ►independence and territorial integrity of ►states. In this sense diplomatic immunity implies both an exemption from rules associated with ►domestic jurisdiction and also an affirmation of them. Rules relating to the special status of diplomats are common to all ►state-systems and are among the earliest manifestations of ►international law. Communication between independent units would have been all but impossible without rules establishing the sacrosanct nature of the emissary or herald. With the development of resident embassies, permanent missions and legations during the late Renaissance period in Europe, this was extended to cover location as well as personnel. It should be noted, however, that diplomatic immunities and privileges are granted not to particular persons but to the states or organizations on whose behalf they act. Customary rules associated with exemptions were codified at the Congress of Vienna in 1815 and more extensively at the Vienna Convention on Diplomatic Relations of 1961. (Incidentally, in both cases the word 'privileges' is preferred to 'immunities'.) The following areas are covered: the inviolability of premises and property, the personal; inviolability of diplomatic officers, freedom of communication and transportation, inviolability of records, archives, documents and correspondence, customs privileges (e.g. the 'diplomatic bag'), exemption from taxation and various jurisdictional privileges. Most of these exemptions also apply to representatives of states to ►international organizations. Representation to the UN and its specialized agencies is covered by the rules established by the General Convention on the Privileges and Immunities of the UN of 1946 and these are premised on an agreement between the United States as the host country and the organization itself.

The functional necessity of diplomatic privileges and immunities as a general rule for the efficient conduct of ►international relations is almost universally recognized. However, this does not mean that immunities are absolute or cannot be waived by the sending state or withdrawn by the receiving state (►*persona non grata*). In general, violation of these rules is considered a serious international dereliction. The near universal condemnation of the Iranian imprisonment of US diplomats for use as hostages in 1979–81, and the widespread public outcry at the US raid on the Nicaraguan ambassador's residence in Panama in 1989, is testimony to this. Indeed, with regard to the latter, President Bush's remark that it was a 'screw-up' clearly implies that the violation was contrary to accepted practice.

**Disarmament** Disarmament is both a process and an end state. As a process it involves the reduction, removal or elimination of identified weapon systems. As an end state it involves the establishment of a disarmed world and the prevention of rearmament thereafter. Disarmament may be regional or global. It may be ►unilateral, ►bilateral, or ►multilateral. It may be partial or complete. It may be limited to certain weapon systems or general to all classes. In this way it may be seen that general and complete disarmament is the most comprehensive of these schemes.

In the modern ►state-centred system disarmament has usually followed defeat in war. A defeated ►state will temporarily be disarmed by the victor(s). Often, a subsequent peace ►treaty or ►truce will confirm this outcome. The vanquished may be prohibited from acquiring certain kinds or certain amounts of stipulated weapons. Negotiated agreements between nominal equals, without the test of strength of ►war, require a different approach and produce a different outcome. These agreements require the parties to recognize that cooperation is to be preferred to the continuation of the ➤arms race. In such bargaining situations the tendency is to proceed by a strategy of ➤incrementalism and to work from areas of agreement towards partial or limited measures. This approach shades off into ➤arms control in many instances and potential confusion is not assisted by the tendency among politicians and diplomats to run these two ideas together.

The arms race, and the appropriate attitude to take towards it, is really what separates the proponents of general and complete disarmament from the proponents of arms control. Whereas arms controllers accept that weapon systems have a function and role in international affairs, general and complete disarmers hold that the dynamics of the arms race exacerbates tensions and leads to violence, in short, that the arms race is a cause of conflict and violence, rather than merely a symptom.

Disarmament is not automatically tension-reducing. There are powerful incentives to 'cheat' on the other party during the process. Indeed, the further disarmament proceeds, the greater these incentives become. The ultimate paradox of the disarmament process is that in an effort to eliminate the tensions caused by the arms race, disarmament creates tensions itself.

As an end state, a disarmed world would require considerable centralized management to avoid these contradictions. State sponsored disarmament clearly implies the internationalization of military ➤force. If this outcome is ever achieved, two issues will immediately arise: what military ➤capabilities will the international force require, and what policy goals will the new institution follow in order to maintain disarmament and prevent competitive rearmament? These are complex and difficult questions, but they indicate the kinds of problems that will arise if the process ever reaches the end state.

It should be noted that states do, on occasions, engage in disarmament negotiations in order to achieve what might be called 'side benefits'. These might include a desire to understand the other side's point of view, in many instances. However, more cynical motives can sometimes be identified. States will talk about disarmament in order to score ➤propaganda points by manoeuvring the opposition into positions where they can be made to appear intransigent and insincere about the issue.

**Dollar diplomacy** Phrase particularly associated with the ➤foreign policy of President Taft (1909–13) and now commonly used to describe US efforts to secure their objectives through financial and economic instruments of control. Initially the target area was Central and Latin America, but the policy was extended to China and the Far East, as well as post-Second World War Europe (the ➤Marshall Plan). The assumptions behind it were that extensive US investments would create economic progress, political stability and compliance in areas that the United States considered strategically important. It also, of course, had the benefit of furthering the interests of US business. Dollar diplomacy does not rule out the option of military or political ➤intervention.

In fact, the establishment of extensive financial commitments abroad might make it more likely in periods of instability and upheaval. This is especially true of the Panama Canal, the completion of which coincided with the origin of the phrase. Other notable examples are Guatemala (1954), Cuba (1961) and the Dominican Republic (1965). This policy, along with its successor 'missionary diplomacy' – the term given to Woodrow Wilson's missionary zeal in attempting to export democracy – has led to considerable 'Yankee-phobia' in Latin America which the ➤Good Neighbor policies of the 1930s were designed to dispel.

Dollar diplomacy is a good example of ➤economic statecraft serving specific and self-regarding ➤goals. During the ➤Cold War era American economic ➤power was extensively used in pursuit of both 'possession' and 'milieu' goals. The results were often mixed but in the case of the Marshall Plan the objectives were realized. The manner in which the Cold War ended has, if anything, substantiated many of the latent assumptions behind dollar diplomacy. As reference to the ➤Clinton Doctrine shows, the United States continues to assert its economic preferences in the post–Cold War period.

**Domain** An ➤actor's domain is a measure of the number of other actors in world politics over which it can effectively exert ➤influence at any one time. The concept is used in the analysis of ➤power relationships. Its utility is considerable because it enables the analyst to look at power relations as a dynamic rather than a static set of occurrences. The term is usually used in conjunction with ➤scope and, accordingly, its explanatory value is enhanced further.

**Domestic analogy** A concept, beloved of traditionalists in international theory, whereby the domestic political, legal and social experience is applied to inter-state affairs. Most commonly used by adherents of the ➤Hobbesian view in which order is achieved in the state of nature by the creation of a Leviathan, or 'a common power' to regulate individual behaviour. The thesis is that ➤international relations can only benefit by reproducing the institutions of domestic society. Since 'absence of government' is a defining feature of the former, its provision as per the domestic analogy ought to be a major goal of international theory and practice. The domestic analogy has always been suspect – even Hobbes himself seems to have resisted it – since the conditions of order among ➤states are not generally regarded as similar to those among individuals. The best of the recent explorations of this idea and its consequences is Hedley Bull's *Anarchical Society*. ➤➤Agent-structure; anarchy; neoliberalism; neorealism

**Domestic jurisdiction** A logical consequence of ➤sovereignty whereby a ➤state rules supreme within its own territorial frontiers. This duty of ➤non-intervention within the domestic jurisdiction of states means that in regard to certain issues, the international legal ➤regime is not deemed valid. Article 2 (7) of the ➤UN Charter provides that 'Nothing contained in the present Charter shall authorize the United Nations to intervene in matters which are essentially within the domestic jurisdiction of any state or shall require the members to submit such matters to settlement under the present Charter.' This article is one of the most controversial in the Charter and its application one of considerable dispute. In ➤international law, domestic jurisdiction refers to those matters where a state's discretion is not limited by obligations imposed by international law unless the state itself agrees. However, the concept is a relative one and the influence of international law is beginning to make inroads in areas hitherto regarded as exclusive to the state and also in areas where internal regulation may have international repercussions. Thus, matters which are not generally regarded as falling within domestic jurisdiction are a breach of international law, an infringement of the interests of other states, a threat to international ➤peace, violations of ➤human rights and questions of ➤self-determination. The range of activities now considered to be within the competence of international law has grown considerably, especially in relation to the latter two categories, as the Republic of South Africa had cause to note over the issues of ➤apartheid and Namibia. ➤➤Humanitarian intervention

**Domino theory** An analogy with the way in which a row of dominoes falls sequentially until none remain standing, the domino theory was particularly popular with ➤decision-makers in the United States in the 1950s and 1960s, although some would still want to defend its cogency today. The cause of the collapsing dominoes, according to this view, was transnational ➤communism which, it was held, had a propensity to expand across state ➤frontiers consuming all before it. After 1949 proponents of the theory looked particularly to the People's Republic of China in this regard. The ideas and precepts of ➤People's War were believed to be widely applicable to many parts of the ➤Third World. Communists had to some extent been contributors to this view themselves because they were wont to emphasize the extent to which revolutionary experience and example can be exported to and acquired by others, particularly when environmental or 'objective' conditions appear to favour it.

President Eisenhower's press conference of 7 April 1954 is usually instanced as one of the earliest and most influential statements of the theory, although some UK commentators have wanted to claim that the theory is descended from UK origins. The genesis of the theory is, however, less significant than its subsequent impact and in this regard no reputable scholar would deny that, as a ➤definition of the situation, the theory is the progeny of US perceptions of post-war communism. In essence, what Eisenhower said in 1954 was that the stakes in Indo-China also included the future of the neighbouring states. However, the idea of 'neighbourhood' was interpreted to cover much of the ➤region, and in this way he spoke of a 'sequence of events' linking Indo-China, Burma, Thailand, Malaya and Indonesia. Subsequently, Eisenhower extended his 'falling dominoes' ideas to Central America and the so-called 'offshore islands' of Quemoy and Matsu.

➤Vietnam in particular, and Indo-China in general, were central to the domino theory. There is considerable documentary evidence now to substantiate the conclusions that both Kennedy and Johnson subscribed to the theory. Indeed, documentation such as the Pentagon Papers suggests that a similar ➤perception was held by many Cabinet members in those two administrations. A notable and interesting exception is the Central Intelligence Agency (CIA) which queried the theory in June 1964 when specifically requested by Johnson to give an opinion on its relevance.

The Presidency of Richard Nixon, and crucially the promulgation of the ➤Nixon Doctrine, signified the waning of the theory as central to the definition of the situation. The event that appeared to query the worst case outcomes predicted by the theory being the failure of the Indonesian communists to prevail during the period of intense civil strife in 1965.

Since Nixon, US leaders have been much more willing to accept that Asian ➤regionalism can provide a counter-balance to hegemonial ➤intervention, from whatever source. The domino theory can still influence US perceptions whenever they contemplate political developments in areas that appear to be highly unstable, particularly if the presence of communists can be detected. Central America was always a favoured setting for these perceptions.

Intellectually domino thinking can be roundly criticized for its often crude and unstructured generalizations about political systems that are quite different. Its failure to apportion sufficient weight to the ➤ideology of ➤nationalism as an alleviation or antidote to transnational communism is almost certainly its greatest error. However, consideration of the impact that the domino theory had upon three successive US Administrations in the ➤issue area of Vietnam is a valuable reminder of the manner by which the images that ➤decision-makers hold can influence their definition of the situation and, thereby, their policy-making.

**Donor fatigue** A term used in the analysis of ➤foreign aid, particularly by advanced industrial countries (➤AICs). The term refers to the development of an adverse and critical climate of informed public opinion about the principles and purposes of Aid programmes. This re-evaluation has been occasioned by the seeming failure of such aid efforts to realize the expectations of the donors that foreign assistance to the ➤Third World has had the same positive impact, both economic and political, as was achieved by the European Recovery Programme. The disappointing economic performance of many recipient ➤states, added to their dogged refusal to allow the donors to buy their political allegiance, is the proximate cause of this eroding support. Other latent factors that have contributed to this re-evaluation include: the adverse economic climate in the AICs during the 1970s and 1980s, particularly the growth of unemployment and the problems of controlling inflation; and the development of a more critical market orientated political economy which tends to denigrate the applicability and relevance of what are seen as collectivist planning ideas.

In the post-►Cold War period, the problem of donor fatigue has been exacerbated in some ►regions, Sub-Saharan Africa in particular, by political and economic marginalization. Thus the 'opening up' of Central and Eastern Europe to Western investment and aid has resulted in much of Africa 'falling off the map' of contemporary world politics. For some analysts, particularly from the realist perspective, donor fatigue is an antidote to the culture of ►dependency.

**Doomsday Machine** The agile and provocative mind of the strategist and ►futurologist, Hermann Kahn, conjured up the idea of the Doomsday Machine in his work *On Thermonuclear War* (1960). Having identified three types of deterrent situations facing a ►nuclear power such as the United States, Kahn argued that, in what he termed 'type one ►deterrence', that is to say, deterring a direct attack on the homeland of the United States, the Doomsday Machine was the near-perfect answer. In brief, the machine, which he postulated could destroy all human life on the planet, would be automatically activated once sensors had detected that ►nuclear weapons had landed on the United States. Kahn argued that if a deterrent threat was a near-certainty and if a deterrent threat posed overwhelming and unacceptable damage when carried out, then no rational ►decision-maker would risk the consequences by challenging the deterrer.

An exegesis of the Kahn argument is probably less important than recognition of the facet of deterrence theory that the Doomsday Machine idea highlights. In particular, by emphasizing the near-certainty of the response, Kahn answers those who have argued that deterrence would fail when it was most needed because the threatener would be 'self-deterred' by the enormity of the threat. ►►Deterrence.

**Double veto** The ►veto or unanimity rule that obtains in the UN Security Council has been interpreted since the Charter Conference at San Francisco in 1945 as applying to the preliminary question of whether a matter before the Council is procedural (where the veto does not apply) or substantive. In effect, then, any of those ►states with the veto can use this facility on the initial issue as well as the consequent and substantive one. Hence the term double veto. ►►P5; veto

**Dove** A colloquial term used in the analysis of ►international relations and ►foreign policy. A 'dove' is a personality type who favours certain approaches to dealing with other ►actors and rejects other approaches. Generally speaking, doves are held to favour ►diplomacy that seeks ►accommodation, ►conciliation and ►conflict resolution. Conversely doves oppose using excessive ►coercion, see the ►arms race as highly dangerous and even view ►deterrence rather critically. Doves often set much store by ►international organizations such as the UN and their intrinsic belief in international cooperation is reflected in this supportive view. The dove or dovish personality is often used as a relative point of reference and contrast with the ➤hawk, who is supposed to be the antithesis of everything the dove stands for. Both terms are often used rhetorically.

**Dual nationality** Simultaneous citizenship of more than one ➤state. In ➤international law citizenship is either acquired *jus sanguinis* (law of blood) or *jus solis* (law of the soil) or else by the legal process of naturalization (which usually involves a minimum period of residence). Thus dual nationality can occur when a person is born in one state (*jus solis*) of parents belonging to another (*jus sanguinis*). It can also occur through nationalization where the original state does not accept rights of renunciation of allegiance. When this occurs, as for example it has among the English-speaking peoples of South Africa, tensions can arise over the question of an individual's duty to perform military service. This is usually, though not always, resolved in favour of the state possessing *de facto* jurisdiction. Dual nationality is a mixed blessing. Although it confers on the individual the rights, benefits and protection of more than one state, it also involves a dual set of duties which may often conflict with one another.

**Dumbarton Oaks conference** A meeting held in Georgetown, Washington, DC, between August and October 1944 to discuss the nature and functions of the UN organization. The main participants were the United States, the Soviet Union, the United Kingdom and later China. The purpose was to hammer out agreement on the framework for post-war cooperation and to establish an effective ➤security community which would supersede the somewhat ineffectual ➤League of Nations. The preliminary draft of Proposals, with some modifications, became the ➤United Nations Charter at the San Francisco Conference in 1945. Between these conferences, the ➤Malta meeting in February 1945 between Roosevelt, Churchill and Stalin confirmed the main outline of the proposals and underlined the need for ➤great power dominance of the new organization. The conference was virtually unanimous on the reasons for the failure of the League of Nations and injected a spirit of ➤realism into their proposals for the new world organization; ➤peacekeeping responsibilities were given to the ➤Security Council where the great powers were to have permanent representation and the right of ➤veto. It was widely assumed by the representatives at the conference that disagreement over the post-war political settlement could be amicably settled in the Security Council, without having to revert to the traditional practices of ➤power politics and regional ➤alliance systems. Because of the two-tier structure, which emphasized great power management of operations, it was fondly believed that by-passing the organization on issues of international importance would be discouraged and that the dangers of reverting to ➤unilateral and ➤bilateral policies that characterized the inter-war years would be averted.

**Dumping** This term is used in two specific respects in ➤international relations:

in political economy and in ➤environmental politics. In the first instance dumping is ➤exporting goods at artificially low prices. It may be engaged in to reduce surpluses and/or to drive rivals out of the market. How low a price has to be to qualify as dumping is often a matter for political judgement since the term has a certain pejorative connotation. Most international economists would be happy with the idea that selling goods below what they would fetch on the domestic market, allowing for transport costs, is dumping.

Dumping can provoke retaliation in the form of anti-dumping duties from target ➤actors. Anti-dumping retaliation is officially condoned by ➤IGOs. Dumping can also provoke responses from third parties who feel that their market share is being unfairly damaged as a result. This tit-for-tat pattern associated with dumping means that it is often the cause of ➤trade wars between states. The EC/EU Common Agricultural Policy (CAP) has produced considerable surplus produce over the years which has been dumped on occasions. This has provoked critical reactions from other producers outside the Union who feel that their agricultural exports have been unfairly damaged as a result.

Dumping is also an ➤issue area in environmental politics as a result of the activity of dumping various wastes in the world's oceans. Clearly the problem here is one of ➤pollution. In 1972 the Convention on the Prevention of Marine Pollution by Dumping of Wastes and other Matter (London Dumping Convention) established a ➤regime to control this activity by prohibition of and permission-giving for ocean dumping.

# E

**East Asian Crisis** This refers to the ➤crisis within the East Asian ➤region which began in the second half of 1997 with a loss of confidence on the foreign-exchange markets which rapidly spread to the corporate banking sector. All the economies of East Asia were affected, including Japan and the so-called ➤Asian Tigers. It is likely that the ➤protectionist traditions within financial services in East Asia will be abandoned or reformed substantially as a result. In the interim there has been significant clawing back of inward investment by these economies in other parts of the ➤North This knock-on effect is predictable given the level of ➤interdepence of these ➤AIC economies and the ➤scope of the ➤globalization of financial markets evident in the closing years of the twentieth century. The broader macroeconomic picture in East Asia is much less optimistic as a result. Triumphalism about an 'Asian model' of capitalism now looks inappropriate and the ➤image of the region within developmental studies is being adjusted accordingly. The downturn has affected employment and growth within these economies since the beginning of 1998. Politiclaly, both South Korea and Indonesia have been ➤destabilized and the opportunity has not been lost to point these systems in the direction of ➤good governance habits as a condition for external assistance. Economic ➤crisis management has been effected through the IMF but its customary conditionality clauses have included political demands for greater accountability in addition to the economic ones.

**Ecology/Ecopolitics** In the context of ➤international relations ecology refers to the relationship between human beings and their biological and physical environment. In particular, it refers to the challenge posed by a combination of world population growth and technological developments which threaten the balance of the world's life-sustaining ecosystems. Ecopolitics, which stresses the interrelatedness of political and ecological matters, is a comparatively recent issue area and owes much to the pioneering work of Harold and Margaret Sprout who in 1971 introduced an important and new dimension into the study of international relations with their acclaimed *Towards a Politics of the Planet Earth*.

Traditional perspectives in world politics have been obsessed with issues of ➤peace, ➤security and economic well-being embedded within the classical framework of the nation-states and the state-system. Ecological issues, such as ➤food and resource scarcities, environmental degradation, climatic changes or technological developments relating to the oceans, the sea bed, the atmosphere and outer space, were generally considered in relation to the bearing they had on the primary issues of national security and economic development. Since they were considered to be marginal or at best, long term in this context, the man/environment issue was relegated to the outer fringes of the subject. In any case, since ecological issues were indifferent to ►boundaries and are intrinsically ►transnational, they were effectively beyond the range of traditional ►state-centric world politics, where self-interest and ►self-help are primary and, perhaps, necessary values. There is now, however, a growing body of concern about the impact of such issues as the disposal of chemical and nuclear toxic waste, deforestation, acid rain, soil erosion and ►pollution which has slowly but perceptibly raised the ecological perspective to a higher level on the agenda of contemporary world politics. This is partly due to the fact that these matters now impinge on traditional areas of ►high policy but it is also partly to do with the increasing awareness that species survival may in the final analysis depend on multilateral political cooperation to ensure the durability of the earth's 'carrying' capacity. Nation-states, renowned as they are for egoism and intro-spection, cannot unilaterally address these problems. Ecopolitics therefore focuses on the symbiotic relationship among political communities themselves and between them and their environment. In so doing, it has provided a new ►definition of the situation.

A term commonly associated with ecopolitics is global 'commons' which refers to natural resources such as the oceans, the sea bed, radio waves, the atmosphere and outer space which were previously regarded as part of the ►common heritage of mankind and are not, as yet, subject to rigid control by international legal ►regime. Advances in technology render these common resources vulnerable to individual exploitation. The 'tragedy of the global commons', a parable popularized by Garret Hardin in 1968, envisages a scenario in which intensive, unrestricted unilateral harvesting of resources could eventu-ally lead to resource destruction on a hitherto unimagined scale. Traditional perspectives involving notions of voluntary restraint are inadequate since the problem of the 'free rider' is always present. Ecopolitics therefore envisages the need for strict communal regulations of the commons based on shared values such as conservation, controlled production and equity. Implicit in the approach is a conviction that ecological issues cannot be resolved on a unilateral basis. Whether or not the international community is willing to abandon age-old preferences and multilaterally develop the embryonic legal infrastructure to enable these problems to be resolved is a matter of considerable debate and not a little hope. ►►Green movements; maritime law

**Economic liberalism** A theory of political economy, economic liberalism is particularly associated with the writings of Adam Smith and the school of thinkers of the nineteenth-century free market persuasion. Internally, the political implications of economic liberalism were that as far as possible government should confine itself to a minimum of tasks and roles within society. Externally, this theory of minimum government stipulated that the primary task of ➤state authorities was to protect the state from external threat. As an international theory economic liberalism was particularly associated with the advocacy of ➤free trade and what would now be called ➤complex interdependence. Free traders believed that such a system of relations would remove important economic causes of conflict from the system and that this was an additional reason – above and beyond its economic rationale – for favouring it.

The failure of newly emerging economic powers such as Imperial Germany and the United States to adopt unequivocal free trade principles and policies threw the assumptions of classical economic liberals into confusion during the last decades of the nineteenth century. Not for the last time, ➤protectionism adopted by key ➤actors in the system was to represent a challenge to the ➤liberal orthodoxy. Gradually liberals began to realize that they would have to reverse the relationship between free trade and international cooperation. If free trade did not lead to international cooperation then perhaps international cooperation could establish free trade. This revision of the relationship was achieved in the post-1945 ➤Bretton Woods agreements and the signing of the subsequent General Agreement on Tariffs and Trade (➤GATT). If the years after the repeal of the Corn Laws in 1846 were the 'golden age' of liberalism then the years after Bretton Woods ran a close second.

At the same time as the free trade order was under challenge from the newly emerging economic powers of Germany and the United States, the principles of liberalism were being directly challenged by writers within the tradition. Hobson was accusing liberalism of being deflected into ➤imperialism while Hobhouse was trying to synthesize traditional liberal commitments to liberty with socialist commitments to equality. This compensatory or Keynesian liberalism emerged full-blown in the twentieth century as a genuine heterodoxy within the tradition. Internally these heterodox liberals argued that the state would have to intervene more significantly and regularly in the economic and social life of the nation in order to prevent significant inequalities from persisting. Left to market forces, it was argued, such readjustment would not occur. Externally the heterodox liberals still looked to greater international cooperation but believed that, again, this must be directed to reducing inequalities as much as increasing liberties.

The rise of the ➤Third World in the post-1945 system has presented the compensatory version of liberalism with the perfect ➤issue area to apply its ideas. The two ➤Brandt Reports have rightly been identified as typical of this genre. According to this view the ➤First World states should be prepared to do much more for the ➤least developed countries (LDCs) by manually overriding the automatic tendencies of the liberal order. Many of the demands made under the aegis of the ➤New International Economic Order (NIEO) and via institutions like the United Nations Conference on Trade and Development (UNCTAD) are favourably received by compensatory liberals. Stabilization of commodity prices – which is anathema to classical liberals – in order to guarantee the LDCs continuity of income, is just one of the types of proposals currently being acted upon under the influence of Third World pressure and compensatory liberal sympathies.

**Economic sanctions** A form of ➤economic statecraft which involves the use of economic ➤capability by an ➤actor or group of actors (the Imposer) in a deliberately coercive manner to pursue certain policy goals. The Imposer will identify a certain actor or group of actors (the Target) against which the sanctions will be directed. The essence of the sanctions attempt is to get the Target to behave in a more compliant way. The means used to secure this compliance will involve denying the Target access to certain goods and services that are controlled by the Imposer. Although in principle sanctions can be either positive or negative, ➤conventional usage of the word in this context is always negative. Thus, when reference is made to economic sanctions, such punitive measures as the embargo, the ➤boycott, the withdrawal of ➤most favoured nation (MFN) status, are envisaged. Reducing ➤tariffs to bribe or reward a Target, although logically sanctions, are not intended to be covered by this definition. Similarly, sanctions can be distinguished from economic warfare where the instruments are similarly negative but the policy goals are different. In economic warfare, the Imposer seeks to deliberately weaken the economy of the Target, either as a temporary or permanent measure. Such measures are usually pursued as part of a general policy of making ➤war against the Target in the military idiom.

Economic sanctions may be directed at the whole Target or at some section of society within the Target. Collective sanctions directed at the Target *per se*, to the extent that they are effective, will punish everybody, weak and strong, guilty and innocent. Indeed it is often the case that collective sanctions hurt those who are least able to withstand the costs. Alternatively, sanctions can be directed at particular groups within society. These would normally be economic groups and, in particular, corporations, businesses and firms. The usual form such individually aimed sanctions take will be to institute a blacklist. This will identify businesses that the Imposer wishes to punish. Such firms may be subject to boycott action, to confiscation of their property and to prosecution of their employees.

Sanctions may be unilateral – applied by one actor against another – bilateral – applied to two – or ➤multilateral. The more actors involved in the sanctions policy, the greater its chances of actually causing the Target some deprivation. However, the more actors involved in the sanctions policy, the more difficult it is to establish and maintain a common front against the Target. In particular, the attraction of defecting from multilateralism can be considerable. The defector may, thereby, steal a march on its trading rivals by replacing them in the markets of the Target. In general terms the role of what might be termed the Third Party – in contradistinction to the Target and the Imposer – is crucial if economic sanctions are to stand any chance of success. If an Imposer cannot secure the cooperation of Third Parties then a policy of economic sanctions can be self-defeating and very expensive. For example, the UN policy of economic sanctions against Rhodesia (now Zimbabwe) between 1966 and 1979 was seriously flawed by the fact that Rhodesia's second largest trading partner – South Africa – actively worked to undermine the policy. The Union was assisted in this 'busting of sanctions' by certain multinational corporations (►MNC)s, notably Anglo-American oil companies.

Economic analysis would suggest that, notwithstanding the role of third parties, sanctions are likely to be more or less effective depending upon a number of variables. First, the Imposer should be in a monopoly or a monopsony position *vis-à-vis* the Target. Moreover, the Target should not be able to overcome the monopoly by ►import substitution, nor the monopsony by finding new ►export markets. The Target may then be said to be highly vulnerable to economic sanctions. Second, the goods and services denied to the Target should supply key sectors of its economy. It is for this reason that oil has been considered a 'strategic commodity' in the sanctions context. The impact that trade dependence upon such a key commodity can have was demonstrated during the 1973–4 ►diplomacy of the ►OPEC and the OAPEC states. Third, the Imposer should be able to avoid self-inflicted economic costs arising from sanctions. In addition to the Third Party issue discussed above, self-inflicted costs will be reduced by substitution. If substitute markets can be found for embargoed exports and substitute goods found for boycotted imports, the costs will be reduced.

Monitoring, supervision and enforcement actions will all be required to implement a sanctions policy. Such activities will require Third Party cooperation and this will normally involve regional or global institutions. *In extremis*, military force may be needed to enforce control over Third Parties and typically this will involve a ►blockade of the territorial ►frontiers of the Target state. If the Target is an island or if the Target can be isolated politically then enforcement procedures should be facilitated. The international institution will serve to legitimize as well as to enforce sanctions. Parties breaking sanctions are, in effect, defying the express purpose of the majority of the membership. As such they may be Targets for punitive sanctions themselves.

The logic of the aforesaid arguments would seem to be that economic sanctions will work best if they are universal and general. This in turn points to the need to institutionalize sanctions through organizations such as the ►League of Nations and the ►United Nations. Thus under Article 16 of the League Covenant the member states were clearly committed to confront international wrong-doing with economic sanctions. If anything the powers of the UN under Chapter 7 are even more extensive than those of the League, and again, in Article 41 of the Charter economic sanctions are specifically stipulated. Finally under Chapter 4 the General Assembly has permissive powers of ➤recommendation. *In toto*, then, the UN has an impressive capability base for both mandatory and voluntary use of economic sanctions.

Until the ➤Persian Gulf War both the League and the UN faced their most important test cases on their sanctions provisions in Africa: the League over the Ethiopian case and the UN over the Rhodesia (Zimbabwe) case. In the light of the above analysis, the failure of the League to include oil exports on the embargo list in its confrontation with Italy was a serious omission. The Suez Canal was never closed to Italian shipping nor were the sanctions ➤implemented until one month after the decision had been taken by the League Council to initiate measures under Article 16. The absence of the United States of America and Germany from these League deliberations weakened the ability of the institution to bring all putative Third Parties into the sanctions exercise. The use of economic sanctions by the League in 1935–6 has passed into conventional wisdom as an exercise in failure which cost both the institution and the policy dearly in terms of ➤credibility.

The Unilateral Declaration of Independence (UDI) by the recalcitrant regime in Rhodesia (Zimbabwe) in November 1965 was a challenge to the United Nations commensurate with that to its predecessor in the 1930s. The UN did not in fact impose mandatory sanctions until December 1966, more than one year after the UDI. Indeed, when it became clear in September 1965 that the voluntary policy was not working, the United Kingdom came under pressure from the ➤Commonwealth to tighten the sanctions policy. The UN had already approved the UK's 'Beira patrol', so the imposition of mandatory sanctions by Resolution 232 of the ➤Security Council was a legal continuation of the same policy. Sanctions were further tightened in the spring of 1968 when Security Council Resolution 253 supposedly closed a number of loopholes. As the diplomatic record now clearly shows, however, a determined and successful operation had been mounted from the outset to circumvent sanctions. The South African government was central to this strategy but, as suggested above, they were able to implement this policy with the help of certain MNCs. It is difficult to isolate the economic effects of sanctions in the Rhodesian example from the economic effects of other inputs into the situation – for instance, the economic dislocation caused by the ➤guerrilla war after 1972. Certainly the attempted 'internal settlement' of the late 1970s was inspired by the belief that it would achieve international ➤recognition and the lifting of sanctions. The eventual collapse of white domination in Rhodesia was multi-causal and sanctions were a variable in the causation.

Although the nature and context of the compliance sought from Italy in the 1930s and from Rhodesia after 1965 by the respective IGOs was quite different – one was attempting to reverse outside ➤intervention, the other to end an internal rebellion against ➤colonial control – the end results were equally disappointing for the advocates of multilateral sanctions. In both the examples cited the unwillingness of leading ➤states to contemplate the use of ➤force to support sanctions reduced their efficacy. Indeed, as E. H. Carr (1946) pointed out, this separation of economic sanctions from other coercive instruments is a false dichotomy.

The Rhodesian example is suggestive of a further conclusion – sanctions tend to be slow-acting. They are more like the war of ➤attrition than the ➤blitzkrieg. Moreover, they have the character of a collective punishment. There was no doubt that the white settlers in Rhodesia cushioned themselves against some of the adverse effects of sanctions by 'passing them on' to the African population. Zambia and Malawi were also damaged by the sanctions policy aimed at Rhodesia. In summary then they are blunt as well as slow-acting instruments. Finally, both the instances cited above show how sanctions depend upon the active cooperation of Third Party parties. If this prerequisite is not fulfilled then the implementation of sanctions may produce a trial of strength with a very uncertain outcome.

The Persian Gulf War again saw the use of sanctions by the UN as a policy instrument. Resolution 661 of the Security Council, passed on 13 August 1990, imposed comprehensive mandatory sanctions against Iraq under Chapter 7. Three weeks later the Council endorsed a naval blockade of Iraq under Resolution 665 and, *inter alia*, resuscitated the Military Staff Committee to co-ordinate the policy. On 13 September the Council under Resolution 666 attempted to distinguish 'humanitarian' supplies to Iraq from the general range of embargoed goods and services, while on 25 September sanctions were extended to include an embargo on air traffic. Following the initiation of Operation Desert Storm, aimed at forcing Iraqi withdrawal from Kuwait, the Council closely monitored the warfare and passed Resolution 687 on 3 April 1991, which stipulated the terms of the cease-fire.

The use of economic sanctions in advance of the military instrument and then latterly in support of full implementation of the cease-fire represents the most extensive use of this instrument by a multilateral body in the post-1945 system. Whether by design or by accident, many of the implications of earlier sanctions policies seem to be verified in this instance. In particular the need to support economic sanctions with military enforcement measures and the need to monitor the 'collective punishment' character of sanctions seem to have been understood by the ➤decision-makers in 1990–91. As a result of the Persian Gulf War it is not too much to say that economic sanctions have been given a new lease of life as an instrument of righteous indignation. Whether the Iraqi case will be *sui generis* remains to be seen. Certainly the circumstances were highly auspicious in 1990 for this type of response to a perceived transgression.

**Economic statecraft**  Economic statecraft is defined by David Baldwin in his

1985 book as 'influence attempts relying primarily on resources which have a reasonable semblance of a market price in terms of money' (pp. 13–14). In other words, economic statecraft is any political act which utilizes economic instruments to achieve compliant behaviour from a Target actor. In Baldwin's discussion the usage is synonymous with the idea of the ➤power relationship because the economic instruments envisaged may be divided into positive and/or negative sanctions. Thus both economic ➤aid and ➤economic sanctions – the two most prevalent instruments – would both be subsumed under Baldwin's definition as instances of economic statecraft.

Economic statecraft may appropriately be regarded as an umbrella term covering all instances where international ➤actors use economic instruments for political ends. It may be usefully seen as a replacement term for such stipulations as 'economic warfare' because it covers all contingencies in one portmanteau idea.

**Eisenhower Doctrine** This US policy initiative was a direct consequence of the Suez affair of 1956 when, on the insistence of the United States, the United Kingdom and France were forced to withdraw their troops from Egypt. Fearful of a ➤power vacuum developing in the oil-rich Middle East, and perhaps having second thoughts about their role during Suez, a Congressional Joint Resolution in 1957 proclaimed the Eisenhower Doctrine which authorized the President to assist any ➤state in the Middle East which was judged to be threatened by ➤communist aggression. Although allegedly directed against the spread of 'international communism', this doctrine was a specific attempt to limit the expansionist ambitions of President Nasser's Egypt. Under the terms of the resolution, US forces and/or economic assistance could be sent to the region under the Mutual Security Programme. Accordingly, in July 1958 Anglo-American troops intervened to assist the pro-Western regimes in Jordan and Lebanon, and subsequent commitments were made to Turkey, Iran and Pakistan. The Eisenhower Doctrine was thus a declaration that the Middle East was to be regarded as an area of vital interest to the United States. ➤➤Persian Gulf War

**Elite** A broad-based term used to identify a minority out of a total population. In ordinary usage the term often connotes superiority. Further precision can be obtained by adding the prefixes 'political', 'economic', 'cultural'. Indeed in most social systems found in the ➤First World observers would expect to find a plurality of elites along these bases. In the above sense, an elite is simply a descriptive term for individuals and groups found at the top of a particular ➤hierarchy.

The term is also used in a more prescriptive sense. Here the suggestion is that such minorities are a natural and positive outcome. It is possible in this usage to talk of 'elitism' having in mind an ➤ideology or value system which assumes that by nature or by nurture the majority in a population are unsuited and unqualified for elite status. However, elitism does recognize that exceptions will occur to this rule and that a 'counter-elite' may arise to challenge the existing elite structure. Whatever the outcome, elitists would still want to insist that in the end the system will resume its hierarchical structure.

Elite theories and the ideology of elitism originated with political sociology. However, the idea of an elite has been applied with considerable ingenuity to the study of ►policy-making and the related issue of ►public opinion on ►foreign policy issues. The early seminal work in this field was Almond's *The American People and Foreign Policy* (1966). Without wholly subscribing to the ideology of elitism, he did clearly distinguish a hierarchy based upon a division of labour and a division of influence. This hierarchy depended upon a fourfold division. At the bottom Almond placed the majority, the mass of the population. Distinguished from the mass was the ►attentive public. Above these two strata Almond locates the policy elites and, finally, at the top what might be termed the formal office holders.

Public opinion polling, which has become increasingly accurate over the last half century, provides the empirical confirmation of the view that the mass of the population, in all systems, lacks either the knowledge or the inclination to exert continuing and consistent influence over the policy process. The idea of ►mood has been developed to identify the manner and content of public attitudes towards foreign policy. Within the fairly permissive parameters set by public moods, the strata above the mass of the population operate. The attentive public then, by default, become the audience in front of which the elites make and justify their policy.

The actual foreign policy elite is divided between formal office holders and organized interests (what Almond calls 'the policy elites'). The formal office holders will occupy authority positions within the system and will be those persons officially designated to act on behalf of the ►state. Surrounding them will be a bureaucracy of departments centred around foreign ministries but including a number of other departments of state. The relationship between the formal office holders and their bureaucracies on one hand and organized interests on the other will differ from system to system. In general terms, whereas the formal office holders are by definition members of the elite, in the case of interest groups only the leaders will be classed unambiguously within the elite structure. In systems where the formal office holders, their senior bureaucrats and the interest groups elites are drawn from the same background the term 'establishment' is sometimes used to describe this broader arrangement. The growth in the number of state ►actors in world politics since 1945 has stimulated new interest in elite theories of policy-making. In many respects the structural analysis of ►Third World states seems to reflect classical elitist characteristics and structures. The actual composition of the elite in Third World states is, of course, a matter for empirical inquiry in particular cases. In all instances, however, a Western education seems a definite advantage – if not prerequisite – for recruitment into the elite. In many areas of the Third World traditional elites have capitalized on these educational opportunities to maintain their influence into the current period of national ►self-determination. This tendency has been particularly notable in Latin America. In other parts of the Third World, elite recruitment reflects a more heterogeneous catchment area. In all instances, however, the findings confirm the validity of the elite approach to the structure of policy-making.

**Enclave** Territory of one ►state surrounded by the territory of another. Thus, Walvis Bay in south west Africa was, until 1993, part of the domestic sovereign jurisdiction of the Republic of South Africa despite being surrounded by Namibia. Similarly, West Berlin was an enclave hemmed in by East Germany, as is the thirty-two square mile Republic of San Marino, in this case surrounded by Italy. ►►Exclave

**English school of international relations** This refers to the supposed existence of a distinct academic tradition of writing on ►international relations, which originated at the London School of Economics and Political Science in the 1950s. According to Roy E. Jones, who first identified the school (in a largely iconoclastic article in the *Review of International Studies* (1981)) its founder members were C. A. W. Manning and Martin Wight but others associated with it include Hedley Bull, F. S. Northedge, Michael Donelan, Alan James, R. J. Vincent and James Mayall. Although there is some disagreement and confusion surrounding the term, especially concerning the epithet 'English', it is now generally accepted that these writers and others constitute a distinct group whose unifying element is the concept of ►international society. The approach is holistic in the sense that it displays a vision of international society where the whole is greater than the sum of its parts, i.e. the sovereign ►states that compose it. In this sense, it is sometimes referred to as the 'international society approach' and its central thesis is that state behaviour cannot properly be explained without reference to the rules, customs, norms, values and institutions that constitute international society as a whole. International relations is conceived as a distinct and perhaps discrete entity and the principle object of inquiry is to examine the nature of this society and its ability to deliver a measure of orderliness and freedom within a predominantly decentralized and fragmented ►state-system. The approach can be viewed as a variant of the realist perspective, especially in its rejection of ►utopian schemes for restructuring the international system and its insistence on the necessary juxtaposition of the concepts of state ►sovereignty and international society. On the methodological level, it lies firmly in the classical or ►traditional mode and is dismissive of the ►behavioural or scientific approach which it sometimes identifies, somewhat pejoratively, as the 'American school of scientific politics'. (The epithet 'English' is, of course, a misnomer since members of the original LSE grouping included Australian, South African, Scottish and Welsh scholars.)

**Entente** Diplomatic term referring to a specific or non-specific 'understanding' between two or more ►states and which is distinct from a formal ►treaty or ►alliance. The phrase *entente cordiale* was first used by French premier M. Guizot in 1843 to denote a ►rapprochement between the United Kingdom and France in relation to matters affecting the general European ►balance of power. A specific entente was signed in 1904 which alarmed Germany and was regarded by some historians as placing unnecessary constraints on the United Kingdom's freedom of manoeuvre in the event of a Franco-German conflict. Ententes, though, however 'cordiale' they may appear, usually fall short of detailed commitment on the part of either side.

**Environment** The global environment has emerged as quite possibly the issue area in world politics to rival the post-►Cold War future for its impact and significance. This virtual exponential growth has propelled the ►politics of the environment from a ►low policy area for two-thirds of the century to a ►high policy area for the final third. The relationship between humankind and the environment is properly the subject of ►ecology. It is now clear that this relationship is in need of redefinition if the most damaging effects are to be avoided. It is not extravagant to claim that environmental ►security is at stake in the way this issue area is handled in the future. Ecologists are now arguing for a ►paradigm shift in the way in which economic growth is viewed as a ►goal for societies and systems. Accordingly, the idea of 'sustainable development' seeks to wean people away from the most rapacious forms of economic ►modernization – which is now seen to have involved high energy consumption and improper resource utilization. A virtual 'ecological shadow' has been cast over the planet by these activities. The idea of sustainable development raises queries not simply about cost/benefit calculations but about ►normative ideas.

The environment is manifestly an issue area where the mixed actor model has relevance. States, ►IGOs, ►international non-governmental organizations (INGOs) and ►MNCs are all ►actors in this case. Moreover as the ►environmental politics approach makes clear, ►state-centrism is explicitly and implicitly questioned. Probably the most crucial areas of the environment are those arising from the ►pollution problem. Other areas include: whaling, trade in endangered species, waste disposal, including ►dumping, privileging the Antarctic and protecting tropical rainforests (and their indigenous peoples). The ►United Nations has been in the forefront of all discussions on the environment since the 1972 Conference on Environment and Development (Earth summit) confirmed the importance of the world body in agenda-setting on this issue. Raising the profile of the environment is testimony to the importance of ►epistemic communities in world politics and pressure group politics. The ecological movement's success in promoting sustainable development and participatory democracy as key organizing concepts in this issue area is beyond dispute.

**Environmental politics** The growth of the ►environment into a major ►issue area in world politics is now having a profound effect upon ➤international relations (IR). In particular what some see as the challenges of the environment are calling into question the ➤state-centric ➤paradigm of IR which has certainly been the dominate one since the early century foundations of the discipline. Environmental politics seems to fit better into a ➤neoliberal rather than ➤neorealist perspective. Thus it can be argued that the key concept of power is perhaps less significant in the analysis of environmental politics than in other areas such as ➤international political economy or ➤security studies. Power may be able to allow states to exercise ➤veto restrictions over the ➤implementation of Environmental conventions but – if the ➤ecologists are right – the veto states 'shoot themselves in the foot' because change in the form of environmental degradation is ongoing and its impact is ➤transnational. Again traditional theories of ➤sovereignty are challenged by environmental politics. The problems of ➤pollution are manifestly transnational. So too should be the solutions, according to this logic. Environmental issues are ➤intermestic, bridging the distinction between domestic and international once again. ➤Green movements recognize this situation and refuse to be hidebound by formalism. The implementation of environmental agreements will again be intrusive upon sovereignty. The impact upon the ➤quasi-states in the system will be to further confirm their uneasy status as 'of' the system but not 'in' the system. As a corollary to the intermestic factor, both ➤globalization and ➤localization processes are evident in the politics of the environment. Within IPE the impact of environmental politics is only just being absorbed. The classic ➤economic liberal ➤IGOs like the ➤World Bank Group, the ➤WTO and the ➤IMF are coming under increasing pressure to incorporate environmental factors into their policy making.

**Epistemic communities** Refers to groups or networks of specialists with recognized expertise in policy-relevant knowledge areas. Since knowledge is an important dimension of ➤power, epistemic communities can and do play an important part in ➤decision-making and agenda setting. Although not a new phenomenon in public policy, the twentieth-century world has witnessed a growing reliance on these pressure groups in an ever widening range of ➤issue areas, more especially those with a strong technical component such as the environment, the economy or matters relating to national ➤security. Thus, epistemic communities are directly and indirectly involved in both ➤high and ➤low politics, though their effectiveness is likely to be greater in the latter where issues do not have an immediate bearing on 'core' interests. For this reason, they are not properly non-➤state ➤actors, though some, like Greenpeace, may aspire to or actually be. A striking instance of the role of experts in ➤regime creation and institution building in international relations is the Montreal Protocol of 1987 which dealt with ozone layer protection. In this instance, scientific evidence of a causal link between ➤pollution and ozone depletion created the ideational framework necessary for international cooperation and policy harmonization involving twenty-five signatory states.

The role of these knowledge collectives in international relations is under-researched (Haas, 1992) but the available evidence suggests that it is not insignificant and is growing. This is not to say, however, that we are witnessing a transfer of decision-making from politicians to experts. The degree to which they can affect or effect outcomes depends ultimately on the nature of the issue area addressed. The broad scientific consensus on the ➤nuclear winter thesis for example, has had little or no impact on theories of ➤deterrence or the desire to possess or acquire ➤nuclear weapons. ➤➤Ecology/ecopolitics; Green movement

**Equality of states** One of the primary values of the modern international ➤state-system is the sovereign equality of ➤states. Since the establishment of the ➤Westphalian system the formal recognition of equality was intimately bound up with the notions of ➤sovereignty, ➤independence and ➤reciprocity. It is enshrined in Article 2 of the ➤United Nations Charter which asserts that 'the Organization is based on the principle of the sovereign equality of all its Members'. However, despite institutional recognition, the role of equality in ➤international law and politics is not at all clear. There is frequently confusion between its descriptive and normative aspects. This confusion is magnified by the obviously hierarchical nature of the multistate system, which assigns particular status and responsibilities to the ➤great powers.

The condition of sovereign equality means that an ➤actor can claim the privileges, opportunities and diplomatic status that derive from statehood. The assertion that all states are equal does not suggest that all states are the same. Indeed, some commentators allege that equality is not a fact but an ideal; that the international community adopted for convenience a Platonic form of equality which, like sovereignty from which it derives, is a matter of degree rather than absolute. E. H. Carr (1946) put it this way: 'The constant intrusion, or potential intrusion, of power renders meaningless any conception of equality between members of the international community.' This observation still forms the basis of most discussions of equality, or the lack of it, in world politics.

Traditional thinking has it that inequality is endemic in a system where differences between actors are more obvious and immediate than similarities. (Compare for example Russia with Lesotho or the United States with Tonga.) Even the formal condition of equality (all states are equally entitled to the rights of sovereignty) is really an expression of inequality in practice, since the right to ➤self-help that this implies will necessarily be dependent on the ➤power that is at the disposal of those who wish to exercise it. ➤Recognition of a formal condition of equality has led inexorably to preserving what were regarded as natural and existing inequalities. Attempts have been made to rationalize the unequal endowments of the states, especially in ➤liberal theories of ➤international relations, but with little practical effect on the process of ►diplomacy. In fact, until comparatively recently, inequality has been taken for granted in world politics not just as a reflection of how things actually are, but also as a valuable asset in a system which has no overall ►authority to regulate demands and resolve disputes. Because states are manifestly unequal, some international disputes are that much easier to settle. In this sense the contribution of the great powers to the maintenance of ►international order can be seen as a direct function of inequality. If all states were equal how could conflicts ever be settled?

The institutions of ►international society, ►war, ►balance of power, international law and diplomatic practice, while paying homage to the sovereign equality of states, nevertheless served to encourage and sustain the hierarchical order which allowed equality only between powers which were evenly matched. ►War, or capacity for waging it, was in this sense the great equalizer. The history of international relations has unfolded largely in these terms and whatever collective procedures for settling disputes existed, they did so because of inequality, not in spite of it. The ►veto power given to permanent members of the ►Security Council of the UN is an explicit recognition of this; and this has always been so. What the Athenians said to the ►Melians – that the powerful take what they can and the weak grant what they must – has thus been the starting point for some, and the stumbling block for others, in the quest for a satisfactory relationship between ►order and ►justice in international relations. For ►Thucydides (1959 ed.) this was an enduring (though not perhaps endearing) fact of international life: 'This is not a law we made ourselves, nor were we the first to act upon it when it was made. We found it already in existence, and we shall leave it to exist forever among those who come after us.'

The question of whether or not this basic condition of equality really is 'to exist forever' is precisely the issue that many people think bedevils statecraft in the last part of the twentieth century. The tension between the advanced industrialized states of the ►North and the ►developing states of the ►South, the demand for a redistribution of wealth, power and status within a ►New International Economic Order (NIEO) which goes far beyond the formal recognition of equality, coupled with the apparent decline in the utility of military power (especially in ►great and ►small powers' relations) has led to a re-evaluation of the traditional hierarchical structure of world politics. The expansion of the role of the ►General Assembly, in particular, has created a demand for a more egalitarian basis for international law and international politics. Though ►Third World claims for greater equality are unlikely to break the traditional mould of diplomatic practice some commentators have noticed a new political sensibility about the issue. The ►non-aligned movement and ►polycentrism are indications of this. However, it is difficult to escape the Orwellian conclusion that in world politics all states are equal but some are more equal than others.

**Espionage** ➤intelligence

**Ethnic cleansing** A modern euphemism for the systematic, deliberate and often brutal forced removal of members of one or more ethnic groups from territory claimed by another ethnic group. In theory, it can be distinguished from ➤genocide, which is the deliberate and systematic extermination of a national or racial group, but in practice the two are often indistinguishable. Other concepts associated with the term are ➤'communal conflict', 'cultural conflict' and 'ethno-national conflict', all of which are said to be variants of a new and virulent form of racism based on the ideology of ➤nationalism. From 1992 to 1996 in the former ➤Yugoslavia, ethnic cleansing was practised by Serbs and Croats against each other, and more especially against Bosnian Muslims. The standard operational procedure was the organized use of intimidation, terror, rape, starvation and murder to effect forced removals. The objective was to alter the map of Bosnia-Herzegovina in favour of the perpetrators. Although this extreme form of ➤human rights abuse has been designated a ➤war crime and apprehended parties have been tried by the ➤International Court of Justice at the Hague, the Dayton Agreement ending the Bosnian War (1995) is widely regarded as condoning the results of ethnic cleansing through ➤recognition of the new ➤boundaries it created.

Ethnic cleansing is regarded as a species of 'postmodern war' where conflict between ➤states has been replaced by conflict between rival militias, factions and other informal ethnic groupings. The victims are overwhelmingly civilians who are often slaughtered without mercy by their former neighbours and compatriots. Recent examples besides Bosnia, include Liberia, Rwanda, Sri Lanka, Sierra Leone, Somalia, Sudan, Haiti, Cambodia, Zaire and ➤Afghanistan. According to Robert Kaplan (1994) postmodern war, genocide and ethnic cleansing are products of the post-➤Cold War phenomenon of ➤failed nation-states which have witnessed 'the withering away of central governments, the rise of tribal and regional domains, the unchecked spread of disease and the growing pervasiveness of war.' In this 'coming anarchy', orthodox political maps are illusory because 'the classificatory grid of nation-state is going to be replaced by a jagged-glass pattern of city-states, shanty states, nebulous and anarchic regionalisms.' The end of the Cold War has exacerbated this process. The removal of ➤superpower competition, and with it economic and military assistance and control, has brought simmering local rivalries and hatreds to the fore in many multi-ethnic states and ➤regions of the world previously under the tutelage of one or other of the superpowers. Ethno-national clashes differ greatly from the anticolonial, ➤secessionist and separatist movements of the past which in the main were conducted within the juridical framework of the persistence of a system of ➤sovereign territorial states. The international community, because of its predilections for the ➤Westphalian presumptions of state sovereignty and its corollary ➤non-intervention, has thus far not been able to develop a coherent response to this phenomenon. ➤Ethnic nationalism; humanitarian intervention; refugees

**Ethnic nationalism (sometimes rendered as Ethno-nationalism)** This refers to the sentiment of belonging to a group identified by ties of ethnicity as well as, or in preference to, those of the ➤nation-state. Most states are in fact multi-national or multi-ethnic and in this way ethnic nationalism may simply be seen as recognizing a fact of political life. On the other hand, it may lead to expressions of ➤irredentism or ➤secession as political goals, in which case it becomes a movement or political tendency. Like any group sentiment, ethnicity is both subjective and objective in its causes and effects. If a people define themselves as different then they will perceive themselves as different, but at the same time this ➤perception will require tangible points of reference such as linguistic, cultural, tribal or religious similarity. This is the in-group/out-group dynamic familiar to sociologists and social psychologists.

Twentieth century ➤international relations has had mixed dealings with ethnic nationalism. The ➤League of Nations was mindful of the problem of ethnic minorities – particularly in Central and Eastern Europe – and this otherwise maligned ➤IGO was at least ready to accept the importance of the ethnic dimension in world politics. The ➤United Nations has been less sympathetic. The post-1945 system has witnessed the process of ➤decolonization and the successor states to the colonial regimes have shown a marked reluctance to query the multi-ethnic origins of their territories. As a result secession and irredentism tend to be bitterly resisted by ➤elites and ➤leaders in the ➤Third World. The implosion of the Soviet Union after ➤nineteen eighty-nine and the violent demise of the state of ➤Yugoslavia show how significant the sentiments of ethnicity are in Eastern Europe. Indeed the ➤communal conflict in Northern Ireland and the existence of ethnically based separatist parties in Western Europe suggest that the continent as a whole is susceptible. Giving due regard to ethnicity as a factor in building political communities may simply shift problems of participation on to a new agenda. One of the few ethnically homogeneous ➤states in Africa – Somalia – has shown great political instability of late. Whatever the outcome in Somalia the general tendency towards great ethnic awareness noted above has called into question the viability of the concept of the nation-state across global politics. The possibility that dissociative methods of ➤conflict settlement may be more feasible than keeping communities locked into an associative nation-state framework must now be regarded as a viable approach.

**Ethnocentrism** This is the tendency to see one's own group, culture, ➤nation in positive terms and, conversely, other groups in negative terms. The term has sociological origins and, with some important exceptions such as Booth's work on strategy (1979), ethnocentrism continues to be a socio-psychological concept which has important implications for international behaviour. The intensity of the attitudes that ethnocentrism gives rise to will vary between groups and over time. Similarly, the specific contents of the favourable/ unfavourable ➤image will also be time dependent. Ethnocentric attitudes may be passed down from generation to generation via the process of socialization. Much of this transmission will be informal but such biases can also infiltrate into the education system where both the formal and the 'hidden' curriculum can become transmission channels for these attitudes. In modern, large-scale complex societies, the mass media can reinforce and reflect ethnocentric views. Contact with out-groups and foreigners, far from 'broadening the mind', can confirm and strengthen these feelings.

Booth has outlined three applications of the term. First, as suggested already, the term is a shorthand means for reference to the near universal tendency of people to perceive others in relation to their own membership groups. Second, he suggests it can be used to refer to a faulty methodology. Booth has suggested, in a highly imaginative text, that ➤strategic studies may be criticized for evidence of ethnocentrism. In particular, the phenomenon of ➤worst-case analysis is at least partially explicable in these terms. Possibly the problem lies in the fact that strategic studies is a 'policy science' and its very proximity to ➤decision-makers leads to these biases. Third, Booth suggests that the term is synonymous with being 'culture bound'. This is the condition where the individual or group becomes locked into its ethnocentrism so that it is unable to empathize with others and, therefore, is unable to see the world from their point of view.

Ethnocentrism is a consequence of the fact that politics is a group activity. Political socialization, which begins in the family, inevitably produces a discrete and distorted image of others. In the modern world ethnocentrism is closely related to ➤nationalism in both its statist and its ethnic forms. These attitudes can undoubtedly be manipulated by political leaders and ➤elites for their own purposes. For this reason ethnocentrism, as a tendency, is often found to be contributing to tension and hostilities that occur whenever groups conflict. Although better communication and closer contact will not of themselves reduce ethnocentrism, the reverse does appear to be the case, namely that communication failures and barriers do increase the scope for ethnocentrism to grow and flourish. ➤➤Deterrence

**European Community (EC)** The European Community came into being in July 1967 thereby ➤implementing the 'Merger ➤treaty' of July 1965. As the name implies this document created a series of common institutions out of the three European Communities which had been established during the phase of so-called 'sector ➤integration' in the 1950s. The most significant common institutions in this merging were the Council of Ministers and the European Commission. In addition the European Community shared a common membership. In 1967 this was the ➤Benelux states, France, Italy and West Germany (technically the Federal Republic of Germany-FRG). In 1992 the signing of the Maastricht Treaty on ➤European Union reclassified the European Economic Community (EEC) as the European Community and the term European Union is now accepted terminology for the collectivity. At the time of Maastricht the membership had doubled from the original 6 to 12 states: Denmark, Ireland and the UK joined in 1973, Greece in 1981 and Portugal and Spain in 1986. The end of the ➤Cold War in Europe freed up the applications from a number of ➤neutrals and in 1995 Austria, Finland and Sweden became members. Even more significantly in 1993 the European Council accepted the principle that membership of the ➤EC/EU would be recognized as a feasible policy ➤goal for all of the Central and Eastern European states that had formerly been in the Soviet ➤bloc.

The European ➤region has witnessed some of the most significant and far-reaching instances of regional integration in twentieth-century ➤international relations. The process was a direct result of the devastation caused by the Second World War and the realization that political, economic and social recovery could be best achieved by abandoning ➤state-centrism in favour of an amalgamated ➤security community through ➤functional sectoral integration in the first instance. The initial step was the creation of the European Coal and Steel Community (ECSC) in 1951 by the Treaty of Paris following the Schuman Plan proposals of 1950. Stipulation of these traditional heavy industries was thought to address the issue of so-called 'war-potential' of states by denying the signatories the ➤capability to use this industrial ➤power for narrowly defined ➤national interests. The ECSC membership was the original six Western European states already identified. The UK – not for the last time – remained semi-detached. Significantly in its institution-building the ECSC was to be the bell-wether for the Rome Treaty organizations.

Plans for a European Defence Community and a Political Community which were laid in the mid 1950s came to nothing but the integrative process in the wealth/welfare ➤issue area was strengthened by the establishment of the European Economic Community (EEC) and the Atomic Community (EUR-ATOM) by the Treaty of Rome in 1957. In institutional terms the Coal and Steel Community provided the role model for the Rome institutions. It was clear that the founding six states were intent upon establishing a ➤customs union which would impact upon a broad range of economic activities. This was achieved – ahead of schedule – in July 1968. At the same time it was clear that a significant number of political ➤elites and ➤attentive publics in the founding six states were committed to closer forms of economic collaboration as a long-term goal. A summit conference of the six at the Hague in 1969 set the next goal for the EC as Economic and Monetary Union (EMU). At the same time the principled stand against UK membership which had been such a feature of ➤Gaullism was removed. The 1973 enlargement, referred to earlier, was substantial in terms of the expansion of the EC's domestic milieu. At the same time both Denmark and the UK were seen to favour ➤intergovernmental-ism as opposed to ➤supranationalism. In the process of becoming wider during the 1970s the Community spirit was undoubtedly diluted.

The decision to move towards a directly-elected European Parliament sig-nificantly revived the supranationalist mind-set. The 1979 vote instituted a rolling commitment to five-year Parliaments, and therefore elections, through-out the Community. The membership (MEPs) have done much to confirm the expectations of the supranationalists and the fears of the intergovern-mentalists that the Parliament would significantly ratchet up the federalist agenda. In essence Parliament became a constituent assembly and in 1984 produced a Draft Treaty for European Union. The European Council had already indicated a similar commitment to the unionist goal the previous year with its Stuttgart Declaration and whilst the Parliament's Draft Treaty was more radical than the summit heads' Stuttgart initiative, both pointed in the same direction. The member states' reaction was to take the form of the Single European Act of 1986. This achieved a number of ends: it codified the European Council and European Political Cooperation as existential facts. It substantially reduced the degree to which ➤decision-making proceeded on the basis of ➤unanimity rules, substituting instead qualified majority voting particularly in respect of moves towards a ➤single market. Finally the goal of economic and monetary union was specifically identified in the Single Act.

The Maastricht Treaty of 7 February 1992 was the most important revision of the treaties that established the EC since its inception in the 1950s. Maastricht represents the fusion of the two tributaries – economic and monetary union and political union – into the confluence that is the European Union. The current union is not simply the Community under another name. It is another stage in the journey to the unknown destination that was first mapped out at the inception of the Community. At the same time the organizational infrastructure of the EC has come to represent the ability of the Community to accommodate change within the parameters first set out in the Paris and Rome Treaties.

The main decision-making body in the EC/EU remains the Council of Ministers. The Council consists of representatives drawn from the governments of the member states. It works under broad policy directives drawn up by the European Council (which is simply the name by which regular summit meetings of heads of state and government are known). The Council of Ministers works closely with the Parliament in preparing budget proposals and with the Commission in implementing policy decisions. The Council is the political hub of the organization and because it represents national interests it is its least integrative component. The aforementioned European Council was never envisaged in the Paris and Rome treaties but has developed from the need for ➤summit diplomacy to resolve issues and point new directions. As noted its existence was codified under the Single Act. Taken together the Council of

Ministers and the European Council may be seen to represent intergovernmentalism within the system.

The European Commission is the secretariat of the organization. The term 'Commission' is used in two senses in the EC. In the first usage the Commission is the 20 commissioners who hold office for five years and superintend a number of portfolios. In the second sense it is the 'Eurocrats', the civil servants who run the organization on a day-to-day basis. Normally the first usage obtains. The Commission is usually seen as the leading supranational player in the organization and the defender of small states' interests against the larger members. It is quite conceivable that the Commission and the Parliament will seek to balance out against the intergovernmental forces of the Council of Ministers and the European Council in the future.

**European Convention on Human Rights** Established since 1953 the Convention sought to create machinery for the protection of ➤human rights among signatory ➤states. To this end it is probably the most sophisticated ➤multilateral treaty in so far that it provides for a Commission which determines the admissibility of petitions and a Court of Human Rights which sits at Strasbourg to provide rulings on the cases presented. Most observers agree, though, that the Convention and the institutions it established tend to favour 'the high contracting parties' (i.e. member states) rather than individuals. The decisions of the Court as to the violation of rights are binding but generally enforcement depends on voluntary compliance since few sanctions, short of outright expulsion from the ➤Council of Europe, are provided for. Apart from its intrinsic importance in the development of human rights legislation, the Convention is significant in that it can and does command wide media coverage and public interest, it does seek to provide outside protection for individuals against national government and it could be seen as a role model for future world developments under the auspices of the ➤UN.

**European Court of Justice (ECJ)** Probably the most integrative institution associated with the ➤European Union (EU). It is now the Union's Supreme Court and as such its findings are binding upon the member states and the institutions of the Union (e.g. the Parliament). The Court was originally established at the inception of the ➤European Community with the ECSC in 1951. Its responsibilities were confirmed by the Treaty of Rome and these have recently been extended by the ➤Maastricht Treaty. The members of the Court are chosen on the basis of one per member ➤state and justices serve for six-year terms (renewable). Although chosen by member governments, the justices have established a reputation for impartiality and ➤independence from political pressures. Since the Court reflects several different legal traditions (unlike the American Supreme Court) and since it notionally works in all the languages of the Union (English and French are the two working languages) this degree of consensus is impressive.

The role of the ECJ is wide-ranging and involves, among other things, rulings on the obligations under the various treaties and instances of non-compliance therewith, judicial review of the Commission, the Council of Ministers and the Parliament, failures to act by member states or by institutions of the Union and preliminary rulings on the validity of EU action in relation to national courts. It is in relation to this last category that the ECJ has been most innovative and some commentators see a 'new legal order' being created throughout the community, superimposed upon national law and superior to it. Its most important achievement in this ➤issue area has been to advance EU law as a ➤'transnational constitution' over and above national ones. In this sense the ECJ may be seen as contributing to the corpus of ➤international law. In other respects however the Court may be seen to be applying the domestic law of the union as laid down by the several treaties and subsequent actions of the institutions.

**European Economic Community**  ➤European Community

**European Union**  The ➤goal of European Union has always been implicit in the ➤treaties which established the ➤European Community in the 1950s. This objective was made explicit in October 1972 at the Paris summit meeting of European ➤leaders and was reaffirmed in Copenhagen in 1973. However it was to be 20 years before the aim of union was enacted into treaty law – 1992 the ➤Maastricht Treaty brought the union into existence.

A European Union or a United States of Europe (and the two are not the same) had been the long held dream of a twentieth century leaders such as Briand and Churchill. The formation of the European Movement in 1948 to lobby on behalf of European ➤integration and the establishment of the ➤Council of Europe can now be seen as important early developments. The Tindemans report of 1975 envisaged the goal of union by the end of the decade and it identified four ➤issue areas: economic and monetary union, reform of the EC institutions, common foreign and ➤defence policies and common regional and social policies. In the 1980s plans for the union emanated from two sources: from the heads of the various governments – the European Council – which produced the Stuttgart Declaration in June 1983 and from the directly elected European parliament which actually produced a Draft Treaty on Union in 1984. This combined pressure, from the more cautious Council and the more integrationist Parliament culminated in the ➤Single European Act of 1986. This gave formal recognition to the European Council and to the procedures under European Political Cooperation. For the first time it explicitly sought to introduce consistency into the foreign policies of the member ➤states in the EC. The SEA also envisaged that complete economic and monetary union would be achieved by the end of the century. It was recognized that the goal of economic and monetary union (EMU) would be a process as well as an end state and the parties accepted the need for 'convergence' of their economies according to stipulated criteria.

The deliberations which resulted in the SEA of 1986 took place in the context of the Intergovernmental Conference (IGC) of 1985. Intergovernmentalism (which is the rationale for the IGC) is simply the EC/EU's version of ▸confederalism. It is both a theory and a procedure. Procedurally intergovernmentalism locates primary ▸decision-making competences within the ▸sovereign state members of the EC/EU. At the same time leaders are aware that within the IGC structure integration must proceed. Thus somewhat paradoxically perhaps intergovernmentalism can be the generator behind ▸supranationalism. This was evident in the SEA and in the Maastricht Treaty of 1992, which was again preceded by IGCs.

The Maastricht Treaty – properly known as the Treaty on European Union (TEU) – was signed in 1992 and entered into force in 1993. The term ▸European Union (EU) is now accepted terminology for the post-Maastricht actor formerly known as the European Community (EC). However because of its historical antecedents it is sometimes well to remember that the EC/EU constitute one generic entity. The TEU was divided into three components or 'pillars': the European Community, Common Foreign and Security Policy (CFSP) and Justice and Home Affairs (JHA). The first pillar concentrates upon political and economic integration (which was the rationale of the EC historically) the second and third on cooperation in foreign and domestic ▸issue areas. Integration under the first pillar remains structurally what it has always been – the issue of balancing powers between the EU centre and the member states combined with the issue of balancing powers within the EU's institutions between federal and confederal (intergovernmental). Supranationalism is the accelerator, intergovernmentalism is the brake. Under the second pillar of CFSP, ▸Yugoslavia has been a chastening experience for the EU, whilst on the security issue area opinion is divided about the ▸scope of the WEU. JHA deals with such matters as ▸immigration policy. These are covered in the Schengen Agreement of 1985 which was negotiated on an intergovernmental basis. Thirteen of the member states of the EU have now acceded to Schengen (only Ireland and the UK have not done so) while Norway and Iceland have found that Nordic solidarity inclines these two outsiders to join Denmark, Finland and Sweden on the inside as far as frontier controls and their abolition are concerned.

The context in which European Union was being pursued as a ▸regional goal was changed totally following the end of the ▸Cold War. For more than three decades the idea of union amongst the states of Europe was essentially a Western European prerogative because of the Cold War divisions. The ending of that particular era in the international politics of Europe has presented the leaders of the EU with the challenge on the type and scale of enlargement they may wish for the union in the next century. It was agreed at the European

Council meeting in Copenhagen in June 1993 that full membership should be extended to any Central and Eastern European state provided it was able to meet the political and economic criteria of being a functioning and stable democracy with a free market system of political economy. At the same time Copenhagen recognized that enlargement should not jeopardize the process of integration amongst the existing members of the EU. What some see as the debate about widening and deepening the Union was thus outlined. It is clear that the majority opinion within the Union's leadership regards enlargement as a procedure whereby aspirants are assessed to see if they come up to standard or not. What is termed the 'acquis' – which the EC/EU has established over the years as its basic constitutional framework – is the touchstone or standard by which aspirants will be judged. At the insistence of Germany, moreover, enlargement looks like taking place on a case-by-case basis. It is already evident that applications of the standards referred to above on the putative new members will be extremely strict.

**Ex aequo et bono** A term in ➤international law which allows decisions to be made on the grounds of fairness or equity rather than applying the rules of positive or customary international law. Article 38 (2) of the Statute of the ➤International Court of Justice (ICJ) indicates that the sources of law described in Article 38 (1) 'shall not prejudice the power of the Court to decide a case ex aequo et bono, if the parties agree thereto'. Although the ICJ has never decided a case of *ex aequo et bono* arbitration tribunals have employed the concept, as they did in two Latin American ➤boundary disputes in the 1930s (Guatemala–Honduras 1933 and Bolivia–Paraguay 1938).

**Ex post ex ante** ➤deterrence

**Exclave** Whereas an ➤enclave refers to a territory of one ➤sovereign state which is surrounded by another, an exclave is the same territory viewed from the point of view of the host state. Thus Walvis Bay was until 1993 an exclave of South Africa, but an enclave of Namibia. So an exclave is usually a relatively small part of the state, administratively integral to it, but separated from it by the territory of another state. In this way the standard joke among political geographers is that an 'exclave is a small foreign territory completely surrounded by trouble'.

**Exclusive Economic Zone (EEZ)** An important, and potentially explosive, development in ➤maritime law which came to the fore at the UN Convention on the Law of the Sea in 1982. It involves claiming functional, though at present not territorial, ➤sovereignty over a 200-mile area adjacent to the coastal ➤state. If universally adopted this would mean that 32 per cent of ocean space (28 million square miles) will be covered by some form of national administration (Booth, 1985). At present fifty-six states claim some form of exclusive rights in these zones, whereas others, including the United States, the Soviet Union and the United Kingdom who have rejected the EEZ concept, nevertheless claim 200-mile Exclusive Fisheries Zones. Technically, the 3-mile territorial jurisdiction limit still applies, but the widespread acceptance of EEZ throughout the 1970s portends some change in law. Also known as 'creeping jurisdiction' or 'territorialization' it represents a movement away from classical notions of *mare liberum* (open seas) towards *mare clausum* (closed seas). This closed sea principle and the doctrine of ➤'Common Heritage of Mankind' which it embraces is not viewed as a welcome development by the older maritime powers and their belief in freedom of the seas and 'finder's keepers'. The conflict of interests is part of the ➤North–South debate although clearly it could find itself on the agenda of world politics if, for instance, a ➤great power backed the claims of exclusive rights advanced by the emerging sea powers of the Southern Hemisphere. The 200-mile limit is an arbitrary one, having been arrived at initially by Chile, Ecuador and Peru in the Declaration of Santiago (1951). In this case, 200 miles happened to cover the productive fishing areas of their coastlines. The EEZ is an obstacle to the mobility of warships and aircraft overflights and is therefore viewed as a serious challenge to established naval 'blue water' strategies. This confrontation between the interests of the maritime powers in navigational freedom and the desire of coastal states to extend the range of their jurisdiction is likely to dominate future discussions on the law of the sea.

**Exile** The banishment of a person or group from one place to another. Exile may be self-imposed (e.g. ex-President Marcos of the Philippines, to Hawaii) or enforced (e.g. Napoleon to Elba and St Helena) but in either case it is usually viewed as a form of punishment. Originally used as such by the Greeks and Romans, it is now a commonplace of world politics and is a special and dramatic variant of emigration. In cases where the ➤legitimacy of a ➤regime is questioned, a government-in-exile may be formed and seek general ➤recognition. Thus, the French government-in-exile was officially recognized by the United Kingdom from 1941 to 1945 and was based in London. The nationalist government of Taiwan was officially recognized by the United States as the legitimate government-in-exile of China from 1949 to 1979. The form of exile which involves loss of citizenship, whether voluntary or enforced, is known as 'expatriation'.

**Export** In the broadest terms an export is something which is transferred from one international ➤actor to another, or from one actor to the global system. Thus, it is possible to describe an intangible – such as ➤nationalism or socialism – being exported. Again it is possible to describe a tangible – such as manufactured goods – being exported.

The term is also used in a narrower, economically based sense. Here the reference is to the movement of goods and services between economic systems. It is important to note that with the growth of ➤common markets and trading

➤blocs the exporting actor need not be a ➤state. Classical economic analysis, drawing upon the concept of comparative advantage, tends to the view that exporting goods and services is an efficient and, therefore, desirable activity. As a corollary, exporting encourages specialization and, left to itself, an international division of labour. Exporting states and trading blocs create wealth by this activity, which in turn provides for growth in incomes and possibly employment. The term *export-led growth* has been a policy goal that many political elites have set for themselves and the systems they administer.

Recently, considerable attention has become concentrated upon the export of ➤technology – known as ➤technology transfer. The argument has been advanced that the ability to export technology is not evenly spread throughout the international system, but, rather, is largely located within the advanced industrial countries (➤AICs). These actors via agencies such as the multinational corporations (➤MNCs) have such an effective control over applied knowledge that they can often dictate the terms and conditions upon which the transfer takes place.

The example of technology transfer highlights another issue about exports and exporting. Success at this activity often provokes resentment and even fear among other actors. The bases for these sentiments are not entirely unfounded. Historically some of the most powerful and influential states in the system have been those which generated a considerable proportion of the GNP from exporting. Pre-eminent in this regard would be nineteenth-century United Kingdom and twentieth-century Japan. During the ➤Cold War era the two ➤superpowers relied less on exporting goods and services for their wealth creation, but, paradoxically, more upon exporting ideas – particularly political ideas – for their influence.

**Expropriation** Refers to the requisition of the property of ➤aliens and the transfer of ownership to the ➤state. A variety of ➤nationalization, although the latter can involve domestically owned property, whereas expropriation usually refers to foreign ownership only. Expropriation is a normal consequence of declaring a war. Under ➤international law expropriation of alien property is legitimate provided certain conditions are met. It must be 'for reasons of public utility' and undertaken with due regard for the legal processes. In addition, 'prompt, adequate and effective compensation' must accompany the action. None of these conditions are precise and it is generally acknowledged that, as in so many other areas, international law is weak in this regard. Expropriation has been an important issue in twentieth-century politics especially as a consequence of the decline of ➤colonialism and the development of ➤communism. The nineteenth-century expansion of Western economies generated capital outflow and heavy investment in ➤developing areas, resulting in large segments of local economies coming under the ownership of foreign nationals. The success of the anti-colonial movement and the nationalization measures demanded by the communist ➤ideology (initially in the Soviet Union) led to conflict both over the right to expropriate and to the amounts of compensation due. Retaliation by the aggrieved state can involve the entire range of diplomatic options – from protest to military sanctions and overt ➤intervention in the internal affairs of the expropriating state (e.g. US reactions in relation to post-1959 Cuba, especially the ➤Bay of Pigs incident). Two considerations dominate international legal thinking on expropriation. First, capital-exporting states require some form of security before they are willing to invest. Second, the targets of such activity are entitled, according to rights associated with ➤sovereignty and ➤independence, to control their own economic destinies and under the doctrine of ➤self-help are empowered to resist undue pressure. These conditions are not always reconcilable since many ➤Third World states do not accept the provisos for compensation even though they may be embodied in ➤treaty form. The general weakness of international law in this regard was instanced in the Ugandan expropriation of Asian property in 1972.

**Extended deterrence** This is a special instance of that class of relationships referred to in ➤international relations (IR) as ➤deterrence. In extended deterrence the Imposer is seeking to get a Target to abandon plans to attack or otherwise ➤coerce a third party. In his work on the subject, Paul Huth (1988) following Patrick Morgan's (1983) distinction, identifies two analytically different extended deterrence situations. In one type-referred to as 'immediate' deterrence – the Imposer/Defender is seeking to deter the Target/Attacker in circumstances where an attack is ➤perceived as highly likely. Extended-Immediate deterrence is thus positively correlated with ➤crisis situations, confrontation and high levels of tension. The second type is referred to by Huth as 'Extended-General' deterrence. Here the perception is of some likely future contingency where the Imposer may be required to confront the Target on behalf of a third party. Although there is perceived to be no immediate threat, the general correlation of forces implies a generalized perception that some form of deterrence relationship between the Imposer/Defender and the third party is required. Clearly, a situation of extended-general deterrence is very likely to precede a situation of extended-immediate deterrence. The second situation might also be seen as a ➤self-fulfilling prophecy of the first.

During the ➤Cold War era much intellectual effort was put into the analyses of both forms of extended deterrence by ➤strategic studies analysts. Historically problems of extended deterrence were not new, but most observers agreed that ➤nuclear weapons had introduced new considerations into these calculations. The ➤NATO alliance was continuously beset with problems between the parties regarding the ➤nuclear umbrella over Europe. It was a basic assumption in these debates that the ➤credibility issue was exacerbated in extended deterrence situations.

Hypothetically extended deterrence can end in one of three outcomes:

deterrence will succeed and the third party will not be attacked, deterrence will fail and the third party will be attacked, deterrence will protect the third party but only to deflect the attack on to the Defender/Imposer. Some see ➤Pearl Harbor as a case of this third outcome.

**Extradition** Legal term meaning the handing over of fugitives from one ➤state to another. A criminal may take refuge in a state other than the one in which the offences occurred. The practice of extradition has evolved to deal with this. It involves a formal request from the injured state that the individual be extradited to be tried or punished for offences against its laws. In the absence of a specific ➤treaty there is no duty in ➤international law to extradite. On the other hand states can, if they wish, extradite without a specific treaty obligation. Mutual interest and ➤reciprocity usually leads states to cooperate in these matters, but certain stringent provisions normally obtain. Thus, political, military and religious offences are usually exempt. The definition of 'political' of course varies and international affairs are replete with examples of controversy over the 'criminal/political' distinction. (UK requests to the United States for extradition of IRA members often fall into this category.) Most extradition treaties are ➤bilateral and share certain provisions to safeguard individual rights. Among the most common are the following:

1 Double criminality principle, i.e. the crimes must be crimes under the laws of both states concerned.
2 Speciality principle, i.e. an extradited individual is not tried for a crime other than that for which he was extradited.
3 *Prima facie* evidence of guilt must be shown.
4 Requests are usually confined to 'serious' crimes (defined either in terms of length of punishment expected or in terms of type of offence).
5 The offence must have been committed on the territory of the requesting party.
6 It is not usual to be expected to extradite one's own nationals.

Extradition is a complex and delicate legal process impinging on the ➤sovereignty and ➤independence of states as well as on individual rights. The procedure is cumbersome and as such is in decline on a world-wide basis. However, ➤deportation has proved to be a useful substitute.

**Extraterritoriality** A vital aspect of ➤diplomacy which refers to the exercise of legal jurisdiction by a 'sender' ➤state within a 'received' state's territory. In modern usage it is bound up with ➤diplomatic immunity. However, extraterritoriality has not been mutual or reciprocal. During the period of European ➤imperialism it was common practice for an imperial state to insist that its own expatriates be subject to their home-based legal system and not that of the locale in which they were placed. With the withering away of empires and colonies this unfair practice has all but disappeared. Apart from diplomats, it is common practice in ➤alliance systems for the armed forces of one state which are present in the territory of another to enjoy the privileges of extraterritoriality. Agreements establishing this are referred to as 'status of forces' ➤treaties (e.g. the ➤NATO Status of Force Act, 1951). Immunity from local prosecution can, of course, be waived by agreement.

# F

**Factor analysis**  A means of analysing events in world politics mathematically by grouping them into clusters or bundles. Factor analysis is thus a statistical means of labelling events – a common enough procedure in all social explanation. The growth of international government organizations (➤IGOs) since 1945 has greatly increased the output and availability of moderately reliable statistical sources and this growth has undoubtedly increased the possible application of research methods such as factor analysis. An area of inquiry that has particularly interested scholars using this technique is the relationship between the occurrence of ➤conflict within states and conflict between states. Leading exponents of factor analysis have been Rudolph Rummel and Raymond Tanter.

**Failed nation-states**  A term indicating a dangerous new development in the aftermath of the ➤Cold War – the breakdown of law, order and basic services in a number of multiethnic ➤states, particularly though not exclusively in sub-Saharan Africa. This phenomenon is accompanied by bitter ➤communal conflict, violent ➤ethnic nationalism, ➤militarism and possibly endemic ➤regional conflict. Examples are Haiti, ex-➤Yugoslavia, Somalia, Sudan, Liberia, Cambodia, Rwanda, Zaire, Sierra Leone and ➤Afghanistan. The end of the Cold War has exacerbated this process since the rival powers no longer extend economic/military assistance to former client regimes which are now unable to survive unaided. According to R. D. Kaplan in a celebrated essay (1994) much of the ➤Third World is experiencing 'the withering away of central government, the rise of tribal and regional domains, the unchecked spread of disease and the growing pervasiveness of war.' As a result, conventional ➤geopolitical maps are highly misleading since 'the classificatory grid of nation-states is going to be replaced by a jagged-glass pattern of city-states, shanty-states, nebulous and anarchic regionalisms.' The increasing incidence of 'failed' states is regarded by many analysts as evidence that the ➤New World Order confidently predicted by optimists after the fall of the Soviet Empire and the unprecedented ➤multilateral cooperation to end the ➤Persian Gulf War, is something to be regretted rather than welcomed (Mearsheimer, 1990). ➤➤Quasi-states

***Fait accompli***  A ➤unilateral act by one ➤state, or group of states that suddenly and dramatically changes the ➤status quo. It usually carries the element of surprise and has the effect of breaking a diplomatic deadlock. In this sense, it can be regarded as an alternative to diplomatic ➤negotiations. It is always a high-risk strategy since the onus is put on the other side to react or to acquiesce.

Correct assessments of the likely responses of opponents are therefore crucial. Examples of notable successes are Hitler's remilitarization of the Rhineland (1935) and the Japanese occupation of Manchuria (1931). Failures include the placing of nuclear ➤missiles on ➤Cuba (1962) and the Argentinian occupation of the ➤Falklands/Malvinas (1982).

**The Falkland Islands (Malvinas)** A group of islands in the South Atlantic which are the subject of a long standing dispute between the United Kingdom and Argentina. Originally, possession was claimed by France, Spain and the United Kingdom, but by 1833 the United Kingdom had gained effective control. Argentina, by virtue of its proximity and also its claim to be the natural successor to Spanish possessions, has consistently claimed ➤sovereignty over the islands since ➤independence in the 1820s. Talks about sovereignty have continued intermittently in the twentieth century, but were bedevilled by the islands' insistence on remaining under British protection. In April 1982 Argentina, without prior warning, occupied the Falklands and South Georgia, landing about 14,000 troops on the islands. The United Kingdom, after exploring a number of diplomatic initiatives including the ➤UN, launched a counter invasion. Argentine troops surrendered on 14 June. The affair, though fairly short in duration, was costly for both sides and Britain in particular faces a difficult task in maintaining its position as the sovereign ➤power and providing permanent defence for the islands. Argentina has not dropped its claim to sovereignty and the dispute continues to disrupt normal diplomatic relations between the two states. ➤➤Decolonization

**Fascism** Now used mainly as a multi-purpose term of abuse, it originally referred to political and ideological systems developed in Italy (1922) and Germany (1933). Historians disagree as to whether it is a nineteenth- or twentieth-century phenomenon, but agree that it is an ➤ideology of the extreme right which encompasses ideas about race, religion, economics, social welfare and ➤leadership which are directly and specifically opposed to ➤communism, socialism and ➤liberalism. It is not a coherent and self-contained political theory although its adherents regard Hitler's *Mein Kampf* as a fundamental text.

In ➤international relations it is closely associated with ➤imperialism, ➤militarism and ➤nationalism. The logic of belief in racial superiority leads to policies of conquest, domination and even elimination of lesser races. ➤International law and ➤morality are subordinated to concepts of national necessity defined by the leadership and so 'might is right' and ➤'justice is on the side of the stronger' are central features of the approach. A semi-mystical belief in the destiny of the ➤nation is also a strong pointer, as is the involvement of the military in deciding national objectives. Political theorists most closely identified with the development of fascist ideas concerning international affairs are Gobineau, Sorel, Herder, Darwin, Nietzsche, Marinetti, Spengler and Chamberlain, although the ideas of more mainstream political philosophers such as ➤Machiavelli, ►Hobbes, Hegel and Treitschke are drawn upon and elaborated. Although usually associated with pre-war Italy and Germany, neo-fascist systems have appeared, among other places, in Spain, Portugal, Greece, Argentina, Brazil, Chile, Lebanon and South Africa, although the absence of a specific definition might render this judgement suspect.

**Federalism** This term is used in two contexts. The first, to describe and explain how legitimate ►power is shared in constituent political units – the federation. Second, as an explanation and perhaps prescription of how ►integration might be achieved between previously separate state ►actors. Although explanation and prediction are linked, this ►linkage is not a necessary one. Thus a federation of previously separate states might be achieved via ►functionalism as much as by federalism. However, both would recognize that the only viable and applicable working model for power-sharing in the newly integrated community was the federal one.

As a means of describing and explaining the division of legitimate power or ►authority in federations, federalism postulates as an initial position a tension or conflict between centripetal and centrifugal forces. This conflict will be settled by the several parties signing a constitutional bargain which will stipulate where the jurisdictions of the centre and the periphery lie. Thus certain ►issue areas will be reserved for the centre, others retained by the periphery. Normally ►defence, ►foreign affairs and macroeconomic policy are handled exclusively at the centre. Conversely, the periphery will retain some revenue raising power, control over social and welfare services and some small discretion regarding penal codes and provisions. Federalism is a favoured system of government in large, culturally diverse states. Most of the largest states in the present system are federations.

Federalism as a balance between centripetal and centrifugal forces should be distinguished from decentralization or devolution in unitary systems. In federalism the centrifugal forces are already in place when the initial constitutional divisions of labour are effected. In decentralization the centrifugal forces come to the surface after the initial constitutional arrangement has been made. If these centrifugal tendencies become very strong and effective, decentralization can lead, by design or accident, to federalism.

Federalism, as a theory of regional or even global integration, derives its inspiration from seeing the positive benefits of federalism as a system of state government. Its proponents argue that the inherent tension between centre and periphery and the 'unity through diversity' dialectic are appropriate working assumptions for inter-state unification efforts. Federalism, as a system of integration at these levels, has a good deal of ideological and prescriptive leaven therefore. In particular, in comparison with functionalist and neo-functionalist approaches, the federalists claim to be able to tackle the issue of legitimate power-sharing head on by proposing an empirically tested system for dealing with it.

The major laboratory testing of federalism in twentieth-century ➤international relations has taken place in the European ➤region. Federalism was espoused as an ➤ideology by politicians and intellectuals who saw 1939 as the nadir of the European ➤state-system and 1945 as an opportunity to replace it. It was necessary to set in train plans to move 'beyond the nation state' in the future. Specifically with the institution building of the ➤European Community (EC) federalists were constantly primed to push for a populist, participatory agenda. The establishment of a directly elected Parliament and moves towards majority voting within the principal organs of the EC were correctly seen as important. The ➤Maastricht Treaty on ➤European Union emboldened federalists to seek to move the Union into the issue-areas noted above as keys to the federal centre. The end of the ➤Cold War era in European relations has presented a window of opportunity for the ➤EU to realize some of the aspirations of an earlier generation of federalist who saw 1939 and the Cold War divisions as such mid-century disasters.

Federalism remains the only empirically tested theory of regional integration that combines unity with diversity. Implicitly it is also a theory of limited government as the Founding Fathers of the United States well understood. Whether it should proceed by the ➤elitist or by the populist modes is a point of debate within its adherents. By tackling the issues of ➤high politics directly, the federalist approach to integration is far more ambitious and controversial than functionalism. This is its latent mass appeal. It confronts the key issue areas of state ➤sovereignty and ➤national interest by proposing a power-sharing arrangement which is enshrined in a constitutional bargain.

**Feedback** A term originating in information theory. It refers to the inter-relationship between an organism and its environment, using these terms in the broadest sense. Thus through the mechanism of feedback an organism reacts to its environment and vice versa. Feedback allows the organism to increase its chances of ➤goal attainment, and/or goal modification, by demonstrating that a particular behaviour pattern is likely, or unlikely, to lead to the desired goal. Feedback, accordingly, can either be positive or negative. The latter is particularly important if self-correction and adjustment of behaviour is to take place. According to information theory, therefore, negative feedback allows organisms to adjust to their environment and maintain stability through adaptation or ➤homeostasis. Homeostatic equilibrium is dependent upon negative feedback, therefore, if 'learning' is to be achieved. A seminal work that sought to apply these ideas to politics, and particularly policy-making, was Karl Deutsch's *The Nerves of Government*. The influence and impact of these ideas can be judged from the extent to which the term feedback is used as a colloquialism.

**Fifth column** Term which originated during the Spanish Civil War (1936–9) meaning an organized and secret body working within enemy ranks which aims to subvert, sabotage and disrupt the ➤war effort. Thus, during Franco's attack on Madrid he was said to have four columns of regular troops preparing for the frontal assault, while a fifth column of rebel sympathizers existed within the city ready to aid the cause. Fifth column activities are especially associated with ideological conflict and as such ought to be distinguished from practitioners of ➤espionage. A term closely associated with the fifth column is ➤quisling, which refers to a group of Nazi supporters who aided Germany's attack on Norway in 1941. This, though, carries pejorative overtones (i.e. traitor), whereas fifth columnists are often regarded as brave honourable people. There is a sense in which both can be regarded as latter-day Trojan Horses.

**Final Act** An abbreviated reference to the document known as the Final Act of the Conference on Security and Cooperation in Europe (➤CSCE) signed in Helsinki, Finland on 1 August 1975. The document is also sometimes referred to as the ➤Helsinki Accords. The document is not a ➤treaty and was, therefore, not binding on the parties. Notwithstanding it was regarded after the event as a key building block in European *détente*, particularly by the ➤leadership of the former Soviet Union.

**Finlandization** A ➤geopolitical term which refers to the extension of a ➤state's ➤influence over contiguous or near neighbours by indirect means. This influence will be directly mediated in the ➤issue area of ➤foreign policy but this is likely to spill over into the domestic agenda as well. As the term implies, it has historically been taken as read that the policy of the former Soviet Union towards Finland was the paradigm example of this type of extension. It should not be thought that finlandization condemns the target state to a totally reactive foreign policy. During the ➤Cold War years Finnish ➤neutrality was certainly a core value in Soviet foreign policy but within these parameters Finland was able to conduct its ➤diplomacy – often to good effect. European ➤security cooperation and the ➤Helsinki Accords are testimony to this.

**First strike** The attempt to achieve strategic surprise by attacking the adversary first. First strike requires both ➤capability and intention. The former requires a level of military technology which enables an offensive strategy to be risked with a feasible chance of success. The latter requires a political and military ➤leadership which is not averse to risk-taking. *In extremis*, failing to strike first may look like political incompetence as the attractions of such a strategy mount. ➤Decision-making operates in a hair-trigger context and the ➤leaderships cannot afford to pass up the opportunity to 'get their retaliation in first'. It has been argued that such a frenetic atmosphere surrounded the decision-makers in 1914.

The advent of ➤nuclear weapons combined with the outbreak of the ➤Cold War increased both the attractions and the risks of a first strike strategy. The burgeoning field of ➤strategic studies set itself the task of manipulating these risks without the Gadarene consequences of 1914. The result was strategies such as ►brinkmanship and the literature of ►crisis management. There remains the possibility that in the absence of a more organized system of ►security relations first strikes may occur if the operational and ►perceptual contexts are ripe.

**First World** As the word 'First' implies this categorization refers to those states that were historically in the vanguard of the ►modernization process following the Industrial Revolution that commenced in eighteenth-century Britain. As a collective expression the terms First World and Advanced Industrial Countries (►AIC) are coterminous. The occurrence of the ►Cold War in mid-twentieth-century ►international relations led to the term taking on a more relativist connotation. It became a requirement of popular analysis to contrast the First World with the Second (meaning the ►communist states) and eventually the ►Third World. The end of the Cold War, the collapse of communism and the weakening of the viability of the concept of Third Worldism has had a ►feedback effect upon the idea of the First World.

Historically the term probably retains relevance as a means of identifying a group of states that espoused ►capitalism and ►economic liberalism. In the account of this development, change occurred as a result of internal processes rather than external pressures. Economic growth led to the development of a bourgeoisie and to demands for political participation to be broadened to accommodate these new classes. Scientific innovation and technological change are important features of these societies and again they tend to be in the vanguard of most of these changes. The multinational corporation (MNC) is the unique non-governmental creation of the First World's value system and it has been the vehicle or transmission belt for distributing these values to the rest of the system. There is growing evidence that the template of First Worldism is being reassessed from within as so-called 'quality of life' considerations are producing a possible ►paradigm shift towards more sustainable development.

**Flag** An indication of affiliation or ownership, the flag typically symbolizes such relationships. Thus all ►states have their own flag as symbols of statehood. It will be carried by state airlines, warships and merchant ships as well as being prominently displayed on public buildings both within the home state and on embassies and missions abroad. The right to fly the flag of the state is embodied in ►international law and is known as *jus banderae*. In ►maritime law this refers to the norm that a ship's nationality is decided by the colours under which it sails and not by the nationality of the owner. Thus it is possible to grant the right to fly the flag of a state to non-nationals – 'flags of convenience'. This refers to a situation where a state will authorize vessels owned and operated by nationals from other states to fly their flags. The attraction of this practice is that it enables operators to enjoy regulations, and perhaps tax ►regimes, that are less onerous than those they would have to operate under in their own state, or else it is done for political/strategic reasons, as was the case in 1988 with the reflagging of Kuwaiti ships during the ➤Iran–Iraq war. The system is not without its critics and in 1958 the Geneva Convention on the High Seas suggested that there should be a 'genuine link' between ship and state. However, the problem of identification persists and in 1982 the shipping committee of the United Nations Conference on Trade and Development (UNCTAD) produced these figures relating to registration: fifty-six countries representing 45 per cent of the world's dead-weight tonnage had a significant degree of control and managerial involvement with vessels that flew their flag, five states (Liberia, Panama, Cyprus, Bermuda and Bahamas) representing 29 per cent of tonnage had open registration, while three states (the United Kingdom, Greece and Saudi Arabia) representing 18 per cent of the world's tonnage had a mixed system that lay somewhere between the open and closed varieties.

International ➤actors other than states may also have flags. Indeed, the most famous example is that of the ➤International Red Cross where the flag has become the title of the institution. In this instance the symbol is the reverse of the state flag of Switzerland.

Flags may also be used as signals rather than symbols. Before the growth of more advanced technologies, flags were widely used by armed forces for signalling instructions or simply allegiance. Various colours indicate different signals, the 'white flag' being widely regarded as a signal of the willingness to ➤surrender or call a ➤truce in situations of armed combat.

**Flexible response** A term that was much used in ➤strategic studies during the ➤Cold War era. It became part of the lexicon of analysis favoured after the election of J. F. Kennedy to the White House in 1960. In the strategic sense, flexible response (sometimes called 'controlled response') grew from the need perceived at the time to abandon ➤massive retaliation for something more controlled and flexible. Events such as the second ➤Berlin crisis and the ➤Vietnam situation persuaded the Democratic administration that America needed to expand its ➤conventional capabilities to meet more contingencies. The subsequent attempt to convince America's ➤NATO allies that the alliance should embrace flexibility was greeted with a mixed reaction. The eventual adoption of flexible response in May 1967 committed the Organization – and specifically the US – to a ➤forward defence of Western Europe in order to avoid the early use of ➤nuclear weapons.

**Foggy bottom** Irreverent American media term for the US Department of State which is said to be located in the foggiest quarter of Washington DC. Sometimes also used as an uncomplimentary synonym for American ➤foreign policy.

**Food** Although the production and provision of food has always been a central concern of political life, it is only in the twentieth century that it has been perceived to be a major ►issue area of ►international relations. The first organization to address the problems of production and distribution on an international scale rather than a domestic one was the International Agriculture Institute established in Rome in 1905. The ►League of Nations, in response to the Great Depression of 1929, established a Food Committee to investigate the problems of mass starvation and hunger. In 1945 the ►United Nations established the Food and Agriculture Organization (FAO), which has now become the central intergovernmental agency dealing with the problems of combating undernourishment and starvation. Since 1965 the FAO has published every three years the World Food Survey, which reviews and monitors developments on a global basis. In 1974 the UN held a World Food Conference which set up a World Food Council meeting annually at ministerial level, and it also adopted a Universal Declaration on the Eradication of Hunger and Malnutrition.

The UN and its agencies have been largely responsible for acknowledging that 'the right to subsistence' is a fundamental ►human right and therefore a duty to which the international community must respond. However, although the problem of deprivation is technically soluble, the international community, especially the relatively rich industrialized ►North, has not so far responded in a generous or even coherent manner.

According to Lester Brown (1990), although the world grain output between 1950 and 1984 more than doubled, the greatest beneficiaries were the wealthiest states, which continue to overconsume. Since 1984 the world production trend has been reversed, and in the 1990s, given the projected ►population explosion, the food crisis is likely to be of systemic proportions. The task of increasing production above consumption is complicated not just by a lack of political will, but also by factors such as ►environmental degradation, global scarcity of crop land and irrigation water, and climatic changes associated with global warming. Most analysts now believe that unless there is a coordinated international response to the problem – which will involve bringing population growth into line with food production – a major international disaster is waiting to happen.

**Football war** Name given to the 5-day military conflict between El Salvador and Honduras which occurred in July 1969 and resulted in the deaths of over 3,000 people. Simmering hostility between the two states (mainly over ►boundary disputes) was ignited by the victory in June of that year of the Honduras national soccer team over that of El Salvador in the preliminary round of the World Cup. After ►OAS (Organization of American States) ►intervention a cease-fire was agreed and the El Salvadorean army withdrew from Honduras territory. The incident illustrates the thesis that the causes of ►war are many and wondrous.

**Force** Force is closely related to ideas about ►power and ►coercion. It is usually connected in international affairs with the use of arms although this need not always be the case. In fact, it is a physical manifestation of how power relationships can spill over into a dimension of violence. Not all power relations involve the use of the threat of force so in this sense power is a much wider and more broadly based set of ideas. However, if power can be seen as covering a continuum of relationships, then force lies at one extreme, with perhaps ►influence at the other.

As a member of the power family, force requires a ►capability as a necessary condition. Normally this capability is expressed in terms of military resources. In ►international relations, as there is no monopoly of force held by a central agency, every ►actor, in theory, can possess the means and capacity to use force should it so wish. Acquiring and maintaining such a capacity is expensive. Accordingly, those wishing to go down this path have to make conscious and continuous decisions about allocation of often scarce resources. ►States, traditionally the actors most likely to seek to acquire such capabilities, have always distinguished themselves by how much of these resources they might be willing to allocate to maintain and increase their force capabilities. Indeed, an important variable in assessing position in the hierarchical structure of states (►great, ►middle or ►small powers) is an estimation concerning the capacity and willingness to use force. One conditional variable in this process may be the state's ►orientation. Clearly a state that is ►isolationist is less likely to feel threatened by others or feel the need to threaten others with the use of force. A second major constraint on the acquisition of force capability is likely to be the overall structure of the system. For example, the ►balance of power was, at its height, based on the assumption that the leading states in the system had the capability, individually or in coalition, to intervene forcefully if necessary to preserve the system and prevent its domination by one or a group of dissident states. These groupings were often referred to as ►status quo and ►revisionist, as they were by E. H. Carr in *The Twenty Years' Crisis, 1919–39*. Again, acquiring a force capability will require leaders within states to make choices as to the allocation of resources and, in particular, with the choice between force capabilities and other goals. The argument about 'guns versus butter' is clearly not confined to Stalinist Russia.

►Technology has affected the role of force in a number of ways. First, the acquisition of a credible force capability is highly expensive. Modern weapons systems place a heavy burden on the economies of even the wealthiest states. Second, modern technology has increased the ►scope and destructiveness of the violence available to the state that practises the use of force. The distinction between combatants and non-combatants is increasingly difficult to sustain and civilian deaths as a proportion of total ►war deaths have increased greatly. Since the gunpowder ►revolution the ultimate technological innovation to date has been the development of ►nuclear weapons. Indeed, the nuclear revolution in international affairs has caused further revisions to be made to our conception of the use of force. In particular, the distinction between force capability and force relationship is now sharper than ever. In nuclear weapons, states possess instruments of force which they would prefer not to use. As a result, ►deterrence theorists have identified the problem of ►credibility as being especially critical. Nuclear weapons have also blurred traditional distinctions between victors and vanquished. Consequently, the use of force, if it is to include nuclear weapons, is now beset by ambiguities and contradictions, the most blatant being the idea of its skilful non-use.

*International law and the use of force*

Restriction on the use of force has always been part of the rationale of ►international law, and the twentieth century has seen the most concerted attempt yet to outlaw violence employed in the private interests of individual states. The ►League of Nations did not ban the use of force altogether but it did attempt to restrict it to tolerable levels and during the inter-war years there was a movement to achieve its total prohibition which resulted in the General Treaty for the Renunciation of War (the ►Kellogg-Briand pact) of 1928. However, even this was not a complete ban, as the right to ►self-defence and ►reprisals remained. ►War, of course, is not an exact synonym for force, and the ►United Nations Charter attempted to address the issue head on. Thus Article 2 (4) declared that 'All members shall refrain in their international relations from the threat or use of force against the territorial integrity or political independence of any state, or in any other manner inconsistent with the purpose of the United Nations.' The reference to 'force' rather than to 'war' was deliberate as it covers incidences where violence may be employed although perhaps falling short of a technical state of war. This is now part of customary international law, yet it is unclear whether the term includes not only armed force but other manifestations; for example economic force. This ambiguity was highlighted in 1973–4 with the use of the Arab oil weapon against states deemed friendly to Israel. It is not possible with any degree of certainty to establish whether economic or other forms of coercion are contrary to the Charter but expert opinion has it that international law is moving in the general direction of widening the definitional scope of the term.

Under the Charter the threat or use of force is illegal except in certain circumstances, and these are broadly the exercise of ►self-defence and the collective use of force by the organization itself. This doctrine of ►collective security led some to expect the UN to play a key role in the post-1945 system. In fact the intrusion of the ►Cold War into the working of the organization weakened the possibility and desirability of its providing a genuine international ►regime for the use of force. The ►Korean War (1950) is an exception to this but only because of the fortuitous absence of the Soviet Union from the ►Security Council when the decision for collective coercive action was taken. Subsequently, the UN has developed a more modest ►peacekeeping competence which seeks to avoid the active use of force and instead rely more on diplomatic techniques. The issue of ►terrorism has not so far produced a specific prohibitive ►treaty mainly because of definitional problems associated with political preference. One man's 'terrorist' is another's 'freedom fighter' and so international law has not thus far been able to encompass the phenomenon.

The centrality of force in international relations has shown the inadequacy of international law, yet its use is hedged about with limitations. States possessing considerable military potential find its actual use more difficult to envisage and to enact. Force potential is not easily transferred into force relationships and when the transformation is made the resulting use of force is often self-defeating and costly. The attempt to establish international institutions which administer quasi-legal force has so far not been successful. As a result, although modern technology has placed enormous putative force into ►policy-makers' hands, they have found its conversion into usable instruments highly contingent.

**Force de frappe** The French nuclear delivery system. The decision to develop an independent nuclear deterrent for France is normally associated with the Fifth Republic and, in particular, the Presidency of Charles de Gaulle. However, the original decision was made under the Fourth Republic. Unlike its UK neighbour, France has maintained a genuine independent force structure. France has land-based, sea-based and air launched delivery systems and has developed ►tactical nuclear weapons as well. Closer nuclear collaboration with the United Kingdom has been actively discussed for a quarter of a century and might become a viable policy option in the future. The term *force de dissuasion* is often used in preference, indicating more appropriately its deterrent intention. ►►Gaullism

**Force majeure** Diplomatic term referring to situations which arise out of unavoidable or unforeseen circumstances or else as a result of irresistible ►force. Failure to comply with known ►international law, e.g. respecting territorial waters, may be excused on the grounds of *force majeure*. Used in this sense, it is the diplomatic equivalent of 'Act of God'. In another sense, it is frequently used to describe the application of superior or overwhelming force to settle a problem which hitherto had been a matter of consent, agreement or legal process. A group ruling through terror or repression alone could be described as ruling through *force majeure*.

**Foreign aid** A technique of ►economic statecraft where ►aid is used as an instrument of policy in order to achieve certain goals. Foreign aid implies a relationship between two ►actors which may be stipulated on one hand as 'donor' and on the other hand as 'recipient', these words clearly implying that the relationship will be seen in positive terms by the participants. Although it will be argued here that aid relationships can become negative and coercive, the initial position will be that the sanctions involved are rewards rather than punishments. In summary, then, foreign aid may be seen as a form of ►power relationship. Accordingly, the donor must possess a ►capability which can be converted into an aid relationship. For example, a ►state may possess large agricultural surpluses which it is willing to dispense to identified recipients. Similarly, the recipient must perceive that the goods and services offered will provide real additional resources. Both parties will look for tangible benefits from foreign aid relationships, therefore. In ►game theory terminology foreign aid expectations are positive sum.

States are not the only actors involved in foreign aid relationships, although they are the most important. International institutions such as the UN, through agencies such as the IBRD (►World Bank Group) and the ►IMF, also play an aid role. Moreover, it is certainly a mistake to see the activities of such bodies as being somehow 'non-political'. To the extent that such agencies get other recipient actors to do things that they would not otherwise do, then they may be said to be exercising political power relationships as donors over their identified recipients.

The precise political functions served by aid relationships are not always easy to uncover. The most overt politically manifest function of aid will be evident from an examination of the conditions laid down by the donor. Indeed, such stipulations as laid down by agencies such as the ►IMF, for example, can specify the kinds of economic policies they expect the recipient to follow. IMF conditionality is rightly regarded as political, as well as economic, in its implications. This political connotation has led some commentators to criticize the Fund accordingly. Similarly, from the outset the ►Marshall Plan had clear political implications. Important among these were: using US economic capability as a weapon in the ►Cold War, increasing cooperation among European states, assisting in the rehabilitation of Germany and boosting US exports in the post-war period.

Knorr (1975) has been responsible for directing the attention of analysts to the coercive function that foreign aid relationships can serve. The explanation for this is implicit in the initial characterization of foreign aid as a form of power relationship. A reward, once offered and accepted, can seem subsequently to be punitive if the donor threatens to withdraw or discontinue rewarding the recipient in the future. Because aid relationships exist over time, the opportunity for the donor to assume an intrusive and even coercive role *vis-à-vis* the recipient will increase. Furthermore, the donor may attempt to link the aid relationship with other foreign policy ►issue areas. Thus the United States used its Marshall aid link with the Netherlands to put pressure on the Dutch to come to terms with Indonesian nationalists in 1948–9.

A more general example of coercive linkage is provided by the Hickenlooper Amendment of 1962, which is a blanket prohibition upon US aid to states that nationalize US assets without offering full and fair compensation. During the Nixon Presidency, when the United States was considering extending ►most favoured nation (MFN) status to the Soviet Union, the US Congress via the Jackson-Vanik Amendment sought to make this offer dependent upon recipient states allowing their nationals freedom of migration to other countries. (This stipulation was specifically aimed at Soviet citizens wishing to settle abroad, especially Israel.)

Whether conditions are stipulated, implied, altered or amended at some later date, the fact remains that donors will want to make some assessment of the aid relationship both with regard to their initial objectives and in order to assess the overall efficacy of the exercise. Judging how successful a particular instance has been in terms of ►national interests is bound to be a subjective exercise. Thus the Marshall Plan was, at the time, regarded as a highly successful example of foreign aid working both in political and economic terms. However, as Baldwin (1985) has recently pointed out, Marshall aid helped European recipients to do things that they would probably have done anyway and its influence declined towards the end of the programme. Additionally, it fostered the habits of European cooperation and, in the long term, created a powerful trading rival to the United States. ►►Donor fatigue

**Foreign Office** Originally a European innovation, it refers to an executive and administrative agency of ►state which is concerned with the formulation and conduct of ►foreign policy. It goes by a variety of names including foreign ministry, ministry for external affairs, ministry of foreign affairs and the state department, but the basic functions remain the same. These are: the gathering of ►intelligence (usually through the diplomatic service), collating and evaluating information received, determining policy options available to government and communicating and explaining chosen policies to other governments and ►international organizations. Since 'defence of the realm' is part of the rationale of politics, this agency is one of the most important in government. Most Foreign Offices are organized on geographical lines (an African desk, an Asian desk, etc.) and on functional lines (commercial, financial and administrative) and are co-ordinated by a Minister or Secretary who holds high rank and status in government and/or party.

**Foreign policy** The activity whereby ►state ►actors act, react and interact. Foreign policy has been termed a boundary activity. The term 'boundary' implies that those making policy straddle two environments: an internal or domestic environment and an external or global environment. The ►policy-makers and the policy system stand therefore at these junction points and seek to mediate between the various milieux.

The domestic environment forms the background context against which policy is made. Thus factors such as the resource base of the state, its position geographically in relation to others, the nature and level of development of its economy, its demographic structure, its ►ideology and fundamental values will form the domestic or internal milieu. The international or external environment is where policy is actually implemented. ➤Implementation of policy immediately involves other actors and their reactions will ➤feedback into the policy-making system, thus forming part of the picture upon which future policy will be made. This attempt to create a reality upon which policy can be made is referred to as the ➤definition of the situation. It is a necessary prerequisite to understanding the environment and therefore to making policy decisions.

For most ➤decision-makers the international environment will be approached from a regional perspective. ➤geopolitics sets the parameters for this ➤regionalism. States have to react to their neighbours in all aspects of policy and therefore this regional dimension will be crucially important. Even the most significant states in contemporary ➤international relations have regional interests. Cooperation and ➤integration often take place on a regional basis. Similarly many ➤conflict situations, including some of the most chronic and persistent, have their origins in regional rather than global politics. The ➤Arab–Israeli conflict is a good example. The actual conduct of policy will be based within the institutional framework of the state. What are defined as vital matters of ➤national interest will be handled by the head of government along with senior advisers. Such questions are normally referred to as ➤high politics and would include matters of immediate ➤peace and ➤security as well as questions vital to the wealth and welfare of the state and its people. Conversely ➤low politics refers to matters of a routine ➤diplomacy. An intermediate category, often called Sectoral Politics has been coined by some writers on foreign policy to cover those areas where particular interest groups perceived that they have vital interests at stake but where these cannot really be called 'national' without distortion. Clearly these categories are not hard and fast and a particular ➤issue area may change in its relative significance. For the United Kingdom this happened in 1982 when the ➤Falklands issue moved rapidly from low/sectoral to high following the Argentinian initiative to occupy the islands ➤unilaterally.

Conventional wisdom might want to suppose that foreign policy is made on the basis of rational calculations of advantage and disadvantage with the policy-makers acting as a unified system. There is good reason to doubt that this view is entirely valid. In recent years the ➤bureaucratic politics approach has sought to emphasize the fact that the organizations that make foreign policy are not unified. Rather, key individuals tend to pursue their own version of the national interest often in conflict with others within the system. As a result the policy that emerges may represent a compromise between various points of view or the triumph of one organizational perspective over another. It is certainly plausible to see the ➤arms race in terms of this view. If this is the case, then the action-reaction model suggested above needs to be modified to allow for the organizational context in which policy is made.

The implementation of policy decisions requires states to utilize instruments such as military and economic ➤capabilities. The military instrument of policy has traditionally been seen as the most important where areas of high policy are concerned. Recently, economic instruments have attracted increased attention. This is partly as a result of increases in ➤interdependence and partly because of some of the problems surrounding the use and the threat of the use of ➤force in contemporary politics. In the last analysis, however well endowed a state may be with capacity to act to advance its interests, the skill and determination of its diplomats and the conduct of its ➤diplomacy may be crucial to the outcome. It is useful to distinguish diplomacy from foreign policy, since they are sometimes used synonymously in the more traditional texts. Whereas diplomacy refers to the manner of conducting one's relations, foreign policy refers to the matter. The latter remains the best term to use to encapsulate a state's relations with the outside world.

**Forward defence** A form of extended ➤defence where a ➤state intends to engage an enemy as soon as its territorial ➤frontiers have been crossed. Although there is a natural assumption that states will want to defend every scrap of their territory, the willingness to withdraw and establish a 'defence in depth' can be more effective as invaders of Russia have found to their cost. Forward defence is more controversial in ➤alliance diplomacy where one state or a group of states will be committed to engaging an enemy not on home territory but in some other identifiable 'forward' location. During the ➤Cold War years the United States was committed to the forward defence of Western Europe, particularly after the Federal Republic of Germany joined ➤NATO. The adoption by the parties of a policy of ➤flexible response meant that perforce if ➤deterrence failed then a forward defence of German territory would be effected. This strategy became the standard operating assumption amongst NATO allies after 1970.

Historically forward defence has often been positively correlated with the idea of the ➤buffer state. For the would-be defender, the buffer state affords an example of forward defence that can be highly cost effective. Anglo-Russian imperial diplomacy during the nineteenth century is a case in point. ➤Aghanistan was ➤perceived in Britain as a buffer state between its Indian possessions and expanding Russian imperial interests. Any intrinsic interest that Britain had in the Afghan situation was secondary to the need to use it as a forward defence of India. Amongst nineteenth-century diplomats in London the term 'forward policy' was often used in the context of Afghanistan.

**Fourteen points** Speech by President Woodrow Wilson to Congress on 18 January 1918 which contained the ideological justification for the US ➤war effort and which subsequently became the basis of the new ➤international order sought by ➤idealists after the First World War. While undoubtedly representing the Wilsonian approach in ➤international relations the speech owed its substance to a group of experts who had been assembled by Colonel E. M. House to draft proposals for the long-term settlement of international disputes. Among these was Walter Lippmann, who was subsequently regarded as one of the foremost American ➤realists. The speech contained a mixture of general and specific issues presented by the war and by the continued international ➤anarchy. It called for new ➤diplomacy consisting of 'open covenants openly arrived at', freedom of the seas in ➤peace and war, removal of ➤trade barriers, reduction of armaments and impartial adjustment of colonial claims. No less than eight points applied to the doctrine of ➤self-determination to political settlements in specific parts of Europe. The fourteenth point, which subsequently became the most influential, was the plea for the formation of a 'general association of nations' which would give 'mutual guarantees of political independence and territorial integrity to great and small states alike'. This ➤League of Nations was the centrepiece of the whole programme, although it is ironic that the state that did so much to create it subsequently refused to join it.

The significance of the speech is that it contains, in a practical form, almost all the elements of a ➤liberal theory of international relations – ➤multilateral diplomacy, the rule of law, the creation of ➤international organizations to mitigate anarchy, ➤collective security, self-determination, ➤free trade and ➤disarmament. Despite the failure of the League of Nations, this programme has had a powerful influence on Western thinking about international affairs and elements of it form part of the general corpus of modern international law. In spirit, if not in substance, it still forms the essence of the liberal approach to world politics and represents the first specifically US contribution to the creation and maintenance of an international order consistent with its basic political philosophy.

**Fourth World** A shorthand term for what the ➤UN has called the ➤least developed countries. These ➤states are distinguished by very low per capita Gross Domestic Products (GDPs), low levels of literacy and low levels of manufacturing development. Geographically, the Fourth World is confined to two continents: Africa and Asia. In Africa, the so-called 'famine belt' stretches across the middle of the continent from Mauritania to the Sudan; in this region the already vulnerable economies have recently been exacerbated by drought. In Asia the ➤paradigm Fourth World state is Bangladesh. States can slip into this category as a result of man-made rather than natural conditions. ➤Afghanistan and Mozambique, states ravaged by revolutionary ➤insurgency and foreign ➤intervention, can be cited here.

In terms of the global ➤hierarchy of states, the Fourth World clearly refers to those actors at the margin of the system. The UN and agencies such as UNCTAD, as well as influential bodies of private interests such as the ➤Brandt Reports Commission, have sought to draw the attention of ➤elites and ➤attentive publics in the rest of the system to the plight of these states. ➤➤quasi-states

*Francophonie* A term used to describe common bonds among those ➤states and communities that share the French language, culture and civilization. Originally a nineteenth-century notion relating specifically to French North

Africa it was revived by President Senghor of Senegal in 1960 and widely publicized in 1962 (the year of Algerian ➤independence) by a special issue of the journal *Esprit*. Its subsequent popularity in the French-speaking world led to the establishment of over two hundred private and public organizations, usually Paris-based, designed specifically to promote the idea of a shared identity and to maintain ties with the thirty-five states which accord some official status to the French language. Four main institutions or areas of activity sustain the idea of *francophonie*: the Agence de Coopération Culturelle et Technique (ACCT, 1966), the annual Franco-African summit conferences, regular meetings of the Francophile States and the French Secretariat of State for *francophonie*. The first occupant of this position, Madame Michaux-Chevy, defined it in this way 'Francophonie is a fight ... for a new international solidarity, for a new intricate and manifold cultural identity and for a common development.' Although its aspirations are vague, it does represent a coherent, if somewhat loose, movement in world politics and serves to demarcate and defend the French-speaking world from possible encroachments from the more dominant Anglo-Saxon civilization. In this sense it has often been described as an agency of French ➤foreign policy or alternatively as an instrument of ➤neo-colonialism.

**Free trade** A trading system between two or more ➤actors. The essence of free trade is that goods are imported without any restrictions, such as ➤tariffs, being placed upon them. From an economic standpoint, free trade increases competition and efficiency. Producers have access to foreign markets, while consumers have access to ➤imports. As a result of free trade the greater specialization occurs in economic activity throughout the system. Individual members become less self-sufficient and more dependent upon others. Consequently, free trade is often associated with the growth of ➤interdependence among actors. As a system of organizing economic relationships it may be directly contrasted with ➤autarky or self-sufficiency.

The advocacy of free trade is usually associated with ➤economic liberalism, at least in its classical phase. Many of these ideas were resuscitated after 1945 under the ➤Bretton Woods system of international economic relations. Under the hegemonial influence of the United States, the major institutional framework for post-war relations was established. Similarly the later negotiations for an international trade ➤regime, under the defunct International Trade Organization (ITO), and the substitute General Agreement on Tariffs and Trade (➤GATT) reflected the same liberal free trade philosophy. The same outlook influenced the ➤Marshall Plan and post-war tariff-cutting negotiations under GATT. Free trade regimes have been most successful in manufacturing (secondary) sectors of economic activity. Agricultural production has rarely been truly free whilst free trade in service industries is technically difficult to ➤implement. As a result the call for 'fair trade' as opposed to free trade is increasingly heard in these sectors.

The philosophical assumptions behind free trade have been criticized by compensatory liberals and others. The rise of the ►Third World has thrown these doubts into sharp relief because the alleged shortcomings are not simply a matter of intellectual fashion or preference. Writers such as Prebisch (1964) have argued that if ►terms of trade penalize certain economies a system of free trade will leave some states permanently at a disadvantage. If those penalized are those that can least afford it, then free trade can exacerbate and widen inequalities within the system. Demands for a free trade regime that ignore such structural inequalities have been opposed by the Third World. The ►New International Economic Order (NIEO) and the United Nations Conference on Trade and Development (UNCTAD) have been used by this constituency to press for changes in the trade regime that will recognize and compensate for these difficulties.

**Free trade area**  A form of economic union between ►states. In a ►free trade area the constituent members agree to abolish ►tariffs and other restrictions on stipulated goods between themselves. However, *vis-à-vis* the rest of the system they continue to maintain the structure of their existing tariffs. A free trade area is therefore a less integrated system than a ►customs union because there is no common external tariff. Although a free trade area is less integrated it may prove to be just as complicated to implement because rules and procedures have to be agreed to prevent goods entering the area from outside via those member states with the lowest range of tariffs. Without clear rules about origin, the states with the lowest external tariffs will benefit most from a free trade area, because ►trade and production will be deflected in their favour. Logic would suggest that a free trade area works best where the members have a similar pattern of external tariffs, or where they agree to substantial ►harmonization of tariffs to reduce differentials. For this reason a free trade area is often seen as the preliminary stage in the formulation of a full customs union.

During the 1950s considerable discussion took place among Western European state members of the ►Organization for European Economic Cooperation (OEEC) about the desirability of forming a free trade area. Agreement was not possible, however, and instead the membership became divided between those states wishing to proceed much further with ►integration in order to form a customs union and the remainder, led by the United Kingdom, wanting to stay with the free trade area idea. The formation of the ►European Community (EC) constituent institution, the European Economic Community under the Treaty of Rome in 1957, seemed to settle the issue. In retaliation the British formed the European Free Trade Association (EFTA) under the Stockholm Treaty in 1959. EFTA was a bargaining chip designed to force the EC to expand its membership and to lower the common external tariff. The EC refused to negotiate with EFTA *en bloc* and in 1961 the British defected to begin access negotiations with the Community.

Free trade areas, as forms of economic integration, were covered by General Agreement on Tariffs and Trade (►GATT). Although it might seem that some aspects of the free trade area idea contradict the GATT principle of non-discrimination, exceptions were made in the Agreement for these types of groupings. Currently the Asia-►Pacific region is following the lead set by Europe in mid-century. Various forms of economic cooperation are under exploration and more specifically the establishment of ►NAFTA exemplifies this trend.

**Free World** A term associated with the ►Cold War era indicating those parts of the world not subject to ►communist influence or domination. Sometimes used as a synonym for the West, although this was erroneous as it was clearly the intention of US ►policy-makers to include non-Western and ►Third World ►states under this rubric. In the immediate post-war period the United States was the architect of a number of overlapping global ►alliances which John Foster Dulles referred to as the 'Free World Alliance'. ►►Containment; Truman Doctrine

**Front** A term that is used in ►international relations in a number of senses:

1 To refer to the scene of fighting, line of battle or the forward position of armed forces. A First World War variation on this was the notion of the 'home' front indicating that the ►war was ►total.
2 Political movements which come together for a specific ►goal such as opposing or toppling a governmental system: e.g. the Patriotic Front (Zimbabwe) and the United Democratic Front (South Africa).
3 A group which is used, or deliberately set up, to feign allegiance to certain acceptable aims or institutions but which in reality is controlled by activists working for another goal. In this sense 'front organizations' have a hidden or latent agenda. This usage was often associated with the ►foreign policy of the Soviet Union, particularly with Leon Trotsky.

**Frontier** A zone of contact between two entities or social systems. It should be distinguished from ►boundary which implies more or less strict territorial limits. Frontier is a much vaguer concept and is projected outwards ('in front') rather than inwards ('within bounds'). A frontier zone therefore refers to an area of delineation between different ►domains. It is often used in a metaphorical sense ('the frontiers of knowledge') but in ►international relations it has tended to signify contact zones between one civilization or culture and another. Thus, the history of European ►imperialism is often presented as a record of pushing forward 'the frontiers of the known world'. Implicit in this notion was the implication that frontiers were not immediately or obviously subject to the post-►Westphalian rules of international contact (►non-intervention, ►sovereignty and ►recognition) that had been established by the boundary-conscious Europeans in their dealings with one another. This double standard has always been a feature of frontier politics especially as practised by, but not in relation to, the European ➤state-system.

The phrase 'frontier thesis' refers specifically to the work of American historian Frederick Jackson Turner who in 1893 argued that the closing of the American West as a frontier in the latter part of the nineteenth century would have important consequences for US politics, especially with regard to overseas expansion. Generally in world politics, frontier has been superseded by boundary, which with its connotations of cartographical territoriality, has brought into play the political and legal conventions associated with state sovereignty. In ➤geopolitics spatial frontiers have been converted into boundaries when two powers begin to approach each other's peripheral territory. This may lead to the creation of ➤buffer states between the two competing systems as was the case, for example, with ➤Afghanistan which straddled the contact zone between Russia and British India. These regions, as the history of Afghanistan illustrates, are often extremely sensitive to sudden shifts in the overall configuration of world politics.

**Front-line states (FLS)** This term referred to those southern African ➤states that shared a territorial border with the Republic of South Africa during the ➤apartheid period, and who were directly or indirectly affected by its policies of ➤destabilization. The FLS were originally an informal grouping of post-➤colonial states who shared a commitment to ending apartheid, securing majority rule in the ➤region and freeing themselves of all forms of ➤dependency. Originally, the term applied only to Zambia, Botswana, Tanzania, Angola and Mozambique, but with the formation of the Southern African Development Coordination Conference in 1980 they were joined by Malawi, Lesotho, Swaziland and the newly independent Zimbabwe. SADCC was a regional ➤integration organization that sought to minimize the region's dependence on South Africa. In 1990 it was joined by Namibia. In 1992 SADCC was transformed into the Southern African Development Community (SADC) in order to play a more powerful regional role and to further economic and regional integration. It was subsequently joined by the post-apartheid South Africa and Mauritius. With the demise of apartheid the term FLS ceased to have any formal meaning. However, given the natural tendency of South Africa, even under President Mandela, to choose national solutions over regional ones, it could be argued that the term still had some relevance. Ironically, the ending of apartheid, for which the FLS have worked so hard, might well serve to legitimize Pretoria's long-standing regional ➤hegemonic ambitions. Although South Africa has formally renounced this aim, many commentators believe that given the sheer relative size of South Africa, the distinction between ➤'leadership' and 'hegemony' will be difficult to sustain.

**Frustration** ➤aggression

**Functionalism** Functionalism was originally conceived, as Claude suggests in his 1971 volume on international organization, as an approach to ➤peace. However, it has implications for ➤integration as well and these ideas have been taken up and developed – particularly by ➤neo-functionalism. Functionalism begins its analysis with the deceptively simple proposition that the provision of common needs can unite peoples across ➤state boundaries. This has produced a concentration by functionalist writers on what has been called the wealth-welfare dimension in ➤international relations and the avoidance of ➤high politics. The functionalist logic, that there are wide and significant areas for the provision of common services and for the meeting of common needs, served to inspire the UN to establish a host of ➤specialized agencies – such as the ➤World Health Organization (WHO). By avoiding the most politically contentious ➤issue areas and concentrating instead upon the wealth-welfare provisions, functionalists tried to focus upon areas of unity rather than disunity between people and states. Functionalists assumed that a natural ➤harmony of interests existed in these matters.

David Mitrany's 1943 book is generally regarded as the first and most persuasive statement of twentieth-century functionalist principles. Mitrany's intellectual milieu was Fabian Social Democracy and his debt to this kind of thinking is clear, in particular his belief that common needs should be met by public provisions of goods and services. Mitrany, in discussing functionalism, sought to draw explicit contrasts with ➤federalism which he saw as being too locked into constitution building and considerations of power-sharing rather than the provision of common needs. In this and in other ways Mitrany anticipated contemporary arguments in favour of ➤transnationalism and ➤interdependence.

Functionalists believed that loyalties could be transferred away from the ➤nation-state towards new functional organizations. This would occur because people would see that the provision of goods and services now depended upon transnational cooperation and, following a kind of utilitarian calculus, they would perceive that their best interests were now being served by the new arrangements. Among political elites also the experience of working in a cooperative framework with others would encourage mutual responsiveness in the future.

Second, functionalists saw 'enmeshment' or 'engrenage' occurring as states increased their cooperation to meet functional tasks. As states became more interdependent it would be increasingly difficult to pull out of these arrangements and increasingly costly to remain outside for any length of time. In this way the functionalists were anticipating the idea of ➤spillover which became a distinctive feature of the neo-functionalist literature in the 1950s and 1960s.

It should not be thought that functionalism, as originally conceived of by Mitrany, was a theory of regional integration. Indeed he was rather hostile towards such developments, believing that they would deflect people's attention away from the true goal of international integration. Moreover, Mitrany saw the possibility that regional ➤federations might simply become superstates or ➤superpowers. The old issues and the old problems of the nation-state would simply be recast in new clothes. Instead, following the dictum the 'form follows function', the true functionalist should not arbitrarily foreclose on any possible arrangements for the future.

**Fungibility** A term used in the analysis of ➤capabilities and ➤power relationships. Literally a thing is held to be fungible if it is transferable or can be used in lieu of another. Thus the inability to achieve such a conveyance is termed 'low fungibility'. Power theorists such as Baldwin (1979) have argued that capabilities or possession suffer from low fungibility and that, as a result, considerable operational restraint will be experienced when ➤actors attempt to use these capabilities out of context. Baldwin has striven hard to establish the point that the attribute of 'powerful' should only be applied in a policy contingency framework.

**Futurology** ➤alternative world futures

# G

**Game theory** Game theory is a formal, mathematical method of studying ►decision-making in situations of ►conflict. Being formal, it expresses its ideas in terms of how things *should* be, given certain assumptions. Notable among these are that those making decisions will act rationally. Being mathematical these ideas are expressed in quantitative, numerate form. Thus it is usually the case in this type of analysis for the decision problem to be represented in the form of matrix with numerical values attached to the outcomes, as shown in figure 1(a). Each player in the game has two choices, giving four possible outcomes. This binary choice situation is, clearly, a simplification of reality. It is a plausible simplification, however. It is possible to include more than two strategies in the matrix and, obviously, to produce more than four outcomes. The numerical values attached to the outcomes are known as pay-offs and it is usual to read one player on the lower left (or south-western) row and the others on the top right (or north-eastern). It is important to note that each player must commit himself to a strategy without knowing what the other has done in advance.

|   | I | II |
|---|---|---|
| **1** | -50<br>+50 | +100<br>-100 |
| **2** | 100<br>100 | 50<br>50 |

(a) *Zero-sum*

Given these ground rules a number of consequences follow. Returning to the point about ►rationality made above, it can be seen that it is necessary to settle upon some agreed definition of what constitutes rationality, at least initially, if the analysis is to proceed. In game theory it is assumed that the players will seek to maximize their gains or to minimize their losses. In other words, in this branch of social analysis rationality is defined in terms derived from microeconomics and with ideas about utility maximization and disutility minimization. In the language of game theory, this rule of rational behaviour is referred to as the ►minimax principle.

Applying the minimax principle can be quite straightforward if the game situation is ►zero-sum. The zero-sum situation can be identified when the pay-offs in the matrix added together equal zero, as shown in the first example. The zero-sum game is the game of pure conflict, there is no cooperation on offer at all and the motives displayed are totally antagonistic. A gain by one party is seen as a loss by the opponent. In these circumstances minimax is a very useful guide to follow and a stable solution, or ►saddle point, will be reached. This is stable because neither player can have any incentive to prefer another strategy.

A second class of games, known by a variety of terms, can be distinguished from the zero-sum game. Using mathematical criteria this second class can be termed non-zero-sum or variable sum games. Using psychological criteria they can be called mixed motive games. The essence of the difference is that the assumption of pure conflict is dropped from the game and the players face outcomes where they can both lose and both win, where coordination and cooperation emerge as alternatives to pure conflict. This switch has the merit, so its proponents allege, of being more isomorphic with reality. The switch has the shortcoming that the notion of minimax rationality can no longer be confidently applied to mixed motive games.

Furthermore, the situational characteristic that game moves are supposed to be made without prior knowledge of what the other side has done appears to be a real handicap when a more coordinated and cooperative strategy is sought. A classic mixed motive game known as the Prisoner's Dilemma (figure 1(b)) raises these central issues in a direct way. Unlike the zero-sum game, this type provides no clear answer to the question 'what is the rational strategy?' As Rapoport (1974) has suggested, the Prisoner's Dilemma actually suggests two types of rationality, individual rationality and collective rationality. Moreover the Prisoner's Dilemma is interesting because it raises psychological issues about being both trusting and trustworthy.

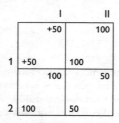

(b) *Prisoner's dilemma*

Another variation within the mixed motive class of games is that known as 'Chicken'. Even the most cursory study of Figure 1(c), which is a matrix for this type of game, will show that outcome 2:II is one which both players would

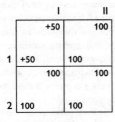

|   | I | II |
|---|---|---|
| **1** | +50      +50 | 100      100 |
| **2** | 100      100 | 100      100 |

(c) *Chicken*

want to avoid. Conversely outcome 1:I, implying some form of cooperation, appears attractive. However, the possibility exists in Chicken to exploit the common desire to avoid 2:II to achieve 2:I or 1:II. The pay-offs in the Chicken game therefore seem to imply that behaving in a deliberately risky, if not reckless, way can be rewarded if the other side gives ground thereby. The temptation to behave in this manner is built into the game situation. Just as the Prisoner's Dilemma has been held to raise parallels with ►arms control and ►disarmament negotiations, so Chicken is held to raise parallels with tactics that are sometimes used in ►crisis situations.

Game theory is not without its critics, as an examination of the works of Schelling (1960) and Rapoport (1964) shows. By remaining a purely formal, quantitative set of precepts game theory retains its purity but in the process has little relevance as an ►ideology or metaphor for certain real-world situations. On the other hand, once the attempt is made to apply game theory to real-world situations its limitations are apparent. Rapoport has argued that in the field of mixed-motive games no unambiguous definition of rationality can be given and that, indeed, the playing out of the mixed motive game involves consideration of factors such as 'trust' which are not encountered in the zero-sum game. Its great value to social science must be as a heuristic device rather than a means of testing or ►verification.

**GATT** The General Agreement on Tariffs and Trade (GATT) was signed by twenty-three ►states in October 1947. From the outset it was envisaged that the Agreement would be an integral part of the putative International Trade Organization (ITO) and that the latter would be an equal ranking institution in the ►Bretton Woods system along with the ►IMF and ►World Bank. When the draft charter of the ITO was not ratified by the USA, GATT became by default the only ►multilateral agreement covering the ►issue area of world ►trade. GATT represents then both a formal international convention and a ►*de facto* ►IGO. The somewhat interim nature of GATT in this latter role was well demonstrated by the fact that member states were properly referred to as 'contacting parties'.

Since 1947 GATT sought to create and maintain a ➤free trade ➤regime. This was implemented by promoting the principle of tariff reductions through multilateral conference ➤diplomacy and by extending the ideas of the ➤most favoured nation and non-discrimination. Exceptions to these ground rules were permitted only in the following circumstances: in states with severe balance of payments difficulties, in ➤customs unions and ➤trade blocs, and where discrimination was intentionally adopted for security purposes, including ➤collective security actions by the UN.

As a forum for trade negotiations GATT promoted what might be termed 'tariff disarmament' at a number of bargaining rounds. The most recent (and significant) of these were the ➤Kennedy, ➤Tokyo and ➤Uruguay sessions. Bargaining behaviour at these meetings followed the ➤reciprocity rather than the ➤harmonization model, as would be expected from parties with often highly conflicting interests and goals. Agreement tended to follow once a consensus on a 'deal' or 'package' emerged. Details were worked out by civil servants, but major initiatives and opening and closing sessions remained the province of ministers and political heads.

Trade issues became increasingly a stage which GATT shared with other parties in the last quarter of the century. In particular the ➤OECD and UNCTAD represented the interests and perspective of the ➤North and the ➤South respectively. Received opinion was coming round to the view that a fresh attempt at something more akin to the erstwhile ITO might be needed to replace the General Agreement. The decision reached at Uruguay to set up the ➤World Trade Organization (WTO) was the natural culmination.

**Gaullism** A loosely structured set of approaches, aspirations and assertions associated with the political life and legacy of the French military and political leader, Charles de Gaulle (1890–1970). Gaullism is derived from three sources: de Gaulle's memoirs, his public utterances, speeches and press conferences and his policies, particularly in the period after he became first President of the Fifth Republic in 1958.

In the language of contemporary analysis, Gaullism may be termed ➤state-centric. It is thus a reassertion of the realist view that ➤states are the primary ➤actors in ➤international relations. In the context of the development of closer integrative ties with Western Europe after the formation of the European Coal and Steel Community (ECSC) and the ➤European Community, Gaullism sought to eschew supranationalism in favour of a more ➤confederal arrangement based upon the state. This conceptualization became known as *Europe des parties*. The peremptory pursuit of these ideas led to considerable stresses and strains within the Community throughout the period of de Gaulle's presidency of France (1958–69).

De Gaulle sought to resist what he saw as the encroachments of the United States by creating Europe as a Third Force between the hegemonial aspirations of the two ➤superpowers. The United Kingdom, seen as part of this 'Anglo-Saxon' tradition, was ironically dubbed as the 'Trojan horse' for US ➤intervention in the Continent. As a result the UK application for membership of the Communities was ➤vetoed by de Gaulle in 1963.

In the context of military ➤security politics, Gaullism provided the rationale for the development of France as an independent nuclear power with the creation of the ➤*force de frappe*. Although the infrastructure for this development was created during the Fourth Republic, it is generally agreed that the elaboration of this into an independent arm was essentially Gaullist. Similarly, the French decision to withdraw from the unified military command structure of NATO in 1966 was perfectly explicable in terms of Gaullist precepts. Indeed the 1966 decision had been signalled a long time before.

Under de Gaulle, France developed a high profile as the leading European critic of US ➤foreign policy. This criticism extended across the whole range of ➤issue areas from the ➤Vietnam War to the role of the dollar in the international payments system, from US ➤intervention in Central America to the role of multinational corporations (➤MNCs).

How far Gaullism endures beyond its founder is a moot point. It certainly constitutes, in its most enduring aspect, a fundamentally different approach to the question of European ➤integration than that represented by supranational enthusiasts and it may be noted somewhat paradoxically that since joining the EC in 1973 successive governments in the United Kingdom have been doggedly Gaullist in their approach to these issues. ➤➤D'Estaing Doctrine; *Francophonie*

**Gender**  In common with other branches of the social sciences and humanities, gender issues entered mainstream ➤international relations via ➤critical theory, ➤peace research and development studies during the 1970s and 1980s. The pioneering work is generally acknowledged to be an article in the influential American journal, *Journal of Conflict Resolution* entitled 'Peace Research: the Cult of Power' by Bernice Carroll, (1972). Carroll argued for a step-level shift in scholarly thinking about ➤conflict away from orthodox centres of ➤power towards the conventionally 'powerless', in this case the role of women in the structure and processes of ➤international society. Re-visioning the ➤scope and ➤domain of conventional International Relations, she argued, would necessitate a re-examination of its key concepts and values. Thereafter, the study of women and ➤war, ➤peace and development began to make inroads on the traditional agenda, culminating in 1988 when the British journal *Millennium* published a special issue on 'Women and International Relations'. Since then, gender issues, gender literature and gender scholars have occupied a highly visible and voluble place in the study, particularly in international political theory. (C. N. Murphy, 1996). Despite this, there is a great deal of controversy regarding the nature of its contribution. Does attention to women and gender address the central research problems of international relations? Or is it properly to be seen as part of a subset of ►human rights issues, such as poverty, ►food, ►migration, ►refugees and so on which, although important, are tributary rather than mainstream? Has it merely added to the range of empirical issues to be addressed (eg the role of women in politics, in ►diplomacy, in warfare, in development, in peace-making etc) or has it made a genuinely substantive impact on how the key concepts of the discipline (►anarchy, ►power, ►sovereignty, the ►national interest, ►security, the ►state ►actors etc.) are conceived, defined and employed? There is no general consensus on this. Unsympathetic critics argue that the extension of the empirical agenda does not require emending existing theories of international behaviour. That is, 'looking for women' adds to, but does not substantially alter, orthodox conceptions of international relations. Moreover, the central thrust of its attack on classical international theory – ►realism's alleged state-centrism – has already been conceded within the discipline mainly as a result of ►interdependence and ►neoliberal theories of co-operation in anarchy. Gender studies may have reinforced this paradigm shift; they did not initiate it. By contrast, others argue that aside from performing the valuable task of identifying international relations as an essentially 'gendered activity' thereby highlighting the marginalization of women, feminist theories have succeeded in recasting IR, especially in terms of its epistemological and onto-logical foundations. Furthermore, they have shifted the boundaries away from the study of juridical states towards the more comprehensive realm of interso-cietal relations, the construction of social identities, the nature of world orders and how these interact with one another. In other words, placing gender at the centre of the subject has changed both its methodology and its content. Whether this amounts to restructuring the subject, making it more inter-disciplinary or abandoning it altogether for a species of developmental sociology and/or social and political theory is the question at issue. Most traditionally trained scholars would agree that gender based studies have helped move human rights ►issue areas out from the subjects' periphery and have highlighted the pitfalls of the conventional 'domestic-international', 'inside-outside', 'private-public' distinctions that have hitherto distorted understanding. But conceding this, they maintain that it is unlikely that greater attention to women and gender will reveal something significant about the issues that are at the core of research in the subject.

**General Assembly** One of the principal organs of the UN. As its main arena for general political debate, the Assembly is the nearest institution to a genuine world forum that exists in contemporary international affairs. Unlike the other organs (the ►Security Council, the Economic and Social Council, the Trustee-ship Council, the Secretariat and the ►International Court of Justice (ICJ)) the General Assembly is the only one in which all member ►states are represented. Its main function is discussion and ►recommendation. Article 10 of the ►UN Charter gives an extremely wide mandate in regard to the scope of its functions.

It can cover 'any questions or any matters within the scope of the present Charter or relating to the powers and functions of any organs provided for in the present Charter.' Despite this seemingly generous remit, there are two important limitations. First, Article 12 confines the Assembly to discussion of, but not recommendation on, any dispute or situation which is simultaneously under consideration by the Security Council. Second, its authority is confined to recommendations that are not binding on individual member states. In addition to discussion and recommendation, the Assembly exercises a supervisory role in relation to all the activities of the UN, and acts as the central coordinating body for all the other organs and agencies. A third major function is financial. It has the ►authority to consider and approve the overall budget and to make recommendations on the budgets of the ►specialized agencies. The Assembly also has sole power to elect the non-permanent members of the Security Council, the Economic and Social Council and the Trusteeship Council and jointly with the Security Council it selects judges for the ICJ. On the recommendation of the Security Council it also appoints the ►Secretary-General. Again, alongside the Security Council, the General Assembly has control over admission to membership of the UN. Finally, the Assembly has a role in the amendment and revision of the Charter, although this is subject to ►ratification by the permanent members of the Security Council.

The very broad range of powers and functions allocated, combined with the tendency to interpret them expansively, have led many observers to conclude that the Assembly is an inefficient and cumbersome body. Suggestions are frequently made on the need for streamlining or slimming down, but the primary rationale of being the only world forum where all members can be heard defeats all efforts at reform.

Despite its apparent impotence in the area of ►decision-making, the Assembly has played a significant role in the maintenance of ►international order, especially during periods of Security Council stalemate. The Charter provides for the calling of 'special sessions' and it is in this area that the Assembly has had most effect. In particular the Uniting for Peace Resolution of 1950, which enables the Assembly to initiate action if the Security Council is unwilling or unable to, has significantly upgraded its importance. There is no doubt that the Assembly has played a larger part in the process of peaceful settlement of disputes than a strict reading of the Charter would indicate. The Uniting for Peace Resolution has been the basis for calling a number of emergency special sessions dealing with ►crises in such divergent areas as the Middle East, South Africa, Eastern Europe, the Congo and ►Afghanistan. It has been estimated that more than 22 per cent of all disputes submitted to the UN have been dealt with solely by the General Assembly, and another 75 per cent have been considered in conjunction with the Security Council. Clearly, while the Assembly is not the primary agency for the settlement of disputes, it has succeeded in interpreting its role in this regard in quite a different way to that envisaged in 1945. ►►UN reform

**Geneva Conventions** ➤conventions on the rules of warfare

**Genocide** This act, or series of actions, is now defined under the 1948 ➤Genocide Convention. The term was first used by Raphael Lemkin in his 1944 study on the occupation of Europe by the ➤Axis states. Prior to the 1948 UN drafting, genocide has been specifically mentioned in the indictments laid against the Nazi ➤leadership at the Nuremberg ➤war crimes trials. Contrary to popular wisdom, genocide is not coterminous with mass murder. Specifically two differences should be noted. First, genocidal behaviour is broader than mass killings. Thus mass deportations, forced resettlement and deliberately induced starvation come under the rubric of genocide. Second, whereas murder can be thought of as behaviour directed at individuals, genocide is directed at groups previously identified by some criterion. Again, conventional conceptions of genocide often expect these groups to be racially distinct. However, as the examples of Stalin's rule in the USSR until 1953 and the genocide in Cambodia/Kampuchea both show, genocidal behaviour patterns can be directed at one's own people – autogenocide. In addition, intentionality to commit the act(s) must be shown in order to substantiate the charge. In this context the ➤nuclear weapons attacks upon ➤Hiroshima and ➤Nagasaki could not be defined as genocide – although they resulted in mass killings of civilians. Controversially the deliberate targeting of civilian populations as proposed under assured destruction doctrines might be so regarded. Certainly the advent of nuclear weapons has raised in an acute form the relationship between mass destruction and genocide. Indeed, some scholars have tried to distinguish such acts as 'omnicide'.

Like other acts of extreme violence, for example ➤war, genocide has increased in both scope and intensity in the twentieth century. Historically genocidal behaviour has a long pedigree and has generally been associated with warfare, ➤colonialism, ➤imperialism, and ➤conflict. Since genocide involves the destruction of particular groups of people, it is particularly associated with ➤nationalism, nation-building and the construction of 'pure' political communities. Thus, its adoption by political ➤elites stems from a nationalistic ➤ideology which emphasizes exclusiveness and a need to disregard conventional morality in pursuit of a particular 'grand design'.

Notwithstanding past performance records, many would concur with the view that genocidal tendencies reached new heights of barbarism combined with bureaucratic zeal under the Holocaust of the 1930s and 1940s when the Nazis sought to eliminate Jews and Judaism from Europe. As the reference above to the events in Cambodia/Kampuchea under Pol Pot shows, genocide has not been eradicated by the passing of the 1948 Convention. Mindful of the psychological and ideological mainsprings behind genocide, few would have expected any other outcome. Unfortunately the failure to use the ➤International Court of Justice to identify responsibility for genocide, as stipulated in Article

9 of the Convention, has severely weakened the efficacy of the ➤regime that was supposedly established in 1948. Furthermore, the failure to regard the Pol Pot leadership as international ➤pariahs *ex post facto*, has increased cynicism about the willingness of ➤states in the system to address politically motivated killings from a truly humanitarian rather than an interest-based perspective. ➤➤Ethnic cleansing; Yugoslavia

**Genocide Convention** The convention was passed by the ➤General Assembly of the ➤United Nations Organization in December 1948 and came into force in January 1951. Genocide is defined in the Second Article as the act of destroying, in whole or in part, a national, ethnical, racial or religious group. Such acts are held to include: killing, seriously injuring or causing mental harm to members of such groups, inflicting upon such groups adverse living conditions so that the physical destruction of the group is threatened, deliberate attempts to prevent members of the group from having children, and forcibly transferring children from one group to another.

In addition to punishing genocide itself, conspiracy to commit genocide, incitement to commit genocide, attempts to commit genocide and complicity in genocide are punishable. Persons held to have committed any of these acts are liable under the convention, whether they are acting in an individual capacity, or as leaders, officials, or agents of governments.

In principle, therefore, the Convention appears to establish a broad based regime for outlawing genocide. It also represents a major extension of international criminal law into an area of world politics highlighted by the Nuremberg trials. It is one of the few instances where 'general principles of law recognized by civilized nations' (see Article 38 of the Statute of the ➤International Court of Justice for details) can be said to have had a major impact on the law-creating process.

In practice, as is the case so often in the most contentious areas of ➤international law, enforcement or ➤implementation of the Convention is more contingent and qualified. In particular, where such acts are carried out as part of government policy, or where such acts have the tacit support of the government of the ➤state concerned, it may be difficult to bring the criminals to account. Furthermore, the charge of complicity may be levelled against other members of the UN, who when confronted with such evidence fail to enforce the standards enshrined in the Convention. ➤➤Ethnic cleansing; Yugoslavia

**Geopolitics** A method of ➤foreign policy analysis which seeks to understand, explain and predict international political behaviour primarily in terms of geographical variables, such as location, size, climate, topography, demography, natural resources and technological development and potential. Political identity and action is thus seen to be (more or less) determined by geography.

According to Harold Sprout in a seminal article (1963) the word 'geopolitics' is a loose translation of the German word 'geopolitik' which meant the exploitation of knowledge to serve the purposes of a national ►regime. In other words, German geopolicy was an overt and subjective policy science designed to further the nationalistic interests of the ►state. In this way, it came to be associated with justifying the aggressive posture of the Third Reich. This identification has had an unfortunate effect on the study of geopolitics, particularly in the English-speaking world, where the concept of ►lebensraum came to be seen as having a malign and sinister effect on German policy. Many concluded that the study of geography in conjunction with politics meant an obsession with strategy, which in turn meant a predilection for ►war and conquest. The German study of geopolitics as a pseudo-science is associated with the work of R. J. Kjellen, Freiderich Ratzel and more especially with the founding in 1924 of the Institute of Geopolitics in Munich under Karl Haushofer. Haushofer had strong links with the Nazi party and after Hitler's rise to power in 1933, he became an influential academic policy adviser. Because Haushofer and the Munich Institute were regarded as exploiting geographical concepts for specific power-political purposes the whole enterprise was frowned upon in UK and US academic circles where the term 'political geography' was preferred to the more value-laden 'geopolitics'.

Nevertheless, a number of important hypotheses have been advanced concerning the geographical dimension of political relationships. These concern the global distribution of land and sea, climatic variations, the distribution of raw materials and the distribution of people and institutions. In relation to the spatial distribution of land and sea, two names in particular stand out, both of whom were writing at the turn of the twentieth century, Mahan (1890) and Mackinder (1919). The gist of Mahan's thesis, which had an important and acknowledged impact on the development of the US navy, was as follows: given that the sea and the great oceans are continuous and uninterrupted and given that sea transport was more efficient and cost effective than land transport, whoever controlled the sea would soon ascend to primacy in world politics. Ability to control the sea depended on the possession of a powerful navy, strategically located overseas ►bases, and an insular and defendable home base. Insular states with these properties (and he saw the United States as a 'continentally insular' state) would therefore play the major roles in establishing the future patterns of world politics. Mackinder, while agreeing with Mahan that the key to understanding world politics is the layout and configuration of the sea, reached the opposite conclusion and saw control of the continental heartland as the vital objective if ►hegemony was to be achieved.

Geopolitical hypotheses connecting climate (i.e. recurring patterns of weather) to political behaviour have a long history stretching back at least to the ancient Greeks. It is known, for example, that both Hippocrates (400 BC) and Aristotle (300 BC) made correlations between climate and human behaviour. It is a commonplace assumption (though no more than that) that the Mediter-

ranean and milder North temperate climates are more conducive to the development of civilization and rapid technological growth than the more equatorial
or Arctic conditions that prevail elsewhere. Therefore, cyclical fluctuations in
climate are important (though not fully understood) variables in predicting
political behaviour. This, of course, is why all states are concerned about the
scientific possibility of effecting weather-controlling schemes; the geopolitical
consequences are potentially enormous. Other hypotheses commonly advanced
concern the distribution of natural resources and population distribution. Again
neither are conclusive although it is assumed as a rule of thumb that the state
power is directly related to the ability to convert raw materials into military
instruments of statecraft, and also that sheer manpower can be decisive ('God
is on the side of the big battalions'). However, technological expertise and
knowledge can and do whittle away at these premises.

The term geopolitics has now acquired some academic respectability although
the subject is still not central to mainline international politics courses. In the
United States especially, it has had a number of outstanding practitioners,
including H. & M. Sprout, J. Hertz and N. J. Spykman. It is still a somewhat
neglected field but it has seen something of a revival in the area of military/
defence analysis. One of the major pitfalls associated with the approach has
been its avowedly determinist character, although its more sophisticated adherents now stress that their hypotheses are 'possibilistic' rather than 'probabilistic'.

In contemporary foreign policy analysis, the ➤realist preoccupation with the
military/territorial dynamic of world politics has largely given way to the
➤neoliberal emphasis on interdependence and an ordering of world politics
based primarily on economic considerations rather than strategic ones. Thus,
'geoeconomics' (or even 'geoinformation') is said to have replaced geopolitics
as the guiding motive in foreign policy formulation and conduct. Nevertheless,
the retention of the prefix 'geo' continues to highlight the importance of
geographical location in international relations. ➤Heartland theory

**Glasnost** Gorbachev Doctrine

**Global governance** Concept and goal associated with the management of
➤international relations in the post-➤Cold War period. Initially associated with
Willy Brandt, the term refers to a perceived need to foster the growth of
multilateral systems of regulation and methods of management to encourage
global interdependence and sustainable development. It thus has ➤North–South,
security and ➤human rights perspectives. Two major reports have been published
in this connection: 'Common Responsibility in the 1990s: the Stockholm
Initiative on Global Security and Governance' (1991) and 'Our Global Neighbourhood: Report on the Commission on Global Governance' (1995).

Global governance should not be confused with ➤world government, which
implies a singular or unitary authority. Nor does it focus exclusively on
intergovernmental relationships. Rather, it involves the participation of non-

governmental organizations (NGOs), multinational corporations (MNCs), citizens' movements, the global mass media and global capital markets. There is no single model or form of global governance; it is envisaged as a dynamic and complex process of interactive ➤decision-making covering a wide range of common problems and ➤issue areas. The concept is a fuzzy one but its central thrust is a movement away from the decentralized ➤Westphalian system with its emphasis on the rights of ➤sovereignty and the duties of ➤non-intervention, towards a more cooperative and consensual system of management based on respect for democratic principles, the free market and a belief in a common humanity and destiny. An important dimension of the idea is reform of the ➤United Nations system. Two recent developments in particular are associated with this idea: an increased emphasis on ➤humanitarian intervention and ➤UN involvement in the spread of democratic values. Regarding the latter, the UN broke new ground in 1989 when it organized and monitored the entire electoral process in Namibia. After the success of this initiative, the UN subsequently monitored elections in Nicaragua and Haiti (1990), Angola (1992), Cambodia (1993), El Salvador, South Africa and Mozambique (1994), and various republics of the former Soviet Union in 1995. An Electoral Assistance Division within the UN's Department of ➤Peacekeeping Operations was created in 1992 and between April 1992 and May 1995 it provided technical assistance in electoral matters to 55 states. This is now regarded as a growth area within the UN and is a significant contribution to global (or 'good') ➤governance.

**Globalism** Globalism has two discrete and analytically separate meanings. First, it is used in the context of ➤foreign policy analysis to characterize an ➤orientation taken by ➤hegemonial ➤states. Second, it is used in ➤international relations to identify a particular approach to issues perceived to be global.

In the first sense, therefore, globalism is the tendency to collapse the distinction between the ➤national interest and ➤issue areas in the rest of the system. Accordingly, there is a high propensity for such 'globalist' states to evince interventionist tendencies when conducting their foreign policy. Globalism requires a significant ➤capability, particularly in the military and/or economic dimensions and the willingness to use such capability to secure perceived goals, often at considerable cost. Ideologically, globalism will be sustained and justified by reference to a world view which sees the global ➤actor as uniquely qualified to pursue interventionist behaviour. This perceptual sense has appropriately been termed 'nationalistic universalism'.

During the ➤Cold War era both the United States and the Soviet Union showed globalist tendencies. Militarily, they were the most significant state actors in the system. Economically, they offered competing 'models' for development. ➤Ideologically US exceptionalism and Soviet attachment to Leninist thinking about ➤imperialism encouraged the ➤leaderships in both states to follow interventionist policies, particularly in the ➤Third World. The collapse of ➤communism has removed that model, whilst American ➤declinism evidenced by such factors as the ➤Vietnam Syndrome has qualified American interventionism. This is now more evident in ➤multilateralism than Cold War globalism.

Globalism in the second sense refers to the viewpoint which holds that such problems as ➤pollution, ➤population and conservation can only be dealt with on a global scale. Moreover, this view sees the state-as-actor approach as being inadequate to the challenge these issues present. Non-state actors must be admitted into the policy process if the global challenge is to be met. This admission will take place at a number of stages. First, in the ➤definition of the situation non-state actors, including individuals, may be able to provide the expertise and the understanding to reach an adequate definition. Second, at the ➤implementation stage non-state actors, particularly ➤international organizations, may be required to establish the ground rules and monitor the subsequent conduct of the participants.

While it does not necessarily lead to advocacy of ➤world government, globalism does emphasize the extent to which cooperation must be conducted among a system of mixed actors. Accordingly it can be regarded as a form of ➤pluralism. Many of the assumptions of globalism are derived from theories about collective goods. It has a strong family resemblance to ideas about ➤global governance.

**Globalization** The process whereby ➤state-centric agencies and terms of reference are dissolved in favour of a structure of relations between different ➤actors operating in a context which is truly global rather than merely ➤international. The implication is that individual actors – and, in particular, ➤states held to exercise ➤sovereignty – have 'lost control' of these processes and therefore of the consequential outcomes. The term is imprecise and its use is often heavily laden with ➤ideological baggage. It has become particularly popular in ➤international political economy (IPE) and in cultural studies. Thus, evidence is sometimes adduced (or an assumption is simply made) in support of a 'global economy' or a 'global culture'. Apart from its lack of precision, globalization needs to be placed in some kind of historical context and it provokes crucial questions about ➤governance. In particular, what evidence is there that some form of ➤global governance exists to manage these processes?

Economists have been aware of the significance of the economies of scale since the development of the modernization of production following the Industrial Revolutions in Europe. Marxist analysis in particular was based upon the essential notion that the intrinsic nature of capitalism was such that entrepreneurial talent would not be constrained by geographical and legal boundaries. The growth of a dynamic ➤trade system and the consequent development of classical payment arrangements like the ➤gold standard have been seen by political economists as early yet decisive pointers towards the globalization of the world economy. At the centre of this process is the idea of the Market and in particular the market for finance, capital, allied with the MNC is seen as a major agent and conduit for the globalization of production. In the ►postmodern world system the essential link has been provided by the development of communications – both physical and symbolic – to a point where major actors in the economic system are thinking and acting upon global assumptions.

In political studies globalization ideas have been significant in thinking about ►ideology and in political behaviour in terms of ►issue areas such as ►ecopolitics and ►human rights. Writers like Huntington (1991) and Fukuyama (1992) have pointed to the globalization of ►liberalism following the end of the Cold War. This political acculturation has reinforced the previously noted tendency to think in terms of capitalism as the dominant paradigm with the IPE and this scholarship within political studies has also identified democratization in places like Eastern Europe and Southern Africa as reinforcement for the liberal paradigm. Meanwhile in terms of the ►environment and human rights clear evidence of the need for global codes of conduct and – in the case of the former – for ►regime creation can be cited to support a developing framework of political globalization.

►Religion is in a profound sense a globalizing belief system and in a more general sense all ideational tendencies evince this characteristic. Secular movements such as Feminism can similarly be shown to have the kind of interconnectedness that is the defining characteristic of globalization. The reactions to the ►AIDS pandemic amongst the Western ►elites and the increasing evidence of global criminal networks and connections are further instances of a burgeoning cultural globalization. Some writers have recently sought to link this into theories of ►imperialism through the concept of ►cultural imperialism (Mazrui, 1977)

It is now a conventional wisdom that the overlapping processes outlined above amount to a seismic shift in ►international relations. They have varied in intensity from place to place and have been highly differentiated in their effects. For this reason some have posed the questions as to whether the term 'global' is wholly appropriate. In IPE, for instance, the global agenda has been set by the ►North and the management IGOs associated with that faction – the G7/G8 and the OECD. Paradoxically, globalization may evince ►regional variations and this may be the key to locating governance responses to these processes. For instance, the creation of a single currency for the ►European Union may introduce an element of management into a system which has been characterized by 'floating' mechanisms since the collapse of the ►Bretton Woods arrangements. The recent call for an economic ►security council under the United Nations aegis similarly reflects the need for management ►capabilities to be effected. For both campus and the chancellery, the existential facts of globalization present challenges that cannot be ignored. ►►Localization

**Goals** A term used in policy analysis to identify the objectives pursued by actors. Indeed in some treatments the terms 'goal' and 'objective' are seen as interchangeable. Traditional analysis in the literature on ►international relations tended to equate the question with the idea of the ►national interest. This tended to skew the subsequent discussion in a ►state-centric direction. Thus non-state actors – though clearly pursuing goals/objectives – could not logically be held to be pursuing national interests. There was also a tendency in traditional analysis to see national interests as immutable and objectively determined. The distinguished writer Arnold Wolfers attacked this approach in his essay on goals (1962). Wolfers argued that goals should be treated as 'significant variables', being susceptible to a wide variety of interpretations. Wolfers in a famous dichotomy discussed goals in terms of two typologies: possession goals and milieu goals. Possession goals are those objectives that relate to the attainment of the actor's values, for example ►security or prosperity. Milieu goals are those objectives that relate to the attainment of values beyond national boundaries, for example ►environmental security or ►UN ►reform. Security can reasonably appear as both a possession and a milieu goal because, as Bull observed (1961) security is both a national and an international objective. Indeed the burgeoning field of ►security studies eschews state-centrism by precisely defining security in both senses here. Wolfers makes a further distinction between 'direct national goals' and 'indirect national goals'. This dichotomy rests entirely upon who is defining the substance of the goal(s) sought after, the former are state interests, the latter sectional or private interests. This raises a further qualification into the discussion of goals: whose ►definition of the situation is critical? Tracking down the sources of goals is an empirical question but in general terms the institutional structure of the particular actor will give the primary clues. Benefits and costs may well be distributed differentially from the pursuit of goals. Thus the policy of ►*détente* – pursued at various instances by the United States during the ►Cold War era – realized differential benefits and costs. Interest groups concerned to maintain a high level of defence spending and ethnic lobbies committed to anti-Soviet ►perceptions did not see *détente* as a goal worth pursuing at all costs or in all circumstances. Political ►leaderships might become embroiled in a particular goal attainment for side benefits – electoral opportunism for example.

The cost factor and the time factor are two important variables in both the formulation and the ►implementation of goals. Goals expressed as core values might be seen as worth paying any price for but in practical terms 'how much is enough?' considerations will always come into play. Even such a central possession/milieu goal as security is not an absolute but a relative objective and cost calculations help to make it so. Time too is relevant as a variable. Many goals are defined in medium or long term contexts. Inis Claude's seminal work on ►IGOs, *Swords into Ploughshares*, is an examination of institutions like the ►united nations against the benchmarker of certain long-run milieu goals – for example ►disarmament. Amongst state actors, long-run goals will often express broad national objectives and will be reflected in a ➤bipartisan approach – for example, the policy of ➤containment was shared as a long term goal by both Democratic and Republican leaderships. Conversely most of the 'great debates' within state ➤diplomacy have been about long-term goals and ➤orientations. For example, in the United States about ➤isolationism (in its various manifestations) and ➤internationalism.

**Gold exchange standard** A system of international payments where individual currencies are tied to a fixed exchange rate with a stipulated currency which is, itself, fully convertible into gold, also at a fixed rate. After 1945 under the ➤Bretton Woods system, a gold exchange standard operated with the US dollar acting as a fully convertible store of value and means of exchange within the system. This system lasted for a quarter of a century and under its aegis international economic relations were rebuilt and rekindled. Impressive growth targets were achieved by individual ➤states particularly amongst the advanced industrial countries (➤AICs) and overall world ➤trade increased significantly as a result. The system collapsed in the 1970s when following the devaluation of the US dollar it became impossible to 'hold the line' on fixed parities and instead currencies were allowed to fluctuate or 'float'.

With hindsight it can be seen that the maintenance of the system was too contingent upon the strength of the dollar and the willingness of other international actors to hold dollars and not to convert them into gold. France, in particular, was reluctant to cooperate in this fashion arguing that, in effect, other major trading states were being invited thereby to underwrite US ➤foreign policy. Economically, it could be argued that the system of fixed parities was too conservative and that it encouraged political and financial authorities to regard a particular rate as sacrosanct. Accordingly, when the adjustments were made in rates the situational context would invariably be one of ➤crisis.

Analytically, the post-war gold exchange standard can appropriately be seen as correlated with US ➤hegemony in the system. This was clearly institutionalized in the ➤IMF and given its first and perhaps clearest expression in the European Recovery Programme or ➤Marshall Plan of 1948 – 52. Similarly, the collapse of the system in the 1970s is also correlated with the relative decline in US ability to maintain the ➤regime. ➤➤Pax Americana

**Gold standard** A system of international payments where individual currencies are tied to a fixed exchange rate with gold. This pricing of individual currencies enables exchange rates between them to be calculated, pro rata, once their gold price is known. This rate, at which it is possible to exchange one currency for another, and/or for gold, is known as ➤parity.

The international gold standard was an important mechanism for underwriting international ➤trade and payments for almost two hundred years up to 1914. Indeed it reached its peak in the decades immediately before 1914, when the United Kingdom was the leading ➤state in the international system under the

➤hegemonial arrangement known as ➤Pax Britannica. The leading states in the system went off the standard during the First World War in order to finance the enormous expenditures caused by this protracted war of ➤attrition.

An attempt was made after 1919 to return to the standard but the recession in economic activity known as the 'Great Depression' caused states to abandon the standard and to allow currencies to fluctuate or 'float'. Thus, the United Kingdom left the standard in 1931 and the United States in 1933. By accident rather than design, therefore, the system became in effect a ➤gold exchange standard during these rather uncertain years. After 1945 a full-blown gold exchange standard was instituted under the ➤Bretton Woods system. Reflecting the hegemonial position of the United States, the dollar became in effect 'as good as gold' as a store of value and means of exchange within the system. Like the old pre-1914 system parities were fixed against the dollar, while that currency had a fixed parity in terms of gold. This system itself collapsed in the early 1970s and, to date, no attempt has been made to reintroduce a system of international liquidity based on gold.

**Good governance** ➤global governance; ➤governance

**Good Neighbor** An attempt to reverse the traditional US policy of protectionism and ➤intervention in Central and Latin America. Under the ➤Monroe Doctrine (1823) and the Roosevelt Corollary (1904) the United States had sought unrivalled hemispheric superiority in the ➤region to the extent that is reserved the right to intervene, by force of arms if necessary, in the internal affairs of sovereign ➤states south of the Rio Grande. This policy, not unnaturally, attracted much criticism and resentment with the result that the United States in the twentieth century began to abandon direct methods of coercive control and moved towards a more subtle mechanism of dominance (➤dollar diplomacy). In 1933 President Roosevelt inaugurated another more dramatic shift in American policy when he proclaimed the Good Neighbor doctrine. In his inaugural address he declared that he 'would dedicate this Nation to a policy of the good neighbor who resolutely respects himself and, because he does so, respects the rights of others'. No geographical region was mentioned, but it soon became clear that this policy initiative was directed at Latin America. Accordingly in 1933, at the seventh conference of the American states in Montevideo, the United States signed a ➤non-intervention treaty, in 1934 it abrogated the Platt Amendment which had placed restrictions on Cuban ➤sovereignty, in 1935 it withdrew troops from Haiti and in 1936 it signed a treaty with Panama terminating its right of military intervention outside the Canal zone. After the Second World War the Rio Treaty, the first general security pact created by the United States, was signed and this process culminated in the establishment of the organization of American states (OAS) in 1948, which sought to draw the states of the region closer together in social and economic matters and deals with ➤security, principally at that time the threat of the spread of ➤communism in the hemisphere.

Most analysts consider the Good Neighbor policy to be somewhat fraudulent. It replaced policies of overt military intervention and financial control with a more indirect form of US dominance, namely the enlisting of indigenous political, military and business ➤elites to maintain US interests. The US Export-Import bank has been used to lock the economic systems of the individual states firmly into the US economy, and the United States has trained and equipped local police and military forces with the specific purpose of suppressing national revolutionary movements which may threaten their dominance. US support for unpopular regimes coupled with instances of military intervention (Cuba 1961, Dominican Republic 1965, Grenada 1987, Panama 1989) have led many to question the ➤credibility of this policy. No one doubts though, that its purpose is to maintain US ➤hegemony.

**Good offices** A technique in ➤international law relating to the involvement of a third party in the peaceful settlement of disputes. The procedure involves attempts by the third party to bring the opposing sides to ➤negotiation. In theory it can be distinguished from ➤mediation which implies the active participation of the third party in the negotiation process itself, but in practice the two approaches often converge. Good offices is generally non-participatory and is limited to providing a channel of communication between the disputants, thus paving the way for direct ➤bilateral ➤diplomacy. It differs from ➤adjudication and ➤arbitration in that its object is to stimulate diplomatic dialogue between the contending parties and not to stipulate settlement provisions or to provide means for their implementation. The ➤Hague Conventions of 1899 and 1907 tended to classify 'good offices' and 'mediation' together. Thus both 'are exclusively concerned with the giving of advice and are never of binding force'. In practice mediation tends to be more activist than good offices. All signatories to the Conventions were accorded rights to offer good offices or mediation in international disputes and the offer was not to be construed by the disputants as an unfriendly act. Examples of good offices would be Switzerland's role in formally ending hostilities between Japan and the United States in 1945, or the part played by France in initiating US–North Vietnamese negotiations in Paris in February 1970. An example of mediation would be the US role in the ➤Arab–Israeli conflict since 1973. In the latter case the third party played a much more ➤interventionist role than in either of the former cases.

It is useful to distinguish between 'good offices' and 'interest sections'. The latter usually refers to situations where diplomatic relations have been broken off and a third party embassy is entrusted with overseeing the interests of one side. Sometimes a ➤state may request that its own diplomats be allowed to operate from a third party embassy. This occurred during the ➤Falklands conflict when the United Kingdom established an interest section in the Swiss Embassy in Buenos Aires. Using the good offices of a neutral third state or establishing interest sections are common devices in a world characterized by extreme ideological hostility. Thus, Israel, Libya, Iran, South Africa, as well as the United States and the former Soviet Union have all at some time found it convenient to establish direct contact with their opponents through friendly third-party intermediaries.

**Gorbachev Doctrine** Western media term for new initiatives, particularly relating to ➤superpower cooperation in Soviet ➤foreign policy after 1985 under the tutelage of Mikhail Gorbachev. The reorientation of Soviet domestic society symbolized by the concepts of glasnost (openness) and perestroika (restructuring) were perceived to have important external consequences. In 1985–6 the Soviet ➤decision-making ➤elite apparently concluded that superpower status and the ideological and political ➤hegemony that this implied carried a heavy economic cost with correspondingly little positive benefit. Despite the ostensible 'success' of the Brezhnev era which witnessed the US débâcle in Vietnam, socialist ➤revolutions in Angola, Mozambique and Ethiopia as well as a heightening of revolutionary momentum in Latin America, the Soviet Union had made few tangible gains. In fact these initiatives proved burdensome. Angola and Mozambique quickly assumed debtor status, Ethiopia was ravaged by famine, and the 1979 invasion of ➤Afghanistan put increasing strains on the Soviet military and economic systems. An energy crisis in Eastern Europe in 1984–5 further exacerbated the problem, as did growing Soviet dependence on Western sources of high ➤technology and vital food commodities. In addition a renewal of the ➤arms race with the United States and more especially disquiet at the proposed US Strategic Defense Initiative (➤SDI) and the economic costs that the installation of a reciprocal system would invoke, resulted in a fundamental reappraisal of the basic ➤goals and directions of Soviet foreign and defence policies. In particular, the Gorbachev doctrine led to the Intermediate Range Nuclear Force (➤INF) ➤Treaty signed in Washington in 1987, which was the most significant ➤arms control measure since the beginning of the ➤Cold War era in 1946. It also led to direction-shifts in Soviet involvement in Afghanistan, southern Africa, the Middle East and the Persian Gulf. In Afghanistan (the invasion of which Gorbachev declared to be a 'mistake') Soviet forces were withdrawn in 1989. In Southern Africa, the removal of Cuban troops from Angola and its linkage with Namibian ➤independence from South Africa was a direct consequence of Gorbachev's 'new thinking' about the Soviet role in the ➤region. In the Middle East it led to new ➤peace initiatives by the former Soviet Foreign Minister Edvard Shevardnadze (a Gorbachev appointee) and a restoration of diplomatic relations with Israel. Similarly in the Persian Gulf region there were attempts at a diplomatic ➤rapprochement with Iran. All these directional changes were perceived to be logical consequences of the 'revolution' in Soviet domestic, social and economic policies signalled by glasnost and perestroika. On the level of ➤ecopolitics the relative openness of the former Soviet authorities regarding the Chernobyl ➤nuclear accident in 1986 was its most dramatic manifestation. It is difficult to assess the depth to which the doctrine penetrated Soviet decision-making circles, but most Kremlinologists argued that a rationalization of the complex, compartmentalized and bureaucratic character of foreign policy formulation was well under way before the sudden collapse of the Soviet Union in 1991. Reconstruction and modernization of its political economy meant a large scale transfer of resources away from the military and into the civil sector. This in turn led to a new spirit of ➤*détente* in ➤international relations which became manifest in the ➤Persian Gulf War which witnessed Soviet acquiescence and indeed tacit support for Allied policies.

Many analysts have argued that the liberalization of Eastern Europe which occurred dramatically in 1989 was a direct consequence of the Gorbachev Doctrine, in particular its departure from the ➤Brezhnev penchant for active interference in the internal affairs of ➤bloc ➤states. While this radical policy shift was welcomed outside the Soviet Union the internal repercussions were a cause of great concern not merely over Gorbachev's own political future, but more seriously over the continued coherence of the Union itself and of the leading role of the ➤communist party within it. For over seventy years the communist party had been the unifying force which kept more than 100 different nationalities together within the largest country on earth, covering about one-sixth of the earth's surface, and with a total population of about 280 million. Growing nationalist unrest, ethnic rivalries and economic dissatisfaction – all of which have been exacerbated by glasnost and perestroika – created ➤secessionist movements in the rimland Republics which led to the disintegration of the Soviet Empire. By the end of 1989 the Baltic Republics (Estonia, Latvia and Lithuania) had already signalled their interest to seek a new relationship with Moscow. The other 'autonomous' republics, Ukraine, Byelorussia, Moldavia, Armenia, Azerbaijan, Georgia and the Muslim republics of Kazakhstan, Kirgizia, Tadhikstan, Turkmenistan and Uzbekistan followed suit soon after. On 19 August 1991 in an attempt to reverse the liberalizing effects of perestroika and glasnost both inside and outside the USSR, a ➤*coup d'état* was attempted by conservative malcontents within the Gorbachev administration. The failure of the coup, ironically, signalled the end of Gorbachev's political career. The role played by Boris Yeltsin who favoured a decentralized ➤Commonwealth of Independent States (CIS) to replace the centralized Soviet Union, effectively scuppered Gorbachev's more limited top-down reform proposals. The failed coup accelerated the dissolution of the Soviet Union and on 25 December Gorbachev formally resigned as President and handed over his functions to Yeltsin, the first elected national leader in Russian history. Thus by the beginning of 1992 the USSR had formally ceased to exist as a ➤geopolitical entity and as a subject of ➤international law. ➤➤Nineteen eighty-nine

**Governance** Governance is not a synonym for government. While both concepts refer to systems of rule, 'government' suggests activities that are regulated by a formal authority whereas 'governance' is much looser and refers to activities that are not necessarily backed by any legal or sovereign power. Governance thus has a wider meaning than government. It embraces governmental institutions, but it also covers more informal regulatory mechanisms which exist in the absence of central authority. In ➤international relations the concept is often used coterminously with institution-building and ➤regime-creation. This culminates in the idea of ➤global governance. ➤Liberal theories of IR are predicated on the notion that while ➤anarchy presumes a lack of government, it does not also presume an absence of governance. The term is thus closely bound up with the concept of 'order', which consists of routinized sets of arrangements which maintain stability and also provide for change.

In current usage, the word 'governance' is often preceded by the adjective 'good'. The idea of good governance is associated with the spread of democracy and free market economics, particularly in the conditionality clauses issued by the ➤World Bank and the ➤IMF. Its evaluative connotations implicitly – and sometimes explicitly – condemn arbitrary and self-seeking rule, corruption and cronyism. ➤Quasi-states

**Great powers** Term associated with traditional, especially realist, analyses of ➤international relations. It refers to the ranking of ➤states primarily in terms of their military and economic capabilities. Hence the hierarchical structure of world politics is often characterized as consisting of great powers (or ➤super-powers), ➤middle powers, ➤small powers and ➤micro-states. The term itself can be traced back to fifteenth-century Italian politics but the first time it was adopted as an orthodox diplomatic concept was with the signing of the Treaty of Chaumont in 1817. As a result of the Congress of Vienna (1815) five states, Austria, Britain, France, Prussia and Russia, had informally conferred on themselves great power status. The intention was that these states acting in concert would adopt a managerial role in relation to the maintenance of order in the European ➤state-system. The Concert system with its emphasis on controlled ➤multilateral management thus replaced the somewhat 'loose' ➤balance of power system that had preceded the Napoleonic Wars. Throughout the nineteenth century there was a self-conscious effort by these states (they were sometimes joined by Italy after 1860) to enforce, in their own interests, the '➤peace and ➤security' of Europe. The interests of lesser powers, for example Poland, were often sacrificed on the altar of great power unity. Outside Europe two other states came to be regarded as having great power status: the United States after its defeat of Spain in 1898 and Japan after victory over Russia in 1904–5. In the twentieth century the tendency to assign special status in diplomatic conferences continued and great power status was institutionalized in both the ➤League of Nations and the ➤United Nations where five states (the

United States, the United Kingdom, France, the Soviet Union and China) were given permanent membership of the ➤Security Council with the power of ➤veto. Since the Second World War the term 'great power' has given way to 'superpower', a word first coined by Fox (1944). The use of the latter term denoted the emergence of a new class of power which is clearly superior in military/economic terms to the traditional European great powers. After a brief flirtation with the term 'superpowers', most analysts now prefer the traditional stipulation. Although the nomenclature may have altered the managerial roles they seek to adopt remain in essence the same.

It is a matter of some dispute in the literature of international relations as to what constitutes great powerhood. In most discussions the military dimension is paramount: great powers are generally those that can maintain their security independently and against all others. They are in the first rank of military prowess. This means, at the very least, a developed strategic nuclear ➤capability. It is sometimes alleged that economic strength alone can confer great power status. Thus, Japan is often spoken of in these terms. But although economic strength is a necessary condition, it is not generally regarded as a sufficient one.

In addition to military and economic strength, great powers normally have global if not universal interests and are usually characterized as possessing the political will to pursue them. The United States, for example, although long regarded by others as a great power, has not always displayed the political will to behave like one, especially during the period until 1917 and between 1921 – 41. It was only after the Second World War that the United States consistently and self-consciously adopted this posture. The United Kingdom and France, on the other hand, have frequently displayed the political will associated with great power status and also sometimes perceived themselves as having world-wide interests, but because they are not in the first rank in military and economic terms they are no longer considered to be members of the great power club. They are more properly regarded as ➤middle or secondary powers even though they are still accorded the formal institutional trappings of membership of this category in the UN. This category has undergone a revival in current usage as a consequence of the collapse of the superpower typology. ➤➤Nineteen eighty-nine

**Green movements** The growth of ➤environmental politics as an ➤issue area in ➤international relations has been correlated with the growing activity of such movements. A broad classificatory distinction can be made between ➤transnational and ➤state-centric movements. Typical of the first type is Greenpeace, whilst Green Parties focus on political activity – and representation – within ➤states. Both types share a non-traditional approach to political activity in the sense that they use non-violent protest activism as a key means of raising the profile of certain issues.

Greenpeace began as a movement against ➤nuclear weapons testing in the early 1970s, but they soon moved into direct action fields including whaling and toxic waste ►pollution later in the decade. At the same time their lobbying activity of political ►decision-making centres became more sophisticated. The movement was granted observer status by the ►United Nations and it became increasingly involved in monitoring agreements such as the London ►Dumping Convention. Greenpeace established a base in the ►Antarctic in 1986 to monitor the activities of the states with territorial claims to the continent. The extent of the efficacy of Greenpeace's campaigning was revealed following the destruction of the surveillance ship *Rainbow Warrior* by French authorities in 1985. Subsequently it became clear that the French ►intelligence and counter-►terrorist organizations had been monitoring the activities of Greenpeace for months before the 'coup de main' in New Zealand. Latterly, Greenpeace has moved more into mainstream political activity and organizational complexity. As a result it has dropped off some of its more radical supporters on the way. There is also evidence that some of their adversaries – e.g. ►oil companies – are willing to take them on.

The movements in Green parties have been primarily a European phenomenon. They are political parties in the sense that they contest national and local elections but they are 'Green' also in the sense that they endorse the same kinds of goals as the transnational versions. In those states with systems of proportional representation (PR) the Greens have sometimes been able to muster sufficient voting power to exercise a 'swing position' on key issues. The growth of the EC/EU has meant that these groups can operate also at the level of the European Parliament. Prior to ►unification, the Green party in the former West Germany was particularly effective at this kind of swing positioning.

There is no doubting the contention that the activities of the Green movements discussed above have contributed to a ►paradigm shift in the last quarter of the twentieth century. Environmental politics is now accepted into the mainstream agenda as both level two and level three activities. Their alternative strategies for global survival into the next century – although they posit a significant shift away from state-centrism – are widely seen to have much cogency.

**Grotian view of international society** Concept employed originally by Martin Wight and developed by Hedley Bull to describe a twentieth-century view of ►international society which appears to bear great resemblance to the classical presentations of Hugo Grotius (1583–1645) in *Mare Liberum* (1609) and *De Jure Belli ac Pacis, On the Law of War and Peace* (1625). Bull's view is that underlying much of the theory and practice of ►international relations since the First World War and enshrined in the Covenant of the ►League of Nations, the Paris Pact, the ►United Nations Charter and the charter of the International Military Tribunal at Nuremberg is a formula for orderly international conduct which is largely derived from the ►domestic analogy as used by seventeenth-century social contract theorists. The central Grotian assumption is that of solidarity, or potential solidarity, of ➤states with respect to the enforcement of ➤international law. The doctrine seeks to establish ➤world order by restricting the rights of states to go to ➤war for political purposes and promotes the idea that ➤force can only legitimately be used to further the purposes and goals of the international community as a whole. In other words, as in domestic society, the private use of violence is severely proscribed. The rules which Grotius devised were biased in favour of the 'just' party and therefore designed to support and encourage a solidarist conception of the international community.

The principle of ➤collective security is the culmination of the neo-Grotian movement in twentieth-century international thought, the idea being that, apart from ➤self-defence, the legitimate use of force is assigned to ➤international society itself and not its separate members. Of course, this formula depends for its success on the common ➤recognition by states of a degree of communality, a willingness to forgo narrower conceptions of the ➤national interest and a desire to promote the wider cause of international solidarity. None of these essential prerequisites operated during the inter-war years with the result that not only was the new Grotian world order not forthcoming but also that older devices for the maintenance of order (e.g. ➤balance of power) were weakened to such an extent that they too failed to keep the ➤peace. Bull's conclusion is that, although the attempt to apply the solidarist formula has failed in the twentieth century, this does not mean that conditions will never arise when it might succeed.

**Groupthink** Groupthink is the tendency, noted in small group ➤decision-making situations, for individuals within a group to cease thinking for themselves and to merge their opinions with the prevailing group viewpoint. As a result, these individuals may fail to voice doubts and disagreements about decisions that are under consideration by the group. This tendency towards conformity and concurrence may so inhibit critical thinking that fundamental, and even fatal, errors will occur. In summary, then, groupthink is a theory of defective decision-making.

The US social psychologist, Irving Janis (1972), first used the idea. In his book, Janis compares and contrasts four ➤foreign policy 'fiascos' with two successes – all the examples being taken from US foreign policy in the twentieth century – and then draws certain inferences about groupthink and how it might be avoided in the future. There is, for Janis, an inverse relationship between the groupthink syndrome and the effective performance of the group.

Janis argues that the primary causal condition for groupthink to occur is group cohesiveness. Loyalty to the group, and in particular loyalty to the leader, is likely to be important. Individuals may feel that taking an independent line will lead them into conflict with the colleagues whose respect and friendship they value. This attitude will make the would-be deviant think hard before challenging the intellectual orthodoxy of the majority.

In the 1972 original, and in the 1982 revision, Irving Janis stipulates other antecedent conditions. The most significant are:

1 That the group is isolated from contradictory and critical opinions that would otherwise significantly criticize the policy.
2 That the leadership within the group is 'directive', that is to say that the group has a strong committed leadership.
3 The existence of a high level of stress within the group caused by a ➤perception that the stakes at issue are high. In short, that the group faces a ➤crisis.

These antecedent conditions are necessary, although not sufficient, conditions for the occurrence of groupthink. The principal defects caused by groupthink can be summarized as:

1 The group fails to survey a sufficient range of alternatives or objectives.
2 The group fails to examine the risks involved due to wishful thinking.
3 The group fails to re-examine courses of action that had been previously rejected.
4 The group fails to work out contingency plans.

Janis's work on decision-making and groupthink syndrome is certainly prescriptive. By contrasting 'fiascos' and 'successes', by stipulating how groupthink may be avoided, Janis is clearly identified as an optimist who believes that errors can be avoided, or at least reduced in number and consequence, by more vigilant attention to process and procedure.

Other approaches to decision-making have avoided the dichotomy between 'good' and 'bad' that emerges from Janis's work. Thus at least one analyst has suggested that policy-making consists not of looking for the best solution, but rather for 'satisfactory' ones, following a procedure known as 'bounded rationality'. If one starts from the position that policy-making is the art of 'muddling through' then Janis's checklist of allegedly defective processes looks uneasily like the norm. Recent work on the ➤bureaucratic structure in which policy is made has suggested that 'standard operating procedures' play an influential role in policy-making within the organizational milieu.

Irving Janis's groupthink ideas remain a provocative and perceptive view of how small groups of key decision-makers may reach decisions. Approaching the question from the very distinguished tradition of US 'group dynamics' ideas, he has pointed to the impact that close loyalties and affiliations can have upon individuals when placed in situations of great stress and strain.

**G7/G8** Acronym for the Group of Seven. These states are: USA, Germany, Japan, France, UK, Canada and Italy. They constitute the seven leading ➤state economic ➤actors or ➤AICs. The Group meets annually to discuss major ➤issue areas in world politics – particularly those pertaining to economic problem-solving. Meetings are held at the Head of State/Head of Government level and can thus be regarded as part of that repertoire of diplomatic instruments referred to as ➤summit diplomacy.

G7 summits began in 1975 at Rambouillet when, at the instigation of the French President Giscard D'Estaing, leaders of six states (Canada was not invited to this first summit) met to address a number of economic issues arising from the first ➤oil shock, the recent devaluations of the dollar and proposed changes to the ➤Bretton Woods system. Seven months later the Six became the Seven with the accession of the Canadians at the Puerto Rico summit. A further innovation in membership occured in 1977 when the ➤European Community began to participate in summits as a single actor. Since the London summit of 1977 the President of the Council and the commission of the EC/EU have participated in G7 discussions on those issues – such as world ➤trade – where it was felt appropriate to regard the EC as a single actor.

The advent of AIC summitry under the G7 aegis can be judged on a number of variables. At the personal level the meetings afford the opportunity for face-to-face contact. This can be further reinforced if the conferences share ideological approaches and assumptions. Since 1980 there has been a clear bias in favour of conservative policies and market orientated thinking amongst the majority of G7 leaders. At the level of decision-making substance, the summits enable at the very least an exchange of views and frequently achieve a great deal more. The style and inclination at G7 meetings is towards consensus formation rather than formal voting, and leaders reach understandings rather than resolutions. Since the early meetings the agenda has broadened to cover many more ➤foreign policy issues such as ➤terrorism, ➤arms control and ➤nuclear accidents.

Structurally G7 confirms the ending of US ➤hegemony in macropolitical economics and the concurrent emergence of Japan as a major actor. Membership of the Group has done much to confirm Japanese status within the system and accordingly has added a new dimension to their ➤diplomacy. Similar opportunities have presented themselves to the unified Germany following the collapse of the ➤communist systems in Eastern Europe and the implosion of the Soviet Union. The G7 has been at the forefront of the process to convert the Russian economy into a free market system. In essence G7 has acted as a gatekeeper for Russian access to such ➤IGOs as the ➤IMF and the ➤World Bank group. It has also been a facilitator for ➤aid and investment into Russia and a validator of the Russian commitment to ➤economic liberalism. The participation of the Russian ➤leadership in G7 meetings points to the possibility of the Group formally becoming G8 (some would say that *de facto* it already is). ➤➤OECD

**Guerrilla warfare** The word 'guerrilla' is derived from Spanish and means literally a small war. Its original use refers to the involvement of Spanish irregular forces in the Peninsular War (1808–14) in support of Wellington. In this instance guerrilla war was adopted after the regular Spanish armies had been defeated by the French invaders. This early nineteenth-century use of guerrilla warfare established many of the ground rules for this type of combat. First, the physical environment of the Iberian peninsula was sufficiently extensive and formidable to afford a suitable context for hit-and-run tactics. Second, the local population were generally supportive of the guerrillas. This provided the Spanish with valuable ➤intelligence as well as material support. Third, the Spanish enjoyed external support from Napoleon's opponents, in particular from Wellington's forces. These factors of isolation, support from the population and external assistance have remained important variables in successful guerrilla campaigns ever since.

Throughout the nineteenth century this type of irregular combat continued to be used as an adjunct to ➤conventional warfare. A defeated ➤army might turn to guerrilla tactics to sustain some kind of opposition to the victors. The Second Boer War (1899–1902) was a precursor of things to come later in the twentieth century with regard to this kind of campaigning. It was truly an asymmetric ➤conflict in the sense used by writers on ➤protracted war. Although not revolutionary in the sense that can be applied to ➤People's Wars of later in the century, the Boers were strongly motivated by ➤nationalism and an opposition to British ➤imperialism. Although they were ultimately defeated, the Boers demonstrated again the principles of mobility and a supportive population in the conduct of such campaigns. On the British side a strategy of isolating the guerrillas from the supportive population was tried and eventually found to be successful. At the same time the prosecution of the Boer War caused serious rifts and schisms within the British political system and between Britain and other states in Europe.

During the First World War, guerrilla warfare was used with some success by the Arab forces who rebelled against the Turkish rule following British encouragement in 1915. The British promised Husain Ibn Ali, the Sherif of Mecca, ➤recognition and support for moves towards Arab independence in return for support for the British war against the Turks. The Arab Revolt that followed was chronicled by the enigmatic T. E. Lawrence in his *Seven Pillars of Wisdom* (1926). Lawrence reiterated the by now standard operating procedures of the guerrilla exponent: mobility and a supportive population, the need for a protracted war and appropriate motivation.

Guerrilla warfare developed most of its technical characteristics between the Peninsular War and the Arab Revolt. Thereafter its character changed as it became the principal *modus operandi* for parties and factions seeking to effect ➤revolutionary changes in a ➤state or a region. In particular, it was with Mao Tse-tung and the ideas of People's War that the ➤paradigm shift took place. Guerilla warfare is now used by insurgents of all descriptions fighting wars against incumbent systems. In the lexicon of protracted war, guerrilla methods occupy the second (of three) stages. The term is often used somewhat loosely when the user really intends to talk about ➤insurgency.

**Gulf War** ➤Persian Gulf War

**Gunboat diplomacy**  The phrase refers to the use of warships as an instrument of ➤foreign policy. It is particularly associated with British ➤imperial policies in the nineteenth century. Britain's general naval strategy was to keep most of the fleet in home waters and occasionally dispatch a squadron to a particular ➤region so as to restore order, to enforce the payment of debts or engage in punitive ➤intervention. The overall purpose was to initiate sudden, limited intervention to defuse a ➤crisis and to discourage repetition of the alleged offence. In this way, gunboat ➤diplomacy is associated with active ➤coercion, albeit of a limited kind, rather than with a passive ➤show of force. The term is a species of 'naval diplomacy' though in contemporary strategic analysis, the latter normally refers to a 'signalling' role rather than one involving actual combat. Naval warships are used as highly visible symbols of ➤power to reinforce policy directives or to deter possible obstacles to their success. Indeed, although the classical period of imperial gunboat diplomacy may be over, the use of warships as instruments of foreign policy short of all-out actual engagement is still considered important. Contemporary naval diplomacy involves a wide variety of tasks including the use of warships to signal intentions to an adversary, deploying them in order to negotiate from strength, or using them for display purposes ('showing the ➤flag') to reinforce or create a more compliant or supportive mood. In this way, the high profile 'presence' of naval forces has become the rationale underlying their peacetime strategic utility.

# H

**Hague Peace Conferences** These occurred in 1899 and 1907 and were self-conscious attempts by a major section of the international community (twenty-six ►states participated in the first conference, forty-four in the second) to clarify and codify rules relating to arms limitation and the occurrence of and conduct in ►war. They were significant in that they were a revival of the conference system that had monitored the ►'peace of Europe' from 1815 to 1854 (►Concert system). But unlike the Concert system, they were not confined to the ►great powers alone and their deliberations were much more specific and particular. They produced no substantive ►arms control measures (except for a rather vague resolution that all states should restrict their ►defence budgets for the 'welfare of mankind') but nevertheless are important as they represent the first general conference on ►disarmament and in this sense laid down the ground rules for subsequent initiatives on arms limitation. The most significant practical innovation produced at the Hague was the establishment of a ►Permanent Court of Arbitration, forerunner of the Permanent Court of International Justice and the ►International Court of Justice. The conferences also produced rules relating to conduct in war, treatment of ►prisoners of war and the rights of neutrals, as well as codifying conventions relating to land and sea warfare. On a political level, the conferences were beset by great power rivalry, especially that between Germany and Britain, neither of whom were greatly interested in ►multilateral across-the-board reductions on ►force levels. Despite this, and despite the fact that the Hague conferences failed to prevent the First World War or even to limit the excesses of the participants in it, they are an important development in ►international relations and law as they prepared the ground for post-war attempts to regularize international behaviour. Participation was virtually universal; it was not confined to one class of state, and deliberations were conducted on the basis of sovereign equality. All these factors, plus the creation of a skeletal ►peacekeeping body, constitute step-level functions in the development of ►international law and ►organization. The Hague conventions created the basis for the modern law of war in the sense that they codified existing state practice and customary international law. The norms and standards embodied therein are still binding as ►treaty rules, except where later treaties (e.g. the ►Geneva Convention of 1949) have superseded them.

**Harmonization** A process whereby constituent ►actors agree to coordinate their policies more closely than in the past, usually in the expectation that the process will be ongoing. Typically ►states will be the actors involved in harmonization measure and the broad expectations will be formally stipulated in ►treaty law. ►Implementation requires an institutional infrastructure to supervise the arrangements and bureaucracies such as the European Commission of the ►European Community are typically involved on the practical details. Normally, states will agree to harmonization in specific ►issue areas and these can be identified as ones showing a high degree of ►interdependence. There is a symbiosis between harmonization and ►integration. The latter cannot proceed in specific issue areas unless and until participants agree to harmonize their actions. The more complex and complicated the integration, the more the need for harmonization. However harmonization is not dependent upon integration and in this sense the symbiosis is not complete. Harmonization may take place in a ►supranational or in a ►state-centric context. The ►European Union is a good example of the former (although that begs the question on how far the union is truly supranational). The ►European Convention on Human Rights exemplifies the latter.

**Harmony of interests** ►liberalism

**Haves and have-nots** Term coined by Cervantes in *Don Quixote* (1605–15): 'There are in the world two families only, the Haves and the Have-Nots.' Universally popularized in the twentieth century and used as a relative or comparative term whenever a commentator seeks to distinguish within a total population, two groups, classes, functions, peoples, ►states or coalitions of states. The classification clearly implies an unequal or ►hierarchical division as when it is used to indicate the great disparities of wealth between states, especially between those belonging to the rich industrial ►North and those belonging to the developing or underdeveloped ►South. The term also implies that due to the division, the system is likely to be unstable. Thus E. H. Carr, in *The Twenty Years' Crisis*, discusses 'haves' and 'have-nots' in the context of peaceful change. Indeed, ►power theorists have often written in terms of ►status quo versus ►revisionist, or 'satisfied' versus 'dissatisfied' actors in order to highlight its unstable characteristics. The ►Brandt Reports have a clear conception of where 'haves' and 'have-nots' can be currently located with regard to political economy. The relationship between ►vertical and ►horizontal proliferation implies a similar dichotomy. The term clearly lacks precision, but it is nevertheless a convenient shorthand.

**Hawk** A hawk is a hard-liner. Like the term ►dove, this is a personality type which can be identified by reference to a number of typical components. The hawk is overly concerned with not appearing to be weak. The rationale for this view is provided by the hawk's ►perception that what counts in ►international politics and ►foreign policy is ►power, and particularly the willingness to use it. According to the hawk, adversaries will only comply with one's wishes if they see firmness and resolution. In particular, the maxim that one should seek to 'negotiate from strength' is essentially hawkish. Hawks are more likely than doves to engage in ➤worst-case analysis and consequently to interpret ambiguous or unanticipated moves by the opponent as malevolent. Hawks are not afraid to look for 'showdowns' that is to say crisis situations that will be approached from a strategy of pure ➤coercion unless and until the adversary retreats to some more compliant position. The importance of correct handling of the showdown ➤crisis is not simply intrinsic to the issues immediately at stake. Hawks see such as tests of resolve and reputation which, with success, will be enhanced for the next time. The hawk's dilemma is that, if he extends his self-➤image to the adversary, then the end result is violence and ➤war. Two hawks, who are not bluffing, can only test each other's resolve by engaging in the reckless ➤brinkmanship. The end result of hawkish behaviour can be the war that nobody wants but which nobody can back away from. The greatest danger with the hawkish mind set is that by being too provocative it produces the classic paradox – the ➤self-fulfilling prophecy.

**Health** ➤World Health Organization (WHO)

**Heartland theory** Probably the most well-known model associated with the ➤geopolitics school illustrating the global relationship between land-based and sea-based ➤power. It was first propounded by Sir Halford Mackinder in 1904 as 'The Geographical Pivot of History' and was subsequently refined in *Democratic Ideals and Reality* (1919) (where 'pivot area' became 'heartland') and added to again in 1943.

Mackinder's original model is drawn from a very wide and sweeping conception of world strategic history. The pivot area (or heartland) he identified as central Asia, from where horsemen dominated Asia and Europe. With the age of maritime discovery in the fifteenth century, however, the balance of forces shifted to the maritime powers, especially Britain. By the end of the nineteenth century this dominance of sea power was coming to an end and Mackinder predicted the reassertion of land-based power. Accordingly, he asserted that the ➤state that could control the Eurasian landmass between Germany and central Siberia would be able to control the world. He expressed it in this way:

> Who rules East Europe commands the Heartland
> Who rules the Heartland commands the World Island
> Who rules the World Island commands the World

In this representation central Asia is the 'heartland' and the 'world island' is Eurasia plus Africa – in all, over two thirds of the world's surface land area.

His theory was widely interpreted as a rationalization and justification for the traditional British policy of maintaining a European ➤balance of power and of preventing heartland ➤hegemony by either Germany or Russia which would pose a direct threat to Britain's Empire. In this way the ➤buffer states created by the Treaty of ➤Versailles (1919) were designed to drive a wedge between Germany and Russia and thus protect the strategic route to the Heartland. In 1919 his concern was to avoid German control of Russia. By 1943 the roles were reversed – Russian dominance now needed to be countered. Although the original work had stressed the strategic dominance of land power, Mackinder's final version in 1943 hinted at a revival of sea power. The US school of geopolitics, led by Nicholas Spykman, took this up and argued that the key area was the 'inner crescent', which was called the 'Rimland', control of which could ➤neutralize the power of the Heartland. US sea and ➤air power therefore had a positive role to play in post-war world politics. The Heartland-Rimland thesis then became the conceptual basis for post-war US policy, ➤containment being the effort to seal up the Rimland in order to hem in the Heartland (Soviet Union). The post-war ➤alliances, ➤NATO in Europe, CENTO in West Asia and SEATO in East Asia, were specific attempts to do this. Most of the post-war conflicts involving confrontation between the ➤superpowers developed in the Rimland – ➤Berlin, ➤Korea, the Middle East and ➤Vietnam being cited as the most dangerous. This thesis has obvious connections with the ➤domino theory whereby the 'fall' of one Rimland state will inevitably lead to the fall of adjacent countries until the 'World Island' itself becomes vulnerable.

That Mackinder's ideas persisted for so long in Western strategic thinking owes much to the fact that his simple spatial model provided a clear and coherent set of policy guidelines to the United States after 1945. The Heartland-Rimland thesis did indeed provide a global perspective to US strategic thought and dovetailed neatly with their obsessive fear of ➤communist expansionism.

**Hegemonial stability theory** A theory developed within the ➤International Political Economy (IPE) by US academics in the 1970s and particularly associated with the writings of Kindleberger (1973, 1978), Krasner (1976, 1983), Keohane (1984) and Gilpin (1975). This scholarship has taken the concept of ➤hegemony as the independent variable and sought to correlate it with the idea of ➤regime as the dependent variable. The hypothesis is that stable regimes, particularly in international economic relations, depend upon a hegemon establishing norms and rules and then superintending their functioning by enlightened use of its ➤capability to encourage other members to work the regime under its hegemonial power. Enlightened use of power requires the hegemon to use positive sanctions to create a structure of incentives for those further down the ➤hierarchy to benefit and therefore stay in the system. This enlightened hegemony will eventually cause the downfall of the regime because ➤revisionist interests will challenge the position of the hegemon, either explicitly or implicitly, and destabilize the regime.

The two examples that, almost without exception, are invariably quoted by hegemonial stability theorists for the purposes of illustration and validation are nineteenth-century Britain and post-1945 United States. In both cases the hegemonial control was short-lived. The UK impact upon the international ➤trade system lasted perhaps through the thirty-year period after the repeal of the Corn Laws in 1846, while US hegemony was seriously starting to wane in the 1970s when the fixed ➤gold-dollar exchange rate system collapsed and ➤OPEC successfully challenged the post-war international petroleum regime.

Hegemonial stability theory is firmly placed within the ➤power tradition. Its leading exponents are clearly committed to the view that putative power or capability is an important variable in both ➤international relations. While recognizing the low ➤fungibility of power as a resource, and therefore the highly contingent nature of power relationships, hegemonial stability theorists doggedly persist in their 'resource-power' perception notwithstanding the significant arguments posed by Baldwin (1979) and others against this somewhat static view.

Hegemonial stability theory is also exclusively concerned with relations within the ➤advanced industrial countries (➤AICs) of the ➤First World. No attempt was made to apply it to relations with the centrally planned economies, while in terms of the ➤North–South dichotomy the theoretical market place is already well stocked with economic ➤liberalism and ➤dependency theory. Finally hegemonial stability theory takes a rather truncated view of one of its central concepts – hegemony. The ideological implications of hegemony, a view stressed within the Marxist tradition, have been largely ignored by hegemonial stability theorists.

**Hegemony** A term which has been used in ➤international relations for some time, although rather intermittently. Its popularity has increased over the last two decades because it is now used by writers on ➤International Political Economy in connection with ➤hegemonial stability theory. Hegemony is a concept meaning primacy or ➤leadership. In an ➤international system this leadership would be exercised by a 'hegemon', a ➤state possessing sufficient ➤capability to fulfil this role. Other states in the system would thereafter have to define their relationship with the hegemon. This they might do by acquiescing, by opposing or by remaining indifferent to its leadership. It is clear that sufficient numbers of states, out of the total system membership, must take the first option in order to establish hegemonial control. This acquiescence can be called 'hegemonic consent'.

Since the role of hegemonial actor depends upon capability, the concept of hegemony bears a strong family resemblance to the concept of ➤power. It is important to remember that power has an ideational as well as a materialistic content. Capability analysis of hegemonial ➤actors needs to be constantly vigilant against crude ➤realism which tends to operationalize the concept in strictly economic and military terms. Although these are important, it should be stressed that a hegemon's ability to lead is derived as much from what it stands for as from how it seeks to achieve its goals.

Writers are agreed that the United Kingdom in the nineteenth century and the United States in the twentieth constitute examples of hegemons. UK hegemony began after the repeal of the Corn Laws and continued for thirty years until it started to wane in the 1880s, when the United States and Germany challenged its industrial supremacy. US hegemony began in 1945 and its ending is charted in the ➤declinist thesis including the ➤Vietnam Syndrome. Japan and the ➤EC/EU have emerged as ➤tripolar rivals at least in terms of IPE.

Ideationally, both ➤states represent similar world views. They can appropriately be seen as standard bearers for what has come to be called the ➤First World and for the values of economic ➤liberalism. Currently some writers on the subject see possibilities for a reassertion of hegemony taking place via ➤trilateralism. Ideationally there is no particular problem here, because the United States, Japan and the EC/EU all subscribe to the same ideas about the nature of economic and political systems. The main departure from the past would be that the assumption that a hegemon was a single state actor would have to be dropped.

**Helms—Burton** A highly controversial US law promulgated on 12 March 1996 which tightens the economic embargo against Cuba and provides for legal recourse against non-compliance by third parties. Properly called The Cuban Liberty and Democratic Solidarity Act it is named after its congressional sponsors Senator Jesse Helms and representative Dan Burton. It was a direct response to the destruction of two US registered aircraft in international air-space by Cuban ground control authorities in February 1996. Helms—Burton is controversial in three specific senses:

i) by seeking to punish any foreign citizen, company or government that does not adhere to the US embargo, it violates accepted codes of conduct in contemporary ➤international law. As with the ➤Monroe Doctrine of 1823 which forms the diplomatic framework within which this law was conceived and executed, it is a unilateral, essentially domestic declaration which has profound, international and multilateral consequences. Its dubiety has been questioned and challenged by a number of states, including post-apartheid South Africa which has insisted on its ➤sovereign right to conduct international relations with Fidel Castro's Cuba in accordance with accepted principles of international law, i.e. freedom to pursue independent foreign and trade policies.

ii) by initiating a tightening of the Cuban embargo the US is continuing to engage in ➤Cold War diplomacy and is out of kilter with the spirit of reconciliation which characterizes the post-Cold War period. This policy is inconsistent with overall contemporary US policy regarding Russia, China, Vietnam and N. Korea. It is thus perceived to be atavistic, punitive and contrary to the spirit of the new world order.

iii) on a more pragmatic level, increased use of the ➤sanctions instrument is unlikely to result in the peaceful transformation of Cuba from a dictatorship to a democracy. It may in fact prove counter-productive. The USA has maintained its embargo since 1960. During the past 36 years economic sanctions have not resulted in regime-change in Cuba. The notion of 'one final push' on which Helms–Burton is predicated, may in fact illustrate the perverse effect of the use of the sanctions instrument in international relations, i.e. to stiffen the resolve of the target state.

In sum, Helms–Burton is widely regarded outside the USA as a retrograde step, both regarding good relations with its allies (especially Europe and Canada) and its former adversaries. It is also perceived to be a challenge to accepted understandings of the ➤scope and ➤domain of international law.

**Helsinki Accords** To some commentators the diplomatic agreement signed in Helsinki in 1975 at the conclusion of the Conference of Security and Cooperation in Europe (➤CSCE) represented, at the time, the highest achievement of ➤*détente* in East–West relations. The conference, which lasted from 1972 to 1975, was proposed by the Soviet Union and was attended by representatives of thirty-three European states (the only exception being Albania), as well as the United States and Canada. The Accords, also known as the Helsinki Final Act, was divided into four areas or 'baskets' of common concern; Basket I covered the questions of ➤security in Europe and the Mediterranean, Basket II dealt with cooperation in the fields of economics, science, ➤technology and the environment, Basket III was concerned with humanitarian matters, ➤human rights, culture, education and the free flow of people's ideas and information throughout Europe, and Basket IV provided the holding of review conferences to oversee progress in these areas and to continue ➤multilateral cooperation. Subsequent meetings took place in Belgrade (1977), Madrid (1980–83) and Ottowa (1985), which was specially convened to review progress on human rights. The Accord was not a ➤treaty as such, but was an agreement which all parties undertook to implement. International agreements which are not law are known as 'Non-binding International Agreements' – the Helsinki Accords was clearly of this genre, since officially it was a political statement of intent rather than a legally binding document. Nevertheless, 1 August 1975 must be regarded as a historic date if only because the agreement signed represented the formal end of the Second World War, in the sense that the political and territorial ➤frontiers of Europe (including the border separating the two Germanies) were formally recognized by all parties. In return for ➤recognition of Soviet domination of Eastern Europe, the West succeeded in putting human rights (Basket III) firmly on the agendas of East–West relations alongside the traditional concerns of ➤trade and security, something which Moscow came to regret. Other matters covered by the Accords included an increase in economic, technical and cultural relations between the two ➤blocs, a specification of prior notification of and the exchange of observers at large scale military operations by both sides, provisions relating to ➤environmental protection and the establishment of monitoring groups to oversee performance in all sections of the Final Act.

The overall configuration of the agreement was characterized by the anxiety of the Soviet Union to legitimize its ➤hegemony in Eastern Europe and the determination of the West to exact a price for this. Thus, while the Soviet Union stressed the principle of ➤non-intervention (Principle VI) as being the crux of the agreement, the West continually focused on human rights (Principle VII) as the heart of the matter. The post-Helsinki debates were conducted largely in terms of these two issues: the Soviet Union insisted that no foreign government or group or individuals had a right to interfere in areas of its own ➤sovereign jurisdiction and the West insisted that the non-intervention principle was not an obstacle to monitoring respect for human rights within the Soviet domain.

After the inauguration of the ➤Gorbachev Doctrine in 1985–6, Moscow became much more amenable to Basket III humanitarian and human rights provisions. The process was further consolidated by the revolutions in Central and Eastern Europe in ➤nineteen eighty-nine. At the 1990 Copenhagen follow-up meeting the ideas of multiparty democracy, political pluralism, minorities protection, and independent judiciaries were unanimously endorsed by all parties as guiding principles of political behaviour. Thus the Helsinki Accords, despite the lack of formal organizational structure was an important diplomatic instrument which contributed to the end of bipolarity in Europe and subsequently to the creation of a new security architecture involving the eastwards expansion of ➤NATO and Partnership for Peace arrangements with Russia.

**Hierarchy** A hierarchy is a system of stratification. All social systems show evidence of stratification although the basis of this will differ. In the ➤international system, stratification is based upon ➤power and status. Taking these two dimensions as independent variables, it is possible to stipulate hierarchies based upon models which take power and status to be factors which are distributed unevenly between member ➤states. As a result the relationships which develop within these hierarchies produce unequal outcomes between member states in the system. When the state actor perspective is modified to include ➤mixed actor ideas then both the ➤IGOs and INGOs serve to confuse the picture but not to invalidate totally the idea of hierarchy. Thus when students of the ➤MNC first began to study it as a 'new ➤sovereign' it was commonplace to compare the gross annual sales of the MNC with the GNP of the state thereby suggesting that – at least in this binary hierarchy – the MNC was further up the ladder than many states.

Recently neorealist writers like Waltz (1979) have sought to contrast the idea of hierarchy with the idea of anarchy. According to this view, because the system is an anarchy it cannot be a hierarchy. As the above discussion shows this ►neorealist dichotomy depends for its rationale upon a rather different definition of hierarchy than common-sense usage might suggest. It might be thought that by defining hierarchy in this way the school of neorealism has denied itself a potentially powerful instrument of analysis widely used within social theory. ►►structural power

**High Commissioner** Term used specifically by ►Commonwealth states to refer to ►ambassadors or heads of mission sent by one member country to another. The use of this term instead of 'ambassador' indicates the ►special relationship that is thought to exist between members of this international sub-community.

**High politics** This term is used in two contexts. First, in ►foreign policy analysis, where it is used as a collective expression for certain ►issue areas of crucial importance. Second, high politics is used in the study of ►integration where, borrowing from the first usage, theorists again identify certain ►issue areas which are highly resistant to integration processes. Both meanings imply a horizontal division and explicit contrast with ►low politics. The idea that foreign policy is structured in terms of hierarchies in this way is also evident in the analysis of elites. Here, of course, the hierarchy is about 'who makes foreign policy?' rather than about issue areas.

In its first usage, high politics implies that in cases of a ►conflict foreign policy issues take precedence over domestic. The idea of the primacy of foreign policy is certainly a tradition within many states. In representative systems this primacy leads to injunctions that 'party politics should stop at the water's edge' and competing political parties are often encouraged to seek out areas of ►bipartisanship, certainly in the high politics areas. At a minimum, high politics involves the maintenance of core values – including national self-preservation – and the long-term objectives of the ►state. Clearly these are not transient or temporary concerns and indeed in many systems they will show remarkable continuity over time. ►Crises situations are, by definition, issues of high politics, because one of the situational characteristics of the crisis is that important values will be threatened. Similarly, significant changes in the ►orientation of the state – for example the UK decision to apply for membership of the ►European Communities, or the ►independence issue of a ►Third World state – will involve high politics.

In terms of elite structures, high political questions will be dealt with by the formal office holders. In some states, notably the USA, formal pronouncements by the national leadership on matters of high policy are often referred to as 'doctrines'. Once a decision has been made in principle and the ►implementation stage has been reached, high political issues will be increasingly handled within the bureaucratic and organizational context. Thus the UK decision to apply for membership of the European Communities, although taken after soundings at the highest levels, was quickly 'bureaucratized' once the decision had to be implemented and access negotiations began.

High politics in the second sense has been used as an implied critique of both ➤functionalist and ➤neo-functionalist theories of integration. The argument here is that by ignoring the distinctive character of high politics, certain integration theories are overly optimistic about their chances of success. Integration theorists have been too willing to assume that economic motives for change would dominate political motives for ➤status quo. In particular, via the idea of ➤spillover, it was thought that a kind of automatic and irresistible momentum would be created. Such high political principles as state ➤sovereignty have proved much more tenacious than was sometimes thought. To their credit the federalists have been instinctively ready to tackle these high policy issues directly and have not assumed that the functionalist/neo-functionalist disregard for high politics was justified or wise.

**Hiroshima** The first ➤atom bomb was dropped on the Japanese city of Hiroshima at 8.15 a.m. local time on 6 August 1945. The device was a uranium-based bomb, in the kiloton range. The bomb was dropped from a single, modified B29 aircraft from a height in excess of 30,000 feet. The weapon air-burst above the city at slightly under 2,000 feet. The death and destruction wrought by the immediate explosion was extensive. Due to the scale of the disruption caused to rescue services, many of the most severely wounded died subsequently. In February 1946 Supreme Allied Headquarters indicated that its estimate of the casualties were: dead 78,150; still missing 13,983; seriously wounded 9,428; slightly wounded 27,997. These figures may well err on the side of caution.

The bomb was not tested before it was used, so Hiroshima could be regarded as reality testing. Most commentators are agreed that, like most difficult decisions, a complex of factors was involved. The United States was certainly anxious to avoid an opposed invasion of the main Japanese Islands and to end the ➤war, if possible, before the Soviet Union carried through its pledge to declare war on Japan. The bomb's use was a demonstration of the awesome potential of ➤nuclear weapons, although at the time the US stockpile was too small to amount to more than a putative ➤capability. It should also be remembered that the United States had total air superiority *vis-à-vis* Japan. The implication that the United States could destroy large urban targets at will was reinforced at Hiroshima.

Since 1945 Hiroshima has come to symbolize the dawn of the nuclear age. Proponents of nuclear weapons regard it as a salutary reminder of the potential ➤power which concentrates the minds of would-be transgressors upon the ➤deterrent threat. Opponents of such weapons see in Hiroshima the need to escape from a system of relations based upon the threats and ➤reprisals which are too costly to carry out.

**Hobbesian** Along with ➤Machiavellian this is probably the most well known and well worn categorization of the ➤realist approach to ➤international relations. It is not difficult to see why. Thomas Hobbes' (1588 – 1679) account of relations between ➤states is drawn largely from his identification of this with the condition of man in the 'state of nature' before the establishment of civil society (*Leviathan*, ch. xiii). Hobbes' state of nature is anarchic and warlike where the life of man is 'solitary, poore, nasty, brutish and short'. Using this ➤domestic analogy he suggests that states, like individuals, are in a state of nature, which is a state of ➤war:

> But though there had never been any time wherein particular men were in a condition of warre one against another; yet in all times Kings, and Persons of soveraigne authority, because of their Independency, are in continual jealousies, and in the state and posture of Gladiators; having their weapons pointing, and their eyes fixed on one another; that is their Forts Garrisons and Guns, upon the Frontiers of their Kingdoms; and continual Spyes upon their neighbours; which is a posture of war (p. 65).

This account of ➤anarchy and the ➤security dilemma each individual (and therefore each state) faces is the conceptual basis of what might be termed the 'pure' realist school. It appears to contain all its essential elements. Man is aggressive and egotistical, the state seeks only its own ends, interest is defined in terms of ➤power, conflict is natural and the social environment is anarchic/chaotic. There is no law or morality to speak of and actions are limited, if at all, by prudence, which in any case is little more than enlightened self-interest.

Following the domestic analogy, the logical way out of this condition is the creation of a 'Leviathan amongst Leviathans', but Hobbes resisted this step towards world empire or ➤world government and most adherents to this view argue that survival ultimately rests on a form of ➤balance of power. Hobbes himself was not concerned with inter-state relations; his observations about them are an offshoot, a subordinate part, of his explanation of domestic politics and his justification for government. It is somewhat surprising therefore that his few and brief references to IR have been so influential. This is partly due to the vivid and forceful style of presentation, partly because it appears in outline to fit the simple realist model, and partly because of the general paucity of philosophical speculation about IR.

However, not a little controversy surrounds this orthodox interpretation of the Hobbesian view. It is possible to argue that Hobbes himself was not a 'Hobbesian' in the traditional sense. Hobbes describes that state of nature where men live without a common power 'to keep them all in awe' as a war of all against all, and then like Locke after him, forestalling the argument that such a condition never existed, he points to the relations between states as exemplifying it. But he adds this sentence, which makes all the difference to his view of international relations. He says of the state of war between states

. . . 'But because they uphold thereby the industry of their subjects; there does not follow from it that misery which accompanies the liberty of a particular men.' Therefore, although he clearly defines the state of nature with relations between the states, the external conditions of the states are not the same as those of individual men (i.e. they are less miserable). ➤International politics is in a state of nature because there is no government, but this anarchy, this absence of government, does not lead to chaos as it clearly does for individuals. Anarchy in its international context is therefore not as intolerable as in its domestic context. It may in fact be compatible with the idea of an ➤international society of states (the 'anarchical society'). In addition, Hobbes specifically identified the laws of nature – which dictate that ➤peace should be sought wherever possible – with the laws of nations. This suggests that far from being a bleak, unrelenting battle for daily survival, inter-state relations are capable of sustaining communal, cooperative endeavours based on reason and mutual respect for law. (See Hedley Bull (1966).)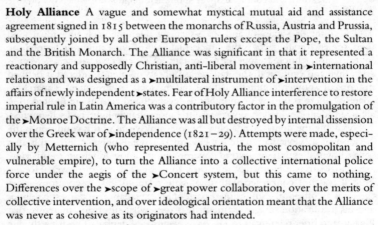

**Holy Alliance** A vague and somewhat mystical mutual aid and assistance agreement signed in 1815 between the monarchs of Russia, Austria and Prussia, subsequently joined by all other European rulers except the Pope, the Sultan and the British Monarch. The Alliance was significant in that it represented a reactionary and supposedly Christian, anti-liberal movement in ➤international relations and was designed as a ➤multilateral instrument of ➤intervention in the affairs of newly independent ➤states. Fear of Holy Alliance interference to restore imperial rule in Latin America was a contributory factor in the promulgation of the ➤Monroe Doctrine. The Alliance was all but destroyed by internal dissension over the Greek war of ➤independence (1821–29). Attempts were made, especially by Metternich (who represented Austria, the most cosmopolitan and vulnerable empire), to turn the Alliance into a collective international police force under the aegis of the ➤Concert system, but this came to nothing. Differences over the ➤scope of ➤great power collaboration, over the merits of collective intervention, and over ideological orientation meant that the Alliance was never as cohesive as its originators had intended.

**Homeostasis** A term used in ➤cybernetics. Homeostasis is to cybernetics what equilibrium is to mechanics; that is to say, it conceptualizes how an organism maintains an even state with its environment. In cybernetics this is achieved by processing information about the environment in relation to the goals being pursued by the organism and adapting behaviour patterns accordingly. Since the flow of information into the system is continuous – this is one of the basic principles of cybernetics – homeostasis is an ongoing process itself. Unlike the term ➤feedback – itself also taken from cybernetics – homeostasis has not passed into the currency of standard political analysis. The major reference work on these ideas remains that of Professor Karl Deutsch (1963).

**Horizontal proliferation** ➤nuclear proliferation

**Hot pursuit** A legal doctrine usually associated with ➤maritime law but now used more widely to cover activities on land, air and sea. It refers to the right to pursue an offender outside the territorial limits of one's own national ➤jurisdiction. The adjective indicates that the exercise of this right is a limited one in circumstances, time and place. Thus, the action must begin within the jurisdiction of the violated party, is undertaken only by its authorized agents, is engaged in until the offender is arrested and broken off when the offender reaches its own territorial area or that of a third ➤state. It is justified as an enabling device for the reasonable exercise of territorial jurisdiction.

**Human rights** The notion that human beings have rights because they are human beings and not because they are citizens of state X or state Y is, in terms of the practice of ➤international relations, a relatively new one. Traditional thinking has it that ➤international law is concerned primarily with states rights – in particular rights associated with post-➤Westphalian ideas about➤sovereignty and its corollary, ➤non-intervention. Human rights, in so far as they were acknowledged, were subsumed under states rights, conventional wisdom being that international law was law between states whereas municipal law was law between individuals. Although the distinction has never been quite as clear as this – the rights of ➤aliens and foreign nationals have long been a matter for concern, for example – orthodox accounts of➤international politics and law have always been more or less ➤state-centric in this way. However, the distinction between the two has become increasingly blurred and contemporary world politics has witnessed a dramatic upsurge in the question of human rights and their place in the ➤state-system. It may be said that whereas the innovation of the seventeenth-century world politics was the creation of a society of states, the ➤revolution of the twentieth century is the creation of a prototype ➤world society in which individuals have equal standing with states and where states themselves acknowledge that issues connected with the fundamental rights of human beings are as legitimate a part of ➤foreign policy concerns as the more traditional preoccupations with ➤peace, security and economic well-being. This process was formally heralded by the establishment in 1946 of the United Nations Commission on Human Rights, and on 10 December 1948 (which was designated Human Rights Day) the ➤General Assembly passed the Universal Declaration of Human Rights. This was unopposed, although South Africa, Saudi Arabia and the Soviet ➤bloc abstained. The Commission worked on two covenants designed to give substance to the general declaration: the first was on economic, social and cultural rights and the second on civil and political rights. The first was passed by the General Assembly in 1966 (although it did not become operative until ten years later) but the second covenant has had a much more difficult ride and the investigatory Committee established has constantly run up against recalcitrant governments insisting on the overriding principle of states rights (Israel, for example, refused to cooperate with its investigations into possible violations in occupied territories after the Six-Day War). Thus, the ►international system has clearly laid down a code of established human rights and attempted to create judicial machinery which can investigate infringements but the problem of enforcement remains a thorny one. States can, and do, ignore them. Yet as a statement of principle, and perhaps of positive world morality, these proposals clearly have an effect on ►world public opinion and the standard they set is used as a yardstick to measure, and also beat, states which consistently fail to comply. Rhodesia and South Africa, the Soviet Union and China have borne this brunt most often in recent times.

On a ►regional level, as distinct from the international, provision for human rights implementation has been more successful. The ►European Convention on Human Rights (1953) sought not only to delineate these rights but also enforce them. A commission and a court of human rights has been established to which individuals can bring action against their own governments. In the American continents there are similar developments. The American Convention on Human Rights (1978) created a commission and a court which again contained provision for individuals to present grievances. In Africa the Banjul Charter on Human and People's Rights (1981) is somewhat weaker than its European and American counterparts, mainly perhaps due to the different African conceptions of human rights – a conception which stresses the rights of collectivities and groupings ('peoples') rather than individual rights as such. In all these incidences, whether provision for enforcement is present or not the power of ►public opinion is an important sanction in the conflict between individuals and the sometimes overbearing ►power of the state. Other regional innovations have not been as successful as those in Europe or the United States. The 1975 ►Helsinki Accords, which included provision for human rights, has not so far made much headway in the Soviet bloc partly because Helsinki is not legally binding on its signatories. The Arab Commission on Human Rights (1969), too, has made little progress mainly because in ►Islam the rights of the community come before the rights of the individual; for Muslims duty to God, from whom all human beings emanate, is logically prior to obligations to individuals.

Of the non-governmental institutions concerned with this issue ►Amnesty International (founded in Britain in 1961) stands out. This group actively specializes in seeking to obtain freedom for prisoners of conscience and has been instrumental in campaigning for the rights of thousands of unfortunates on a world-wide basis. Other specialist organizations in this field are the Minority Rights Group, the Anti-Slavery Society and the ►International Committee of the Red Cross – all of which are concerned with specific aspects of individual rights.

Clearly, although the twentieth century has seen a greater movement towards acceptance of human rights as an integral part of world politics than at any other time, there is a great deal of debate as to where the emphasis should be placed. In the West the rights of individuals to be free from the interference of others is paramount, whereas in the East economic and social rights took precedence over civil and political rights. Liberty in socialist states was expressed primarily in social and economic terms: in liberal states it is largely a civil and political affair. Therein perhaps lies an important dimension of the tension between the two systems, and because of its emphasis on economic development rather than the legal protection of civil liberties the ➤Third World tends to prefer the socialist view. After all, subsistence and basic needs are often a more immediate and pressing concern than constitutional niceties and protective legal procedures (R. J. Vincent, 1986). Whatever ideological differences can be delineated, though, no one doubts that the human rights issue has altered, probably for ever, the classical conception of international relations.

**Humanitarian assistance** Traditionally associated with acts of assistance undertaken by ➤states in response to natural disasters of a temporary kind: that is earthquakes, floods, fires, famines and so on. In classical international legal theory it is associated with the idea of *offices d'humanité* developed in particular by Vatell. It is not regarded as a duty under ➤international law, rather is it rendered as a matter of 'grace or bounty'. Some modern theorists have argued that the concept should be extended to cover not just natural and temporary disasters, but also social and endemic disasters. In addition, the rendering of humanitarian assistance should be regarded as a positive duty and consequently could be demanded by sufferers as a right derived not only from the doctrine of 'shared humanity', but also as a logical consequence of membership of the international community of states. Thus the provision of, for example, minimum subsistence to all should be viewed not as a voluntary act of charity, but as a legal requirement under the doctrine of distributive ➤justice. ➤➤Human rights

**Humanitarian intervention** The coercive intrusion into the internal affairs of a state to protect large-scale ➤human rights violations. As such, it is to be distinguished from humanitarian 'assistance' which does not involve coercion and usually occurs with the consent of the target ➤state. In other words, humanitarian intervention (HI) involves the use of armed forces by a state, a group of states or an ➤international organization on the grounds of humanitarianism with the specific purpose of preventing or alleviating widespread suffering or death. As with other varieties of ➤intervention this is the subject of dispute in ➤international relations and ➤law on the grounds that it is subversive: it threatens the institutional basis of ➤international order. Specifically, it is regarded as a threat to the foundational ➤Westphalian principle of ➤sovereignty and its corollary, ➤non-intervention.

Since the creation of the modern ➤states system, scholars and practitioners have struggled to define the conditions under which ➤actors could intervene in each other's affairs. The general assumption is that since non-intervention is the norm in this decentralized system, all interventions must be justified. Not surprisingly therefore, the idea of intervention in theory and practice is fraught with political and legal difficulties. This ambiguity is reflected in the Charter of the ➤United Nations which is premised on the idea of non-intervention (Articles 2,4 and 2,7) yet specified certain conditions under which intervention is admissible ('threats to the peace,' Chapter VII). Thus, the UN itself can be seen to be hedging its bets; trying to strike a balance between the claims of state sovereignty and those of international authority. Or as some allege, between the claims of order and the desire for justice. Recently, this balance appears to be shifting towards a 'softer' interpretation of sovereignty which recognizes the saliency of the human rights argument for intervention.

The first authoritative statement of the principle of humanitarian intervention occurred in the writings of ➤Grotius (in 'De Jure Belli ac Pacis', 1625) who presumed a right of intervention to prevent maltreatment by a state of its own subjects. For Grotius, this right was embedded in classical theories of the ➤just war. During the modern period of international relations, from the seventeenth century to the end of the ➤Cold War, the doctrine was marginalized in favour of the much more compelling Westphalian case for non-intervention as the basic behavioural principle of international order. However, some interventions on broad humanitarian grounds did occur. (Greece in 1827, Lebanon 1860, the Balkans 1877–8 and in the multinational expedition to Macedonia in 1905). But as these examples illustrate, it is very difficult to distinguish these European interventions from traditional ➤realpolitik practice since they were invoked against the Ottoman Empire for real or perceived oppression of Christian subjects. Generally, during the modern period, the international community appeared unwilling to promote human rights by enforcement. This was not merely because of a systemic presumption in favour of order, it also stemmed from a fear, particularly expressed by developing states, that it could become a 'Trojan horse' for ➤great power interference in their internal affairs.

In the post-Cold War period, the doctrine has witnessed a resurgence both in international theory and in state practice. The watershed was the establishment of 'safe havens' in northern Iraq in 1991 in the aftermath of the ➤Persian Gulf War. Since then there have been a succession of humanitarian-based interventions in Somalia, Haiti, Liberia, Rwanda and Bosnia. In an operational sense, none of these were successful. Nevertheless, the issue is now high on the international agenda. Reasons for this are the absence of ➤superpower conflict, the spread of human rights awareness, the ➤globalization of information and the tendency of the UN ➤Security Council to interpret 'threats to the peace' expansively. Though as yet there is no legal right of humanitarian intervention comparable to the traditional rights of states, there is a growing international consensus that the Westphalian system is too restrictive (G. M. Lyons and M. Mastanduno, 1995). Certainly the privileged status enjoyed by sovereignty in international law is now under attack, and as the six UN authorized interventions above show, there is now a qualified but evolving right of intervention on humanitarian grounds along with an emerging practice.

In international theory, the general movement away from ➤realism has reinforced this tendency. However, the continued reluctance of states to put their forces at risk for objectives other than national ➤security ones is still a powerful constraint as illustrated by the US withdrawal from Somalia in 1992. Without a clear entrance and exit strategy ➤decision-makers will still hesitate before committing themselves to intervene. So despite a growing predilection in favour of intervention (usually arising from a public clamour to 'do something') these operational problems have yet to be resolved.

Sometimes referred to as 'second generation ➤peacekeeping', humanitarian interventions have not yet developed standing operating procedures, although the general tendency appears to be to aim for the establishment of a secure environment for the provision of humanitarian assistance, rather than to engage in humanitarian ➤war. Whereas the traditional debate over humanitarian intervention was a legal one, the current debate is primarily political/diplomatic/military. It consists of a search for the optimum conditions upon which they could be carried out without leaving the door open to abuse and/or without exacerbating conditions on the ground. Despite these difficulties, it is clear that international relations is now in limbo. Sovereignty continues to be eroded by human rights yet international society has not entirely abandoned the Westphalian framework. Without doubt it is under siege from this doctrine but it is still proving remarkably resilient and adaptable. ➤➤International Red Cross, Médecins Sans Frontières

**Hydrogen bomb** The hydrogen bomb is the most powerful weapon invented by man – to date. Its energy is generated by the fusion of hydrogen isotopes. Hence it is sometimes referred to as the 'fusion' bomb, although the weapon as developed actually combines fission and fusion processes. A small ➤atom bomb is exploded to act as a trigger for the fusion of the hydrogen. This two-stage process has led some to refer to 'thermonuclear' weapon instead of hydrogen weapon. The size of the hydrogen weapon is limitless – at least in theory – and larger yielding weapons are measured in the ➤megaton range. This exponential increase in destructiveness has led some to argue that the real ➤revolution is thermonuclear rather than nuclear. The difference between fusion weapons and fission weapons is greater than the difference between fission and ➤conventional weapons.

Although scientific interest in the fusion process dates from 1942, the political impetus to development came from the ➤arms race. In particular, the Soviet testing of an atomic weapon in 1949 provoked the United States Administration into serious consideration of the research and development implications of thermonuclear weapons. The Soviet atomic test, achieved several years in advance of their anticipated ➤capability, had so alarmed the United States that they felt unable to stand aside from the possible development of fusion weapons themselves.

# Hydrogen bomb

Policy discussion over the so-called 'super' took place within the Truman Administration between three agencies: the Defense Department, the State Department and the Atomic Energy Commission. Unanimity between the three over the development of the 'super' was far from complete. Indeed there were powerful voices inside the Administration and outside in the scientific community arguing against development of hydrogen weapons. In particular it was felt by many that if the United States went ahead with development and production of these weapons any remaining chances for an international control ➤regime would be lost. Additionally many critics of the hydrogen bomb argued that such a destructive weapon used against civilian targets would be quite indiscriminate in its effects. In a remarkably prescient anticipation of the debates over mutual assured destruction (➤MAD) these early fears warned against the development of such a 'countercity' ➤capability by the United States.

The decision to go ahead with the development of fusion weapons led to the first test in 1951, further testing in 1952 and the Bikini test of March 1954 which confirmed the power of the weapon. By the time of the Bikini test, the Soviet Union had already commenced their programme. In retrospect the decisions over the 'super' in the early 1950s look tantalizingly like a window of opportunity situation; one which unfortunately closed almost as soon as it opened.

# I

**Ibn-Khaldūn** An influential Arab philosopher (1332–1406) who anticipated many of the themes of modern international theory – particularly those associated with Machiavellian/Hobbesian ➤realism. His writing on 'universal history' shares similarities with ➤Thucydides and modernists such as Hegel and Toynbee. Principally known for his work *The Muqaddima* in which he develops a 'science of cults' his work has been largely neglected in the Anglo-American world, but is still influential in Middle Eastern social and political philosophy.

**IBRD** ➤World Bank group

**IDA** ➤World Bank group

**Idealism** Sometimes called 'utopianism', and with less accuracy, 'rationalism' or '➤liberalism', it refers to an approach to ➤international relations that stresses the importance of moral values, legal norms, ➤internationalism and harmony of interests as guides to ➤foreign policy-making rather than considerations of ➤national interest, ➤power and independent ➤state survival within a multi-state decentralized system. According to E. H. Carr (1946), its foremost critic, the central fallacy of idealism was its tendency to indulge in wishful thinking at the expense of rigorous empirical analysis, to the extent that it was characterized by 'the inclination to ignore what was and what is in contemplation of what should be' (p. 11). Thus, excessive emphasis on abstract principles rather than factual realities led, according to Carr, to an inability especially in the Anglo-American world both to comprehend and to control international events during the inter-war period. Theorists such as Arnold Toynbee, Norman Angell and Alfred ➤Zimmern, as well as practitioners such as Woodrow ➤Wilson, consistently failed to grasp that the mainsprings of state action and behaviour revolved around considerations of power and national interest rather than ethics and universalism. Policies based on such fallacies (e.g. general ➤disarmament, international cooperation and internationalism) were bound to fail because 'these supposedly absolute and universal principles were not principles at all but the unconscious reflections of national policy based on a particular interpretation of national interest at a particular time'. In fact, although Carr was among the first to identify 'idealism' as a particular school or approach which dominated thinking in the period following the First World War (and which, in effect, created international relations as a separate academic discipline) the tradition was well established in the history of international thought long before the twentieth century. Thus Locke, Bentham, Rousseau, Kant and J. S. Mill were all regarded as 'idealists' of one sort or another since all of them, albeit on various levels and with varying degrees of conviction, expressed faith in 'reason' and conscience' as harbingers of perpetual ►peace and universal harmony. The doctrine of the ►domestic analogy, whereby conditions which created order within the state could be reproduced on the international plane, was a central assumption of the approach and this led directly to the advocacy of ►collective security and the creation of a ►League of Nations which would forever resolve the ►security dilemma associated with an unstructured and untutored international ►anarchy. For the idealists, therefore, peace was both indivisible and achievable.

The 'realist-idealist debate' which dominated the discipline (especially in the United States) in the late 1940s and early 1950s has largely been superseded in academic commentaries, but is now regarded as a suitable (if somewhat naive and dated) general introduction to the outer parameters of the subject. ►►neo-liberalism

**Ideology** An ideology is a set of assumptions and ideas about social behaviour and social systems. Its application to political studies has been far-reaching, particularly since the French Revolution. In politics these assumptions and ideas are often referred to as doctrines. Thus a political ideology can be defined as a set of doctrinal assumptions and ideas about the past, present and future states of affairs in political systems, including the ►international system and the world system. Political ideologies are usually thought of as being very explicit philosophical systems such as ►Marxism/Leninism. This is almost certainly too narrow a view. ►Nationalism is quite clearly an ideology in the terms used above, yet it is often much less explicit than Marxism/Leninism and it is certainly more specific and relative to a particular political culture. All political ideologies will contain components which seek to describe and explain how a particular state of affairs came into being; sometimes in addition a political ideology will seek to stipulate what ►foreign policy analysts would call long-term goals for the future. In this sense political ideologies are also predictive and prescriptive. Ideologies fulfil a number of functions:

1 Ideologies are a source of ►conflict in ►international relations. Rosecrance (1963), in his study of nine European systems from 1740, found that four, including the two most recent, showed elements of ideological conflict. Ideological conflicts show great intensity between the parties, unwillingness to compromise and marked tendency to become total. Many of the post-war regional conflicts have had ideological dimensions, usually nationalism. The ►Arab–Israeli conflict is a good example.

2 Ideologies as a source of ►capability in international relations. The realist tradition of separating ►power and ideology has tended to obscure the possibility that ideology may be a source of putative power. Ideology contrib-

utes towards what Speigel calls motivational power. Although neither a necessary nor sufficient condition for an active foreign policy, a high level of ideological self-righteousness will be conducive to active ►interventionist foreign policies. Ideology is also a source of capability within the ►state and this internal dimension can 'spill over' into the external environment. States come to represent a particular ideology within the international system as a reflection of their internal beliefs and values. Charismatic ►leadership relies upon an ideological base. This type of leader derives considerable power and influence from the success with which she or he appears to encapsulate in their personality the aspirations of particular classes or peoples. Classic twentieth-century examples would be Lenin, Mao, Gandhi and Mandela. The routinization of charisma occurs when the principles and practices of the leader outlast the life of the individual and become part of an ideological tradition.

3 Ideologies as an influence upon policy-making. In this use of ideology, the concept becomes much more subjective. Ideology becomes a kind of lens through which policy makers perceive their various environments and react accordingly. The process of reaching a ►definition of the situation will bring ideological influences to bear upon the policy process. These ideological influences will be generalized rather than specific but in the process of specifying their relevance to a particular ►issue area differences may arise between the individuals and groups. Explanations of US foreign policy have often been sought in terms of the ideologies of ►isolationism and ►interventionism/internationalism. In terms of the current discussion these would become the 'lenses' through which policy ►goals, particularly in the long term, would be defined. The decision after 1919 to reject Wilsonian ►idealism is sometimes presented as a reversion to the politics of self-interest. The ideological approach instead would see it in terms of isolationism suggesting one course and interventionism/internationalism another. These ideological influences are a product of socialization influences as much as intellectual fashion. Socialization, both in childhood and adult life, is important in two ways. Manifest socialization, including indoctrination, occurs in all social systems and begins in the family. Latent socialization, by placing individuals in a particular milieu, occurs throughout life. Political sociology has tended to concentrate upon totalitarian societies when examining the role of socialization in the creation and maintenance of ideological factors. Totalitarian systems are, however, only the most overt and extreme instances of what is a general tendency.

4 Ideologies as ways of looking at the subject. In this aspect intellectual preferences come to the fore. Little and Mckinlay (1986) approach ideology in this way. They identify three ideal types: liberalism, socialism and realism. Gilpin (1975), in writing about political economy, has identified the same three although his terminology is different and his exemplification is some-

what narrower. Writers in an earlier period have spoken of realism and idealism/utopianism. Recently a ➤World Society perspective has become fashionable. In this usage ideology is perhaps interchangeable with 'perspective' or 'intellectual tradition'. It is a way of looking at politics both domestically and externally. Indeed, in the World Society perspective it is a way of collapsing that distinction. It is more concerned with the subject as studied on the campus rather than the subject as conducted by the ➤Foreign Office, but the two activities are interdependent.

**IFC** ➤World Bank group

**IGO** Intergovernmental organizations. Sometimes rendered as international governmental organizations. To all intents and purposes, the meaning is the same. IGOs are founded by governments representing ➤states. These organizations are established to engage in problem-solving in the interests of, and possibly on behalf of, their member states. The specificity of the problem(s) to be solved will have a bearing upon the ➤scope and ➤domain of the organization. The broader the range of problems, the more multi-purpose the organization must be. Thus, the best known contemporary IGO is the ➤United Nations (UN) established by a multilateral ➤treaty known as the Charter. The UN aspires to universal membership and in this regard has been far more successful than its predecessor, the ➤League of Nations. It is made up of a number of organs plus the ➤specialized agencies, Commissions, Funds and Programmes. It has attempted problem-solving in all the major ➤issue areas in contemporary ➤international relations.

The greatest proliferation of IGOs since the inception of the UN in 1945 has been at the regional level. Regional cooperation and regional ➤integration have produced a host of IGOs in all the major identifiable regions of the world. Unlike the UN, most of these organizations are single purpose. They may operate in the area of military security, economic integration and cooperation, cultural exchanges, ➤human rights questions and so on. The possibility of 'regional arrangements' of this kind was anticipated in the UN Charter, although the scale of the proliferation almost certainly was not.

Finally in the categorization, there are those IGOs which seek to articulate and aggregate the interests of a particular class of states within the total ➤state system, but which cut across ➤regional demarcation lines, e.g. the Organization of Petroleum Exporting Countries (➤OPEC) and the ➤Commonwealth. Both of these IGOs draw members from a number of regions, yet neither can claim to be universal within its class – there are oil exporting states outside OPEC and there are former British colonies outside the Commonwealth. Both are fairly 'loose' ➤associations by comparison with the types mentioned above but both have been sufficiently successful to encourage emulators, rivals and opponents.

IGOs of all types are important channels of communication between representatives of their member states and governments. Particular importance is attached to the potentialities and possibilities for informal face-to-face contact. The cloakroom conference and the cocktail bar bargain are valuable activities which often go unreported by journalists and unrecorded by historians, but which enable ➤diplomats to talk about talks and exchange information with others. More publicly IGOs can sometimes attempt to mediate in conflicts that occur between their members.

Thus ➤NATO has attempted to ameliorate differences between Greece and Turkey, while the ➤Organization of African Unity (OAU) has sought to mediate in a number of African conflicts including the protracted ➤civil war in Nigeria. This kind of internal conflict may, hypothetically, occur in any IGO. In the special case of the UN, because it is near universal, all ➤conflict between member states can be seen as internal. In another sense, though, if the UN is viewed as an autonomous ➤actor conflict between the UN and a state or group of states can occur. Some of the most controversial moments in the UN ➤peacekeeping record have left the IGO as one of the parties to the conflict with member states in opposition to the Organization.

The above discussion raises the most fundamental question about IGOs. To what extent can they be regarded as autonomous actors in international relations? Realists are inclined to deny the IGO any ➤autonomy. For them, the organization is little more than the sum of its constituent parts and is particularly susceptible to domination by the most powerful and influential state members. The IGO thus becomes an expression of and an extension of the ➤foreign policy of the dominant state or coalition. This rather limited view of IGOs is questioned by those who argue that the very existence of these organizations can affect, mould and even modify the policies of state members. Moreover the fact that states are concurrently members of a plurality of IGOs may mean that a cumulative impact will be generated over time which, effectively, sets limits upon what a state can or cannot do, or even say, on an ➤issue area. In this respect IGOs become what Pentland (1973) has called 'systemic modifiers' of state behaviour. To what extent are they autonomous actors?

There are two ways of looking at the autonomy question; one is institutional, the other issue orientated. Institutionally, if an IGO develops a secretariat which can act independently of governments then this can lead to greater autonomy. This happened to the UN under Dag Hammarskjöld but it was controversial and produced a reaction from, amongst others, the Soviet Union, which proposed to replace him with a troika system of international civil servants. This autonomy is more prevalent in economic IGOs such as the ➤IMF and the United Nations Conference on Trade and Development (UNCTAD), a reflection of the greater amount of ➤interdependence in economic relations. Genuine independence in the secretariat, as opposed to the quasi-independence above, is evident in regionally based IGOs such as the

➤European Union (EU). Since the EU has ➤supranational implications, the role of the secretariat is bound to be more significant in this case.

IGOs may gain autonomy because there are issue areas in world politics which can only be dealt with on a ➤multilateral basis. These issue areas tend to be Prisoner's Dilemma situations where there are strong collective motives for cooperation, ➤pollution, ➤proliferation of ➤weapons of mass destruction and access to the world's oceans being examples. If states are to act collectively in these areas with any likelihood of success then they must establish a system of rule-governed relations, including a system of sanctions, that can be implemented by IGOs. By definition this will involve allowing the organizations a degree of autonomy. ➤➤Regime

**Image** An image is a subjective assessment made by an individual or a group of its physical and social milieu. An image is a pyschological construct that is an amalgam of cognitive and affective processes. For this reason, there will always be a sense in which the image can be distinguished from 'reality'. This discrepancy may be trivial or it may be critical to any subsequent behaviour patterns. An image, moreover, contains elements of past, present and future.

The most basic image identifiable in ➤international relations is the image that a people have of themselves expressed through their concept of nationality and the ideas of ➤nationalism. Thus the first tangible images that most people have are of their own national or ethnic reference group. As with so many political attitudes, these self-images will be the result of upbringing and socialization. In most nation-states these images are reinforced by the mass media and sometimes manipulated for ➤propaganda purposes. As suggested above, images are affective as well as cognitive; they can therefore arouse feelings of amity or enmity. Hostile and/or friendly images of other national and ethnic groups are an important factor in the impact thay can have upon world politics. Indeed, a number of studies have shown the tendency for images to be reciprocated: hostility begets hostility, friendliness begets friendliness. This tendency is referred to as the ➤mirror image.

The study of national images has been wholly advanced within the ➤social science approach. K. E. Boulding's 1956 work is widely regarded as the first, and now seminal, contribution to the literature. Subsequently, images have been particularly studied by those favouring a psychologically orientated approach to the subject and by students of ➤public opinion.

**IMF** The International Monetary Fund (IMF) was established as part of the ➤Bretton Woods system in 1944. Subsequently it became part of the UN structure. In conjunction with the ➤World Bank, the IMF was regarded as one of the central institutions for the management of post-war economic relations.

The IMF, as the name implies, was intended to supply international liquidity to member ➤states finding themselves in ➤balance of payments difficulties. In addition the Fund was to manage a system of stable (rather than fixed) exchange rates. A particular currency would have a 'par value' which was expressed in terms of dollars. Alteration of that rate would be effected, with the approval of the Fund, if the state's external payments balance was held to be in 'fundamental disequilibrium'. As already stated, in addition to its supervision of the exchange rate ➤regime, the Fund lends money to member states in balance of payments difficulties. It is always assumed that the monetary authorities of the recipient state would take appropriate measures to correct such imbalances and indeed it has become a feature of the IMF lending that so-called 'conditionality' stipulations would be part of the 'rescue package'. Recognition of the right to lay down such conditions is indicated by the recipient government issuing a 'letter of intent' to the IMF. This whole procedure – of laying down conditions which are then accepted in the letter – is clearly a significant erosion of state ➤sovereignty. Although an accepted and expected feature of the IMF's conduct it is not without controversy. The IMF has a tradition of requiring states in receipt of its loans to make structural adjustments to rectify the disequilibrium. Thus raising taxes and interest rates and cutting public expenditure, including subsidies, are typical IMF-preferred policies.

The linchpin of the original Bretton Woods arrangement was the US dollar. The gold/dollar exchange rate had been fixed at 35 dollars per ounce in 1934 and it was assumed that this exchange rate was, to all intents and purposes, fixed and immutable. During the early post-war period of reconstruction the principal concern about the dollar was its shortage. Although the US balance of payments began to move into deficit during the 1950s it was not regarded as serious. As long as the dollar shortage remained other states in the system were willing to see the United States running deficits which were financed by the export of dollars. The IMF system was, in fact, a ➤gold exchange standard with the dollar regarded as being 'as good as gold' for these purposes. The IMF system of stable exchange rates established as a fundamental principle of the system after 1944 began to be seriously questioned towards the end of the 1960s. By 1961 the great emerging problem was the US deficit. By running a deficit the United States was funding the system but equally was running the risk that, if confidence collapsed, then a forced devaluation of the dollar would be necessary.

When the collapse of confidence in the dollar eventually came in 1971 it was both spectacular and momentous. Speculative attacks upon the dollar were encouraged by a series of poor ➤trade figures which seemed to suggest that the link between gold and the dollar might have to be suspended or ended altogether. In August 1971 the US President announced that the convertibility of the dollar into gold was temporarily suspended. At the end of a year a joint meeting of the Group of Ten (G10) and the Executive Directors of the Fund agreed to devalue the dollar 10 per cent against the other currencies in the Group. These decisions effectively brought down the Bretton Woods system of stable exchange rates. Following a second dollar devaluation in February 1973 the system was abandoned and the new era of 'floating' rates replaced it.

Cautious and considered deliberations of these changes were reduced by the first ➤oil shock in 1973–4. Suddenly states were moving massively into credit or debit on their balance of payments. Any chance of structured reform was abandoned and floating continued into the future. The Jamaica Agreement of January 1976 amended the Articles of Agreement of the Fund to legitimize floating. In reality there has been a good deal of 'management' of the float by the central banking authorities of the principal G10 states since. The Jamaica Agreement also confirmed that for the future the ➤Special Drawing Rights (SDR) would be the principal reserve asset of the Fund.

The ➤debt crisis of the 1980s was a significant ➤issue area in IMF management strategies. The IMF-Mexico rescue package of November 1982 extended almost 4 billion dollars of IMF credit lines in return for structural adjustments such as reducing the budget deficit and subsidies from the Mexican government. Further IMF conditionality included a 5 billion dollar credit from commercial banks to match the IMF monies. The Mexican agreement became the model for other IMF-sponsored rescue packages. These attempts at debt crisis management proved to be a Faustian bargain for many recipients. Growth rates significantly deteriorated as debt as a proportion of GNP rose. IMF structural adjustment demands were the object of party political attacks from opposition groups. Eventually a new initiative under the so-called Brady Plan allowed for debts to be re-negotiated to reduce interest payments and, in some cases, to rescind the debt totally. Throughout the IMF has continued to insist upon structural adjustments as condition for debt relief.

**Immigration** Refers to the movement of people from their home ➤state to another state, usually to seek employment, to improve wages, to join family members or to escape from adverse living conditions. The immigrant is distinct from the ➤refugee in that the move is voluntary rather than forced. The issue of international migration impinges directly on central concepts such as ➤sovereignty, ➤nationality and ➤human rights and as such has important implications for ➤international relations. For example, migrants may be a source of conflict between sending and receiving countries (as is the case between ➤Afghanistan and Pakistan). Immigration may also pose security problems in the receiving state, especially where cultural and ➤ideological differences between host and sender are great. In addition, movement across ➤international boundaries can have unsettling economic and financial consequences arising from the international flow of capital, savings and investments. Most discussions of immigration centre on economic conditions as the main initiator of population movement but political factors are also crucial. Population movement is often impelled or encouraged by governments (e.g. Kenyan Asians after independence, or bourgeois Cubans after Castro's ➤revolution); it is often prevented by governments (e.g. Jews in the former Soviet Union) and of course, it is governments who decide whether immigrants should be allowed to enter the state of their choice. Political determinants are therefore crucial. Forced emigration has often been used as a means of achieving cultural homogeneity or ethnic dominance and can be linked with the rise of ➤nationalism in Europe and the rise of post-colonial new states in Africa and Asia. Remittance from migrant workers is often of great importance for the economies of many ➤Third World and developing states. Zimbabwe, Botswana, Lesotho, and Mozambique are, in varying degrees, dependent on such sources of returning income. The host state (in this case South Africa) was never reluctant to use this economic weapon to gain leverage over the sending states. Indeed in post-apartheid South Africa the problem of immigration has become acute. Despite its formal commitment to a ➤human rights based ➤foreign policy, President Mandela's Government of National Unity has been forced to adopt measures to curb the influx of migrants from neighbouring states across the Republic's porous borders.

➤International law relating to human migration has tended to defer to the good will of sovereign states or else is bound up with specific ➤treaty commitments. Generally, states have no legal duty to admit all immigrants, and most impose selective restrictions on entry, most of which relate, at least ostensibly, to possible threats to the public safety, security, welfare or institutions of the recipient state. Often these restrictions serve to mask racial or geographical discrimination. However, there is a growing body of opinion that the moral duty of states to admit immigrants under certain conditions is incontestable. Greater concern for human rights may lead to more open boundaries but as yet, each state jealously guards its sovereign right to adjudicate such issues.

Approximately half of immigrants are properly ➤refugees driven out of their country of origin by government persecution or ethnic violence or both. In recent years ➤ethnic cleansing in Bosnia and Rwanda, in particular, has highlighted the plight of these unfortunate victims. In the case of Bosnia, the ➤European Community drew up a hasty quota system amongst neighbouring states in order to manage and absorb those fleeing the violence in the former ➤Yugoslavia. The immigration permits were invariably temporary though and under the terms of the Dayton (Ohio) Agreement in 1995 it was envisaged that most Bosnian migrants would return home. This did not happen voluntarily and enforcement measures were subsequently adopted by many states.

The issue of immigration is bound up with the ➤Westphalian concept of IR and the division of the world into separate ➤sovereign states. Immigration control is therefore a fundamental attribute of sovereignty, mainly on ➤security grounds. All political communities have some limit on membership (citizenship) therefore restrictive immigration policies are virtually universal. An exception was the USA in its early years but even there the right to enter the country was never absolute. Even the ➤European Union, which has gone furthest down the road of border elimination, still allows for exceptions. The Schengen Convention which came into force in March 1995, is widely regarded as a model on how frontier controls could be eased or abolished. However, although this allows for the free movement of persons its objective is economic not humanitarian. The aim is to assist the logic of the ➤single market, not to extend civil liberties. Thus the contradiction between the right to leave one's country and the absence of a corresponding right to enter another one, has not been resolved in inter-state practice or international law. ➤➤Migration; orbiters

**Imperial overstretch** ➤declinism

**Imperialism** Derived from the Latin word *imperium* it refers to the relationship of a hegemonic ➤state to subordinate states, ➤nations or peoples under its control. An imperial policy therefore usually means a deliberate projection of a state's power *beyond* the area of its original jurisdiction with the object of forming one coherent political and administrative unit under the control of the ➤hegemon. This assertion of dominance is associated with, but can be distinguished from, ➤colonialism. An empire can result in full economic and political integration of its subjects in the form of a ➤supranational entity whereas colonies are separate and subordinate by definition. In practice though, the two concepts often overlap.

Territorial expansion is an age-old phenomenon but in the modern world it is usual to identify two distinct phases: (a) mercantilist or dynastic imperialism which dates roughly from 1492 to 1763 and which saw the Western hemisphere and much of Asia come under European control and (b) 'new' imperialism 1870–1914, which witnessed the subjugation by Europe of most of Africa and part of the Far East. The period between is dormant in the sense that domestic issues such as ➤balance of power, ➤free trade, ➤nationalism and the industrial revolution were the major preoccupation's of the European states. In the development of theories of imperialism it is the second phase that has attracted the most attention. The first major effort in this direction was J.A. Hobson's *Imperialism* (1902), which linked the phenomenon with the demands of maturing capitalism for markets, investment opportunities, raw materials and cheap labour. Hobson's thesis was revived by Lenin in *Imperialism: The Highest State of Capitalism* (1916), which subsequently formed the basis of the ➤communist view of ➤international relations and the causes of ➤war. The competitive urge generated by monopoly capitalism would inevitably result in generalized imperialist world wars which would in turn destroy capitalism itself, thus preparing the way for the establishment of socialism. The equation capitalism = imperialism = war has had enormous influence in the twentieth-century world, although its explanatory power is rather limited. Many analysts have disputed the necessary connection between capitalism and imperialism and point to the frequency of imperial conquest and war long before the development of modern capitalism (see Schumpeter, 1951). Furthermore, it is difficult to subsume the expansionist record of the former Soviet Union under this formula (i.e. 'socialist imperialism') as it is the apparent lack of imperial drives in advanced capitalist societies such as Switzerland or Sweden.

Alternative explanations, casting doubt on the ➤Marxist/Leninist insistence on the link between capitalism and imperialism, abound in the literature on the subject. Thus, the demands of ➤power politics, strategic imperatives, diplomatic manoeuvrings, the search for honour and prestige, the rise of assertive ➤nationalism, changes in military ➤technology, the shift in sea-power from sail to steam, developments in communications, the growth in the power of the media, the extension of the railway system, the invention of the telegraph – all these have been identified as factors in the rise of modern imperialism, as indeed have humanitarian or missionary impulses and racial ➤ideologies (a phrase which neatly couples the two is 'white man's burden'). Clearly, the phenomenon is not susceptible to a mono-causal or deterministic explanation; it is more likely to result from a combination of a number of often disparate elements which existed in some imperialisms, but not in others. Besides the Marxist/Leninist view, another which emphasizes the determinist nature of imperialism is the ➤realist school where imperialism is regarded as a natural, and if not curbed, inevitable consequence of the anarchic, multi-state ➤international system

In contemporary usage the word has become politicized and now denotes *any* form of sustained dominance by one group over another. 'Cultural', 'economic' or 'structural' imperialisms are phrases frequently used to describe more subtle forms of relationship that do not involve overt political control. Notions of neo-imperialism, neo-colonialism and ➤dependence have accelerated the process of moving the term away from its traditional meaning, to such an extent that to many the term is now a political slogan so vague and wide-ranging that it is devoid of any practical or theoretical utility in the study of international affairs. ➤➤Structuralism

**Implementation** Implementation is a facet of decision-making. While not every decision requires implementation – for instance, a decision to do nothing – every implementation act presupposes a previous decision. Thus when the United States decided in October 1962 to institute a ➤quarantine during the ➤Cuban missile crisis, this decision required implementation by their military forces. Implementation may be seen as a set of discrete acts or as a process. Either way, it involves the agents of a particular ➤actor in carrying out certain behaviour repertoires at the instigation of the ➤decision-makers themselves. Of course, in the limiting case the decision-makers may implement their own decisions. This is more likely to occur in cases of ➤high politics where core values and long run goals are at stake in a particular policy outcome. Again in the example of the Cuban missiles, the US and Soviet leaders communicated directly with each other in order to manage the ➤crisis successfully.

Analytically, then, the implementation is that stage of a policy decision that comes after formulation. Additionally, the results of the implementation process will constitute ➤feedback into the decision system. Policy-makers should be enabled to decide thereby whether their policy is likely to achieve the goals they set when the initial formulation took place. For the decision system to work in this way it is necessary for what Halperin (1974) calls 'faithful implementation' to take place. Only very rarely is implementation a 'one-shot' affair. Usually it requires coordination between a number of departments of the government and cooperation between a number of governments, and non-state actors, if it is to stand any chance of working as intended.

The UK government's decision to enter into negotiations to join the EC in 1961 was a highly complex decision to implement, because it involved the departmental interests within the government and several different external interests – including the ➤Commonwealth – at the same time. The French ➤veto cut short an implementation process that was proving extremely difficult to effect in the way the policy-makers had intended.

In large organizations – such as those involved in implementation of ➤foreign policy decisions – the process is treated as a standard operating procedure (sop). Sops may be highly resistant to change because they represent the routines of the organization. They can also lead to a certain rigidity with the result that policy formulation may not be perfectly transferred into policy implementation as desired by the decision-makers. Halperin comments that this flexibility means that large organizations find it difficult to develop new plans quickly or to implement plans developed in a different context.

The possibility that faithful implementation may not occur because officials are unwilling to implement in the manner requested must be faced. In those political systems where the leadership is subjected to regular and routine electoral scrutiny the tendency is very apparent for senior bureaucrats to regard themselves as permanent fixtures and their political masters as transient and temporary occupants. In this way a bureaucracy can create its own ethos, rules of the game, procedures and so on. These will effectively reduce and constrain the initiatives available to decision-makers freely to implement their own policy decisions.

**Import** In the broadest terms an import is something which is introduced into an international ➤actor from the external environment. Thus it is possible to describe an intangible – such as democracy, ➤nationalism, feminism – being imported into a ➤state, or ➤region from outside. It is equally possible to describe a tangible – manufactured goods – being imported.

The term is generally used in a narrower, economically based sense. Here the reference is to the movement of goods and services for which there is an identifiable demand into a specified economic system. Again with the growth of ➤common markets and trading ➤blocs the importing actor need not be a state.

Common sense indicates that one actor's imports are another's ➤exports and, consequently, the level of imports into any system has to be monitored by policy makers and their advisers. At any one time there will always be some actor in the system seeking to alter the balance between its imports and its exports. This disequilibrium may be short-term and temporary or long-term and structural. ➤Policy-makers may seek to remedy this by discouraging imports and/or encouraging exports. The former policy is known as 'import substitution'.

Import substitution has a number of political advantages. If the market within the system is actually or potentially very large then import substitution will increase the self-sufficiency of the system *vis-à-vis* the external environment. For example, the establishment of ➤customs unions such as the ➤European Community has led to extensive import substitution in the agricultural sector of the economy. In this example import substitution has led to over-production and to such measures as ➤dumping of surpluses in other markets. Import substitution has the important additional advantage of reducing the actor's ➤dependence upon the external environment. Because it can lead to great uncertainties and vulnerabilities, dependency is often held to be an undesirable state of affairs. It can certainly place an actor that is so dependent in a situation where leverage, pressure and even coercion can be exerted by those providing goods and services. Thus, although import substitution is sometimes inefficient and is contrary to ➤free trade ideas, it does have considerable political advantages and attractions.

**Incrementalism** A theory of ➤decision-making first developed by David Braybrooke and Charles E. Lindblom (1963). This was then incorporated into later works by Lindblom in 1965 and 1977. In the original discussion by the two authors the theory – called therein a 'strategy' – was termed 'disjointed incrementalism' but the shortened version is widely used. The essential arguments for incrementalism are outlined in the fourth chapter of the joint work. The authors, using the idea of a continuum, suggest that decision-making can be analysed using two variables: the degree of information that is available at the time of the decision and the degree of change that is effected by the decision. Combining the two variables four typologies emerge: decisions effecting large change where the available information is good, decisions effecting small change where the available information is good, decisions involving small change where the available information is poor and decisions involving large change where information available is poor. What is termed 'incremental politics' is identified as type three above: decisions effecting small change made with a low level of information.

It is suggested that incrementalism is typical or 'normal' decision-making. ➤Policy-making is seen as solving problems, issues are approached on a step by step basis, the evaluation of alternatives is restricted and the goals sought after are short-term rather than long-term.

Incrementalism has been well described as like moving away from outcomes that are undesired, rather than towards outcomes that are desired. Policy-making, according to the incremental model, proceeds through a series of approximations which is why it is characterized as 'problem solving'. Where long-term change is effected it comes about through sequential rather than sudden movement.

Although the above-mentioned texts were not written specifically with ►foreign policy-making in mind, the theory of incrementalism has recognizable features with this context. In general terms it has served to direct attention away from what have been called rational actor models of policy-making towards viewing the organizational and bureaucratic contexts as important to the policy process. Graham T. Allison (1971) pays due respect to the innovations of the earlier books.

**Independence** This term has normally been used in two senses in the analysis of ►international relations. First, it is used in a quasi-legal sense to indicate that a ►state exercises exclusive authority over a tract of territory and that, moreover, this exercise of authority is recognized by other ►actors in the system. In this first sense, independence is a corollary of ►sovereignty. Second, the word is used to describe a policy ►goal pursued by individuals, interests and factions which seek independence or ►self-determination for an identifiable group which will often comprise a ►nation or a putative nation.

The two usages become fused when a state is declared independent. This has been a common occurrence in twentieth-century international politics, particularly as former ►colonial powers have relinquished control over peoples and territories that were previously part of their imperial systems. This process is known as ►decolonization. Thus the term independence marks a historical turning point in the political history of the majority of state members of the contemporary system. In most cases this transition was marked symbolically to demonstrate the transfer of ►authority. In ►Third World states the history of the period is often referred to as the 'struggle' – as in the idea of the struggle for independence – while the mobilization of people in support of these goals produces the 'movement' – as in the idea of the independence movement. Some analysts have pointed to the dangers of being too easily seduced by these symbols and have argued that in many important respects – particularly economic – ►dependence not independence was the reality. This idea that colonial control continues in other forms is known as neo-►colonialism.

The quasi-legal use of the term independence is exclusively reserved for state actors. It is therefore part of that approach to the subject known as ►state-centrism. Discerning analysts of this approach accepted that political independence had to be safeguarded in a system that was ►sub-system dominant. Traditionally this was achieved by ►balance of power ►diplomacy which was dedicated to the preservation of the political independence of, at least, the dominant actors in the system. Complete political independence was probably only available to those states committed to ➤isolationism. Even then it was difficult to sustain in all ➤issue areas of policy, particularly in the field of international economic relations where the benefits of ➤interdependence were demonstrated by the classical economic ➤liberals of the nineteenth century. As the system has become more of a mixed actor structure, the applicability of the term independence – in the first sense outlined above – has been reduced. The term ➤autonomy is certainly more appropriate for the non-state actors.

**INF Treaty** This convention, signed on 8 December 1987 between the United States and Soviet Union, eliminated a class of missiles variously described as Intermediate Range Nuclear Forces (INF) or Long-Range Theatre ➤nuclear weapons (LRTNW). The agreement was the culmination of some six years of ➤arms control negotiations instigated by the United States with a set of proposals known as the 'zero option'. The momentum generated by these events produced further agreements under the ➤START process.

The events following ➤nineteen eighty-nine, including the collapse of the ➤Warsaw Pact system amongst the former Communist regimes of the Eastern ➤bloc, has meant that much of the strategic significance of the INF has been lost. What was in effect a unilateral ➤disengagement of forces from central Europe removed the ➤perceived threat that had made the deployment of Cruise and Pershing missiles seem necessary in the first instance. INF is historically important as a pointer towards the ➤*détente* policy that was initiated as part of the ➤Gorbachev Doctrine, which culminated in the end of the ➤Cold War. The system of on-site ➤inspection incorporated in the Treaty was rightly seen as a breakthrough at the time but these facilities are now regarded as essential if inspection is to be enforced.

**Influence** A term which has strong connotations with ➤power, influence is used in two senses. First, it is used as a non-coercive form of power. Like power it can be analysed both as a ➤capability and as a relationship. Influence relationships, moreover, are similar to power relationships in the sense that they seek to 'cause' someone to do something that he/she would not otherwise do. In the case of influence relationships, however, sanctions are not overtly employed. The target is persuaded to change its mind instead of being coerced into doing so. Influence relationships, in this non-coercive sense, are likely to be particularly prevalent among ➤actors that are accustomed to expecting and receiving a high level of responsiveness in their relationships. ➤Allies rather than adversaries, coalition partners rather than ➤conflict parties, actors with ➤'special relationships'; it is in these situations that influence rather than power will be the preferred way of securing agreement. What has been called sensitivity ➤interdependence is often thought of in terms of responsiveness within an existing relationship and the two concepts – influence and interdependence – may be linked in this way. Alternatively influence relationships may be identified in a ►hierarchy, provided that the actors further down the 'pecking order' accept the leadership of the 'top dog'; then the latter will be able to exercise influence over the rest, but conversely will be susceptible to influence in return. Again the responsiveness will be present but the relationship will be closer to what has been called 'vulnerability interdependence'. In a hierarchical system influence will be prone to shade off into power when and if actors seek to manipulate perceived vulnerabilities in a coercive manner.

Second, influence may be identified within the power relationship itself, rather than as an alternative to it. The term can thus be used to describe power relationships which fail to produce compliance, but do produce some reaction from the target to the imposer's attempts. Because influence is seen as a kind of power failure, in this second usage the two concepts are much less distinct. 'He failed to get the target to do what he (imposer) wanted, but he still caused the target to change its behaviour' would be an example of influence in this way. In this second context the ►capabilities for influence and the capabilities for power are identical. 'He thought he had power but he only had influence', could plausibly be said of someone in this second sense. Thus any actor that is unable to overcome resistance and to secure its goals is merely 'influential', but not 'powerful', the distinction between this use of 'influence' and the use discussed earlier being in the role played by sanctions. In one use of the term influence sanctions play no role whatsoever, in the other they are present in the relationship but fail to secure compliance.

*Influence without power* and *influence within power* are difficult ideas to oper-ationalize and to observe empirically. Many distinguished authorities have not even tried. Dahl (1984), one of the foremost writers on power within political science itself, lumps 'power' 'authority' 'control' all together as 'influence terms'. In this way influence truly becomes the paradigm 'portmanteau' term. This approach has been avoided here by defining influence in two ways which are admittedly close to power but which can, at least analytically, be distinguished from it.

**Innocent passage** The right of foreign sea-going vessels to traverse the territorial waters of another ►state without interference provided 'it is not prejudicial to the peace, good order or security of the coastal state' (Article 19 of the 1982 ►UN Convention on the ►Law of the Sea). This includes the right to stop and anchor but only in accordance with the ordinary navigational requirements or if occasioned by ►*force majeure* or distress. The 1982 Convention initiated a twelve-mile innocent passage ►regime for all vessels, although some states (e.g. the former Soviet Union) require prior authorization for passage of warships. In ►international law, vessels in innocent passage are subject to the laws of the coastal state and the usual rules relating to transportation and navigation. Submarines must normally travel on the surface and show the ►flag. However, the Convention was somewhat ambiguous in the provision for underwater vehicles since the problem of inspection and detection is difficult even for the most technologically advanced coastal states. Sweden and Norway, for example, were known to be particularly concerned about the difficulties of tracking the illegal submerged passage of Soviet submarines in Scandinavian waters.

The exact meaning of 'innocent passage' has never been clear but the Convention did attempt to clarify it and provide specific criteria for assessment. Thus, the character of the mission must be understood (is it threatening or dangerous or contrary to international law?). Secondly, the activities of the vessels during passage must conform to certain standards (are they engaged in weapons practice or information gathering?). Thirdly, the passage must comply with environmental, fishing and research requirements (are they engaged in wilful ➤pollution or illegal sea-bed exploitation?). All these criteria were intended to strengthen the hand of the coastal state and to ensure that only activities which had a direct bearing on passage were permitted. Critics have argued that the concept is a vague and ambiguous one and that it seriously impedes global naval mobility. In particular, the territorialist trend towards greater coastal jurisdiction of adjacent waters caused some concern to the larger naval powers. Nevertheless, most commentators agree that in relation to innocent passage, the Convention achieved a fine balance between traditional naval interests and coastal states' aspirations towards greater control of the sea. ➤➤Law of the Sea

**Inspection**  Inspection is a form of ➤verification. It is that form of verification that takes place onsite. Inspection thus differs from surveillance. Surveillance is also a form of verification but it involves observing rather than inspecting. In an efficient verification system, inspection would properly follow surveillance. The latter would suggest that something was wrong, inspection would either confirm or deny this assumption. Inspection is thus a means of providing information and ➤intelligence. It helps to establish that an actor is doing something. Inspection may be carried out by the parties to a relationship or by a third party – such as the ➤United Nations – brought into the relationship because of its perceived ➤neutrality and impartiality. In a relationship of total cooperation and trust, inspection would not be regarded as either appropriate or necessary. In a relationship of pure ➤conflict and total hostility, inspection would not be possible. Inspection functions essentially along a continuum between these two polar positions.

Inspection is important to most ➤arms control and ➤disarmament agreements. In addition to providing the information and intelligence function referred to above, inspection helps to deter evasion of arms control and disarmament agreements. If it is impossible for parties to agree to a system of inspection then they may find it impossible to agree to arms control and disarmament *per se*. Alternatively, and in the absence of agreement about inspection, the parties will have to rely upon other means of verification, such as the so-called national technical means. Thus, when it proved impossible to get agreement on the number of on-site inspections that would be permissible, the United Kingdom, the United States and the Soviet Union agreed to a partial ➤test-ban treaty in 1963. The only kinds of ➤nuclear weapons tests needing inspection were those conducted underground (to avoid confusion with earthquakes) and this class of testing was left out of the final agreement. Inspection systems are normally institutionalized in the terms of the agreement between the contracting parties. For example, under the ➤non-proliferation treaty which came into force in 1970, the International Atomic Energy Agency (IAEA) was empowered to make periodic and *ad hoc* inspections of national facilities in order to maintain the safeguards ➤regime. The ➤Persian Gulf War and the subsequent denucleariz-ation of Iraq showed up the shortcomings of this consensual 'gentlemen's agreement' approach to inspection. It is now widely seen to be necessary for an international inspection regime to be more intrusive if states are to be ➤deterred from cheating. This system of what is referred to as 'challenge inspections' is a feature of the ➤Chemical Weapons Convention. If a full-blown agreement to initiate general and complete ➤disarmament became possible, it would require an international inspectorate, among other things, to ensure that agreements were being kept. Inspection is part of the family of international institutional repertoires that includes fact-finding, observation and supervision duties. All of these quasi-diplomatic functions require some measure of support and cooperation from the parties being inspected or supervised if they are actually to be efficacious.

**Insurgency** Insurgency is an armed insurrection or rebellion against an estab-lished system of government in a ➤state. If the violent challenge by the insurgents is forcefully resisted by the incumbents, and it normally is, a ➤civil or internal ➤war situation will result. Such outcomes lead to ➤protracted violence between the parties. Insurgencies are normally aimed at one of two goals. Centripetal insurgencies seek to replace the incumbent ➤regime with a system of government more conducive to the interests and inclinations of the insurgents. Typical within this category are movements for the independence of colonial peoples and territories which seek via the insurgency to end formal colonial control. Because colonial systems relied upon coercion rather than consent as their principal means of social control, even a fairly low level of insurgent violence will be perceived by the authorities as a threat which has to be resisted. Centripetal insurgency is also a typical form of violent opposition to authoritarian regimes within states that are formally independent. In this sense the term is isomorphic with the idea of ➤revolution – although not all revolutions take the form of insurgencies, of course. Centrifugal insurgencies, on the other hand, are aimed at ➤secession from the incumbent state and the formation of a new entity. In the present system centrifugal insurgencies are likely to be associated with the expression of ➤ethnic nationalism. Although less common historically than centripetal insurgencies, contemporary instances such as Eritrea and Southern Sudan show the salience of this category.

Individuals and groups are recruited into insurgency movements by two principal appeals: (a) to their sense of ethnic identity and (b) to their political allegiance. These two appeals may fuse, as they did in the case of the Malay Communist Party after 1948, if affective and cognitive attitudes come together. Social groups that are recruited into insurgency movements include the intelligentsia and the rural peasantry. This fusion was explicitly recognized in the idea of ➤People's War and the Chinese and ➤Vietnamese revolutions which exemplified this model.

Insurgencies proceed by using the strategy of unconventional warfare, including ➤guerrilla war, particularly in their earlier stages. Centripetal insurgencies normally move beyond this guerrilla mode in their later stages when it becomes necessary physically to 'liberate' areas of the disputed territory from the control of the incumbents. Eventually the violence may become essentially ➤conventional if there is no short cut available to removing the last vestiges of the ➤status quo. Anti-colonial insurgencies usually succeeded well before this point of finality was reached. In all cases insurgency situations are paradigm instances of the ➤Clausewitzian tradition of viewing the military instrument as the means of achieving political goals.

Since insurgencies are protracted conflicts, external or third party ➤intervention is the norm rather than the exception, certainly in the macropolitical system post-1945. Third party intervention tends towards one of three typologies. First, a third party may attempt to mediate between the insurgents and the incumbents. Diplomatically such intervention requires giving at least ➤*de facto* ➤recognition to the insurgent movement. Second, intervention may occur because the external actor has been drawn into the violence as an ally or protector of one of the parties. If this intervention is made on the side of the insurgents then they will look to the ally to provide them with a sanctuary or base area, safe and secure, from which operations against the ➤status quo regime can be conducted. For the latter, on the other hand, the most important role an ally can play is diplomatic support and economic ➤aid to assist in prosecuting their campaign against the insurgents. During the 1960s this prosecution came to be called ➤counter-insurgency. Third, an outside party can use an insurgency to penetrate the state concerned militarily and/or economically for its own interests. This can occur as a ➤spillover from alliance links or it may be quite independent of the parties. As a result the target state becomes in effect a client or satellite, whatever the outcome of the civil war.

**Integration** Integration is both a process and an end state. The aim of the end state sought when actors integrate is a political community. The process or processes include the means or instruments whereby that political community is achieved. There is an important proviso which must be entered immediately. The process of integration should be voluntary and consensual. Integration which proceeds by ➤force and ➤coercion is ➤imperialism. Although historically empire-building has some of the characteristics currently attributed to integration, modern scholarship has been insistent that the process of integration should be regarded as non-coercive. Taking a historical perspective, the most significant attempts at building political communities in the past have been directed towards the creation of ➤nation-states. Nationalist sentiments have often preferred to describe this as unification rather than integration. Current scholarship, with its emphasis on integration between ➤state actors, can present a truncated view of the process if due regard is not paid to the nation-building purposes of earlier eras.

An integrated political community must possess certain structural characteristics. Thus typically among states integration will produce a collective configuration of ➤decision-making that will be closer to ➤supranational ideal type rather than the ➤international. For instance, collective decisions might be taken by a majority of the membership and the strict ➤unanimity principle would be abandoned. The need for policy integration will be particularly important if the nascent community is responsible for the allocation of goods and services between the constituent units. This will certainly be the case in those instances where political community building is predicted upon economic integration via ➤customs unions and ➤common markets. This aspect of community building has particularly exercised the interest and attention of students of integration in the post-1945 period.

At a minimum, integration presupposes the existence of a ➤security community, that is to say a system of relationships which has renounced force and coercion as means of settling differences. Beyond this requirement, economic ➤interdependence will encourage the putative participants to engage in the kinds of collective action referred to above in order to promote mutual interests. ➤Regionalism – expressed both in terms of similarity and proximity – will further enhance these tendencies. As integration proceeds new tasks, responsibilities and mandates will be taken on by the central institutions. This 'organizational task expansion', as it has been called, will be positively correlated with the integration process.

In an integrated community, political processes will take on characteristics often associated with intrastate, rather than interstate, politics. For instance, political parties and interest groups will start to press demands and articulate interests at the centre as well as at the periphery. Indeed, eventually they will prefer to concentrate upon the former locus of ➤power. Groups representing economic, social, environmental and religious interests will develop in addition to more traditional party arrangements. If economic integration has been a key preliminary to political community building then these groups may well be associated with wealth-welfare issues. The 'rules of the game' for these groups will broadly include a willingness to work within the system in order to achieve their goals and specifically a commitment to ►pluralism as a political style. This pluralist characteristic of the political processes will give rise to ►transnational politics as an increasingly significant section of the population within the member states perceive that more and more of their expectations and aspirations are being met within the integrated structure.

A political community must command the loyalties and affections of the majority of the population of its constituent units. Historically in the formation of nation-states, ►nationalism provided the ►ideological and attitudinal infra-structure for this loyalty transfer. Contemporary efforts at building communities 'beyond the nation state' have the task of providing a new focus for centripetal growth while confronting the centrifugal tendencies of nationalism. ►Function-alism and ►neo-functionalism, ►federalism and ►confederalism have all sought to address this crucial aspect of integration in their own ways.

Integration is a highly persuasive process in the contemporary world political system. Its development since 1945 has been largely on a regional basis with the greatest advances being made within Western Europe. The development there of a security community following the Second World War was an important prerequisite. Externally the active encouragement of the United States from the ►Marshall Plan onwards was an important contributory factor in the emergence of new entities in the continent. As the number of actors involved in the European experiment has increased some observers have seen the dynamic being diluted. On the other hand the ►scope of integration – as measured by the number of sectors/issues involved in the integration process – has increased.

**Intelligence** Since knowledge is ►power, the gathering of information about another's ►capabilities and intentions is a vital aspect of ►state behaviour, both internally and externally. It can be open or covert, strategic or non-strategic. In all cases, its purpose is to acquire, analyse and appreciate data in order to facilitate ►policy-making. While the acquisition of confidential information is the prime function of the intelligence community, other roles associated with it are counter-intelligence (to prevent others acquiring information), deception (the spread of disinformation) and covert action (political warfare or subversion). Intelligence is gathered in two ways, technical and human. Technical intelligence is referred to as *sigint* (signals intelligence) and *elint* (electronic intelligence); human intelligence is called *humint* and refers primarily to espionage. It is a mistake to assume that technical intelligence (through the use of spy satellites, sensitive listening devices, early warning aircraft and spy ships) has rendered human intelligence obsolete. There are some kinds of information (classified documents or likely intentions of ►decision-makers) that are not externally detectable, however sophisticated the ►technology involved. An 'agent in place' or a highly trained individual on the spot who is able to eavesdrop, purloin or otherwise glean sensitive information, is still an essential instrument of intelligence services. In any case, since the problem of avoiding strategic or political surprise lies more in analysis than in gathering information, human intelligence will always be paramount. Faulty analysis of relevant information has resulted in some spectacular and well known political and strategic disasters. Among them are the following: the German attack on the Soviet Union in 1941 (Operation Barbarossa), ➤Pearl Harbor 1941, the North Korean-Chinese offensive 1950, the ➤Bay of Pigs 1961, the Tet Offensive 1968, the Yom Kippur War 1973 and the ➤Falklands/Malvinas War of 1982. Intelligence failures of this kind are often followed by political upheaval and measures of organizational reform, but given the complexity and volume of data available, as well as the constraints of time, it is doubtful that they can be eliminated altogether. Scholarly analysis of these events suggests that the problem usually lies with the consumer of intelligence rather than with the producer. Bureaucratic inertia, complacency, internal rivalry and above all, a fixed ➤image of an adversary's likely behaviour, are the most common faults.

Intelligence is often referred to as the 'missing dimension' of diplomatic history and ➤international relations. Apart from the very nature of the enterprise, one of the reasons for this is that intelligence successes are rarely made known outside the professional circles involved in them, and then only when the outcome cannot be affected. One of the outstanding successes of modern intelligence was undoubtedly the deciphering of German wartime codes (the Enigma machine). This, it was subsequently claimed, considerably shortened the Second World War. However, we have no means to substantiate this: in matters of intelligence failure is easier to gauge than success.

**Interdependence** Interdependence in world politics implies that ➤actors are interrelated or connected such that something that happens to at least one actor, on at least one occasion, in at least one place, will affect all the actors. Thus in any given system of relations the more actors, the more places and the more occasions, the greater the interdependence. As Keohane and Nye (1977) point out, interdependence always implies sensitivity, in the short term at least. Thus, the above definition is congruent with this idea of sensitivity. Whether all actors in a system are affected equally will define whether the interdependence is symmetrical or not. Symmetry is usually seen as a benchmark against which actual instances may be judged. In reality it is not likely to be perfect. Conversely if one actor in a system is relatively indifferent about some change in the relationships while another is crucially affected by it, then the interdependence is asymmetric. This can lead to a highly manipulative set of relations with one actor or a group being totally dependent on some other actor or group. This highly vulnerable position is again recognized by Keohane and Nye as a longer-term and structurally determined effect of interdependence. It also bears a strong family resemblance to ➤power analysis.

Since interdependence is a neutral term, it can convey both positive and negative connotations. For ➤neoliberals a high degree of interdependence leads to greater interstate cooperation and is therefore a force for stability in the ➤international system. ➤neorealists (such as K. N. Waltz) on the other hand, argue that since states seek to control what they depend on or to lessen their dependency, increased interdependence leads to conflict and instability. Part of the difference between the two positions relates to the degree of symmetry/dependence/vulnerability in the relationship: the general rule being the greater the symmetry the greater the likelihood of cooperation and stability. Conversely the greater the asymmetry the greater the likelihood of conflict and system instability. ➤Dependency theorists incline to the latter view. In South America and the ➤Third World interdependence is often regarded as a synonym for 'structural' or 'neo-' ➤imperialism since it is perceived that the ➤North has imposed (and benefits from) the dependence of the ➤South on its capital, ➤technology and markets. The transformation of the international system from a predominantly ➤bipolar one to a ➤multipolar system in the post-➤Cold War period has led many neoliberals to argue that this inevitably leads to greater symmetry. In particular, the demise of the ➤superpower-client phenomenon and the substitution of economically based relationships for military-based ones results in greater degrees of interaction especially at the institutional level. For 'neoliberal institutionalists' therefore the mechanism of cooperation is enhanced at both regional and global levels: regular contact leads to policy coordination and to the progressive elimination of extreme asymmetries.

Although ideas about interdependence became very fashionable during the 1970s, more discerning writers recognized that interdependence, as a characteristic of relationships, could be identified with one of the most persistent features of the ➤state-system – the ➤alliance. It is quite clear that the activities of ally seeking and alliance construction presage interdependence. In the alliance situation the degree of interdependence will depend upon how much the allies need each other and how dependent they are upon each other's ➤capability to meet the external threat. In the twentieth century recognition of the importance of interdependence in military-security ➤issue areas was taken a stage further with the idea of ➤collective security. In terms of the concept of interdependence, collective security took the motivation that produces ally seeking a stage further and sought to establish a ➤security regime which would be more organized than the traditional alliance. At the same time both institutional responses recognized the significance of interdependence.

As the Keohane and Nye book (1977) shows, more recent scholarship on the idea of interdependence has tended to focus primarily upon wealth-welfare economic issue areas rather than those referred to above. The explanation for this is not hard to find. As a general rule interdependence increases directly as industrialization and ➤modernization take place. Moreover, if and when these processes commence, regular and routine access to markets will be required to achieve and sustain economic growth. Interdependence increases further and a complex ➤feedback loop is set up between certain economic goals and the consequences of interdependence. The ➤trade system is usually taken as the paradigm example of this process of economic interdependence. The larger the ratio of trade to GDP the more dependent the state is upon the international trading system.

Recent scholarly interest in interdependence is a reflection of this economic fact of life rather than the military-security issue area mentioned earlier. Indeed, a whole perspective or paradigm on ➤macropolitics – the ➤pluralist – has been built upon the recognition of this as a persistent and pervasive process in the system. Ideas about ➤regimes and empirical analysis of regime construction have, again, been primarily influenced by this sector of macropolitical activity. ➤➤complex interdependence

**Intergovernmentalism** ➤confederalism

**Intermestic** A term coined by Manning in an article in *Foreign Affairs* (1977) specifically in the context of American ➤foreign policy. The author was seeking to encapsulate the extent to which traditional boundaries between 'international' and 'domestic' issues had broken down in contemporary analysis. The expression may be separated from its American origins to achieve wider applicability wherever policy making in pluralistic communities involves ➤issue areas that amalgamate ➤actors from domestic/international contexts. Drugs, ➤immigration and ➤pollution can be cited as examples of issue areas that are by definition intermestic. Recent controversies in the United Kingdom over food safety involving the export of beef products and the need to take remedial measures at the behest of the ➤European Union can be categorized as intermestic. ➤trade policies are by common understanding intermestic because significant interest groups within the negotiating ➤states will be involved in lobbying in favour of or against certain proposals.

In the intermestic issue area both executive and legislative branches of the government will be involved in the policy process. The legislature provides a focal point for lobbying activity from within the state whilst the executive mediates differing interests in the ➤bureaucratic politics paradigm. Policy tends to emerge from a series of deals that might have to be cut and traditional axioms favoured in some types of analysis about the ➤national interest have to be abandoned or modified. Intermestic politics invariably concerns diverse interests and different priorities. Likewise any expectation that policy can be significantly conducted through ➤Foreign Offices will not apply here. Intermestic issues concern a variety of operating agencies/ministries within the governmental structure.

**Internal colonialism** This term is used in two senses in IR. The first sense is largely economic, the second political. Economically, internal colonialism refers to underdevelopment within a ➤state or ➤region as a result of unequal exchange between the periphery and the core. First employed by Gramsci and Lenin it highlighted the discriminatory economic policies of the central state (Italy and Russia) and the consequence of this for regions within them. Basically this involved a marked contrast between the wealth of urban core areas and the poverty of peripheral rural ones. It is particularly associated with theories of ►development and was frequently employed by ►Marxist and neo-Marxist analysts of ►apartheid in South Africa to explain the wide disparities of wealth and privilege between whites and blacks. In the second sense of the term, it is used to describe cultural and political divisions, rather than purely economic ones (though these are all related). Thus, in the UK for example, internal colonialism refers to the relationship between England (the core) and the Celtic fringes, Scotland, Ireland and Wales. These three countries tended to develop specialized export economies which were directly related to the needs of the core and instead of political assimilation all these maintained separate cultural and political traditions. Politically therefore, the term is closely allied to theories of ►imperialism, ►nationalism and ►secessionism.

**International** The word was coined by Jeremy Bentham and first appeared in *An Introduction to the Principles of Morals and Legislation* (1780). He invented the word to give a more accurate rendering of the Latin phrase *ius gentium* or 'law of nations':

The word 'international', it must be acknowledged, is a new one; though, it is hoped, sufficiently analogous and intelligible. It is calculated to express, in a more significant way, the branch of law which goes under the name of the law of nations; an appellation so uncharacteristic that, were it not for the force of custom, it would seem rather to refer to internal jurisprudence.

There has been some scholarly dispute as to whether Bentham was actually translating the Latin term, but what is beyond dispute is that he believed that a new adjective was needed to describe the system of law between ►sovereign ►states – 'international' ►law thus contrasts and ought not to be confused with, 'internal' or 'municipal' law.

**International civil society** A fashionable but somewhat shadowy term indicating the demise of the ►Westphalian concept of independent ►sovereign states and its replacement by a system of overlapping communities, jurisdictions and loyalties centred around a recognition of global interdependence. It is thus closely associated with ideas about ►functionalism, ►New World Order and world ►society perspective, where the ►state-centric approach is rejected in favour of a more ►pluralist emphasis on ►transnational and ►transgovernmental ►actors and processes. The existence of a civil society in ►international relations, like its domestic counterpart, assumes the presence of a complex web of autonomous organizations and institutions which transcend the state and monopolistic ideas of territorial sovereignty. Again, like its domestic counterpart, it is associated with the democratization of politics and is regarded as a bulwark against the authoritarianism and ►power politics. Part of its rationale involves a rejection of established power structures and the creation of formal and ►informal regimes to promote stability, economic development and environmental protection. As concept and as fact, it is still in an embryonic state.

**International Court of Justice (ICJ)** This was established by the ►UN as its 'principal judicial organ' and as such is the most far-reaching attempt yet to apply the rule of law to international disputes. Its Statute, which is annexed to the Charter, is similar to its predecessor the Permanent Court of International Justice (PCIJ) and all members of the UN are automatically members of it. The Court consists of fifteen judges who are elected by the ►General Assembly and the ►Security Council voting separately. The elections are staggered to ensure continuity, and the judges are elected for a period of nine years. Permanent members of the Security Council always have a sitting judge, but if a ►state appearing before the Court does not have a judge of its own ►nationality on the Court, it may appoint an *ad hoc* judge. The Court elects a president and vice-president for a three-year term, and it sits in the Hague.

The jurisdiction of the ICJ is twofold: settling international disputes and giving Advisory Opinions. Only states may be party to cases before the Court but non-state actors, such as private individuals or international organizations, may be able to obtain advisory opinions. States which are not members of the UN, for example Switzerland, Liechtenstein and San Marino may under certain conditions accede to the Statute. The so-called Optional Clause (Article 36) was designed to strengthen the Court's competence and required that all signatory parties recognize the compulsory nature of the Court's jurisdiction. This has not proved very successful. It has been estimated that up to the 1980s less than half the members of the UN accepted this 'compulsory' jurisdiction.

Article 38 of the Statute of the Court stipulates that the law to be applied should be: international conventions (i.e. ►treaties), international custom and 'general principles of law recognized by civilized nations'. In practice, the Court has been extremely cautious about applying this last source of law to disputes that have been referred to it. In mitigation it has to be recognized that as the membership of the UN has more than trebled since the inception of the Court, the chance of any positive consensus emerging about these general principles has receded. Because the Court has cautiously based its judgments on convention and custom, the Court's main impact upon litigation has been to clarify existing law-creating processes rather than to boldly push for judicial innovation. The rather different situation on Advisory Opinions is referred to below.

A number of contentious cases have been heard and ruled upon by the ICJ but its decision has not always been complied with. For example, in the dispute between the UK and Albania over damage to ships and loss of life in the Corfu channel (1946), the Court awarded nearly a million pounds damages to the

UK against Albania. Albania, though, has consistently refused to accept this judgement and pay the damages awarded against her. Although doubts abound as to the value of raising major international disputes before the ICJ (partly because of the difficulty of enforcing decisions), the Court has had many successes in laying down principles by which disputes may be judged.

Notable in this context are the principles for drawing base lines concerning territorial waters, fishing rights and the method of calculating the continental shelf beneath the sea. Generally, though, the record of the Court is a mixed one in contentious cases.

Besides these, the Court has given a number of important Advisory Opinions which have helped set the tone for post-war international affairs. The most important of these was that concerning South West Africa/Namibia. In 1971 the Court, revising an earlier decision, gave an opinion to the effect that South Africa's presence in Namibia was illegal and that other states were under an obligation to take no action which recognized South Africa's legal authority there. South Africa continued to dispute this view, arguing that the UN did not succeed to the League's power of supervision over the mandate which was given to South Africa. In 1989, however, South Africa finally agreed to accept the UN Resolution 435 which called for the Namibian ➤independence. In this instance extraneous political factors, such as the ➤Gorbachev Doctrine and the US policy of ➤constructive engagement, rather than the pressure form the ICJ, produced the policy change.

The General Assembly of the UN is charged with the responsibility for 'developing' ➤international law (Article 13) and there can be little doubt that the ICJ is a crucial component in this process. However, a number of important criticisms and constraining factors have mitigated against its development. Only a limited category of cases are brought to the Court – in general, those that do not affect fundamental interests. On issues likely to give rise to international conflict – issues connected with the ➤Cold War, for example – the Court was brought into play. The lack of enforcement power is clearly a basic handicap and although under Article 94 the Security Council has power to give effect to the Court's judgments, it has never done so. In the work and even in the composition of the ICJ the 'political' and the 'legal' elements often appear to be at odds. In this connection, developing states in particular have been critical of the Court, seeing it an instrument to further the interests of the ➤First World or Western European states. Notwithstanding these criticisms, few would doubt that the ICJ is one of the most important attempts in international history to establish the rule of law in the settlement of international disputes.

**International law** The term was coined by Jeremy Bentham in 1780 and refers to the system of rules that are regarded as binding on ➤states and other agents in their mutual relations.

It is usual to distinguish between two branches, 'public' and 'private'. Private international law, which is sometimes called 'conflict of laws' has to do with the rights and duties of individuals as they are affected by overlapping jurisdictions so is an adjunct of law within states rather than between them. Public international law on the other hand sees states themselves as legal entities and consists of the sum total of the rules, principles, customs and agreements that these entities accept as having the force of law in their relations. It is public international law that is dealt with here.

There is a great deal of confusion and often dismay concerning international law since the tendency to compare it with municipal law is often irresistible. International law has not been able to solve the problems of ➤conflict, ➤aggression and ➤war despite the hopes of ➤idealists of the 'peace-through-law' approach who believe that law and institutions could form the basis and inspiration for a ➤commonwealth of states. It is clear that international law differs in many respects from other types of law, so much so that some allege that it is not 'law properly so-called', but is at most 'positive morality' (Austin, 1832). Since the international system is characterized by an absence of legislature, judiciary and executive, it is argued that there cannot therefore be a legal order. There is, of course, the ➤General Assembly of the ➤United Nations (UN) comprising delegates from all member states, but their resolutions are not legally binding except on certain UN agencies. There is no system of courts and although the ➤International Court of Justice exists it can only decide cases where both sides agree and it has no enforcement powers. There is no governing body in ➤international relations since the ➤Security Council – which is the nearest institutional equivalent – is handicapped by the veto possessed by five states (the United States, Russia, China, France and the United Kingdom).

Notwithstanding these ultra-realist objections, international law does exist even if it has limited applicability in the high profile areas of controlling aggression, conflict and war. It has over the centuries played a vital part in shaping the character of ➤international society, having developed an elaborate system of rules and procedures covering the land, the sea, the air, outer space, ➤diplomacy, ➤neutrality, warfare, ➤human rights and so on – almost every aspect upon which one state's existence impinges upon another.

*Sources*

As may be expected given the absence of a written constitution and an international legislative body, the sources of international law are varied. They can be divided into four categories in order of importance: (a) agreements or ➤treaties; (b) custom; (c) reason; (d) authority. With regard to (a) treaty law is founded on the principle of ➤*Pacta sunt servanda* which means that treaties which are in force should be observed. There is a rider to this ➤*rebus sic stantibus*, which does allow a party to nullify a commitment if there have been significant changes in the conditions existing at the time the agreement was originally entered into. Under international law a treaty normally prevails over a national law which may conflict with it. Regarding (b) an important part of contemporary law arises from the customary practice of states over many centuries. This may or may not be translated into ➤multilateral treaties or codes of conduct. Categories (c) and (d) above are invoked when appeals to agreement and customary practice fail to indicate the rights and obligations of states. In this case recourse is made to logical deductions from established principles or opinions of legal authorities and jurists. Underlying all this is the principle of ➤reciprocity – the notion that it is in the mutual interest of all states to follow the established conventions.

*History and development*

It is something of an exaggeration to say that Hugo ➤Grotius (1583 – 1645) is the father of international law as paternity suits can be served at least as far back as the Romans, but it is generally acknowledged that, as with so many concepts in international relations, it was seventeenth-century Europe that cradled, nourished and developed modern international law. Grotius certainly played a vital part in this process as it was his *De Jure Belli ac Pacis* (1625) that put international law on a secular basis and made the somewhat daring assertion that law between states was based not on theology but on reason. The emergence in Europe of ➤independent and powerful ➤nation-states with incessant local rivalries and insatiable appetites for territorial expansion increased the need for legal demarcation of rights and duties and an important area of law which was refined during this period was that relating to the occurrence of, and conduct in, warfare. Theories of the ➤just war abounded and although this has now disappeared from modern treaties on international law it still underlies approaches to aggression and ➤self-defence.

Two predominant schools of thought evolved concerning the foundations of law: the 'naturalist' school, which identified international law with the law of nature based on reason, and the 'positivist' school, which held that law is man-made and therefore the consent of states is its sole basis. Positivist theories dominated the nineteenth century, the idea being that international law depended upon the will of the sovereign states and its purpose was to establish order and stability in an anarchical society rather than to promote values such as ➤justice or fair play. In the twentieth century, especially as a result of experiencing two world wars, these assumptions began to be questioned and the ➤natural law tradition made something of a comeback. The ➤League of Nations was created in 1920 and although it was a lamentable failure in the prevention of continuing international conflict, it did help to break the untrammelled authority claimed by the sovereign states and prepared the way for the establishment of the United Nations in 1946. The ➤Permanent Court of International Justice was set up in 1921 (succeeded by the International Court of Justice in 1946), the International Labour Organization was also established at this time and many other inter- or supranational bodies were created which in theory at least were designed to water down the purer notions of ➤sovereignty which had hitherto dominated the field.

International law is now in a state of flux. It appears to be moving away from being premised on a system of sovereign states towards the development of a common law for a world community of individuals. In the past states were the sole legal persons; in the twentieth century this hard shell has been breached and international law now concerns itself not just with states but also with individuals. This development was substantiated by the Allied Tribunals of 1946 which found enemy personnel responsible for 'crimes against humanity'. The process has continued to this day, most notably with recent multilateral declarations and conventions on ➤human rights.

However, although international law appears to be moving in the general direction of ➤world law it is important to remember that the absence of a supranational enforcement agency, coupled with the continued insistence on state sovereignty and states rights, means that a radical revision of the basis of international law is unlikely in the near future.

*Communist views*

The emergence of the Soviet Union in 1917, wedded to ➤Marxist/Leninist notions of the relationship between law and politics, has surprisingly had little effect on the orthodox system of international law described above. Since classical international law was founded on 'the state', this revolutionary ➤ideology appeared to demand that it, too, should 'wither away'. However, Soviet attitudes to international law amounted to a modification rather than a denial of traditional practice. Soviet realism under Stalin suggested that the international legal order could not be changed overnight, however desirable that goal might be. Therefore, as a temporary expedient, the Soviet Union would recognize the validity of the system yet reserve the right to view it as a strategy of capitalist exploitation. In the Khrushchev era this 'transnational stage' was replaced by the international law of Peaceful Coexistence, which was based on five principles: renunciation of war, ➤non-intervention, respect for territorial integrity and sovereignty, development of economic and cultural cooperation and recognition of the principle of ➤equality. This package was not so far removed from Western notions and it indicated that the Soviet Union had abandoned the notion that 'capitalist' and 'socialist' international law were radically different from one another. Yet since these declarations were accompanied by a firm commitment to the continuance of the international class struggle and the willingness to use violence to this end ('wars of liberation'), the idea of peaceful coexistence met with a high degree of scepticism in the West.

*The Third World*

Given the ➤imperial and ➤colonial background, which incidentally was legitimized by the prevailing international legal system, it is hardly surprising that the principles and practices associated with international law would be challenged. The Christian and Eurocentric nature of this legal order would not, at first sight, appear to suit the needs of these newly independent states. However, traditional international law has proved to be remarkably resilient and pliable, and in recent years the new states have embraced the concepts of sovereignty, territorial integrity, non-interference, non-aggression and equality with all the fervour of the original participants at ►Westphalia in 1648. The interests of the new states are often in direct conflict with the older members of the international community but so far they have been anxious to work within the existing framework rather than create a new one. The quest for a ►New International Economic Order (NIEO) has not so far been accompanied by a formal quest for a New International Legal Order, although some inroads have been made on past practice, especially in the direction of ideas associated with collectivism and 'common heritage'. These notions are at the forefront of the Third World approach and are a frontal assault on the more individualist and libertarian foundations of the older order.

*Effectiveness*

Despite widespread scepticism, most states obey international law most of the time. It may indeed be a weak legal system, but it is not violated more often than municipal law. States accept international law because it is in their interests to do so. It reflects the need felt by virtually all state actors, for order, stability and predictability in their dealings with one another. Since states themselves are the lawgivers in international society, consent underpins its efficacy. Moreover, it can and does reflect changes in international mores, norms and values. Although states are still the principal legal subjects, international law is a dynamic process and a number of recent developments are beginning to challenge their privileged position. These include the growth of international organizations as law-giving bodies, the increasing tendency towards regionalization and crucially, the increased emphasis on human rights in international relations. ►►Law of the Sea; International Law Commission; Common Heritage of Mankind

**International Law Commission** A subsidiary organ of the ►United Nations. The Commission was established in 1947 with fifteen members elected by the ►General Assembly. Since then the membership has been steadily expanded to reflect the growth in states in the Organization in general. Thus in 1956 the Commission was increased to twenty-one members, in 1961 to twenty-five and in 1981 to thirty-four. These members are distinguished legal authorities who sit in a personal capacity, not as representatives of governments.

The commission is intended to implement Article 13 of the ►UN Charter which speaks of 'the progressive development of international law and its codification'. Codification refers to the process whereby existing conventions and customs may be stipulated in a more systematic form. Progressive development implies the extension of the international legal ►regime to areas where the law is nascent. It could be argued that it has been in the area of codification that the Commission has been most successful. For example, the Vienna Convention on Diplomatic Relations (1961) had its origins in the work of the Commission, as did the various conventions on the ➤Law of the Sea. In respect of the codification process, the Commission may be seen as working in the same tradition as the Committee of Experts for the Progressive Codification of International Law established by the ➤League of Nations in 1930.

The existence and activity of the International Law Commission raises fundamental questions about the law-creating processes in the ➤international system. Perhaps an appropriately cautious view would be to say that, in comparison with the judgements of the ➤International Court of Justice, the reports of the Commission are of secondary importance as evidential value. As these proposals have the status of recommendations, it is unlikely that any radical reform of ➤international law will arise *directly* from the work of the Commission. Rather, it is a more plausible conclusion to see this body working indirectly to change the parameters within which international law and its development are assessed.

**International morality** A traditional term, closely related to the notions of ➤international order and ➤international society, which implies that ➤international relations are, or should be conducted on the basis of certain shared ethical values, assumptions or norms which are not necessarily embodied in ➤international law. The issue has been a contentious one throughout the history of international thought; indeed, the question of whether or not there are ethical limits to political action is central to the ➤traditional or classical approach to ➤world politics. At one extreme, political ➤realism, taking its cue from the ➤Machiavellian or ➤Hobbesian, models, argues that ➤international politics is essentially amoral; that notions such as ➤justice or ➤equality or freedom can only have proper application within the ➤state. The ➤international ➤anarchy dictates that ➤self-help and self-interest are key values in ➤decision-making. To think otherwise would not just be unwise or foolish, but irrational. In this view states create their own morality and the highest morality of all is the ➤national interest and ➤*raison d'état*. A watered down version of this extreme sceptical view is the relativist argument that moral obligations do impinge on world politics, but that the context within which it takes place renders it imperfect. The stress here is on the issue of national survival and on the instrumental value of order; in matters of policy formulation the outcome of order is more important than the principle of justice. Pursuit of ➤balance of power therefore takes priority over the pursuit of justice, equality, ➤human rights or freedom. This is the view adopted by most modern realists, including E. H. Carr, H. J. Morgenthau, R. W. Tucker and Henry Kissinger; order is a necessary precondition of justice and since the unrestrained pursuit of the latter could well lead to disorder and chaos, prudence rather than moral principle should guide state policy. Sometimes known as the 'morality of the lesser evil' this position rests on the belief that the moral requirements of states, existing as they do with no common political superior, are of a different and perhaps lesser order than those of individuals within an orderly civil society. This is not to say that they do not exist or are not important; it is just that other more pressing values and considerations, usually revolving around ➤security issues, are always likely to intrude.

In contrast, the ➤idealists or universalists hold that if human beings have moral obligations to one another, then so too must states, which after all are social collectivities. The idea of context is irrelevant, right conduct is universal and therefore what is considered good or evil in one context is, *ipso facto*, good or evil in another. This view identifies 'absolute' values such as the promotion of universal justice, human rights or ➤self-determination which override parochial concerns with interest or self-advantage. The society of states is in reality a society of people; boundaries exist but this does not diminish or alter the moral position. Rights of subsistence, for example, are universal, therefore traditional ➤state-centric doctrines evolving around ➤sovereignty and ➤non-intervention are barriers to progress which must in the end be breached. Adherents to this approach, or variants of it, can be found in a tradition which included Kant, Woodrow Wilson and some of the more modern ➤world society theorists. Underlying it is a belief in the idea of a common humanity which brings with it a common set of rights, duties and obligations. Accompanying this there is a corresponding belief that the present social and political institutions that characterize the ➤international system are seriously defective: global unity and planning are therefore essential if the moral issues of peace, security, harmony and environmental well being are to be resolved.

Between the two basic realist/idealist positions there are innumerable variations and mutations on the meaning and significance of international morality, and the most contemporary commentators take their stand on a compromise or synthesis between the two extremes. That is, that ➤transnational obligations and rights are important and certain obligations of common humanity undoubtedly exist, but their realization is circumscribed by the character of the international political system. An international community of sorts exists, but it is not cohesive enough to generate operational definitions of rights and obligations. Poverty, hunger, starvation and natural catastrophes elicit genuine international concern and action, but this is never undertaken at the expense of serious deprivation in the home base. Altruism is not entirely absent from world politics, but the political significance of state boundaries inevitably takes precedent over universal moral claims. ➤➤Normative theory

**International Non-Governmental Organization (INGO)** INGOs are ➤transnational, non-profit-making organizations. Thus the multinational corporations (➤MNCs) are specifically excluded at the outset, since they are profit making, and merit special attention on their own. INGOs are particularly prolific in the following issue areas: economic and commercial, ➤environmental, arts and leisure, medicine, science, ➤technology and education, youth and women's organizations and humanitarian relief work. Although INGOs' constituent members are states, the state representatives are non-governmental. Although some government representation may be allowed within the definition, the majority of the members should not be agents for any governmental interest. The separation from the ➤state-centred perspective is further enhanced by the fact that INGOs will necessarily have their own secretariat which will be internationally recruited – but from outside governmental structures.

Some relative assessment of the size and significance of INGOs can be obtained by applying the criteria of ➤domain and ➤scope. Domain will give an indication of the membership size. Scope will give an indication of the issue areas covered by these organizations, and therefore of the functions which they perform. Over the post-1945 period the domain of INGOs has increased by an average of 5 per cent per annum. The increase in the state membership of the system over the same period is, undoubtedly, an important contributory factor. However, increases in the scope of INGOs over the same period have had a ➤feedback effect upon domain. The most significant increases during this period have been in the economic and commercial sectors, ➤environmental politics, humanitarian relief, youth and women's movements. The distribution of INGOs within the regions of the world is highly uneven. Thus the advanced industrial countries (➤AICs) are heavily represented. Among ➤Third World states, Latin America is the most prolific participant. Conversely the lowest levels of participation come from the formerly centrally planned economies of Eastern Europe and from Asia. The majority of the headquarters offices of the INGOs are located in the AICs. The conclusion would appear to be that a high level of political and economic development is a necessary condition for effective participation in INGOs. Political development leads to ➤pluralism and the growth of interest groups within societies. These groups may then seek to establish links across state boundaries, thereby creating the basic prerequisites for INGO development. At the same time economic development creates the conditions wherein this development can take place. In summary, then, political development provides the ideological nexus, while economic development provides the infrastructure.

The growth of INGOs since 1945 has forced analysts to re-examine the extent to which the state can still be considered the dominant actor in ➤international relations. If the system is indeed a ➤mixed actor model then INGOs share the stage with the states, MNCs and intergovernmental organizations (➤IGOs). Detailed analysis of the political role of the INGO probably requires a case study, policy-contingent type approach. The majority of INGOs are not political ➤actors *per se* but rather functionally specific groups which may 'cross over' into politics when the opportunity or the need arises. The limiting case is probably that of ➤Green movements and environmental politics. In this case INGOs do not really function independently from the international political system. There is a qualitatively significant difference between Greenpeace and the World Council of Churches in this regard. INGOs collaborate with or conflict with governments on a case-by-case basis. In theory the growth of INGOs is limitless. There are not the territorial restraints evident with the growth of states. If present trends are maintained the continued growth of INGOs will have far-reaching implications for the future of international relations.

**International order** Sometimes used as a synonym for ➤international system it usually refers to the pattern of activities or the set of arrangements that characterizes the mutual behaviour of ➤states. In this sense it has a number of formal attributes – political, diplomatic, legal, economic, military – which provide method and regularity to ➤international relations. The contemporary international order is based on the European ➤state-system established at ➤Westphalia in 1648: a multiplicity of sovereign states coexisting in a condition of ➤anarchy which nevertheless recognize common standards of behaviour and interaction. There have been other international orders, such as empires, suzerainties and tribute systems with different components and attributes, but the contemporary order, which is now global, is premised on a rejection of ➤world government and a presumption in favour of state ➤sovereignty. It is said to display 'order' in the sense that it recognizes regulating elements (e.g. ➤balances of power, ➤diplomacy, ➤law) which provide a framework within which interaction takes place. The periodic resort to armed ➤conflict is not compatible with this order since violence itself is circumscribed by known rules. However, in any type of international order stability is a key value. This does not necessarily mean that the order is static. Change and development (for example the emergence of new states) can and do occur, but these are generally accommodated by the process of adaptation or adjustment. Some commentators argue that the rationale of order is ➤security; that the purpose of the regulating arrangements is to provide protection for the states themselves and for the system of which they are a part. This ➤realist or conservative view favours the ➤status quo and is generally adverse to claims that order is or ought to be synonymous with ➤justice. Others again argue that no international system can be legitimate without the just ordering of affairs. Thus, pressures for a ➤New International Economic Order stem from a belief that the contemporary arrangements are inequitable and should be changed. In the present order, this demand stems principally from the ➤Third World or developing states. The argument for justice as the central value is often accompanied by the idea that the international order (order between states) should give way to a world order (order between individuals or non-state groupings of people). In this way, emphasis on diplomatic-strategic issues are viewed as inseparable from global, social, cultural, economic and ➤technological issues. Instead of relating primarily to matters of national and international security, order is organically bound up with the issues of human suffering, poverty, hunger, social justice and ecological balance. The conditions for ►peace rest on the fulfilment of basic human needs and in relation to this the present arrangement of ►power and ►authority in world politics is hopelessly inadequate. Yet another use of the term concentrates on the establishment of ►international organizations and central institutions as being characteristic features of order. Order cannot properly exist between states until central authoritative institutions commanding the loyalty of all have been created. However, as some commentators have pointed out, the use of the term 'international order' in this context is inappropriate since with the establishment of ►world government, the bases for order would be internal not international. ►►Neorealism; neoliberalism

**International organizations** Formal institutional structures transcending national ►boundaries which are created by ►multilateral agreement among ►nation–states. Their purpose is to foster international cooperation in areas such as ►security, law, economic and social matters and ►diplomacy. They are a relatively recent phenomena although many commentators, from the Ancient Greeks onwards, have advocated their creation in one guise or another. In fact they began to emerge in the context of the nineteenth–century European ►state system where there were specific and self-conscious attempts to facilitate international intercourse and to provide a functional enabling procedure for common international endeavours. The first of these was the Central Commission for the Navigation of the Rhine in 1815 and the most well known was the International Telegraph Union of 1865 which was the precursor of the modern International Telecommunications Union (ITO). In the twentieth century these organizations have proliferated to such an extent that on almost every issue, over and above the traditional state-to-state diplomatic network there exists a more or less permanent framework of institutions through which collective measures can be realized.

Modern international organizations are of two basic types, the 'public' variety known as intergovernmental organizations (►IGOs) and the 'private' variety, the ►international non-governmental organizations (INGOs). Foremost examples of the former would be the ►League of Nations and the ►United Nations and of the latter, the ►International Red Cross and ►Amnesty International. Common characteristics of both types are voluntary membership, permanent organization, a constitutional structure, a permanent secretariat and a consultative conference. IGOs are established by ►treaty thus their competence is initially limited to the specifics of the convention, but organizational task expansion to meet new contingencies will commonly follow if the IGO is to respond to change. In this way, although states retain ultimate ►authority, international organizations not only provide a means for cooperative action but also multiple channels of communication which on varying levels overlie traditional diplomatic structures. For example, it has been estimated that at present over 380 public and 4,700 private international organizations are operative on a day-to-day basis in ➤world politics.

The theory of international organization has evolved from developments in such areas as ➤internationalism, transnationalism, ➤complex interdependence, the study of ➤regimes, ➤functionalism, ➤federalism and ➤integration. The central focus of all these concerns is an attempt to get beyond the political, social and economic fragmentation which has traditionally characterized the more parochial and individualistic views of classic ➤realism. While it is not easy to access the extent to which international organizations have contributed to the growth of internationalism, two basic views can be identified. On one hand, they are seen as early prototypes for an emerging ➤global governance, and on the other they are regarded as ineffectual and largely symbolic subterfuges for ➤unilateralism, which is the 'real' or 'proper' source of international behaviour. Neither extreme adequately captures the role of international organizations in contemporary world politics. Although doubts persist as to whether they are autonomous international ➤actors with a defined legal personality, few deny that they have made an enormous contribution to the management of ➤international relations.

**International Political Economy (IPE)**  IPE is now a major field of study within ➤international relations (IR) with an impressive body of literature built up in the second half of the twentieth century. As the name implies it relies for its rationale on accepting that the interstices between economics and politics merit consideration in their own right. By implication therefore studying international economics without considering the political milieu and studying international politics without the economic constraints is an unnecessary form of self-denial. IPE is thus the study of the confluence of these two subjects with special reference to structures, processes and interactions at the international level. As will be suggested below IPE is eclectic in terms of its approaches or perspectives (as is IR of course). It also has close family ties with political economy. Both fields can be said to show an almost congenital recognition of the importance of ➤ideology in the way their subject matter is analysed and explained. The concept of the 'market' elucidates this point. The market is both an existential reality and an ideologically informed perspective on how economic activity should be organized. Thus commitment to the market idea is both a recognition of its efficiency and of its eminence over other arrangements. Unlike other branches of IR, IPE has never struggled to prove itself as somehow 'value free'. Cox (1981) in a seminal article in the journal *Millennium* distinguished 'problem-solving theory' from ➤'critical theory' in IPE. In advocating the second Cox implicitly rejects notions of value-free study. Unlike ➤strategic studies (as it operated during the ➤Cold War era at least) IPE has been willing to include critical theory within its remit.

Given the growth of IR in the decades after 1945 it was always highly predictable that theoretical attention would turn to the interstices referred to above. Knorr's 1956 work on ►war potential is an early instance of an author looking at the economic aspects of national ►security policy. Wu's study of *Economic Warfare* came out in 1952, Schumpeter's essay on ►imperialism in the early 1950s. At the same time developments in world politics focused new interest upon what was at the time called 'The Politics of International Economic Relations (PIER)'. The ►Bretton Woods system and the new statecraft of ►aid concentrated minds on the importance of economic factors in ►foreign policy-making.

IPE was still locked into Cox's problem-solving theoretical approaches at this stage. Joan Spero's standard text on PIER (1977) rather than IPE took a heavily policy-orientated approach balancing relations within the ►North and between the North and the ►South. In retrospect perhaps Spero's work looks very conventional but a start had to be made somewhere and conformity has its merits. At the same time as PIER/IPE was taking off pedagogically, ►hegemonial stability theory was born and raised within the IPE. Whereas earlier theoretical excursions had been hybridized, stability theory was throughbred within political economy. Again as the name implies, hegemonial stability theory was a theory of equilibrium rather than a theory of change. Moreover stability will be enhanced to the extent that the hegemon encouraged cooperation even to the extent of tolerating 'free-riders' in the system. Stability theory was always a top-dog view of the IPE. ►Dependency theory on the other hand could justifiably claim to be a Southern viewpoint on the subject. Meanwhile the growth of ►declinist literature seemed to signal the end of ►hegemony. Keohane recognized this in 1984 in *After Hegemony* but argued that habits of cooperation could be continued through ►regime building. Cox (1987) and Strange (1988) made highly original contributions to the power literature by stressing the importance of ►structural power as against the prevailing ►social science tradition of viewing power as being about relationships. At the same time both authors have contributed to an attack on the ►state-centric approach within IPE, Strange (1996) taking this on a stage further to examine a range of non-state actors in the international economic system. ►Globalization as a prevailing tendency has further enhanced this mixed actor point of view. In 1994 in the first edition of the *Review of International Political Economy* the editors pointed to six influential aspects of globalization: finance, knowledge, production, economic diplomacy, culture and geography. However, stipulating complexity is easier than providing an intellectual framework to analyse it. IPE like IR is currently engaged in a period of broad-based speculation including ►neorealist, ►neoliberal and critical approaches.

**International politics** This term is used to identify those interactions between ►state ►actors across state ►boundaries that have a specific political content and character. These interactions will be handled by governments directly or by their accredited and accepted representatives. The term 'international' rather than 'interstate' is used because the latter has confusing connotations with ➤federalism and federations. The term may immediately be compared with ➤international relations. It is generally accepted usage to regard international politics as a class or category of international relations. The relationship between international politics and ➤foreign policy is also close. If the former is concerned with interactions, the latter is concerned with actions and reactions. From the foreign policy perspective, international political relationships are created by states engaging in the activity of making policy.

International politics implies that states are the dominant actors in the field. If other actors are identified then their ability to 'act' autonomously must be seriously questioned. The moment the assumption about state primacy ceases to be possible, then the term 'international' begins to look seriously deficient and some other designator – such as 'world' or 'global' – has to be used in conjunction with politics in its stead. Considerable confusion has been caused over recent decades because this terminological requirement has not been observed and authors have persisted in using 'international politics' when they mean ➤world politics.

Discussions on international politics are also made more difficult because there is no agreed definition of what the word 'politics' means. Indeed, some writers have wanted to define politics very narrowly in terms of the 'polity'. Without the polity one cannot have politics. Since there is no international polity, there is no international politics. This, albeit briefly, is the nub of the argument. Other definitions of politics, which stress the centrality of ➤power considerations, are much more compatible with international politics. They are also intuitively acceptable to the extent that they confirm the importance of the power variable in international politics and foreign policy. Some definitions of politics favour a more ➤decision-making approach. Thus, in one famous aphorism, politics has been defined as 'who gets what when why and how?' In terms of state behaviour this definition certainly re-establishes the links between foreign policy and international politics. However, it is necessary in this instance to insist on the ➤state-centred character, otherwise an ➤international organization deciding to lend money to a state becomes an international political actor.

**International Red Cross** Initially known as the International Committee for Aid to Wounded Soldiers, it was founded in 1863 by a group of Swiss citizens who were influenced by Henry Dunant (see H. Dunant, 1947). Formed a year before the first ➤Geneva Convention its role has been to work for the application of the principles of humanitarian conduct agreed at the various international conventions on the rules of warfare. It began with the care of the sick and wounded on the battlefield, extended its operations to ➤prisoners of war

(1929) and twenty years later achieved a major breakthrough in international cooperation when the Red Cross Convention, designed to protect civilians in occupied territories, was adopted (1949). In 1977 its scope was again widened to include humanitarian protection and assistance to victims of interstate or internal conflicts and other disasters.

The movement consists of three sections – the International Committee of the Red Cross (ICRC) which is its official title, the Red Cross or Red Cross Crescent Societies (139 in all) and the League of Red Cross and Red Crescent Societies formed in 1919. These three meet once every four years as the International Conference of the Red Cross. The ICRC is a neutral and independent institution (membership being confined to Swiss citizens) and performs an intermediary role in situations of armed ►conflict. For example, it was in place during the most dangerous phase of the conflict between Federal Nigeria and Biafra (1967–70) when it lost fourteen delegates in the fighting. Suggestions were made that the ICRC should supervise the withdrawal of Soviet missiles from Cuba in 1962 under the auspices of the ►United Nations but this was defeated by the refusal of Cuba to allow ICRC inspection of its ports. The main task of the ICRC, besides being an impartial intermediary, is in providing medical supplies and personnel during wartime and in attempting to protect civilians and non-combatants. To this end it seeks to establish 'hospital' or 'neutral' zones in the battlefield areas. It also provides assistance to prisoners of war and attempts to oversee treatment of political detainees. Given the ubiquity of armed conflict in twentieth-century ►world politics, the humanitarian role of the ICRC cannot be underestimated and virtually all states recognize its value (see D. P. Forsythe, 1977).

**International relations (IR)** This term is used to identify all interactions between state-based ►actors across ►state ►boundaries. The term can immediately be compared with, though is broader than, ►international politics. Indeed, the latter is subsumed as one, and certainly one of the most important, sub-fields of international relations. Thus ►international law is part of international relations but not international politics. Law is, after all, certainly in its customary form, created by interactions between state-based actors. Similarly international economic relations are part of international relations but not international politics. This is not to say that political calculations will not intrude into these areas, but only that they can be separated for the purposes of analysis.

International relations (IR) is thus an interdisciplinary and heterogeneous area of study. It has no unifying methodology because, taken with three examples mentioned above, international economics is an empirical social science, international law is far more normative than most social sciences while international politics is eclectic, borrowing from a number of traditions and divided in many minds into a rather unruly flock of activities. It should also be noted that the above listing is illustrative rather than exhaustive, diplomatic history, which again has its own methodology, being an obvious omission.

Despite its multidisciplinary and fragmented nature, most students of international relations view it as a sub-discipline of political science, broadly conceived. Although the main professional societies in the Anglo-American world have specifically and deliberately avoided using the term IR in order to indicate its multidisciplinary character (The International Studies Association and the British International Studies Association) the majority of members are in fact drawn from the study of politics. Indeed the domain of IR is often still referred to as 'international politics' despite the differences noted above. This terminological imprecision can also be noted in related labels such as 'world politics', 'foreign affairs', 'international affairs' and more recently 'international studies' and 'global politics'. ➤Foreign policy analysis, ➤security studies, ➤International Political Economy and ➤normative theory are the most vibrant subfields and these also are dominated by political scientists.

## History and approaches

As a separate field of academic inquiry distinct from International Law, Political Theory and Diplomatic History, IR effectively began with the establishment of its first chair at the University of Wales, Aberystwyth in 1919. The first general theoretical perspective was popularly labelled ➤idealism and was characterized by a belief in progress; that the international system could be transformed into a fundamentally more peaceful and just world order.

From the start therefore IR was policy-orientated. Thereafter the subject underwent a succession of waves of theoretical activity which inspired a number of 'great debates' within the discipline. In rough chronological order (mindful that these 'schools' are not exclusive and do overlap) these are: ➤realism, ➤behaviouralism, ➤neorealism, ➤neoliberalism, ➤world systems theory, ➤critical theory and ➤postmodernism. These perspective shifts often involved bitter disputes about methodology, epistemology and ontology. However, there is now general acceptance within IR that given the range and complexity of the subject matter, a wide variety of theoretical approaches might be an asset rather than a liability. Most of these ➤paradigm controversies were centred on the work of analysts in the USA and Europe (sometimes, inaccurately referred to as the 'Anglo-American tradition') which tended to concentrate on ➤great power/ ➤superpower issues. IR students in the ➤Third World or ➤South by and large, by-passed these debates and not unnaturally focused on particular policy problems with their states or ➤regions. Overall theoretical perspectives, if developed at all, usually had their origins in ➤Marxist/Leninist theories of ➤imperialism, in ➤dependency theory and ➤structuralism. With the ending of the Cold War, IR like its subject matter is in a state of flux. The two dominant perspectives are neorealism and neoliberalism but the general uncertainty about the continued validity of the state as the key actor in world politics, has led to doubts about the ability of IR in its present form, to survive as a separate area of academic study.

**International society** Ever since ►Grotius posited his concept of a 'great society of states' as the bedrock upon which ►international law, order and cooperation would be built, scholars have debated the very existence of a genuine 'society' or 'community' beyond the ►nation-state. There is no hard empirical evidence that the practice of international relations has generated a society or community in the usual senses of the words at all, and most scholars cautiously preferred to speak of an ►international system of ►states which, although displaying a regularized pattern of interaction within a specified environment, did not attain the degree of integration necessary to warrant the appellation 'society'. However, to theorists in the classical tradition, the notion of an international society which forms the basis for ►international order is fundamental. The misnamed ►English School of International Relations is predicated upon it: its principal members, Charles Manning, Martin Wight, F. S. Northedge, Hedley Bull, James Mayall, John Vincent and Alan James are all alleged to belong self-consciously to the 'international society' or 'international community' approach. That is, they all assert that the proper object of study is the conditions of social order present and possible within the prevailing international ►anarchy. As such, the approach is regarded as a variant of the ►realist school which focuses on the 'state-as-actor' axiom within a broad framework of institutionalized 'unity-in-diversity', i.e. the anarchical society. Thus Hedley Bull (1977), its most prominent advocate, asserts that 'a society of states (or international society) exists when a group of states, conscious of certain common interests and common values, form a society in the sense that they conceive themselves to be bound by a common set of rules in their relations with one another and share in the working of common institutions' (p. 13). The institutions which are said to create or foster this order are international law, ►diplomacy, ►international organization and ►balance of power. In this way the autonomy of international relations as a separate field of forces is alleged to be established as is the distinction between this and a 'system' which merely involves contact and interaction without the concomitant communal values, mutuality or ►reciprocity involved in the society approaches. The theories advanced are primarily ►normative although great pains are taken to establish their empirical relevance. Further, and in contrast with the systems approach, it is not ►sub-system dominant; that is, in many important respects the international society itself conditions the behaviour of the actors within it.

Whether or not international society is fictional or exists only in the mind, few would doubt that its image has underpinned mainstream classical international theory since at least the Second World War. The behavioural/systems movement, which for a short period dominated US approaches, is now beginning to acknowledge the vitality and persistence of the older traditions of political philosophy, jurisprudence and diplomatic history which first identified and elaborated the societal perspective. The US concept of 'international ►regimes' could therefore be seen as an implicit acknowledgement of this, since 'regime' in this context is a specific attempt to identify the intervening and perhaps autonomous institutional structures which sometimes have decisive effects on national strategies and perspectives.

**International System** This term, which is derived from ➤systems analysis, is used in two contexts in international relations; first as a description and second as an explanatory ➤level of analysis.

As a descriptive idea, international system is another way of referring to the ➤state-system. At the level of the state, groups and interests within it may be regarded as sub-systems. ➤Foreign policy is made against an external environment which is the international system. Because the activity of making and ➤implementing foreign policy will have a significant effect upon the system, the system is sometimes referred to as 'sub-system dominant' (Kaplan 1957). Traditional analysis of the international system has tended to place particular emphasis upon the ➤goals and ➤orientations of ➤great powers as being highly influential upon processes and outcomes. In systemic terms a great power is a ➤state ➤actor of such significance that its removal from the system would change the structure – e.g. from ➤multipolar to ➤tripolar.

Two fundamental systemic processes have usually been identified by scholars looking at international systems, past, present or future. These are the processes of ➤conflict and cooperation. Because these are so pervasive at the system level individual states in effect take them as 'givens' in their policy making and respond accordingly. In an effort to confront these systemic processes states have engaged in ➤regime creation and institution building. ➤International organizations like the ➤League of Nations and the ➤United Nations and ➤regional counterparts have proliferated in the twentieth-century system. The extent to which these organizations can be regarded as actors has been hotly debated. Certainly their existence has substantially modified the nature of the system and has led some to speak of a ➤mixed actor model.

The second sense in which international system is used is to locate the appropriate level of analysis at which explanations should be pitched. Waltz (1979) and Gilpin (1981) are examples of writers who have argued that the international system fundamentally determines the behaviour of individual state actors within its field. The first task of analysis is to discover the law-like characteristics of the system that all individual actors have to take account of. Thus ➤security is often seen as a primordial goal of states because of the ➤anarchic nature of the system. ➤➤Agent-structure

**Internationalism** Refers to a wide variety of doctrines and ➤ideologies which aim to transcend ➤state-centred politics and focuses instead on universal, or at least, ➤transnational interests. It is usually associated with ➤idealism or utopianism in international thought and as such is presented as a rational and moral alternative to the narrow conception of ➤nationalism alleged to pervade ➤realist thinking. However, the ➤national interest and the international interest are not always presented as alternatives. Under the liberal ➤harmony of interests doctrine the two are coterminous. American ➤liberalism, for example, has often asserted that 'what's good for America is good for the world'. This somewhat spurious identification of individual interests with those of the wider community is not confined to the United States. Most ➤states, whatever their professed ideology, have at one time or another asserted if not believed similar sophistries. Indeed, a major theme of E. H. Carr's seminal text, *The Twenty Years' Crisis* (1946), was the exposure of the use of the concept of internationalism to justify the ascendancy of the ➤great powers in the nineteenth and twentieth centuries.

Besides liberalism, other important examples of internationalist doctrines are ➤Marxism/Leninism and ➤pacifism. For the Marxist the end product is 'the withering away of the state', for the pacifist it is the abolition of ➤conflict and warfare, but both are premised on the obstructiveness and volatility of state-centred political behaviour. In this sense, internationalism could be seen as ➤revolutionary creed, not just in terms of ultimate goals, but also in terms of the strategies envisaged to achieve them. Whereas state-centred theories could be said to be horizontal (i.e., state-to-state relations), internationalism is primarily vertical, appealing as it does to a universalist conception of the human condition. In the study of international affairs, its most recent manifestation is in the ➤world society and ➤world law approaches where concepts of a common humanity and universal ➤human rights replace more traditional perspectives. Internationalism is by no means a recent phenomenon in ➤world politics and the history of international thought is replete with examples, mostly drawn from the ➤natural law tradition, of universalism or cosmopolitanism. Erasmus (1466–1536) is perhaps the most well-known example, but Kant (1724–1804), too, is central to this tradition.

**Internment** Properly, the forced detention of ➤aliens and ➤prisoners of war during wartime, but the term has also been used to describe the enforced resettlement, encampment or imprisonment of dissident nationals in peacetime. The ➤Hague Convention of 1907 obliged neutrals to intern alien troops, vessels and military aircraft. Specific conditions governing the treatment of internees were outlined in the Geneva Conference on Prisoners of War and the Protection of Civilians in August 1949 and were subsequently developed by the ➤International Red Cross Conference at New Delhi in 1968. Cases of internment which fall outside the scope of the Hague and ➤Geneva Conventions are now regarded primarily as ➤human rights issues.

**Intervention** A portmanteau term which covers a wide variety of situations where one ➤actor intervenes in the affairs of another. The relationship has been the source of much scholarly interest. Lawyers, basing their arguments on the starting point that there is an international norm of ➤non-intervention, have sought to establish operating rules which allow intervention to be successful. Diplomatic historians have sought to understand why particular interventions, usually of a controversial and possibly of an influential nature, took place, while political scientists have sought to identify and stipulate the characteristics that link these discrete events into that class of conduct we call intervention.

Under the classical sovereign ►state-system, established after ►Westphalia, interventionism as a behaviour pattern had to be restricted and hedged about with legal and diplomatic restraint. If►states and statesmen intervened willy-nilly in each other's affairs then the very idea of sovereign ►equality and territoriality would be undermined. Accordingly the ►billiard-ball model of the state actor developed to enshrine and enhance the idea that what lawyers called ►domestic jurisdiction would prevail. This meant that certain matters and concerns were 'off limits' to the society of states. Key areas where this prohibition was held to apply were referred to by terms such as 'territorial integrity' and 'political independence'. In essence these ideas attempted to safeguard the territorial and governmental ►status quo in the sovereign state. Territory and governmental structure were both intrinsically and symbolically important to states and statesmen. Thus intervention in these matters was supposedly prohibited by the sovereignty principle.

How far behaviour had to go to constitute 'intervention' is a moot point. Certainly, under the classical system military ►force was the most widely available instrument for this purpose. It can be used to gain admittance to both the territory and the political structure of a target state. Its impact in this respect is often dramatic and sometimes decisive. Once the force option has been taken, it becomes difficult to retreat from it. ►Influence, having been established by force, is subsequently maintained by force. Because force was such a threat to the exclusivity of state sovereignty an antidote had to be found. Conceptually, as we have seen, this was the doctrine of non-intervention. Diplomatically if this proved to be inadequate, then recourse was taken to the ►balance of power. Although the balance of power sometimes involved interventionist tactics, it also served to inhibit and restrain intervention, or was supposed to. This preventive function was achieved through the mechanism of ►deterrence. States in the system could act to prevent others from intervening in their affairs, as well as those of third parties, by threatening some credible sanction. Such sanctions were, again, usually manifested in military terms. The balance system is often held to have reached its fullest expression during nineteenth-century European ►diplomacy, in particular in the period after the defeat of France in 1815 and before the First World War. During this time frame other developments were taking place in international affairs which were to significantly increase the potentialities and possibilities for states to intervene in matters essentially within the parameters of domestic jurisdiction.

First, the rise of the ►liberal-democratic state in western Europe and North America created a type of political system which was much more open to intervention. Ideas about ►free trade implied the free movement of goods and services across states. Ideas about political freedom and representative democracy implied the free movement of ideas. The availability of more rapid and effective means of communication and transportation assisted these developments. Writers characterize these systemic changes as ►interdependence.

Second, the growth in the number of actors in the ►international system has created an environment where intervention might flourish. It should not be thought that these actors are exclusively states, either. The development of intergovernmental organizations (►I G Os), particularly in the twentieth century, means that these actors can adopt interventionist policies and attempt implementation thereafter. The persistent intention of the majority membership of the ►United Nations to discuss ►apartheid, notwithstanding the invocation of ►domestic jurisdiction defences by the state government, being a case in point.

The growth in actors also presents an increase in the number of targets for intervention. Many of the newer ►Third World states are polyethnic arrangements often with fragile and a corrupt governmental structure. These fragmented states are, clearly, more susceptible to intervention. It is often not difficult to find an interest group or faction within the ruling ►elite willing to collaborate with the outside party and, in this way, access to the policy centre is achieved. The paradigm example is the civil strife situation where authority is actively and openly contested and where ally-seeking activity with external parties is endemic. The intervener's objectives will thus be predetermined by the factions themselves while the instruments of intervention will run the gamut from diplomatic support to economic assistance to military operations. US involvement in ►Vietnam is a good example of this process.

Thus, starting off from an initial position in favour of non-intervention, the ground has shifted to the present position where intervention is endemic among international actors. Clearly, instruments of intervention cover a continuum from the use of force at one extreme to most conventional forms of ►diplomacy at the other, but how confidently can we stipulate the objectives of intervention? At the outset the intervener believes he can materially alter the situation from becoming more disadvantageous by his actions. However, it is important to remember that intervention is rarely a one-shot operation and that having embarked upon interventionist policy a threshold is crossed and the tendency is to continue with more of the same rather than to be constantly reassessing the rectitude of the original decision. Moreover, the reaction of the Target can affect the perception of objectives. Original objectives may be altered, entirely new ones may be undertaken as a result of the dynamic between an intervention initiative and a Target response. Again, the point about the time frame within the intervention is to be implemented appears to be crucial to understanding objectives.

Reference was made at the outset to scholarly conceptions of intervention. One of the most ambitious attempts to provide a synoptic view was that made by political scientist, J. N. Rosenau. In a series of influential papers, Rosenau (1968, 1969a) stipulated that intervention had two characteristics: it appeared as a break from conventional or normal behaviour and it was intentionally directed at the structure of political ➤authority.

Viewing intervention as a sharp break from previous behaviour has much to commend it. It reflects the legal tradition, already referred to, which tended to take non-intervention as the norm. Seen from this perspective intervention is a break. Unfortunately, contemporary behaviour by international actors appears almost to argue the opposite. Intervention is now the norm, but not vice versa. Moreover it has been argued that the instruments are much more refined and sophisticated than in the past. This makes intervention more pervasive and insidious. Emphasizing intervention as a break diverts attention from the point of view which stresses gradualism and ➤incrementalism as characteristics of interventionary behaviour. It would avoid the rather contentious, not to say dubious, argument advanced by Rosenau that US intervention in Vietnam began with the bombing campaign of February 1965.

Stipulation that the target for intervention should be the *structure* of government looks more promising. A plausible starting point might be to say that intervention occurs when the authoritative allocation of values within an actor's internal environment is made by, or made with, the assistance and approval of persons and parties representing other international actors. This definition covers such activities as the ➤IMF team arriving in the state capital and insisting on a more balanced budget before they open a credit line. It covers the activities of the ➤PLO in Beirut as well as the substantial American funding of the French ➤counter-insurgency war in Indochina fifteen years before the commencement of overt US bombing. Events in the post-➤Cold War period have focused attention on intervention in ➤communal conflicts where state structures are minimal or absent altogether. The growth of ➤environmental politics has concentrated minds on the possibility that environmental ➤regimes can only be sustained at the expense of state sovereignty. ➤➤Humanitarian intervention

**Iron curtain** A phrase usually associated with Winston Churchill but actually first used by Nazi ➤propaganda minister Joseph Goebbels, to describe the deliberate isolation of Eastern Europe from the West by the Soviet Union. It was popularized by Winston Churchill in his famous Fulton, Missouri speech of March 1946 where he said: 'From Stettin in the Baltic to Trieste in the Adriatic, an iron curtain has descended across the Continent.' The speech, and the implications of Soviet expansionism it appeared to contain, made a powerful impression particularly in the United States and many commentators allege that the image it projected underpinned Truman's policy of ➤containment and that it provided justification for ➤hawkish Western policies during the ➤Cold War. In fact the speech was less pugnacious than popularly believed and Churchill went on to say '. . . I do not believe that Soviet Russia desires war. What they desire is the fruits of war and the infinite expansion of their power and doctrines'. This observation clearly echoed the thoughts of the more ➤liberal US supporters of containment who argued that the Soviet Union should be opposed by diplomatic, ideological and political means rather than straightforward military confrontation (►X). This speech served to increase Soviet fears of ►encirclement and effectively ended any hope of a revival into the post-war period of East–West cooperation.

**Irredentism**  A term derived from the nineteenth-century Italian movement for national ►unification. In this context it referred to territories such as Trente, Dalmatia, Trieste and Fiume which had cultural and ethnic ties with Italy but which lay outside the physical control of the new Italian ►state. They were thus waiting to be 'recovered' or 'redeemed' for the nascent national community.

The term has passed into general political discourse in the twentieth century. Mayall (1990) considers irredentism (rendered irridentism, p. 57) to be a ►revisionism of the idea of national self-determination. It is certainly widely used, sometimes pejoratively, to characterize policies which seek to alter the ►status quo in a particular territory on the basis of nationalistic or ethnic criteria. Irredentism is particularly likely where state-based ►frontiers straddle and divide an ethnic group, or where they represent the imposition of external (for example ►colonialist) control over a previously unified system. The 'irridentia' then becomes, as it were, the 'lost' territory. As a result irredentism is a source of potential or actual ►conflict between international ►actors. Examples abound in the contemporary ►macropolitical system. Thus, Argentinian claims to the Malvinas and Spanish claims to Gibraltar represent the anti-colonial version of irredentism. Ethnic irredentism can be identified in the claims by Somalia to incorporate Somali peoples in Ethiopia and Kenya into a Greater Somalia, and in the claims for *enosis* or union with Greece made in the immediate independence era by some Greek Cypriots.

**Islam**  Islam is one of the three great monotheistic ►religions of the world. Founded in the seventh century A D it is also the most recent and, some would say, the most vital. It rapidly expanded from Mecca and Medina in the Arabian Peninsula throughout the Middle East, North Africa, Central Asia and Southern Europe in the century that followed the death of Mohammed, the Prophet. Uniquely among the three religions, Judaism, Christianity and Islam, its founder showed great political skill as well as great spiritual commitment. This fusion of political, legal and spiritual into one complex system is the singular achievement of the Islamic tradition. The Christian dichotomy of sacred/secular, Church/State, rendering to Caesar and rendering to God, is not really recognized as such within Islam. Certainly in its classical period Islam was a total expression of allegiance to a way of life that impinged upon all aspects of society.

Islam is sectarian, the main division being between Sunni – orthodox – and Shia – heterodox. These divisions date from the fourth Caliphate and are as much political as spiritual in origin. The breakdown of Islamic unity thereafter allowed the Ottoman Turks to succeed to the Caliphate and for ►state-centric tendencies to manifest themselves. When Shiism became the official religion of Persia (Iran) in the sixteenth century this established a trend which has continued as the ►state-system developed from its European nexus to cover the world. In the contemporary system it is thus possible to identify Islamic populations within particular ►states as being either predominantly Sunni or Shia and also to define followers of Islam within a particular state in relation to other religious groups. In the modern Lebanon indeed a whole political system was devised which recognized this confessionalism and sought to reflect it in a 'spoils system'.

In terms of ►international relations Islam can be identified as operating at two levels: that of the state and that of the state-system. At the former level there are a number of states which by affiliation and tradition can be termed as 'Islamic' whether their integral arrangements are sacred or secular. A fairly basic form of identification of this category would be membership of the Islamic Conference Organization. The sacred/secular dichotomy is important within this group and can be used as a benchmark of trends and tendencies. There is general agreement that secularism has lost ground of late and that 'Islamization' has taken hold both at the elite and mass public levels. In states which are predominantly Islamic this has led to the growth of 'back to basics' movements usually referred to as 'fundamentalism'. Because of the inherent ►transnationalism of Islam this fundamentalism has spilled over ►boundaries and impacted across frontiers.

Recognition of the fundamentalist tendencies referred to above brings in the second level; the state-system. Reactions to Islamic fundamentalism – particularly in the West – have been profound. Visions of the ►leaderships of Islamic states – notably Iran – wielding the sword of 'Jihad' and confrontation have been widely canvassed. Death threats to authors, assassinations, hostage situations, economic warfare, state-sponsored ►terrorism and inter-state ►war are included in the litany of fears. Islam can counter with the evidence of ►colonialism and ►imperialism over a long period of time during the modern era and of ►intervention during the ►Cold War. Recently the American scholar Samuel Huntington (1993) gave a significant section of his clash of civilizations thesis specifically to Islam's relations with other 'civilizations'. (The distinguished Middle Eastern historian Bernard Lewis had in fact used the term 'clash of civilizations' – in the context of Islam – in a widely circulated article in 1990.)

**Isolationism** An ►orientation used to describe and analyse ►foreign policy. Literally it implies a low level of involvement with the world outside the ►state and accordingly it requires certain operational criteria to ensure its ►implementation. In particular: geographical separation from the main power centres in the ►international system, substantial self-sufficiency and a political ►leadership which eschews national self-extension as a significant policy goal. In action isolationism avoids political, diplomatic or military commitments to other states. The term has been applied to the foreign policy of a number of states historically, including China and Japan. In the modern era it has been particularly associated with the foreign policy of the United States, but it has also been used to describe phases of UK policy. In the latter it was seen to enhance diplomatic flexibility following the dictum 'no permanent friends, no permanent enemies, only permanent interests'.

The United States provides the best example of isolationism becoming a political dogma and a touchstone of American exceptionalism. Following the Washington Administrations (1789–97) it was believed that the first President had set out the parameters of isolationism in his valedictory. Urging his fellow Americans to avoid 'permanent alliances' but recognizing the need in extremis for temporary alignments, Washington was held – wrongly – to be arguing for a blanket ban on outside arrangements. The waters were further stirred when the third president, Thomas Jefferson, inveighed against 'entangling alliances' in his inaugural in 1801. Isolationism in the United States was thus bound up with its insulation from the main centres of political activity, with its uniqueness as a ➤liberal state and with its belief in the moral superiority of the American way of life. In this way it was always ➤regionally specific-directed against Europe rather than the Western Hemisphere, the Pacific or the Far East. Indeed in the Americas, the ➤Monroe Doctrine presaged ➤interventionism more than anything else. Even in relation to Europe it did not imply commercial, cultural, or intellectual separation as it clearly did in the cases of China and Japan referred to earlier.

The use of the term has aroused much debate among US diplomatic historians, political leaderships and ➤public opinion in general. As indicated earlier the 'Washingtonian' and 'Jeffersonian' versions of the isolationist impulse differ subtly, the one pointing towards a ➤realist, ➤national interest version, the other towards a liberal, exceptionalist ➤ideological specification. Mainstream diplomatic historians have argued that US foreign policy from 1783 onwards can be best understood in terms of a more or less permanent tension between the forces of 'isolationism' and the forces of 'interventionism' but this begs the question about the relative significance to be attributed to the two versions of isolationism suggested above. Many have seen the high-water mark of twentieth-century isolationism in the Senate's rejection of the Treaty of ➤Versailles in 1919 and 1920. However, US foreign policy during the 1920s can hardly be called isolationist given its prominent role in ➤arms control and ➤reparations diplomacy which involved all the leading ➤great powers. Following the Great Depression and New Deal of the 1930s policy became more principled in its opposition to interventionism and ➤multilateralism. This culminated in the ➤Neutrality Acts of 1935–7 and the lobbying of interest groups like 'America First'. As a result of World War II America was placed in a leadership role in world politics which spilled over into the ➤globalist policy of ➤containment during the ➤Cold War era. The rhetoric associated with isolationism continued to be used often reproachfully until the defeat in ➤Vietnam and the evidence adduced by ➤declinism led to a ➤neo-isolationist revival. Isolationism remains America's first and most enduring orientation and it is not surprising to note its longevity.

**Issue area** Sometimes rendered issue-area, this classificatory term was first introduced into empirical political science by Robert Dahl (1961a). In what was fundamentally a piece of political sociology, Dahl sought to show how the composition of key local ➤elite groups was crucially dependent upon the issue area chosen. Dahl identified the three key issue areas in New Haven as: public education, urban redevelopment and party nominations for local elective offices. Dahl used his research to argue for a ➤pluralist conception of elite structures but later in the decade the concept of issue area was taken up by writers on ➤foreign policy analysis.

James Rosenau is generally agreed to have broken new ground in applying these ideas. In his chapter in R. Barry Farrell's 1966 volume and then in his own 1967 edition on domestic sources of foreign policy Rosenau sees the concept of issue area as a vertical ➤boundary in politics. The stipulation of an issue area thus enables the researcher to link discrete ➤actors, processes and outcomes into one functionally significant whole. In the Farrell volume Rosenau suggested four issue areas in his 'pre-theory': territorial, status, human resources and non-human resources. In the 1967 work he attempted to reach an assessment of the validity of distinguishing domestic policy issues from foreign policy issues.

The term issue area has now passed firmly into the lexicon of policy analysis. It is, for instance, difficult to envisage any study of UN voting patterns proceeding very far without a primary designation of key issue areas in the organization. Again, approaching the ➤Arab–Israeli situation as an issue area immediately sensitizes the researcher to the need to establish an early identification of who the parties are in that particularly complex situation.

# J

**J-curve** Term employed by J. C. Davies (1969) of the University of Oregon to indicate graphically the de Toqueville notion that ➤revolutions are more likely to take place when a period of prolonged rising expectations is followed by a period of sharp reversal. The frustration which is generated by the gap between expectations and gratifications is, at its most intolerable point, likely to result in violent regime change. As a broad generalization it has proved useful in analysis of revolutionary situations, but the problem of uniqueness and its general inability to distinguish between 'revolution' and 'rebellion' (which does not necessarily involve change of regime) has severely curtailed its predictive capabilities. In addition, it is primarily a psychological explanation and as such does not address itself directly to the political, social and economic milieu within which change takes place.

**Jingoism** A general term indicating ➤hawkish or bellicose policies in dealing with other ➤states. It has been suggested that the term is of Basque origin ('Jainko' is the name of the supreme god of the Basques) and was first used by mercenary Basque soldiers in the employ of Edward I in his thirteenth-century Welsh campaigns. It was popularized in an English music hall song by G.W. Hunt in 1878: 'We don't want to fight, yet by Jingo! if we do/ We've got the ships, We've got the men, and got the money too.' In this instance, it became a rallying cry for those who supported armed British resistance and the use of ➤gunboat diplomacy against the Russian advance into Turkey in that year. Now generally used as a synonym for chauvinism or extreme and pugnacious patriotism. It is sometimes associated with a variety of ➤isolationism as when J. F. Kennedy spoke of 'belligerent jingoism and narrow isolationism' as characterizing a periodic and unhealthy trait in US ➤foreign policy.

**Johnson Doctrine** Sometimes known as the Johnson–Mann Doctrine, this was formulated in 1965 by President Johnson and his Under-Secretary of State for Latin American affairs, T. C. Mann. It stated that the policy of giving support only to those ➤states in Latin America with representative governments (i.e. those formed through general elections) would cease and would be replaced by a pledge that the United States would henceforth support any Latin American government whose interests were deemed compatible with those of Washington. It was composed in the wake of US military ➤intervention in the Dominican Republic and in this sense was a revival of the Dulles–Eisenhower policy preferences in relation to Latin America. Its general purpose was to reassert US willingness to combat the 'clear and present danger of the forcible seizure of power by the Communists'.

**Junta** Originally a Spanish term referring to a ruling committee or administrative council such as those established in Spain in 1808 during the Peninsular War in opposition to Napoleonic rule. Now more generally used to refer to military government (*junta militar*) especially, though not exclusively, in the Hispano-American world. In Latin America during the period of liberation from Spanish and Portuguese ➤imperial rule, representative governments were frequently established by military conspiracies. Usually the junta consisted of several officers drawn from all the services and was in effect a joint ruling cabal, but in the twentieth century the term is most often used in relation to the dictatorial rule of a single dominant military commander, as it did in relation to the administration of General Pinochet in Chile after September 1973.

***Jus ad bellum/jus in bello*** These mean literally 'justice in going to ➤war' and 'justice in the conduct of war'. This distinction between the ends for which it is fought and the means by which it is conducted is an essential part of the ➤just war doctrine. *Jus ad bellum* was of more concern to the ancient and medieval worlds, whereas in modern times *jus in bello* receives more emphasis, perhaps because of the greater acceptance of the ➤act of war as a necessary consequence of the establishment of secular ➤sovereign states. The ➤Geneva and ➤Hague Conventions, for example, were concerned with identifying precise conditions of *jus in bello* rather than with occasions on which *jus ad bello* operated. The recent ➤Islamic revival of the Jihad, or Holy War, is in this sense a return to premodernist conceptions of *jus ad bellum*.

***Jus cogens*** Refers to a body of principles or norms in ➤international law which override or supersede others and 'which cannot be set aside by treaty or acquiescence but only by the formation of a subsequent norm of contrary effect' (I. Brownlie, 1973a). According to this, which has its origins in the writings of ➤Grotius, a ➤treaty or commitment would be void if it was contrary to certain basic principles of international law. The technical name given to these (unspecified) principles is 'peremptory norms of general international law' and is enshrined in Article 53 of the Vienna Convention on the Law of Treaties, 1969. Examples of such overriding rules would normally include the outlawing of ➤genocide, the principles of ➤self-determination and the banning of piracy. During the ➤apartheid period, radical international lawyers argued that *jus cogens* applied in relation to the Republic of South Africa. They argued that, notwithstanding laws relating to the rights of ➤neutrality or non-interference in internal affairs, ➤apartheid was such an affront to the public interest of the world community that all ➤states had a positive and active duty to oppose it. The precise application of *jus cogens* is not universally agreed upon, but its revival in international law is an indication of its evolution from the notion of law based on the consent of states, to a ➤world law established on certain fundamental principles which are considered binding and not discretionary.

**Just war** The attempt to justify ➤war in one set of circumstances and not in another has its origins in Christian ethics, in particular in the fourth century AD which witnessed a transition from ➤pacifism to beliefs in the right or duty to fight for a just cause. The early Christians did not bear arms but by the time the Roman Emperor (Theodosius I, in AD 38) declared that Catholic Christianity was the state ➤religion of the empire, canon law began to move in the direction of a just war doctrine. St Augustine (AD 354–430) is commonly held to be the first major propagandist for these ideas, which in essence have remained part of a western civilization ever since. Definitions of the Just War have periodically altered but the general purpose remains the same: that is, to give some wars legal and moral justification, to condemn those that do not comply with the requisite specifications and also to impose restrictions on the actual conduct of war.

The formal terms given to this enterprise are ➤*jus ad bellum* and ➤*jus in bello*. Emphasis on the latter, referring to right conduct in warfare, indicates that an important aspect of the Just War doctrine is that just wars must not be pursued by unjust means, e.g. the indiscriminate slaughter of non-combatants. The medieval view of the Just War is best represented by St Thomas Aquinas (1225–74), who wrote that war may be justified if three conditions are satisfied: (a) it must be waged by a proper sovereign ➤authority; (b) there must be a just cause and (c) the intentions must be pure, so that they intend to promote good and not private aggrandizement. Further conditions which were generally agreed upon later were that in wars which were not fought strictly in ➤self-defence there must be a reasonable prospect of victory and that every effort must be made, prior to the use of ➤force, to resolve the issue by peaceful means. In relation to conduct in war, the innocent (i.e. the non-combatants) should be immune from direct attack and the amount of force used should not be excessive. The legal dimension of this doctrine owes more to ➤Grotius than to any other single theorist. His *De Jure Belli ac Pacis* (1625) is still regarded as the classic statement on the just war and the means of waging it. Against the backdrop of natural law and the customary law of nations, Grotius delineated four causes which make a war just: (a) self-defence; (b) to enforce rights; (c) to seek ➤reparations for injury; and (d) to punish a wrong-doer. Grotius held that a war cannot be just on both sides and also warned that even a just war can become unjust if intentions are wrong and if unjust acts are committed. Grotius' main contribution to the development of this theory was to put on a secular, pragmatic basis what had previously been considered to be a matter of theology or ethics. He accepted that a multi-state ➤international system would inevitably mean the occurrence of wars. His purpose was to limit their incidence and to limit the damage or harm that was bound to occur. These twin purposes have subsequently been that rationale for the various international conventions on the rules of warfare in the nineteenth and twentieth centuries as well as ►international organizations such as the ►League of Nations and the UN. In modern times a number of problems have arisen in relation to the doctrine. In particular, the following ought to be considered: the ►preventative war or the pre-emptive strike, can this be justified on a principle of extended self-defence? (Israel, for example, justified its actions in June 1967 on these grounds); counter-►intervention, is it permissible to intervene against the prior intervention of other ►states? (the United States sometimes used this pretext in relation to ►Vietnam); ►humanitarian intervention, is it justifiable to intervene against acts that are morally reprehensible (for example against ethnic cleansing or genocide in ►Yugoslavia or Rwanda/Burundi)? These and other issues such as ►guerrilla warfare and ►terrorism raise doubts about the continued validity of rules and principles drawn up in more civilized periods of international history. Indeed, it might be claimed that the decline of the Just War doctrine in the twentieth century, especially in the nuclear age where the concept of ►deterrence rests on the threat of deliberate mass slaughter of the innocent, is related to technical developments in warfare, which at least blur and at most obliterate traditional distinctions between combatants and non-combatants. One area where the doctrine, or an extreme bastardization of it, has been revived is in the notion of the Holy War. This is a war which, because it is commanded by God or his earthly representatives is, without question, just. ►Islamic fundamentalists, especially under the leadership of the Ayatollah Khomeini, were specifically committed to a Jihad on behalf of Allah. President Reagan too, when he railed against the evil empire of ►communism, especially in Central America, seemed to be reviving the spirit of the early Christian crusades and their sacred duty to uphold the spirit of righteousness. Indeed, political ►realists have long been critical of the dangers involved in the application of varieties of the just war doctrine in world politics. A. J. P. Taylor (1979) summed it up well: 'Bismarck fought "necessary wars", and killed thousands; the idealists of the twentieth century fight "just" wars and kill millions.' Apart from these extreme manifestations, in the twentieth century the doctrine of the Just War, for reasons given above, has tended to be rather muted and confined to Christian (usually Catholic) theology, although the Vietnam War and the uncertain basis on which the United States was involved did generate some soul-searching on the issue (see Walzer, 1977, 1978).

**Justice** As with other subjective terms, there is no widespread agreement either on the meaning of justice in the international context or even on its general applicability to ►international relations. For the ►Hobbesian, the recognition of a decentralized international ►state-system characterized by an absence of a single legitimate ►authority inevitably means that justice takes a back seat to considerations of ►order. Indeed, its very existence on this view is structurally dependent on the prior realization of orderly relations. For ►idealists, on the other hand, not only can justice be defined but it is also a prerequisite of a stable and lasting order. The question of order versus justice therefore is a central and often divisive issue in traditional international theory. On one hand, ►realists argue that the issue is secondary and derivative while on the other, non-realists argue that it is primary and constitutive.

The term 'international justice' usually refers to moral standards over and above those prescribed by law which confer rights and duties on ►actors irrespective of size or importance. They may be embodied in ►international law (e.g. the rule on ►non-intervention or sovereign equality) but this is not necessarily the case. Demands for justice, for example, can refer to the redistribution of the world's resources based on criteria which are not yet embedded in contemporary international law (e.g. the notion of the ►'Common Heritage of Mankind' and its implications for ownership or possession of resources which are not covered by established rules of territorial jurisdiction). Sometimes the terms 'international justice' and 'inter-state justice' are used synonymously, though clearly the latter is more specific and may even exclude from its purview considerations of fair play to non-state actors.

The right of ►self-determination, for example, can and does frequently clash with the rights associated with ►sovereignty. Indeed, a major feature of the development of the international legal ►regime is the present tension between ►state-centred considerations of justice derived from customary or positive law and the individual or human justice derived from the ►natural law tradition. It is often asserted that the natural law tradition, in so far as it challenges the positivist conception, is potentially subversive in the sense that it is designed to erode the principle of sovereignty upon which international order ultimately rests.

In contemporary IR, dissatisfaction with the traditional state-centred views (which reach their extreme manifestation in phrases such as 'justice is on the side of the stronger' or 'might is right') has led to a growing body of opinion that justice must be cosmopolitan and universal. Supporters of ►ecopolitics, for example, argue that since ►technology has outgrown the limits of its state boundaries and since ►interdependence is now a fact and not an ideal, considerations of justice should be tied to concepts of a common humanity and should entail at least minimum standards of welfare and ►environmental concern. 'World' justice on this view must take precedent over the interstate or individual varieties. However, there is yet no evidence of substantial inroads into the traditional view expressed most forcibly in, for example, the ►Melian dialogue in ►Thucydides' fifth-century BC account of the Peloponnesian Wars. The persistence and intrusion of questions of ►power and order into considerations of justice appears to be endemic and will remain so for as long as states are the main actors in world politics.

**Justiciable/non-justiciable disputes** Terms used in ►international law to distinguish between those disputes that are capable of legal resolution through, for example, ►adjudication or ►arbitration and those which are resistant to it. The distinction reflects the lack of autonomy of international law and the existence of two basic categories of international disputes, the legal and the political. Political disputes sometimes involve matters of ►high politics and ►national interests which, although often capable of settlement, are not usually thought of as susceptible to legal resolution. International law may be applicable to such disputes, but the party or parties involved may not wish to be bound by such decisions. In such cases, where a settlement is sought the means employed are generally non- or quasi-legal, e.g. ►bilateral or ►multilateral ►diplomacy, mediation, ►good offices or in the last resort, war. The distinction between the two categories rests ultimately on the importance ►states attach to the issues involved. Generally, the more important the issue the less likely its justiciability.

# K

**Kellogg–Briand pact** Also known as the General Treaty for the Renunciation of War or the Pact of Paris. It was a ➤multilateral ➤treaty signed in 1928
initially by fifteen signatories which later rose to sixty-eight. It began life as an
attempt by French Foreign Minister Briand and US Secretary of State Kellogg
to bring the United States, which had refused to join the ➤League of Nations,
back into the ➤internationalist quest for world ➤peace. It contained two main
proposals. First, that all signatories renounce war as an instrument of national
policy and secondly that all disputes should be settled by peaceful means.
However, a number of ➤states, including the United Kingdom, insisted on
reservations regarding the right to take military action in cases of ➤self-defence.
For the United Kingdom this right extended to protection of the British
Empire.

The United States, for their part, did not envisage the enforcement of the
➤Monroe Doctrine to fall within the terms of the treaty. Although the pact
was an attempt to strengthen the League's position on the issue of ➤collective
security, its articles were far too general and hedged about with too many
reservations for it to have any significant impact on developments in ➤intern-
ational relations, either between the signatory states themselves or between
them and the non-signatories.

The failure to distinguish operationally between wars of ➤aggression and
wars of self-defence allowed the pact to be interpreted permissively. As one
contemporary observer put it 'to a much greater degree than is true of most
treaties, it is a scrap of paper binding no one to anything' (Schuman, 1933).
Nevertheless, violations of the Pact of Paris were integral to the prosecution
cases at the ➤war crimes trials in Nuremberg and Tokyo after the Second World
War.

**Kennedy Round** This is the name given to the sixth session of ➤multilateral
➤tariff ➤negotiations held under the aegis of the ➤GATT since 1947. The
round lasted from May 1964 until June 1965. Fifty-four states participated in
these negotiations including the ➤European Community, which negotiated as
a single ➤actor. Although the US President who gave his name to these
deliberations was dead before they even started, conventional usage has retained
this reference.

The round remains significant in terms of tariff-cutting ➤diplomacy because
for the first time tariffs were reduced across the board on a 'linear' method.

This method was seen as preferable to the item-by-item approach by those seeking to liberalize ➤trade by the most efficacious method. The cuts in industrial tariffs eventually negotiated during the round averaged out at 35 per cent and were ➤implemented over a five-year cycle from 1968 to 1972.

Kennedy represents the last session of GATT rounds where the primary agenda setting was effected by the ➤First World states. It was initiated to address a particular set of issues arising from the EC's ➤customs union. Demands from the ➤Third World states for non-reciprocal tariff cuts in their favour were first being voiced during the time frame covered by Kennedy. The round was also criticized for doing nothing to tackle the issue of ➤non-tariff barriers (NTBs) to trade and that of temperate agriculture.

**Korean War** The Korean War began in June 1950 and ended in July 1953. It originated as a ➤civil war and thereafter expanded to draw in the ➤United Nations (UN) and the People's Republic of China (PRC). Hostilities commenced when a substantial incursion of North Korean forces across the 38th parallel occurred. Korea had been divided since 1945 following the defeat of the Japanese forces in Asia (the Japanese had annexed the territory in 1910). The somewhat arbitrary line of the 38th parallel thus divided what were a single people with a strong sense of territorial identity. It is certain that in 1945, given a free choice, the majority of the Korean people would have chosen national ➤independence and ➤unification. Like Germany, Korea became divided as a result of being occupied by the ➤superpowers after 1945. As a result their division became caught up in the ➤Cold War rivalry between the two sides.

The sequence of events which began on 25 June 1950 may be termed a surprise attack within the meaning of that concept, at least as far as US ➤perceptions were concerned. It is evident from recent documentation available since the ending of the Cold War that the Soviet ➤leadership gave general encouragement to the Kim Il Sung regime in the North to attack the South. It was assumed that large sectors of the population in the South would support such an incursion since the leadership of Syngman Rhee was widely rejected by the population at large. The Truman Administration viewed Rhee as at best capricious and at worst perfidious. Although America continued to supply the South with ➤aid following the withdrawal of US forces in June 1949, doubts about the extent of American commitment were fuelled in January 1950 when Secretary of State Acheson appeared to exclude both Korea and Formosa (Taiwan) from the defence perimeter that the United States was seeking to establish in Asia under the policy of ➤containment.

If the US government was surprised by the events of the last week of June 1950 in the Korean peninsula, then the Soviet Union was equally surprised by the US response. Soviet thinking appeared to be that Kim's initiative would present the US with a ➤*fait accompli* to which they would have no answer. As Paige shows in his study (1968), the United States responded to what was a classic ➤crisis situation with a sequence of rapid decisions in the days that followed. By the end of the month the Administration was committed to the reintroduction of ground forces back into Korea and the UN was committed to significant enforcement measures under Chapter 7 of the ➤UN Charter. The Truman Administration never perceived the Korean War as purely or essentially a civil war. Rather, the United States became convinced that the Soviet Union was behind the North Korean moves and that the United States was being 'tested' to assess its ➤credibility to resist perceived ➤aggression. Parallels with the 1930s and the 'lessons' of the ➤appeasement period were frequently drawn by the US leadership who would have been particularly influenced by that inter-war decade. Given that the United States was being 'tested', therefore the appropriate response was resistance. The only question remaining was whether this should be ➤bilateral or ➤multilateral. As Paige demonstrates, the decision to take the Korean crisis to the UN was made very early in the first week.

The involvement of the UN in the Korean War was controversial. Meeting in emergency sessions on 25 and 27 June, the ➤Security Council passed a series of resolutions fixing the blame for the commencement of hostilities on the North Koreans, called for a ceasefire and the withdrawal of forces to their original positions and, when compliance was not forthcoming, recommended enforcement action under Chapter 7 of the charter. It is now generally accepted that the Korean vote was *sui generis*. The Soviet Union was absent from the Council throughout these proceedings (it was protesting at the refusal of the organization to accept the credentials of the PRC). The Soviet absence undoubtedly enabled the Council to take a number of decisions, at the height of the crisis, which served to legitimize what was, in truth, a US-inspired response to the Korean War. The Council did, however, side-step the legality of its ➤decision-making by making recommendations to the membership. At the time of the Korean situation the United States and its allies commanded considerable voting support in the UN. It should be remembered that the bulk of the ➤Third World States had still to join the organization and many states in the organization were at that stage in post-war politics still orientated towards the West. The fact that both Cuba and China voted in support of the US-sponsored resolutions on Korea in the June crisis is instructive of how far the institution was dominated by these interests.

The UN decision to extend the war into North Korea in the autumn of 1950 provoked the second major crisis of the war. If the original involvement of the UN was controversial because the Organization was seen to be taking sides in a Cold War confrontation, the extension of the fighting across the 38th parallel clearly exceeded the spirit if not the letter of the first Security Council resolution '. . . to repel the armed attack and to restore international peace and security in the area'. Moreover, in implementing that decision the UN provoked Chinese ➤intervention in support of the North Koreans. As a result there was a significant escalation of the war. Far from achieving the unification of Korea by this adventure, the UN forces were repulsed from the North with significant losses and the North Koreans and the Chinese 'volunteers' drove the UN forces back to the original 38th parallel dividing line. Initially, it seemed as if they were going to repeat the stunning gains of June. The intervention of the Chinese locked the conflict into a ➤stalemate situation until a permanent cease-fire was agreed in 1953.

The Korean War has provided valuable case study material for research in a number of areas. Obviously, its relevance to ➤crisis literature is apparent. Students of ➤foreign policy analysis and of ➤strategic studies have used Korea to examine certain ideas. In the policy analysis field particular interest has been shown in the decision to escalate the war in the autumn of 1950 when the UN forces crossed the 38th parallel into North Korea. Janis (1972), writing in the context of ➤groupthink ideas, has called this decision Truman's ➤Bay of Pigs. ➤Deterrence theorists have also looked at these events in the light of the seeming failure of the PRC to deter the UN from this step. The Chinese Communists issued repeated warnings that if the 38th parallel was crossed they would assist the North Koreans. In summary, studies of this period in the Korean conflict, aimed particularly at the US decision system, seem to suggest the following conclusions: (a) the Truman Administration took excessive risks in their escalation decision; (b) they held stereotypes of the Chinese leadership which seemed to suggest that the latter's capacity for independent judgement was limited and, following on from this, that the Soviet Union, the PRC and the North Koreans could be regarded in effect as a single ➤actor where decisions on the war were concerned; (c) the escalation decisions were bitterly opposed within the Administration by some of the most senior and respected foreign policy-making staff, including George Kennan (➤X).

Halperin (1963) has suggested that Korea was a paradigm of ➤limited war in the post-war system. This conclusion is rather contingent upon where the analyst stands. From the perception of the United States, the Soviet Union and the PRC, perhaps Korea was a limited war fought for limited ends. From the perspective of the Koreans, however, the war was comprehensive in its impact and significant in its implications. This is because the war was a civil conflict and these situations are by nature total.

# L

**Land reform** A policy whereby the ownership and use of land is changed. The changes associated with land reform involve the redistribution of land held in large estates – *latifundia* – to small farmers and tenants and/or to landless farm workers. A variation of land reform, particularly favoured in centrally planned economies, was to redistribute land to cooperatives and collectives rather than to individual farmers. Politically, land reform is seen by its proponents as weakening or even destroying the ➤power base of the traditional landed oligarchy or *rentier* class. As a policy therefore land reform is particularly associated with radical and reformist ideas. Alternatively it may be seen as a means whereby a traditional system can avoid violent upheaval by instituting change in order to mitigate the worst excesses of the system. Such a judgement might appropriately be made of the attempts at land reform in Russia before 1917.

In contemporary ➤international relations land reform is certainly seen in reformist if not ➤revolutionary terms. There are many examples from the ➤Third World of land reform programmes being initiated by ➤less developed countries (LDCs) since 1945. Ideologically, these measures are usually seen in these ➤states as representing the desire to place land ownership in the hands of those who actually work the land. Widespread support for these changes has come from organizations such as the ➤United Nations, particularly in those organs of the UN where Third World concerns are well represented.

Economically, land reform can make a great deal of sense. It leads to a redistribution of income in favour of groups who might reasonably be expected to spend their money at home rather than abroad. It can lead to a redirection of land use in favour of producing cash crops for domestic urban markets rather than internationally marketed commodities, which is a feature of the *latifundia* system.

**Landlocked states** Those ➤states that do not possess a coastline. Prior to the disintegration of the USSR these were: ➤Afghanistan, Andorra, Austria, Bhutan, Bolivia, Botswana, Burkina Faso, Burundi, Central African Republic, Chad, Czechoslovakia, Hungary, Laos, Lesotho, Liechtenstein, Luxembourg, Malawi, Mali, Mongolia, Nepal, Niger, Paraguay, Rwanda, San Marino, Swaziland, Switzerland, Uganda, Vatican City, Zambia, and Zimbabwe. Most of these states have felt disadvantaged by the traditional ➤Laws of the Sea which for obvious reasons favour those states with coastlines. The revision of the Law of the Sea in 1982, UNCLOS III, attempted to give even landlocked states some maritime rights, especially concerning the resources of the sea-bed, under the ➤'Common Heritage of Mankind' doctrine. However, UNCLOS III has not been universally ratified.

Landlocked states are susceptible to economic warfare techniques as a result of their geographical position. Thus the entrepôt position of the state controlling access to the sea can be used to apply pressure to the landlocked state by withholding or reducing the availability of goods and services. Zambia and Zimbabwe were certainly aware of this type of economic leverage during the ➤apartheid era, while Lesotho is double landlocked, in so far as it is totally surrounded by the Republic of South Africa, in addition to its geographical position as a landlocked state.

**Law of the Sea (maritime law)** The attempt to apply general rules to cover over two-thirds of the earth's surface has always been fraught with difficulty, no less so in the twentieth century than in the seventeenth when this issue was first systematically tackled by jurists. From the outset the matter of control and jurisdiction of the seas was a power-political affair. Throughout this period the major maritime ➤nations have oscillated between attempting to claim huge tracts of the high seas as part of their proper territorial domain and devising a principle of 'open seas' which would preclude appropriation and give free access to all. The latter view (freedom of the seas) eventually prevailed mainly because of the interests of the European maritime states in exploration and commercial exploitation of the Orient and elsewhere. The Dutch scholar Hugo ➤Grotius, in his *Mare Liberum* (1618), is generally credited with elaborating the first systematic doctrine of 'the freedom of the seas'. Grotius' brief was to sustain the right of Dutch navigation and commerce in the East Indies against Portuguese claims to monopoly. From the outset the Grotian doctrine was regarded as a permissive one by the major ➤states who saw themselves as having virtual *carte blanche* over the great oceans. On the other hand, it was regarded as an oppressive and pernicious doctrine by the smaller, weaker states who were concerned with the expansion of their territorial rights rather than with free passage. This division between the interests of the more powerful and less powerful states has remained a fundamental one in maritime law to this day.

Once enunciated, freedom of the high seas rapidly became one of the basic principles of ➤international law. This freedom was not unlimited, however, for it was regarded as permissible for a coastal state to claim a maritime belt around its shores ('territorial waters') which was treated as an integral part of its territorial jurisdiction. The subsequent history of the law of the sea from the seventeenth century onwards has largely to do with finding precise demarcation lines to establish these limits of control. Originally limits were based on the 'cannon-shot rule' which meant in effect that the dividing line between the high seas and territorial waters was the extent to which the coastal state could exert military domination. Modern practice favours a 12-mile territorial sea, although this was not universally the case, as some states claim 3, 4, 6, 15, 20, 30, 50, 70, and even 200 nautical-mile limits defining their territory. Given this, it is hardly surprising that many commentators refer to the chronic untidiness of the law of the sea. In addition to the 'territorial waters', other aspects which comprise the basic principle of freedom are 'belligerents' rights' and the right of ►hot pursuit, both of which purport to give states temporary privileges in certain defined circumstances, though this is often a matter of dispute as it is sometimes claimed that the 'right of ►innocent passage' takes precedence.

The trend in maritime law has been in the direction of extending ►jurisdiction over portions of the high seas and this has resulted in the elaboration of special claims to 'Contiguous Zones', 'Economic Exclusion Zones', 'Maritime Exclusion Zones' and even ►'Pollution Zones'. This shift in emphasis is clearly a reflection of the increased awareness of the economic and ►ecological potential of the sea and the anxiety of some states and some multinational companies (►MNCs) to exploit this to the full.

However, alongside this tendency towards ►annexation of the sea a counter-movement has developed, particularly among ►Third World states, which proclaims the seas and the riches therein to be part of the ►'Common Heritage of Mankind' and therefore beyond the range of the individualistic aspirations of the more acquisitive states. This phrase and the sentiments it expresses were popularized in 1967 by Ambassador Arvid Pardo of Malta and was quickly endorsed by the ►General Assembly of the UN. The fear was that with the discovery of raw materials in the sea-bed and with the rapid growth in ►technological capability that renders these materials extractable, the poorer, less developed states, not to mention the ►landlocked states would once more lose out if there was a general free-for-all of the kind implied in the original doctrine of freedom of the sea. Combined with increasing concern about the depletion of the world's resources this has led to a demand for a fresh look at the underlying philosophy of the law of the sea.

The result is that at present two competing ideologies – freedom of the sea versus common heritage – vie for general approval by the international community. A number of recent conferences on the law of the sea, UNCLOS I (1958), UNCLOS II (1960) and UNCLOS III (1974–82), have attempted to resolve the differences between the two positions. Indeed, UNCLOS III has come so close to revising the traditional approach that it is regarded by some observers as being the first significant step in the direction of a ►New International Economic Order. So far, over 120 states have appended their signatures to the new maritime ►regime. But the old divisions remain and major maritime users, such as the United States, the United Kingdom, Japan, Germany and Italy, among others, have so far rejected the proposals. It remains to be seen whether this minority of traditionalists eventually accede to the collectivist view or whether they will continue to cling to the libertarian and permissive principles of the Grotian tradition.

**Leadership** Considerations of leadership occur in two contexts in ➤international relations. At the level of ➤macropolitics, certain actors seem to enjoy ➤*de facto* positions of leadership. In this usage, the term is coterminous with ➤hegemony. In the second sense, leadership is used in ➤foreign policy analysis to direct attention towards the personalities holding leadership roles at the head of organizations. The remaining discussion will concentrate upon this latter usage.

Studying the influence of personality raises methodological issues. Historians are inclined towards a contextual analysis of particular individuals and time periods, while psychologists prefer to stipulate personality types in general before looking at individual cases. The two approaches become synthesized in the so-called 'psychobiography' which attempts to correlate an individual case study with more general ideas about the relationship between personality, upbringing, self-perception, etc., and the individual. The Georges' 1964 study is a good example of this approach.

Personality types have been more overtly synthesized with policy preference in Eysenck's (1954) two-dimensional, tough-minded versus tender-minded and conservative versus radical treatment. Barber (1985), likewise, used the two-dimensional idea in his discussion of US Presidential personality. Looking more explicitly at foreign policy outcomes, Stoessinger (1985) identified two types of policy maker: the crusader and the pragmatist, while Paige (1977), taking the variable of change, argued that this produces three attitude types: conservative, reformist and revolutionary.

An overly psychological orientation to the issue of individual leadership is probably inevitable. Certainly, as the above citations show, it is a popular approach. It is well to remember that leadership is exercised within an organizational context. In many political systems, moreover, leadership roles and positions are competitively sought after. Thus for every group of power holders there may be an identifiable group of power seekers as well. This competitive environment will affect the leaders' perceptions of issues and how they handle them, particularly if the leadership is likely to face electoral judgement upon their ➤decision-making in the future.

Leadership also implies 'followership'. The consequential question, 'what causes followers to respond positively rather than negatively to a leadership?' can appropriately be raised. Here Weber's (1947) seminal trichotomy of charismatic, traditional and rational-legal ideal types may point towards an answer. Charismatic leadership is derived from the kind of individual, personality characteristics discussed already. The charismatic leader is the revolutionary, the warrior, the prophet, the demagogue, the national hero, etc. Such leadership styles surface during times of great social change to confirm or challenge the ➤status quo and to provide an inspiring vision of the future. This ability to mobilize the followers is clearly an important facet of leadership and, in the case of the charismatic type, it seems to inhere in the individual. On the other hand, Weber's other two types depend upon the social and legal nexus for their leadership capabilities. Recent studies of ►Third World polities has done much to increase interest in the traditional or patrimonial leadership types. ►►hegemony

**League of Nations** Probably the most significant innovation of twentieth-century ►international relations, the League was created in 1920 with the specific object of establishing procedures for peaceful resolution of international disputes and conflicts. The immediate catalyst for its formation was the First World War and the Treaty of ►Versailles which followed it but its origins go back to ►idealist and ►liberal dissatisfaction with the international ►anarchy, ►balance of power and the concept of ►self-help which had hitherto characterized the ►state-system. It was intended to be a global organization though it was handicapped from the outset by political and ►ideological realities. The United States refused to join, the Soviet Union was ostracized by the others, France and the United Kingdom gave only lukewarm support and Germany, Italy and Japan operated outside the principles established in the Covenant. Nevertheless, its brief history (1920–46) is testimony to the break-up of the old system and the almost universal desire in the twentieth century to establish international institutions which would go some way towards establishing a legal ►regime for the orderly conduct of international affairs. The ►United Nations is its successor and between them these organizations have added a new dimension to world politics.

The League consisted of three main organs: the Council (fifteen members, including France, the United Kingdom and the Soviet Union as permanent members) which met three times a year, the Assembly (all members) which met annually, and a Secretariat which functioned as an international civil service. All decisions had to be by unanimous vote. The underlying philosophy of the League was the principle of ►collective security which meant that the international community had a duty to ►intervene in international ►conflicts: it also meant that parties to a dispute should submit their grievances to the League or the ►arbitrators. If the League or the arbitrators failed to reach a unanimous decision within six months the disputants could, after a further delay of three months, go to ►war. The ►Permanent Court of International Justice, although separate from the League, acted in concert with it. The centrepiece of the Covenant was Article 16, which empowered the League to institute ►economic or military ►sanctions against a recalcitrant ►state. In essence, though, it was left to each member to decide whether or not a breach of the Covenant had occurred and so whether or not to apply sanctions. This is regarded by commentators as a major weakness, yet although the League failed in respect of German, Italian and Japanese ►aggression in the 1930s, it did succeed in resolving some disputes in more minor cases (notably in the Balkans and South America). The settlement of international conflict was its rationale but the League also concerned itself with other matters and subsidiary bodies were set up dealing in areas such as ➤mandates, ➤disarmament and economic and social cooperation.

History might have dealt harshly with the League's overall record of achievement but none can doubt that its very existence was a major and radical step in the development of modern international relations. The argument that it failed in its purpose has to be balanced against the notion that it was never really tried. The member states, particularly the more powerful European ones, were locked into traditional concepts of ➤sovereignty and ➤diplomacy and in matters of ➤high policy bypassed the League system altogether. However flexible the provisions of the Covenant might have been, unless it received the full cooperation of the major powers in implementing decisions it was bound to be something of a non-starter in the matter of resolving international conflict.

**Least developed countries (LDCs)** This term has been used for some time within the ➤United Nations to describe those ➤states at the bottom of the ➤hierarchy, at least in terms of economic criteria. The UN defines these states as those having the lowest per capita GDP, the lowest levels of literacy and the smallest share of secondary or manufacturing industries input into GDP. The colloquial term ➤Fourth World is sometimes used to refer to these states. Bangladesh, with something like one-quarter of the total population of the LDCs is a ➤paradigm of this class of states. In many instances they show negative growth rates of per capita income annually and they run the real risk of 'dropping out' of the system altogether if their prospects cannot be improved.

**Lebensraum** German ➤geopolitical term meaning 'living space'. The term can be credited to General Haushofer (1869–1946) and his team at the Institute of Geopolitics in Munich, but was popularized by Adolf Hitler in *Mein Kampf*. Originally, it was an adjunct of the ➤Heartland theory and referred to control of central and eastern Europe. Hitler used it as part of his thesis that it was Germany's destiny to control the East and therefore other ➤states must accede to her request for lebensraum. Territorial expansion was deemed necessary because of Germany's overpopulation and need for foodstuffs; therefore, the Ukraine, for example, was seen as a German 'granary'. Lebensraum also has overtones of racial superiority, the Aryan master race having a mystical right to dominate those around it.

**Legalistic—Moralistic** Term that gained wide currency as a description of American ➤foreign policy after publication of George Kennan's *American Diplomacy, 1900–1950* (1957) where he stated that this approach 'runs like a red skein through our policy over the past fifty years'. Kennan argued that in the twentieth century, unlike the nineteenth, American ➤policy-makers tended to lose sight of ➤power considerations and a limited conception of the ➤national interest and substitute instead a belief in legal and moral contractual engagements as the solution to ➤world order problems. The ➤domestic analogy (arguments drawn from the internal American experience) plus a feeling of moral righteousness, encouraged a serious misunderstanding of the realities of ➤international relations. Woodrow Wilson's policies and speeches are said to be the best illustration of this approach.

**Legation** Originally an ecclesiastical term denoting someone deputed to represent the Pope but now more commonly used to indicate a ➤diplomatic mission of the second order where the head of mission does not hold the titular rank of➤ambassador. Thus, while it is usual to style an ambassador as 'Ambassador Extraordinary and Plenipotentiary', the head of a legation is likely to be called 'Envoy Extraordinary and Minister Plenipotentiary'. The term is also used to refer to the building in which the minister resides and the area surrounding it. In this sense, the legation is usually immune from the ➤jurisdiction of the host ➤state and subject only to the laws of the sending state. It can, and frequently does, therefore serve as a place of refuge. For example, black political activists in South Africa used the UK and West German legations as places of sanctuary during the apartheid era. ➤➤Diplomatic immunities and privileges

**Legitimacy** In ➤international relations this is bound up with notions of ➤recognition and as such is more often a political matter rather than a strictly legal one. The doctrine of legitimacy is sometimes called the 'Tobar Doctrine' which takes its name from the Foreign Minister of Ecuador who elaborated the idea in 1907. The suggestion was that governments which came to ➤power by means other than those laid down in the constitution should not be recognized by the international community. Thus a ➤*coup d'état* or a ➤revolution would render a ➤state illegitimate and therefore beyond the range and scope of ➤international law and the conventions of ➤diplomacy. The concept is especially associated with American ➤foreign policy in relation to Latin America which, in accordance with the ➤Monroe Doctrine, it regards as a special area of interest and concern. Under President Woodrow Wilson this was given added precision through the policy of 'democratic legitimacy'. This was a refinement of the Tobar method in that it invoked the idea of popular support: if the ➤regime was popular, it would be granted legitimate status; if it was not, it would not. Although this principle and the ➤ideology associated with it is still a feature of American foreign policy it is generally regarded as an unsatisfactory and unrealistic way of determining full membership of the international community.

The term is also used in a more general sense referring to the framework of the ➤international system. Thus Henry Kissinger (1964), for example, writes of a 'legitimate international order' implying that all the major powers have accepted established conventions of dealing with one another and agree on the parameters of foreign policy aims and methods. A legitimate order is stable, as contrasted with a revolutionary system, where a major power or powers is dissatisfied and seeks to rearrange the ➤status quo. The period from 1789 to 1815 was a revolutionary one, whereas the system that was established between 1815 and 1914 was legitimate.

**Lend–Lease** The Lend–Lease Act was inaugurated in March 1941 and was designed to render assistance to the Allied powers fighting the Second World War through a system of deferred payment for goods. This programme, inspired by F. D. Roosevelt, effectively ended the ➤neutrality of the United States even though it was nine months before the United States actually entered the ➤war. Roosevelt felt that the United States should become 'the great arsenal of democracy' and to this end proposed that it should 'lease, lend or otherwise dispose of' arms and supplies to the amount of seven billion dollars to states whose ➤defence was regarded as vital to America's interests. From 1941 to 1945 it has been estimated that the United States provided more than fifty billion dollars' worth of weapons, raw materials, food, machine tools and other strategic supplies to aid the hard-pressed Allies in Europe – the bulk going to the United Kingdom and the Soviet Union. In the post-war period repayment of Lend–Lease became a contentious issue particularly between the United States and the Soviet Union and contributed to the climate that produced the ➤Cold War.

**Less developed countries (LDCs)** A term of relative economic development which is normally used with reference to the ➤Third World of Africa, Asia, and Latin America. In this context it has become widely accepted by analysts and commentators. It would be possible to identify an LDC using such economic indicators as gross domestic product (GDP), *per capita* GDP, *per capita* growth and so on. LDCs tend to be recipients of ➤aid rather than donors. They tend to play a disproportionately small role in world ➤trade. In short they tend to be dependent upon advanced industrial countries (AICs). Identification of this grouping has led to the characterization of economic relations as being divided on a ➤North–South axis with the LDCs corresponding to the South.

It should be acknowledged that the term is a blanket one and covers a large number of states with a fair degree of imprecision. Thus some writers have attempted to characterize the very poorest as the ➤Fourth World while others have identified a small group of rapidly growing economies, in Asia, as Newly Industrialized Countries (➤NICs). These sub-divisions are tacit recognition of the imprecision referred to above.

**Level of analysis** A term that was introduced into the vocabulary of ➤international relations analysis in April 1960 when David Singer reviewed K. N. Waltz's (1959) volume on ➤war. Subsequently Singer elaborated on these ideas in his 1961 article in the same *World Politics* (Princeton) journal. What Singer was in essence recognizing was that the burgeoning literature in the IR discipline needed to be aware of the units of analysis being studied. In this respect the field showed commonality with other social sciences which had similarly sought to distinguish the wood from the trees and the trees from the forest. In the two references cited Singer varied between a micro/macro dichotomy and the individual/►state/system evinced by Waltz.

Over subsequent years the value of explicit and prompt recognition of the operational level of analysis was generally recognized by scholars. It was testimony to their efficacy that they became good habits rather than self-conscious decisions. The fields of ►conflict research and ►integration studies can be exemplified in this regard. The publication twenty years after the volume on war of a systems analysis of IR by Waltz (1979) resuscitated the issue of levels since the ensuing debate between Waltz and his critics over ►neorealism implicitly raised these matters. Waltz was seen to have struck out in favour of the ►macropolitical level in this highly influential study, although his preferences in this regard had been well flagged up two decades earlier.

Recently Buzan (1995) has sought to review and reconstitute the discussion on levels by in effect suggesting that the term has two meanings: one is the aforementioned idea of units. Here Buzan suggests five: system, subsystem, unit, bureaucracy, individual. The other meaning is as sources of explanation. Here Buzan suggests three levels: structure, process and interaction capacity. In effect Buzan wants to talk about *horizontal* and *vertical* levels corresponding to units of analysis and sources of explanation. Whether Buzan's excursion into what he terms 'intellectual history' has clarified or muddied the waters remains to be seen. As with the original distinction of Singer's custom and practice within the discipline will be the ultimate judge. ►►Agent-structure

**Liberalism** The liberal tradition in international affairs can be traced back at least as far as John Locke (1632–1704) but it is in the nineteenth and twentieth centuries that liberalism has had its most enduring impact. Indeed, the development of modern ►international relations would be incomprehensible without an appreciation of the part played by the liberal approach. For example, the role of ►international organizations such as the ►League of Nations and the ►United Nations can be directly attributed to the liberal quest for the elimination of the international ►anarchy and the inauguration of the rule of law. It could be argued that the success of liberalism in the twentieth century is due to the influence in world politics of its most powerful proponent, the United States, but this would be to deny one of the basic tenets of its belief system – the idea that progress is inevitable and that the ►realist responses to the question of ►world order are atavistic and inherently dangerous.

The liberal theory of international relations contains a number of propositions, most of which derive from the ►domestic analogy concerning the relationship between individuals within the state. Among the most important are the following:

1 ►peace can best be secured through the spread of democratic institutions on a world-wide basis. Governments, not people, cause ►wars. ►Democracy is the highest expression of the will of the people, therefore democracies are inherently more pacific than other political systems. An ►international system composed of democratic ►states would, in consequence, lead to a condition of perpetual peace, where ►conflict and war would disappear. This is self-evident and based on reason. Best known proponents of this view are Kant and Woodrow Wilson, both of whom believed that the solution to the problems of world order and security lay in the spread of the democratic ideal. In this connection 'consent' is the only legitimate grounds for government, therefore ►imperialism is immoral. ►Self-determination is a condition of democracy, just as the final bar at the court of world judgement is ►public opinion which in the last resort is the safeguard of peace.

2 Bound up with this, and underpinning it, is a belief in the 'natural ►harmony of interests'. If people and states make rational calculations of their interests and act upon them, something akin to Adam Smith's 'invisible hand' would ensure that the ►national interest and the ►international interest would be one and the same. The free market and the perfectibility of human nature would encourage ►interdependence and demonstrate conclusively that 'war does not pay' (Angell, 1910).

3 If disputes continue to occur, these would be settled by established judicial procedures, since the rule of law is just as applicable to states as it is to individuals. An international legal ►regime based on common voluntary membership of international organizations would begin to fulfil the functions of a legislature, executive and judiciary, while still preserving the freedom and ►independence of the states.

4 ►Collective security would replace notions of ►self-help. The assumption here is that just as it must always be possible to identify an ►aggressor so also must it be possible to organize a preponderant collective coalition of law-abiding states to oppose it. The League of Nations and the United Nations were founded on this premise; ►security being conceived of as a collective, communal responsibility rather than an individual one.

These are core beliefs of liberalism but liberals themselves often disagree as to the advisability of particular courses of action. In this context, it is instructive to distinguish between ►interventionist and ►non-interventionist liberals. The former, among whom Woodrow Wilson figures prominently, believe that although 'progress' is historically inevitable, it is sometimes necessary to help it along. Thus, war on behalf of the liberal ideal may occasionally be required to rid the world of illiberal and persistent opponents. The ►just war or the crusade are perfectly permissible policies provided the object is to further the cause of democratic liberalism. This attitude to war was put most succinctly by R. H. Tawney: 'Either war is a crusade, or it is a crime. There is no half-way house.' The non-interventionists, on the other hand, believe that a liberal ►world order is implicit in history and that the virtues of liberalism itself would spread without any active prodding by its adherents. Nineteenth-century American traditions of ►isolationism were often expressed in these terms; the new politics of the New World would, by dint of its own obvious superiority, sweep all before it. However, the emergence in the twentieth century of two powerful anti-liberal ideologies, ►fascism and ►communism have rendered the non-interventionist stance somewhat anachronistic. Since the Second World War and the defeat of fascism, the liberal stand has been taken on the ground of ►containment which argues that the future of liberal democracy rests on its ability first, to stop the spread of communism and second, to eliminate it altogether. Containment, can thus be seen as a compromise between interventionism and non-interventionism, but it is as well to stress that liberalism, whether active or passive, on the battlefield or in the market place, envisages the eventual defeat of the force of illiberalism in whatever garb it decks itself. It is this self-righteousness and spirit of moral omnipotence that is one of the weaknesses of contemporary liberalism, as it all too easily leads to policies of sustaining the ►status quo almost at any cost. US foreign policy, in particular, has come under repeated criticism for supporting regimes with appalling records on ►human rights on the sole grounds that these regimes were anti-communist. Nevertheless, the 'victory' of the liberal democratic ideal in the Cold War has led many to believe that, for the foreseeable future at least, this now is the only game in town. The triumphalism that greeted what Francis Fukuyama called 'the end of history' is testimony to this.

The dark side of liberalism is its chronic inability to come to terms with the use of ►force for particular and specific ends. ►Realists have never been slow to point this out. The brighter side is that it honestly and self-consciously intends to work for a brave new world where human rights and the well being of individuals are given a higher priority than state's rights and the narrower conceptions of ►national interest which characterize the more traditional approaches. Whether this is regarded as unduly idealistic and utopian depends upon one's own general, political orientation. ►►Democratic peace theory; economic liberalism; neoliberalism

**Liberation theology** A branch of Christian theology which emphasizes the important role that the Church can play in the achievement of social justice and ameliorating the conditions of the poor and oppressed. Employing a ►Marxist or socialist view of social, economic and political conditions, it calls for activist ►intervention on the part of the clergy in the struggle against exploitation both from internal and external sources. It has had a profound impact on ►Third World politics generally, but it is in Latin America that it has achieved its greatest political impact. At a conference of Roman Catholic bishops of Latin America at Medellín in Colombia in 1968 there was near-unanimous support for the aims of the movement despite opposition from the ➤Vatican, which considered it to be a dangerous intrusion into politics and perhaps an unwitting instrument of communist ➤propaganda. Outside Latin America, it has had an important effect on the developments in southern Africa and the World Council of Churches has on a number of occasions publicly endorsed its general aims. In South Africa in particular, Archbishop Desmond Tutu (Nobel Peace Laureate in 1984), and Dr Allen Boesak (president of the World Alliance of Reformed Churches) gave liberation theology a high international profile in the general opposition to ➤apartheid. Liberation theology is also sometimes known as 'revolutionary theology' although most of its adherents have tended to shy away from this appellation due to its connotations of condoning violent change. ➤➤Religion

**Limited nuclear war** Using ➤nuclear weapons in a ➤limited war situation will always have attractions for ➤states that perceive themselves facing an adversary that can overwhelm them conventionally. It is essentially a particular instance of the general proposition about substituting ➤technology for man-power. The problem is that using such ➤capabilities demolishes a clear and unambiguous limit without replacing it with another of equal clarity.

Limited nuclear war between nuclear armed adversaries is a development made possible by ➤nuclear proliferation. With the end of the ➤Cold War era this kind of nuclear-to-nuclear exchange could occur under two contingencies. One would be that the United States would ➤intervene against a ➤perceived ➤pariah/rogue state as some kind of ➤crisis manager (albeit in a very coercive mode). The other contingency would be a nuclear exchange between regional powers which would be limited rather than total, e.g. India and Pakistan.

Limited nuclear war remains a possibility in the post-Cold War world. The most likely ➤scenarios geographically, other than the above, would either be in the Middle East or the Korean peninsula. The American policy of ➤non-proliferation is intended to address this particular risk but as the ➤Persian Gulf War seems to show the difficulties of ➤regime building and maintenance are daunting.

**Limited war** A term used in strategic analysis. Limited ➤war is the deliberate exercise of restraint by parties engaged in military operations. As Brodie (1965) has emphasized, the qualification of intentionality is crucial. If a party lacks the ➤capability to fight a ➤total war then this is not an example of limited war within the definition. Empirically establishing that restraint is deliberate is not easy. One method might be the case study as approached by Paige (1968) in the ➤Korean War decision. Clearly evidence that ➤decision-makers eschewed certain options in order to observe limits would constitute a reliable test. Colloquially, limited war is akin to someone fighting with one hand tied behind their back – they have a capability which remains potential rather than actual.

Restraint leading to deliberate war limitation may be observed in a number of dimensions. First, restraint may operate with regard to means. Certain weapons available to a party are not used or are used in moderation. Schelling (1960), probably the foremost contemporary thinker on limited war, has argued that 'break-points' or 'fire-breaks' should be qualitatively distinct and salient. Thus 'no nuclear weapons' or 'no gas' are objectively distinct. Limits within classes are less easy to operate than limits between classes. This is particularly important if such limits are to be reached by tacit understanding rather than explicit convention. Over time, Schelling argues, it should be possible to establish such limits or 'thresholds'. In bargaining terms, deliberate war limitation is a way of signalling or communicating with the adversary. Schelling can also be credited with establishing the idea that many forms of conflict behaviour are instances of bargaining. Establishing limits of war limitation is an example of this genre.

Bargaining in a limited war does not stop at the establishment of initial limits because, by raising or lowering the limits, the parties are attempting to communicate with each other. In the ►worst-case situation, if a party perceives that the war is going badly it will want to review the limits and revise them upwards. The United States' conspicuous failure to realize any of its policy goals in ►Vietnam after 1961 led to the steady revision limits, specifically by using ►air power and then by introducing ground forces.

If means are one type of limit, ►domain and ►scope are others. By domain here is meant limitations on the number of parties, limits on the commitment of parties and limits on the geographical area of operations. By scope is meant limits on the issues at stake and ultimately limits on the objectives being pursued by the parties in fighting the war in the first place. Schelling argues that ►unconditional surrender is a limit, 'unconditional annihilation' is not. If this is not trailing the coat, it is certainly stretching what most would intuitively regard as the boundary between limited/unlimited. Schelling is surely right to argue, however, that tacit limits are often more viable than explicit agreements.

Establishing limits to war by tacit bargaining depends in the final analysis upon the ►perception of the parties. If there is sufficient overlap then collaboration and even coordination is possible. If perceptions do not overlap then tacit bargaining may fail to establish the parameters for limitation. In the Vietnam War the limiting process failed to work. This highly speculative and imaginative writing about limited war depends upon certain fundamental assumptions about the ►definition of the situation between the parties.

**Linkage** The term is used in two senses in ►international relations; first in ►foreign policy analysis, second in ►diplomacy. Analytically, linkage theory argues that hard and fast ►boundaries cannot be drawn between, for instance, domestic policy and foreign policy: between what happens at the national level and what happens at the global level. Foreign policy is a 'boundary' problem in the sense that there is a lack of clarity about where the boundary should be. Through a system that communication theorists would call a ➤feedback loop events internally influence events externally and vice versa.

Linkage ideas have influenced ➤pluralists and those writers currently arguing for a ➤world society perspective. The idea of the ➤state as clearly defined unit is seen to be redundant as a result of, among other things, the erosion of the concept of external ➤sovereignty because of the linkage between national systems and other ➤actors. State actors are seen as being 'penetrated' to such an extent that they often cease to be effective operating units. Linkage ideas were first advanced in a significant way in the 1960s by James Rosenau (1969b). They form part of the pluralist perspective which questions the validity of traditional models of state-based politics.

Linkage may often be used in the diplomatic sense where during ➤negotiations one side may seek to 'link' concessions in one field for those in another. For example, in the ➤Helsinki Accord process western negotiators specifically linked ➤arms control measures to ➤human rights issues in their dealings with the Soviet Union. In southern Africa in the late 1980s US negotiator Dr Chester Crocker successfully connected the withdrawal of Cuban troops from Angola with the retreat of the South Africans from Namibia, thus paving the way for Namibian independence in 1990. ➤➤Constructive engagement

**Localization**  Localization is often seen in an ➤action–reaction dynamic as the antithesis of ➤globalization. The trends and tendencies which have assisted globalization in ➤international relations have released countervailing tendencies towards localization. Although localization may be seen thus as a kind of 'small is beautiful' rejoinder, it is a process with intrinsic values. The ➤world society literature has pointed to the demands that individuals and groups make of social systems for greater participation and it is this participatory dynamic which is behind the process of localization in many cases. Indeed in democratic ➤states, localization is the outward and visible sign of a participatory democracy. In the United States – where these localization processes have been particularly identified – the movement for a more participatory democracy coincided with the social and political unrest of the 1960s, in particular with movements on civil rights and against the ➤Vietnam War. The two movements that came out of that period – ➤Green and ➤peace – are testimony to the felt need for greater participation by individuals and groups. Both have succeeded in mobilizing opinion at the local level against national policies – for example on the nuclear freeze issue – and they represent the kinds of centrifugal characteristics of localization. Thus localization is often associated with 'fragmentation'.

It is important to recognize therefore that localization is not simply a reaction to globalization. The phenomenon of ➤ethnic cleansing can also be seen as the product of these tendencies. Indeed more broadly, movements towards the recognition of ethnic differences and ➤ethnic nationalism are manifestations of localization. In this sense the relationship between localization, violence and war is quite different from that suggested in the earlier example. ➤➤Subsidiarity

**Lomé Convention** ➤ACP

**Low-intensity conflict (LIC)** A relative term used predominantly by American strategic analysts to identify a class of ➤conflicts where the commitment of ➤capabilities by the United States is finite and limited. The term has always been used with the ➤Third World in mind historically but recently its remit has been expanded to cover a wider range of contingencies including drug control and anti-➤terrorist measures. Typically the kinds of forces required for ➤intervention in low-intensity conflicts are held to be highly mobile, functionally specific units with perhaps a commitment to self-reliance beyond the conventional norm. The support capabilities required for this kind of force structure again emphasizes flexibility and mobility. The airlift and sealift requirements for this kind of force projection are only really available to a limited number of ➤actors of which the United States is the principal example.

There is more than a passing sense of *déjà vu* about recent interest in LIC situations. American interest in ➤counter-insurgency which was the hallmark of the J. F. Kennedy Presidency and British scholarship on the subject (Kitson, 1968) dates back to the ➤Cold War era in ➤international relations. America's involvement in the ➤Vietnam situation can be analysed as a LIC which escalated to a higher level of intensity. Indeed Krepinevich's (1986) critique follows this line of argument. In the interim, the end of the Cold War and the collapse of ➤communism has changed the parameters in which LICs are now ➤perceived particularly in Washington. Avoiding – rather than confronting – the ➤Vietnam Syndrome is an additional benefit which conflict intervention at the low-intensity level provides for American leaders.

**Low politics** A term used in the analysis of ➤foreign policy. Issues are held to be low politics if they are not seen as involving fundamental or key questions relating to a state's ➤national interests, or those of important and significant groups within the ➤state. Low politics issues tend to be dealt with by the bureaucracy employing standard operating procedures. In the last analysis, whether an issue is perceived as low politics depends upon the ➤definition of the situation and how other key ➤actors similarly 'define their situations'. The ➤Falklands prior to 1982 and post-1982 is a good example, from the UK context, of how an issue traditionally defined as 'low' can suddenly escalate to take in the most fundamental values of ➤high politics.

# M

**Maastricht Treaty** ➤European Union

**Machiavellism** Term which symbolizes the ruthless pursuit of objectives regardless of conventional moral values. Niccolo Machiavelli (1469–1527), in his best-known works *The Prince*, the *Discourses* and the *Art of War*, outlines a theory of ➤*raison d'état* whereby the use of any technique is permissible so long as it achieves the desired end. Associated with a cynical, pessimistic view of politics and ➤international relations, it is often and incorrectly identified with the realist view with which it shares family resemblances. The essence of Machiavellism is that every other value is subordinate to the survival of the ➤state:

Where the very safety of the fatherland is at stake there should be no question of reflecting whether a thing is just or unjust, humane or cruel, praiseworthy or shameful. Setting aside every other consideration, one must take only that course of action which will secure the country's life and liberty.

The absence of a moral dimension is linked to the concept of 'necessity': the state is necessary, ➤power is necessary to its survival, and in order to secure power it may be necessary to act immorally. 'A prince must also learn how not to be good; this is the demand of necessity which rules the whole of human life' (see F. Meinecke, 1957, p. 49).

**Macropolitics** A term used to identify a ➤level of analysis. The prefix 'macro' connotes the 'whole' and is often used in contradistinction with the prefix 'micro' connoting individual or several parts. This distinction is widely used in the social sciences and is particularly favoured by economists where the macro/micro dichotomy is well known. Given a particular field of study, macroanalysis therefore begins with the field *per se* and works inwards thereafter to examine individual case studies. Macroanalysis has been particularly favoured by ➤systems theorists as part of the ➤social scientific approach to the field. Morton Kaplan (1957) was one of the first scholars within this burgeoning tradition to apply macroanalysis, while the distinguished political geographers Harold and Margaret Sprout (1971) must be credited with much of the earliest, ground-breaking work on the relationship between man and his milieu.

Macropolitics is, then, that study of politics which centres upon the milieu or the ➤environment rather than the individual ➤actor. As such it is coterminous with world politics. Unlike terms such as world or ➤international politics, macropolitics is uncommitted on the central issue of whether the state is any longer the most significant actor in the system. Used in this way macropolitics may be taken to be as 'value free' as any expression can be in the analysis of social systems.

**Maghrib (sometimes rendered as Magreb)** An Arab term variously translated as 'the West', 'the Occident' or 'the land of the sunset'. Historically it was first applied to all those territories to the west of the Nile valley across to the Atlantic coast of North Africa. In the context of the modern ➤state-system this inclusive definition covers five: Libya, Tunisia, Algeria, Morocco and Mauritania (which has no Mediterranean coast). ➤*Francophonie* scholarship has sometimes used the term 'Maghrib' more exclusively as coterminous with the three former French territories of Morocco, Algeria and Tunisia. These definitional differences well illustrate how arbitrary the concepts of ➤region and regionalism can be.

However defined, the Maghrib is ➤geopolitically and historically quite distinct from the other Arab lands. Indeed in pre-Arab times the North African littoral was sucked into ➤power struggles between Rome and Carthage and between Byzantium and Persia. Following the expansion of ➤Islam the area came under both Arab and Ottoman ➤influence. Mediterranean influences were reasserted through ➤colonialism and the establishment of settler societies. ➤Decolonization was prompted by the 1939–45 World War and in the case of Algeria at least it produced a classic ➤insurgency movement as the vehicle for the expression of anti-colonialism.

All five Maghrib states are engaged in the process of institution-building. In the spring of 1958 the three francophone states produced a call for a United Maghrib, and somewhat hesitant attempts at creating a framework for cooperation have continued since this inception. In November 1989 the five states formed the Union of Maghrib states (UMA – Union du Maghrib Arabe). This alignment is a response as much to the Mediterranean dimension of Maghrib politics as to the Arab one. In particular the need to find a structure for a coordinated response to the ➤EC/EU produced this latest attempt.

**MAD** An acronym for Mutual Assured Destruction. The term was used by strategic analysts during the ➤Cold War era with particular reference to US policies of nuclear ➤deterrence. MAD implied a situation of ➤parity between the ➤superpowers where both possessed such offensive ➤capabilities as to be able to credibly threaten each other's homelands with devastation levels that would be ➤rationally unacceptable. Thus the term 'mutual ➤vulnerability' could be seen as a more accurate, if less dramatic, alternative to MAD.

It is important to understand that MAD was a declaratory policy, not an action policy. MAD described a state of affairs which could arise after a nuclear exchange. Moreover because it seemed to offer national suicide as the alternative to national ➤surrender it raised issues about ➤implementation when and if the nuclear threshold was crossed. Its implication that each side should retain the ultimate ability to destroy the others population centres – the so-called 'hostage cities' situation – seemed to be the ultimate paradox of this logic.

The end of the Cold War and the significant reductions in strategic nuclear weapons made *ex post* and *ex ante* under such ►arms control measures as START has prompted a fundamental reappraisal of strategic thinking at all levels. Inclinations towards a ►security studies rather than ►strategic studies paradigm shift thought towards less provocative theories of nuclear deterrence than MAD. Nuclear arsenals are no longer virility symbols and concepts like ►minimum deterrence are now more relevant.

**Maginot Line**  The Maginot Line was a system of ►frontier fortifications built by France after 1929 to defend their borders with Germany. The principal fortifications covered the area from Luxembourg to the Vosges. South of the Vosges, secondary fortifications stretched down the Rhine valley towards the Swiss frontier. Although the Line bears the name of the French Minister of War at the time, the idea of fortifications along the north-eastern borders had been favourably discussed for some years previously. The Line was completed in 1934. In construction it represented an elaborate system of gun emplacements, underground bunkers, storage and living facilities and transportation networks.

The strategic thinking behind the Maginot Line was derived from the French experiences during the First World War. It was argued that heavy and concentrated fire power plus determined resistance would always check and then defeat an enemy offensive. In ►deterrence terms, the Maginot Line, and indeed the Maginot mentality, was a nearly pure example of deterrence by denial. By making an enemy attack too expensive to contemplate in terms of manpower and material losses, the enemy would be deterred from launching it in the first place.

In the event, the Line proved to be an expensive irrelevance in 1940. Using ►blitzkrieg tactics, and fighting a war of great movement and bold offensive, the German invading armies swung north of the line through Belgium. The line remains testimony to the fallacy of refighting the last war and ignoring strategic and ►technological changes in the interim. The term 'Maginot Line mentality' is sometimes used – usually in the pejorative way – to describe over-reliance upon the defensive techniques and approaches.

**Mandate system**  ►administered territory, trusteeship

**Manhattan Project**  The code name adopted after August 1942 for the project to build an ►atom bomb. Scientific research thereafter came under the aegis of the political and military control of the US Government. The normal rules of academic research were abandoned and the strictest secrecy prevailed. The fact that the team was headed by a professional soldier, General Leslie Richard Groves, is indicative of the primacy of military/security issues over the usual canons of scientific scholarship.

Notwithstanding the reference to New York in the code name, research on the bomb project was conducted at three centres: Oak Ridge, Hanford and Los Alamos. Oak Ridge was an enrichment plant, Hanford a ➤plutonium reactor and Los Alamos in New Mexico was chosen by Groves and J. Robert Oppenheimer as the location for the testing and production of the actual bomb. This test took place in July 1945 at Alamogordo, New Mexico.

**Maoism** A system of ideas and assumptions about politics, economics and society in general associated with the life and thought of the Chinese ➤nationalist and ➤communist leader Mao Tse-tung (1893 – 1976). Mao was the popular, indeed charismatic, leader of the Chinese ➤revolution which eventually overthrew the Kuomintang in 1949, thereby establishing the People's Republic of China. It should be understood at the outset that Maoism is not specifically a corpus of ideas about ➤international and/or ➤world politics; rather like ➤Marxism/Leninism, it is a system of ideas which has implications for the field.

Maoism has made two distinct contributions to world politics. First, in the period up to 1949 Mao developed and applied a theory of revolution which emphasized the fusion of ➤guerrilla warfare as an instrument with the mobilization of the peasants as the mainspring of the revolutionary movement. It was this fusion which was unique about Maoism. Previously guerrilla warfare had not been specifically seen as the means whereby an ➤insurgency could overcome an incumbent ➤regime, nor had the rural peoples been seen as the appropriate basis of support for such changes. It was Mao's genius that made the connection. Mao's theories of guerrilla warfare are often referred to as ➤people's war and the distinctive historical experience of the Chinese under his leadership led to the belief in the positive benefits, as well as the dire necessities, of a ➤protracted war.

The second contribution of Maoism was to develop a world view and ➤foreign policy orientation that was distinctly different but which still had roots in the Chinese tradition. These ideas were developed in the period of power after 1949 when the People's Republic of China (PRC) had to respond to the putative ➤leadership of the Soviet Union and the considerable hostility and suspicion of the United States. At the same time the process of ➤decolonization in Asia presented the new Chinese leadership with the opportunity to implement theories about the 'intermediate zones' and the 'three worlds' in the decade of the 1950s. Maoism, among other factors, was instrumental in creating a new self-consciousness among ➤Third World elites while at the same time establishing a definite role for the PRC within the Third World movement.

Maoism also developed a ➤tripolar configuration between the ➤PRC, the Soviet Union and the United States after 1949. Indeed, Chinese orientations towards these two ➤superpowers underwent a full 180-degree about-turn between the establishment of the ➤PRC and the death of Mao in 1976. An initial period of amity with the Soviet Union, when Mao himself personally negotiated the Sino–Soviet Treaty of 1950, and hostility towards the United States, when China intervened in the ►Korean War in the same year, had by 1976, changed into hostility towards the former ally and ►*détente* with the former enemy. The split with the Soviet Union under Mao and the ►rapprochement with the United States during the Nixon presidency were significant aspects of this orientation towards a more ►tripolar relationship.

**Maritime law** ►law of the sea

**Marshall Plan** The Marshall Plan, or European Recovery Programme, takes its popular name from the US Secretary of State, George C. Marshall, whose address at Harvard in June 1947 contained the original idea. Marshall proposed that the United States establish a programme of economic assistance to help European governments and peoples rebuild their economies that had been shattered as a result of the Second World War. By the summer of 1947 it was clear that the early post-war optimism about European recovery was not justified. ►Bilateral US ►aid to states such as the United Kingdom had been rapidly dissipated and existing international institutions, such as the International Bank for Reconstruction and Development (IBRD) were not appropriate for the task. Marshall specifically proposed a ►multilateral regional initiative rather than a variation of the previous ►bilateral programmes. To this end the US Government stipulated that the European states should immediately consult together to assess their needs and provide the donor American government with specific statistically based requests.

The consultation that took place among European states during the summer of 1947 was important for two outcomes. Economically, it provided an early example of cooperation in an ►issue area which was to become increasingly important to Europeans, particularly in the West, in the decades ahead. The Organization for European Economic Cooperation (OEEC) was formed for this purpose in 1948. Politically it showed that there was a clear division of opinion between the free market approach led by the United Kingdom and France and the centrally planned approach led by the Soviet Union. As a result effective Soviet consultation and cooperation in these matters ceased after July 1947.

The Soviet perception of the Plan was that it constituted an infringement upon their economic ►sovereignty. There is no doubt that the Marshall scheme would have meant that outside parties would have been able to pass an opinion on the Soviet economy and on the manner in which it was run. A tradition had been established under Stalin of planning for self-sufficiency, with a particular emphasis upon manufacturing industry and a managed market. The whole tradition established under US ►hegemony was the very antithesis of this. Whatever the intentions of its framer, the Plan undoubtedly became caught up in the ►Cold War. By the time that the Plan had been approved by Congress in the spring of 1948 attitudes had hardened on both sides and the programme had become politicized into part of the repertoire of instruments available in the United States and its friends. By exerting counter-pressure upon Eastern European states to reject the Plan, the Soviet Union confirmed its own hegemonial intentions in the East and helped to confirm the division of Europe and the consequent demolition of European ➤interdependence which had been a feature of the region before 1938. The Soviet Union responded to the specific challenge of the Marshall Plan by the Molotov Plan which led to the formation of ➤Comecon in January 1949. The formation of these rival economic institutions, outside the competence of the UN Economic Commission for Europe – which was the only pan-European institution – signifies the importance that the Cold War was to have in the politics of international economic relations after 1945.

It is beyond dispute that Marshall assistance was directed towards a very real and pressing economic need. The Second World War had turned Europe from a creditor into a debtor within ten years. ➤War damage was considerable and the transition from a war economy to a peace economy was daunting in its implications. Additionally, Germany, the engine room of the European economy before 1938, was divided and if the Soviet Union had its way would be subjected to an onerous ➤reparations programme. At the same time Europe had been the continent which had pioneered economic development in the previous centuries and thus the infrastructure for recovery was present. Although generous, nearly three-quarters of all Marshall aid was spent on purchasing goods from the United States, so that the US economy was indirectly subsidized as a result. The long-term recovery of the economies of western Europe was such that with the formation of the EC, the region became a serious trade rival and competitor to the United States. Notwithstanding these somewhat mixed results for US interests, the Plan must be regarded as one of the major successes of post-war economic assistance policies.

**Marxism/Leninism** A number of commentators have remarked on the difficulty of establishing a Marxist/Leninist theory of ➤international relations. Martin Wight (1966), for example, asserted that 'neither Marx, Lenin nor Stalin made any systematic contribution to international theory; Lenin's *Imperialism* comes nearest to such a thing, and this has little to say about international politics.' While this may be so, it is possible to provide an outline of the main thrust of the ➤communist approach, especially in relation to ➤imperialism, war, social conflict and ➤revolution. The essential elements of Marxism are as follows:

1 All history is the history of class struggle between a ruling group and an opposing group.
2 Capitalism gives rise to antagonistic classes, the bourgeoisie and proletariat, with the bourgeoisie in control.
3 Capitalism uses war to further its own ends.
4 Socialism, which destroys classes, must also destroy war.
5 Once the state has withered away, so too must international politics.

On this view all political phenomena are projections of underlying economic forces. So whereas ►liberal and ►realist theories are *horizontal* (relations between states) the Marxist/Leninist view is *vertical* (relations between classes). In this sense, many argue that Marxism/Leninism is a theory of domestic politics rather than international relations. Certainly, the approach denies the separateness of international relations and views it as an extended manifestation of the quest for economic gain or advantage. Given that 'capitalism' and the 'state' are both seen as the villains of international affairs, it is not clear from the Marxian analysis if one or both must be abolished to bring about permanent peace. K. N. Waltz (1959) points to this as a major ambiguity and argues that socialist theory in the twentieth century has had to adapt or revise the original all-encompassing propositions. Lenin (1870–1924) is a major figure in this process, so much so that the official orthodoxy is now termed Marxism/Leninism rather than simply Marxism.

Lenin's *Imperialism: the Highest Stage of Capitalism* (1916) owes much to the pioneering work of J. A. Hobson in 1902. For Lenin, imperialism is an inevitable consequence of capitalism. It is 'decaying' capitalism where competition has been replaced by monopolies, and at this stage states come to live more and more on capital exports; because of lack of opportunity within the capitalist countries themselves, the export of capital to achieve a high rate of investment return is essential. The drive towards political or military control of markets and sources of raw materials results in a general capitalist scramble for colonies. This has the added bonus of providing cheap sources of labour and guaranteed market for surplus goods. The general result is that advanced capitalist states are driven through imperial policies into conflict with one another over possession of underdeveloped areas. Because markets and sources of raw materials are not unlimited, international conflict between capitalist states is endemic and although there may be temporary agreement between these exploiting states as to the ownership of territories or ►spheres of influence, in the end these states are bound to clash. The First World War is seen as proof of this thesis. The solution to the problems of continuing international conflict and the establishment of ►peace is the elimination, through revolution, of capitalist states themselves. A peaceful ►world order can only be achieved through attacking the domestic economic systems of the states. 'World proletarian revolution' is thus the means to effect this change.

Capitalist states will not 'wither away' overnight, so socialist states are established in the interim, and the conviction is that an international socialist system of states would be free of conflict since socialists agree on basic questions of resource allocation and are not tainted by the ►militarism which characterized the old order. (Many critics, however, have pointed out that this does not seem to have occurred in quite the same way the theory suggests, as the Sino-Soviet conflict of the 1950s and 1960s was just as bitter as any between capitalist states.) An associated idea is the notion of encirclement which Stalin in particular saw as a likely strategy of the capitalist world, and indeed this took on a new significance with the adoption of the policies of ➤containment by the United States in the post-1945 era. Eventually, though, according to Khrushchev, this would give way to socialist encirclement as the forces of capitalism weakened. Another important revision of Marx's original thesis is the idea of peaceful coexistence which was first used by Lenin and Trotsky in relation to the Treaty of Brest-Litovsk (1917) and which came to signify ➤accommodation with capitalist states, but did not altogether abandon the commitment to undermine them through ➤wars of national liberation.

Lenin's analysis of imperialism is the backbone of the communist theory of international relations, and although modifications have been made in the face of the changing patterns of world politics in the twentieth century it is likely to remain as the theoretical prism through which socialist states view the outside world. Critics of the equation Capitalism = Imperialism = War are legion and most point out that Lenin built a universal system out of a limited set of historical experiences. While the theory throws light on the period between 1870 and 1914, it lacks explanatory power both before this time and after it. Very little attention is given to the causes of international conflict other than the economic one (e.g. political, psychological, cultural, ideological, religious or personal causes). The assertion that a world of socialist states would be non-imperial and peaceful has been questioned. The element of the 'inevitability of war' with the capitalist world remains but the increasing importance of ➤détente and ➤arms control agreements between the two camps has the effect of watering down this bastion.

However, while many criticisms may be made of the internal coherence of the arguments and of their external application no one can doubt that Marxism/ Leninism has had an influence on the twentieth century. The charge that Western capitalism and imperialism deliberately suppressed the economic development of the Third World has been reiterated and restated by ➤dependency theory. The Marxist/Leninist shift of attention away from the sovereign state towards an emphasis on non-state ➤actors and the commitment to ➤hierarchical/ vertical relationships is reflected in ➤structuralism and in some notions of ➤structural power. Marxism/Leninism may not amount to a theory of international relations, but its observations on world politics have succeeded in restructuring the focus of the discipline to the extent that for some scholars historical materialism is now one of its central ➤paradigms. Marxism/Leninism may be defunct as a political movement but this does not detract from the validity of much of its analysis nor does it gainsay its continuing influence. The subfield of ➤international political economy demonstrates this as well as any other.

**Massive retaliation** Part of the 'New Look' ➤defence policy of the first term of the Eisenhower Presidency (1953–7), massive retaliation was the first serious attempt to elaborate a strategic doctrine for the nuclear age. It was designed to meet the needs for a ➤deterrent posture that would capitalize upon the technical advantages the United States then possessed over the Soviet Union, in particular in its offensive bomber capabilities. At the same time it was intended that the policy would operate within the budgetary constraints which would allow the United States to put most of its strategic eggs in the air force basket while running down expenditure on the army and navy as a corollary.

Although the administration never formally renounced the doctrine, by the second term it had become more symbol than substance. In any event the new ➤technology of ballistic missiles, dramatically demonstrated by the launching of the Soviet ➤Sputnik suggested that the future lay with these systems rather than the manned bombers which had been the basis of the doctrine when it was first announced. Meanwhile the analytical inconsistencies behind the doctrine had been ruthlessly exposed by strategic studies academics such as Kaufmann (1989).

**Médecins Sans Frontières (MSF)** Established in 1971 by a group of former ➤International Red Cross (IRC) medics, MSF is now the world's largest ➤non-governmental organization (NGO) providing emergency medical relief. Consisting mainly of doctors, nurses, surgeons and logistical experts it has six operational sections in Europe and twelve branches world-wide. It is an independent body but it often works in conjunction with other humanitarian agencies, notably the IRC and the ➤United Nations High Commission for Refugees (UNHCR). It maintains a strictly impartial status and believes in the cosmopolitan notion of an absolute right to humanitarian assistance. It scorns the ➤Westphalian principle of ➤non-intervention and, if necessary, is prepared to work clandestinely with people in need, and to speak out publicly against ➤human rights abusers. Apart from providing medical relief in man-made conflicts or in natural emergencies, the bulk of MSF work is in primary ➤health care. It is therefore not a one-shot operation; an important part of its remit is reconstruction and long-term amelioration of local conditions. In 1997 the MSF's largest relief effort was in Rwanda where it had 360 expatriate volunteers and over 1,500 support staff in Burundi, Tanzania and Zaire. Other recent major emergency missions include Bosnia, Angola, Sudan and Afghanistan. ➤humanitarian intervention

**Mediation** This is a form of ➤accommodation which is directed at ➤conflict settlement and possibly ➤resolution. Mediation as an ongoing activity presupposes a mediator and it is axiomatic that a certain typology of the latter can assist a successful outcome to the former. The would-be mediator is primarily a facilitator who seeks to establish or restore communication between the parties. In the process the identity of the parties and the nature of the issues will be clarified. In effect, the mediator reaches a ➤definition of the situation with and between the parties. Since the settlement/resolution process will normally involve face-to-face ➤negotiations, the putative mediator must bring the parties into contact with this expectation in mind. Timing can often be crucial. Zartman (1989) has spoken of conflicts being 'ripe for resolution' when the parties reach a 'hurtling stalemate'. An alteration in the relative ➤power positions of the parties such that the 'top dog' starts losing and the 'underdog' starts gaining may be another precondition. In such instances the ➤perception is widespread that the ➤status quo is unacceptable and that 'things cannot be allowed to continue like this'. The role of the mediator may be crucial at this stage both in establishing agreed procedures and in defining viable solutions. Impartiality and ➤neutrality may be seen as essential prerequisites.

In ➤international politics effective mediation often comes from other ➤states in a particular ➤region or from ➤great powers in an ➤anarchical system. The latter in particular may be able to exercise leverage over the parties and can additionally underwrite a settlement with guarantees and side payments. ➤International organizations such as the ➤United Nations have superficial merit as mediators since they evince impartiality and neutrality.

Empirically, the promise of such IGO's has not been matched by the performance. Custom and practice has seen the ➤Secretary-General's office playing the role of facilitator but this intervention critically depends upon the support of the ➤P5. Indeed, on occasions the Secretary-General has assisted one or several of the permanent members to 'save face' themselves – Suez in 1956 and ➤Afghanistan in the 1980s being instances. Notwithstanding, some see significant structural problems in the UN's mediation abilities in the post-➤Cold War system. The complex ➤decision-making process within the ➤Security Council means that building and then maintaining a consensus behind a particular mediatory stance may be difficult. The nature of the consensus may simply reflect the lowest common denominator of agreement amongst the membership. This is hardly the most auspicious infrastructure for a sustained mediation effort between conflicting parties. Additionally, some of the most difficult and intractable conflicts have been 'dumped' upon the organization and as a result the UN's track record has not improved.

**Megaton** A measure of the destructive power of ➤nuclear weapons. The megaton, or MT, is held to equal one million tons of TNT. This measure is usually applied to fusion weapons. As a general tendency the Soviet Union tended to produce more missiles capable of carrying heavier warheads than the United States.

**Melian dialogue** A much quoted section of ➤Thucydides' *Peloponnesian War* (Book V, ch. 7) which is used by many commentators to illustrate the indifference of ➤power politics to moral argument. Ignoring a desperate plea from the Melians that they wished to remain ➤neutral in the conflict with Sparta (431–404 BC), the Athenian envoys asserted that 'the standard of justice depends on the equality of power to compel and that in fact the strong do what they have the power to do and the weak accept what they have to accept.' The Athenians then besieged Melos and eventually executed all the men of military age and sold the women and children for slaves. In a chilling rider to the idea that ➤justice is on the side of the stronger the Athenian diplomat added: 'This is not a law that we made ourselves, nor were we the first to act upon it when it was made. We found it already in existence, and we shall leave it to exist forever among those who come after us.' The idea that the powerful take what they want and the weak grant what they must has been a pervasive one in ➤international relations and has constantly intruded into discussions on the ➤equality of states in the ➤international system. Preventing this law from existing 'forever among those who come after us' has been the main purpose of ➤normative theories of I R in twentieth-century international thought.

**Mercantilism** A school of thought connected with International Political Economy. Mercantilism flourished in Western Europe in the centuries between the Renaissance and the Industrial Revolution. Its impact upon the developing system of ➤international relations was considerable because its basic contention that foreign economic policy should reflect ➤state interests was compatible with the trend towards ➤state-centred thinking evident at the time. Mercantilism may be contrasted with ➤economic liberalism which, as originally articulated by Adam Smith, was a frontal assault upon the assumptions and implications of the mercantilists. Whereas the liberals emphasized policies and philosophies that favoured cooperation, the mercantilists were wholly self-centred and self-regarding in their approach. In particular mercantilists argued that state policy should seek to increase ➤exports and decrease ➤imports relative to a given level of economic activity. Since one state's exports are another state's imports, this doctrine of seeking selfish advantage has come to be called 'beggar-my-neighbour' policy.

Mercantilism is also associated sometimes in the popular mind with so-called 'bullionist' theories. This line of reasoning argued that great significance was attached to the accretion of precious metals as a source of wealth and a store of value. Accordingly the self-centred pursuit of a favourable ➤trade balance was important because it enabled the payments balance thereby generated to be converted into bullion. Again the economic drawbacks of frankly hoarding precious metals and not recycling them through the system was easily demonstrated by the subsequent liberal critique.

It should not be thought that mercantilism is completely archaic because of the above remarks. ➤Protectionism and ➤neo-mercantilism as practices and policies show that this is not the case. Moreover, the mercantilists' fundamental ideological commitment to the view that foreign economic policy is about the accretion of wealth, ➤capability and putative power is still valid today. Their belief that economic capabilities provided the 'war potential' for the state was widely accepted within the ➤strategic studies tradition as a fundamental tenet.

Their contention that international economic relations were, at bottom, insepar-able from political considerations continues to receive much endorsement today.

**Mercosur** A regional economic organization linking Argentina, Brazil, Para-guay and Uruguay, established by the Treaty of Asunción in 1991. After the North America Free Trade Association (NAFTA) it is the second most important economic bloc in the Americas. In 1996 Chile gained associate status and Mercosur now embraces a population grouping of over 220 million people stretching from the Atlantic to the Pacific oceans. It is the fourth largest economic grouping in the world behind NAFTA, the ➤European Union (EU) and the Association of South East Asian Nations (ASEAN). The basis of the organization is the Iguazú Declaration of 1985 which established ➤bilateral economic links between South America's two traditional rivals, Argentina and Brazil. The model for this ➤rapprochement was the Franco-German experience after World War II. The catalyst was the restoration of democracy and the quest for economic liberalization in both states. As with the European example, the binding together of the two most powerful antagonists in the ➤region was followed by a process of expansion to include neighbouring states. Thus, Bolivia now has observer status and other regional states are likely to follow. At present Mercosur is primarily a ➤free trade area but through the process of ➤functional ➤spillover it may well develop more European-style ➤supranational institutions, including a central decision-making body and a community legal ➤regime. The first stage in this process would be the inauguration of a ➤Customs Union which involved not merely the elimination of tariffs and quotas between members but also a common external tariff.

**Micro-state** Micro-states, according to UN and ➤Commonwealth defi-nitions, are those ➤states with under one million inhabitants. Of the Common-wealth's fifty-three members, twenty-seven have been officially identified as micro-states. These are as follows: *Europe*, Cyprus and Malta; *Caribbean*, Guyana, Barbados, Bahamas, Belize, Antigua-Barbuda, St Lucia, Grenada, St Vincent, Dominica, St Kitts-Nevis; *Africa*, Mauritius, Botswana, Gambia, Swaziland, Seychelles; *Asia*, Brunei, Maldives; *Pacific*, Fiji (present status uncertain), Solo-mon Islands, Western Samoa, Vanuatu, Tongo, Kiribati, Tuvalu and Nauru. In all, there are over forty of these very small states dotted around the globe sometimes occupying strategically important locations. The problems of defence and avoiding outside ➤intervention are acute, particularly so for island micro-states in the Caribbean, Indian and Pacific oceans. The (1983) US invasion of Grenada spawned great interest and concern that these micro-states were not economically viable and are potential trouble-spots in world politics. What is 'viable' is often a reflection of one's own prejudices but certainly the possession of full voting rights in the UN and its agencies by these states is something that the international community as a whole will soon have to monitor. The

United States, in particular, is beginning to question the wisdom of granting equal rights to all states regardless of size or development.

**Middle powers** Middle powers are those ►states which are generally regarded as secondary only to the ►great powers. Martin Wight (1978) defines them in this way:

. . . a power with such military strength, resources and strategic positions that in peacetime, the great powers bid for its support, and wartime, while it has no hopes of winning a war against a great power, it can hope to inflict costs on a great power out of proportion to what the great power can hope to gain by attacking it.

France, with its ►*force de frappe*, clearly belongs in this category, as perhaps does the United Kingdom. But because of Wight's emphasis on military ►capability this definition appears to rule out other states, such as Japan and Germany whose military capability may be limited but whose economic strength, in particular, is vast. The problem of definition is a complex one and C. Holbraad (1984), looking mainly at GNP, population and armed force levels for 1975, lists eighteen states as belonging broadly in this category: France, the United Kingdom, China, Japan, Germany, Canada, Italy, Brazil, Spain, Poland, India, Australia, Mexico, Iran, Argentina, South Africa, Indonesia and Nigeria. The list is a controversial one and reasons for inclusion or exclusion might not always be clear but these states and perhaps others, such as Israel, Syria, Pakistan and South Korea, may be regarded as sharing some minimal common characteristics. They usually have large populations, they are relatively ►developed, they possess credible armed forces and are reasonably wealthy. They are also ►regional powers of some stature. Yet any characterization that groups Spain alongside Germany, or Poland alongside Canada, or Mexico alongside the United Kingdom is imprecise. In recognition of this middle powers are sometimes subdivided into 'upper middle powers' (the first five in Holbraad's list) and 'lower middle powers'. Other commentators prefer a separate categorization for those in the upper bracket and use the terms 'secondary powers' or 'regional great powers' to distinguish them from middle powers. In this way S. Speigel (1972), identifies secondary powers as 'those states which are able to challenge the superpowers in particular areas of activity'. Middle powers are then 'those states whose level of power permits them to play only decidedly limited and selective rôles in states and regions other than their own'. The fact that, for example, the United Kingdom could reasonably be slotted into both these categorizations indicates the difficulty of the enterprise. In most assessments of position in the international ►hierarchy five elements of capability are usually considered: material or economic power, military power, motivational power, achievement and potential. Since some, if not all, of these indices involve subjective evaluations, agreement on particular classification will always be contentious.

**Migration** The mass movement of people has always had an obvious, though

perhaps unpredictable, effect on ➤international relations. The impact of the
New World on the twentieth century, for example, was a direct consequence
of the 'Great Atlantic Migration' of earlier epochs, which is to say European
(mostly 'voluntary') and Afro/Asian (primarily 'enforced') migration. However,
although cross-boundary and intercontinental movements of immigrants has
always occurred, it is only recent years that the ➤issue area has been ➤perceived
to be a first order problem in IR, in the sense that it begins to impinge directly
on its core concepts – ➤sovereignty, national ➤security, order and stability.

The idea of the free movement of peoples has long been an integral part of
the Western conception of ➤human rights. The Kantian notion of 'universal
hospitality' (which in any case did not confer automatic rights of citizenship)
and the American presumption in favour of acceptance of 'the tired, poor and
huddled masses yearning to be free' can be regarded as ➤idealist propositions
reflecting broad spectrum ➤liberal assumptions about IR. They were converted
into practical propositions by the ➤technology of mass communications (beginning with steam transport) and the ➤globalization of markets (particularly for
labour). Historically mass migrations have been correlated with the incidence of
➤communal conflict, ➤ethnic cleansing and ➤genocide and economic recession.
The prospect of significant ➤environmental migrations in the twenty-first
century cannot be dismissed, particularly if the major issue area of climate
change is not effectively addressed by building a ➤regime to control damaging
forms of ➤pollution.

Empirically the occurrence of large-scale migrations has severely tested the
kind of assumption made earlier. As a consequence the idea of Fortress World
with a presumption in favour of 'closed' rather than 'open' borders has always
attracted adherents, especially in the developed ➤North. Immigration control
has historically been politicized within these societies by ➤leaderships and parties
seeking to link this issue with other actual or potential policy areas. America is
a case in point. The first target for immigration quotas and controls was the
Chinese workers brought in to construct the transcontinental railways after the
Civil War. Following the conclusion of the First World War, a nativist backlash
encouraged legislation on quotas in the 1920s. In Britain, steps were taken to
restrict ➤Commonwealth immigration in the 1960s. Although contested at the
time, this legislation enjoyed bipartisan support afterwards. Within the European
➤region the implosion of the Soviet Union and the collapse of the ➤Cold War
structures in the East has precipitated the threat of the mass movement of
economic migrants to the West. Germany, in particular because of its wealth
and central location, is a favoured destination for these peoples. German
reluctance over the issue of Turkish membership of the ➤European Union is
in part at least fuelled by fears of significant Turkish migration. In addition, the
chronic structural problems of much of the ➤Third World, which continue to
engender mass displacement of peoples, are beginning to affect both North–
➤South and South–South relations. Overlying this, and giving the issue greater

urgency, is the relentless ►population explosion in the developing world and the threat that this poses to the integrity of national borders. Increasingly, then, analysts are recognizing that mass migration threatens the stability of the ►state-system itself, not just subordinate parts of it.

Immigration control is now a priority issue area globally. As indicated above, the European Union, which is now a net *receiver* rather than a *sender* of migrants, faces migratory pressures from several directions: the aforementioned Eastern Europe and North Africa being the most pressing. In the USA the quota restrictions induced by the nativist backlash had the paradoxical effect of enhancing migration from within the hemisphere with the result that the various Hispanic–American communities (notably Mexican, Cuban, and Puerto Rican) have grown in significance in the twentieth century.

While the international community has long since established an embryonic legal ►regime for dealing with the issues of ►refugees and ►asylum seekers, as yet there is no coherent or systematic attempt to deal with the causes or consequences of large-scale migration. Since 1980 the ►United Nations has been examining immigration prevention ('International Cooperation to Avert New Flows of Refugees') and in 1982 the Commission on Human Rights prepared a study on 'Human Rights and Mass Exoduses', but the policy implications have not been widely followed. It remains to be seen whether the problem of migration becomes sufficiently pressing to be considered as a key issue on the agenda of the UN Population Conference.

Given that the control of boundaries and the granting of asylum impinge on issues of national ►sovereignty, long-term solutions depend upon the extent to which the international community is willing to jettison ideas and practices established by the ►Westphalian regime (see Widgren, 1990).

**Militarism** Militarism is the subordination of civil society to military values and the subordination of civilian control of the military for military control of the civilian. Typically the two processes may occur together whenever the military institutions take over the political system. A necessary condition for the emergence of militarism is the establishment of armed forces – particularly armies – of sufficient size and complexity to play a significant and lasting role in the political system. One reason in the past for resisting large permanent military establishments has been the awareness that this can lead to militarism. In what might be called the Anglo-American tradition, political leaders and commentators sought to eschew large armies, in particular, to avoid this kind of occurrence. In other traditions – notably European socialism – the ►militia was seen as an acceptable alternative to the standing army, which was perceived as reactionary and ►status quo orientated.

The growth of ►states and ►international systems combined with the ►technological changes associated with the Industrial Revolution has increased the scope for militarism. States usually establish and maintain standing armies and the military is the one sector in society which, perforce, will be technologically orientated. Additionally, the ►modernization process has further enhanced the relative importance of the military in society. Obsolescence of ideas, equipment and training is the Achilles heel of the armed forces. In all states the military, as an interest group, will fight its corner, campaigning for more equipment, better pay and an expanded complement. In some instances this activity may lead to the growth of a ►military-industrial complex (MIC). In unstable political systems it may lead to the growth of militarism. In short, militarism thrives on political instability. ►Intervention by the military will often be justified, to both domestic and international audiences, on the grounds that it will promote stability in a system that would otherwise decay.

Militarism in contemporary international/world politics is particularly associated with the ►Third World. Within that very broad classificatory grouping, the Latin American region is probably the paradigm example of the phenomenon. Militarism has been virtually endemic in much of Latin America since the Wars of Independence at the start of the nineteenth century. Where military leaders have taken power over the last centuries it has usually been with the assistance of or in ►alliance with the more conservative social forces in the ►region. Alternatively the military has remained more in the background, exercising ►veto power in the system by the constant threat of intervention.

External developments have also influenced Latin American militarism. In the 1920s and 1930s ►fascism in Italy and Spain provided contagious role models. After 1947 the ►Cold War was a new justification for intervention – to prevent or check the spread of ►communism, a move which, additionally, re-established the militarists' alliance with the conservatives. On many occasions – for instance in Argentina and Chile – the military have seemed to regard themselves as above the law, or at least outside it, in their suppression of opposition and infringement of ►human rights. The military may be indicted on the grounds of widespread corruption and excessive personal enrichment – even populist regimes like Perón's (1945–55) in Argentina were susceptible to this failing.

**Military–industrial complex (MIC)** A term given wide currency by US President Dwight Eisenhower when he issued a warning about the 'unwarranted influence' of the military–industrial complex in his farewell address in 1961. Intellectually the idea can be seen as having two derivations: political sociology and political economy. Political sociology provides the idea of ►elite and in particular C. Wright Mills's (1956) characterization of political economic and military circles in the United States forming 'overlapping cliques'. Mills saw the ►Cold War having an important causal connection with the ►power elite and in this respect he shares with the political economists the view that the 'permanent war economy' established in the United States after 1945 created the infrastructure for the MIC.

The leading figure in the political economy tradition is undoubtedly Melman (1985). He argues that between 1941 and 1945 what he calls an 'ideological consensus' emerged in the United States about the relationship between military expenditure and economic activity. In brief this consensus holds that military expenditure generates employment and prosperity, boosts the economy and reduces unemployment. This creates a permissive climate among the mass public for maintaining high levels of ➤defence expenditure during peacetime. As a result the 'overlapping cliques' about whom Mills wrote in the *Power Elite* are able to manipulate and dominate the system.

The idea of the MIC firmly locates the explanation for ➤arms races within the domestic structure of the states concerned. In this respect it is a distinct break with those ➤action-reaction theories that have rested upon the external, state-to-state behaviour patterns. A particular difficulty with the MIC is deciding whether it is *sui generis* to the United States or whether it can be applied to other social systems.

Critiques of the US version of the MIC have come from two directions. First, political sociologists writing within the ➤pluralist tradition have suggested that the power structure is not as monolithic as the elitists suggest and that considerable competition for power and ➤influence goes on at the top. Political economists, meanwhile, have attacked the permanent ➤war economy on the grounds that it is inefficient. There are considerable direct and opportunity costs for society in supporting the MIC. Evidence is adduced from the recent experience of states such as Japan which would appear to show that fast economic growth is not correlated positively with high, but rather with low, levels of defence expenditure. Indeed, according to this view there is very little statistical evidence to substantiate a positive link between growth, employment, inflation or favourable external payments accounts and high levels of military expenditure.

**Militia** Locally raised, part-time forces used to supplement or to replace the regular ➤army in an emergency situation. This might be an external threat to the ➤state, such as that posed by an invasion. Alternatively civil strife and even ➤civil war can pose an internal threat of such magnitude as to require the ➤intervention of the militia. Allowing the local population to bear arms in this way requires a considerable act of confidence by any political ➤leadership since an armed population may defy the civil authorities rather than support them. At the same time the principle of the nation-in-arms has attracted considerable support and carried considerable appeal over the centuries from ➤nationalists and ➤communists alike. For some advocates of the militia, the right to bear arms is regarded as almost 'inalienable'.

Strategists have been interested in the role of the militia since ➤Machiavelli and debate has continually raged about the relative merits of professional armies versus locally raised forces. The development of ➤Marxism/Leninism added a further ➤ideological dimension to the issue. Many communists, following the lead provided by Engels, have argued that the militia is the best type of military organiz-ation for this type of political system. With the establishment of the Soviet Union the debate had an empirical point of focus. In this case the issue was decided in favour of the regular army and the term 'militia', although still used in the Soviet Union, now refers colloquially to sections of the civilian police forces.

Among other European states, a similar kind of debate took place in the years between 1919 and 1939. Again the principle of the 'nation-in-arms' was central to French thinking. Additionally it was felt that the milita was essentially a defensive system and that, in conjunction with the ➤Maginot line, its existence would send appropriate signals to the Germans about French intentions. Other European states with a tradition of relying upon militias include Switzerland and Finland, both states with a neutralist ➤orientation in their ➤foreign policy.

**Minimax** A term derived from ➤game theory. It is sometimes written as *maximin*. Either rendition means the same. It refers to the assumption that, in the game, the players will seek to maximize their gains in the abstract but that given an opponent who is seeking the same outcome, i.e. maximization then it becomes ➤rational to seek the best *available* solution. In a ➤zero-sum game this best available solution is minimax. Mathematically minimax becomes a theorem of zero-sum game strategy.

Although seemingly arcane, minimax approximations are sometimes resorted to in policy-making when ➤actors faced with an absence of attractive alternatives seek to pursue what is ➤perceived to be the least worst outcome. As with the formal game structure, these strategies do rely upon certain assumptions about the motivations of putative adversaries. In the short term these can often be made. In the long term they may be more contingent.

**Minimum deterrent** A term used in strategic analysis. It refers to the special case of ➤deterrence where an ➤actor rejects notions about superiority or even ➤parity of force ➤capabilities in favour of a force posture that is sufficient to create doubts and uncertainties in the mind of a putative opponent such that this adversary will be deterred from the behaviour that is deemed unacceptable in the first instance. Sometimes referred to as 'finite' deterrence, this minimalist posture may be the only available ➤rational strategy for a ➤state actor confronted by threats from an adversary perceived to be more powerful than itself. Just how 'minimum' such a deterrent has to be to retain ➤credibility remains a moot point. It depends upon the relativities in the relationship between the parties and the terms of their ➤conflict situation. These relativities will themselves change over time.

It is generally agreed that the advent of ➤nuclear weapons in the ➤international system after 1945 placed new forms of deterrent capability in the hands of states and their political ➤leaderships which had not been available before. During the ➤Cold War era it was common for analysts to see both the British nuclear forces and the French ➤*force de frappe* as minimum deterrents *vis-à-vis* the Soviet Union. The end of the Cold War and the growth of a very different ➤security complex in Europe has left these two states with capabilities which looked minimal set against the former Soviet Union but which seem luxuriant now.

**Mirror image** Sometimes rendered as 'mirror percept'. The term is clearly derived from the psychological idea of ➤image and ➤perception as important dynamic qualities affecting the way individuals and groups 'see' their world, particularly their social world. The necessary conditions for the mirror image effect are: first, a situation of social ➤conflict within or between groups and, second, a situation of ➤polarization about the cause and conduct of the conflict. Given these antecedent conditions, mirror-imaging occurs when antagonistic groups attribute exactly the same 'diabolical' characteristics to their opponents. Thus the two groups may come to the independent judgement that the other is attempting to 'surround' or 'encircle' them. They may be equally convinced that the other is 'cheating' or 'dissembling'. During ➤negotiations they may present data which appear to suggest that while they are negotiating in good faith the adversary is not. In short, mirror-imaging is a form of perceptual distortion or ➤misperception.

The American psychologist Bronfenbrenner (1961) is generally credited with some of the earliest social scientific work on mirror image effects. His publications in the early 1960s seemed to substantiate the phenomena in Soviet-American relations both among mass and informed publics. More recently J. W. Burton's interest in the possibility of 'controlling communication' between adversaries via third party activities has resuscitated the mirror image effect. In the context of ➤conflict resolution, of course, mirror images stand in the way of self-sustained solutions. Unless and until they can at least be substantially modified, if not totally altered, these perceptions will exacerbate hostilities and antagonisms between parties in conflict.

**Misperception** A misperception is a misinterpretation or misunderstanding. Its usage assumes that there is a 'correct' or more 'accurate' ➤perception from which a deviation has occurred. Since both terms – 'perception' and 'misperception' – are subjectively defined concepts, it may be quite difficult to establish what is 'accurate' or 'correct' in these matters. On many occasions such a conclusion can only be reached after the event when, with hindsight, it can be said that certain ➤actors 'misperceived' the situation. Like the term perception, misperception directs the analyst to individual and small group levels of ➤analysis. It probably makes little sense to speak of a ➤nation misperceiving a situation and it certainly makes no sense to speak of a ➤state doing so, since the latter would be an unwarranted reification.

There are a number of causal factors which can be identified as increasing the probability that an actor will misperceive the aims and intentions of others when conducting ➤foreign policy. Situationally, information that reaches

➤decision-makers is often ambiguous and susceptible to a number of interpretations. In extreme circumstances other actors may deliberately seek to enhance this ambiguity and uncertainty by deliberate deception. Second, political leaders are often under time pressure to make up their minds and given this time pressure, and the inherent ambiguity already referred to, ➤policy-makers may 'rush to judgement'. This can lead the policy-makers to foreclose prematurely on fresh information, particularly if it appears to be contradictory, and to make decisions without sufficient reference to it. A potentially unsatisfactory occurrence will then be made worse as psychological defence mechanisms come into play and fresh information is distorted to fit into the existing picture. If this becomes the 'official view' it may be hard for diplomats and advisers to break through an increasingly inappropriate ➤definition of the situation with dissonant arguments and ideas. A spiral of misperception is then built into the decision-making process. Sometimes it is only possible to break out of this situation by some traumatic event, such as change of ➤leadership. In retrospect it becomes clear that serious misperception has occurred and this becomes part of the 'why?' factor in subsequent explanations.

Misperception is also causally related to ➤images. Actors' images, both of themselves and of others, will enhance the chances of misperceptions affecting policy-making. In particular, images may encourage actors towards certain tendencies which produce misperceptions. Actors sometimes overestimate their own ability to influence outcomes and they wrongly attribute a change of policy by another actor to their own efforts. Actors sometimes show a tendency to see discrete happenings as an overall plan, to apply a crude 'conspiracy theory' where none may be justified. In strategic relations there is the tendency to assume another actor's intention upon the basis of his capabilities – known as ➤worst-case analysis.

Misperception, like perception, is affected by emotional factors as well as cognitive factors. Stress and strain may build up within a decision-making group, particularly in a ➤crisis situation, and this can increase the extent to which decisions are made in an atmosphere that is emotionally charged. In particular the tendency towards 'wishful thinking' has been noted by a number of psychologists as being positively related to an increase in affective as opposed to cognitive factors.

Recent research by historians and social scientists has sought to direct attention towards the relationship between misperception and the occurrence of ➤war. Taking the distinction between capability and intention as central to the analysis, researchers have examined how misperception of capabilities and/or misperception of intentions are causally related to the decision by actors to go to war. In many of these studies the issue of where misperception begins and perception ends is, unfortunately, not always clarified. This problem was identified at the outset of the discussion and it remains the case that such distinctions can often only be established *ex post*.

**Missile** A rocket or projectile with its own propulsion and guidance systems. Its payload would normally be a warhead but unarmed missiles could be used for reconnaissance purposes. Modern missile ➤technology was first developed during the Second World War when Germany produced the so-called V1 and V2 weapons. The V1, or 'flying bomb', was a small pilotless aircraft. It would now be called an 'air-breathing' system and was a precursor of the ➤cruise missile. The V2 was a ballistic missile with a range slightly in excess of 200 miles, which would make it a short-range system by contemporary standards.

Since 1945 advances in missiles have been made with regard to propulsion systems, guidance mechanisms and warheads. When combined with ➤atomic and ➤hydrogen bombs, the offensive missile is a potent system indeed. Defensive technologies have not, generally speaking, kept pace with offensive systems since 1945. Thus the advent of modern missiles has had the tendency to tip the balance in favour of the putative attacker.

**Missile Gap, The** The Missile Gap – written with capitals and the definite article – refers to a particular period in the ➤Cold War confrontation between the United States and the Soviet Union. The development by the latter of the ➤technology of long-range missiles evinced by their launching of an earth satellite – ➤Sputnik – in 1957 thoroughly alarmed the American political and military ➤leadership. Fanned by a good deal of ➤worst-case analysis and politicized by Democratic opponents of the Eisenhower Administration the 'missile gap' became an issue in the 1960 election. It was subsequently made clear to the incoming Kennedy Administration by the ➤intelligence community that the United States enjoyed a favourable gap rather than an adverse one. There can be little doubt that President Eisenhower had been provided with intelligence showing that the Soviet Union was not ahead during his tenure of the White House. The ➤capability of the United States to monitor Soviet missile sites from reconnaissance satellites which became available after August 1960 enhanced the view that no adverse 'gap' existed. At a press conference in November 1961 Kennedy gave perhaps the most objective analysis of the period from autumn 1957 to autumn 1961, tacitly conceding that the adverse version of the 'gap' was a myth.

This episode is typical of the kinds of alarmist thinking that was present during the Cold War era and that parties to ➤conflicts are often prone to. Like the testing of the Soviet ➤atomic bomb in 1949, the post-Sputnik speculation led to demands for a reaction which subsequent events showed to be too alarmist. Domestic interests in America fed off these ➤definitions of the situation during the Cold War to exacerbate these estimates.

**Mixed actor model** A term used by Oran Young (1972) in a seminal contribution to a book of essays appropriately dedicated to Harold and Margaret Sprout. Young's argument was that it was no longer possible or desirable to base the analysis of ➤macropolitics upon a single ➤actor model – such as the

➤state-centric idea of ➤international relations – and accordingly that hetero-geneity was the order of the day. In this way Young also challenged the idea that the concept of ➤hierarchy could usefully be applied to the field of macroanalysis. Again, no doubt in part under the influence of the Sprouts, Young suggested that questions of domination and submission should be settled on a policy-contingency, ➤issue-area basis rather than by deductively stipulating that certain actors were intrinsically dominant. Young's mixed actor perspective also enables a basic distinction to be made analytically between relations contain-ing actors of the same type and relations between different types of actors – for instance between states and intergovernmental organizations (➤IGOs) or between IGOs and ➤international non-governmental organizations (INGOs). However, unless these mixed relationships are demonstrably growing in impor-tance much of the force of Young's argument is weakened.

In some respects the mixed actor idea leaves something to be desired. In particular it leaves open the question of how a relative comparison is to be made of the different actors if an idea of their ranking or 'weighting' is to be achieved. What Young achieved was to point scholars towards an increasingly significant perspective – usually referred to as ➤pluralism – which appeared to influence macropolitical thinking in the 1970s.

**MNC** An abbreviation of Multinational Corporation. The term ➤Trans-national Corporation is sometimes used. Recently, Hirst and Thompson (1996) have suggested that the MNC has not reached sufficient ➤globalization of its functions and operations to be truly transnational. The abbreviation 'Multi-national' is sometimes used, in singular or plural forms. Finally the MNC sometimes appears as 'Multinational Enterprise'.

Although they are in one sense ➤international non-governmental organiza-tions (INGOs) MNCs are usually excluded from the category of INGOs because they are profit-making. Their growth and contemporary significance in world politics also merits special and separate treatment from the INGO. The ➤scope and ➤domain of their operations have led some commentators to welcome their activities, while others have warned against their self-regarding pursuit of corporate ➤influence. The UN and some of its ➤specialized agencies, the governments of ➤states, interest groups such as trade unions have all conducted analyses and investigations into MNCs in general or into specific cases. These inquiries are a measure of the seriousness with which informed opinion in world politics takes the Multinationals. An early collection of academic essays on them was subtitled 'the New Sovereigns' (Said and Simmons, 1975). Others have seen the MNC as one of the main corrosive agents attacking the ➤state-centred view of the system. The arrival of the MNC on the stage of world politics has clearly provoked much activity.

MNC may be defined as a profit-making organization which controls assets in at least two states. These may be identified as the home state (the state where the company is incorporated) and the host state (the state where the company has branches or affiliates). The activity of establishing or taking over branches/affiliates is referred to as a *direct foreign investment* (sometimes rendered as foreign direct investment) and is a further characteristic of the MNC. Direct foreign investment is now a crucial means of pump-priming the global economy and it has to some extent replaced the role of ➤trade in this regard. This investment is not distributed evenly throughout the economy, most goes between AICs with a smaller proportion going to NICs and BEMs.

Gilpin (1975), among ➤hegemonial stability theorists, has sought to establish a link between the hegemonial position of the United States after 1945 and the rapid growth of the MNC thereafter. In the decades immediately after 1945 the link between US domination of the system of political economy and the burgeoning of the MNCs was close. This domination has now declined, but MNCs are still predominantly incorporated in one of the states in the advanced industrial countries (AIC) region. This domination is now ➤trilateral, with the EU and Japan emerging as important home bases for their own respective MNCs. Indeed if the AICs can be regarded as an economic system, then a considerable amount of inward investment is evident within it. Paradoxically, at present the United States is almost as important as a host state for others' investment as it previously was a home state from which others could invest.

MNCs can be identified operating in primary, secondary and tertiary sectors of economic activity. The classic primary sector MNC is the ➤oil company. MNCs have also been important in extractive industries, notably in bauxite/aluminium production. Historically, the primary sector was the first to develop prominence, the impulse to develop on a transnational basis being largely dictated by geography, the natural location of the raw materials determining the move abroad. Extractive industries have often been seen by critics of the MNC as the most exploitative. Their impact upon the local economy of the host state may be minimal and their managerial structure may tend to be ➤ethnocentric. MNCs operating in primary sectors of economic activity tend to invest in ➤Third World hosts rather than AICs. The history of ➤OPEC shows that these host states need not be passive recipients of this kind of investment system. Provided that the market conditions are favourable, host states can do much to combat the worst excesses of the MNC by requiring more local participation in production, by acquiring a greater share in profits generated from local activity, by negotiating an agreed and guaranteed price for the products and even by nationalizing some or all of the locally based activities of the MNC. (Clearly they can do little about the MNC's activities outside their ➤frontiers.)

Manufacturing, or secondary economic activity, was traditionally the most important area of MNC activity. The growth of manufacturing has increased the relative importance of the AICs or the ➤North as recipients for corporate investment. In the Third World this kind of manufacturing investment is very selective indeed in its location, with the newly industrialized countries (NICs) predominating. In many areas of manufacturing investment ►technology transfer is a key subsidiary factor in the MNC's operations. The first ►Brandt Report highlighted the extent to which, via control of patents, the MNCs exercise control over technology.

The location of manufacturing activity is not controlled and constrained in the same way as extractive industries are by geography. In deciding where to locate a foreign subsidiary, an MNC can 'shop around' to some extent. Moreover, if there are strong vested interests in the putative host state that would welcome this investment, the MNC may be offered positive inducements by the national government to come into the state. This naturally increases the bargaining power of the MNC and may mean that 'side benefits' – such as a favourable arrangement with the labour unions – can be obtained as part of the final agreement. In general terms, manufacturing activity tends to be more integrated into the economic and social life of the host state. It should not be thought from the above discussion that the MNCs experience a complete free choice situation. In the case of an integrated market like the EU, for instance, MNCs from Japan and North America may be very anxious themselves to establish subsidiaries in such a buoyant ►region.

With regard to their activities in the Third World, concern has been expressed that the technology exported with manufacturing investment may not be the most suitable. Systems of production that encourage high productivity of labour may be less appropriate for an economic system where there is no shortage of labour and where wages rates are, comparatively, low in any case. The recent attempts by the UN and its agencies to establish a code of conduct for the MNCs have been particularly concerned with this 'appropriate technology' dimension.

MNCs are increasingly important in the tertiary or service industry sector, banking, insurance and other financial services being one growth point, leisure and tourism being another. Service industry expansion overseas tends to follow manufacturing as would be natural with a 'service' sector. Investment is concentrated in the AICs and selected Third World states. Service industry direct foreign investment is now the fastest growth sector of MNC activity.

The impact of the growth and development of the MNC upon world politics in the second half of the twentieth century has been considerable. This growth is likely to continue into the twenty-first if present trends obtain. Adherents to the view that globalization has fundamentally altered the relationship between the state and the MNC may have to wait a little longer to be confident about their predictions that the ►sovereign state is simply a local authority in the global economy increasingly dominated by these 'new sovereigns'.

**Mobility** A term used in military strategy. Mobile forces are regarded as important for both ►defence and offence. Defensively, mobility makes it harder for an adversary to seek out a defender's forces in order to destroy and defeat them. Ships at sea rather than in harbour, aircraft on patrol rather than on the ground, armies on the move rather than encamped are all more elusive. If an ►actor fears a surprise attack then mobility will reduce the damage that can be caused even if warning time is very short.

Distinction may be made between ►conventional force mobility and nuclear force mobility. In conventional modes, mobility is partly a function of the kinds of weapons possessed. This in turn depends upon procurement decisions taken years in advance of the actual contingency. Thus acquiring airlift mobility means, in the first instance, having sufficient transport aircraft and helicopters ready and available to lift men and materials into or away from a particular area. Even something as elementary as maintaining equipment at a high state of readiness can enhance mobility. In general terms a good defensive strategy should combine fixed and mobile ►capabilities. Mobile forces can plug gaps and breakdowns that can occur in fixed positions and prevent the total collapse of the defence that can happen if a fixed position is breached or circumvented. The experience of France and the ►Maginot Line in 1940 is surely instructive here. Nuclear mobility is inversely related to ►vulnerability. That is to say the more mobile the nuclear forces, the less vulnerable they are. The submarine-launched ballistic missile (SLBM) Polaris system was the first delivery system to be specifically recommended and required in order to enhance mobility.

Issues of mobility play an entirely different role in ►guerrilla warfare. One of the defining characteristics of this type of combat is the need for the guerrilla forces to practise mobility in order to trade space for time. Guerrilla war, at least in its more prevalent 'countryside' version, seeks by employing a strategy of ►protracted war to harass and wear down the adversary. Once guerrilla war ceases to employ mobility it ceases to be guerrilla war and moves instead into the more conventional idiom already discussed. Classical guerrilla war literature accepted that, if the method was to be used to achieve political change, then such a transition to the conventional mode was inevitable. ►►Rapid reaction force(s)

**Modernization** The term modernization is used to identify certain processes of social change that historically first occurred in Western Europe and which have subsequently become ►global. Modernization as a type of social change is not specifically political in its character. Rather the argument is that as societies become more modern these antecedent conditions will produce changes in the structure and function of their polities. In particular modernization will produce demands for increases in political participation which will be met by changes in the character and availability of political institutions. Modernization is indeed a multi-faceted process involving, in addition to politics, changes in economic, cultural, technical, psychological and intellectual aspects of human relations.

Examples of such changes often cited include: the weakening of the extended family in favour of the nuclear, increased importance of money as a means of making payments and settling debts (as opposed to payments in kind) an increase in secular as opposed to sacred values, the replacement of cottage industries with large-scale mass production, the spread of literacy and the growth of urbanization.

These changes are certainly not uniform, nor are they inevitable. Moreover, the somewhat simplistic view that they represent 'progress' has certainly been rejected by most discerning observers. What does, however, seem to be the case is that, as trends over the last two centuries indicate, these modernizing characteristics appear to be highly significant and near universal.

Since modernization is a global process which all social systems experience to some extent it has tended to increase levels of ➤interdependence and even ➤integration across ➤state ➤frontiers and between different peoples. Among individuals and groups these changes appear to have the most impact upon ➤elites and ➤leadership groups. These sections of society seem to embrace a more cosmopolitan attitude towards modernization tendencies and, as a result, their ➤power and status is often enhanced because they seem to be in the vanguard of these changes. The more far-sighted of these modernizing elites see modernization as supplementing rather than supplanting traditional society and there is considerable evidence, particularly from the ➤Third World, of modernity and tradition coexisting in the same social system. The growth of ➤Green Movements in some of the advanced industrial countries (AICs) of late shows that modernization is not perceived by all as an irreversible process.

During the ➤Cold War era in world politics modernization processes became politicized into ideas about 'development' and '➤nation-building'. The competing blocs saw the Third World as in some senses a testing ground for competing models. The results were mixed. In some states and ➤regions modernizing elites have been in the vanguard of the kinds of changes discussed above. Indeed the most successful instances have combined modernization with ➤globalization to integrate economies into the global market economy. Elsewhere modernization has failed to encourage change and states and regions have regressed into a cul-de-sac of traditionalism.

**Monroe Doctrine**  Originally intended as a warning to European ➤states not to intervene in the New World, it has become the conceptual basis of US policy in Central and Latin America. In 1823 and for a considerable period afterwards it was little more than wishful thinking, as the United States did not possess either the naval ➤power or the diplomatic status to enforce what Bismarck came to call 'this extraordinary piece of insolence'.

Throughout the nineteenth century it was the convergence of US and UK interests in the region and, in particular, UK sea power in the Atlantic and Caribbean that permitted a 'free' Latin America and prevented a resurgence of political and military ➤intervention from the European imperial powers. In fact the early violations of this ➤non-intervention doctrine were by the United Kingdom, as when UK troops occupied the ➤Falkland/Malvinas Islands in 1833, despite protests from the Rio de la Plata (Argentina). It was not until the end of the century that the United States acquired the military, diplomatic and economic power to act as the self-appointed guardian of the southern half of its hemisphere. In 1904 the Roosevelt corollary took the doctrine an imperial step further and declared that misgovernment (or 'chronic wrongdoing') within the Latin American republics themselves would invite active armed US intervention. Henceforth, the United States took upon itself the roles of both moral tutor and policeman in the area south of the Rio Grande (➤➤Wilson Doctrine).

Outside the United States, the doctrine has not been a popular one and they have been anxious to disguise its rather obvious hegemonic character (➤➤dollar diplomacy, ➤good neighbor). However, within the United States the Monroe doctrine has been revered as an article of faith akin to the notion of 'manifest destiny'. In fact, the two beliefs are coupled in the national psychology; just as the United States was destined for continental westward expansion, so too did it seem predestined to dominate the entire hemisphere. The ➤unilateral projection of US power into Latin America has legal as well as moral overtones. For example, it was used to justify the ➤blockade of Cuba in 1962 to force the withdrawal of Soviet missiles and although Khrushchev dismissed its validity most Americans continue to believe that it is now part of the general corpus of ➤international law relating to the region. After the Second World War it became ➤multilateral in character with the formation of the Organization of American States (OAS) and the Rio Treaty. The reference in the UN Charter to 'regional arrangements' being kept apart from UN jurisdiction appears to reinforce the idea that outside intervention in hemispheric matters is not permissible.

When President Monroe first proclaimed it, the doctrine was ➤isolationist in character and appeared to offer a *quid pro quo*; that the Europeans keep out of Latin America and the United States for their part would not interfere in Europe. Since the formation of NATO the United States have been actively involved in Europe, therefore many believe that, apart from US power, there is no legal or moral justification for continued outside exclusion. Because of these changes Dexter Perkins (1955), echoing Bismark, urged that the doctrine should be discarded as its words 'convey a definite impression of hegemony, of supercilious arrogance, of interference'. It is extremely unlikely that this will happen as the United States continues to demonstrate that the Western Hemisphere is firmly within its own ➤sphere of influence. Whether Latin Americans themselves will continue to accept the strictures of the 'Colossus of the North' is another matter and it may well be that in the long term the Monroe doctrine becomes the United States' Achilles heel.

**Mood theory** A term used in ➤public opinion analysis. It refers to what has been called 'the mass public' and seeks to establish links between attitudes and inclinations among this group and the ➤decision-makers. The term was originally discussed in Almond's (1966) standard work on the subject. The word 'mood' clearly implies a generalized and somewhat imprecise set of predispositions. Clarification is possible through such techniques as opinion polling, of course. Care must be taken not to build too many hopes upon public opinion polling. It might tell us what the prevailing mood is on a particular issue. It cannot explain how those opinions came to be held, nor can it describe what relationship there might be, if any at all, between opinion and policy.

Writers on the subject of public opinion, particularly within the ➤social scientific approach, have been considerably exercised by the fact that the majority of the adult population, even in democratic systems, do not appear to hold consistent, coherent or informed opinions about ➤foreign policy, ➤international or ➤world politics. On particular issues the precise percentage will clearly vary, but Holsti (1983) talks of '70 per cent or more'. Rosenau (1961a) speaks of estimates varying from 75 to 90 per cent. In purely quantitative terms, then, it seems that the mood theory applies to a very sizeable majority of the population.

Examples of public 'moods' on issue areas most often cited include: the apparent '➤war weariness' of many people in the United Kingdom after the First World War, the so-called '➤Maginot mentality' in France during the inter-war period, the '➤isolationist impulse' in the United States after Woodrow Wilson, the alleged 'Kith and Kin' sympathies with Rhodesian Whites after the Unilateral Declaration of Independence (UDI) in 1965 shown by UK citizens, the '➤Falklands Factor' in 1982, the '➤Vietnam Syndrome' in the USA, and so on. In these examples public mood seems to be a distillation of recent historical experiences, particularly those of perceived national triumph or tragedy, plus a somewhat impressionistic concept of the fundamental ➤orientations and long-range goals of the ➤state. The mood sets permissive limits beyond which decision-makers may be reluctant to go, at least in the short term.

Mood theory clearly implies that membership of the mass public does not mean that people are totally passive *vis-à-vis* ➤policy-making processes. Mood theory also leads to the tentative rejection of the view, favoured by many ➤idealists, that mass public opinion on these issues is inherently pacific. Although most of the examples quoted above might seem to suggest a non-belligerent mass public – apart from the Falklands case – this conclusion should not be drawn. Mood theory implies that innovative thinking about foreign policy and the external environment will not come from the mass public. In a sense this is tautological because it is built into the idea of the 'mass' as opposed to the ➤attentive publics. Nonetheless, it is worth reiterating that mood theory is reactive rather than innovative. It seems valid to conclude that the mass public will tend to favour the ►status quo and, in consequence, be one step behind the policy-makers when it comes to agreeing changes in a state's policy ►goals and orientations.

**Moratorium** A temporary suspension of relationships or activities by ►actors in order to give one or more parties a respite or 'grace period' in which to effect changes. The moratorium may be legally binding or *ad hoc* and persuasive. The device is particularly used in political economy where creditors give debtors more time to repay debts by declaring a moratorium. It is hoped thereby that during the moratorium measures will be taken to reschedule the payments or take other steps to alleviate the debtor's circumstances.

Moratoria may, in principle, be declared in any relationship. Thus ►states ►negotiating ►arms control agreements may stipulate a moratorium on some activity which they consequently hope to include in a more permanent agreement. The ►Partial Test Ban Treaty was preceded by a moratorium on testing in 1958. Although the moratorium was subsequently broken, it did demonstrate that the three states concerned – the United States, the Soviet Union and the United Kingdom – were potentially amenable to such an agreement. After a further round of testing, the treaty was eventually signed.

**Most favoured nation (MFN)** This fundamental principle of international trade seeks to establish and advance the principle of ►equality of treatment and non-discrimination among trading ►states. The principle may be illustrated by taking a ►bilateral situation thus: under mfn principles the parties will extend to each other the same advantages that they have extended to other third parties in the past, or are extending to others concurrently, or intend to extend in the future. Most favoured nation principles are typically applied to ►tariffs and if these principles are applied consistently, they should lead to mutual and balanced tariff reductions.

It is generally agreed that the mfn principle began to be applied to international trade in the eighteenth century, reaching its peak in the last decades of the nineteenth. The First World War and the events thereafter led to the weakening of its application but with the formation of the General Agreement on Tariffs and Trade (GATT) in 1947 a concerted attempt was made to resuscitate these ideas by writing them into the first article of GATT. At the same time GATT allows important exceptions to the mfn principle. Crucially ►trade blocs, ►free trade areas and ►common markets are all exempt. The emergence of the United Nations Conference on Trade and Development (UNCTAD) in the 1960s further weakened the mfn principle because the ►Third World called for a system of positive discrimination in their favour to replace it. This call has been recognized system of preferences between advanced industrial countries (AICS) and the Third World.

The mfn principle remains a testament to those who believed in a liberal, equal, non-discriminatory international trading system. ➤➤Multilateralism; reciprocity

**Multilateralism** Multilateralism refers to a system of coordinating relations between three or more ➤states in accordance with certain principles of conduct. As a policy, multilateralism is deliberate action by a state, in concert with others, to realize objectives in particular ➤issue areas. Because generalized principles or codes of conduct are a defining characteristic of multilateralism, it is often assumed that multilateralism equals institutionalism. Although this has certainly been a familiar correlation in the twentieth century, in the nineteenth examples like the ➤Concert system, the ➤gold standard and ➤free trade were not formalized into ➤international organizations but they were examples of multilateralism within the definitional terms above. States participating in any one, two or all three accepted the rules of the game as far as they were concerned. In this sense multilateralism requires its adherents to seek diffuse rather than specific ➤reciprocity and to regard the outcomes from their collaboration as being indivisible as between them (although arguments about an '➤imperialism of free trade' might seem to reject this). As noted earlier twentieth-century multilateralism has been akin to institution-building. The increased ➤interdependence of states in economic, political and military matters coupled with rapid industrial, scientific and technological developments led directly to the growth of multi-purpose, universal organizations like the ➤League of Nations and the ➤United Nations. In the area of military-➤security, the concept of ➤collective security in its various guises has called into question the ➤bilateral notion of ➤alliances. In the collective security system – at least as understood by purists – ➤peace is most definitely indivisible. With regard to ➤disarmament, multilateralism argues that progress towards the ➤goal is most likely if arms reduction is undertaken by all states simultaneously and in concert – again the idea of indivisibility.

As a policy multilateralism is often associated with ideas about ➤hegemony and ➤leadership. The United States of America has been particularly thought of in these terms in its twentieth-century ➤diplomacy. In this case multilateralism is strengthened by American ➤perceptions of its own exceptionalist nature. American leaders have been predisposed to issue clarion calls for new world orders – often at the conclusion of a ➤war in which America has emerged victorious. Certainly the most successful instance of American multilateralism in the twentieth century emerged after 1945 when the ➤Bretton Woods and the ➤Dumbarton Oaks conferences produced systems of highly coordinated relations in the post-war world. President Bush's calls for his version of a new world order are from the same multilateralist stable. Some see American policy after the ➤Cold War as 'pick-and-mix' multilateralism.

**Multipolarity** A type of system structure with at least three 'poles' or ➤actors being identified as predominant. This domination is dependent upon the idea of ►capability or ►power potential as the essential defining possession of the 'poles'. The actors that dominate a multipolar system need not be ►states; ►blocs or coalitions may qualify. Historically, the classic example of a multipolar system was the ►balance of power. As Walt (1987) has shown the act of balancing against a perceived threat in this type of system leads to the formation of ►alliances. Conversely if states do not balance against a threat, then they may bandwagon behind it. Waltz (1979) has argued that multipolarity increases uncertainties between the polar actors and therefore enhances instability. Polar actors may resolve this uncertainty by committing themselves to another party come what may – as Germany did to Austria–Hungary before 1914. Alternatively they may 'pass the buck' onto another party – as Britain and France attempted to embroil the Soviet Union against Germany before 1939. Since both these multipolar systems collapsed into systemic ►war, the empirical implication is clear–multipolarity is less stable.

The end of the ►Cold War era has provoked some analysts to dust off the multipolar model of ►international relations. Certainly in the sub-field of ►international political economy (IPE) multipolarity with admittedly a ►tripolar hue looks very plausible. The United States, Japan and the ►European Union being generally seen as the 'poles'. In military-►security contexts the United States looks more dominant but seemingly lacks the will to prevail, preferring instead ►multilateralism which allows for 'permissive enforcement' on occasions such as the ►Persian Gulf War. The attitude of states that are 'near-poles' can be crucial. India's position as a 'near-polar' actor in the Asia-►Pacific region seems to have influenced its recent ►nuclear weapons assertiveness. The removal of the Soviet Union from the regional front rank has left India bereft to face a Sino–Pakistan special relationship that is perceived as threatening within the regional system. Mearsheimer (1990) famously speculated about a similar multipolar system emerging in Europe following the end of the Cold War era.

Multipolarity is sometimes loosely used to characterize any system which is diffused and discontinuous. Whilst not exactly a debasement it certainly weakens the ties that bind this structural term to the idea of 'poles' that can be stipulated as the actors that give the system its character.

# N

**NAFTA** The North American Free Trade Agreement was negotiated between the United States, Mexico and Canada between 1991 and 1993. It supplements the earlier US-Canada accord which had been in operation since 1 January 1989 and extends the principle of the free movement of ➤trade and financial services to Mexico as well. In a sense the agreement simply formalizes the extensive economic ties that Mexico and Canada have with the United States. Over 80 per cent of Mexican manufacturing ➤exports go to the American market and any resurgence of American ➤protectionism would be profoundly damaging. For the Mexican political ➤leadership NAFTA means that the United States now has an overt ➤national interest in Mexican stability and economic development. At the same time it lays to rest Mexican paranoia about American ➤interventionism which has been evident since the 1840s.

Canada, which had already been operating the Canada–US Free Trade Agreement (CAFTA) since 1989, responded to the Mexican/US initiative of June 1990 by opening up the negotiations for a ➤tripolar solution. Like Mexico, Canada is crucially dependent upon the American market and again like the Mexicans, Canadians have had to overcome traditional ambivalence about their powerful neighbour. Moreover the benefits of expanding free trade area status to Mexico were less apparent for Canada. Rather like the United Kingdom with the ➤European Union (EU) Canada has perforce participated in NAFTA because of an absence of attractive alternatives. The danger of course was that NAFTA would diversify trade away from Canada rather than create trade anew. Within the United States, opposition to NAFTA came from the unions (seeing American jobs being exported to Mexico) and from the environmental lobby (which feared that Mexican ➤pollution standards might be lower than those operating in the United States). The eventual outline agreement was piloted through the US Congress with the assistance of ➤bipartisan support because the Democratic party was deeply divided for and against the Agreement.

The reaction of other Latin American ➤states to NAFTA may be crucial for the future. Already Chile is being spoken of as a putative member. Alternatively a more confrontational response might be seen in the ➤Mercosur grouping. Whether such trade regionalism is to be preferred to a more ➤multilateral approach remains to be seen. The difficulty with trade regionalism – at least from the perspective of ➤economic liberalism – is that it produces cooperation at one level but inhibits it at another.

**Nagasaki** Three days after ➤Hiroshima, a second atomic weapon was used against the Japanese industrial city of Nagasaki. Unlike the first device, the fissile material in the Nagasaki bomb was ➤plutonium. A similar device had already been tested at Alamogordo, New Mexico in July 1945. The Nagasaki bomb could not be justified on 'testing' grounds in quite the same way as Hiroshima, therefore. Like the first weapon, the Nagasaki bomb was in the ➤kiloton range and was air-burst over the target. The United States had originally intended to use the second bomb on Kokura but poor visibility over the area caused them to bomb Nagasaki instead.

The decision to use the second bomb on Japan so soon after the first indicates that having made the decision in principle to begin atomic bombardment of Japan, the United States intended to continue with that policy as long as bombs were available and until Japan surrendered. How far the use of the ➤atom bomb against Japan actually caused its surrender remains to be debated. Controversy has continued ever since over these two incidents and their implications.

**Nation** Although probably the most pervasive concept of the contemporary world, this is a vague notion which refers to a social collectivity, the members of which share some or all of the following: a sense of common identity, a history, a language, ethnic or racial origins, religion, a common economic life, a geographical location and a political base. However, these criteria and characteristics are often present in different degrees and combinations. None is either necessary or sufficient for definition. Nations can exist without a distinct political identity (eg the Jewish nation during the Diaspora) and they can exist without common linguistic, cultural, religious or ethnic components (eg the Indian nation). Usually, though, there is a strong sense of common identity and unity. Yet even this apparently most basic requirement may be lacking (hence the emphasis on 'nation-building' which is widely regarded as a vital ingredient in the ➤modernization process and developmental politics relating, in particular, to post-➤colonial Africa). The difficulty of definition is compounded by common political usage which tends to blur the distinction between the social and legal aspects of the term. Thus, membership of the ➤United Nations refers specifically to political entities defined by spatial terri-torial ➤boundaries. Those peoples or groupings who fall outside this rubric (eg the Kurds) appear therefore not to possess the relevant criteria. In this connection the term ➤nation-state may be more precise though even here some states (eg the United Kingdom) may comprise several nations. In the modern world everyone 'belongs' to a particular nation (the word itself derives from the Latin verb *nasci* – to be born) and so ubiquitous is the concept that it is even employed to convey ideas which to some extent run counter to its general meaning (eg ➤international, supranational).

**Nation-state** The nation-state is the dominant political entity of the modern world and as such can be considered to be the primary unit of ➤international relations. However, it is a comparatively recent phenomenon. It developed in Europe between the sixteenth and nineteenth centuries after the collapse of the Holy Roman Empire and the emergence of the centralized ➤state claiming exclusive and monopolistic ➤authority within a defined territorial area. Absolute political power within the community and ➤independence outside it are characteristic features. With the emergence of a number of such political formations the modern framework of international relations began to take shape, that is, separate political units interacting within a context where no final arbiter or authority is recognized or indeed present. Historically, the fusion of 'nation' and 'state' post-dated the process of political centralization and it was the nineteenth century that witnessed the dovetailing of political organizations with a political social grouping which constituted the 'nation'. The people comprising the nation became the ultimate source of the state's ➤legitimacy and the national idea itself became the natural repository of, and focus for, political loyalty. Thus, it was during this period that the coincidence of the ➤boundaries of state ➤jurisdiction and the characteristic elements that made up 'nationhood' took place. In the twentieth century this process became a universal one, though it should be noted that nations can exist without states and that states are not always composed of ethnically homogeneous social, cultural or linguistic groups. The nation-state, which is commonly regarded as the 'ideal' or 'normal' political unit, is in fact a particular form of territorial state – others are ➤city-states and empires – and many commentators regard it as a disruptive force in the modern world. In particular, its obsessive emphasis on ➤nationalism, on ➤sovereignty and on ➤*raison d'état* has tended to mitigate against the development of a cohesive and pacific international community. The twentieth century has witnessed what appears to be a growing trend towards ➤supranational forms of political organization, especially on a ➤regional basis, yet the nation-state is still a potent force in international relations. However, its detractors have argued that although it may have been the most effective political formation in terms of providing economic well being, physical security and national identity, there is no guarantee that this will continue. After all, the nation-state is an artificial, not a natural, construct and it may well be that despite its near-universality, it may already be something of an anachronism. However, some post-Cold War developments, especially secessionism and ethnic cleansing, may indicate a resurgence and malign refinement of the idea, as events in Somalia, Rwanda and Bosnia indicate. ➤➤Nation; ethno-nationalism

**National interest** Used generally in two senses in IR: as an analytical tool identifying the goals or objectives of ➤foreign policy and as an all-embracing concept of political discourse used specifically to justify particular policy preferences. In both senses it refers to the basic determinants that guide ➤state policy in relation to the external environment. It applies only to sovereign states and relates specifically to foreign policy: the internal variety usually being characterized as 'the public interest'. According to Charles Beard (1934), the first scholar to produce a sustained analysis, the term entered the political lexicon in sixteenth century Europe and began to replace the older notion of ➤*raison d'état* in harness with the development of the ➤nation-state and ➤nationalism. It expressed no particular dynastic or state-familial interests but the interests of the society as a whole and as such was linked with the idea of popular ➤sovereignty and the ➤legitimacy of the state. Thereafter it came to represent the entire rationale for the exercise of state ➤power in ➤international relations.

As an instrument of political analysis it is particularly associated with the school of political ➤realism and its most influential advocate was Hans Morgenthau (1951), for whom the concept was of central importance in understanding the process of international politics. Morgenthau's thesis that the acquisition and use of power is the primary national interest of a state had a profound effect on a generation of scholars in the 1950s and 1960s and consequently on the development of the discipline as a whole. For Morgenthau, the idea of national interest defined in terms of power as the central motif of state behaviour had an objective and therefore discoverable reality. However, his emphasis on military and economic dimensions to the virtual exclusion of other factors (especially the notion that principles or moral values could play a dominant part in formulating policy) led to a reappraisal of the concept and a rejection of the presumption that it was synonymous with the pursuit of power. Since then the idea of the national interest as the key to foreign policy analysis has largely been superseded; ➤decision-making theorists in particular argued that far from having objective reality the interests that guide foreign policy are more likely to be a diverse, ➤pluralistic set of subjective preferences that change periodically both in response to the domestic political process itself and in response to shifts in the international environment. The national interest therefore is more likely to be what the policy-makers say it is at any particular time. Its value in ➤analysis has been further eroded by the move away from ➤state-centrism and the strategic-diplomatic milieu and the emergence of models of ➤complex interdependence and ➤world society. The term has consequently been largely ignored in recent literature on ➤international relations. Indeed, in much contemporary theory it is the 'sin that dare not speak its name' because of its symbiotic relationship with ➤realpolitik and political realism.

In essence, at the root of the idea of the national interest is the principle of national security and survival. The defence of the homeland and the preservation of territorial integrity is basic to it. It is presumed that all other policy preferences are subordinate to this one. The term 'vital interest' is often used in this connection, the implication being that the issue at stake is so fundamental to the well being of the state that it cannot be compromised and so may result in the use of military force to sustain it. However, vital interests may not relate solely to questions of national survival. The ➤Vietnam War, for example, was

345

regarded, at least by some administrations, as involving a vital interest of the United States yet at no time was the territorial homeland threatened. Other considerations involved in the concept which are equally if not more value-laden are the ideas associated with economic well-being, the promotion of ideological principles and the establishment of a favourable ➤world order or ➤balance. All these, either singly or in combination, could be regarded as vital depending (among other things) on the dominant perceptions of the decision-makers at the time. Attempts have been made to develop models or matrices of the varying levels of intensity an interest may be expected to generate (eg is it a 'survival' issue, a 'vital' issue, a 'major' issue or a 'peripheral' issue?) but these have floundered on the bedrock of subjectivism. One ➤actor's peripheral interest may well be a matter of survival to another. In sum, the concept does highlight important factors in foreign policy analysis and continues to be used in political discourse, but its value as a research tool is extremely limited. ➤Goal

**Nationalism** This term is used in two related senses, first, to identify an ➤ideology and secondly, to describe a sentiment. In the first usage, nationalism seeks to identify a behavioural entity – the '➤nation' – and thereafter to pursue certain political and cultural ➤goals on behalf of it. Pre-eminent among these will be national ➤self-determination. This may be empirically defined in a number of ways, ➤irredentism, ➤independence, ➤secession are all goals that may be sought under its rubric. In its second usage, nationalism is a sentiment of loyalty towards the nation which is shared by people. Elements of cohesion are provided by such factors as language, ➤religion, shared historical experience, physical contiguity and so on. In the last resort such bonds must be integrated into a perceptual framework which subjectively defines a group of people as different from their neighbours and similar to each other. Empirical instances continually show that it is perfectly possible to create such a sense of national identity in the absence of some of the above factors. In short, it is difficult to stipulate convincingly that there is any cohesive factor that is necessary or sufficient for the creation of such sentiments.

The ideological origins of nationalism are to be found in the political history of Western Europe after the collapse of feudalism. It first became manifest during the French ➤Revolution and thereafter the nineteenth century saw it reach its zenith in Europe. The Italian Risorgimento was perhaps the precursor of the twentieth century phenomenon of nationalism as a resistance movement against foreign domination. In general, intellectual opinion in the nineteenth century was inclined towards the view that the nation represented a 'natural' bond amongst humans and that, accordingly, nations should form the basis for ➤states. This fusion of the nation and the state into the ➤nation-state idea became such an influential factor that it gave rise to a whole category of relations – ➤international relations – and a complete perspective on activities – that of ➤state-centrism.

Nationalism as an ideology was exported during the nineteenth and twentieth centuries from Europe to the rest of the world. The fact that European ➤imperialism hypocritically failed to extend to others what it was willing to claim for itself – the right of national self-determination – meant that the nationalist ideology was turned against European control and used as a weapon of national liberation. In addition to turning against the foreigner, nationalists turned against their own parents and made the issue one between generations as well as between rulers and ruled. This sense of grievance created by Europeans among their subject peoples and the discrepancy between theory and practice produced what historically came to be called the nationalist movement. As a form of protest anti-➤colonial nationalism began as an ➤elite expression of dissatisfaction and spread downwards thereafter to the masses. The immediate demand in all instances was for independence and the turning over of control of the territory to the indigenous elite. In the process of using nationalism to wrest authority away from external control a subtle change in the relationship between the idea of 'nation' and the idea of 'state' occurred. The ➤Third World states that were turned over to their own fates with the ending of formal colonial control were not homogenous nations at all. Most contained at least two ethnic groups – for example the tribal system in Africa – and many contained three or more. As a result the fusion of the nation with the state was not carried over into the non-European context. So prevalent is this characteristic in Third World nationalism that most writers on the subject make a clear distinction between state nationalism and ➤ethnic nationalism. The classic European assumption that nations must have states and that, if possible, states must have one homogenous nation, has been completely abandoned in the process of diffusing the nationalist ideology from Europe to the rest of the world. This distinction is often referred to in the literature as the difference between nation-states and state-nations. (➤➤Quasi-states)

Nationalism in the second sense – as an attitude or sentiment – varies between individuals and groups within the extant or putative nation. Elites – intellectuals, political leaders and the military especially – are likely to show clear evidence of nationalist attitudes. Among the rest of the population nationalism will vary along a number of dimensions. Recent research by ➤social scientists into extreme forms of nationalism such as ➤fascism seems to show that there is often a positive correlation between certain personality types and extreme nationalist sentiments. Nationalism, like other political ideas, is diffused and spread among a population via the mechanism of socialization. The growth of mass education and the mass media in the twentieth century has created important transmission belts for this process but socialization processes start in the family and it is reasonable to assume that in many instances nationalistic attitudes are transmitted in this primary group setting.

Nationalism is often encouraged and enhanced by contact with foreigners. This contact may take place at the personal level or it may be mediated via the media and other channels. It is clearly possible to manipulate these sentiments to create a climate of ➤public opinion favourable to a political ➤leadership, faction or party. Once mobilized these attitudes are often difficult to control and a particular leader or leadership may become permanently invested with a kind of aura as a result. The term 'charismatic' is often used to identify this fusion of a people's aspirations in one individual. Although over-used it can be applied to a number of twentieth-century figures.

Many political analysts see nationalism as a divisive force in IR. Indeed, ➤idealists of many sorts have argued that nationalism was a temporary phenomenon and with the imperative of economic ➤interdependence would be replaced by ➤internationalism and cosmopolitanism. In particular, the Marxists argued that nationalism was primarily a bourgeois ➤ideology and that the rise of the nation-state was inseparable from the requirements of early capitalism. As capitalism developed and became more international, nationalism would be replaced by the 'class struggle' which would in turn break down national boundaries. These assumptions were not borne out by political developments and the First World War, in particular, destroyed the idea of class solidarity against the nationalist principle. Thereafter, Marxian analysis of nationalism has associated it with anti-colonialism and the struggle against imperial or foreign domination and exploitation. As such the first major revolution that combined nationalism with revolutionary socialism was the Mexican revolution (1910–17) which subsequently was regarded as the model for the anti-colonial movement.

Liberal analysts have warned of the inherent dangers of unrestrained nationalism. Whereas in the first half of the nineteenth century it was associated with democracy and ➤liberalism it later took on an aggressive, militaristic form and came to be identified with imperialism, fascism and totalitarianism. This form of 'integrative nationalism' according to liberal thought, is a distortion. There is no necessary connection between nationalism, ➤conflict and ➤war. In fact nationalism, properly understood and fostered, is a positive development in world politics leading to the liberation of colonial peoples and subject national minorities.

Although there is no general theory, there is a broad consensus that nationalism both as a form of consciousness and as a political ideology has been the single most important factor shaping the structure and the process of the modern world. The ideas of the nation-state and self-determination, from which it is inseparable, have formed the recognized foundation for the practice of international relations and although there are movements towards supranational forms of cooperation and political organization, few doubt that its effects have yet to be fully worked out. Indeed, the end of the ➤Cold War witnessed a revival of nationalism, albeit of a particularly aggressive kind (eg ➤Yugoslavian).

The process of nation-building and emancipation from the old dynastic, multinational and imperial states has redrawn the world political map, first in Europe and the Americas between 1815 and 1920 and then in Asia and Africa after the Second World War, so that now, with the exception of Antartica, all the earth's land surface is divided into nation states. Up to 1914 the international system consisted of about fifty sovereign states in all. By the end of the war ten new states emerged. When it was founded in 1920 the ➤League of Nations had forty-two members. The ➤United Nations in 1945 had fifty-one but membership rose to 135 in 1973 and to 159 in 1988, and 185 in 1997. Estimates vary, but such is the continued force of the ideas of nationalism and national self-determination that by the end of this century it is likely that the international system will comprise some 200 sovereign states. Since there are no optimum requirements concerning size or population (most of the new states will in fact be ➤'micro-states') it is impossible to assess what the ultimate number of independent political units will be. Clearly, nationalism is not only the most potent force in world politics, it is also, judging by mere numbers, the most successful.

**Nationality** Often described as the connecting link between the individual and ➤international law, nationality indicates the status of belonging to a particular ➤state. By virtue of this, an individual may be entitled to certain benefits and obligations under municipal and international law. There is no universally accepted definition of nationality, and as a general rule each state is free to define who its nationals are though this discretion can be circumscribed by specific ➤treaties (eg treaties concerning the elimination of ➤statelessness). Thus, Article 1 of the 1930 Hague Convention on the Conflict of Nationality Laws stated that:

. . . it is for each state to determine under its own law who are its nationals. This law shall be recognized by other states in so far as it is consistent with international conventions, international custom and the principles of law generally recognized with regard to nationality.

The most important of these principles concerning the acquisition of nationality are first, descent from parents who are nationals (*jus sanguinis*) and secondly, the territorial location of birth (*jus soli*). Nationality may also be acquired by marriage, adoption, legalization, naturalization or as a result of transfer of territory from one state to another. It should be noted that since international law recognizes the primacy of the state in this regard, the practice of acquiring nationality varies considerably. As well as being acquired, nationality can also be lost or denied. Thus denial of nationality to blacks in South Africa prior to 1994 can be seen either as deprivation on racial grounds by Pretoria or as the result of the transfer of territory (ie as a consequence of the creation of the 'homelands'). As with most concepts in international law, the political element is the dominant one, and the condition of statelessness is not uncommon. Conversely, and by the same token, ➤dual or multiple nationality, usually arising from overlapping applications of the *jus sanguinis* and *jus soli* rules, has long been accepted practice. In addition to individuals, companies, ships and aircraft are regarded as having nationality, usually relating to the state in which they are registered. The practice of ➤flags of convenience has grown to exploit the lack of uniformity in this regard.

**Nationalization** An act of economic policy by a ➤state ➤actor whereby foreign owned economic assets are expropriated by the authorities of the state concerned. Nationalization has always been recognized under ➤international law as an appropriate and proper exercise of ➤sovereignty provided always that fair and prompt compensation is offered. Failure to make such restitution makes the act of nationalization tantamount to confiscation.

It should not be thought that governments necessarily resort to nationalization as a result of any commitment to collectivism or socialism. Although this may on occasions be a factor in such policies, it is more often the case that such measures are an expression of ➤nationalism and spring from a desire to curb and control the activities of foreign interest and to seek preferment for one's own nationals. Expropriation, or at least the threat of it, is seen as an effective way of controlling the activities of multi-national companies (MNCs). ➤➤Oil companies.

**NATO** An acronym for the North Atlantic Treaty Organization. The North Atlantic Treaty was signed in Washington DC in April 1949. The original parties were: Belgium, Canada, Denmark, France, Iceland, Italy, Luxembourg, Netherlands, Norway, Portugal, the United Kingdom, and the United States. Greece and Turkey joined in 1952, the Federal Republic of Germany in 1955 and Spain in 1982. In 1966 the French Government informed the Organization that it was withdrawing its forces from assignment to the Organization and as a corollary requested that all units, ➤bases and headquarters not controlled by the French be removed from its territory. France did not, of course, repudiate the ➤treaty.

NATO is sometimes identified as a ➤collective security organization, although this is a misuse of the original idea behind the concept. It is more accurate to regard NATO as a military ➤alliance and as such it is typical of an important class of ➤international organizations that have been a characteristic of the ➤state-system. In keeping with the stipulations of the UN Charter, NATO is a defensive arrangement and, like the ➤Warsaw Pact of 1955, it is an ideological alliance. That is to say it represents a grouping of like-minded states with similar political and economic systems. Given this ideological connotation, it can be seen that the ➤Cold War and the policy of ➤containment of Soviet ➤power and ➤influence in Europe was the essential rationale for the formation of NATO. The proximate cause for NATO was the ➤Berlin Crisis of 1948–9 and the ➤perception among UK and French leaders in particular that some antidote to the conventional military capability of the Soviet Union was needed if Western Europe was to avoid Soviet coercion or worse in the deteriorating relations after 1945.

Like most alliances, NATO is based upon the idea of ➤deterrence. Article Five of the North Atlantic Treaty states that: 'The parties agree that an armed attack against one or more of them in Europe or North America shall be considered an attack against them all'.

Since an attack upon North America was not considered a significant possibility in 1949, it is clear that the framers of the Treaty intended that the main deterrent effect of their convention would be a US pledge to defend rather than liberate Western Europe in the event of war. The United States assumed that Europeans would be willing to engage in a good deal of ➤self-help as well but the onus to provide the deterrent ➤capability lay across the Atlantic in 1949.

As a result of this arrangement NATO took on two characteristics which have remained permanent features: first, the most powerful and influential member of the Alliance is not a European state and second, that the Alliance would be strong in those military capabilities in which the United States was strong: ➤air power and ➤nuclear weapons. This left NATO with a strategy which was based upon nuclear deterrence of conventional attack from the outset. The lack of symmetry was recognized very early in the Alliance's history and strenuous efforts were made, notably by setting ➤conventional force levels at Lisbon in 1952 far in excess of existing capabilities to persuade NATO members to redress the balance within the alliance between nuclear and conventional in favour of the latter.

It has to be said that, apart from a brief period after the second Berlin crisis, NATO never looked like matching Warsaw Pact conventional numbers. Indeed, among the European states there was a marked reluctance to do so. NATO military commanders were forced by the circumstances to devise strategies that would allow for this gap between available conventional forces and desirable conventional forces. This was achieved, often very successfully, in two ways: by relying upon the first use of nuclear weapons and by substituting ➤technology – particularly air power – for ground forces. ➤Geopolitically, if ➤war was to occur between NATO and the Warsaw Pact, Germany would be the first and most important area of land operations. Having regard to German interests, therefore, NATO became committed to the '➤forward defence' principle in order to prevent, if at all possible, the devastation of German territory by a conventional campaign. The twelve German divisions which it was planned to add to NATO's conventional capability following German membership were envisaged as part of the conventional 'shield' for the nuclear 'sword' but not as the means to fight a purely conventional war.

NATO's nuclear addiction, as it has been called, was the defining characteristic of the alliance. The development of so-called independent nuclear forces by, first, the United Kingdom and then France (two of the most important European members of NATO) only served to enhance this trend towards nuclearization. Under Robert McNamara the United States tried to wean NATO away from this addiction with ideas about ►flexible response only to find these notions being reinterpreted to suit nuclearization in 1967. The North Atlantic Council's decision in 1979 to introduce new long range theatre nuclear weapons into Europe raised the issue of nuclear weapons anew. The response of a number of European publics was critical and the deployment of these theatre weapons was the subject of successful, if protracted ►arms control negotiations which produced the INF ►treaty.

Institutionally, NATO is a complex of civil and military organizations. The highest political ►authority in the Alliance is the North Atlantic Council. The Council provides a means whereby fundamental issues concerning the organization can be discussed. All member states are represented on the Council by their ambassadors and, in this way, the Council can remain in virtually permanent session. Meetings of the Council are chaired by the ►secretary-general who is, like the UN counterpart, an international civil servant. Although formal voting in the Council is not used, in reality a ►de facto ►unanimity principle operates through the need to reach a consensus. The Defence Planning Committee, despite its name, is more than simply a committee of the Council. It would be better to describe it as a collateral committee. The Nuclear Defence Affairs Committee and the Nuclear Planning Group, established in December 1966 under the aegis of the Defence Planning Committee, reflect the nuclearization of the alliance and the need to establish some consultative machinery whereby all the members can have an input into nuclear ►decision-making even though they do not possess nuclear weapons themselves.

The military organization of the alliance is headed by the Military Committee. The command structure is tripartite: European, Atlantic and Channel. Allied Command Europe is located in Belgium, Allied Command Atlantic at Norfolk Virginia and Allied Command Channel at Northwood, United Kingdom. In 1966, France withdrew from the military command structure (it rejoined in 1996). Iceland, having no military forces, is represented by a civilian observer.

*Post-Cold War changes: NATO's enlargement*
The first Secretary-General of NATO, Lord Ismay, in a memorable phrase described its pre-1989 objectives in this way: it was designed 'to keep the Soviets out, the Americans in and the Germans down'. Events since the end of the Cold War have brought fundamental changes in at least two of these areas (the disintegration of the Soviet Union and the unification of Germany) and in the third – US commitment to the defence of Europe – a fear of an American return to neo-►isolationism. Since NATO formally declared the end of the Cold War in the Declaration of Turnberry in June 1990 (seven months after the fall of the Berlin Wall) there has been understandable speculation about the future of the Alliance. For some, its ►*raison d'être* had gone: alliances are formed in response to a perceived common threat and alliance cohesion is a

function of the intensity and duration of this threat. Given the collapse of the USSR and the Warsaw Pact therefore, it could be argued that NATO has outlived its usefulness. This argument has particular resonance for some opinion makers in the USA, where NATO is viewed essentially as a 'foreign' commitment. ➤Neorealist K. N. Waltz, for example, in evidence before the US Senate Foreign Relations Committee in 1990 said: 'NATO is a disappearing thing. It's a question of how long it's going to remain a significant institution even though its name may linger on.' Countering these views, a prominent British ➤hawk, former Premier Margaret Thatcher argued forcefully that 'you don't cancel your insurance policy just because there have been fewer burglaries on your street in the last twelve months' (McCalla, 1996). In other words, Russian behaviour may have changed, but concern over Russia's residual military capability remains; to abandon NATO would be premature and dangerous. Most analysts and policy-makers within the Euro-Atlantic ➤security community concur and the main issue in the 1990s concerns the transformation of the alliance not its demise.

NATO has always been more than a military alliance. During the Cold War it was also a political instrument; a means of ensuring cooperation amongst its members in socio/economic matters as well as military/diplomatic ones (Article 2). In 1990 the London Declaration formally recognized that the changed circumstances had made reliance on the nuclear option less important and since then the debate about adaptation has revolved largely around the political, social and economic aspects of Euro-Atlantic cooperation. This covers two broad areas; institutional realignment with indigenous European organizations (➤EU, WEA and OSCE) and geographical expansion into Central and Eastern Europe. Expansion has proved controversial in at least three ways: the question of which states to admit as new members, the attitude of existing members and above all, the likely reaction of Russia. Regarding new membership, NATO has produced a check list of five basic criteria: an established democracy, respect for ➤human rights, a market-based economy, armed forces under civilian control and good relations with neighbouring states. Ten countries (Bulgaria, the Czech Republic, Estonia, Hungary, Latvia, Lithuania, Poland, Romania, Slovakià and Sloveniâ) have submitted membership requests and two others, Albania and Macedonia have declared an interest, bringing the total number of potential candidates to twelve. In the first expansion round, three of these (Poland, Hungary and the Czech Republic) are likely to be admitted. The Clinton Administration favours enlargement, but some European members are cautious fearing that the widening process might be a prelude to eventual US withdrawal. Regarding Russia, which is potentially the biggest stumbling block to enlargement and diversification, NATO has proceeded gingerly mindful of the deep sense of grievance felt at the 'loss' of Central and Eastern Europe and the historic fear of encirclement. NATO has accordingly offered Russia a number of inducements including the Partnership for Peace

(PFP) proposal which envisages closer cooperation between the alliance and Moscow, including 16 + 1 meetings at which Russian foreign and defence ministers would have regular contact with their NATO counterparts. This arrangement was formalized at Paris in May 1997 – the 'Founding Act on Mutual Relations, Cooperation and Security between NATO and the Russian Federation'. This agreement ensures consultation on aspects of alliance policy but crucially, does not give Moscow a veto on policy making. The precise contours of enlargement and the character of the Russian relationship will be the subject of NATO's summit meeting in Madrid in June 1997. It is expected that this will consist of a revised version of the ➤Clinton Doctrine outlining the President's vision for a new world order in the post Cold War period. The centrepiece of this is likely to see 'enlargement' and 'open door policies' replace ➤containment and coexistence as bedrocks of America's Euro-strategy into the new millennium.

**Natural law** Refers to the idea of a natural system of law existing independently of customary or positive law. Thus human beings, and by extension states, are subject to a universal set of rules which are derived from nature (or God) and which are discernible through reason. The natural law tradition underlies the formative period of ➤international law and although its antecedents can be traced to Roman and Greek thought (especially in the idea of *jus gentium*) it is during the period from the fifteenth to the seventeenth century that it exerted most influence. International legal theorists associated with this school are Vitoria (1480–1546), Suarez (1584–1617), Gentili (1552–1608), ➤Grotius (1583–1645), Zouche (1590–1660) and Puffendorf (1632–94). All these writers agreed that the essence of ➤international society was a respect for mutual social rights and duties which were not man-made but were implicit in the natural order of things. However, despite its apparent universalism, the natural law tradition and the values associated with it were basically Christian (although Groitus, arguing that natural law was the main source of the law of nations, conceded that this law would remain valid even if God did not exist). In this way, differentiations were made between Christians who shared a common conception of the divine origins of law and those such as the Ottomans who did not. The essence of the doctrine was that law was derived from universal principles of ➤justice and therefore natural law was accorded primacy over conventional or positive law. In the eighteenth and nineteenth centuries the positivist conception that law was man-made and that as a result law and justice were the same thing became the accepted orthodoxy and the natural law school faded away except in the Roman Catholic Church, where it is still held to be the official philosophy of law. In the twentieth century there have been a number of secular attempts to revive it as the basis for international law (see especially J. L. Brierly, 1958, and H. Lauterpacht, 1950). The fact that this doctrine does not distinguish between states and individuals and is consequently ambiguous on the question of membership of the international society has made it especially attractive to ►human rights theorists and those who regard the doctrine of ►sovereignty as an obstacle to the achievement of social justice in IR.

**Natural resources**  These are normally thought of as the physical assets of the planet which can be divided into land-based and sea-based categories. The most basic of the former is the land itself. Sea-based assets may be divided between those pertaining to the ocean – such as fish stocks – and those pertaining to the sea-bed. Natural resources are territorially divided between ►states and are legally owned as public or private goods. The major exception to this state of affairs is the oceans. Under the traditional principle of the freedom of the seas and under the contemporary idea of the ►common heritage of mankind the seas were made exceptions to this ►state-centrism. Whereas the principle of the freedom of the seas was exclusive, that is to say, that beyond the territorial waters nobody had control, the principle of the common heritage is inclusive; that is to say, beyond the jurisdiction of the coastal states the natural resources of the oceans belong to all. (►Law of the Sea)

On land there is no equivalent to the common heritage principle, although significant moves are currently being made to provide a more global perspective on such issues as the tropical rain forests. Deforestation of the land is a serious problem in much of the ►Third World. It is becoming increasingly clear that a purely self-centred ►national interest approach to these problems is no longer appropriate and that solutions must be sought that reflect legitimate global as well as state-centred concerns.

Natural resources are allocated in an asymmetric way between states in the system. In the past, and indeed at the present, this produced and still produces disparities rather than equalities. Theorists interested in such concepts as ►capability and ►power tend to try to build these disparities into their analyses. In this way resource allocation becomes part of the explanation for what many see to be a situation of ►hierarchy and stratification. This tendency is especially marked when more traditional analyses based upon ►international politics are involved.

The endemic disparities in resources between states have often been held to be a precipitant cause of ►conflict in international politics. Quarrels between actors over land are among the most fundamental and prevalent. These disputes do not only or always involve natural resources. Indeed, land can have an important symbolic significance quite separate from its inherent resources. However, where quarrels over land are pursued for largely economic reasons it is plausible to assume that the parties are disputing access to and control over natural resources. (►Resource wars)

**Negotiation**  Negotiation is the process whereby ►macropolitical ►actors interact in order to effect a number of goals that can only, or most effectively, be realized by joint agreement. If an actor has the ►capability and the willingness to effect an outcome independently then no negotiation is required. To this extent entering into the negotiating process is a tacit recognition by the parties that their interests are complementary.

Fred Charles Iklé (1964), in his standard work on the subject, suggests that it is possible to establish five analytical categories when looking for reasons why actors negotiate to effect outcomes. First, in order to extend an agreement that is already in force between them where the original understanding had a time limit. In this way the Salt II agreement was an extension of Salt I. Second, to normalize relationships as when two actors re-establish diplomatic relations. Third, a redistribution agreement involves situations where parties agree to change a particular ➤status quo. Redistribution agreements are common after the ending of a ➤war situation. The parties to the ➤conflict may make such arrangements. Fourth, innovation agreements may be reached to establish new actors. The San Francisco Conference approved the establishment of the UN. The Balfour Declaration viewed with favour the establishment of a home for the Jews in ➤Palestine in 1917. Finally, negotiations may be entered into for what Iklé calls 'side-benefits'. Parties may negotiate simply in order to establish a clearer ➤perception of each other's goals, and to make ➤propaganda for themselves and their position.

These categories are made for purposes of analysis and empirically they may be combined. Thus a cease-fire agreement can be said to normalize a situation. However, to the extent that during such ➤armistice negotiations the acceptance of a cease-fire line involves a change of territory, then redistribution has taken place. Equally it is possible for parties renewing an agreement to introduce new clauses thus innovating. It is also possible to redistribute values when renegotiating agreements. This is particularly likely when actors are involved in ➤tariff bargaining; the essence being to renew an agreed tariff position but to redistribute at the same time. The process of negotiating for side benefits may be implicit in any of the other four processes.

Formal negotiating begins with the statement of positions by the parties. Sometimes these formalities are preceded by negotiations about who are to be included as parties and even about the physical arrangements for the meetings. Once all sides are in possession of the other's demands then three basic choices are available: to accept agreement on the available terms, that is to say upon the terms other parties put forward; to attempt to improve the available terms by bargaining; to break off negotiations because neither of the previous choices are acceptable.

The essential tactic in negotiation is for a party to convince all others that its current offer is the best available and that there is no point in bargaining around the terms in order to improve them. The actual behaviour whereby terms are modified and outcomes evolved is the essence of the bargaining process. There are a variety of stratagems that parties can use to reach the bargain. It may be possible to reach agreement by setting a deadline or dateline for the terms offered or by giving the impression that these terms may harden if agreement is not reached.

An essential variable in the process of negotiation will be the way the issues are defined by the parties. This perception of the issues can determine the likelihood of negotiations ever taking place, let alone whether they succeed or not. As a general rule the smaller the issue difference the greater the chance of negotiations succeeding. Conversely, the more issues are seen as fundamental matters of principle, the harder compromise becomes. Sometimes parties deliberately manipulate the issues to make agreement easier or harder, the deliberate widening of issues into matters of principle being the most obvious. If all parties can agree in principle at the outset, that impediment is removed and details can be filled in during the bargaining. Sometimes parties will couple issues together. This may be done in order to be constructive, for example by offering to reciprocate concessions, or it might be destructive, widening the agenda of discussion in order to exert pressure. The way in which issues are perceived by the parties is likely then to have an important bearing upon the outcome of the negotiations. The broader the structure of the ➤issue area the smaller the chances of success but the greater the pay-offs if the negotiations do succeed. Conversely reducing the issue area increases the chances of success but reduces the significance of what is agreed. If the negotiations fail in the latter case, the chances of reviving the negotiations at some later date is almost certain to be greater. This kind of ➤incrementalism stands frequent repetition.

The whole question of the relationship between capability and negotiation is a complex one. It is sometimes simplified into the aphorism that parties should seek to 'negotiate from strength'. This view has much superficial validity, and appears to be intuitively sound. Upon closer examination, however, the injunction looks flawed. Kenneth Boulding (1962) has observed that parties 'dictate' rather than negotiate from positions of strength. A position of ➤parity is more likely to be conducive to success in negotiations than great diversity in strength.

It is often necessary to differentiate between amity and enmity as background conditions in negotiations. It seems intuitively valid to suggest that between friends the parties are likely to be more accommodating than between foes. Whereas ➤accommodation between friends is likely to be the outcome, at least in part, of positive values between the parties, accommodation between foes is more likely to be dictated by expediency. In particular, negotiations between friends are more likely to evince the attitude of 'negotiating in good faith'. In essence this carry-over from an international legal concept means to negotiate with a real desire to reach agreement rather than to negotiate for 'side-benefits'. More specifically, 'negotiating in good faith' involves not maintaining a dogmatic position that precludes agreement and accepting the principal rule of accommodation, which is the willingness to make concessions in order to secure agreement.

Agreements are most usually reached through compromise if negotiations are not to break down. In order to compromise parties agree to a partial withdrawal from their initial positions. This withdrawal need not be symmetrical and it is not infrequent that one side will appear to submit to demands made of it without seeking an adequate *quid pro quo*. The essential point about compromise, as Kenneth Boulding has pointed out, is that all parties must appreciate that the price of continued conflict is higher than the costs of reducing demands. Compromise is, in fact, a two-step process, the first being that all sides withdraw some of their demands in preference for a continuation of the status quo and, having made this move, the bargaining for the actual terms of the compromise can take place. These two stages can be termed 'the commitment to compromise' and the 'compromise bargain', respectively.

The physical environment against which negotiations take place can be significant. Under this rubric such factors as the venue, the number of parties and the degree of secrecy or openness can be significant. The choice of venue will often be dominated by considerations of ➤neutrality. Other considerations may be good access to communications and the nature of the issues to be negotiated. ➤Bilateral negotiations are, for obvious reasons, more manageable but run the risk that by excluding third parties, important interests will not be consulted and will therefore not feel constrained to support any agreement. Conversely ➤multilateral negotiations are more unwieldly but have the advantage of allowing all parties to be represented. The debate between open and secret negotiations is an old problem about which strong views were held by both ➤idealists and ➤realists. The dichotomy is empirically overdone. No contemporary negotiation is completely open or secret. In this respect the open/secret categories mark the ends of a continuum between which actual negotiations can be ranged. Factors that are likely to affect the movement towards one end or the other will include: the level of amity/enmity between the parties, the reasons for the negotiations and the perceived need for public support during the process itself. The CODESA negotiations which resulted in the successful 1994 multi-party elections in South Africa exemplified virtually all the conditions mentioned above.

**Neo-colonialism** ➤Colonialism

**Neo-functionalism** An academic theory of ➤integration originally suggested by Haas (1958) as a result of his work on the European Coal and Steel Community. As the term implies, neo-➤functionalism is a modern variant of functionalism. Both theories are based upon the view that integration proceeds best by working from areas of mutual and overlapping interest in a piecemeal fashion. This is often referred to in the literature as the 'sector approach'. Both theories assume that these sectors will in all probability be located in the ➤issue area of political economy. Both theories assume that people's loyalties to their existing ➤nation-states will be steadily eroded as they see that integration has many positive benefits and that these can best be obtained, and sustained, by the new nexus.

Neo-functionalism differs from functionalism in a number of important respects. First, it is a theory of regional rather than global integration, and specifically a theory of how this process has been achieved in Western Europe since 1945. By concentrating upon a region in this way the neo-functionalists have been able to achieve great parsimony of concepts and theories. The main weakness inherent in the regional concentration is that a certain breadth of vision is thereby lost. Second, neo-functionalists have been much more concerned with institution building than were the original functionalists. With this in mind, Mitrany (1975) dubbed them 'federal-functionalists'. Notwithstanding, neo-functionalism is distinctly orientated towards the political aspects and implications of integration. Central to this view is that once commenced, sector integration will lead to a ➤spillover effect into other cognate areas of activity. In particular, in those issue areas where high levels of ➤interdependence actually or potentially exist, spillover integration will be difficult to resist. Moreover, as interest groups within the member states begin to see the positive benefits of the process, they will actually initiate moves for further integration. Spillover, therefore, may be semi-automatic or manually operated.

The events in Western Europe in the 1950s seemed to confirm the explanatory significance of neo-functionalism. The formation of the European Coal and Steel Community (ECSC) was followed by further attempts at the sector method of integration. Although the European Defence Community failed to secure the ➤ratification of all its putative members, the formation of the ➤European Economic Community and of Euratom in January 1958 seemed to confirm the logic of neo-functionalist thinking. Within the institutional structure of the Community, neo-functionalists place their greatest confidence in the Commission. Although nominated by the member states, the Commissioners represent the ➤supranational rather than the ➤state-centric tendencies in the arrangement. Fresh initiatives for integration and recognition of spillover tendencies are likely to come from the Commission. The initiation of a directly elected European Parliament after June 1979 further strengthened the neo-functionalist institutions within the Community.

Neo-functionalism comes from the same intellectual stable as the US school of political sociology known as 'Pluralism'. Like the pluralists, they assume that politics is a group activity and that in advanced industrial societies ➤power and ➤influence will be diffused among a number of competing groups. Because competition rather than ➤conflict is the norm, the nature of the political activity will be circumscribed by a basic underlying consensus. Differences of degree rather than differences of kind will identify these groups and politics will be a bargaining process often identified as ➤incrementalism. These pluralist assumptions fit well together with the point mentioned above, that neo-functionalism tends to concentrate upon the issue area of political economy as particularly susceptible to integration. Since advanced industrial societies tend to be preoccupied with wealth/welfare questions, the whole set of assumptions are self-reinforcing. It is not surprising to find that the neo-functionalists expect politics at the supranational level to be similar to politics at the national level. Both are dependent upon the same pluralist conceptions.

In the 1960s Western European neo-functionalism encountered ➤Gaullism. As a result the assumptions, particularly about the dynamic tendencies of spillover, were called into question. It became clear that the ideas derived from pluralism, referred to above, were in themselves dependent variables and that political ➤elites with fundamentally different perceptions would not be able to work the same system in the same way. Moreover, to the extent that these elites exercised constitutional authority within their own states, they were able and willing to exercise ➤veto power over groups such as the commission. It is now accepted by neo-functionalists that the Council of Ministers and the European Council represent this veto power and that, with the accession of the United Kingdom after 1973, a further enhancement of Gaullist tendencies took place.

What many see as the relaunching of European integration in the 1980s was not accompanied by a significant resuscitation or redefinition of neo-functionalism. Instead the recent history in Europe has been a melange of ➤confederalism, federalism and neo-functionalism. It is clear that in the European instance a 'union of states' rather than a 'united states' is being created. This eclecticism has a place for neo-functionalism but it is not exclusive to that theory.

**Neo-isolationism** Unlike its derivative ➤isolationism, this term refers exclusively to the ➤foreign policy ➤orientation of the United States of America. In the American context, isolationism has been seen as her oldest and most enduring orientation but one about which debate has raged and dubiety felt. In the twentieth century the impact of ➤Pearl Harbor was believed to have removed isolationism from the agenda of public debate and even civilized discussion. Pearl Harbor seemed to invalidate the policy assumptions of a generation that had sought to pursue ➤unilateral ➤goals and to put America first. The events of the 1970s, and in particular the outcome of the ➤Vietnam War, restored isolationism, which was now increasingly dubbed neo-isolationism, to public debate. In particular the growing impact of ➤declinism on American attitudes to ➤international relations sent many back to America's roots in search of an alternative ➤paradigm to ➤internationalism.

In keeping with its derivative, neo-isolationism is a broad spectrum of aspirations, assumptions and attitudes. Realists tend to take their cue from the idea of the ➤national interest as the benchmark in their assessment of America's role. Taking a broadly 'Washingtonian' view the national interest version of neo-isolationism argues that America can no longer afford to define its security in ►globalist, internationalist terms. The end of the ►Cold War in particular should suggest that permanence is a vice and flexibility a virtue. America's engagement with the world outside its own hemisphere should be selective and dictated by national priorities above all else. 'Pactomania' is a Cold War syndrome which America no longer needs. Writers like Carpenter (1992) have argued for America to make a strategic declaration of independence in the post Cold War world, whilst Tonelson et al (1991) have combined neo-isolationism with neo-mercantilism to pick up on themes discussed in Kennedy (1988) about the economic costs of a global security policy. ►Liberalism has joined forces with realism in the neo-isolationist paradigm. Picking up on themes that are deeply embedded in American exceptionalism the liberal neo-isolationist sees America's involvement in 'entangling' security commitments as a means whereby the United States was inexorably drawn into fighting others battles on terms which compromised the role of being an exemplar nations for others to follow. The antiwar movement during Vietnam and the ►Vietnam Syndrome thereafter are organizational and ideational indicators of the extent to which foreign involvements produce domestic costs. The thesis of the Imperial Presidency (Schlesinger 1974) is a salutary warning of the impact that foreign entanglements have upon the balance of the American constitution.

As McGrew has pointed out (1994) neo-isolationism involves an *ad hoc* approach to military engagements and a new concern with economic and social regeneration inside America. In this sense the Neo-Isolationist paradigm rejects Cold War triumphalism in favour of a more sober assessment of the winners and losers in the Cold War. ►Public opinion studies seem to confirm a strong latent sense of isolationism amongst mass publics in the United States which confirms the enduring impact of this orientation upon American ►diplomacy.

**Neoliberalism** Sometimes referred to as 'neoliberal institutionalism.' This term distinguishes neoliberalism from earlier varieties of ►liberalism such as 'commercial' liberalism (theories which link ►free trade with ►peace), 'republican' liberalism (theories linking democracy and peace) and 'sociological' liberalism (theories of international integration). Neoliberalism which is inclusive of all the above is generally understood to be the most comprehensive theoretical challenge to the ►realist/neorealist orthodoxy in mainstream international theory (see Baldwin 1993).

The principal charge levelled against political realism is its obsession with the ►war/peace, and military/diplomatic dimensions of international relations and its fixation on the ►nation-state as key ►actor. While not denying the ►anarchic character of the international system, neoliberals argue that its importance and effect has been exaggerated and moreover that realists/neorealists underestimate the varieties of cooperative behaviour possible within such a decentralized system. Concentration on the ►security dilemma they argue, severely limits the ►scope and ►domain of ►international relations and renders it anachronistic as a model of global relations. Indeed, neoliberals define 'security' in much broader terms than neorealists: moving away from a ➤geopolitical/military reading of the term, they emphasize wealth/welfare and environmental issues as equally valid considerations. Thus, they focus on institution-building, ➤regime creation and the search for 'absolute' rather than 'relative' gains as mitigating strategies in a quasi-anarchic arena. Although nation-states continue to be important actors, they have declined in their ability to effect outcomes, particularly on the plethora of issues that transcend political ➤boundaries Instead of a single agency, neoliberals favour a ➤mixed-actor model which includes ➤international organizations, transnational organizations, NGOs, MNCs and other non-state players. The dynamics of international relations arise from a multiple sources involving a mix of interactions not captured by the simplistic (albeit elegant and parsimonious) theories of realism/neorealism. Keohane and Nye (1977) refer to this process as ➤complex interdependence and argue that the exclusiveness of neorealism fails to capture the complexities of international behaviour and in particular distorts reality by ignoring the institutions, processes, rules and norms that provide a measure of governance in a formally anarchic environment. In sum, neoliberals contend that the IR agenda has been greatly expanded in the twentieth century, particularly in the non-military wealth/welfare/environmental arenas. Therefore theories that concentrate on military/diplomatic ➤issue areas are bound to be one-dimensional, since they are wedded to the past and incapable of dealing with systemic change.

Neorealists for their part argue that neoliberals exaggerate the extent to which institutions are able to mitigate anarchy, and they underestimate the potency of ➤nationalism and the sheer durability of the nation-state. Although they agree that cooperation is possible under anarchy it is much harder to achieve and maintain than neoliberals allege. In this connection, the future of the ➤European Union is regarded as an important test for both theories. For ➤critical theorists and ➤postmodernists, both approaches are faulty, since both are located in the 'anarchy problématique'. The much vaunted differences are in fact minimal. Neorealists tend to study security issues; neoliberals tend to focus on economic issues. Both are similarly obsessed with conflict and cooperation within a ➤self-help environment and therefore critically assume that actors behave as egotistic value maximisers. Most importantly neither approach critically addresses the ➤normative presuppositions of the anarchical order they work within. In this sense, both accept the prevailing ➤definition of the situation and both are embedded within a privileged, ➤status quo conception of international relations and eschew explanations of approaches not based on rational choice theory.

**Neo-mercantilism** Neo-mercantilism or new mercantilism is, as the term implies, the resurgence of ➤mercantilism. Historically, two examples of this regeneration are usually cited. First, the period between 1919 and 1939 and, within that time frame, the period after the Great Depression of 1929–33. Second, the period since 1970 when the ➤Bretton Woods system of ➤trade and payments began to break up as the US ➤hegemony looked more questionable. The link between these two periods is that in both instances ➤states used ➤protectionism in various forms as an economic instrument to insulate themselves from external events and circumstances; the aim, as ever, being to produce a surplus on the current account trading position by exporting more than is imported at a given level of economic activity.

Since the idea of mercantilism was first promulgated and a link was thereby established between foreign economic policy and overall ➤goals and ➤orientation, important changes have taken place in the conventional expectations that individuals and groups have about the proper role of the state, both internally and externally. In particular, the growth of the ideas about the welfare state and the growing acceptance that wealth/welfare issue areas are central tasks for governments to tackle and central aspirations for peoples to have, caused a quantum shift in the ➤scope and ➤domain of governmental activity. Whereas in the sixteenth century protectionism was seen as a means of increasing state power, it is now often seen as a means of protecting the standard of living, the employment prospects and the growth targets of states. Mercantilism, or the new mercantilism, serves more masters than it did and, therefore, is seen as more benign than it once was.

The first twentieth-century neo-mercantilist experiment ended with the Second World War and the emergence of the United States as the hegemonial actor immediately afterwards. The consensus at the time of the Bretton Woods negotiations was that ➤economic liberalism was positive and that any deviation from the norm – such as might be implied by a move towards protectionism/neo-mercantilism – should be resisted. In general terms the General Agreement on Tariffs and Trade (GATT) system ought to encourage these liberal tendencies but by allowing states to form ➤customs unions and ➤common markets under the same ➤regime, GATT was strengthening the protectionist tendencies within the system.

The GATT dispensation weakened ➤liberalism and encouraged neo-mercantilism in two respects: First, it promoted the formation of ➤blocs of states based upon regional affinities and secondly, within the bloc structure, it allowed the participating states to discriminate against those outside the ➤trade bloc/common market. This discrimination reached its height in the Common Agricultural Policy (CAP) of the EC/EU. CAP is a ➤paradigm example of neo-mercantilism on a number of counts: it seeks to protect domestic interests and lobby groups from external competition, it artificially raises prices within the market *vis-à-vis* world prices, it leads to overproduction by marginal/uneconomic units, and it encourages ➤dumping which further distorts the world market. In terms of what might be called 'classical' mercantilism, CAP encourages people to think in terms of security of supply rather than economy of production and efficiency of price. At the same time it provides stocks of surplus food which can be distributed in the form of economic ➤aid for political purposes.

It should not be thought that the European Union is the only standard-bearer of neo-mercantilism in the present system. One of the characteristics of this type of political economy is that it provokes retaliation, tit-for-tat measures and even trade wars. From the perspective of the economic liberal, neo-mercantilism becomes a bad habit which others quickly learn to emulate.

**Neorealism** Sometimes called 'new' or structural ➤realism, this theoretical perspective is associated with the writings of K. N. Waltz, especially his influential *Theory of International Politics* (1979, see especially chs. 5–6). While retaining many of the basic features of 'classical' realism (e.g. ➤states as key rational unitary ➤actors and ➤power as a central analytical concept), neorealism directs attention to the structural characteristics of an international system of states rather than to its component units. The concept of 'structure' here refers to the 'ordering' or the 'arrangement' of the parts of a system, and in Waltz's formulation it is the structural constraints of the global system itself, rather than the attributions of particular component units, that to a large extent explain state behaviour and affect international outcomes. In Waltz's words: 'By depicting an international political system as a whole, with structural and unit levels at once distinct and connected, neorealism establishes the autonomy of international politics and thus makes theory about it possible. Neorealism develops the concept of a system's structure which at once bounds the domain that students of international politics deal with and enables them to see how the structure of the system, and variations in it, affect the interacting units and the outcome they produce. International structure emerges from the interaction of states and then constrains them from taking certain actions while propelling them toward others' (Waltz, 1990).

In other words, it is 'structure' that shapes and constrains the political relationships of the component units. The system is still anarchical, and the units are still deemed to be autonomous, but attention to the structural ➤level of analysis enables a more dynamic and less restrictive picture of international political behaviour to emerge. Traditional realism, by concentrating on the units and their functional attributes, is unable to account for changes in behaviour or in the distribution of power which occur independently of fluctuations within the units themselves. Neorealism, on the other hand, explains how structures affect behaviour and outcomes regardless of characteristics attributed to power and status.

Waltz argued that the international system functions like a market which is 'interposed between the economic actors and the results they produce. It conditions their calculations, their behaviour and their interactions' (pp. 90–91). Not all neorealists accept his image of the market as the primary force field of international relations, but all accept the basic propositions regarding the centrality of the state as rational, unitary actor and the importance of the distribution of power (i.e. overall systemic structure) in the analysis of inter-state behaviour, outcomes and decision-making perceptions. Waltz's reworking of political realism has attracted much critical attention, especially from ►neoliberals and, in a more dismissive fashion, from ►critical theorists and ►postmodernists, but few would deny that *Theory of International Politics* is the most sophisticated defence of realism and the theory of ►balance of ►power in contemporary international theory. (►Agent-structure)

**Nesting** Term associated with ►neoliberalism which argues that advanced democracies share a cluster of common interests and therefore are well placed to seek 'absolute' rather than 'relative' gains, since their economic arrangements are 'nested' in larger political – strategic ►alliances. 'Nesting' thus promotes cooperation and compliance since allies take comfort in each others' economic successes as this strengthens their combined military ►capability. This contrasts with the realist view that states can never be indifferent to the gains of others: in cooperative arrangements they will always worry that their partners might gain more than they do. Theories of nesting are thus located in the ►neorealist/neoliberal debate about the nature and consequences of ►anarchy (see Keohane 1984)

**Neutralism** Increasingly replaced in the vocabulary of IR by the term ►non-alignment, neutralism refers to a declaration of non-participation in specific conflicts and of treating all parties impartially. Such a policy need not necessarily apply to all international conflicts since neutrals can belong to ►regional ►alliances; it is therefore possible to be neutral *vis-à-vis* a particular conflict and an active participant in another one. India, for example, declared itself neutral in the ►Cold War yet maintained strong regional commitments. Neutralism is often regarded as a useful posture to serve the security interests of new and relatively weak ►states in the ►international system. Not taking sides may maximize the possibilities of genuine ►independence in a ►bipolar world. It may also serve an important domestic function in that ►decision-making ►elites can avoid the charge that they are tools of one international faction or another and of course it also has the advantage of giving freedom of action and flexibility to the practising state. Indeed, one of the benefits of noncommitment during the Cold War was that it helped to undermine rigid bipolarity and force the ►superpowers to widen the ►scope of their policies. In particular, economic, social and developmental issues have been highlighted at the expense of narrower confrontational policies. This has been especially evident in the ►General Assembly of the ►United Nations Organization.

Neutralism should not be confused with ►neutrality which has a specific legal connotation nor should it be confused with ►isolationism which, nominally at least, involves complete separation from and perhaps indifference to, international affairs.

**Neutrality** Unlike ➤neutralism with which it is often confused, neutrality is a legal concept which involves established rights and duties, both for the ➤state which refrains from taking part in a ➤war and for the belligerents themselves. Like other international legal concepts, the laws of neutrality were formed mainly by ➤treaties in the seventeenth and eighteenth centuries, subsequently entered customary law and were then codified by judicial rulings and international conventions in the nineteenth and twentieth centuries. Under the UN ➤Charter, although neutrality is recognized no member can assume the posture of a neutral if the ➤security council has sanctioned a proposed action against an aggressor. In this sense, it can conflict with notions of the ➤Just War. Generally, a state is presumed neutral if by word or deed it has not declared support for one or other of the belligerents. In that case certain specific rights and duties are delineated. For example, belligerents must not violate the territorial integrity of neutrals. Their commercial activites on land, sea and in the air are to be respected so long as they are sanctioned by ➤international law. In return, neutrals are to remain impartial, they are not to aid any of the belligerents directly or indirectly and they are expected not to allow their citizens to do so. In particular, they should not permit neutral territory to be used for war purposes. Clearly these rights are always enjoyed precariously and neutrality must not be confused with ➤demilitarization. In fact, because of the conditions imposed by international law, neutrality involves the ability to defend one's territorial integrity.

Neutrality can be proclaimed in unilateral declarations, as the United States did in 1793, but also in multilateral treaties. In 1815, for example, The Perpetual Neutrality of Switzerland was guaranteed by the Congress of ➤Vienna. This was later reaffirmed by the ➤Versailles Treaty in 1919, and by the ➤League of Nations in 1933. In 1830 the London Conference proclaimed the neutrality of Belgium (it was in violation of this that the United Kingdom formally entered the First World War). In 1907 the Second International Hague Peace Conference reaffirmed the territorial inviolability of neutrals and codified their rights and obligations at sea. Difficult areas in this respect involve the laws of ➤blockade, the definition of contraband and the whole process of neutral shipping plying between ports of the belligerents. The issues of trade and commerce are notoriously thorny and the general rule of thumb is encapsulated in the phrase 'free ships give freedom to goods'. In other words, the nationality of a ship determines the status of its cargo. Enemy goods on a neutral ship, if they do not fall into the category of contraband, are thus not subject to seizure. However, as with so many things 'contraband' often lies in the eye of the beholder, and belligerents have rarely hesitated to intervene if there is any possibility at all of neutral activity giving aid and succour to the enemy. The rights of neutrality have been largely ignored in both World Wars and few states – with the continuing exceptions of Switzerland and Sweden – saw neutrality as a viable policy for maintaining ➤independence. In ➤total or ➤nuclear war conditions, neutrality appears a very quaint proposition. However, in 1955 the Austrian Peace Treaty provided for the perpetual ➤neutralization of Austria. Although technically this was self-neutralization, it was directly promoted by the Soviet Union and agreed to by the United States, the United Kingdom and France. The extent of Austrian ➤autonomy rather than mere acquiescence in this regard is difficult to assess.

Other concepts associated with neutrality are 'neutral territories' and 'neutral zones'. The former usually refers to uninhabited territories that divide two states and which are under joint supervision, for example, the desert territory on the borders of Iraq and Saudi Arabia or that between Saudi Arabia and Kuwait (which was in fact divided in 1965 after the discovery of oil pools). 'Neutral zones' refer to sanitary or security zones formed during a war, to protect civilian populations under the supervision of the ➤International Red Cross. These were first established at Madrid during the Spanish Civil War of 1936 and have since become common practice especially in ➤conflicts in the Middle East. Article 14 of the Geneva Convention of 1949 provided for the establishment and recognition of sanitary and security zones which were specifically designated for the wounded and the sick (whether they were combatants or non-combatants) and for the protection of civilian populations. In similar fashion, 'safe havens' were declared by the UN and the Allies in Bosnia and Iraq respectively during the conflicts in ➤Yugoslavia and the ➤Persian Gulf War.

**Neutralization** Neutralization is permanent ➤neutrality. It is a status concept and is usually applied to ➤state ➤actors, although in principle any territory can be neutralized. Since the requirement of neutrality is permanent in this instance, the diplomatic ground rules extend into ➤peace as well as ➤war. Thus a status of neutralization may, in exceptional circumstances, be regarded as totally incompatible with membership of some intergovernmental organizations (IGOs) even though they are not ➤alliances. The ➤paradigm example of this limiting case of neutralization is Switzerland. In addition to eschewing alliances, that state has also regarded full membership of the ➤United Nations as incompatible with its neutral status.

Neutralization is usually implemented by an agreement between a number of interested state actors – often referred to as guarantors – and the state that is to be the subject of the neutralization understanding. Occasionally neutralization can be self-imposed – as in the case of Austria after 1955 – but again the tacit support of outside parties is still required. As such neutralization may be regarded as the assumption of reciprocal rights and duties. The particular state actor declares itself neutral and in return the outside parties agree to respect this situation. It can be seen that from the perspective of extraneous interests, neutralization can be an effective method of insulating disputed territory and deterring outside ➤intervention. It may appropriately be regarded as a system of ➤conflict management as a result. It should not be confused with ➤demilitarization and in fact neutralized states have rarely been demilitarized.

Demilitarization involves deprivation of organized military force; it does not necessarily involve external guarantees about independence or territorial integrity. ➤Neutralism, too, is a different phenomenon although it does share family resemblances. Unlike neutralization, a posture of neutralism can involve external military, diplomatic and political commitments.

Neutralization was a popular method of conflict management under the ➤balance of power system. In particular, during the nineteenth century a number of agreed initiatives were taken to establish states as permanent neutrals. Switzerland was the first but the example of Belgium is possibly better if a specific instance of balance of power consequences is sought. Belgian neutrality and independence was established in the 1830s. This status was seen, particularly by the United Kingdom, as constituting a ➤buffer state, first to French and then to German interests in the region. Indeed it was the violation of Belgian neutrality in 1914 that led to the British intervention in the continental violence of that summer.

Neutralization has continued to have its proponents in the contemporary system and the example of Austria demonstrates how this technique can be applicable in a ➤bipolar rather than in a balance of power system. Probably the most significant drawback with this status is that it imposes severe restraints upon the ➤foreign policy makers in the neutralized state. As the case of Switzerland indicates it can inhibit full participation in IGOs and more generally it requires a good deal of consensual agreement among the foreign policy ➤elite about the fundamental orientations of the state. With the exception of Laos, it has not been popular in the ➤Third World where the more dynamic orientation of ➤non-alignment is preferred.

**New International Economic Order (NIEO)** The NIEO is a ➤Third World manifesto for revision of the global system of economic relations. It was first mooted by the leaders of the ➤non-aligned movement at their Algiers summit in the autumn of 1973. Subsequently the issue was taken up by a Special Session of the ➤General Assembly of the ➤United Nations in May 1974. The Assembly adopted a Programme of Action for the establishment of a NIEO. At the autumn meeting of the regular Assembly Resolution 3281 on the Economic Rights and Duties of States was passed by 120 votes to six (the opposition including the United Kingdom and the United States) with ten abstentions. Both the Action Programme and the Charter on Economic Rights reiterated ideas about revision and restructuring which had been under discussion in the United Nations Conference on Trade and Development

(UNCTAD) since its inception in 1964. The whole package produced by the ➤conference diplomacy of the period 1973−4 might appropriately be regarded as a series of basic negotiating demands or bids from which more detailed and specific agreements could follow.

The tabling of the demands for a NIEO concurrently with the first ➤oil shock and the emergence of OPEC was no coincidence. The possibility that the oil weapon presaged a more fundamental shift in bargaining power away from the ➤North towards the ➤South could not be ignored. The emergence of clear divisions within the Northern States − particularly between the United States and France − in 1975 seemed to confirm this.

The reforms demanded under the aegis of the NIEO can be grouped into the following classes: (a) reforms in the terms of ➤trade and in access to the markets of the advanced industrial countries (AICs); (b) reforms in the major global economic institutions, particularly the IMF; (c) recognition of the burgeoning problem of Third World debt; (d) demands for greater economic assistance and recognition of the issue areas of ➤technology transfer; and (e) recognition of the rights pertaining to economic ➤sovereignty of states particularly with regard to ➤nationalization and the control of the activities of multinational companies (MNCs).

International trade reform has been called the priority item on the NIEO agenda. Specifically, two demands have been made, first, for a system of pricing for primary products or commodities which would, at a minimum, even out adverse fluctuations so that the export earning of less developed countries (LDCs) are not damaged by adverse movements. A Common Fund agreement was eventually worked out under the auspices of UNCTAD in June 1980 which seeks to stabilize commodity prices on stipulated items. Second, deliberate and intentional preferences should be granted in favour of the LDCs to secure their access to the market economies of the AICs for their manufacture. Since this runs counter to the whole principle of the General Agreement on Tariffs and Trade (GATT), and particularly the ➤most favoured nation (MFN) idea, its implementation into a generalized system of preferences represents a major departure from the strategy of trade liberalization.

Judgement on the NIEO should not entirely rest with its implementation. Like any manifesto this is certainly one criteria for evaluation; however, it is also profitable to assess the documents in terms of the ideas lying behind them. As Cox (1979) argued in his review article in *International Organization*, while the NIEO is at one level a set of negotiation demands − or a manifesto − at another it is about the fundamental structure of the global system of economic relations ('global' rather than 'international' because non-state actors are involved). At a third level it is about the kinds of analytical frameworks that should be used to address these issues. Frameworks such as ➤economic liberalism, mercantilism, ➤neo-mercantilism, ➤realism and ➤Marxism. In this sense the NIEO is about ➤ideology and ➤power.

**New medievalism** Concept associated with the later writings of Hedley Bull, in particular his exploration of alternative forms of world order in *The Anarchical Society* (1977). Rejecting the idea of ►world government as a likely (or indeed desirable) alternative to the ►Westphalian ►states-system, Bull makes a powerful case for envisaging the emergence in contemporary world politics of a secular reincarnation of a neo-medieval system of overlapping jurisdictions, segmented authorities and multiple loyalties. In such a system for example, the government of the United Kingdom would share its authority with administrations in Wales, Scotland, Yorkshire, Wessex and elsewhere, and with a European authority in Brussels as well as world authority in New York and Geneva. In this scenario, the power/authority structure would be horizontal rather than vertical. To this extent the notion of a single ►sovereign authority residing in London becomes obsolete. If such a state of affairs prevailed globally, this would constitute a 'new medieval order', the essential characteristics of which are criss-crossing jurisdictions, dispersed loyalties and the absence of a single overacting territorially-based authority. In Bull's words:

It is conceivable that sovereign states might disappear and be replaced not by world government but by a modern and secular equivalent of the kind of universal political organisation that existed in Western Christendom in the Middle Ages. In that system no ruler or state was sovereign in the sense of being supreme over a given territory and a given segment of the Christian population; each had to share authority with vassals beneath, and with the Pope and (in Germany and Italy) the Holy Roman Emperor above. The universal political order of Western Christendom represents an alternative to the system of states which does not yet embody universal government. (p. 254)

According to Bull five features of contemporary world politics give some substance to this back-to-the-future scenario: the emergence of ►regional integration, the disintegration of ►states, the restoration of private international violence, the growth of ►transnational organizations, and the accelerating process of ►globalization. All of these centrifugal/centripetal trends challenge classical international theory which because of its commitment to state-centrism and the ►international states-system as primary behavioural and ideational referent points, cannot properly encompass developments 'beyond the state'.

Despite Bull's scepticism concerning the absolute decline of the state system and his commitment to the continuing vitality of traditional rules and institutions associated with it, many contemporary theorists have suggested that his vision of a new medievalism in world politics is now in the process of being realized. Building on these insights, ►critical theorists and ►postmodernists in particular, have challenged the 'tyranny' of concepts and principles associated with the Westphalian compromise which through the principle of *cuis regio, eius religio,* (who rules, his religion) effectively ring-fenced the territorial state and purchased domestic order at the expense of more-or-less permanent international disorder.

The perspective underlying this view is that the new forces at work in international politics, which Bull correctly identified, cannot be understood within his essentially 'modernist' framework. Therefore the task of students of international relations is to focus on these trends and crucially, to accelerate them. In this sense, the idea of a new medievalism represents not merely a radical critique of classical theory, but also something of a utopian, post-Enlightenment project which re-visions the bases of a universal political order, premised on something other than ►sovereignty and ►anarchy. This subversion and dislocation of traditional thinking is clearly at odds with Hedley Bull's original position.

**New World Order (NWO)** In contemporary usage the phrase is associated with President George Bush who popularized it in the aftermath of the Iraqi invasion of Kuwait on 2 August 1990. Bush was anxious that the American reaction to this act of ►aggression should not be, or be seen to be, a ►unilateral one, but should be viewed in the context of a re-emergence of ►collective security in the post-►Cold War era. In a speech to a joint session of both houses of Congress on 11 September 1990, President Bush outlined five 'simple principles' which should form the framework of an evolving international order: 'Out of these troubled times, our fifth objective – a new world order – can emerge: a new era – freer from the threat of terror, stronger in the pursuit of justice and more secure in the quest for peace, an era in which the nations of the world, East and West, North and South, can prosper and live in harmony.' As this quotation indicates, President Bush's conception of the NWO did not rise much above the rhetorical and it clearly lacked operational precision (what's new? which world? whose order?), but most analysts argued that at the very least the phrase referred to greater ►great power cooperation, a strengthening of the ►United Nations and a more robust role for ►international law. Many in the triumphalist West believed that with positive US ►leadership a new more stable and more just international order could arise out of the straitjacket of Cold War rivalry and hostility. Although the term is associated in the popular mind with the ►Persian Gulf War, the ideas it embodies are by no means new; calls for a 'new world order' have regularly accompanied significant events – usually the ending of general ►wars – in international relations. Similar calls were made in 1815, 1918 and 1945–46. In essence, these ideas are a re-embodiment of traditional ►idealist or Kantian ►liberal notions concerning inter-state cooperation, perpetual peace and harmony of interests.

The remarkable events in world politics between ►nineteen eighty-nine and the early 1990s led many to believe that international relations was now in a period of profound transformation. The collapse of ►communism in Eastern Europe, the demise of the Soviet Union, the end of the ►Warsaw Pact, the unification of Germany and the ending of ►apartheid in South Africa were events that encouraged the idea that a 'new age' of international relations had arrived. Among the elements associated with this supposed transformation are increased evidence of ➤interdependence and cooperation, ➤globalization, integration, regionalism, the disutility of ➤military force and importantly, a possible new role for the UN. Indeed, much of the discussion of a NWO centred on reforming the UN, strengthening the machinery for collective action and laying down the groundwork for ➤global governance. For optimists therefore the 1989−91 period marked a watershed in world politics, producing conditions of unheard of political, economic and military cooperation. Pessimists, (usually drawn from the ➤realist/neorealist perspective) have taken a much less sanguine view. Indeed one analyst has suggested that the end of the Cold War has released long-repressed ➤ethnic and ➤communal conflicts on a global scale and that far from eradicating conflict altogether, the NWO will be characterized by a ➤clash of civilizations, of which the conflict in ex-Yugoslavia is but a prelude. The ➤proliferation of ➤nuclear weapons accompanied by ➤failed states, ➤resource wars and ➤environmental decay may in fact make the original Cold War something that 'we will soon miss' (Mearsheimer, 1990). For realists NWOs are always false dawns since continuity not change is the fundamental feature of international relations. On this view, there are no grounds to assume that the future will be any better than the past.

**NIC** An acronym for Newly Industrialized/Industrializing Country (both terms are found in the literature). There is some debate and discrepancy about the membership of this grouping but four unequivocal NICs can be identified in the ➤region of East Asia: South Korea, Taiwan, Hong Kong and Singapore. Other putative NICs in other regions of the system are referred to below. In passing it should also be noted that of the above four, Hong Kong is *sui generis*. Its status was that of a dependent territory, not a state: it has now been repatriated to China. Nor does its undoubted economic prosperity make it typical of the NICs. Unlike the other three, Hong Kong has developed as a key financial and business centre, playing an entrepôt role *vis-à-vis* China and East Asia in general.

Notwithstanding the Hong Kong case, the NICs have been able to expand their manufacturing sectors because they have enjoyed advantageous comparative costs *vis-à-vis* the market leaders, the advanced industrial countries (AICs). They have a high level of entrepreneurial skill amongst their populations, an open economy regarding foreign investment and stable, if undemocratic, political regimes. The emergence of the NICs exemplifies a real shift in productive resources from the ➤North to selected sites in the ➤South. Typical examples of manufacturing growth can be cited in such fields as: cars and trucks, consumer electrical goods, shipbuilding, steels and textiles. Among ➤Third World states the NICs stand out for their achievement of self-sustained, export-led economic growth. They have, moreover, avoided the kinds of ➤debt problems associated with the recent economic performance of the putative NICs of Latin America.

The evident success of these NICs has had two effects upon the relations in the field of political economy. First, their success has weakened the concept of Third World solidarity. Ideologically the NICs have achieved their impressive economic performance by applying the principles of ►economic liberalism and by following the example of Japan. They have been willing to see multinational companies (MNCs) investment in their economies and have often facilitated such capital flows by offering a permissive taxation ►regime to corporations. Their political systems, if stable, have poor ►human rights records and limited and restricted opportunities for participation.

The second consequence of NIC success has been that it has provoked a backlash amongst the AICs. One form this has taken has been for increases in ►protectionism on the grounds that 'cheap' imports are flooding into home markets from these areas. A second response, particularly favoured in the United States, is to argue that the NICs have 'graduated' into the first division and that henceforth they should cease to regard themselves, or be regarded by others as Third World states requiring special consideration. Institutionally their appropriate destination would seem to be the ►Organization for Economic Cooperation and Development (OECD) according to this perception.

Four unequivocal NICs were identified earlier. Overlapping membership with the colloquial ►Asian Tigers is evident. Putative membership for the next decade and the new century must include many – if not all – of the recently identified ►big emerging markets (BEMs). ►►East Asian crisis

**Nineteen eighty-nine (1989)** The political and ideological map of ►international relations – especially but not exclusively in the northern hemisphere – was altered, probably for ever, by the events that occurred during 1989. The nerve centre for this *annus mirabilis* was Central and Eastern Europe where the two halves of Germany were united (or more accurately Eastern Germany folded into the arms of its larger Western compeer) and where the ►communist system of states in Eastern Europe collapsed. Institutionally the CMEA and the ►Warsaw Pact were fatalities, while structurally the ►Cold War division of Europe ceased to have any *raison d'être*. The whole complex of events and sequences was symbolized by the extemporaneous destruction of the Berlin Wall, two hundred years after the storming of the Bastille (14 July 1789).

Although some commentators have claimed to see the cause of these changes lying with the Western ►alliance's resolute ►containment of communism, most opinions that are not totally blurred by the ideological wishful thinking chart the changes from within the communist system itself. It is ironic that an ►ideology which saw contradictions in capitalism should have produced so many of its own: an economy run on the basis of bureaucratically determined input and output figures rather than demand and supply, a polity based upon a fear-framework rather than popular legitimacy, a culture intolerant of intellectual free thinking and dissidence, and a ►military-industrial complex which overcompensated for the ►security dilemma. It is now clear that Hungary (1956), Czechoslovakia (1968) and Poland under Solidarity were pointers towards the break-up. ►Polycentrism was not accompanied by enough liberaliz-ation. Instead the ►Brezhnev Doctrine showed the mind-set of the ruling ►elites. Even those regimes lacking internationally recognized opposition factions and tendencies – such as Bulgaria and Romania – fell to an Eastern European version of the ►Domino theory.

Finally the ►Gorbachev Doctrine's refusal to follow a policy of ►intervention was crucial. Indeed the clear indication that the internal arrangements for ►states such as Hungary and Poland was a domestic matter (jocularly referred to as the Sinatra doctrine) was a blank cheque to reform movements to take the initiative. Soviet domination of Eastern Europe and the consequent division of Germany had previously been regarded as the principal fruits of victory in 1945, and the ►Yalta system had been the bed-rock on which the post-1945 Soviet security policy had been built. Instead the liberalization under Gorbachev fed back into the Soviet system itself so that the centrifugal tendencies amongst ethnic groups began openly to challenge control from Moscow. Beginning in the Baltic provinces, a ►mirror image process of breakdown took place within the former Soviet Union.

The ending of the Cold War and the irrelevance of the Soviet system as a model for ►Third World states terminated the ►bipolar system. Notably in Africa there has been a general movement away from post-independence one-party autocracies towards greater ►pluralism. ►Civil wars in Angola and Mozambique have ended, Namibia has become independent and South Africa has entered its post-apartheid phase. In the Middle East the new cooperation between the former Cold War adversaries facilitated a multilateral response to the Kuwait crisis of 1990. New attempts at ►conflict resolution in the Middle East followed the initiatives of Secretary James Baker and showed a new American willingness to take on the 'Jewish lobby' in Congress in order to confront the Israeli government publicly.

The ►United Nations, the IGO constitutionally charged to have regard to matters of peace and security, enjoyed a renaissance following the removal of Cold War considerations from its decision-making structures. In particular, the unanimity of the ►Security Council voting procedure now functions in a more consensual environment among the veto powers. Thus the UN was able to maintain an impressive ►collective security consensus in relation to Iraq's ►annexation of Kuwait. The twelve Security Council resolutions passed between August 1990 and February 1991 formed the legal and moral basis for Western intervention in the ►Persian Gulf War.

Intellectually the events of 1989 and its aftermath have spawned fresh scholarly appraisal of the structures and processes of IR. All the elements which comprise the post-1989 ►New World Order – the disutility of military force, the reduction of ideological ►polarization, increased economic interdependence, new emphasis upon wealth/welfare dimensions, an enlargement in the ➤scope and ➤domain of ➤international law and ➤international organizations and new awareness of the ➤environment as an ➤issue area – have been on the agenda since the 1970s. Structurally the events of the *annus mirabilis* throw into relief the key question: what will replace bipolarity? Some commentators now see the USA as the only ➤superpower, but this conclusion ignores totally the fundamental inability of the American economy to sustain a world role commensurate with this status. Others see ➤multipolarity, particularly in terms of ➤political economy, as more plausible. However, neither model should gainsay the possibility that the system will evince greater ➤regionalism and a tendency towards ➤bloc politics. As a category of states the ➤Third World now stands in contradistinction to the ➤First World of leading states, the Second World of the command economies being henceforth redundant. Notwithstanding its different manifestations, capitalism now stands alone as the benchmark form of economic organization. Gorbachev's own reluctance to grasp this particular nettle quickly enough in the former Soviet Union may, in retrospect, be seen as his greatest failure.

➤Security matters which have traditionally been seen as the first-order concern of states may now be redefined in broader terms to take account of pressing concerns in issue areas traditionally regarded as fringe events of world politics: ➤migration, ➤population, ➤human rights, environmentalism and ➤ecology/ecopolitics. The elevation of these issues challenges the fundamental premises of the ➤state-centric system. Although this may not amount to what Francis Fukuyama called 'the end of history', it certainly points to the end of a particular kind of political geography. At the very least, 1989 altered the landscape of world politics even if it did not altogether eradicate the incidence of surface collisions upon it.

The optimism that initially greeted the events of 1989 and the 'triumph' of ➤liberalism and ➤democracy it supposedly symbolized quickly subsided as the epicentre of the ➤revolution, Central and Eastern Europe, witnessed the rise of militant ➤nationalism, ➤communal conflict, ➤ethnic cleansing, ➤failed states and economic collapse during the early 1990s. The ➤new world order confidently expected did not materialize in quite the way that many analysts had hoped. As a result, policy makers and scholars alike have struggled to grasp the nature, ➤scope and ➤domain of world politics in the post-1989 period. The 'post-Cold War era' has not acquired an identity or label of its own. Given that it is characterized confusingly both by the forces of ➤integration and fragmentation, the discipline of IR is now in a state of flux. Indeed according to some 1989 signalled the 'bankruptcy' of IR since it failed both to predict the revolutionary nature of the events that occurred and the disintegrative consequences that followed. ➤Cold War and the discipline of IR ; Clinton Doctrine.

**Nixon Doctrine**  Originally known as the Guam doctrine since in outline it was first articulated in a number of informal statements at Guam in the Philippines in July 1969. Although rather vague and ambiguous, these briefings about the future US global role received world-wide media coverage and subsequently the Nixon Administration elevated these policy guidelines into a full-blown presidential doctrine. According to Henry Kissinger (1979) the President's ►Vietnam address of 3 November 1969 deliberately re-echoed these themes in order to ensure that the doctrine was named for the President rather than for the location in which it had first been expressed. In essence the doctrine contained three major policy themes:

1 It pledged that the United States would maintain all existing ►treaty commitments.
2 It promised to 'provide a shield' should a nuclear power threaten an ally or any other state whose survival was deemed important to US interests.
3 In cases involving other non-nuclear types of ►aggression, the United States promised to provide military and economic assistance with the important proviso that 'we shall look to the nation directly threatened to assume the primary responsibility of providing the manpower for its defense.'

The doctrine should be viewed in the context of the desire for disengagement from Vietnam and its central purpose was to reaffirm the primacy of US global commitments while simultaneously avoiding further activist participation in future land wars in ►Third World regions. The immediate antecedent of the doctrine was Nixon's article (1976) entitled 'Asia after Vietnam' where the two major policy initiatives of the new administration were clearly foreshadowed: the emphasis on the development of indigenous regional security systems and the ►rapprochement with China. However, from a larger philosophical and intellectual perspective few doubt that the main architect of the new policy perspective was Dr Henry Kissinger. His central ideas were formed from his studies of nineteenth-century European ►diplomacy and as such were anchored in the notions of ►balance of power, ►multipolarity, ►pluralism, ►status quo, orderly change and resisting ►revolution (see especially *A World Restored*, 1964). In particular, his conception of a 'legitimate order' and a 'stable structure of peace' involved a radical reappraisal of the traditional ►bipolar and very muscular US conceptions of the modalities of ►containment as expressed in the ►Truman Doctrine. Thus, in the new doctrine, although the overall objectives of containing the main adversaries and promoting US interests on a global scale remained intact, the means-ends formula was altered. Containment was to be sought through multipolar ►negotiation rather than through direct bipolar confrontation. Clearly the rationale of the Nixon doctrine was to restore operational flexibility to US ►foreign policy after the disastrous adventure in Vietnam, while at the same time redistribute the burdens of the global security commitments that the nation had to support.

**Non-aggression pact** As the name implies, an agreement between two or more ➤states not to engage in hostilities, usually for a specified period. The ➤actors involved normally share a border or are in dispute over issues which could involve the use of armed force in their resolution. The issues of contention are not resolved by the agreement. The Nazi-Soviet pact of 1939 is a good example. This was specified to last for ten years (in fact it lasted less than two years) and contained a secret ➤protocol which divided Eastern Europe into Russian and German ➤spheres of influence. For both sides the pact represented a convenient breathing space. For Germany it offered security on the Eastern front. For the Soviet Union it bought valuable, albeit temporary, time for rearmament and strengthening its Western defences. Non-aggression pacts are often regarded as a useful means of reducing international tension while not deviating from basic positions. They have also been used as a means of inducing small or weak states to comply with the wishes of a regional ➤hegemon. Thus in 1970 South Africa, seeking to combat a perceived regional ➤communist threat offered non-aggression pacts to its black neighbours. In return for an assurance of non-interference from Pretoria, South Africa expected its neighbours to deny insurgent facilities for operations against it. At the time there were no takers, but in the early 1980s P. W. Botha revived the offer as part of his efforts to create a 'constellation of states' around South Africa. In 1984 the Nkomati accord was signed between South Africa and Mozambique. The essence of this was that while South Africa committed itself to end support for 'Renamo', Mozambique agreed to end the ANC military presence in its territory. This accord and a similar accord signed with Swaziland in 1982, was regarded by Pretoria as a blueprint for a series of regional non-aggression pacts with surrounding black states, which as well as creating a 'Pax Pretoriana' would considerably ease the internal security problems of the South African government.

It should be noted that non-aggression pacts do not commit signatories to the active defence of the other party. The only commitment is to forgo the military option as a means of resolving a dispute. They are not 'treaties of friendship' though given time and mutual compliance, they could conceivably develop into them. However, as in all treaties, the principle of *rebus sic stantibus* is deemed to apply as it clearly did in the German case.

**Non-alignment** A ➤foreign policy ➤orientation that has been widely adopted within the current ➤international system by ➤states of the ➤Third World. Non-alignment, as the term implies, seeks to avoid ➤blocs, coalitions and ➤alliances. Specifically it is a rejection of the system of competitive groupings established around the ➤Cold War confrontation zones in the post-1945 system. In particular non-alignment was a resistance movement against attempts by the United States and its allies to produce carbon copies of NATO in the Third World after 1949. More generally, non-alignment is an assertion of the ➤independence of the state and its immediate attraction to those new members of the system produced by the ►decolonization process should be apparent. Having recently thrown off the ►colonial yoke, the newly independent were concerned to maintain a respectable distance from alliances dominated by the ►First World. At the height of the Cold War some in the West saw this orientation as equivocal and even immoral. More relaxed attitudes now prevail and non-alignment has come to be accepted as the standard operating ►perception of their external environment by the overwhelming majority of Afro-Asian ►elites. Latin American commitment is less evident or total.

Non-alignment differs from traditional policies of ►neutralization by being an orientation that is assumed or taken up by the parties themselves, rather than being guaranteed and assured by outside interests. Moreover, non-alignment is not essentially a form of ►conflict management like neutralization. By insulating themselves from ►superpower conflicts the non-aligned sought to be part of the solution rather than part of the problem. Non-alignment neither requests nor requires outside guarantees beyond the accepted commitment towards 'peaceful coexistence' a principle established at the ►Bandung Conference.

During the 1950s the term positive ►neutralism was sometimes used as an alternative for non-alignment. The prefix 'positive' is instructive here. Far from opting out of the system − like a traditional neutral state − the non-aligned enthusiastically exercised their ►sovereignty, immediately asserting a more independent role diplomatically in events such as the ►Korean situation and enhancing their influence in intergovernmental organizations (IGOs) such as the UN. The early ascendancy of Asian leaders was reflected at the Bandung meeting but thereafter African and Middle Eastern elites became more involved. Following the Belgrade meeting in 1961, the Non-Aligned Movement was established and agreement was reached on triennial meetings. ►conference diplomacy, indeed, has been a specific characteristic of non-alignment. By combining their voting power into blocs such states can command effective working majorities in organizations such as the UN.

By definition the non-aligned position is inappropriate in the context of wealth-welfare, ►North and ►South issues since the non-aligned are one of the poles in the ►bipolar structure. As a result non-alignment as an orientation is only relevant to military security questions and, even within that category, to threats posed externally from outside the state by the activities of the superpowers and their allies. Accordingly, the value of the term 'non-alignment' as an explanatory device is reduced and it reverts to being a taxonomy or label for a large, but divisive, group of states.

In the post-Cold War era, the ending of bipolar rivalry has robbed the movement of much of its rationale. The international consensus in favour of liberal ►democracy allied to free market economics means that in effect there is now no division to be aligned against. This in turn is likely to lead to dramatic loss of political leverage in the South and to a realignment of its position *vis-à-vis* the North. This will inevitably result in heightened marginalization. The ideological and emotional pull of non-alignment however remains: one of the first foreign policy acts of the 'new' South Africa in 1994 for example, was a commitment to uphold the values and interests of this movement.

**Non-intervention** A pivotal notion in the ►Westphalian ►state-system where rights associated with ►independence and ►sovereignty logically implied corresponding duties of non-intervention. Thus, the claim to exclusive ►domestic jurisdiction represented by the principle of *cuius regio eius religio* extended to its corollary – freedom from external interference. Primarily an eighteenth century European idea, the rule of non-intervention in ►international law and public diplomatic practice is especially associated with the writings of Wolff (1740) and Vattel (1758). Most early writers on the subject tended to regard it in absolute terms, seeing it as an indispensable prop to ►state sovereignty and therefore an argument for liberty against earlier ►hegemonic and ►imperial claims. However, just as the rights of sovereignty are not absolute, so the duty of non-intervention is circumscribed by reservations and qualifications (even Wolff, for example, claimed that it could be compromised by collective action – the *civitas maxima*).

While non-intervention is now widely regarded as a rule which states ought to adhere to, it is often thought to be more honoured in the breach than in the observance. Indeed, many scholars have noted that in the post-1945 period ►intervention appears not only to be endemic in ►international relations (to the extent that it can be regarded as 'structural' in character), but may even be coterminous with it. That is, if all states complied all the time with the requirements of non-intervention, international politics as we know it would disappear. In this way, modern debates centre not around the existence of the rule, but rather the nature and ►scope of exceptions.

The legitimacy of intervention in the internal affairs of another state clearly depends on a number of factors including purpose or cause, means employed and the authority under which intervention takes place. Generally, unilateral intervention is regarded as suspect although intervention by 'invitation' (e.g. the Soviet intervention in ►Afghanistan in 1979), or counter-interventions (e.g. Cuban assistance to Angola up to 1989 to counter South African aid to UNITA forces), or even pre-emptive intervention on the ground of ►self-defence (e.g. the Israeli bombing of a nuclear installation in Baghdad in 1981) are often regarded as more or less justifiable exceptions to the rule. Again, interventions in support of ►self-determination or ►wars of national liberation are often advanced as legitimate exceptions, especially from the ►Third World perspective. In addition, ►humanitarian intervention either unilaterally or collectively, is a right that is frequently invoked especially by supporters of the emerging law of ►human rights. To many the doctrine of non-intervention, representing as it does the ultimate expression of states' rights, is not just inimical to the development of ►international organizations but also to the general acceptance of human rights as an integral feature of international relations. The rigidity of the doctrine, at least in its original form, allows ➤pariah or ➤rogue states such as pre-1994 South Africa to survive behind quasi-legal technicalities associated with the most exclusive versions of sovereignty and domestic jurisdiction.

Clearly, non-intervention is bound up with the idea of a decentralized state-system composed of sovereign, independent units who are nominally equal. The survival of the rule is therefore linked to the survival of this particular form of ➤world order. The concentration or centralization of ➤power and ➤authority in one source, or else in a number of regional centres, would severely limit its scope and effectiveness. For the present, despite a number of corrosive forces eating away at its edges, non-intervention is still acknowledged to be a bulwark against unwarranted outside interference. As such, it seeks to define the ➤frontier between internal and external affairs and to express, however hazily, the proper and permissable limits of contact between one state and another. ➤Calvo Doctrine; humanitarian intervention

**Non-Offensive Defence** Non-offensive ➤defence stands or falls on the ability of the policy-makers to effect a sustainable distinction between the two types of military ➤capabilities – defensive and offensive. Provide that the distinction can be made then NOD (which is the accepted acronym) can be seen as a system that should reduce tensions between states by enabling them to engage in defence policy-making which is inherently less provocative than the traditional offence/defence mix. Moreover proponents of NOD argue that it is compatible with achieving ➤deterrence provided that the deterrence relationship is one of 'denial' (see Snyder 1961). NOD is not necessarily a system of ➤disarmament however but rather a system of what has been called 'transarmament', that is to say one where the emphasis moves exclusively towards procuring weapons systems that are defensive and ➤implementing defence policies and postures that are less threatening than offence/defence combinations. NOD is probably incompatible with the possession of ➤nuclear weapons and indeed ➤weapons of mass destruction in general because these systems are inherently threatening and, as the name implies, inherently destructive. The essential message of NOD is 'I will not threaten you if you do not threaten me' and in that logic there is no place for this class of weapons. NOD therefore has a family resemblance to disarmament in that some weapons would be incompatible with its implementation yet it does not go the whole way in rejecting the idea of a 'weapons culture'. Like the ➤arms controllers rather it accepts that weapons can provide ➤stability but that this requires the additional recognition of the defensive–defence criterion. As Buzan noted (1987) if all the ➤states pursued a policy of NOD the ➤security dilemma would be removed virtually from ➤international relations.

**Non-proliferation** A policy ➤goal which aims at halting, preventing or reducing the ➤proliferation of weapons and technologies which are available to ►actors as a result of ►arms races and ►arms trade. During the ►Cold War era most attention was concentrated upon obtaining agreement to a non-proliferation ►treaty (NPT) which would control the proliferation of ►nuclear weapons. Policy makers and strategists would distinguish ►horizontal proliferation (that is of weapons to new members of the nuclear club) and ►vertical proliferation (that is improvements in the weapons profile of extant nuclear powers). The implication of ►haves and ►have-nots in these distinctions was apparent and in retrospect was a near fatal flaw in the NPT ►regime. The revelations following the ►Persian Gulf War that states had signed up to the NPT and then contravened both the letter and the spirit of the agreement has produced a new conventional wisdom which argues for a more intrusive ►inspection system. Actual or potentially recalcitrant states will only be ►deterred by such 'challenge' inspections, according to this logic. The non-proliferation regimes for ►chemical and ►biological warfare have been designed with the experience of the NPT in mind to be more intrusive. United States' policy *vis-à-vis* Iraq since 1991 has continued to insist upon total access to any and all evidence that might be germane to the effectiveness of such a regime. The recent decision of India and Pakistan (1998) to 'come out' of the nuclear closet testifies to the difficulty of enforcing the non-proliferation regime. At present, South Africa (1993) is the only nuclear ►state to have voluntarily acceded to the full implications of the ►treaty. In this case though, the motivation was almost certainly domestic (i.e. white fears of the ANC) rather than a concern with international proliferation among the ►have nots.

**Non-tariff barriers (NTBs)** Non-tariff barriers to trade fall into two categories. First, there are ►quotas, quantitative restrictions deliberately designed to protect domestic interests. These are a clear breach of the principles behind the General Agreement on Tariffs and Trade (GATT), although there are certain exceptions to this prohibition. The secondary category of NTBs is not always or intentionally a form of ►trade restriction. The impact of these upon trade will often be latent rather than manifest so their separation from quotas can be justified. The discussion of NTBs that follows will concentrate exclusively upon this second category.

Under this rubric, NTBs are of four broad types: internal taxes, administrative barriers, health and sanitary regulations and government procurement policies. An internal tax can be used to discriminate against ►imports if a deliberate differential is exercised between domestic and imported products which, to all intents and purposes, are the same. Routine and regular administration of importing, as an activity, can become discriminatory if importers appear to be required to submit to excessive and time-consuming paperwork, delay due to documentation problems, etc. Health and sanitary regulations which are perfectly legitimate in themselves can be used to discriminate against imports. Government procurement policies, by deliberately encouraging individuals and institutions to, eg, 'buy British' or 'buy American' not to 'export jobs', can have a discriminatory effect.

This rather heterogeneous category of activities is subsumed under the idea of NTBs which have a latent rather than manifest impact upon trade. In many instances – such government procurement policies – the original articles of GATT were virtually silent in identifying and prohibiting the discriminatory impact of these activities. It has only been since the ➤Kennedy Round of GATT negotiations that increasing attention and concern has been directed at the NTBs. It is reasonable to assume that this ➤issue area will continue to exercise WTO negotiators.

**Normative theory** Accounts of international theory are generally said to be either 'empirical' or 'normative'. Empirical international relations is taken to be descriptive, explanatory and prescriptive. Normative theory by contrast, is concerned primarily with the moral and ethical dimensions of international affairs. However, this distinction is a very broad one since it is difficult in practice to conceive of accounts of IR that are either non-empirical or non-normative. In addition, both approaches concern themselves with epistemological/ontological issues which are common to the activity of theorising in the humanities and the social sciences. (see Brown, 1992). Bearing these caveats in mind, normative theory addresses questions relating to standards of behaviour, obligations, responsibilities, rights and duties as they pertain to individuals, ➤states and the international ➤state system. In particular, normative studies focus on such contentious issues as the moral significance of states and borders, the ethics of ➤war and ➤peace, the nature of ➤human rights, the case for ➤intervention and the requirements of international distributive justice. Normative theory then, is about norms, rules, values and standards in world politics and as such ranges over all aspects of the subject area – including ➤international law, ➤international political economy and ➤diplomacy, where settled, more established procedural norms are more common.

These issues have always been of central concern to students of IR. Indeed, the establishment of IR as a specific field of academic inquiry was driven by normative considerations. The subject was first constituted as a quest for 'solutions' to the problem of the persistence of war in an ➤anarchic state system. This first phase of normative theory is characterized variously as ➤idealist, liberal or utopian. It consisted of attempts to eradicate war and international violence by means of the ➤domestic analogy – the 'peace through law' approach. The second phase of theorising was a reaction to this and was more self-consciously empirical, it sought to look at the world 'as it is, not as it ought to be.' Thus, ➤realism was explicitly positivist and empirical, although it did contain normative implications. The intellectual dominance of political realism in IR from the 1940s onwards, led one scholar to characterize this period as a 'bizarre forty year detour' away from normative issues. (Smith, S. 1992). This is not entirely accurate since many self-proclaimed realists, including such luminaries as E. H. Carr, Reinhold Niebuhr, Hans Morgenthau and Arnold Wolfers specifically addressed the moral and ethical implications of the ➤power politics approach.

This period also saw the rise of the ➤English school and normative investigations into the bases of ➤international society and order. However, realism and its variants did succeed in marginalising normative theory and this tendency was reinforced by the third identifiable wave of theoretical activity – the methodological 'debate' between the classicists and the behaviouralists (➤social science approach). An important dimension of this debate concerned the place of values in social inquiry, but the ideological framework within which the debate was conducted (the ➤Cold War and the perceived need to respond to ➤security issues) meant that conceptions of order, stability and co-existence took precedence in the discipline over considerations of justice or fair play. ➤deterrence occupied central place in IR and theory became obsessed with technical questions relating to ➤nuclear stability and maintaining the ➤superpower ➤status quo. As an American social science, which IR had now become, perhaps it is not surprising that the discipline came to reflect the concerns, interests and values of the West and its leading ➤actor.

The fourth phase of international theory, which began during the final throes of the Cold War and extends to the present, witnessed a revival of normative issues to the extent that they now re-occupy central place in the discipline. This was partly inspired by real-world events, in particular ➤Vietnam and the ➤Persian Gulf War, both of which raised first order normative questions concerning the ➤Just war and the ethics of intervention. The rise of ➤neoliberalism and in particular ➤critical theory and ➤postmodernism has led to widespread questioning, not merely of the dominant paradigms of IR, but to its very status as a separate, distinct area of inquiry. Connecting IR with parallel debates in social and political theory, this 'new thinking' centres on a concern with 'human emancipation' and accordingly relocates human rights, ➤humanitarian intervention, ➤ecological and ➤environmental concerns and distributive justice away from the peripheral terrain they occupied during the period of state-centic dominance. The centrepiece of contemporary normative theory is the dialogue between the 'communitarians' and the 'cosmopolitans'. The basic distinction between these positions in the words of one influential theorist, rests on our double existence as 'men' and as 'citizens; as members of particularist communities and/or universalist communities. (Linklater, 1990). More specifically, this involves examining the nature of human obligation to one another and probing the moral significance of the autonomous state. The radical assault on the Enlightenment project that this has involved is an indication that international theory has now come full circle and is in the process of re-thinking the philosophical basis upon which the disciplinary enterprise was founded.

**North** The term 'North' is a loose, portmanteau concept used in the advanced industrial countries (AICs). It is particularly popular in political economy and, in terms of developmental models, it may be regarded as being synonymous with the growth of the ►First World. ►Systems analysis tends to juxtapose it with the equally amorphous concept of the ►south. Indeed, the popular title of the first ►Brandt Report was 'North–South?'

**North–South** A dichotomous term used in ►international relations to identify one of the most pervasive ►bipolar divisions in the twentieth century system. Relationships between the ►North and the ►South have grown in significance since the collapse of ►colonialism and the emergence of the ►Third World in the 1950s. The visceral commitment of these new states to ►foreign policy ►orientations variously described as positive ►neutralism or ►non-alignment meant that in the ►issue area of security politics – often thought of as ►high politics – the South would rigorously oppose attempts by the North to secure their adhesion to Northern dominated ►Cold War coalitions.

The South's attempt to throw a cordon sanitaire around the Cold War was not totally successful. The United States, in particular, sought on occasions through policies of ►intervention to carry these issues into the Third World. Justification was found, for example, in the bipolar ►perception of the ►Domino theory. On other occasions it must be conceded that factions and tendencies within the South sought and encouraged Northern intervention in violent ►conflict situations. The Soviet ►bloc – not usually thought of as part of the North – also played the interventionist card and during the 1970s in particular it was clear that the ►*détente* relationship between the United States and the Soviet Union was not inhibiting the latter from pursuing such strategies.

Many commentators argue that, notwithstanding the above analysis, the true issue area for the North–South dichotomy is to be found in wealth/welfare political economy. Certainly in this context a very different picture emerges from that already discussed. The dependence of the South upon the North for ►AID and ►trade in order to generate income to meet developmental goals has meant that in this context the term 'North–South' refers to the ►bilateral and ►multilateral relationships that are entailed. It should not be thought, moreover that these relations are exclusively ►state-centred. The multinational companies (MNCs) based in the North and involved in primary or secondary industrial production in the South are an equally valid picture of North–South interactions. These relationships have been variously analysed using different models and the ►dependency or dependencia perspective is one of the most compelling

From the early 1960s onwards the Southern states began to use their burgeoning majority in the ►United Nations to press for greater attention to be paid to their aspirations and concerns. It was pressure from the South that largely created the United Nations Conference on Trade and Development

(UNCTAD) in 1964 and it was Southern economists such as Prebisch that provided the intellectual framework for the series of demands for a new deal on world trade that accompanied the UNCTAD process. Until the success of ►OPEC in the early 1970s, the terms upon which North–South economic relations were conducted were very unequal. The OPEC cartel seemed to point to new possibilities for strengthening the bargaining position of the South and a comprehensive checklist of demands was presented under the rubric of the ►New International Economic Order (NIEO).

Retrospectively, OPEC and the first ►oil shock would seem to have been a window of opportunity which was not entered. Conservative forces within OPEC collaborated with the Northern financial system to recycle petrodollars and oil-importing advanced industrial countries (►AICs) were able in the short term to finance their debts accordingly. Other commodity cartels were not established and indeed, by accident, the OPEC action hit Southern oil importers harder than their Northern counterparts. The petrodollar recycling exercise, moreover, was a precipitant cause of the subsequent ►debt crisis.

The unintended consequence of OPEC and the first oil shock was to drive a line between oil producers in the South and the rest. The growth of the newly industrialized countries (NICs) constitutes another break in Southern solidarity. Antithetically, the realization that a ►Fourth World of extreme poverty and deprivation existed in an identifiable 'famine belt' removed a further prop from the homogeneity of the South. The OPEC exercise of commodity cartel ►power remains the best instance, to date, of the South being able to back their demands for change with something more substantial than a rectitude based upon perceptions of equity. Realism would suggest that unless and until the South can produce more bargaining chips of the OPEC genre they will have a difficult time wringing agreement from the North on structural change.

Within the North the main systemic changes are associated with the loss of US hegemonial ►capabilities to determine systemic outcomes. The United States now shares predominance with the ►European Union and Japan. This has meant that on certain key occasions the North has spoken with a number of voices vis-à-vis the South. This was notable in the aftermath of the first oil shock, when the United States wanted to pursue a more confrontational policy than either the Europeans or the Japanese. With regard to the continuing area of trade reform, the North has shown a clear preference for the GATT/WTO system rather than the UNCTAD.

The end of the Cold War era in world politics has had less effect on North–South relations than has been the case elsewhere. As has been argued above, the former communist states had less impact here – certainly in the political economy issue area – and changes in the North–South configuration are attributable to other developments. In particular the growth of ►regionalism in the North has meant that approaches to the South are more specific and less global. On the Southern pole, solidarity has been eroded by differential growth patterns. The picture is indeed complex with NICs, BEMs as pacemakers at one end of the continuum with ➤failed states and the Fourth World at the other. The term North–South has probably now lost some of its precision and value. More emphasis is now placed upon internal reform measures within the South as a means of breaking into a virtuous circle rather than relying on redistribution from the North.

**NPT** An acronym for the Treaty on the Non-Proliferation of Nuclear Weapons. This multilateral ➤arms control agreement was opened for signature in July 1968 and came into force in March 1970. The NPT seeks to achieve three principal goals. First, to stop the ➤horizontal proliferation of ➤nuclear weapons from states possessing them to states that do not have this ➤capability. The first and second Articles of the NPT cover this contingency. Second, to allow for the continuation of ➤technology transfer regarding ➤nuclear power facilities. The signatories established a safeguards system allowing the proliferation of peaceful nuclear ➤technology under the aegis of the International Atomic Energy Agency (IAEA). Included in the NPT safeguards system is the notion that the Agency will have full and open access to the civilian nuclear programmes of all non-nuclear states, including the right to conduct periodic ➤inspections of their plants and facilities. Third, the NPT sought to control the trend towards further ➤vertical proliferation by enjoining the signatories to 'pursue negotiations in good faith on effective measures relating to the cessation of the nuclear arms race at an early date and to nuclear disarmament'. Article Seven of the Treaty encouraged the establishment of ➤nuclear-free zones. Article Eight committed the contracting parties to meet at five-yearly intervals to review progress made in establishing and extending the ➤regime.

Structurally the NPT was always flawed by the dichotomy between nuclear ➤haves and non-nuclear ➤have-nots. Unlike the recently concluded ➤chemical weapons convention, the NPT cannot escape this criticism. The revelation in the wake of the ➤Persian Gulf War that the ➤inspection system had failed to detect the clandestine Iraq programme has further eroded confidence. The ➤foreign policy behaviour of the one remaining nuclear ➤superpower – the United States – does not inspire confidence in the NPT Regime. American policy ➤perceptions have moved towards ➤bilateral initiatives to keep ➤pariah/rogue states in the regime. The ➤START II agreement and the moves towards a ➤comprehensive test ban are positive signs and should certainly be set against the above pessimism. Evidence that the existing nuclear states are moving towards policies of ➤minimum deterrence is also significant. The point remains that the NPT Regime was drafted for a world which no longer exists. The parameters of the agreement have shifted so substantially that further changes – which the quinqennial reviews of the NPT stipulate in any event – may have to be made to retain relevance into the twenty-first century

**Nuclear accidents** Nuclear accidents fall into two categories: first, civilian accidents, which invariably mean accidents in nuclear reactors; and second, military accidents, which involve malfunction and breakdown of nuclear devices, including nuclear powered systems, during peacetime conditions. Excluded from this discussion are those 'accidents' (such as the accidental launch of a missile) that might lead to ➤war or ➤accidental war.

The main risks with both civilian and peacetime military accidents is that innocent third parties will be affected by environmental ➤pollution and degradation. The increasing use of ➤nuclear power to generate energy for industrial and domestic purposes has meant that such facilities have proliferated. As a result serious breakdowns often cannot be controlled or restricted to an area within the confines of the power plant. Worse still, they cannot be confined within the territorial borders of the ➤state wherein the plant is situated. Thus the Chernobyl accident of April 1986 was not confined to the Soviet Union and pollution and contamination spread outside its borders. The first inclination that something significant had occurred came when Swedish and Finnish monitors reported high levels of radioactivity two days after the explosion. Truly the Chernobyl impact has been to confirm the extent to which ➤interdependence is a key characteristic of contemporary ➤international relations.

Accidents in nuclear reactors have been depressingly regular occurrences since 1952, when the first reactor accident occurred at Chalk River, Ottawa, Canada. Significant contamination of the environment occurred in 1957 at Windscale in the United Kingdom, while a catastrophic local incident took place in the Kasli/Kyshtym area of Chelyabinsk region of the Soviet Union in the same year as Windscale. The Three Mile Island incident at Harrisburg, Pennsylvania in March 1979 was the most serious, to date, in the United States and, in company with Chernobyl, it showed the importance of human error as a factor in explaining such malfunctions.

Incidents of a military kind are more difficult to uncover and therefore assess. All the ➤nuclear weapon states tend to be very reluctant to admit such incidents occurring or to ask for international assistance thereafter. Particularly drastic are naval accidents. Controlling pollution may be difficult or impossible if a vessel sinks to the sea-bed. The ending of the ➤Cold War confrontation between the two ➤superpowers has left a major problem of decommissioning nuclear powered warships and nuclear warheads.

**Nuclear-Free Zones (NFZ)** A NFZ is a ➤region of the world where the states in the area and/or extra-regional states with territorial interests in the area agree not to test, manufacture or stockpile ➤nuclear weapons. The term 'nuclear-free' is something of a misnomer, therefore, and it is more accurate to call these agreements Nuclear-Weapon-Free Zones. Indeed intergovernmental organizations (IGOs) such as the ➤United Nations have specified that peaceful nuclear developments should be allowed to take place under the rubric of the NFZ/NWFZ idea.

Three specified zonal agreements have, to date, been reached and these are all currently operating in their respective parts of the globe. Historically, the first such zonal agreement was the ➤Antarctica Treaty of 1959. In some ways the most far reaching and comprehensive of the three extant treaties, the Antarctica Treaty demilitarizes as well as denuclearizes the continent. This was followed in 1967 by the Treaty of Tlatelolco which seeks to prohibit the introduction of nuclear weapons into Latin America. Tlatelolco was the first NFZ/NWFZ convention to cover inhabited areas of the globe. Following the UN principles, as well as the inclinations of the parties, no attempt was made to extend the provisions to cover peaceful nuclear development. Indeed the official name of the treaty was changed from 'Treaty for the Denuclearization of Latin America' to 'Treaty for the Prohibition of Nuclear Weapons in Latin America' in order to allow for such peaceful nuclear developments.

All the states in the region, save Cuba, have adhered to Tlatelolco. The strength of the commitment of Argentina, Brazil and Chile is in some doubt since none of these states have signed the ➤treaty on the Non-Proliferation of Nuclear Weapons (NPT). Moreover, since the contracting parties can repudiate the treaty after only 3 months' notice, the possibility of a 'break-out' of the Tlatelolco system by one of these 'threshold' states is always possible. Two ➤protocols to the treaty enabled states with international responsibilities for territories within the region: the United Kingdom, France the United States and the Netherlands – referred to above – to adhere to either or both Protocol I and Protocol II. There is some evidence to suggest that during the subsequent ➤Falklands crisis of 1982 the United Kingdom infringed both the spirit and the letter of the Tlatelolco system by introducing naval forces carrying nuclear weapons into the region.

The third NFZ/NWFZ agreement currently in operation is the Treaty of Rarotonga which established a South Pacific Nuclear-Free Zone in August 1985. Membership of the South Pacific Forum is a necessary condition for signing the Treaty of Rarotonga. In some respects Rarotonga seeks to improve upon Tlatelolco. It is unequivocal in banning 'peaceful nuclear explosions' (which Tlatelolco is not) and it prohibits the dumping of nuclear wastes. Conversely the Latin American treaty is ➤geopolitically more feasible because it covers large areas of land which are, in principle, susceptible to the control of the contracting parties. Rarotonga covers vast stretches of ocean and high seas which the contracting parties are unable physically or legally to control. Moreover, the attachment of the most powerful state in the South Pacific, Australia, to the ➤ANZUS agreement with the United States has meant that such existing security arrangements must necessarily weaken the commitment of any Australian government to a radical interpretation of Rarotonga. Thus the contracting parties have been unable to take a united position on the issue of visits to home ports by ships believed to be carrying nuclear weapons.

The most contentious aspect of Rarotonga has been and remains the continued use by France of its territories in the area for nuclear testing. France has tested both in the atmosphere and underground since 1966. These tests have mainly been conducted at Mururoa Atoll and there is no sign that the conclusion of the Rarotonga Treaty will produce a change of direction of this issue from France. Failure to persuade France to abandon testing within the area covered by the treaty must be regarded as the major failure of Rarotonga.

From the systemic perspective, proposals for NFZ/NWFZ can be seen as assisting the moves to check ►horizontal proliferation. This linkage was formally acknowledged in the NPT. Article Seven of that Treaty specifically encouraged the establishment of such zones. It is surely no accident of ►diplomacy that all the working examples of such zoning have been confined almost completely to the southern hemisphere. The major challenge facing supporters of such zonal agreements must be to extend the process into the North in the decades ahead.

**Nuclear power** A term used for the generation of electricity by a nuclear power plant or station. It was recognized very early in the nuclear age that the heat produced in a nuclear reactor could be converted into steam to run turbines. The world's first nuclear power station was established at Calder Hall, United Kingdom in 1956. At the time great optimism was evident about the future possibilities for nuclear power, particularly among ►attentive publics in the advanced industrial countries (►AICs). It was seen as preferable to oil on the grounds of cost and preferable to coal on the grounds of political economy. The 1956 Suez crisis had shown how easy it was to interrupt oil supplies following a crisis in the ►region.

Since the 1950s nuclear power has become an important energy source for some ►states but overall the early optimism has not been justified. Approximately 15 per cent of the world's electricity is now generated in this way. Three-quarters of this capacity is situated in the ►OECD states. In the ►Third World, the Asian newly industrialised countries (►NICs) have major power programmes, as does India. For the rest of the Third World nuclear power has proved to be too expensive an option to contemplate. The cost-saving expectations of the earlier period are now seen as to be too sanguine. Within the OECD group, France stands out as the state most dependent upon nuclear power for its energy requirements. More than two-thirds of French electricity is generated by nuclear power plants.

The developments in nuclear power referred to above have raised two ►issue areas within ►macropolitics: first, that of ►nuclear proliferation, and second, that of ►nuclear accidents. Of the two issue areas, the proliferation question shows considerable commitment to norm-acceptance and institution-building. As such it is valid to regard the nuclear proliferation concern as a ►regime – in particular with the International Atomic Energy Agency (IAEA) and the Treaty on the Non-Proliferation of Nuclear Weapons (►NPT) in mind. On the other hand, no similar stipulation could be made about nuclear accidents.

Accordingly it seems reasonable to assume that ➤international and ➤transnational cooperation on this aspect of nuclear power must soon be faced.

**Nuclear proliferation** During the ➤Cold War era in world politics the proliferation or spread of ➤nuclear weapons was regarded as one of the most significant ➤issue areas on the ➤arms control agenda. A portmanteau term, it covered two interrelated developments: ➤horizontal and ➤vertical proliferation. In truth the idea of 'spread' really only applied to the first version, the horizontal. The ➤non-proliferation treaty (NPT) which was opened for signature in July 1968 sought to address this problem in the first instance. However during the discussions on the treaty the issue of vertical proliferation became locked into the deliberations. Vertical proliferation identifies the spread of nuclear weapons ➤capabilities within the existing nuclear ➤states. In particular, following the signing of the 1968 Treaty the development of multiple independently targeted re-entry vehicles – 'MIRVs' by the United States and the former Soviet Union seemed to many to show cynical disregard for the obligations enshrined under the Sixth Article of the NPT. Many would see the conclusion of the ➤START I and the ➤START II Treaties as signs that vertical proliferation has at last been addressed by the leading nuclear players. Accordingly the attention of most arms controllers and political ➤leaderships has been redirected back to the horizontal version of the proliferation issue.

Between 1945 and 1964 horizontal proliferation proceeded steadily taking in the United States, the Soviet Union, the United Kingdom, France and China. Following the Chinese development and the conclusion of the NPT, horizontal proliferation began to occur in areas outside the Cold War confrontation zones. The ➤paradigm remains the Indo-Pakistan case. India did not sign the NPT and instead, under the so-called Sarabhai Profile, conducted a peaceful nuclear explosion (PNE) in the Rajasthan desert at Pokhran in 1974. Clandestine nuclear weapons projects were also initiated by Israel and South Africa (under the ➤apartheid regime) during these years. From the viewpoint of proponents of the NPT regime, worse was to follow after the conclusion of the ➤Persian Gulf War. In the aftermath of the violence it became clear that Iraq had had an ongoing nuclear weapons programme throughout the previous decade (1980s). Combined with a somewhat basic missile technology, Iraq was rapidly reaching the capability to threaten nuclear escalation in 1990.

➤Worst-case analysis currently views nuclear proliferation as a sub-plot to a wider drama involving the proliferation of ➤weapons of mass destruction to states and non-state actors including ➤terrorist groups. The release of a nerve gas (sarin) into the Tokyo subway system by the Aum Shinrikyo movement in March 1995 once again indicted the ➤intelligence communities of the state concerned (as some see the case with the Iraqi bomb project). Nuclear proliferation has not been removed as an agenda item in ➤international relations, following the end of the Cold and Persian Gulf ➤wars. It has been transmogrified in a new less sophisticated ➤mixed actor format in the last decade of the twentieth century.

**Nuclear umbrella** A form of ➤extended deterrence. In this instance a ➤state possessing ➤nuclear weapons ➤capability pledges to extend to another state or group of states the protection perceived to be afforded by these weapons. Usually this extension will take the form of an ➤alliance commitment. The ➤paradigm example of a nuclear umbrella situation is the NATO commitment undertaken by the United States of America after 1949. At the time the commitment was undertaken the implications had not been fully thought through either by political ➤leaderships or by intellectuals working in the ➤strategic studies tradition. When this thinking got underway it was soon evident that this particular nuclear umbrella system rested upon a deterrence relationship pure and simple without any ➤defence provision at all. The corollary was that the nuclear umbrella was no substitute for ➤conventional capabilities if a defence as well as a deterrent function was required.

**Nuclear war** Notwithstanding the use of ➤nuclear weapons against Japan in 1945, ➤war between ➤states possessing nuclear weapons has never occurred. During the ➤Cold War era nuclear thinkers, working within the ➤strategic studies tradition, argued that the threat of nuclear war could be manipulated to secure its prevention. Unfortunately, the deadly logic of ➤bipolar nuclear ➤deterrence was complicated by the ➤proliferation of nuclear weapons to states involved in significant ➤regional conflict situations – such as Israel and India. As a consequence, the ending of the Cold War has not removed the likelihood that nuclear war will occur. It is plausible to suppose that a ➤conventional conflict could become 'nuclearized' as one side initiated the use of these weapons – as happened in 1945. A variation on this scenario might be that other ➤weapons of mass destruction would be utilized and a nuclear response would follow. Alternatively, the presence of weapons of mass destruction amongst a number of ➤actors in a region could trigger the use of nuclear weapons as a policy of strategic surprise or first strike. Finally, a nuclear war might be initiated by a terrorist attack which could then precipitate a counter-thrust against states perceived to be sponsoring the ➤terrorism.

Because of the very great destructive potential of nuclear weapons, a full-scale nuclear war would be difficult to control. It is widely accepted that the use of such weapons would result in civilian casualties of pestilential proportions and the wholesale breakdown of social control. The occurrence of a nuclear war – even on a confined regional basis – would be a further erosion of both the letter and the spirit of the humanitarian principles of the laws or war. Deterrence theorists may want to argue that, as long as the threat system works, the potential illegality of nuclear war can continue to be debated. Those who survive such an event may have more pressing concerns than the legal status of the disaster which has befallen them.

**Nuclear weapons** Weapons that employ the fission/and or the fusion principles to destroy their targets. The only two nuclear weapons that have actually been used in ►war are the two ►atom bombs dropped on Japan in 1945. The development of the fusion or ►hydrogen bomb has added a whole new dimension to these types of weapons. In theory the destructive power of the fusion weapon is limitless, although in practice, the production and installation of very large weapons may be of dubious value. Nuclear weapons are now designed for all contexts from the battlefield to the intercontinental. Thus a broad, if somewhat arbitrary distinction is often made between ►strategic and ►tactical weapons. These distinctions tend to be justified upon two criteria: technical and functional. Thus technically, tactical weapons would be thought of as a single-shot systems, of a very limited range, with a small warhead. Functionally such weapons, as their name implies, would be used on or close to the battlefield in support of more ►conventional types of forces. Tactical weapons are highly mobile and thus very easy to conceal. At the other extreme strategic weapons are now usually thought of as multiple warhead, long-range systems which operate at intercontinental distances. Functionally, there is a considerable dispute about whether these strategic systems have any effective or plausible end other than to be used to threaten an adversary.

This last point is held by some commentators to be one of the most significant points of departure in thinking about strategic nuclear weapons. As Professor Glenn Snyder (1961) argued in his seminal work, nuclear weapons have led to a new emphasis upon ►deterrence at the expense of ►defence. Thus nuclear weapons, particularly of the strategic genre, can inflict great punishment upon an adversary but, unlike more traditional types of weapons systems, they cannot deny a potential enemy from inflicting great costs in retaliation. They have great offensive potential but little defensive potential, at least, so it has seemed until recently. The so-called Strategic Defence Initiative (►SDI) was an attempt to redress this imbalance between offence and defence.

This paradox has been termed the 'nuclear revolution', the term being intended to convey the radical way in which nuclear weapons have changed the system of relations, at least between those possessing them. In the language of ►game theory nuclear weapons have greatly increased the incentives to cooperate – to avoid a totally destructive war – but at the same time, have increased the incentives to manipulate this threat to force the adversary to be the one to make the necessary concession. This threat manipulation is elegantly analysed in such classic games as Chicken and the Prisoner's Dilemma.

In terms of the long history of ►international relations, therefore, nuclear weapons have profoundly altered the costs and benefits which, rationally considered, states could expect to gain or sustain from the use of ►force. Moreover, in the language of ►power analysis they appear not to be very fungible. That is to say, states possessing them seem to have difficulty in making their nuclear ►capabilities freely available to support and sustain foreign policies in areas other than those most obviously governed by nuclear ➤diplomacy. It would appear to be the ultimate paradox of nuclear weapons that they confer great potential or putative power but little effective or usable power beyond the deterrent relationship already identified. Attempts to realize the potential of nuclear weapons are often referred to as 'conventionalization', that is, the attempt to think of these weapons in terms of familiar traditional canons of strategy that would have been used prior to ➤Hiroshima. In short, to deny or overcome what was earlier called the nuclear revolution.

The end of the ➤Cold War era in world politics has left a difficult legacy for the ➤leaderships of both nuclear and non-nuclear states. Because the end of the confrontation coincided with the implosion of the Soviet Union the issue of the denuclearization of the successor states – particularly the Ukraine – has been raised. The break-up of the Soviet Union implied a ➤proliferation almost by accident rather than by design. Second, the ➤Persian Gulf War revealed the extent to which ➤pariah/rogue states could sign up to the NPT without committing themselves to its disciplines. Third the link between ➤terrorism and nuclear weapons continues to be a plausible nightmare ➤scenario.

**Nuclear winter** Often rendered as 'nuclear winter thesis' for reasons suggested below, the concept postulated that a significant and potentially catastrophic change in the climate of the earth would follow upon a large scale nuclear exchange between the ➤superpowers during the ➤Cold War era. The argument ran that the smoke and dust raised into the atmosphere by a series of nuclear explosions would obliterate the sun's rays and cause a lowering of the surface temperature of the earth. The idea of the nuclear winter was not an established and tested scientific fact but rather a series of hypotheses which had been derived from research on the impacts of conventional bombing of cities and volcanic activity, hence the qualificatory term 'thesis'. Notwithstanding its ambiguity the nuclear winter idea raised widespread concerns with both ➤attentive and ➤mass publics amongst the ➤AICs during the 1980s. Its promulgation coincided with other movements perceived as 'protests' against the level of nuclearization of the military in both America and the former Soviet Union. It was against this rising level of public concern that the Reagan Administration trimmed back its assertive ➤diplomacy and responded to the ➤Gorbachev Doctrine after 1985.

# O

## OAPEC ➤OPEC

**OAS** The Organization of American States was formed in April 1948 when twenty-one ➤states signed its Charter at Bogota, Colombia. Technically this meeting was termed the Ninth International Conference of American States and was thus part of a tradition of ➤pan-nationalism going back to the 1890s. Amendments to the Bogota Charter were made under the ➤protocols of Buenos Aires (1967) and Cartagena (1985).

At the time of writing the member states are: Antigua and Barbuda, Argentina (founder member – hereafter 'f'), Bahamas, Barbados, Belize, Bolivia (f), Brazil (f), Canada, Chile (f), Colombia (f), Costa Rica (f), Cuba (f), Commonwealth of Dominica, Dominican Republic (f), Ecuador (f), El Salvador (f), Grenada, Guatemala (f), Haiti (f), Honduras (f), Jamaica, Mexico (f), Nicaragua (f), Panama (f), Paraguay (f), Peru (f), St Kitts and Nevis, Saint Lucia, Saint Vincent and the Grenadines, Suriname, Trinidad and Tobago, United States of America (f), Uruguay (f) and Venezuela (f).

The Bogota pact attempted to stipulate certain ground rules for the future conduct of inter-American relations, most notably in its 15th and 16th Articles which explicitly prohibit external ➤intervention in the affairs of member states as well as the use of economic and political ➤coercion. These constraints were specifically aimed at the USA which had developed interventionist inclinations – particularly in Central America – after 1898. The idea that the Americas were an area of special interest for the United States went back certainly to the ➤monroe doctrine, but a more assertive gloss had been put upon this policy with the so-called Roosevelt Corollary of 1904. There followed a period of largely unfettered American interventionism which was checked – but not repudiated – by the ➤Good Neighbor policy of the 1930s.

The advent of the ➤cold war after 1945 and the clear emergence of the United States as the one unequivocal ➤superpower in the system were important situational factors which inhibited rather than enhanced the chance of the Organization working as a bastion against interventionism by the ➤hegemonial state. US inclinations could now be justified in terms of the global ➤ideological struggle with international ➤communism. The emergence of a revolutionary regime in Cuba after 1959 simply confirmed this ➤perception (and produced the ill-fated ➤bay of pigs episode). The United States saved its most contentious interventions for Central America: notably the CIA-inspired toppling of

Arbenz in 1954, the aforementioned Cuban adventure of 1961, the Dominican Republic operation of 1965, the Grenada mission of 1983, the attempted ►destabilization of Nicaragua under the aegis of the ►Reagan Doctrine and the post-Cold War apprehension of Manuel Noriega from Panama in 1989.

In retrospect Dominica proved to be a watershed as far as the OAS was concerned. Diplomatically the United States now finds itself in a minority or in isolation on key issues involving the letter and spirit of Articles 15 and 16. Thus during the ►Falklands/Malvinas crisis of 1982, the majority of OAS members supported the Argentinian position. The following year, the Organization refused to support the Grenada operation launched by the Reagan administration. The intervention in Panama found the US without a friend in the Organization – notwithstanding the earlier OAS condemnation of Noriega for failing to be bound by election results. There is no doubt that under the surface of inter-American unity a significant bifurcation exists between the United States and the other members of the Organization. The United States has tended to see OAS as a means for collectively legitimizing US policy in the region, while the Latin states see it as a means of restricting and restraining US interventionist tendencies by obtaining US adherence to the code of conduct in the Charter.

Structurally the OAS is a typical intergovernmental organization (►IGO) with a small permanent Secretariat and a ►secretary-general elected by the General Assembly for a five-year term. Increasingly in recent years the Organization has turned to ►functionalism and to encouraging regional economic cooperation between member states. At the same time its ideological commitment to democracy has increased with the end of the Cold War.

**Observer status** A quasi-legal term associated with ►conference diplomacy. It extends to neutrals and non-►state ►actors certain rights and privileges falling short of voting powers. In ►international organizations this facility is accorded to those groups or movements which the international community has informally recognized as governments-in-waiting. Recent examples include the ►PLO and SWAPO (►United Nations) and the ►ANC (►Commonwealth).

**Oceania (Pacific islands)** The Pacific islands region in the ►Pacific Basin comprises three entities: Melanesia, Polynesia and Micronesia (exclusive of Australia and New Zealand). It consists of some 10,000 islands and has a total ►population of about 7 million of which Papua New Guinea comprises half. All of these islands are former ►colonial possessions and in most cases the transition to independence was smooth (notable exceptions being Vanuatu and New Caledonia). In 1987 a military ►coup in Fiji deposed the democratically elected government and Fiji (which has a history of ►communal conflict) was suspended from the ►Commonwealth. Papua New Guinea has also been subject to internal unrest, particularly on the copper-rich island of Bougainville. Since 1985 the region has been declared a ►nuclear free-zone. France in particular has been reluctant to acknowledge this ►regime. Most of the island-states are ►microstates but following the ►UN ►law of the sea treaty in 1979 all have declared 200 ►exclusive economic zones around their shores in order to protect valuable marine and mineral resources. This has considerably enhanced their economic potential and viability as separate states.

**Oil companies** The paradigm example of a primary industry multinational corporation (►MNC) for many members of both informed and mass publics is the ►transnational oil company. The mid-twentieth century corporate structure of the oil company was first developed in the United States in the last two decades of the nineteenth century and the first decade of the twentieth. Oil companies are vertically integrated economic ►actors specifically and essentially involved in three activities: exploration for and production of crude oil, transportation and refining of the same and, finally, marketing of finished oil products. In the past this has resulted in great ►structural power accruing to the companies and enhancement of this position was possible by individual companies cooperating to maintain their market position. Consequently, free market principles have never really applied in this industry and instead oligopoly has been the typical and accepted structure.

Oil companies are divided into three groups: majors, independents and nationals. The majors are, as the term suggests, the biggest. Seven corporations are always included in this category: Standard Oil of New Jersey, Standard Oil California, Texaco, Gulf Mobil, Royal Dutch/Shell and British Petroleum. The French CFP (*Compagnie Française des Pétroles*) is also sometimes included in this grouping. The independents are the late entrants, smaller, privately owned companies such as Amoco or Occidental without the same extensive vertical integration outlined above.

The ability and willingness of these independents to employ 'spoiling' tactics by offering host states more favourable terms that the other majors was to prove a crucial variable in breaking the ►power of the latter to control the market after 1970. As a result when the ►OPEC challenge was made to wrest control from the majors the presence of the independents assisted OPEC and weakened the 'seven sisters'.

The final group of companies, the nationals, are as the term suggests those state-owned enterprises established by ►nationalization and ►expropriation. Examples here would be Kuwait Petroleum Company, Petrobras of Brazil or Petroleos de Venezuela. Nationalization of foreign-owned oil assets was first attempted in Mexico before the Second World War. The most celebrated pre-OPEC instance after 1945 was the Iranian nationalization of the UK assets in 1951. Expropriation is now accepted as an effective and legitimate method for increasing local and national participation while reducing or at least curbing the putative power of the majors and independents.

The structure of power in the oil industry is now tripolar. The majors are no longer able to set production and pricing targets as in the past. The independents are increasingly important, particularly in so-called 'downstream' operations. The nationals represent a resurgence of ►state-centred attitudes and a desire to counterbalance the archetypical ►MNC represented by the 'sisters'.

**Oil shocks** A convenient shorthand term for a number of significant changes in the supply, and therefore the price, of oil. The first shock occurred in 1973/4 when, as a result of ►OPEC/►OAPEC action, price increases and supply interruptions were coordinated. The second shock emanated from the Iranian revolution of 1979. OPEC was able to seize this opportunity to substantially raise prices over the period 1979–81. The third shock followed the abandonment by Saudi Arabia of its role of 'swing producer' within the cartel in 1985. The OPEC gains of 1979–81 were expunged and for a brief period the price plunged to 1974 levels (which in real terms meant that it fell even lower).

In all instances adaptive behaviour by other members of the oil ►regime followed in the wake of each shock. The two price rises have encouraged exploration and the development of non-OPEC reserves and the search for alternative energy sources. The events of the first shock also produced institution building, notably among the advanced industrial countries (►AICs) through the formation of the OECD-sponsored International Energy Agency (IEA). The price fall after 1985 confirmed the trend away from OPEC manipulation towards a more ►mixed actor situation. These reductions were welcomed for their deflationary effects amongst consumers, while the producers hardest hit were those with large and growing populations. Their per capita incomes were reduced accordingly.

It would be unwise to be too sanguine about the future. Further shocks– whether deliberately manipulated or accidental – cannot be ruled out. Oil will continue to play an important role in the global political economy for the future. The reserve position still favours OPEC. The world's major reserves are situated in the Middle East which continues to evince political instability. At the same time these reserves are not situated close to the main areas of economic activity. Transportation of oil will also continue to be a major potential political and ►environmental hazard. The experience of the three extant shocks is a reminder of how relative political outcomes can be – one person's shock is another's opportunity.

**Olympic Games** Contrary to popular myth, organized sport has always had an intimate link with politics. At the domestic level, the relationship has generally hinged on 'class'. For example, the idea of 'amateur' sport was an invention of Victorian Britain and was first used to distinguish those who engaged in rowing for the love of it, from the likes of sailors or fishermen who did it 'professionally'. In 1867 the UK Amateur Athletics Association's constitution specifically excluded 'mechanics, artisans or labourers', resulting in a clear division between 'gentlemen' (the moneyed, leisure classes) and 'players' (those who participated for gain). This distinction became an integral part of English political culture and by the end of the nineteenth century, via the process of ►imperialism, was carried over into the colonies established in Africa, Asia, the Americas and Australasia. Thus elitism developed on 'the playing fields of Eton' became part of the organizational structure of modern sport in many areas of the globe.

At the international level, the relationship between sport and politics, by dint of revolving around competition between nations, quickly developed into a variant of ►power politics. The Olympic Games themselves bear eloquent testimony to this.

The modern games began in Athens in 1896 – being a revival of the ancient Greek games held every four years from 776 BC to 394 BC. Although the founder, Baron Pierre de Coubertin, maintained that the purpose was to promote peaceful competition and friendship among nations, from the very first meeting the Games became a forum for political action and dispute as well as a focus for inter-►state rivalry. At the first Olympiad, for example, Irish athletes in the Great Britain squad raised the Irish tricolour instead of the Union Jack on the victory rostrum. (In 1896, of course, Ireland was not a ►sovereign state and was therefore not a member of the International Olympic Committee or IOC.) Thereafter, inter and intra-state tensions have invariably bedevilled the Games, as the following examples show: in London (1908), US athletes refused to lower their ►flag in deference to the British King during the ceremonial march-past; in Stockholm (1912) the Finnish team refused to march under the banner of Tsarist Russia; In Berlin (1936) Adolf Hitler, intending to use the Games as a demonstration of Aryan racial supremacy, was visibly furious at the unqualified success of North American black athletes; in Mexico (1968) US black athletes raised their fists in acknowledgement of 'Black Power' rather than the 'Stars and Stripes'; in Munich (1972) seventeen people died, including Israeli athletes, as a result of a Palestinian attack.

In addition to these specific incidents, the Olympic Games quickly became part of the structure of ►Cold War politics. The USSR did not compete until 1952 but thereafter successive Games were exploited by both camps for ►propaganda purposes: in 1976 Taiwan withdrew because the IOC did not recognize it as representing China; the Moscow Games of 1980 were ►boycotted by a number of Western states in protest over the Soviet invasion of ►Afghanistan; and Los Angeles (1984) suffered a similar fate in reverse. Apart from ►superpower rivalry, the other great issue that has dominated the Games in recent times has been the issue of ►apartheid: the Republic of South Africa did not compete from 1960–1994.

Further, the medal tallies achieved at the Games have invariably been viewed as 'evidence' of national superiority not merely in an ethnic sense but also with regard to rival social and economic systems. Thus, the spectacular successes of

Eastern ➤bloc athletes led to the demand, principally from the Western states, that 'professionals' be allowed to compete since the distinction between professional and amateur status is unknown in ➤communist systems. Analysis of medal tables demonstrates that success is a function of how much resources states are prepared to spend on preparation, the general rule being that the richer ➤North predominates over the poorer ➤South, despite the latter containing well over two-thirds of the world's ➤population (see *Third World Guide*, 91/2).

Despite (or perhaps because of) its overtly political character, the Olympic competition remains an important feature of inter-state affairs. Its growth parallels the growth in the ➤state-system itself. At the first modern Games thirteen states participated. Now virtually all states compete in the Games and view this participation as a vital part of their external projection and prestige.

In sum, it can be seen that sport is not, as some ➤idealists would have it, a substitute for politics. It is an integral part of it. The Olympics illustrate this *par excellence*.

According to some, the Olympic flag itself is a symbol of its link with the world of politics: five interlocking circles representing five continents in the following order of precedence and colour – on top, Europe (blue), Africa (black), and America (red); below, Asia ( yellow) and Australia (green). Although this configuration may have meant something to Baron de Coubertin's nineteenth-century mind-set, it is clearly of only marginal relevance to twentieth century categories of ➤power and dominance.

**OPEC** An acronym for the Organization of Petroleum Exporting Countries. OPEC was established in 1960 by five ➤states: Iran, Iraq, Kuwait, Saudi Arabia and Venezuela. It is an intergovernmental organization (IGO) with a small headquarters staff in Vienna headed by a ➤Secretary-General. In economic terms its intention was to establish a cartel arrangement between the commodity producers in the oil industry to maintain a price structure that would reflect the perceived interests of its member states, rather than the ➤oil companies which had set prices and production levels hitherto.

OPEC was established at a time when the ➤balance of power within the oil industry preponderantly favoured the consumers. The unilateral initiative by the Iranians to nationalize UK oil interests in 1951 had failed. During the Suez crisis of 1956–7 an attempt at concerted action to use the 'oil weapon' against the West had been foiled by the oil companies and their home governments. Rationing oil and bringing supplies in from the Americas had diffused the situation. In real terms, oil prices were declining throughout the 1950s. Economic recovery, rapidly under way in Western Europe and Japan, was considerably assisted by this cheap, non-renewable energy source.

In 1968 the OPEC issued their 'Declaratory Statement on Petroleum Policy' which identified two ➤issue areas between themselves and the oil companies.

First, OPEC wanted more control over pricing policy. The membership rejected the role of price-taker in favour of that of price-maker. Second, OPEC rejected the existing participation agreements. The traditional role of the host states, as tax collectors in respect of their oil concessions with the companies, no longer sufficed. In the same year that OPEC issued their declaration of intent, three conservative Arab states: Kuwait, Libya (prior to the revolution) and Saudi Arabia formed the Organization of Arab Petroleum Exporting Countries (►OAPEC) to shadow the multi-ethnic OPEC.

Within five years from the OPEC statement and the formation of OAPEC a series of actually discrete but potentially interrelated events occurred which served to redress the bargaining power of the oil producers and the companies in favour of the states and against the majors. In chronological order rather than order of significance, these events were as follows.

1 The revolution of September 1969 in Libya which replaced the conservative monarchy with a Revolutionary Command Council.

2 The radicalization of OAPEC following the Libyan changes and the admissions of Algeria and Iraq.

3 The increasing dependence of the advanced industrial countries (AICs) as a whole and crucially the United States within that group, upon Middle Eastern oil. This meant that any significant interruption in supply and/or significant rise in prices would have a most damaging multiplier impact upon the economies, and the polities, of these ►developed states.

4 The increasing instability of the dollar as a reserve currency and a store of value. Oil prices are quoted in dollars and any weakening or devaluation of the dollar had an adverse effect upon the dollar export earnings of the OPEC states. The dollar devaluations of 1971 and 1973 meant that the oil producers had to raise prices simply to prevent a deterioration in their earnings.

5 A further round of international violence in the unremitting ►Arab-Israeli conflict signified another attempt by the Arab states through OAPEC to use the oil weapon against those among the AICs perceived to be sympathetic towards the Israeli position. This led to an ►embargo being instituted against the West which had some effect in producing a more sympathetic attitude towards the Arab position in general and the Palestinian position in particular. It is important to remember that, although the embargo occurred at the same time as the OPEC initiative on prices (which is discussed below), from a causal perspective the two events can and should be kept separate.

OPEC's move into the centre ground as the price-maker for crude oil came in two stages. Following a successful Libyan initiative in the autumn of 1970, OPEC as a group negotiated increases with the companies at Teheran during the early months of 1971. Further increases, necessitated by the falling value of the dollar, were negotiated at Geneva a year later. Agreement was reached later that year on the question of participation which had not been covered in the talks at Tripoli, Teheran and Geneva. It was anticipated that majority participation by the host states would be achieved by 1982. Although it was not clear at the time, this agreement was the end of the first stage of OPEC's assumption of the price-maker's role. Thereafter price increases would be imposed *unilaterally* by the OPEC membership rather than bilaterally via negotiations.

Approaching the watershed events of 1973–4, OPEC had increased its membership from the founding five to include Abu Dhabi, Algeria, Dubai, Ecuador, Gabon, Indonesia, Libya, Nigeria, Qatar and Sharjah. (Abu Dhabi, Dubai and Sharjah later became the United Arab Emirates (UAE)). Within the OPEC membership two state oil-producer profiles may be discerned. First, there are those states with large oil reserves and small populations who can afford to adjust their production downwards if required without experiencing significant and unpleasant domestic consequences. Typical of this category are Saudi Arabia – often referred to as the 'swing producer' – Kuwait and the UAE. Second, there are those states such as Algeria, Iran, Iraq and Nigeria with high populations, smaller reserves per capita, and a vested interest in maximizing their production.

In October 1973 OPEC acted for the first time to raise oil prices unilaterally. A second rise was announced in December to take effect from January 1974. The domination of the Western-based oil companies and the era of cheap non-renewable energy based upon this industry was ended in less than twelve weeks. Equally rapid and sweeping changes were effected on the issue of participation. Nationalization and ➤expropriation measures have been used, not in pursuit of some collectivist commitment to socialism but rather as an expression of ➤nationalism. National-owned oil companies now play an important role in the industry as a result.

The four-fold increase in oil prices to more than eleven dollars per barrel as of January 1974 is often referred to as the ➤oil shock experienced by the world system during the 1970s. Reactions to these events were vigorous. The ➤North-South dichotomy can conveniently be used to identify these repercussions.

Among the Northern states, the United States took the initiative in re-tabling a proposal that those states in the OECD should act in concert to confront the producers' cartel with a countervailing consumers group. These ideas were subsequently to culminate in the establishment of the International Energy Agency (IEA). Although this IGO is not exclusively concerned with petroleum, this is indubitably its original rationale and main function. Indeed, other energy sources are seen as means for reducing dependency on oil and oil products. Japan and the leading Western European AICs (except France) subsequently succeeded in modifying the confrontational ➤image of the IEA and directing it towards a more cooperative ➤perception of its relations with OPEC.

The greatest economic damage from the OPEC initiative on prices was felt by the oil-importing ➤Third World. These states did not have the ➤capability to cushion the fall-out or make adjustments in the way of the AICs. These were long-term effects, however, and immediately OPEC seemed to the rest of the Third World like nemesis. Other commodity producers were encouraged to look towards the OPEC experience and form their own producer cartels. To date none have achieved the successes enjoyed by OPEC in the 1970s.

OPEC also encouraged the Third World to go onto the offensive in the ➤United Nations by presenting a whole raft of proposals and initiatives under the rubric of the ➤New International Economic Order (➤NIEO). The 1970s was officially stipulated the Second UN Development Decade and many of the ideas presented under the NIEO were familiar from the first decade and the early debates within the United Nations Conference of Trade and Development (UNCTAD) in the 1960s. It would be a mistake to attribute too much weight causally to OPEC in these matters. The demand for fundamental restructuring of the world political economy had a much longer and more diverse pedigree. What OPEC did give the Third World's leaders was a new sense of confidence in themselves and the rectitude of many of their arguments. It should be noted also that some of the leading members of the Third World movement – such as Algeria – were also influential in OPEC.

Oil prices continued to rise throughout the 1970s and then after the second oil shock they peaked during the winter of 1980–1 at three times their January 1974 level. Subsequently the price has fallen steadily towards the marker put down by OPEC after their second unilateral move. Statistically the period 1970–90 looks like a classic cyclical pattern. The rising price throughout the first part of the cycle encouraged the exploration and development of the marginal oil producing area – such as North Sea – and the content of non-OPEC oil now traded by the industry has increased accordingly. Collateral effects have been to increase interest in energy saving and alternatives to oil as an energy source. As a result OPEC's share in the industry has been almost halved since 1973–4.

The world's oil industry has entered the last decade of the century evincing many characteristics of a ➤mixed actor model. There are a number of key ➤actors but none can individually restore stability. Cooperation depends essentially upon an agreement about ground rules and if parties are pursuing mutually exclusive goals this may be impossible. OPEC's relative importance has slipped from what now looks like the peak of the mid-1970s, yet no other group exists to replace it. On the company structure, nationals now account for three-quarters of all production, replacing the pre-OPEC domination of the majors. Centrifugal tendencies would seem to be ascendant at least for the present.

**Open door** Used in a general sense it refers to policies that favour the encouragement of ➤free trade. More specifically, the Open Door doctrine refers to a series of notes issued by US Secretary of State John Hay in 1899 and 1900 which invited various governments-principally Britain, France, Germany, Italy, Japan and Russia – to adhere to the principle of equal economic opportunity in China. The notes stated that while the United States recognized the existence of ►spheres of influence in China, it did not accept that this should lead to a discrimination against US interests in respect of railway tariffs, harbour dues and other commercial matters. American foreign economic policy had for some time been seduced by the lure of the 'China market' and the Open Door policy was supported by the Committee on American Interests in China, an influential lobby group which claimed that US business interests in the potentially lucrative Chinese markets were damaged by the spheres of influence system. At the same time increasing interest was being shown in the market for Chinese souls by missionary activists in America. In an instance of what would be termed 'cultural imperialism', Christian missionaries implicitly confronted aspects of Chinese society – notably the treatment of women. In summary it is possible to identify a triangle of interests or constituencies: business, spiritual, and political within America during these years which favoured the Open Door doctrine and its ►implementation in the context of China.

The emergence of the United States as a significant ►actor in world politics dates from this period. The acquisition of the Philippines following the United States' victory over Spain in 1898 was a watershed in this process. The Open Door principle thus provided the rationale for US interests in the area and indicated a new role for the rapidly developing US naval power. US military participation in the international expedition that retook Peking from Chinese revolutionary and anti-foreign forces – known as 'Boxers' – in 1900 confirmed that US interests would be advanced or protected by the use of ►force if necessary. Theodore Roosevelt's reference to the ►region as 'America's Achilles heel' was indicative of the new ►ideological framework within which American foreign policy was now being made. The strategic, economic and spiritual lure of China remained an important twentieth-century ►definition of the situation and it helps to explain why the victory of the ►communist forces in 1949 was perceived as a 'loss' of China in America.

The term Open Door is also used in the historiography of American foreign policy. Essentially associated with the writings of William Appleman Williams and in particular the provocative 1959 publication, *The Tragedy of American Diplomacy*, the 'Open Door thesis' argues that the search to open doors was an informal ►imperialism. The history of American foreign relations shows an inherent contradiction between self professed beliefs in ►self-determination and the strongly held preference that other peoples should follow the American way. Williams argues that the Open Door's transmogrification from a policy ideal into an ideology is the key to understanding US expansionism and the informal American empire that took off at the end of the nineteenth century (however in later works Williams sought to argue that America had been expansionist from the Founding Fathers onwards). Although he disclaimed credit, Williams founded an informal 'school' of revisionist writers, exemplified by LaFeber's 1963 volume *The New Empire* and Parrini's 1969 work *Heir to Empire*.

**Operational environment** A term used in ►foreign policy analysis. 'Milieu' is sometimes substituted for 'environment' in this usage. The essence of the concept is that a distinction can be made between the perceptual world of the ►decision-maker and the unperceived context within which these essentially psychological processes take place. This latter contextual factor is what is meant by the term operational environment/milieu. The term psychological environment is reserved for the former and the symmetry is thus complete.

The idea of the operational environment was introduced into the literature by the US political geographers Harold and Margaret Sprout. In their 1956 essay, and later in their 1965 book, the idea formed part of an extended discussion of environmental factors in both geography and ►international relations. The UK academic Frankel (1963) incorporated it into his analytical text, while Brecher (1972) used the distinction in his 1970s study of foreign ►policy-making in Israel.

The operational environment can best be seen as a constraint or limitation upon what the policy-makers can or cannot achieve. Although it is not perceived as relevant at the time of decision, at the ►implementation stage its impact will be felt. If the operational environment then begins to spill into the psychological via the process of ►feedback, adaptive behaviour by the decision-making system should be possible. Adjustment and correction can be made and a closer correlation between the two milieu should be achieved. Conversely continued lack of congruence between the two environments leads to ►misperception.

**Orbiters** ►Human rights jargon for refugees unable to find a state willing to accept them. The United Nations High Commission for Refugees (UNHCR) reported an upsurge of refugees seeking political asylum in the late 1980s, particularly among Eritreans, Somalis, Sri Lankans, Kurds, Iraqis and Iranians. Many are held by local immigration authorities and subsequently sent back to their last place of call or put on forward flights to other destinations. Under the terms of its remit, ►UNHCR can award 'mandated' status to such refugees and assume responsibility for resettlement, but in practice this has proved difficult to enforce. Efforts to nominate Austria (because of its traditional hospitality and geographical location) as a central pooling point for orbiting refugees has so far failed since ►UNHCR cannot obtain the necessary international guarantees that the Austrian government demands. The term was first used in connection with the expulsion of 50,000 Ugandan Asians in 1972, but in that case the United Kingdom was ultimately responsible for resettlement. The problem became acute when immigration quotas and movement restrictions began to tighten up on a world-wide basis. ►migration, immigration

## Organization for Economic Cooperation and Development (OECD)

The OECD grew out of the ►OEEC. Both the membership and the tasks of the new body were expanded in the process. The OECD includes three significant economic ►actors excluded from the OEEC: the United States, Japan and Canada. The functions covered by the intergovernmental organization (►IGO) were similarly expanded. Development was stipulated at the outset as a central concern of the new organization. Since its inception in 1961 further task expansion into more specific ►issue areas such as multinational companies (►MNCs), ►technology transfer and relations with groups such as ►OPEC have been taken on.

The OECD was established by a convention signed by twenty states in Paris on 14 December 1960. The original signatories were: Austria, Belgium, Canada, Denmark, France, Germany (Federal Republic), Greece, Iceland, Ireland, Italy, Luxembourg, the Netherlands, Norway, Portugal, Spain, Sweden, Switzerland, Turkey, the United Kingdom and the United States. Japan joined the organization in 1964. Currently the membership includes, in addition to the above, Australia, Finland and New Zealand.

Unlike the ►European Union, the OECD was intended to be and remains an ►international rather than ►supranational organization. Provision for binding ►decision-making is extremely hedged about and in reality OECD makes recommendations to its members. Article 6 of the Convention of voting can only be interpreted as a restatement of the ►unanimity principle, albeit *sotto voce*. The Organization has a small permanent secretariat headed by a ►Secretary-General whose powers are stipulated under Articles 10 and 11.

In terms of its economic principles, the OECD may be said broadly to reflect the ideas associated with the term ►economic liberalism of the compensatory, reform or Keynesian kind. Its clear commitment in the Paris convention to such ►goals as economic growth, trade liberalization and development show this. As such it stands in opposition to ►neo-mercantilism and ►protectionism. Its expansion to include Japan in 1964 meant that all the most significant advanced industrial countries (►AICs) were among its members. The admission of Australia and New Zealand has neatly rounded this off.

Internally the OECD works to assist its member states to coordinate their policies to achieve the goals set out above. It is an invaluable source of economic and statistical information for its members and ►attentive publics. It works efficiently at the ►transgovernmental level where high officials seek ►harmonization of policy. All this presupposes a commonality of interest, of course, but it was suggested above that such a broad ideological consensus could be discerned within the Organization.

The formal equality of its members is somewhat contradicted by the existence of the so-called Group of Seven (or ►G7) states. These are: Canada, the United States, the United Kingdom, France, Germany, Italy and Japan. The political ►elites of these ►states meet periodically under the auspices of the OECD in what are popularly referred to as 'economic summits'. Although substantive issues of political economy are covered at these meetings, topics such as ➤terrorism have also concerned the leaders.

Externally, the OECD states represent a powerful interest group in global bargaining. It was felt quite appropriate, therefore, that when the perceived OPEC challenge was made the OECD members should coordinate their energy policies through the International Energy Agency (IEA). In ➤macropolitical terms this might be seen as an attempt at the restoration of ➤hegemony. Certainly with the ➤North-South dichotomy in mind, the strategy was consistent with the need to confront Southern solidarity with an equally united front. Currently the Organization is showing great interest in the newly industrialized countries (➤NICs), other middle income economies (referred to within the Organization as 'Major Developing Economies'), and the conversion of the Russian economy to capitalism. Again the ideological link with economic liberalism is apparent. Membership of the OECD for Russia and for selected major developing economies (MDEs) is now widely anticipated.

**The Organization for European Economic Cooperation (1948–61)** This regional international institution was established on 16 April 1948 when the Convention for European Economic Cooperation was signed by the foreign ministers of sixteen ➤states. The original members were: Austria, Belgium, Denmark, France, Greece, Iceland, Ireland, Italy, Luxembourg, the Netherlands, Norway, Portugal, Sweden, Switzerland, Turkey and the United Kingdom. West Germany and Spain acceded to the Convention in 1949 and 1959, respectively. The United States and Canada became associate members in 1950.

The OEEC was the institutional expression of the ➤Marshall Plan or European Recovery Programme. The Truman Administration had stipulated that US aid under this scheme would be conditional upon suitable multilateral coordination being evinced by European states and peoples. The existing United Nations Economic Commission for Europe was ignored in the process. The US leadership had also expressed the hope that the Plan would act as a catalyst for closer European cooperation and even ➤integration. In summary, therefore, the OEEC may be said to have had two broad functions: the implementation of the ERP through the years 1948–52 and the ➤implementation of agreed schemes for freeing European ➤trade and establishing closer coordination, leading to actual integration.

The principal ➤decision-making organ within the OEEC was the Council on which all member states had equal representation and equal voting rights. All obligatory decisions required ➤unanimity. Under the broad aegis of the Council there was a series of Committees, headed by the Executive Committee. The organization was staffed by an internationally recruited secretariat, headed by a ➤Secretary-General.

Given its area of discretion, the OEEC was more successful in implementing the task of superintending the ERP than in furthering integration. A major ideological division became evident from the earliest days of the OEEC between the UK position on integration and that of France. The British decision to remain outside the European Coal and Steel Community (ECSC) and to absent itself from the discussions on the formation of an EEC was substantive evidence of this division. Indeed the formation of the EEC in January 1958 drew the OEEC into a series of abortive discussions in the so-called 'Maudling Committee'. These meetings, at the behest of the United Kingdom, explored the possibility of a ➤free trade area in industrial goods.

The division within the OEEC membership between the six states in the EEC and the eleven outside meant that the Organization had contradicted its basic rationale. In January 1960 it was agreed that the original Convention had to be revised and after a period of consultation a new Convention was agreed at the end of 1960 establishing the ➤Organization for Economic Co-operation and Development (➤OECD) which came into being on 30 September 1961.

**Organization of African Unity (OAU)** The OAU was founded in 1963 at Addis Ababa to promote unity and solidarity among African ➤states. From the outset it reflected a tension between two views on solidarity: the 'Pan-Africanist' ideas of Ghana's ➤leader Kwame Nkrumah who advocated a 'United States of Africa' that would transcend colonial ➤boundaries, and the more realist view which favoured a fragmented ➤sovereign state system. The OAU Charter adopted something of a compromise in theory, but in practice Article II accepts the colonial legacy and the existing boundaries. The OAU is committed to ➤recognition of states' borders at independence and according to some critics, has thereby frozen the political map of Africa along the lines of the 'artificial' demarcations established by European cartographers and their political masters in the nineteenth century. Established at the height of the ➤Cold War, the OAU is committed to ➤non-alignment. In its history the OAU has not bridged the gap between its promise and its performance. It has been in the forefront of ➤conflict resolution, ➤settlement and ➤mediation in African disputes. However it has failed to exert sufficient moral, political, economic or military ➤coercion on recalcitrant regimes and leaders with appalling ➤human rights records. It was at the forefront of the anti-colonial and anti-➤apartheid movements, but since there is no enforcement mechanism to give its resolutions binding force, it has rarely been able to act effectively in the face of Africa's chronic problems of ➤war, political unrest and famine. In the post-Cold War period, with the accession of South Africa to full membership, there are signs of a renaissance in the pan-African idea, especially in the fields of human rights, ➤defence and economic expansion.

**Orientation** Part of the vocabulary of ➤foreign policy analysis, orientation is used in ➤international relations to describe and explain in the broadest terms how and why ➤policy-makers approach issues in the external environment. An orientation may be viewed as a frame of reference or ➤paradigm which exerts a broad directional ➤influence upon policy. This influence is generalized rather than specific and, accordingly, it may be difficult to extrapolate a ➤state's orientation from a specific policy decision. Occasions will arise when an issue is seen as a watershed, and in these circumstances policy will be made with clear implications for the orientation. Thus the United Kingdom's decision to seek full membership of the ➤European Community, first announced in the summer of 1961, implied a change in orientation away from the relationship with the United States and with the ➤Commonwealth towards its neighbours in Europe. Similarly, US membership of ➤NATO after 1949 represented an orientation towards membership of an extra-hemispheric ➤alliance which remained a US commitment for decades afterwards.

K. J. Holsti (1992) uses the idea of orientation as an explanatory variable in his standard text. He suggests that there are 'at least' three orientations: ➤isolationism, ➤non-alignment, coalition making and ➤alliance construction. Holsti's triad is extremely broad and the categories are not mutually exclusive. However, his subsequent discussion tends to substantiate the idea suggested above that orientation may be seen as a portmanteau, frame of reference term.

Orientations are important for ➤diplomats and statesman as well as for scholars. Practitioners tend to use them to establish a tradition with the past, or as a point of reference for the future. A particular political ➤leadership can be expected to imbibe these ideas as part of the socialization process and they may be invoked at times of perceived ➤crisis when a state's fundamental ➤goals and prevailing perceptions will be challenged or confirmed.

**Outer Space Treaty** Signed in 1967. Its full title is the Treaty on Principles Governing the Activities of States in the Exploration and Use of Outer Space, including the Moon and Other Celestial Bodies. The main provisions of the ➤treaty are that the contracting ➤states agree not to place weapons of mass destruction, such as ➤nuclear weapons, in space or on celestial bodies. It also envisages that the exploration and utilization of this environment should be for peaceful purposes. Some ninety states have signed the treaty since it was opened for signature on 27 January, 1967. There are no provisions in the Treaty for institutional ➤verification that the provisions are being respected, nor is there any machinery for the ➤adjudication of disputes between the parties. The latter can repudiate the Treaty after 12 months' notice.

International space law is still in its infancy but now that the monopoly position enjoyed by the USA and the former Soviet Union has been eroded by other space powers and interested parties, a more comprehensive and equitable legal ➤regime awaits development. In particular since the developing states have now entered the debate about space law, there is a growing consensus that as with laws governing other areas beyond national jurisdiction, (the high seas, the deep sea floor and ➤Antarctica) the general framework adopted should be related to the ➤Common Heritage of Mankind principle.

**Overkill** A term used with reference to the destructive capacity of ➤nuclear weapons during the ➤Cold War era. Specifically it referred to the ability to destroy one's opponent more than once. It was thus testimony to the self-generating processes of the nuclear ➤arms race and to the conservative inclination to go for a margin of safety in the acquisition of such weapons. The term was always imprecise and was often used in a polemical sense by critics of the arms race, implying thereby that the stockpiling and projected use of nuclear weapons was susceptible to diminishing returns.

The end of the Cold War, the demise of ➤communism and the implosion of the Soviet Union have changed the context within which nuclear weapons are now perceived by political ➤leaderships and ➤public opinion. The burden of ➤arms control policies are now directed towards building down nuclear systems, denuclearization of former Soviet forces and preventing ➤nuclear proliferation. deterrence remains a persistent feature of ➤international relations and ➤world politics notwithstanding. At the same time ideas about finite or ➤minimum deterrence are becoming more relevant to the post-Cold War strategic environment.

# P

**P5** ➤United Nations' shorthand for the five permanent members of the ➤Security Council. Of the fifteen members, five are 'permanent' and enjoy the right of ➤VETO. These are China, France, the United Kingdom, the United States and Russia. In a technical sense there have been seven P5s since before 25 October 1971 the Republic of China (Taiwan) and until the end of 1991 the USSR, were occupants of the Chinese and Russian seats respectively. This privileged group is made up of the 'winners' of WWII plus China (in 1945 China was not a communist state and was perceived to be within the foreign policy orbit of the USA). The provision for a special class of membership on the Security Council, the pricipal decision-making organ of the UN, was insisted upon by the USA and the USSR at the San Francisco Conference in 1945. The possession of the ➤veto was seen to be a safety valve by both parties since it could prevent a majority combination going to ➤war or resorting to punitive ➤sanctions against one or more of the others. While this implied lack of faith in the ➤collective security provisions of the Organization it also represented the realist view that if the UN was to manage international relations successfully, it would need the combined support of all the ➤great powers. Although this provision contradicts the egalitarian spirit of the Charter, its inclusion was welcomed by many as a major advance on the ineffectual decision-making arrangements contained in the Covenant of the ➤League of Nations. However, the fact that the P5 states appear to possess these privileges in perpetuity has caused great disquiet both amongst ordinary member states and theorists of international organizations anxious for development towards more representative forms of governance. The question that is increasingly posed is this: why should five states that derive their primacy from events that took place fifty years ago still hog the top table at the UN? This 'closed shop' at the functioning heart of the organization raises serious concerns about its ➤legitimacy especially amongst states of the ➤South, not one of which has permanent representation. Of course, from time to time China has portrayed itself as the voice of the ➤Third World, but this is universally regarded as an ideological rather than an authentic posture. Reform proposals relating to the P5 are of two kinds; those that severely circumscribe the use of the veto or abolish it altogether and those that propose formulae for increasing the number of permanent members to render the Security Council more representative of the world's peoples/➤states/➤regions. A popular proposal, advanced by the Commission on Global Governance (1995) is that a new class of 'standing' membership be established. In this category two should be drawn from advanced industrial countries (Japan and Germany?) and three from the 'larger developing countries' (India, Brazil, South Africa/Nigeria?). However, as one would expect there is no general consensus on this and the issue is fraught with difficulties affecting as it does questions of national honour and prestige. The original P5s virtually selected themselves (war is a long-established decision-making mechanism in interstate affairs) but fifty years on in the absence of such a clear-cut natural selection procedure the issue of reform is a delicate one, to say the least.

**Pacific Basin** A term originally used by geographers to identify the area of the earth's largest ocean. The boundaries of this ocean basin are marked off to the west by the Asian land-mass and off-shore islands and to the east by the west coast of the Americas. The ocean itself covers a greater area of the earth's surface than all of the land continents. The international dateline runs longitudinally through the Pacific, while the greatest ocean depths in the world have been recorded in its troughs. The sheer size of the ocean inhibited travel across its breadth for much of recorded time. This obstacle began to erode when Iberian explorers started to venture across and around the Basin in the fifteenth and sixteenth centuries. When these were followed later by the Dutch, British and French explorers and entrepreneurs, the Basin became increasingly penetrated by European interests and Eurocentric ➤perceptions. It was not until the twentieth century that these extra-hemispheric tendencies were challenged.

Contemporary interest in the Pacific Basin stems therefore from the political, economic and military changes that have taken place among the rimland states and the challenges that have ensued as a consequence. For the purposes of more detailed analysis a basic trichotomy can be made between the Americas, Asia and Australasia.

The Americas can be regarded as the eastern rim of the Basin. Stretching from the Bering Strait to Cape Horn, this ➤region is markedly Eurocentric. The political, economic and cultural institutions of the Americas are wholly derived from the European tradition, and indeed the history of European penetration here includes some of the worst examples of ➤colonialist ➤genocide. Within this area the USA dominates on any criteria of ➤power and ➤influence. Within the Basin *per se* the USA has enjoyed – albeit briefly – hegemonal status. So much so that the Pacific was once thought of as an 'American lake'. There are good grounds for supposing that few Americans regard this view as having much contemporary validity.

Asia stands in marked contradistinction to the Americas. Once an area of great European domination, Asian peoples have asserted themselves in the twentieth century and stamped their own identity and authority on the region. The challenge to European penetration was led by Japan, first in the military and then in the economic sphere. Japan is now the dominant economy in Asia

411

and, as such, is a significant counterweight in the Basin to the USA. As a late developing economy, Japan has evolved important indigenous characteristics which have made its growth pattern quite distinct from that of nineteenth-century America. Stipulating both economies as 'market' or 'capitalist' should not obscure the differences. In China, Asia has a continental power of great potential. In the military–security ►issue area China has challenged American ►hegemony following the defeat of Japan in 1945. China actively opposed American ►foreign policy objectives in both ►Korea and ►Vietnam. China is a significant, if second rank nuclear power, whilst ideologically Maoism and Chinese attachment to the ►Third World have taken that state's foreign policy into a quite different ►orientation from Japan.

In Australasia the Basin has a somewhat disparate area that is Eurocentric, like the Americas, but not dominated by one state ►actor. Sparsely populated and geographically isolated, Australia, New Zealand and the Pacific islands of Polynesia, Micronesia and Melanesia operate at a disadvantage in world politics in any system that is structurally determined by others. The relative decline of America within the Basin has afforded these states more opportunities for economic diversification, while the attempt to enforce a ►nuclear-free zone in the Southern Pacific is a pointer towards greater regional collaboration and cooperation.

The foregoing would seem to suggest that the Basin cannot be regarded as a single ►region within the conventional usage of that term. Indeed the increasing use of the term Asia Pacific in both ►international relations and in world politics would seem to confirm this point. Economic ►pluralism is apparent in the emergence of the ►NICs, while economic ►integration tendencies are evident in ►ASEAN, NAFTA and proposals for Asia Pacific Economic Cooperation (APEC). In comparison with Europe, Asia Pacific/Pacific Basin shows much weaker integrative tendencies. Leading economic actors like Japan have shown in their direct foreign investment decisions a strong inclination to put funds 'out of area'. In the military–security ►issue area, East Asia is often seen as a ►zone of turmoil within the Basin. The end of the ►Cold War has not produced the ►peace dividend familiar to the Europeans. Indeed ►arms sales into East Asia from outside actors and ►defence spending within the zone are buoyant. Similarly ►nuclear proliferation is more contentious than in Atlantic/Europe relations. Conventional analysis always points to North Korea in this regard but Japan and South Korea are other putative 'threshold states'. The greater imponderable remains China, in both the issue areas noted already. It is now beyond peradventure that China will become the dominant state actor in the Asia-Pacific area in the twenty-first century provided it maintains its integrity as a state actor. The end of the Cold War has seen America reducing its commitments in the zone. In this respect its conclusion turned a chapter in American foreign policy which began with the defeat in Vietnam and the redefinition of operational strategies implied in the ►Nixon Doctrine. Saving the Washington Treaty system of the 1920s American ►multilateralism has been less auspicious in the Basin than elsewhere. Given its size and complexity, the Basin exemplifies both amity and enmity – the cooperative as well as the conflictual facets of world politics.

**Pacifism** This refers to the bundle or mosaic of attitudes, ideas and opinions concerning the indictment of ➤war and the use of violence or physical ➤force on human beings. It is not a coherent political ➤ideology or doctrine. Rather two distinct but related meanings can be identified: (a) the 'absolutist' notion which rejects war and the use of physical violence under all circumstances as a means of settling conflicts; (b) the 'relativist' notion which is more discriminating and specific in its rejection of violence. It was, for example, in the second sense that International Socialists rejected the First World War but participated in the Second. Pacifism, in both its uses, is associated with non-violent resistance as a means of implementing its aims. However, in the absolutist use non-violence is a matter of principle in all circumstances. In the relativist use it is not regarded as immutable. Again the absolutist will regard the opponent with respect, good will and even love; the relativist on the hand, may be indifferent or even hostile. We may note that pacifism, in both senses, has been embedded in international thought since earliest times.

In ancient China the writings of Lao-Tzu and Confucius are said to belong to this tradition and in the western world, Judaism and Christianity, on some interpretations, question the validity of the need for violence and warfare. The Christian pacifist tradition is somewhat controversial and most commentators agree that by the fourth century the early absolutist strain of pacifism which forbade Christians joining the Roman Army began to die out. In the Middle Ages, the doctrine of the ➤Just War, while retaining some pacifist elements, saw the religious or spiritual aspect move from the personal to the public domain.

In the modern world, from the seventeenth century onwards, it became particularly associated with the Society of Friends or Quakers which established, in line with these ideas, a disarmed colony in Pennsylvania. However, it was in the nineteenth and twentieth centuries that the pacifist ideas began to spread widely, partly because of the new practice of conscription into national ➤armies. During the period when ➤states employed small professional military forces it was relatively easy for pacifists to avoid compromising their beliefs, but with the development of mass armies from the Napoleonic Wars onwards, pacifism and conscientious objection became a persistent response to conscription and an important feature of contemporary political discourse. Most pacifists since have shown a willingness to cooperate with the authorities to the extent of fulfilling non-combatant duties within the armed services, or taking positions in civilian life vacated by the conscripts.

The impact of the twentieth century on pacifism has been profound. As noted earlier, the First World War was attacked by many International Socialists using ➤Marxist/Leninist ideas about the connection between capitalism and war. Their refusal to participate in it marks their protest as being within the pacifist tradition, although in other respects this group was, and still is, highly selective in its approach to non-violence.

In the aftermath of the First World War, the development of ➤international institutions dedicated to the search for non-violent solutions to conflict and the encouragement given to moves towards ➤disarmament have family resemblance to pacifism. This period saw pacifism at its height. For example, the so-called 'Oxford Oath' when thousands pledged never to fight for King and Country was its greatest public success. One of the criticisms of the movement made later by writers in the realist tradition was that by promulgating these ideas, especially in the United Kingdom and the United States, conditions of military and psychological unpreparedness were developed which served to encourage Germany, Italy and Japan to pursue policies of aggrandizement and conquest. The movement was attacked on the grounds that, as it was blind to the ubiquity of evil and ➤power politics, it served to foster illiberalism and tyranny (see Reinhold Niebuhr, 1940).

Perhaps the most eminent twentieth-century pacifist was Mohandas K. Gandhi (1869–1948). Although Gandhi supported the United Kingdom in the First World War on the grounds that this might accelerate Indian independence, failure to achieve this led him to organize the Satyagraha (truth-force) campaigns of non-violent resistance to continued UK rule. Between 1919 and 1947 under Gandhi's leadership the Satyagraha captured the world's imagination and demonstrated that pacifist ideas were not confined to matters of individual conscience but could be successfully organized at the level of group relations. Under Gandhi, non-violent resistance and mass civil disobedience became powerful tools for the conventionally powerless in their quest to change the prevailing order. His success in gaining Indian independence in 1947 led to a reappraisal of the techniques of non-violence and a stress on planning, organization and discipline, all of which Gandhi possessed to a high degree. It was Gandhi, more than anyone, who demonstrated how civil disobedience could be utilized by the dispossessed and disaffected as an effective sanction. In so doing it became an instrument of mass political protest and direct action.

The heirs to this tradition can be identified in mass political and social protest movements in both the West and the East. Thus the American civil rights movement under Martin Luther King and the African National Congress (➤ANC) movement in South Africa in the 1950s owed a direct and acknowledged debt to Gandhi. The Solidarity movement in ➤communist Poland showed that even in non-democratic states, the techniques of civil disobedience and non-violent direct action could have significant results.

The advent of ➤nuclear weapons in 1945 and the new era of potential ➤nuclear war has not surprisingly evoked a strong response. Pacifists of both the absolutist and relativist varieties have united to oppose these developments and to propose alternatives to the nuclear ➤status quo. As a result they have become part of the peace movement, that loose confederation of interests which seeks radical change in ➤international relations. The first concern of these 'nuclear pacifists' has been to halt the ➤arms race.

Some have suggested that this can be assisted by states acting in a unilateral way – for example by ➤unilateral disarmament – others have stressed ➤bilateral and ➤multilateral measures. Many see the first as a step towards the second, in any event. Second, pacifists have sought to reduce international tensions and encourage structures and processes that would improve international cooperation. Third, they have been prominent in the encouragement of more academically orientated studies of how to encourage strategies for ➤peace rather than war. The growth of peace studies and peace research has resulted from this new emphasis. It should, of course, be understood that pacifists are not alone in championing some or all of the above trends.

It is clear that pacifism is not a uniform, coherent or formal doctrine. Its origins as well as its manifestations are diverse. It has spiritual, theological, humanitarian and utilitarian aspects. In addition, it encompasses a refusal to countenance all forms of violence. Thus, it embraces civil disobedience, peace movements, nuclear disarmament, strikes, ➤boycotts and a wide variety of alternative schemes for replacing ➤force as an arbitrator of ➤international relations. Despite this eclecticism, pacifism is a vital feature of contemporary world politics and is likely to continue to be relevant in the future.

**Pacta sunt servanda** Probably the oldest principle in international law, this asserts that ➤treaties are binding on the parties to them and must be executed in good faith. This proposition is often regarded as the basic and validating norm of the international legal ➤regime and it is not difficult to see why. Without a minimal belief that the agreements will be carried out the very existence of communal law is placed in doubt. The principle asserts that a ➤state cannot release itself from the treaty obligations at will: if this was so the already fragile structure of ➤international law would all but disintegrate. Provision is made for the termination of treaties but this itself is rule-bound. The Vienna Convention on the Law of Treaties 1969, which is the most ambitious attempt yet to codify customary treaty law, reaffirmed both the importance of the rule of *pacta sunt servanda* and the need to clarify provisions for termination. Thus Article 26 asserts: 'Every treaty in force is binding upon the parties to it and must be performed by them in good faith'. Article 42 (2) of the Convention contains the proviso that: 'The termination of a treaty, its denunciation or the withdrawal of a party, may take place only as a result of the application of the provisions of the treaty of of the present Convention.' In fact, most treaties contain provisions for termination or withdrawal either by the inclusion of a time factor or else through extenuating circumstances (➤*rebus sic stantibus*).

**Pan-nationalism** A type of ➤nationalism which is ➤transnational in its implications. This apparent paradox arises because in pan-nationalism the idea of the 'nation' as a defined group is larger than the existing political units. In other words pan-nationalism seeks to unite a number of supposedly separate units into a greater whole. Like other varieties of nationalism, pan-nationalism uses certain cohesive factors to establish this unity. Elements such as language, ➤religion, shared historical experience and physical contiguity, familiar ties to nationalists in general, are used by pan-nationalists in the same way. For example, in the case of pan-Arabism, language binds whereas religion divides. Thus a Christian Arab can aspire to the ideal by speaking Arabic as his first language and living in the Arab lands.

Because pan-nationalism cuts across ➤nation-state boundaries it should be considered closer to ➤ethnic nationalism. Both these types erode the ➤state-centricity of the nation-state matrix. Politically pan-nationalism produces ➤ori-entations and goal-seeking behaviour which seeks to unite disparate territories into larger communities. Sometimes pan-nationalism leads to ➤irredentism but this is not its most usual format. It is more likely that pan-nationalism will be conducive to ➤regionalism, regional cooperation and even ➤integration. It can also be used as a ➤foreign policy instrument by individual political ➤elites for expansionist or ➤hegemonial ends. Imperial Russia was often thought of as using pan-Slavism in the nineteenth century in order to advance Russian claims to protect the Slav-speaking peoples under the aegis of the Ottomans. Finally, pan-nationalism has been linked to ➤decolonization in both the Arab and African instances. Pan-Arabism and Pan-Africanism were part of the resistance movement against the foreign rule which culminated in the ending of formal ➤colonial control in the twentieth century.

**Para bellum** This refers to the age-old idea that 'if you want ➤peace, prepare for ➤war'. The doctrine assumes that military preparedness is a prerequisite of security and stability in a hostile environment. Notwithstanding its dubious validity in the history of ➤international relations *para bellum* has undergone a revival in strategic theory, especially in ➤deterrence and ➤worst-case scenarios. It is usually associated with ➤realism, its most extreme variation being 'the best form of defence is attack'. Beloved of militarists and ➤hawks throughout time.

**Paradigm** A term imported into ➤international relations from the philosophy of science, particularly from Kuhn (1962). A paradigm on this view is a theoretical framework, a set of hypotheses, or a model that serves as an organizing principle and as a guide for research. According to Kuhn a particular scientific era is characterized by a dominant paradigm: this constitutes 'normal science' within which the majority of scholars work. Thus the chronological development of IR as an academic discipline is often presented as a series of 'paradigm shifts' – from ➤idealism and ➤realism to ➤behaviouralism and so on – interspersed by times of 'paradigm crisis' when one dominant approach is challenged by another. These periods are often represented as 'great debates' in the discipline, as in the inter-paradigm debate occasioned by the challenge that ►critical theory posed to orthodox accounts of IR (Hoffman 1987). In contemporary IR, no single paradigm dominates. With the ending of the ►Cold War (itself a ►hegemonial paradigm) the field contains a host of competing paradigms which vie to become the accepted general theory of international relations. ►►Neorealism, neoliberalism, critical theory and postmodernism

**Pariah/Rogue States** Also referred to as 'outlaw' states, these are international state ►actors which by virtue of their political systems, ideological postures, ►leaderships or general behaviour suffer from diplomatic isolation and widespread global moral opprobrium. Their ►legitimacy is in question since they are perceived to defy established rules and conventions of ►international law and ►diplomacy and/or behavioral norms generally associated with membership of ►international society. The classic example of this type of actor is South Africa from 1948 to 1994: ►apartheid and the domestic and ►foreign policy practices it entailed clearly and unambiguously contravened established norms relating to ►human rights, ►self-determination and ►colonialism. Other states in this category might include Israel, Taiwan, North and South Korea, Syria, Iraq, Iran and Libya. However, as this list indicates, pariah status is often conferred subjectively, reflecting the interests and values of a dominant section or sections of the ►international system. Thus, for the USA, Fidel Castro's Cuba has been a pariah state since the ►revolution of 1959.

Pariahood is by no means a contemporary international phenomenon. The Ottoman Empire for example, was regarded as an outcast by European states from the Renaissance to the nineteenth century, primarily on religious grounds (►*res publica christiana*) Bolshevik Russia and the German Weimar Republic were accorded this status in the 1920s, both being excluded from membership of the ►League of Nations. However, the contemporary phenomenon is distinctive because of the problem of potential ►nuclear weapons acquisition. Given the acute and often severe ►security dilemma arising from diplomatic isolation, pariahs are strongly motivated to acquire a nuclear 'equalizer' as a last-resort deterrence against their opponents. This through the ►action-reaction dynamic, could lead to a nuclear ►domino effect where the pariah's regional rivals follow suit. As the ►Arab-Israeli dispute illustrates, this is a major problem for the establishment of a viable nuclear ►nonproliferation ►regime.

Although the terms 'rogue' and 'pariah' states are often used synonymously (along with other epithets such as 'outlaw', 'outcast' or 'crazy') it is possible to distinguish between them. Thus the term 'rogue' states properly refers to leaderships rather than political systems, peoples or nations. In particular, leaders who appear irrational, unprincipled, dishonest, troublesome, mischievous or just plain mad. Examples might include Uganda's Idi Amin and Iraq's Saddam Hussein. 'Pariah' on the other hand implies more than leadership deficiencies.

It signifies those states whose origins, legitimacy, demeanour or ideology is widely questioned by the international community. Recent examples would certainly include Rhodesia (1965–80), South Africa, Kampuchea, Taiwan and Republika Srpska. Clearly the two descriptions may overlap (Hitler's Germany for example) but the essential point of difference remains. Whereas rogue states can be altered by single bullet or ►war crimes trial, pariahs are much more durable. Their demise involves considerably more than the removal of a head of state or a dominant elite.

**Parity** Parity is equality or essential equivalence. It has two uses in ►international relations. In the context of international monetary relations it refers to the rate at which it is possible to convert a currency into gold or a national currency, such as the dollar. Under the ►gold standard parities were fixed against gold and therefore exchange rates could be calculated between national currencies, *pro rata*. Under the ►Bretton Woods system, instituted after the Second World War, parities were again fixed. This time, since the system was not a pure gold standard, they were usually quoted in dollars. The dollar parity was, of course, still quoted in gold. In effect the dollar was 'as good as gold' until the system collapsed in the 1970s.

Under the current system of floating exchange rates, parities may now be quoted in any fully convertible currency, or against a collection or 'basket' of currencies. Within important economic blocs like the ►European Union a system of fixed parities may operate. Normally in these regional arrangements a dominant currency will be the benchmark for the rest. Fixed parity regimes are usually associated with periods of relative political and economic certainty, as, for example, under a hegemonial ►actor system.

Parity is used in a second sense in IR in ►strategic studies in particular in the acquisition and control of arms. Discussions of the idea in this context lack the quantitative foundations that they have in international economics. The attempt under the ►salt processes to compare dissimilar weapons systems under the aegis of 'parity' are a case in point. Allegations that such conventions were 'fatally flawed' were made as a result.

Strategic parity also depends upon a system that is ►bipolar. Of course this bipolarity can obtain between two alliances just as well as it can be between two states. Parity, however, cannot tolerate third or fourth parties of equivalent ►capability acting as independent units because *ad hoc* coalition formation will demolish parity very quickly Indeed in tripolar or multipolar worlds seeking and maintaining parity is a recipe for great instability.

The advent and spread of ►nuclear weapons would appear to have created special problems for the application of ideas about parity. The concept is wholly dependent upon relativities. Nuclear weapons, and indeed nuclear ►deterrence, are in some respects absolutes. Their possession by states such as France does not depend upon ideas of parity for its rationale. Indeed these conceptions of

➤minimum deterrence recognize and accept the asymmetry with more powerful nuclear states and look instead to nuclear weapons as a means of overcoming their lack of parity.

**Partial test-ban treaty** This convention, properly known as the Treaty Banning Nuclear Weapons Tests in the Atmosphere, in Outer Space and Under Water, entered into force on 10 October 1963. Its prohibitions were clear from the full title of the agreement. It contained no provision for periodic review, unlike the Treaty on the Non-Proliferation of Nuclear Weapons (NPT). It contained no provision for ➤inspection and for this reason underground tests were specifically excluded. The treaty contained an escape clause. The parties, after three months' notice, could resume testing if they thought that vital interests were at stake.

The treaty failed to stop nuclear testing since China and France, which were not signatories, continued testing in the atmosphere. By implicitly sanctioning the testing of nuclear weapons underground it encouraged the process known as ➤vertical proliferation. Although almost excessively modest, the partial test-ban treaty can be seen as the first step towards the initiation of a ➤security ➤regime in nuclear weapons. This expanded later into more comprehensive ➤bilateral agreements and into ➤multilateral regimes like the NPT. Diplomatically the 1963 agreement was seen as part of the post ➤Cuban missile crisis atmosphere of ➤*détente*.

**Partisan** A partisan is an irregular soldier conducting ➤guerrilla warfare on behalf of a ➤revolutionary, ➤Marxist/Leninist cause. The term originates from the ➤civil war in the Soviet Union that followed the Bolshevik Revolution of 1917. Partisan warfare was a neglected subject after the Revolution but it was resuscitated following the German invasion of the Soviet Union in 1941. During the same time period the ➤Yugoslav resistance to the ➤Axis invasion of their territory was expressed through partisan tactics. Under the ➤leadership of Tito, the Yugoslav partisans fought off both the invading Axis and their own royalist opponents. No other ➤state-based ➤Communist party succeeded in gaining and holding power in the manner of the Yugoslav partisans. In this one instance ➤intervention by the Soviet Union, and in particular the Red Army, played no part in the outcome after 1945. The infusion of ➤nationalism with revolutionary Communism, which was a feature of the Yugoslav partisan movement, produced a genuine war of national liberation. The subsequent break with Stalin after 1948 and Yugoslavia's successful resistance to Soviet ➤economic sanctions served to strengthen this sense of uniqueness.

Partisan tactics are generally similar to the basic principles of guerrilla warfare: avoid pitched battles, trade space for time and attack the enemy where he is weakest – for instance, his lines of supply. The existence of partisan forces in an area will deter the local population from collaborating with the enemy and, if partisans can win over the 'hearts and minds', the local population can provide additional ➤intelligence about enemy dispositions as well as material support for the partisans. As the case in the former ➤Yugoslavia shows, the partisan forces may go even further in 'liberated' territories, actually establishing the infrastructure of political control. In the case of the former Soviet Union, partisans were auxiliaries operating on the fringes of the regular forces.

**Pax Americana** Literally means ➤peace imposed by America. Most scholars who use the term date the period 1941–5 as a watershed in the emergence of America to pre-eminence. Of the principal protagonists of the Second World War only the USA was neither occupied nor extensively bombed. Indeed the expansion of economic activity following American rearmament after ➤Pearl Harbor had a significant multiplier impact upon its economy. America led the way in the development of ➤nuclear power for military purposes and was the only one of the victorious Allies to have its troops in occupation of both Germany and Japan following the final surrender of the ➤axis in 1945. Post-war America was militarily a maritime and air power of awesome ➤capability. It possessed a 'blue-water' Navy without peer or rival and an offensive Air Force that destroyed Japanese cities and was the putative delivery system for its nuclear arsenal. Economically America dominated the system. The US dollar became the basis for a ➤gold exchange standard, while America developed a significant ➤aid role in the period of post-1945 reconstruction. Ideologically America appeared to symbolize the vitality of market economics and the liberality of participatory democracy. Truly the optimists who had dubbed the twentieth century the 'American Century' seemed free of the charge of hyperbole.

The incidence of the ➤Cold War produced a ➤bipolar configuration, at least in military terms after 1945. Lacking the maritime and aerial capabilities of the USA, the Soviet Union possessed in the Red Army a military instrument that dated back to earlier centuries and epochs. The Cold War stand-off therefore set the ➤geopolitical limits to the Pax Americana. As events in Hungary in 1956 and Czechoslovakia in 1968 showed, America tacitly recognized that ➤spheres of influence delimited its power. America was never called upon to use its military capability in Europe after 1945 and instead the USA provided a ➤nuclear umbrella under which those Western European states that were members of ➤NATO could shelter. Direct challenges to American leadership in Europe were publicly exemplified by ➤Gaullism, neutralism and attendant ➤peace movements.

Outside Europe the Cold War was extended to Asia following the outbreak of the ➤Korean War. As a result the ➤Truman Doctrine of 1947 became the precursor of a generalized policy of ➤containment, and America policy ➤goals became increasingly ➤globalist. The outcome of America's Korean ➤intervention – an inconclusive draw – presaged the far more disastrous ➤Vietnamese episode – a conclusive defeat. Taken together these two major ➤conventional wars of the 'post-war' period sets limits upon America's military capability and created dubiety in the minds of many about the utility of the term 'Pax Americana'.

Economically the post-1945 system set a quite different configuration from the military. In economic terms the USSR was not a significant rival to the USA, although this fact was not immediately appreciated. In particular intellectual opinion and received academic scholarship was briefly dazzled by Soviet ➤propaganda and its own intellectual sympathies into thinking of the Soviet system as some kind of appropriate model for ➤Third World ➤states to follow. Instead the most powerful economic rivals to the USA after 1945 were those states and systems that followed similar market economics. In the wealth/welfare ➤issue area it was conscious copying rather than Cold War confrontation that provided the greatest challenges to Pax Americana.

Under American domination of the ➤political economy of the post-war ➤state-system a range of economic institutions were established known collectively as the ➤Bretton Woods system. Intellectually the system was based upon the principles of ➤economic liberalism, while structurally it has been identified by ➤hegemonial stability theory functioning under American ➤leadership if not domination. The rise of the ➤European Community/European Union and Japan gave this system a ➤tripolar configuration. Institutionally the most important vehicles for the adjustment of these interests are now the ➤G7 and the ➤OECD. Rule-setting still takes place within the Bretton Woods structures – plus the WTO – and America, while exercising considerable veto power, can no longer be said to dominate.

Some have argued that the decade of the 1970s saw the beginning of the end of the Pax Americana. In the military-security field ➤parity with the former Soviet Union was recognized under the ➤salt accords, while economically the ending of the gold exchange standard in 1971 can be taken as an end-of-era decision. In the language of the hegemonial stability theorists, hegemons emerged as a result of major conflicts but hereafter it was downhill all the way as others hitched 'free rides' off the hegemon. Gilpin (1981) and Keohane (1983) seemed to provide academic validation for the view that this ineluctable process had overtaken American domination. Kennedy and the so-called ➤declinists made the ending of the Pax into a best seller.

The ending of the Cold War and the collapse of ➤communism have raised again the issue of Pax Americana. Following a somewhat simplistic logic the argument runs that with the ending of ➤bipolarity the USA enjoys a moment – however fleeting – of ➤unipolar restoration. This 'two-minus-one-equals-one' logic was enhanced by the success of the American-led coalition in the ➤Persian Gulf War. Intellectual help was at hand in the ideas of the ➤structural power theorists like Nye (1990) and Strange (1994) who saw America as the top-dog in these terms. Nye argues that whereas Britain faced new challengers to its Pax, the USA faces new challenges in the 21st century. The form these take and the responses they require may ultimately determine the scope and significance of the Pax Americana.

**Pax Britannica** Literally means ➤peace imposed by British dominance. Used correctly therefore it can only refer to that period in the recent past when Britain was the dominant ➤state in the ➤state system. Most scholars are agreed that this domination began in the wake of the defeat of France in 1815, was at its peak in the middle decades of the nineteenth century and declined thereafter. The decline was disguised for the reason that no other state immediately emerged to replace Britain as the dominant ➤actor. Eventually, the United States did, but this occurred in the 1940s after a long period when the system lacked a dominant state.

The bases of Pax Britannica were military, economic, diplomatic and intellectual. Militarily, Britain was a naval power. The possession of huge naval forces and the concomitant insistence upon the 'two-power standard' – whereby the British navy was able to cope with the combined strength of the next two ranking powers – were the outcome. As a result of this ➤power base, Britain established a vast global network of naval bases. Particularly important, in addition to the home bases, were those in the Mediterranean, in South Africa and in Singapore. Possession of such a powerful ➤capability was an important ➤deterrent to other European powers to move into areas of perceived British interest. For example, there is no doubt that, without the British navy, the ➤Monroe Doctrine would have been merely a declaratory statement of future intentions.

Economically, Pax Britannica was possible because Britain was the first state to adopt modern techniques of industrial production. The wealth created by this revolution enabled Britain to establish a commercial system of banking and foreign portfolio investment based upon the capital, London. A system of international ➤trade and payments was thereby created in the nineteenth century, a system based upon ➤interdependence in economic relations. Intellectually this was justified by a belief in ➤free trade and by the advocacy of ➤liberal ideas about individualism and free enterprise. Diplomatically, the Pax Britannica was dependent upon the European ➤balance of power working to prevent the rise of hegemonial challenges from the continent. To assist this Britain sought to advance and protect its interests either by seeking direct control over territories or through ➤spheres of influence policy. Paradoxically, the European states that sought to challenge this system, France and Russia, became in time Britain's chief allies in European politics. Intellectually this system was an affront to the liberal/individualistic and democratic/nationalistic tendencies in British political life in the nineteenth century.

Like any system based upon a single dominant actor, the Pax Britannica was dependent upon Britain maintaining that position. By the end of the nineteenth century Britain's economic domination had been lost, for good, to the United

States and Germany. The great financial strains placed upon the British economy by the First World War further exacerbated this decline. Britain's imperial system was challenged by the Boers and the Irish. Finally, the intellectual ideas of individualism and liberalism were contested by collectivist thinking, which in some manifestations manipulated or rejected parliamentary democracy altogether. ➤Hegemonial stability theory; spheres of influence

**Pax Nipponica** ➤Yen Power

**Peace** Absence of ➤war. Broadly, three conditions of world politics can be identified: war, non-war and peace. The first indicates a condition of actual hostilities whereas the third signifies either their cessation or absence. In this sense the word carries a negative connotation although popular usage, as well as ➤international law, assume it to be a positive value and indeed regard it as the prevailing or orthodox expression of inter-state relations. Accordingly, peace is simultaneously the fundamental assumption upon which international law is based as well as being both the subject and object of the institutions associated with it. The second condition, non-war (which is sometimes rendered as 'the condition of neither war nor peace'), is by no means a new one in ➤international relations, although it gained considerable impetus as a result of post-war ➤superpower postures. Thus, the ➤Cold War and the development of ideas associated with peaceful coexistence reflected a belief that while the advent of ➤nuclear weapons had rendered war as irrational as an instrument of policy, ➤conflict and competition between the major ➤actors would continue to form the framework of relations. The fact that a condition of actual ➤belligerency did not exist did not mean that, by default, peace could be said to be established. The idea of non-war is an implicit recognition that an absence of organized armed conflict is a necessary, but by no means sufficient, part of the definition of peace. In classical international theory this is often expressed in ➤Hobbesian terms: 'So the nature of War, consisteth not in actuall fighting, but in the known disposition thereto, during all the time there is no assurance to the contrary. All other time is Peace.' (*Leviathan*, ch. 13).

When accompanied by the definite article the word 'peace' is often used as a synonym for ➤treaty. For example, the treaties of Munster and Osnabruck in 1648, which are widely regarded as marking the beginnings of the modern international ➤states-system, are more commonly referred to as the Peace of ➤Westphalia. It is not unusual, either, to speak of 'peace treaties', indicating the ➤ratification of a treaty ending a particular war and distinguishing this type of international agreement from others. Associated with this kind of usage is the Latin word *pax*. This normally denotes an *imposed* settlement (usually by means of conquest or the exertion of superior power) as it did, albeit in different ways, in the following: Pax Romana (2 BC), Pax Ecclesiastica (AD 12), ➤Pax Britannica (nineteenth century) and ➤Pax Americana (post-Second World

War). In these instances, the idea of 'pacification' by a hegemonic power is central to its meaning.

Notwithstanding the difficulty of a positive definition in IR, the quest for peace has dominated international thought, if not practice, since the earliest times. According to F. H. Hinsley (1963) (whose *Power and the Pursuit of Peace* is a seminal study of the search for conditions of peace in the modern state-system), although 'the aim cannot be much less old than the practice of war', it was in the late nineteenth century that for the first time, peace proposals proliferated as a consequence of the fear of the destructive power of war rather than simply the result of its outbreak. This tendency has continued into the twentieth century when the avoidance of war and the maintenance of peace became a first-order problem of political thought rather than, as hitherto, being relegated to its outer edges. An important exception to this is Kant's *Perpetual Peace* (1795) which is widely regarded as the most coherent statement of the ►liberal or ►internationalist approach to the problem of causes of war and the mechanics of the maintenance of peace. The Kantian emphasis on republicanism, constitutionalism, law, civil liberties and judicial methods of settling disputes has been described as representing par excellence the bourgeois or Western view of the establishment of peace and as such is wholly consistent with the continuation of capitalism and its social, economic and governmental manifestations. Indeed, Kant's idea of 'a federalism of free states' as well as his commitment to universal ►human rights could conceivably be regarded as an early prototype of the charter of the ►United Nations for which 24 October, the day it was founded in 1945, is now officially designated as a Peace Day. The ►Marxist/Leninist notion of peaceful coexistence should not be seen as an endorsement of the Kantian view, since although it rules out violent conflict between the major ►states it envisages the continuation of violent conflict between classes as well as legitimizing the propagation of ►wars of national liberation and ►revolution. In this way, its focus is on 'relative' or 'comparative' peace rather than on the somewhat idealistic 'absolute' variety sought by the Kantians. ►►Pacifism; peacekeeping; peace movements; peace research

**Peace movements** ►pacifism

**Peace research** Peace research is that branch of human inquiry which seeks to improve the prospects – in the present and in the future – for the establishment of ►peace. Peace research is thus not a value-free branch of inquiry; indeed, values intrude into peace research in two distinct ways. First, those engaged in the activity ('peace researchers') are philosophically committed, a priori, to the view that peace is both attainable and desirable. Second, the peace researcher eschews strict empiricism in favour of social engineering. Thus by simply conducting peace research the goal of peace may be moved closer to realization. In this way peace research can be seen as an applied study rather than the pursuit of knowledge for its own sake.

Intellectually there are two broad approaches to the subject matter of violent ►conflict and its eradication within the peace research tradition. First, there are those who concentrate upon the psychological environment and take an essentially subjectivist view of the subject matter. This is the 'war begins in the minds of men' tradition. Emphasis is placed upon the ►perception and ►misperception and the relationship of these psychological processes to the tensions that cause violence. It is often assumed that if the parties to a conflict can be made to review their ►definition of the situation non-violent resolution is attainable. This approach tends to concentrate upon ►elites and informed publics as the crucial target populations wherein redefinitions must be effected. Sometimes, peace researchers argue, this is only possible by changing a whole ►leadership structure.

The second approach concentrates upon structures at the outset rather than as a consequence. This view may be said to look towards the ►operational environment, therefore, as the main locus of inquiry. Structures within the state actors and within the ►international system are emphasized in the belief that it is the objective conditions within systems of interaction that produce violent conflict behaviour.

Both approaches are agreed, however, that violence is only the most extreme manifestation of conflict and that a valid self-sustaining condition of peace must begin by an understanding of conflict *per se*. In this respect, at least, peace research and conflict research are interested in the same basic processes. The modern peace research tradition has been dependent upon the insights of the social scientific conflict researcher for its own resuscitation. ►►Security studies

## Peace support measures ►peacekeeping

**Peacekeeping** As a general expression peacekeeping is a third party role played by an ►actor in a violent ►conflict situation. The putative peacekeeper, by using a repertoire of behaviour, attempts to stabilize the conflict at least to the extent of eliminating violence from the relationship. Thus typically a peacekeeper will assist in the establishment of a ►truce or a cease-fire. Peace-keeping then, is an activity engaged in by military and/or civilian actors operating in a neutral and impartial way, with the consent of the parties and using force strictly in ►self-defence: the object being the cessation of violence, through such measures as supervising the withdrawal of forces, the repatriation of prisoners and perhaps the imposition of its own contingents into a 'cordon sanitaire'. In this way peacekeeping can be viewed as a function of ►diplomacy. When the ►United Nations began to develop a significant instrumental capacity for peacekeeping activities during the 1950s the then ►Secretary-General coined the phrase 'preventive diplomacy' to characterize this approach. As such, strictly speaking, it is a species of ►conflict management rather than ►conflict resolution, although the distinction between the two is often blurred. Thus 'peacemaking' or 'peace enforcement' is a different type of activity from peacekeeping but via the process of 'mission creep' the latter often merges into the former. 'Keeping the peace' does indeed imply a more active role for the peacekeeper. Here the third party may attempt to suppress or deter parties to violence from continuing with their behaviour. In this activist usage peacekeeping is more akin to law enforcement and less to diplomacy as traditionally conceived. These two 'ideal types' – one diplomatic the other more a compellent or a deterrent – as indicated often merge into one as the situation develops. Part of the controversy surrounding the UN operation in the Congo after 1960 was that *model one* peacekeeping shaded off into *model two* when the operation was faced with the ►secession of Katanga. Peacekeeping therefore suffers from a great deal of conceptual and operational confusion. In the lexicon of the UN it is part of a bundle of activities referred to as 'peace support measures'. These include ►collective security, preventative diplomacy, peacemaking, peace enforcing, peacebuilding, ►humanitarian intervention, ►crisis management, conflict management and conflict resolution. It is important to note though that 'peacekeeping' is properly concerned only with the ending or abating a conflict. This is its true and original designation.

Peacekeeping, symbolized by the blue helmets worn by the peacekeepers is now virtually synonymous with the UN. However, the strict legal validity of peacekeeping is doubtful as it is not mentioned at all in the UN Charter. It was invented by Canadian Minister of Foreign Affairs, Lester Pearson and the UN Secretary-General Dag Hammarskjöld in response to the need to supervise troop withdrawals from Suez in 1956. Hammarskjöld famously quipped that peacekeeping was Chapter 6½ of the Charter, falling between the pacific resolution of disputes (Chapter 6) and coercive measures to deal with acts of aggression (Chapter 7). But despite being a complete innovation in respect of the UN Charter, peacekeeping has become the most common popular image of the UN. Since 1988 there has been an extraordinary growth in the number and size of UN peacekeeping operations. In the period 1945–87, the UN undertook 13 operations; from 1988 to 1997, 28 new operations were mounted. Among them were missions dealing with such long-standing disputes as those in Cambodia, Namibia, Angola, and parts of Central America. In addition, the end of the ►Cold War was accompanied by new crises in Liberia, Rwanda, ►Yugoslavia, Somalia and the Persian Gulf region. This meant that the ►scope of peacekeeping has increased along with its ►domain. Since 1988 the UN has been forced to address what are primarily intra-state rather than inter-state conflicts. The increased incidence of ►complex emergencies and ►failed nation-states has led to new operational tasks for UN peacekeepers, including conducting elections, civil administration, repatriation of ►refugees and protecting humanitarian convoys. Indeed, for some observers, the UN had travelled so far from the original conception of peacekeeping by the early 1990s that this function was now in danger of becoming an '►imperial' rather than an impartial one.

The question of whether peacekeeping is adequate to meet the problems generated by ➤communal conflicts, ➤civil wars, ➤complex emergencies and ➤failed or collapsing states, is hotly debated. According to some, peacekeeping within states rather than between them is inherently dangerous: the pressures towards mission creep are likely to prove irresistible, particularly on humanitarian grounds (e.g. to prevent ➤genocide or ➤ethnic cleansing). The argument is that 'wider' or more 'robust' peacekeeping is likely to be counterproductive: in these situations the UN becomes part of the problem rather than part of the solution. (e.g. Bosnia and Somalia). The international community has yet to resolve the problems, conceptual, operational, and financial of peacekeeping in the post-Cold War period. Doctrinally the key issue is this: are peacekeepers intended to *create* the peace they are charged to keep? In 1992 Secretary-General Boutros-Ghali entered this grey area with his 'Agenda for Peace' where he defined peacekeeping as 'the deployment of a UN presence in the field, *hitherto* with the consent of all parties concerned' (para 20). Here, the Secretary-General clearly implied that the notion of 'consent' should be an elastic one. He went on to argue that in these new conflict situations, it might sometimes be necessary for the UN to try to *restore* a cease-fire. Thus he was calling for a new conception of peacekeeping; one that goes for beyond the traditional consensual impartial and interpositionary role of monitoring a cease-fire or controlling a buffer zone.

The debate about peacekeeping as a sub-species of peace support measures continues. The traditionalists argue that peacekeeping should remain within the limited remit established in the 1950s. Others argue that it must traverse to no man's land between a defensive posture and a warfighting one. They argue that traditional peacekeeping is inherently ➤status quo orientated, therefore it cannot address or contribute to any lasting political solutions to the problems of the post-Cold War era. The humiliations experienced in Bosnia (where the UN eventually handed over to ➤NATO) and Somalia (where the peacekeepers were forced to retreat) are powerful arguments for a re-evaluation of the aims and objectives of peacekeeping. In terms of continuing UN credibility in the ➤New World Order then, the strategic and doctrinal requirements of peacekeeping urgently need to be reformulated. Additionally, the fictional Chapter 6½ needs to be re-written and incorporated fully into the main body of the UN Charter. Otherwise, the confusion will grow and the humiliations continue. ➤Humanitarian intervention

**Pearl Harbor** The Japanese attack on the US naval base at Pearl Harbor, Hawaii, on 7 December 1941 ensured that the United States entered the Second World War on the Allied side. The term has come to symbolize, at least in Western eyes, both the inherently treacherous nature of ➤international relations and the constant need to guard against the surprise attack. The slogan 'no more Pearl Harbor's' for the post-war US ➤defence establishment was at least as effective in increasing global US military expenditure and commitments as the cry 'no more ➤Vietnams' in the 1970s was in curtailing them. In the two-hour raid the Japanese sank seven battleships, killed 2,403 citizens, wounded another 1,178 and destroyed or put out of commission most of the US air-strike force parked on the runways of the island of Oahu. As a consequence of what Roosevelt called this 'dastardly' attack which would live on in history as 'a day of infamy', the United States declared ➤war on Japan. Three days later Hitler honoured his pledge under the Tripartite Pact (signed by Germany, Italy and Japan on 27 September 1937) and joined the fray against the United States. This gave the Roosevelt Administration justification for converting an informal ➤alliance with the United Kingdom into a formal one, and led indirectly to his 'Europe first' policy – that the European war would take precedence over the war in the Pacific.

Since 1941 historians and ➤decision-making analysts have disagreed both concerning the reasons for the high-risk Japanese attack and concerning possible US presidential complicity in it. Regarding Japanese motivation, most concede that domestic factors, especially the rising influence of ➤militarism within Japanese society in the 1930s, had a decisive effect on the growing militancy of Japanese ➤foreign policy. However, it has been suggested that regardless of domestic factors, developments in the international economic and strategic order meant that Japan as a late industrializer had to accelerate the process of acquiring cheap resources of raw materials and guaranteed markets in a ➤region already crowded with established imperial actors. Thus, Japanese fears of an 'ABCD' (American, British, Chinese and Dutch) ➤encirclement led directly to Pearl Harbor. With regard to possible US high-level complicity, revisionist historians argue that since Japanese codes had been deciphered long before the event, the US government in effect encouraged the Japanese to attack in the interests of manoeuvring the United States into the European war. A variant of this is that it was the United Kingdom which had prior knowledge of the attack and that UK decision-makers had deliberately not informed Washington of it in the sure hope that, as a consequence, the United States would be forced to join them in their battle for survival against Hitler's Germany. Other analysts, especially Roosevelt's biographers, have tended to deny these charges and allege that the attack contained all the elements of 'surprise'. In an innovative and influential study, Wohlstetter (1962) clears Roosevelt of complicity but argues that the US decision-makers, inundated with a wealth of information from the decoded Japanese messages, failed to identify the 'signals' (the worthwhile information) from the general 'noise' (the mass of conflicting reports) and were therefore caught cold.

**Penetrated state**  Term associated particularly with James N. Rosenau (1969b) and is a corrective to the traditional concepts of the 'territoriality' and 'imperme-ability' of the ➤sovereign state. The separation of domestic and ➤foreign politics of a state, for so long a cardinal feature of the classical approach to ➤international relations, is now regarded as naïve and myopic since few, if any, states are completely shut off either from the outside world or from domestic consequences of their own foreign relations. All states are to some extent 'penetrated' by actors from the outside. This may range from overt military support for a particular ➤regime (e.g. the United States and the Philippines) or it may refer simply to the activities of foreign lobbyists on behalf of governments or multinational firms. In either case, the virginal purity of the traditional 'hard-shelled' state has been compromised.

**People's War** A term used in the analysis of ➤revolution which is specifically derived from the experience in China under the ➤leadership of Mao Tse-tung (Zedong). It would be hard to dispute the contention that the defeat of the Japanese invaders and the overthrown of the Kuomintang by the Chinese ➤communists ranks as one of the ➤paradigm examples of revolutionary change. The very essence of this significance stems from the appreciation that the Chinese actually *changed* the paradigm in effecting their revolution. The Chinese revolution has often been referred to as the 'countryside' version, in contradistinction with the Soviet example. This is because, in the former case, the peasants were actively mobilized in support of the Communist leadership and the programme of economic and social change. This was both possible and desirable because the instrument of change was the campaign of ➤guerrilla warfare conducted by Mao and his followers against the incumbent regime and the Japanese invaders. The successful conduct of this campaign required a supportive population, hence the emphasis upon the need to mobilize the countryside. Traditional ➤Marxist/Leninist dogma had been based on the assumption that it would be among the urban proletariat that the main engine of change would come. The Chinese revolution appeared to suggest that an alternative paradigm was viable.

The Chinese Communists were able to broaden the nature of their appeal after the Japanese invasion and claim to represent the only effective vehicle for the expulsion of the interventionist forces and the achievement of national liberation. This represented the fusion of the class struggle with the national struggle. With the increasingly open identification of the United States with the Kuomintang position, the Communists were able to claim that their struggle was against the resurgence of ➤imperialism and ➤colonialism from the West as well as from fellow Asians.

People's War is thus a sort of ideological shorthand for this historical experience. In addition it came to be regarded as a model for others to follow, or at least to refer to in their own revolutionary endeavours. For scholars of international and comparative politics it became a set of analytical benchmarks which could be used to compare and contrast. For the forces of the ➤status quo, People's War became a phenomenon to be resisted and, if possible, defeated. In order to achieve this goal understanding it was the first prerequisite.

The decade of the 1960s became the decade of People's War because of two factors: the ➤Vietnam war, or the second Indo-China War, and the Cultural Revolution in China. The latter led to the vigorous assertion by, in particular Mao and Lin Piao, that the concept was universally valid where all subject peoples, particularly in the ➤Third World, were attempting revolutionary changes against incumbent regimes supported by the West. The former, the Vietnam War, is widely regarded as a test case of People's War. In retrospect, most analysts are agreed that it diverges from the Chinese model in a number of important respects. Vietnam was a much more 'internationalized' conflict than the Chinese revolution. In particular through the phenomenon of ➤intervention outside parties were drawn in to give aid and assistance, and even to act as allies. Second, more attention was perhaps paid by the Vietnamese to the potentialities for psychological warfare and the need to erode the adversaries' will to fight. In particular, a distinctive feature of the Vietnamese version of the People's War was the high profile initiative which would publicize the conflict and, perhaps by achieving strategic surprise, prove to be militarily damaging or even decisive. Such an initiative was the Tet Offensive of 1968. The Vietnam War was not a vindication of guerrilla warfare seen as a means of overthrowing an incumbent regime; after Tet, the fighting became increasingly conducted between ➤conventional units. Rather, Vietnam appears as a vindication of the theory of ➤protracted war which is often seen by strategists as having a family resemblance to guerrilla war.

Like so much of the language of political discourse, People's War begs the important question: to whom does the term 'People' apply? Politicians, for their own purposes, might wish to claim that almost any insurgency that appeared to have a popular basis was, therefore, a 'people's' conflict. An historically circumscribed alternative has been offered here. People's War – with capitals – is another way of talking about the Chinese Revolution and certain stipulated successors and emulators. ➤➤Maoism

**Perception** Perception is a basic psychological process whereby individuals relate to their environment. A distinction is usually made in psychology between the perception of things and the perception of people, the latter process being referred to as 'social perception'. It is a fundamental characteristic of the act of perceiving that selection is involved. Certain stimuli are noted and others ignored. A variety of factors will affect this discrimination including the individual's past experiences, his current physical and psychological state and the frequency and familiarity with which cognate experiences have occurred. How people perceive each other clearly has a considerable bearing upon how their behaviour towards each other is determined.

Taking account of perceptions in world politics involves the study of behaviour at the individual ➤level of analysis. In particular, the investigation of

➤decision-making and how key 'players' perceive their situation will form a large part of the analysis. As such, perception is the basic psychic process that leads to the ➤definition of the situation. All perceptions in decision-making are conditional assumptions or inferences about another person or persons. These inferences will seek to attribute certain intentions to the other and, upon that basis, certain responses will be made. Perception of another's intentions is a difficult procedure because there are states of mind which can only be inferred by indirect evidence.

Psychologists argue that individuals seek to maintain cognitive consistency or balance and that, accordingly, person-perception tends to assimilate new information into existing ➤images. Jervis (1976), in his work on the subject of perception and ➤misperception, argues that this tendency to seek consistency in perceiving is inevitable: 'intelligent decision-making in any sphere is impossible unless significant amounts of information are assimilated to pre-existing beliefs' (p. 145). The policy maker in world politics faces potential inundation by the complexities of the environments in which policy is made if this kind of perceptual screening is not effected. These pre-existing beliefs will be both immediate, contingent concerns ('evoked sets') as well as more deeply held attitudes and images.

The study of perceptions in world politics has been wholly advanced under the ➤social science approach in the post-1945 period. As Jervis points out in the opening chapter of his book such approaches depend upon recognition of the decision-making level of analysis as relevant. A complete picture of why particular decisions were taken requires scholarly reconstruction which will necessarily have to take account of how those authoritatively placed to take decisions 'saw' the situation. At the same time a total commitment to subjective phenomenalism should be avoided. As the distinction between psychological and ➤operational environments suggests, there is a world beyond the perceptual horizon.

**Permanent Court of Arbitration** This was set up by the Hague Convention for the Pacific Settlement of International Disputes in 1899 and revised in 1907. The name is misleading since it is not really a permanent or fixed court. It is rather a panel of jurists who are ready to act as arbitrators in particular cases referred to them. Each ➤state party to the convention nominates four persons to serve and each party to a dispute selects two of these, only one of whom may be a national. The four arbitrators chosen then select one more from the panel to act as an umpire. The Permanent Court of Arbitration, because it is not a standing court and because its composition varies from case to case, has been criticized since for these reasons it cannot develop a coherent body of case-law. However, its value, like most international institutions, lies in its very existence; its provision of a machinery to settle disputes should the parties desire. Its most active period was between 1900 and 1932 when twenty cases were decided, but since then its use has been limited and it has been largely superseded by the ➤permanent court of international justice (1921) and its successor the ➤international court of justice (1946).

**Permanent Court of International Justice (PCIJ)** This was formed under the auspices of the ➤League of Nations in 1921. It was the first systematic attempt to create a world court to provide judicial settlement of international disputes, and unlike the ➤permanent court of arbitration its judges were chosen not by the parties of the dispute but were elected by the League. The PCIJ was superseded in 1946 by the ➤international court of justice which has virtually the same statute and jurisdiction.

**Persian Gulf War** The proximate cause of the Persian Gulf War of 1991 was the Iraqi ➤annexation of Kuwait from 2 August 1990 to 28 February 1991 and *inter alia* the proclamation of 28 August 1990 that Kuwait was henceforth Iraq's 19th province. A coalition of interests acting under the aegis of the ➤United Nations and with the ➤leadership of the United States proclaimed the initiatives to be a threat to international ➤peace and ➤security. The collective response known in America as 'Desert Shield/Desert Storm' resulted in the expulsion of Iraqi forces from Kuwait in 1991 and the imposition upon the defeated Iraqi state of a highly intrusive monitoring ➤regime regarding their weapons acquisition ➤capabilities.

As a definable ➤region in world politics, the Middle East reflects four tendencies which although not strictly causal are certainly contributory factors in the ➤conflict: the region is a significant ➤importer of arms, the region is a significant ➤exporter of ➤oil, the region shows a strong propensity towards authoritarian political systems and the region was deeply penetrated by ➤imperialist interests and ➤spheres of interest politics. During the ➤Cold War era the region was bifurcated between the ➤superpowers and their ➤blocs. Conversely the events following ➤nineteen eighty-nine reduced the likelihood of competitive ally-seeking and increased the potentiality for United States/Soviet cooperation as will be argued below. Relations between Iraq and Kuwait had been damaged following the Iran-Iraq War of 1980–88 (known as the Gulf War). Iraq's quarrel with Kuwait centred around the issue of war debts owed by Iraq to Kuwait and the conflicting oil-pricing and quota policies of the two OPEC members.

It is clear in retrospect that the Iraqi leadership under Saddam Hussein miscalculated badly in pursuing this policy. In particular they ➤misperceived American intentions in the run-up to the August events. In mitigation for Iraqi ➤diplomacy there is evidence that America was rather equivocal in its dealings with the Ba'thist regime. In particular, the so-called 'green light' interview between Saddam Hussein and April Glaspie, the US Ambassador in Baghdad, seems to have left the Iraqis thinking that America might seek ➤appeasement rather than ➤brinkmanship in the dispute with Kuwait. Following the Iraqi invasion the Bush Administration moved swiftly to bolster the Saudi regime. 'Operation Desert Shield' was rapidly mounted to effect a ►deterrent posture should Iraqi ►revisionism spill over into Saudi Arabia itself. Thereafter the USA pursued a determined ►multilateralist counter-offensive at the head of a coalition of some 35 states. An immediate response was forthcoming through the United Nations in the form of comprehensive, mandatory ►economic sanctions. A build-up of forces in the area was also undertaken and by November 1990 this had assumed sufficient complexity to give Desert Shield an offensive capability. Following the expiry of the ►ultimatum in UN Resolution 678, which authorized the use of force if occupation continued, 'Desert Shield' became 'Desert Storm' and after an intensive air campaign a short (approximately 100-hour) land offensive dislodged the Iraqis from Kuwait.

The Persian Gulf War is significant for a number of reasons besides the successful liberation of Kuwait. First, although the war was prosecuted within the remit of twelve United Nations ►Security Council resolutions it depended upon the American military capability and diplomatic leadership. This point was seized upon after the event by the so-called ►renewalist school, to suggest that announcements of American decline were premature. Second, for the first time since the Suez ►crisis of 1956, the United States and the Soviet Union stood together on a major international issue. Third, for the first time since the ►Korean War, the ►collective security provisions (Article VII) of the United Nations were successfully brought into play in the use of ►force. The precise terms of the twelve resolutions circumscribed the ►scope of coalition action, whilst setting out their aims and objectives. The Security Council legitimized the action and the enabling vehicle for international consensus-building. Fourth, Saddam's incursion in Kuwait served to unite the international community in condemnation and to cut across traditional and established alignments in the area. Syria dropped its anti-Western stance in favour of support for the coalition, Turkey became actively involved in regional affairs, Iran remained positively ►neutral whilst Israel displayed uncharacteristic restraint in the face of Iraqi attempts at escalation. Fifth, the Persian Gulf War was the occasion for a revival of public debate concerning the conditions necessary to justify the prosecution of a ►Just war. A general consensus emerged in the West that, although there was an overlap between ►national interest (access to oil) and international interest (to punish aggression), the war and the limited, though devastating, manner in which it was prosecuted conformed with established principles.

The US response to the invasion of Kuwait was necessary to the success of the venture, but it was by no means sufficient. Washington relied throughout on political and financial support from other sections of the international community. Burden-sharing was important from the outset, and non-combatant states such as Germany and Japan made large financial contributions. This awareness of collective responsibility, albeit under American leadership, combined with superpower cooperation, led President Bush to proclaim that the aftermath of the War heralded the beginning of a ➤New World Order predicated on the notions of collective security and a tutored ➤international order. At the regional diplomatic level new efforts were directed at arriving at a settlement (as opposed to a resolution) of the long-running ➤Arab-Israeli conflict. Despite President Bush's claims, the War did not eradicate the ➤Vietnam syndrome from American mind-sets. Nor did it resolve the debate within American foreign policy making about the locus of the 'War Powers' of the Executive and the Legislature.

With regard to Iraq itself, the devastation wrought by high-tech precision bombing on its civil society once more highlights the indifference of modern weaponry to traditional distinctions between 'combatants' and 'non-combatants'. Whereas there exists an international legal ➤regime pertaining to entering into a state of war (➤*jus ad bellum*) and conduct in war (➤*jus in bello*), as yet, despite proclamations of a new world order, in the absence of a specific ➤peace treaty there is no legal duty, or shared sense of obligation, towards the defeated peoples after the belligerency has ceased. The Fourth ➤Geneva Convention, in theory at least, serves to protect the civilian population while war is fought, but is silent in relation to its aftermath. The plight of the Kurds in particular has raised the question of whether Security Council Resolutions limiting the objectives of the action to a reversal of the invasion were counter-productive. The continued force of the doctrine of ➤non-intervention in the internal affairs of ➤sovereign states can only serve to exacerbate the plight of beleaguered ethnic minorities such as the Kurdish people. Until and unless the new world order confronts the thorny issue of ➤humanitarian intervention, the ground rules of international life established at ➤Westphalia in 1648 will continue to penalize the dispossessed and the innocent victims of inter- and intra-state violence.

**Persona non grata** Term normally associated with ➤diplomacy whereby a receiving ➤state declares that it is unwilling to accept or receive a diplomatic representative of another state. This may occur at the initial stage of appointment (*agréation*) or more usually it may occur some time after the granting of *persona grata* (acceptability) when the diplomat concerned has violated the rules of normal diplomatic behaviour. The declaration of *persona non grata* represents a serious diplomatic initiative since it involves expulsion or at least a request that the diplomat be recalled to his country of origin. Tit-for-tat expulsions are not an uncommon feature of contemporary ➤international relation.

**Pivotal states** A ➤geopolitical term applied to those (conventionally periph-eral) states whose fate may well determine ➤regional and/or international stability. The maritime equivalent would be ➤choke points. The classic nineteenth-century examples are Turkey, simultaneously 'the sick man of Europe' and the epicentre of Russo-British imperial rivalry over respective ➤spheres of influence in the Eastern Mediterranean, and Belgium. Regarding the latter, Napoleon, who had good reason to be well versed in these matters, described Antwerp as 'a pistol levelled at the very heart of England'. In recognition of this, after separation from Holland in 1830, the new Belgian state was granted permanent ►neutrality status and thereafter (until 1945) its continued territorial integrity was considered a vital ►national interest by Britain. During the ►Cold War with the widespread acceptance of the ►Domino theory, virtually all peripheral states were potentially 'pivotal' since the 'fall' or 'loss' of one necessarily involved the collapse of others resulting in a threat to international stability. According to some recent commentators (Chase, Hill and Kennedy, 1996) in the post-Cold War era the new, holistic ►security agenda with its emphasis on non-military/diplomatic threats such as overpopulation, environmental degradation, ethnic conflict, ►migration, ►aids, hunger, poverty, ►narcotics etc., necessitates a 'new pivotal strategy' for the USA. Identifying these states then becomes an important policy planning task for Washington policy-makers. Identification criteria are notoriously fuzzy and subjective but at least four sets of factors are crucial; a large population, an important geographical location, developing status as a ►big emerging market and of course, the capacity to affect regional and international stability. From the US strategic perspective the following might therefore be considered pivotal; *Central* and *South America* – Mexico and Brazil, *Africa* – Algeria, Egypt and South Africa, *Near* and *Far East* – Turkey, India and Pakistan, *Asia-Pacific* – Indonesia and Taiwan. While these states may be pivotal from the American perspective, Russian, Chinese, Japanese and European policy makers would no doubt draw up a different list of candidates for inclusion.

**PLO** An abbreviation of the Palestine Liberation Organization. The PLO was formed in 1964 following an agreement in principle the previous year at an Arab League Summit. The Charter of the Organization adopted at the time envisaged that the liberation of Palestine from Israeli occupation would be achieved in conjunction with the Arab states of the Middle East and North Africa rather than by independent action. This strategy, which might appropriately be called 'Pan-Arabism', was later to be challenged and rejected following the comprehensive defeat of a number of Arab ►front line states following the June 1967 war with Israel. The original leadership of the PLO under Ahmed Shukairy was removed in 1967 and a more radical and independent (independent of the Arab states) group of leaders emerged thereafter to take control of the Organization. As a result the PLO underwent a fundamental change of ►orientation.

The PLO became in the late 1960s what it remains to date – an umbrella organization for a variety of resistance movements to the ►status quo in the Middle East. Indeed some of the more radical elements in the PLO, such as George Habash's Popular Front for the Liberation of Palestine (PFLP) wanted to see radical changes in some of the Arab states – notably Jordan – as well as in the territory known diplomatically as Palestine since 1917. The principal resistance movement in the PLO is El Fatah (the Palestine National Liberation Movement). El Fatah was formed under the leadership of Yasser Arafat to pursue a policy of 'liberation' via Palestinian ➤self-help rather than by relying upon Pan-Arabism to achieve Palestinian demands in its 'coat-tails.' In 1965 Fatah established a military wing – Asifah – and began *fedayeen* (commando) operations against Israel. At the fifth session of the Palestine National Council (PNC) at Cairo in February 1969 Fatah gained majority control of the PLO and Arafat became Chairman of the Executive Committee.

Since the eclipse of the old guard and the take-over of the Organization by the *fedayeen* groups the PLO has enjoyed mixed fortunes. As a ➤guerrilla warfare operation the Organization has never had more than a nuisance value. High profile hijack operations, armed incursions into Israel proper and/or the occupied territories on the West Bank and the Gaza Strip, and out-and-out ➤terrorism have been the typical methods of operation. The PLO faces a powerful adversary in Israel; the occupants of the West Bank have not been able to provide the supportive infrastructure for guerrilla operations while the Arab states have not always proved reliable, the crushing of the PLO in Jordan in September 1970 and the ➤Camp David negotiations between Egypt and Israel being instances where ➤national interest was put before support for the PLO. Militarily the Organization's greatest defeat came after the 1982 Israeli incursion into the Lebanon, which was intended to remove PLO bases from Lebanese territory and the Organization's influence upon Lebanese politics.

Diplomatically the PLO under Arafat's leadership has worked assiduously to compensate for its military track record. This diplomacy has had mixed results. On occasions the Chairman has shown a willingness to 'trim' to prevailing circumstances and, as ever, a flair for publicity. Recently his touch has looked less assured. ➤recognition of the PLO as a legitimate party to any ➤settlement ➤resolution of the ➤Arab-Israeli conflict has been steadily achieved since 1969. The Rabat summit of Arab states in October 1974 recognized the Organization as the sole legitimate representative of the Palestinian people, effectively ending any Jordanian hopes in that direction. During the autumn of 1974 the UN ➤General Assembly accepted the principle of Palestinian ➤self-determination and national ➤independence (Resolution 3236) and admitted the Organization to the UN on ➤observer status (Resolution 3237). In 1980 at the Venice summit of the ➤European Community leaders, the Palestinians were recognized as parties. In the closing weeks of the Reagan Presidency the United States moved towards a dialogue on an official basis following Arafat's declaration that the PLO accepted the right of Israel to exist within secure borders. In effect the PLO became committed to a 'two-state' solution to the conflict (as set out in UN Resolution 242) and by the implication it renounced the position set out in its Charter on the continuation of the state of Israel.

This 'two-state' position was legitimized in September 1993 in the Israeli-Palestine Declaration of Principles. This DOP agreement in effect ➤implemented the 'land-for-peace' formula by a phased Israeli withdrawal from the Gaza and selected areas of the West bank in return for Palestinian recognition of Israel. Following the initial withdrawal from Gaza and Jericho in June 1994 the Palestinian authority (PA) was created to administer these territories. Although Israeli political ➤leaders have eschewed the use of the term 'State' to identify the lands under PA ➤autonomy, ➤de facto this is now the position. The major issues identified in the DOP but still unresolved include the status of Jewish settlements in areas outside the 1948 borders and the status of Jerusalem. Israeli/PA relations continue to be fraught with destabilizing possibilities particularly over the vexed question of ➤security. At the same time these relations have become caught up with domestic party politics in Israel and with radical Islam. ➤Hawks can be found on both sides setting the parameters for the main protagonists to operate within. The DOP and its subsequent hesitant implementation exemplifies ➤conflict settlement rather than ➤conflict resolution.

It is clear that the achievements of the PLO have been realized at some cost, both personally and diplomatically. In effect the DOP agreement means that the leading representatives of the Palestinian Diaspora now accept the partition of the former mandate territory of Palestine – a solution proposed by the UN in 1947 and rejected by the Arab side at the time. The PA enjoys considerable autonomy even within the existing parameters. This authority has not always been exercised wisely since 1994. Indeed Arafat has been variously accused of authoritarianism within the PA and cronyism within the leadership. On the Israeli side the need is still evident for that state's leaders and its ➤public opinion to recognize that eventual Palestinian statehood is highly probable.

**Pluralism** This term is used in two senses in ➤international relations. First, as a perspective on the structure of the system. Here pluralism may be taken as a portmanteau term covering all those who reject the assumptions of ➤state-centrism in preference for some kind of ➤mixed actor model. Second, pluralism is derived from political sociology where it is used to identify political systems where power is shared among a plurality of competing parties and interest groups. Pluralism is thus a theory both of inter-state and intra-state politics.

Pluralism in the first sense argues that the assumptions of the traditional state-centred view of world politics were derived from a period when the level of interconnectedness between ➤states was significantly lower than at present. Pluralists argue that there has been a massive erosion in the impermeability of the state during the twentieth century in a number of directions. This erosion is explained in the pluralist literature by reference to the idea of ➤interdependence, particularly in the ➤issue area of economic relations. Pluralists indeed believe that certain economic goals – often bundled together as 'wealth/welfare issues'

– can only be realized by states becoming more collaborative with other state and non-state ►actors. Thus the state is seen as more integrated into the global system by pluralists than by ►realists. Because the system is one of mixed actors, the defining characteristic of the actor becomes ►autonomy rather than ►sovereignty. The pluralists argue that actors such as the IMF or the PLO can be said to enjoy a measure of autonomy and should therefore be included in any model of world politics. For pluralism the concept of actor is relative: it cannot be fixed by some legal principle such as sovereignty; rather, it depends upon the context of the issue area. Pluralists also hold that the billiard ball metaphor gives a distorted picture of intrastate politics. Black-boxing or reifying the state misrepresents the domestic political process. Because pluralism is also a theory of how domestic politics works – at least in those systems which are pluralist – then holding to this perspective produces a rather different picture of ►policy-making as well as ►macropolitics. In particular, pluralists are far more willing to build the bureaucratic and organizational context of the policy system into their modelling and, conversely, to abandon or modify ideas about ►rationality.

The growth and development of ethnic self-consciousness and the emergence of subnational and ►transnational interests associated with the same have, according to the pluralists, had important implications for the idea of the ►nation-state as the typical actor in macropolitics. Any idea that there is a neat and tidy fit between the state and the nation must be revised in the light of widespread evidence of ►ethnic nationalism as a centrifugal force working in many states against state-centred ►nationalism. Some conception of the ethnic diversity of many states can be demonstrated by an examination of language as a variable. On this criteria only a small minority of states are ethnically homogeneous. If loyalty to and identify with the state, through the instrument of nationalism, is not guaranteed in the present system then, at minimum, the billiard ball model needs revision, if not abandonment.

Pluralists argue that many problems in macropolitics, such as combating ►pollution or ►proliferation, cannot be resolved by states taking a narrow, self-centred view. If these problem-solving tasks are so approached the result will be self-defeating. Instead states must recognize a common interest and engage in cooperation, ►harmonization and even sectoral ►integration in order to produce positive-sum solutions. States may engage in institution-building which will further erode their autonomy. ►►Liberalism; neoliberalism

**Plutonium** An artificially created fissile material. Plutonium was discovered in 1941 when it was produced by bombarding ►uranium 238 with neutrons. Plutonium 239, as it is known, is a fissile material like uranium 235, but unlike the latter its production is easier and cheaper. This facility has undoubtedly contributed to the ►proliferation of nuclear weapons since 1945.

**Polarity** A concept used in ►systems analysis, polarity implies that within a definable system certain ➤actors are so important that they constitute 'poles' against which other actors have to respond (by joining coalitions or remaining ➤non-aligned). Thus a polar actor is one which is so significant that its removal would alter the contours of the system. Conversely a new polar actor would be one which, by entering the system, also altered the contours. In the past entry and exit from polar positions has usually been effected as a result of ➤war. Polarity is a relatively new term in the analysis of IR and is often used in conjunction with the term power. Thus a ➤bipolar system would consist of two powers, a ➤tripolar of three, and so on.

Use of the concept of polarity can only proceed with confidence if the term is explicated further to uncover the preconditions that appear necessary and/ or sufficient. Traditionally, military power was regarded as a necessary precondition for stipulation as a 'pole'. Although military potential is not easily or cheaply converted into effective instruments of ➤influence, its possession does give the actor considerable negative or ➤veto power. For this reason, no satisfactory discussion of the bases of polarity can avoid taking into account the military factor.

Economic potential as a determinant is important, both for its own sake and as a contributory factor in the 'war potential' of actors. Economic power is more malleable than military since it can be used for both positive and negative sanctions. ➤Interdependence, although identifiable in the military security ➤issue area, is far more prevalent and pervasive in economic relations.

The determinants of polarity should include an ideational factor. Such factors may be explicit statements akin to ➤ideologies, or they may be implicit and imprecise 'ground rules'. Indeed, the two are different facets of the same thing. Thus in the contemporary system, the ➤Third World states have sought to change the ground rules of the international political economy through such demands as those contained in the call for a ➤New International Economic Order (➤NIEO). At the same time, there is a more structured set of ideas about the nature of economic power, institutions and relationships behind these demands.

In discussions on polarity in the literature the issue of stability is often raised in order to facilitate comparison between different configurations. Some writers have seen bipolarity as more stable, others argue for ➤multipolarity. In these discussions stability is often defined by the limiting condition of an absence of war between the polar actors. In any event, given that in all systems change is endemic, stability is at best a relative not absolute term.

**Polarization** A process that occurs during ➤conflict situations, particularly if the conflict is violent, or threatens to become so. Polarization leads to divisions being established within a system of relations so that parties to the conflict tend to coalesce together to form coalitions. The most usual form of polarization is the straight bifurcation of a system into two competing groups. In ➤international relations this is what is meant by ➤bipolarity and is also the limiting case of polariz-ation. Once a system has become polarized in this way contact between within the 'poles' increased while the contact between the 'poles' decreases; thus polarization can lead to the exacerbation of conflict over time. Polarization is particularly likely if the conflict is perceived to be about fundamentally different ➤ideologies or value systems. In such circumstances the parties conflict over what the other 'stands for' rather than what the other wants out of the dispute. ➤Accommo-dation and ➤compromise become increasingly difficult as a result.

It should not be thought that polarization always or of necessity produces an approximate equality between the 'poles'. Thus in the bipolar case one side may be clearly superior to the other in size and significance. Ideologically one may be defending the ➤status quo, the other seeking to change it. Polarization may lead to greater stability or it may be unstable. In IR academic opinion has been firmly divided between the proponents of bipolarity on one hand and ➤multipolarity on the other. One of the key variables in this dispute has been the relative stability of the systems under review. ➤➤Polarity

**Policy-making** An ➤actor that is a collectivity makes policy. Thus the UN, through its organs such as the ➤Security Council or the ➤General Assembly, makes policy. The PLO makes policy. State actors, most obviously, make policy. The IMF makes policy. Policy-making is, in short the decision to embark upon certain programmes of action (or inaction) in order to achieve desired ➤goals. Policy-making is the activity of individuals and groups holding role positions within organizations. Because of this behavioural connotation with policy-making, the activity is crucially dependent upon a ➤definition of the situation. Since the policy-maker's environment is itself a complex of other actors, potentially also making policy, ➤feedback processes are crucial and must be ongoing if the policy process is to have a point of reference with this environment. The actual process of carrying out policy decisions is referred to as ➤implementation.

It can be said that policy-making is one of the basic processes of ➤international relations. Methodologically students of the subject have sometimes wanted to regard it as a 'policy science', accordingly. This move has been resisted by scholars wishing to maintain a discrete distance between the campus and the cabinet room. In short, the policy science approach, although valuable, is not everybody's taste or inclination. One of the best working examples of the 'policy science' approach is ➤strategic studies. Its students have never been shy of close relationships with the chancellery.

**Political asylum** This refers to the granting of a place of refuge. It is a contentious issue in ➤international law since it is generally thought that the rights of asylum referred to the rights of ➤states to grant, rather than the rights of individuals to demand it. However, Article 14 of the Universal Declaration of ➤human rights appears to give individuals the right of political asylum as a general principle of international law. To strengthen this approach, a declaration on the Right of Asylum was prepared by the UN Human Rights Commission in 1960 which asserted that it was a duty of states to accept people demanding asylum except for 'overriding reasons of national security or safeguarding population'. However, this has not been formally adopted by the ►General Assembly. There are special and legally complex problems associated with the asylum in embassies and warships (see D. R. O'Connell 1970, pp. 808–15) and international law has not, as yet, a universally agreed norm.

**Pollution** Pollution is the contamination, degradation and eventual destruction of vital parts of the environment of the planet. In all instances this polluting process is caused by the activities of man, predominantly in the economic sphere. Because pollution makes such activities more costly it makes them less sustainable. Pollution in this way can be said to have a negative ►feedback effect upon its originators. Unfortunately pollution also affects third parties. In this sense controlling or eliminating pollution may be regarded as a collective good – similar to ►disarmament – that requires cooperation. In contemporary world politics, pollution is increasingly seen as a global ►issue area requiring ►regime formation if it is to be controlled/eliminated. The territoriality of the ►state is irrelevant at all stages in causing, controlling and eliminating pollution. In this way pollution issues may be seen to directly challenge the ►state-centric approach to ►international relations. It is customary to divide pollution into: air (atmospheric) land (terrestrial) and water (aquatic). In fact the three environments are linked and the separation below is purely to assist exposition.

Atmospheric pollution has increased substantially over the last hundred years and more gradually over the last three hundred. Atmospheric pollution occurs as a result of the discharge of gases into the environment. Thus historically two of the oldest pollutants have been methane and carbon dioxide. Such gases are produced by both primary and secondary production. In particular, the mining and burning of fossil fuels, rice cultivation and animal breeding (both sources of methane) and deforestation. The familiar picture of such atmospheric pollutants is the so-called 'smoke-stake' industrialization process associated with the industrial model of Western Europe and North America. Industrialization as a process has been positively correlated with increases in energy consumption. In the past the ►AICs have been the main polluters, now the picture is more confused as former ►communist states and ►Third World countries have joined the transgressors.

The issue area of atmospheric pollution includes three main topics: global warming, acid rain and ozone depletion. Global warming (sometimes rendered as the 'greenhouse effect') is caused by the build up of so-called 'greenhouse gases', particularly carbon dioxide in the atmosphere. This process is predicted to cause significant changes in global climate patterns with feedback effects upon natural vegetation and sea levels unless significant steps are taken to slow it down. Controlling global warming would require a deliberate move away from the use of fuels such as coal and oil in the decades ahead in favour of renewable energy means. Already ►green movements are campaigning for the ending of exploration for new oil fields because of the deleterious effects of oil use. Scientific opinion is now confident: global warming is a validated ►paradigm and the onus is on states to create a regime that will control the production of 'greenhouse gases'. The leading ►veto states in this issue-area have been the United States, China and OPEC.

Acid rain is an example of how the atmospheric and aquatic environments interact. Oxides of sulphur and nitrogen combine with moisture in the atmosphere to fall as sulphuric and nitric acids. Acid rain is also an instance of how third parties can be affected by pollution. Prevailing winds carry the pollution across state ►frontiers with regularity. This problem is particularly severe downwind of major industrial concentrations. In Europe the Nordic countries were amongst the first to argue for the significance of ►transnational pollution through acid rain, with the United Kingdom and Germany as the leading transgressors. In North America, the Canadian government has similarly argued its case as a victim of transboundary pollution from the United States. Attempts have been made since to create a regime to reduce emissions of these oxides but again the United States has been the leading veto power.

Recent studies have shown that the emission of chlorofluorocarbons (CFCs) into the atmosphere is resulting in the depletion of the earth's ozone layer. CFCs are used in refrigerants, aerosols, solvents, and foams. Their damaging impact was first noted over the Antarctic and the term 'ozone hole' has been used to model this depletion. Ozone is the atmospheric gas that prevents solar radiation in the ultraviolet band from reaching the earth's surface. The effect of increased ultraviolet radiation resulting from this depletion would be to increase skin cancers and to depress the human immune system. The effects would be undiscriminating and global. Regime building on the issue area of ozone pollution has perhaps proceeded further than in the two previous cases. The 1985 Vienna Convention for the Protection of the Ozone Layer and the 1986 Montreal Protocol on Substances that Deplete the Ozone Layer now requires the AICs to reduce CFC production by 50 per cent of the 1986 figures by the end of the century.

The major forms of land pollution are desertification and deforestation. In 1984 the United Nations Environment Programme survey suggested that some 35 per cent of the land surface of the planet was threatened with desertification. Deforestation is certainly a significant cause but additionally overgrazing and over-cultivation and salinization of irrigated lands are others. Underlying these causal factors is a more fundamental ►conflict between population and available land. It may be that the 'carrying capacity' of the land in insufficient for the population or it may be that ►land reform is needed to establish greater equity. In the special case of deforestation commercial and developmental interests of governments and logging operations conflict with the holism of the Green Movement which sees the tropical forests as a complex ecosystem which should be protected rather than 'developed'.

The quality of water is degraded in two ways: by organic and by industrial waste. Organic waste has been discharged into rivers, lakes and seas for centuries. Industrial pollution is more serious. Heavy metals and pesticides are not easily degraded; instead they persist and accumulate in the global water cycle. Pollutants enter this cycle in one of three ways: by deliberate discharge (often referred to as '➤dumping'), by leaching through the soil into the water table, and via the atmosphere. Oil pollution of the oceans by deliberate discharge or as a result of accidents at sea is a highly visible instance of water pollution which again affects the ecosystem of the seas. Developments in ➤nuclear power have produced instances of deliberate dumping at sea of low-level nuclear waste, whilst accidents to nuclear-powered submarines can again result in hazardous waste being left in the oceans.

Pollution issues in world politics involve a classic ➤mixed actor approach with states, ➤IGOs and ➤INGOs all involved. In a number of the cases referred to above, scientific opinion has been important in querying and re-establishing a paradigm or effecting a paradigm shift. Regime formation – although primitive – is in evidence in a number of instances of which CFC production is probably the best. Within the AICs pollution issues have been widely taken into mainstream political discourse by the Green Movement. In this respect pollution bridges the problematic divide between domestic and foreign environments. As already noted the territoriality of the state is irrelevant to both the causes of and the responses to pollution issues. State-centrism truly is part of the problem rather than part of the solution. ➤Environmental politics, epistemic communities

**Polyarchic** Literally 'government by the many'. The term is usually employed as a description of ➤states which are not 'centrist' (one-party authoritarian states) or 'personalist' (personal dictatorships). Thus, Western democracies would be regarded as polyarchic states. These terms are often used in discussions of the relationship, if any, between the type of regime and external behaviour. In this way it is often argued that polyarchic states are more pacific than centrist or personalist states, since domestic opinion will exercise a restraining influence on adventurous ➤policy-makers. Contemporary research, while emphasizing that that type of regime does not appear to affect ➤foreign policy actions, in no way affirms the absolute validity of such generalizations.

**Polycentrism** A structural expression used historically in connection with the ➤international relations of the former ➤communist states during the ➤Cold War era. Polycentrism literally meant that a plurality of ➤decision-making centres had emerged within the Soviet bloc. Implicitly polycentrism challenged the ➤perception evidently held in some Western minds of a communist 'monolith'. The term itself was generally credited to the Italian Communist leader Togliatti in 1956, but as an existential reality it began almost a decade earlier. The year 1948 and the break in relations between the Soviets and the former ►Yugoslavia was the point at which most observers retrospectively dated polycentrism. Under Tito's ►leadership, Yugoslavia went further than any other so-called 'people's democracy' in establishing a clear and genuine ►non-aligned ►orientation.

The event which was historically of the greatest significance in confirming polycentrism as a major factor in communist international relations was the Sino-Soviet split. The schism between the two most powerful and influential communist states in the system had a qualitatively different impact from anything that had gone on before. The Chinese provided a completely different point of reference and intellectual tradition from that of the Soviet Union and the other Eastern European states. Indeed the schism between the two states became so wide, public and hostile that by the end of the 1960s a genuine ►tripolar system between the Chinese, Soviets and the Americans was evident. The promulgation of the ►Brezhnev Doctrine in 1968 greatly alarmed the Chinese about the possibility of further Soviet ►intervention in the 'socialist camp' and encouraged the former's polycentric tendencies. Between the ninth Congress of the Chinese Communist Party in April 1969 and the tenth in 1973 a major ►rapprochement between the Chinese leadership and the Nixon Administration in Washington was under way.

As a process polycentrism was seemingly dependent upon the emergence of independent national communist parties free from overt ties with Moscow. In this respect it demonstrates again the point often made in foreign policy analysis of the need to take account of domestic factors in foreign policy outcomes. The Yugoslav and Chinese examples both point to this conclusion. In both these instances national ►elites came to occupy positions of political power without the intervention of the Soviet Union. Thus in Western Europe polycentrism was perceived as taking policy positions that were independent of Moscow. The Italian Communist acceptance of national membership of ►NATO and the French party's willingness to support the ►*force de frappe* being instances of what commentators referred to as 'Eurocommunism' in the 1970s.

**Population**  Population has always been recognized as an important ►capability of ►actors in systems of ►macropolitics. With the development of the ►state as the dominant actor, population became part of the resource base of states. Analysts influenced in particular by ►geopolitics have tended to see a large population (large at least in relation to putative adversaries) as an important facet of national ►power profiles. In the military-security context population was important because it provided manpower, while fiscal implications of having a people whom one could tax to pay for ►war was not lost on ruling

➤elites. Economically population became increasing▮
advent of industrialization. The proportion of the popul▮
economic activity became a crucial factor in production.

The advent of industrialization – which occurred first in Britain –▮
be positively correlated with the growth of population in systems that ca▮
identified as industrial societies. Indeed one of the most persistent features of
➤modernization has been the 'demographic revolution'. What appears to happen
is that, as societies modernize, public health facilities are improved and their
impact is felt immediately in the mortality rate. Birth rates (which are traditionally high in pre-modern societies) remain constant and population increased as
a result of the differential between fertility and mortality. Statistically this appears
to have been the case in the last two centuries. From 1000 to 1750 world
population increased by approximately 14 per cent per century, but since the
mid-eighteenth century world population change has been more rapid. Indeed
in the twentieth century world population grew from 1.65 billion to 5 billion
between 1900 and 1980. Once a society has reached a certain level of economic
development, population increases start to tail off. In this latter case it is
birth rates that show the downward adjustment. Explanations for population
stabilization are multi-causal, but while birth control methods are a necessary
factor, they are not sufficient. Sufficiency is more dependent upon socio-
economic factors than medical techniques. Since these modern societies are
generally characterized by improvements in the status of women, it may be
that the greatest contribution to reductions in fertility lie in this direction in
the long run. Having children is now only part of the women's life cycle in
these societies.

Population change is thus endemic. Differences occur over the rate of change
not over the reality of it. Three factors affect population change within societies:
the aforementioned birth and death rates and, in addition, ➤migration. Not
only will these factors influence the size of the population over time, but they
will affect the numbers within specific age cohorts (under 18 and over 65 and
so on). Thus an 'ageing' population (where the over-65 cohort is increasing
relative to younger ones) will present quite different wealth/welfare challenges
from a 'youthful' population (where the under-18 cohort is relatively large).
Population profiles within the ➤AICs tend towards the former typology, while
profiles within the ➤Third World tend towards the latter.

Population changes can have important implications in multi-ethnic societies.
Differential adjustments in the three factors cited above can alter ethnic distri-
butions. The political implications of these trends can be significant if power-
sharing arrangements do not or cannot reflect population relativities. Disaffected
populations within multi-ethnic societies might be the targets for ➤irredentist
or ➤secessionist appeals, and modern forms of communication mean that state
authorities are often unable to prevent this happening. Contagious influences
from outside can exacerbate these centrifugal tendencies.

445

t of rapid population growth, intellectual
t position and see unrestrained growth as
st enunciated in the writings of Thomas
thinker who was the father of intellectual
wth and resources. His basic tenet was that
the means of sustaining it. Stabilization might
nt, but it is more likely that population stability
ve checks of famine, pestilence and war. Such is
endency statements that in the twentieth century
sm still tends to pervade thinking about population
andt report spoke of a 'vicious circle' between high
birth ... the Third World. Malthus is now, however, presented
with a hu... ..e. Population management is the twentieth-century
extension of Malt... an 'positive' checks. There is no gainsaying the point that
since 1950 the ➤South has experienced a population explosion. Infant mortality
rates in these regions fell by half between 1950 and 1980. Famine and malnutrition are more likely to be caused by political mismanagement and the fall-out
from war than by some kind of Malthusian inevitability. Paradoxically population management has been least successful where it is needed most – in the
➤Fourth World. Lack of resources and conservative cultural traditions again
emphasize that population dynamics are not easy to control or manage.
➤➤Resource war

**Postmodernism** (➤Critical Theory)

**Power** Power is one of the essentially contested concepts in the study of
➤international relations. Unfortunately its usage in the past and at the present
often betrays ambivalence and confusion. As a term it has affinities with
➤coercion, ➤influence and so on. It has been described by one author as a
portmanteau concept and accordingly it is difficult, if not impossible to define
with any precision. Rather it is seen as a something covering a range of
eventualities from the ➤force/coercion mode to the influence/➤authority mode.
Baldwin (1979) has argued that greater clarity and precision had been achieved
in recent years by regarding power as a causal concept. McClelland (1966) saw
fresh hope in the possibility of borrowing from the community power literature.
Unfortunately, political sociologists are not in any more agreement among
themselves than any other discipline about power, as Waste (1986) has shown.

The power tradition in international relations, at least, is now indelibly
associated with the realist tradition and the writings of Morgenthau (1948).
➤realism is covered elsewhere but two points should be noted in passing.
First, Morgenthau defines power in the broadest possible terms. This catch-all
approach is definitely *de rigeur* today. Second, Morgenthau was not without his
critics within the realist tradition and that, accordingly, his qualification to be
their spokesperson should not go unchallenged. Much of the realist discussion

of power has consisted of a debate between Morgenthau and his critics.

Most post-realist discussions of power now begin by making a basic distinction between power meaning a ➤capability or possession and power meaning a relationship. Thus Knorr (1973) speaks of putative and actualized power. Some writers have suggested indeed that confusion might be reduced if the term capability was used in the first sense above and that 'power' be reserved for the relational usage.

Capability analysis has a long and distinguished tradition informed in particular by political geography and political economy. Factors such as GNP and GNP per capita, ➤population size and land area, level of literacy and size of armed forces, skill and morale of the ➤leadership and the diplomatic service come to mind whenever people engage in capability analysis. The idea of ➤hierarchy depends upon a differential spread of capabilities. The Sprouts (1971) sought to emphasize that capability analysis should always take place within 'some framework of policies and/or operational contingencies actual or postulated' (p. 176). Dahl (1984), with his stress on ➤domain and ➤scope, adds the reminder that power relations operate over someone (domain) with regard to a particular ➤issue area (scope). Baldwin has argued in the above-cited article that this approach to the capability/power idea is based upon recognition that capabilities have, generally, low ➤fungibility and that it is for this reason that attention needs to be paid to domain and scope.

Capability is a necessary condition for the power relationship. Without such possessions it is impossible for an ➤actor to obtain compliant behaviour and the aim of the power relationship is to seek and secure compliance. Compliant behaviour may consist of doing something different or it may consist of continuing with a behaviour pattern than an actor really wishes to drop. Moreover, in power relations the expectation is always made that the compliance will have to overcome resistance from the target. In summary then, power relations involve one actor or group of actors in overcoming the resistance of another actor, or group, and securing compliance thereby. Power relationships are confined to situations of social opposition. Their distinguishing characteristic is that sanctions will be used to secure compliance. A sanction can be either positive or negative, that is to say, it may offer rewards or it may threaten punishments. To make either, or both, these contingencies available the actor(s) must possess the capability, which is why it was stated earlier that putative power is a necessary condition for actualized power.

Because power relationships involve the use of sanctions to overcome resistance they can properly be seen as coercive. In this way it is possible, at least analytically, to distinguish, for instance, the power relationship from the influence relationship. Influence is then, in one sense, a non-coercive form of power. Because power relationships involve coercion they can have unpredictable results on the actor(s) being coerced. Rather than securing compliance, sanctions can stiffen resistance and make a target actor determined to 'tough it out' in the face of threats and/or bribes. Moreover, threats cost more if they fail while rewards cost more if they succeed. A threat that fails to produce compliance has to be carried out in order to maintain ►credibility. A reward that succeeds has to be carried through for the same reason. It can be seen, then, that positive and negative sanctions do no work in the same way or within the same psychological framework. On this latter point ►perceptions play an important role in determining how a target actor will respond. Rewards can be seen as punitive in certain circumstances. A state which has been receiving foreign ►aid can see a sudden suspension or reduction in its aid quota as a punishment if the cessation is linked to demands for compliant behaviour.

Power relations exist over time and perceptions of the past can influence reactions in the present or anticipation for the future. Moreover this mixing of past, present and future will be multidimensional. Actors will generalize about experiences with each other and with third parties in a form of 'learning theory'. The UK reaction to the proposed ►economic sanctions against ►apartheid was not solely a desire to protect vested interests. Following their perceived and controversial failure over Rhodesian UDI, sanctions were seen by some received opinion as being slow working and misdirected. US anguish during the ►Vietnam ►intervention was in part explicable in terms of their failure to be seen to be securing any of their objectives but also in terms of their perception that failure would adversely affect their 'standing' as a loyal and trustworthy ally. In both these examples it would seem that generalizations about power in one relationship can, as it were, 'cross over' into other relationships. ►Structural Power

**Power politics** ►Realism

**Pre-emption** Pre-emption occurs when an ►actor commits itself to a course of action that is crucially influenced by anticipation of what another actor intends to do. It has been widely applied to the area of ►strategic studies where it is envisaged that an actor might pre-empt an attack upon itself by striking a putative adversary first. In effect, therefore, pre-emption is a special case of a surprise attack. Writers like Richard Betts (1982, 1987) have argued that US policy-makers and defence planners were attracted to the logic of this strategy during the period of greatest ►Cold War tension and that in certain crisis situations – notably over Cuba – it would have been initiated. Betts argues that pre-emptive attack is easier to justify politically than ►preventive war but that the latter may be more viable militarily.

Like all decision-making situations, pre-emption relies upon good ►intelligence about an enemy's capabilities and a shrewd assessment of its intentions. Conversely ►misperception of either or both can be damaging. Stalin's desire not to provoke a pre-emptive strike from Germany in 1941 led the Soviet Union into a level of military unpreparedness which was most detrimental when the German preventative strike actually came.

Recent discussions of how ➤state actors should react to ➤terrorism have included suggestions that pre-emption must be available to the target states as part of their repertoire. It may be concluded that pre-emption is akin to the old sporting adage that you should 'get your retaliation in first'.

**Preventative Diplomacy** ➤peacekeeping

**Preventive war** Preventive ➤war is the deliberate decision to initiate military violence because the initiator perceives that he has a preponderance of ➤capability in his favour. Furthermore, the initiator believes that this favourable imbalance is purely transient and that, if he delays, his putative adversary may catch up and even overtake him in the future. In effect, then, initiating preventive war is a deliberate, premeditated action based upon a perception of temporary advantage. In general terms preventive warfare involves the use of an ➤actor's military capability in an offensive rather than defensive mode.

Two points may be noted about this definition. First, preventive warfare is one of that class of actions – ➤massive retaliation being another – which depends upon what might be called the 'cult of the offensive'. Second, preventive warfare is in broad terms illegal under the charter of the ➤United Nations and is out of line with the general twentieth-century trend to sanction the use of force only for individual and collective ➤self-defence purposes.

Preventive war is based upon two assumptions about relationships and circumstances. The first is that war is in some senses inevitable. The second is that striking first will be decisive. The inevitability of war may be described as a particularly pessimistic ➤definition of the situation which politicians, ➤diplomats, strategists and military leaders sometimes hold about the future. Such pessimism is deeply entrenched in thinking about ➤international relations and, until the advent of ➤nuclear weapons and ➤deterrence in the nuclear age, adherents to ➤realism as a ➤paradigm were inclined in general towards such views.

The concept of ➤first strike is dealt with elsewhere. Suffice it to add here that preventive war will be plausible in those circumstances where putative adversaries have a significant first strike capability yet lack an active and/or passive ➤defence against each other. Feasibility is enhanced by possessing good ➤intelligence about the disposition of the opposing forces and by achieving surprise.

The constraints upon preventive war are formidable. As defined above, it is certainly illegal under present concepts of ➤international law. It places key ➤decision-makers in the unenviable position of having to strike first, which is morally and psychologically difficult to justify, and it requires political leaders to make a considerable act of faith in their intelligence communities and their military establishments. ➤Pre-emption

**Prisoners of war** Throughout the history of warfare the issue of the appropriate treatment of those taken captive as a result of the hostilities has been a thorny one. The most fundamental problem arises because the captives are under the effective ➤power of a hostile actor. The captor may thus dispose of them in the most convenient way. Thus, death or slavery were frequent fates suffered by captives. Wealth and/or status could sometimes buy a ransom, of course. In the last analysis the main traditional restraint upon gratuitous bestiality was ➤reciprocity. Captors would be constrained by the probability that the enemy would wreak retribution upon their own people if and when they fell into his hands.

Through the process of reciprocity, therefore, the issue of a code of conduct was developed on an *ad hoc*, local and specific basis; that is to say that agreements were undertaken by specific ➤belligerents in particular wars as to the treatment of captives. In 1758 the French lawyer Vattel suggested a minimum standard of treatment when he proposed that '. . . as soon as your enemy has laid down his arms and surrendered his body you no longer have any right over his life'. The next two centuries have witnessed attempts to establish a more humanitarian ➤regime for the treatment of prisoners of war. An attempt which finds its parallel in other aspects of the laws of war.

The treatment of prisoners of war was considered at the Brussels Conference of 1874 and at the ➤Hague Peace Conferences of 1899 and 1907. The Hague meetings were important for establishing the principle that prisoners of war are the responsibility of the hostile government which therefore becomes responsible, in law, for their subsequent treatment. It also established a series of recognized rules for the appropriate treatment of prisoners during hostilities and for their speedy ➤repatriation afterwards. These provisions were supplemented in 1929 by the Geneva Convention on the Treatment of Prisoners of War.

The events of the Second World War, especially but not exclusively in relation to prisoners held by Japan, showed that the regime required further elaboration. The result was the 1949 Geneva Convention on the Treatment of Prisoners of War. Running to 143 Articles it represented the most detailed attempt to stipulate a code of conduct for those authorities detaining captives. It remains, at the time of writing, the major contemporary statement of ➤international law on this question.

Two areas of recent controversy should be noted in conclusion. First, the question of repatriation. Events in Korea in the 1950s, in ➤Vietnam in the 1960s and 1970s and in the ➤Falklands in 1982 have raised certain questions about repatriation. Principally these concern a possible clash of interests between a state wanting its prisoners to be repatriated and the captives not wanting to return. The Falklands raised issues of third parties wanting prisoners to be detained as law-breakers where repatriation to their home state might allow them to escape justice. In brief, speedy repatriation of able-bodied prisoners might not be quite as unambiguous as the 1949 Geneva Convention suggests.

The second area of controversy relates to the increasing use of ►guerrilla warfare, ►insurgency and ►partisan operations either in support of ►conventional methods or in their stead. These operations are, by definition, irregular and unorthodox. As such they raise the question of what should be the appropriate treatment for members of such forces captured during hostilities. The tendency since the advent of guerrilla warfare as a recognized mode has been not to extend to captured persons the protection of the prisoner of war regime. The return to less civilized methods in respect of this category can be justified on a number of grounds. First, the guerrilla often uses deception and concealment; in short, he does not carry weapons openly. Second, the guerrilla does not, himself, observe the rules on the humanitarian treatment of captives. Third, the guerrilla does not wear a recognized uniform. Because the irregular insurgent is usually the standard bearer of a revolutionary ►ideology it is unlikely that state actors and their authorities will ever be able to incorporate this kind of warfare under the aegis of the 'civilizing' tendencies referred to earlier. As such its import is that a significant type of intrastate violence will not be so rule-governed as regards the treatment of captives.

**Proliferation** Literally meaning 'diffusion' or 'spread', proliferation as a process amongst ►actors in ►international relations is usually associated with ►weapons of mass destruction and ►ballistic missile technologies. As a policy ►goal, preventing or stopping proliferation is customarily referred to as a ►non-proliferation. Traditionally this process/policy dynamic has concentrated upon ►nuclear weapons, but the widespread availability of the ►capability to threaten ►chemical and biological warfare has broadened the agenda, particularly since the ►Persian Gulf War. As a process proliferation is technologically driven, but politically inspired, and efforts aimed at halting or reversing these trends invariably concentrate upon ►regime creation around agreed norms and procedures. The ►haves versus ►have-nots dichotomy is implicit in the process and often explicit in the policy making. Actors are required to sign self-denying agreements whilst others retain extant capabilities on the tendentious argument that 'our' weapons are held in 'responsible' hands.

**Propaganda** Propaganda is an instrument of policy. It is potentially available to any actor having the means to promote and disseminate it. Propaganda is the deliberate attempt at persuading people, either as individuals or in groups, to accept a particular ►definition of the situation by manipulating selected non-rational factors in their personality or in their social environment, the consequent effect of this attempt being to change and mould their behaviour into a certain desired direction.

►Technology has been of great assistance to the propagandist. The development of printing, which allowed the propagandist to use newspapers, leaflets, pamphlets and books, was the first. The twentieth-century development of wireless telegraphy enabled propagandists to broadcast actual sounds, including the spoken word, across state frontiers and to 'target' whole populations. The Nazi ➤regime that came to power in Germany 1932 was one of the first twentieth-century leaderships to appreciate the importance of having radio receivers widely available to target a particular population. Picture transmission via television has been a further development in telegraphy since 1945. Film propaganda, intrinsically important in urban societies, has also been further enhanced by television.

There are a number of techniques and factors inherent in the propagandist's methodology. First, propaganda simplifies issues. This is partly to make things more intelligible but in the process of simplification censorship and distortion can be effected. Second, propagandists will appear to exercise a 'cultural proximity' judgement. Propaganda will concentrate upon issues in the external environment where people have some identification; geographic, cultural or political. Third, the propagandist will sensationalise. Sensationalizm is literally appealing to the senses. Propaganda is thus emotionally arousing or disturbing. This involves presenting issues which are personalized, dramatized, nationalistic and often immoderate. This sensationalism is particularly prevalent during ➤conflict situations where tensions are heightened in any event. The propagandist will be greatly assisted by being able to manipulate stereotypes that a target audience holds of other groups, societies and nations. Stereotypes of out-groups are widespread within social systems. They tend to be over simplified in content and not amenable to change in response to changes in the ➤operational environment. These stereotypes, which are present in all social groupings, are therefore amenable to the influence of propaganda.

The classic instance of the kind of sensationalism referred to above is the *atrocity story*. The essence of this event, or series of events, is to manipulate the target audience into the ➤perception that the instigators of the atrocity are inhuman. This will be easier if there is already a high level of tension and hostility between the groups – such as would be expected during ➤war. An atrocity can be defined as a behaviour sequence which so violates the norms as to shock and arouse a sense of horror among those witnessing or hearing the incident. For the propagandist the first requirement is to convince the audience that the atrocity was actually committed. This can be facilitated greatly if independent witnesses are available to corroborate. Thereafter the propagandist must present the atrocity in such a way as to arouse the active concern and implied condemnation of the target audience. Normally the more the victims appear to have been defenceless and without military or political significance, the easier is the propagandist's job. If an atrocity appears to be racially motivated or if a whole group of people appear to have been indiscriminate victims – all the inhabitants of a village, for example – the atrocity will look worse. If the victims suffered other indignities before death – such as rape – the sense of outrage may be greater.

Propaganda is more likely to prove effective if the propagandist is the sole or major source of information for the particular target audience. Propaganda is more effective when directed at a population which shares, at least in part, the attitudes of the propagandist. It is easier to confirm existing attitudes, to strengthen prevalent beliefs than to effect radical change. Propaganda is more effective if it can be directed through agencies of socialization, such as the family or the education system. These agencies can reinforce the message and provide a socio-cultural matrix which supports the propagandist. There is considerable evidence to suggest that people are more susceptible when in crowds, political rallies, etc. The manipulation of the non-rational side of the personality, which is the essence of the propaganda influence attempt, appears to be assisted in these circumstances.

**Protectionism** The use of ➤tariffs and ➤non-tariff barriers (➤NTBs), such as ➤quotas, to 'protect' a market that might otherwise be vulnerable to ➤imports. Traditionally tariffs had been the most widely used instruments for protectionism, but latterly NTBs have been increasingly preferred particularly since the establishment of the General Agreement on Tariffs and Trade (➤GATT). Protectionist measures may be taken by ➤states acting individually, or in concert, as in a ➤trade bloc or ➤common market system. Accordingly, political economists have tended to see states, and their leaders, faced with a choice between ➤free trade or protectionism. Classical ➤economic liberalism came down firmly in favour of the former. Complete free trade has in point of fact always been an 'ideal type' to which the actual policies of states more or less approximated at particular times. ➤Hegemonic stability theorists have recently pointed to a positive correlation between free, or freer, trade and the presence of a hegemonial actor in the system willing and able to support the establishment of ground rules leading to this state of affairs. By implication, therefore, the absence of such an actor leads to the growth of protectionist sentiments and policies.

Protectionism is advocated by those thinkers favouring ➤neo-mercantilist approaches to political economy. This tradition, like the ➤mercantilist approach beforehand, endorsed a ➤state-centred approach to such ➤issue areas as trade and payments. Accordingly it is quite appropriate for the leaders of states to think and act in these self-regarding terms. Liberals argue that if all actors in the system behave in this 'beggar my neighbour' manner then all will lose out since protectionist measures in one state will be cancelled out by reciprocal measures in another.

In contemporary world politics protectionism is a favoured policy among ➤Third World leaders. These states, their leaders argue, face a trading system that favours the established advanced industrial countries (➤AICs). Without countervailing measures they will find it difficult to redress the balance of disadvantage. Operation of such schemes as the generalized system of preferences amounts to explicitly recognizing this structural disadvantage and shows a willingness to modify the liberal orthodoxy towards what is variously called 'compensatory' or 'Keynesian' liberalism.

Protectionist pressure is also likely to be strong in those states where important and influential interest groups can successfully lobby for their particular needs to be met by a policy of protectionism. The Common Agricultural Policy (CAP) of the ►European Union illustrates how a small but well-organized group can lobby in defence of its perceived interests.

**Protocol** A term associated with ►diplomacy which carries a number of meanings. It can refer to the original draft of a ►diplomatic document or ►treaty or it can refer to a record of agreement between ►states which is less formal than a treaty or convention. Thus the agreement signed in 1920 at Geneva to establish the ►permanent court of international justice was described as a 'protocol'. In modern usage the word is universally employed as a generic term for diplomatic etiquette and rules of procedure. (Although the eminent diplomatist Harold Nicolson (1950) argues that the proper term in this second sense is 'protocole' meaning 'correct form of procedure' or 'ceremonial'.) An important ingredient of protocol is rank or precedence since matters of prestige and honour have always been central to diplomatic communications. At the Congress of ►Vienna in 1815 four diplomatic ranks were established and subsequently formally adopted by the European diplomatic system. The hierarchy of rankings was, and is, as follows: (a) ambassadors and papal nuncios; (b) envoys extraordinary and ministers plenipotentiary; (c) ministers resident; (d) *chargés d'affaires*. At the Congress of Aix-la-Chapelle in 1818 it was further established that among diplomats of the same rank precedence was to be established on the basis of length of service in a posting rather than on the ►power or importance of the government the diplomat represented. The 'doyen' or dean of the diplomatic corps, regardless of state affiliation, thus heads ceremonial processions. Protocol in this wider sense embraces procedural matters, diplomatic language and formal aspects of the negotiating process and although modern developments in diplomacy have tended to bypass traditional courtesies it still has an important part to play in the business of communication between states.

**Protracted war** This term has two distinct meanings. Almost any war can become protracted if a ►stalemate occurs between the parties. In this sense it is the antithesis of ►blitzkrieg. However, the term can also be used in a second sense to refer to a deliberate strategy. In this usage the protraction is caused not by stalemate arising from symmetry of forces but stalemate arising from an inferiority of forces. It is thus closely related to the ►guerrilla war situation. Indeed, the deliberate extension of the violence by the inferior guerrilla or insurgent forces is a standard response. The inferiority of the insurgents forces them to opt for the indirect approach; trading space for time, harassing the incumbent's forces and denying them the chance of a decisive engagement, eroding their morale, physically exhausting them and so on. The essence of protracted war is encapsulated in the familiar dictum that the guerrilla wins if he does not lose: the conventional force loses if it does not win.

The most influential articulation of the importance of protraction in the guerrilla war is that of Mao Tse-tung in his writings on the Chinese experience of ►people's war. He argued that in their struggle against their opponents the Chinese Communists made a virtue of necessity by organizing resistance in the most remote rural areas, avoiding potentially decisive engagements, 'liberating' areas from their opponents' control and gradually encircling the urban areas from the countryside; all this in the expectation that, faced with a long campaign, contradictions and fissures would appear in the ranks of opposition. There is no doubt that by employing these methods with skill and determination, a force of insurgents can tie down a conventional force, many times its own size, for an indeterminate period of time. Mao himself saw the balance of forces between incumbents and insurgents gradually changing over time until the latter were in the position of taking the offensive, across the board, against the incumbent forces. It is important to a full understanding of protracted war, therefore, to appreciate that it is a dynamic and malleable instrument which, if effective, will eventually lead to the defeat of the incumbent forces and the downfall of their ►regime. It is part of the means for implementing revolutionary change.

Protracted war thus arises from a situation that has been defined as 'asymmetric conflict' (see Mack, 1975). It has been widely employed by statesmen and strategists since the Chinese ►revolution and an examination of its several applications – both successful and unsuccessful – would have to cover the cases of ►Vietnam after 1959, Malaya, Algeria, Cuba, and a number of instances in Africa, south of the Sahara.

**Public opinion** Public opinion is a key variable in the domestic or internal environment of ►state ►actors, particularly those which have some core value commitment to pluralist ►democracy. Notwithstanding these democratic norms, there is considerable empirical evidence available to confirm the view that even in such participatory systems the mass of the population, in whose name policy is made, are not actively involved in the process in any regular and routine way. In the area of foreign ►policy-making the vast majority of the population are probably ruled out from exercising any effective or significant influence. This is primarily because they simply do not know enough about what is going on, when it is going on, to have any influence.

There are a number of situational reasons for this lack of information and therefore lack of ►influence. First, in all political systems ►foreign policy is widely perceived as an area of executive predominance. Foreign policy or statecraft was traditionally regarded as the prerogative of rulers from the inception of the ►state-system. Notwithstanding the attempts of twentieth-century

➤idealists to democratize the process, this influential tradition is still significant in the contemporary system. In some states indeed this executive bias is strengthened by the amount of secrecy and confidentiality which surrounds policy-making. Second, it must be recognized that, particularly in the field of ➤low politics, many foreign policy decisions are made on the basis of rather specialist knowledge which is not available to the general public and which would probably not interest them if it was available. Third, some foreign policy decisions are essentially reactive in character. Time may very well be at a premium and decisions may need to be made quickly with the minimum of consultation. Fourth, the tendency in many democracies for foreign policy issues to be approached from a ➤bipartisan perspective means that the customary ➤definition of the situation provided by party politics is not available. In all systems the mass of the electorate do not have access to sufficient information to develop and then maintain sophisticated attitudes about foreign policy issues. The mass media often contribute to this relative ignorance by reducing their coverage of foreign affairs, or by presenting issues in a highly simplified form.

It can be concluded, therefore, that public opinion tends to be structured in a hierarchical fashion with an ➤attentive public mediating between the mass public and the policy-making ➤elite. Two communication patterns therefore become evident in public opinion terms. First, there is horizontal communication within the elite and between the elite and the informed public. Second, there is vertical communication between the ➤leadership and the mass of the population. Thus bureaucrats in the elite and interest or lobby groups in the informed public will have regular and routine channels of communication. Provided that there are no significant divisions within the elite this consensual communication pattern can be maintained. If, on the other hand, significant cleavages emerge within this structure the mass public may be mobilized in support of one or more factions and parties within the elite.

The foregoing discussion shows that the mass public need not remain passive on foreign policy questions. The mass of the population are likely to become mobilized when a split occurs within the policy-making elite. Second, the idea of unrelieved passivity is contradicted by the ➤mood theory. This argues that the mass public can exert a negative and constraining influence by their prevailing mood, setting limits beyond which the leadership cannot easily go.

# Q

**Quadruple Alliance** ➤holy alliance

**Quaker** ➤pacifism

**Quarantine** Term referring to the compulsory separation or isolation of people, animals, plants or merchandise arriving from abroad at sea or airports, usually for a specified period, its general purpose being to guard against the spread of contagious disease. Until the First World War, customary ➤international law decreed that the period of quarantine should be forty days on board a ship anchored away from other ships in port. In 1926 and 1933, partly due to the relatively new practice of air travel, new regulations were introduced by the Sanitary Convention; these were amended by the ➤protocol of 1946 and by the Convention of the Cooperation in Quarantine and Protection of Plants of 1959. These in effect diversified the practice to include long-stay isolation hospitals and temporary observation centres.

The term has also been used in a metaphorical sense as in Roosevelt's Quarantine Doctrine of 1937, where he declared that the ➤war-like ➤fascist ➤states of Europe and imperialist Japan should be quarantined by the international community since 'war is a contagion, whether it be declared or undeclared'. The effects of the imposition of total mandatory ➤economic sanctions on a state is often described in these terms: that the outside world should impose total isolation on an offending state until such time as the 'contagion' (for example, ➤apartheid) is cleared. In this sense the term is used to signify punishment rather than precaution, and is therefore less accurate than ➤boycott or enforced isolation. The term took on a novel meaning in 1962 when the US government, under J. F. Kennedy, instituted a naval quarantine around the island of Cuba as a deliberately coercive move in the course of the ➤Cuban missile crisis of October. One of Kennedy's biographers (Schlesinger, 1967) says of the decision: 'Since a blockade was technically an act of war, it was thought better to refer to it as a quarantine' (p. 624). This American finesse of the distinction is now the most commonly cited example of the use of the quarantine instrument.

**Quasi-states** A term used by Bull and Watson in *The Expansion of International Society* (1984) and later popularized by Robert H. Jackson (1990). It refers to ex-colonial ➤states of Asia, Africa and ➤Oceania, which through the process of ➤decolonization have achieved 'juridical' statehood but lack many of the attributes of 'empirical' statehood. They possess all the trappings and formal qualities of ➤sovereign independent statehood – in particular the rights and responsibilities stemming from full membership of the international community – but are deficient in 'the political will, institutional authority and organized power to protect human rights or to provide socio-economic welfare' (p. 21, Jackson). In effect, quasi-states are states in name only; they are able to survive despite being inefficient, unstable and illegitimate by operational rules implicit in the new international order established after 1945. They are protected from the traditional fate of weak, fragmented states – foreign ➤intervention – by new international norms such as anti-colonialism, the right to ex-colonial ➤self-determination and racial sovereignty; ideas which are underwritten by the spread of egalitarian and democratic values which have their origins in Western social and political movements. In other words they escape the classic ➤security dilemma by virtue of the existence of a 'nanny' ➤international society which fosters a culture of entitlement (to sovereignty and its attendant rights) and a culture of dependence (protection and foreign aid) which enables them to survive despite their malformations. Whereas in the past, such entities if they survived the ➤power struggle at all were subordinated in the ➤international system, today they enjoy equal status with all others. According to Jackson, quasi-states and their external support structures – which amount to the international communities version of 'affirmative action programmes' – reflect a new doctrine of 'negative sovereignty' which was created expressly for the independence of the ➤Third World. Thus, post-colonial international society has sheltered these new entities from the harsh ➤balance of power and ➤self-help rules associated with traditional criteria for state-creation and maintenance.

The dire consequences of economic inviability, social/ethnic fragmentation and ➤human rights abuses have been highlighted by Robert Kaplan in his influential article 'The Coming Anarchy' (1994). For Kaplan, these quasi-states all too often become ➤failed states. In the post-➤cold war period the pivotal rule which upholds quasi-states, the rule of ➤non-intervention is now under threat. Increased global concern with human rights, the movement towards ➤good governance, the increased popularity of the idea of ➤humanitarian intervention as well as simple ➤donor fatigue may serve to restrict the political space enjoyed by quasi-states. But for so long as the values of ex-colonial self-determination and sovereign equality are regarded as 'groundnorms' of post-➤Westphalian international relations, these entities will continue to be a settled feature of the international landscape.

**Quisling** Synonym for collaboration with an occupying power, taken from the name of the Norwegian Prime Minister, Vidkun Quisling (1887–1945), as a result of his active acquiescence and cooperation with Nazi Germany. The word quickly passed into the vocabulary of ➤international relations. In 1946, for example, a ➤UN ➤General Assembly Resolution recognized 'the necessity of clearly distinguishing between genuine refugees and displaced persons on the one hand, and war criminals, quislings and traitors on the other'. The term Vichy is also sometimes used in this connection, being derived from a French resort which from 1940 to 1944 was the seat of Marshal Petain's collaborationist government.

**Quota**  A ►non-tariff barrier (►NTB), the quota is a quantitative restriction upon ►trade. It works by setting a physical limit beyond which ►imports cannot go and it is ►implemented by the central authorities of the ►actor concerned – which may be a ►state, ►customs union, ►common market and so on. Quotas are highly protectionist because, unlike tariffs, they work to completely remove goods from the markets and leave the ground free for the preferred products – if any are available. In extremis they can be used as one of the weapons of economic control in a so-called 'siege economy'. That is to say, in an economic system that is run on highly autarkic, self-defensive lines. Siege economies are sometimes forced upon states during ►war conditions, but in addition they may be deliberately chosen goals by states by states following an ►orientation of ►isolationism. A situation of internal war or ►revolution may, perforce produce a siege economy.

As Baldwin (1985) notes, quotas are accepted instruments of ►economic statecraft to be used, for instance, as part of a package of ►economic sanctions. Support for such coercive measures may additionally come from vested economic interests within the actor that willy-nilly benefits from such impositions. Quotas have been particularly favoured as policy instruments by agricultural interests and can be used to combat perceived policies of ►dumping by other actors. Quotas are widely used to control ►balance of payments deficits. Unfortunately they can provoke retaliation and simply store up demand for goods and services which spills out once they are removed.

The General Agreement on Tariffs and Trade (►GATT), while containing a general prohibition upon quota restrictions, made an exception in the case of signatory states with balance payments difficulties. Quotas are restrictions upon ►free trade and therefore the GATT position on this issue was fully congruent with its ►economic liberal assumptions. GATT was not the only intergovernmental organization (►IGO) to face the issue of quotas in the post-1945 system. Both the OEEC and the ►European Community worked to liberalize trade between member states. On the other hand the growth of such trade ►blocs and common markets has led to the use of quotas against third parties outside the arrangement.

# R

**Radiation** The most common form of radiation is electromagnetic: infra-red, ultra violet, and cosmic radiation being examples. Radiation occurs naturally on earth and in outer space. The ozone layer in the stratosphere has functioned to protect the earth and in outer space. The ozone layer in the stratosphere has functioned to protect the earth from damaging radiation from the sun. The recent depletion of this layer by ➤pollution from chlorofluoro-carbons (CFCs) is now a major agenda item in ➤international relations. In 1976 the ➤United Nations Environment Programme highlighted ozone depletion as one key ➤issue area in ➤environmental politics. Subsequent attempts in the 1980s to establish a ➤regime to secure the phasing out of the use of CFCs led to the Vienna Convention of 1985 and the Montreal ➤protocol of 1987.

The example of ozone depletion shows that the most damaging effects of radiation are produced by the activities of human beings. The twentieth-century revolution in nuclear physics has greatly enhanced these processes. Irradiation caused by ➤nuclear power accidents, by the testing of ➤nuclear weapons and by their potential use in a ➤war situation threatens pollution of the planet on a scale that some find unacceptable. The activities of the leading ➤states in the ➤Cold War confrontation was the principal cause of this state of affairs. The harmful radiological effects of weapons testing encouraged the conclusion of the ➤partial test-ban treaty but scientific opinion is dubious about the ability of underground testers to entirely eliminate radiation effects. The worst impact would actually follow the deliberate use of nuclear weapons in ➤conflict. The actual explosion of an ➤atom or ➤hydrogen bomb produces immediate radiation. The longer term irradiation, or fallout, can result in the release of isotopes which can continue to irradiate for centuries or even millenia. This irradiation time scale is known as the 'half-life' of the isotope and is a measure of the time it takes the substances to irradiate half of its energy. Some of the isotopes used in the production of nuclear weapons such as plutonium have very long half-lives.

**_Raison d'état_** Reason of state. This doctrine is intimately bound up with political ➤realism, ➤power politics and ➤realpolitik and is concerned with the primacy or centrality of the ➤state. It asserts that the question of necessity overrides ordinary considerations of morality; that where the well-being of the state is deemed to be at stake all other considerations are subordinate to its interests. As such, it is organically related to the concept of the ➤national interest and its natural tendency is towards a utilitarian calculation of advantage for the state. According to Friedrich Meinecke's (1957) classic study of the idea the phrase was first used in the works of Archbishop Giovanni della Casa in 1547 where it was rendered as *ragion di stato*, but it was ►Machiavelli who developed the first modern exposition of the idea in *The Prince* and *Discourses*. Machiavelli's central proposition was that every other value is subordinate to the survival of the state. In *Discourses* III, 41, for example, he captures its essence in this way:

Where the very safety of the fatherland is at stake, there should be no question of reflecting whether a thing is just or unjust, humane or cruel, praiseworthy or shameful. Setting aside every other consideration, one must take only that course of action which will secure the country's life and liberty.

In the world of practical politics, as distinct from political philosophy (assuming such a distinction can exist in this case where 'practice' clearly created 'theory'), it is particularly associated with the policies of Cardinal Richelieu in seventeenth century France. Domestically it justified the assertion of central ►authority over powerful local interests and in ►foreign policy it allowed France to form ►alliances against, rather than with, the Habsburgs with whom they shared a general religious–cum–ideological affinity. In its utilitarian guise, it reached its fullest expression in the expansionist policies of Bismark (though here the distinction between *raison d'état* and realpolitik is somewhat blurred).

Apart from rational calculation of interests in the service of the state, the idea can be seen to have an ethical dimension, given a particular view of the means–ends formula. If the end to which policies are directed (e.g. the survival of the homeland) is itself deemed to be a moral one, then the tensions between public and private morality which have so damned the doctrine in the eyes of modern ►liberalism disappear: reason of state is then simultaneously reason of God or of the moral ideal. However, as a number of commentators have pointed out, although on occasion 'doing what is right' and 'doing what is in your own interests' might happily coincide, there is no certainty that this will be so, nor is there a built-in guard against its unscrupulous employment. For these reasons, coupled with the fact that in the first half of the twentieth century it tended to speak French with a pronounced German accent, the doctrine has been generally discredited, at least in public. However, in so far as the state is still central (though by no means unique) in IR, the idea of *raison d'état* can never be totally discounted.

**RAND Corporation** ►think tanks

**Rapid reaction force(s)** A product of that type of thinking which sees political problems in terms of military solutions, rapid reaction capabilities are usually thought of as military forces which – as their name suggests – have the facility to move with speed and dispatch into situations that actually or potentially threaten ►national, regional or global ►interests. These situations will often be violent ➤conflicts or instances where violence is threatened and the force is thought of as a ➤deterrent or an insurance. ➤mobility is an asset in all force structures but in this instance it is a defining characteristic. Within ➤strategic studies the distinction is often made between 'offensive' and 'defensive' modes, rapid reaction forces are firmly within the offensive mode. As ➤intervention forces they may be the prologue for 'heavier' commitments, as monitors they may supervise and symbolize a settlement between parties.

Recent policy orientated thinking in the United States has seen rapid reaction capabilities in three specific contexts; as part of an ➤IGO force structure, such as ➤United Nations ➤peacekeeping or ➤NATO intervention forces, as essential to providing a capability for ➤low-intensity conflict, and as a precursor or advanced guard in so-called Major Regional Conflicts (MRCs). This represents the adaptation of early ➤Cold War thinking about 'rapid deployment forces' to the post-Cold War environment. The minimum ground rules for such a capability to operate at all will include: having sufficient contingents trained and equipped, and airlift and sealift facilities, having the political support of parties in the 'target area', having a clear political ➤decision-making centre with a defined and feasible set of ➤goals and a mandate for achieving them. ➤UN reform

**Rapprochement** Diplomatic term of French origin meaning the renewal of normal relations before a period of disharmony or ➤conflict. Thus, US–Chinese relations after 1979 could be described as 'rapprochement'. ➤➤*Détente*

**Ratification** Usually refers to the treaty-making process. A ➤treaty is not confirmed or valid until the procedure for ratification is complete. This process can vary according to the constitutional requirements of the signatory states. In the United Kingdom ratification is by the Crown, in the United States the President negotiates treaties but under the provisions of the 'separation-of-powers' doctrine they cannot be ratified without the approval of a two-thirds voting majority in Senate. Most treaties are duly endorsed but an important example of non-ratification was the Senate's failure to approve the ➤League of Nations Covenant in 1919, thus preventing US participation in the organization. Since treaty-making is vital to the development of ➤international law and is regarded as one of the great achievements of ➤diplomacy, instruments of ratification are regarded as crucial. A treaty is not in force until such instruments have been exchanged or deposited in a specific location. The twentieth century has seen enormous increase in bilateral and multilateral treaties (the United Kingdom and the United States are parties to over 10,000 each) and the treaties registered with the UN extend to over one thousand volumes (see Adam Watson, 1982). Ratification therefore has the effect of creating a new body of rules for those involved, and is part of the general dynamic of ➤international society.

**Rationality** Considerations of rationality frequently arise in the context of the study of ➤international relations, particularly when the ➤decision-making ➤level of analysis is influencing description and explanation. The question 'are decision-makers rational?' is really fundamental to this approach. Indeed, many would argue that this question is one of *the* fundamental challenges facing any study of human behaviour, whatever approach is being used.

Discussions of rationality now usually take as their starting point the view, derived from economics, that rationality can be defined as utility maximization. This is sometimes presented as the way in which 'efficient' decisions should be made. Such stipulations are clearly prescriptive and still leave open the empirical question of whether in actual cases efficient choices are made. ➤Game theory in particular has sought to build upon a series of generalizations based upon this utility maximization approach. Here 'being rational' means following the ➤minimax precept one maximizes gains or minimizes losses. To do anything else would be irrational. When game theoretical approaches are broadened to include mixed-motive games the problem of stipulating rationality becomes more complex. In particular the classic Prisoner's Dilemma game actually involves two concepts of rationality. Individual rationality prescribes to each player the course of action most advantageous to him under the circumstances, while collective rationality prescribes a course of action to both players simultaneously. The 'dilemma' intrinsic in the game is that if both act on the basis of collective rationality, then each is better off than the individual would be if acting on the basis of individual rationality. One of the key variables in resolving the dilemma in this game is the extent to which each player can 'trust' the other, but clearly considerations of trusting and being trustworthy take the analysis beyond the concept of rationality. If efficiency of choice as a criteria for evaluating rationality leads to paradoxes such as the Prisoner's Dilemma then this approach to the question of what constitutes rationality may be a mixed blessing.

An alternative view is taken by those who look at the way decision-makers reach estimations about the choices they have to make. If these individuals and groups can make an optimum estimation of the outcomes of all available courses of action then they can be said to be acting rationally. This idea of optimum estimation has been attacked by organization theorists such as Herbert Simon (1965). Simon developed the idea of 'bounded rationality' as an alternative to optimum rationality in these situations. He argued that decision-making problems are so complex that only a limited number of aspects of each problem can be attended to at any one time. Indeed, psychologically decision-makers identify and formulate problems within a particular framework so that the perceived solution, if there is one, is built into the framework.

Additionally, Simon argued that decision-makers rarely seek optimum solutions. They do not consider all the alternatives and pick the best one; rather, they find a course of action that is good enough for present purposes that satisfies. Simon called this 'satisficing' and said that this is more plausible than the idea of maximization. Simon's thinking about rationality implies that terms like 'finding the best possible policy' have little operational meaning because the search for alternatives is always limited and finite. It is impossible to consider all alternatives so ➤policy-makers tend to consider the most obvious, most attainable, most reasonable, etc. Of course, as the actual decision process proceeds other alternatives may occur or originally conceived alternatives may disappear.

It would appear that confident stipulations about rationality in the field of study are set about with qualifications. Deductive approaches such as maximizing subjective utilities are flawed by inductive, empirical studies which often show that in the particular event these requirements were not followed. The Prisoner's Dilemma shows that such deductive approaches may not produce stable solutions. Any discussion of rationality has to take account of the factor of subject ➤perception if it is to be empirically relevant and Simon's studies have shown how much this perspective can lead to modifications.

**Reagan Doctrine**  A term used to describe the foreign policy of the Reagan Administration from 1980 to 1988. This 'doctrine' was never officially promulgated as a series of coherent policy initiatives in the sense of the earlier ➤Truman or ➤Nixon Doctrines. Rather it emerged from the writings of right wing Republican supporters of Reagan and in the pronouncement of ➤think tanks like the Heritage Foundation. The term itself was popularized in 1985 by Charles Krauthammer of the *New Republic* and *Time*. The essence of the doctrine was the active ➤destabilization of selected target ➤states held to be following policies and ➤ideologies which were ➤Marxist/Leninist and pro-Soviet. From the outset of his term in the White House Reagan had been determined to halt the 'perceived' expansion of Soviet ➤power which had occurred during the so-called 'decade of neglect' of the 1970s. The latent purpose of the doctrine was thus to confront this expansion by ratcheting up the ➤Cold War confrontation to a new level of intensity. This was reflected in the Reagan rhetoric, the rearmament programme and selected ➤intervention in the ➤Third World.

Particular targets for destabilization under the terms of the doctrine were ➤Afghanistan and Nicaragua. In the former case the immediate ➤goal of sucking the Soviet military machine into a ➤mirror image ➤Vietnamese-type of situation worked to America's advantage. In the longer term Afghanistan remains a ➤polarized society with an almost congenital commitment to violence and warlordism. In Nicaragua the active destabilization of the Sandinista regime was to produce the background for the controversial 'arms-for hostages' diplomacy conducted by the National Security system which resulted in the so-called 'Irangate' scandal. Confronted with the initiation of the ➤Gorbachev Doctrine after 1985, the Reaganite policy lost much of its force and thrust as the two ➤superpowers moved firmly towards a ➤*détente* relationship during Ronald Reagan's last years in the White House.

**Realism** Sometimes called the 'power-politics' school of thought, political realism in one form or another has dominated both academic thinking on ►international relations and the conceptions of ►policy-makers and ►diplomats, certainly since ►Machiavelli contemplated the subject.

The ideas associated with it can be traced to the ancient Greeks and ►Thucydides' *History of the Peloponnesian War* is widely regarded as the first sustained attempt to explain the origins of international conflict in terms of the dynamics of power politics. Machiavelli in *The Prince* (1513) and ►Hobbes in *Leviathan* (1651) also provided crucial components of this tradition, especially in their conceptions of interest, prudence, and expediency as prime motivators in the essentially ►anarchic context of international relations. As a theory, or a set of propositions about the individual, the ►state, and the ►state-system, it reached the height of its appeal, especially in the Anglo-American world, in the years after 1940 when it appeared to explain the 'lessons' of ►appeasement and the inception of the ►Cold War era. Thereafter it was challenged on essentially methodological grounds by the ►behavioural or ►social science approaches but it reappeared in the 1980s in the guise of ►neorealism. Among its most prominent early adherents were: E. H. Carr, R. Neibuhr, J. Herz, H. J. Morgenthau, G. Schwarzenberger, M. Wight, N. Spykman and G. F. Kennan. Despite the basic weakness of some of their methodology, this group spawned a generation of distinguised scholars who continued the ►power-orientated approach of their predecessors. Among these were: R. Aron, H. Bull, H. Kissinger, R. E. Osgood, R. Rosecrance, K. W. Thompson, R. W. Tucker, K. N. Waltz and Arnold Wolfers. The restatement of its central concepts, albeit in a highly deductive, systemic presentation (Waltz, 1979 and Keohane, 1986), testifies to its enduring appeal both on the campus and in the chancellery. Without doubt, political realism is the most successful and perhaps the most compelling of the classical ►paradigms that shaped the development of the discipline.

The tradition focuses on the ►nation-state as the principal ►actor in international relations and its central proposition is that since the purpose of statecraft is national survival in a hostile environment the acquisition of power is the proper, rational and inevitable ►goal of ►foreign policy. ►International politics, indeed, all politics, is thus defined as 'a struggle for power'. 'Power' in this sense is conceptualized as both a means and an end in itself, and although definitions are notoriously loose and slippery its general meaning is the ability to influence or change the behaviour of others in a desired direction, or alternatively the ability to resist such influences one one's own behaviour. In this sense a state's ability to act and react is a function of the power it possesses. The idea of ►self-help is central as is the notion of ►sovereignty, which emphasizes the distinction between the domestic and external realms. The addition of an 's' to the word 'state' creates not just a plural, but involves crossing a conceptual boundary. States answer to no higher authority and so must look to themselves to protect their interests and to ensure survival. The

465

national interest therefore is defined in terms of power, to the virtual exclusion of other factors such as the promotion of ideological values or of moral principles. The nature of the anarchic state-system necessitates the acquisition of military capabilities sufficient at least to deter attack, and the best means of self-preservation is a constant awareness and reiteration of the worst-case scenario. Since all states seek to maximize power, the favoured technique for its management is balance of power. Stability and order are the result of skilful manipulations of flexible alliance systems: they do not stem from the authoritative force of international law or organization, which in any case is minimal. The approach is system-dominant in the sense that state behaviour is seen as a derivative of anarchy, but some adherents also claim that since the quest for power and self-interest is inherent in human nature, the states-system is a logical consequence as well as a reflection of it. The realists emphasize the persistence of conflict and competition in international affairs; cooperation is possible but only when it serves the national interest. The structure of the international system gravitates towards a hierarchy based on power capabilities and the notion of equality is at a discount, except in the formal sense that all states are equal states.

Criticisms of the realist paradigm have been legion. It has been attacked for lack of methodological consistency, imprecision on the definition of key terms and for all its ethical implications and overall policy costs. Its obsession with high politics and its presumption about the impermeability and centrality of the state had led to alternative approaches where non-strategic diplomatic issues and non-state actors are highlighted. Critics have also pointed out that political realism did not accurately describe, let alone explain, some of the major developments in the post-Second World War period, in particular the cooperative and integrative movements in Western Europe and elsewhere, as well as the apparent disutility of military force in increasingly larger issue areas of international politics. However, it remains an important theoretical perspective and one which for generations of scholars and practitioners best captures the essence of the international political system. The states-system is still anarchic, states are still the central actors and the great powers are still the most dominant. Recognition of this as well as a keen appreciation of the methodological shortfalls of traditional realism led some scholars to re-examine the role of power in the system, in particular its role in achieving cooperation under conditions of anarchy. K. N. Waltz's (1979) influential *Theory of International Politics* is the most far-reaching theoretical attempt so far to re-establish, albeit in a more rigorous form, the central tenets of realism. For Waltz, the central feature of a theory of international politics is the distribution of power. It is the structural constraints of the global system itself which to a large extent explain state behaviour and dictate outcomes. This 'structural realism' argues that changes in actor behaviour are explained in terms of the system itself rather than in terms of a variation in attributes that actors may display. This concentration on the level of the international political system rather than its component units has become part of the 'neo-' or 'structural' realist revival. While concentration on ►transnational relations and ►complex interdependence challenges key assumptions of political realism (especially that nation-states are the only important actors) the ideas associated with power and its distribution are still central to any sophisticated understanding of IR. The nature of power may have changed, but not the uses to which it has traditionally been put. ►►Neorealism, neoliberalism

**Realpolitik** A nineteenth-century German term referring to the adoption of policies of limited objectives which had a reasonable chance of success. It gained popularity as a result of the disillusionment felt in some quarters with the lack of ►realism in policies pursued by the liberals during the 1848–9 ►revolution. It has been most often used to describe Bismarck's policies and indicates a shrewd attention to detail, an inclination to moderation and a willingness to use ►force if necessary. It is often wrongly used as a synonym for ►power politics and in twentieth-century literature it carries negative connotations because of its association with non-negiotiable demands of the Third Reich.

**Rebus sic stantibus** Refers to a fundamental change of circumstance, normally used in relation to ►treaty law. If such a change is deemed to have occurred then a party to an agreement may withdraw from or terminate it; if circumstances remain the same (*rebus sic stantibus*) then the treaty is binding (*pacta sunt servanda*). This doctrine has been subject to much criticism by international lawyers since it can operate as an escape clause and may be used to evade all sorts of treaty obligations. Modern practice is to severely limit its ►scope. The notion of 'fundamental change' is a slippery one and Article 62 of the Vienna Convention has confined it to changes 'not foreseen by the parties' and changes which 'radically transform the extent of obligations'. Thus, for example, the election of a ►communist government in Britain might be regarded as a 'fundamental change of circumstances' in relation to membership of NATO, whereas the election of a Labour government would not, since the Labour Party was in office when the treaty was signed.

**Reciprocity** Keohane (1986) defines reciprocity as 'exchanges of roughly equivalent values in which the actions of each party are contingent upon the prior actions of the others in such a way that good is returned for good, and bad for bad' (p. 8). Colloquially this is the principle of give-and-take or 'quid pro quo' (something for something). Three points should be noted about the Keohane definition: the importance of equivalence, the idea of contingency and the fact that 'reciprocity' subsumes both good or bad behaviour being reciprocated. Equivalence is inherent in the idea of reciprocity, but is broadly defined as approximate rather than exact. Keohane distinguishes 'specific' reciprocity where an equivalent outcome is expected for both/all parties from 'diffuse' reciprocity where parties are less concerned about the need for clear and prompt 'quid pro quo' in favour of a more cooperative, group-centred gains. Diffuse reciprocity is closer to ideas about ➤regimes and ➤multilateralism than specific versions. Contingency simply means that reciprocity is conditional upon both/all parties fulfilling the bargains, struck or implied. Again this is more explicit in specific reciprocity. ➤Game theories like the Prisoner's Dilemma demonstrate contingency effectively. Cooperation is contingent upon cooperation, defection upon defection. Indeed in the Dilemma game, tit for tat is an accepted strategy. The Dilemma also illustrates the point about good/bad behaviour made earlier. Reciprocity is value free. States may launch reciprocal nuclear attacks as they may bargain about reciprocal nuclear force reductions.

Reciprocity is used in three contexts in ➤international relations. As a fundamental premise of ➤international law. As an important practice in ➤trade and commercial relations. As a building block for ➤international regimes and ➤multilateralism. The logic of reciprocity has been regarded as essential to the development of international law over the centuries since it tends to inhibit unreasonable ➤unilateral claims as these set precedents for others. Reciprocity is an important factor in the observance of international law since self advantage is never confined to one state. Indeed as the concept of diffuse reciprocity suggests, in the long term the benefits accrue to all as the example of ➤diplomatic immunity has shown.

Reciprocity has been regarded as the basis for negotiating mutual trade concessions, especially in relation to ➤tariffs. The Reciprocal Trade Agreements Act of 1934 in the United States was an attempt to break growing economic ➤nationalism and ➤protectionism in the name of ➤free trade using the instrument of the ➤most favoured nation (➤MFN) principle. Indeed the MFN is the ➤paradigm of diffuse reciprocity since it is open-ended in its applicability. The abandonment of specific reciprocity and the adoption of diffuse reciprocity became an important operating principle of American foreign economic policy thereafter. These ideas of ➤economic liberalism became embedded in the global economic system after 1945 under American ➤hegemony. Reciprocity is an essential building block in creating and sustaining international regimes, including those in the ➤security field. Caporaso (in Ruggie 1993) argues that diffuse reciprocity is one of the principles behind the institution of ➤multilateralism.

**Recognition** One of the most difficult and complex issues in ➤international law. It is at once a legal and a political condition. The act of recognition or non-recognition of a ➤state or government is clearly a political matter (eg for ➤ideological reasons the United States refused to recognize the People's Republic of China, 1949–79), but it also has legal consequences (in this case Taiwan legally became China). Deciding whether to recognize a new state or government involves a pledge to deal with the new entity as a full member of the international ➤diplomatic community and in this sense can mean conferring

➤legitimacy. It does not, though, necessarily convey approval. Thus, Britain recognized the People's Republic of China on the principle that the ➤communist government had effective control over the territory and fulfilled the factual requirements of being a state and a government (the so-called Lauterpacht doctrine), yet this did not mean that Britain approved of the 1949 revolution. Britain has generally been realistic in its approach to the question, whereas the United States has tended to be idealistic; one basing its judgement on an assessment of factual situations, the other on moral or ideological grounds.

There are two broad doctrines relating to this issue: the 'constitutive' theory and the 'declaratory' theory. The former maintains that the international community endows a state with legal personality, thus conferring recognition, while the latter believes that it is the factual situation of the existence of the state itself that matters. These two views correspond closely to ➤idealist theories of ➤international relations (which ascribe particular functions to ➤international society as a whole) and ➤realist theories (which concentrate on states and assign a minimal role to the wider community). Modern practice involves an admixture of the two approaches: international law tends to view community acquiescence and empirical reality as proper guidelines for conferring recognition. But it must be emphasized that the whole process is highly political and therefore contingent. Most commentators now regard the 'declaratory' approach as the better since non-recognition for ideological or constitutive reasons could logically infer that the non-recognized state has no obligations at all under international law. For example the refusal of the Arab world to recognize Israel could entail Israel not being bound by international rules covering, say, ➤aggression or the laws of warfare. This has not in fact happened so that even those states which adopt the constitutive view have recognized its limitations.

Recognition is bound up with ➤*de facto* and ➤*de jure* interpretations. The issue is also an important consideration in relation to territorial claims and recognition of ➤belligerents in a ➤civil war. In these matters, political considerations intrude to such an extent that international law itself can offer no hard and fast rule of procedure (see M. Akehurst 1984).

**Recommendation** A non-binding decision. The hallmark of ➤decision-making within the intergovernmental organization (➤IGO) is that such outcomes have the status of recommendations and that, accordingly, member states need not feel bound by them. Thus the statute of the ➤Council of Europe is replete with references to the making of recommendations by the principal organs of that institution. The ➤United Nations charter clearly stipulates that the ➤General Assembly is a body which will essentially recommend and deliberate rather than make binding decisions. Furthermore, under Article 18 of the Charter, recommendations of the Assembly on important issues have to be approved by a two-thirds majority. Like any decision-making competence, recommendations may be made by simple majority or by some system of weighted voting.

**Refugee** Someone who is forced to move from his or her country of origin or of residence. Refugees are an anomaly in ►state-centred ►international law since they are technically '►stateless' until ►asylum is granted. Although not a twentieth-century phenomenon, the refugee problem has multiplied alongside the increase in ideological warfare and ►terrorism. The ►League of Nations created a High Commissioner for Refugees in 1921 to help displaced persons, mainly those who had fled from the Soviet Union after 1917. The Nansen passport was introduced during the League period to enable refugees to cross national boundaries. Since the Second World War, the UN has taken over responsibility for the welfare of refugees and a UN High Commission for Refugees (UNHCR) was established in 1951. UNCHR can only afford temporary protection and the office is mainly concerned with liaising with member states to find more permanent solutions. In addition, a UN Relief and Works Agency (UNRWA) is dealing with the massive task of providing respite and relief for over a million Arab refugees in the Middle East who have been displaced as a result of the ►Arab-Israeli conflict.

Many commentators argue that the 1951 UN definition of refugee is too restrictive. This confines the condition to those fleeing their home states for reasons of persecution (or a reasonable fear of it) because of their 'race, religion, nationality, membership of a particular social group or political opinion' (Brownlie, 1981, p. 51). In addition, the criteria apply only to individuals, not to groups, and exclude economic migrants and the victims of armed combat. Increasingly the distinction between enforced and voluntary movement is difficult to sustain. In the case of the ►Vietnamese boat-people, for example, it is extremely difficult to distinguish between fugitives from political despotism rather than economic hardship since the quest for a better life often involves the implicit belief that political freedom and prosperity are bound up together. The 1951 definition is the only one to have gained widespread international acceptance but recent transformations in ►international relations, especially the demise of ►communism, have led to greater emphasis on the economic and humanitarian categories. Thus, West Germany recognized the migration rights of East Germans and the ►Organization of African Unity has specifically recognised the humanitarian category of refugee (ie victims of wars, famines, communal violence and other social or ecological upheavals). Rigid adherence to the 'pure' refugee criteria of 1951 may make the screening process easier for reluctant governments, but this serves to conceal a problem which actually and potentially is vast in ►international relations. For example, it has been estimated by the US Committee for Refugees that at present the world contains over 15 million people who could conceivably be labelled refugees, though only a very small proportion of these conform to the original definition. In 1951 the refugee problem (mainly the result of the Second World War) seemed containable, especially as most non-European and non-communist fugitives were not a matter of great concern to the West. Since then however the explosion of migrancy on a worldwide basis has created a problem which the international community is at present woefully ill-equipped to deal with. ➤Immigration; migration; orbiters

**Regime** This term, derived from ➤international law, has increasingly been applied to the study of ➤macropolitics. Keohane and Nye (1977) linked the concept of ➤interdependence to the idea of regime and sought to examine regime change in stipulated ➤issue areas. Krasner's (1983) work, a substantial reprint from the journal *International Organization*, developed these ideas in a broad-based, multi-faceted treatment.

A regime is a framework of rules, expectations and prescriptions between ➤actors in ➤international relations. This framework is based upon recognition of a common perceived need to establish cooperative relations based upon the principle of ➤reciprocity. A regime operates within a clearly defined issue area and behaviour patterns will be regulated through common membership of special purpose organizations. This membership will potentially be open to all relevant actors – whether they are ➤state actors or not. In fact most of the empirical examples of regime discussed in the literature are based wholly or predominantly upon state actor membership. Decisions upon appropriate membership will depend upon the policy contingency framework and cannot be identified a priori and in advance.

Regime analysis is analytically dependent upon the concept of interdependence because interdependent units require cooperation and coordination of policies to produce a positive sum outcome. Conversely, once a regime has been established, a complex ➤feedback loop is created and maintenance of the regime may require further policy decisions which have the effect – even unintended – of increasing levels of interdependence. As a results, regime creation can lead to instances of functional ➤integration between actors. The greater the ➤scope of the regime, the more likely is this outcome to occur.

Regime analysts have been concerned to explore three facets of the subject: how regimes are created, what institutional actors can do to maintain the regime and how, in the long run, regimes are transformed or abandoned. Because regime analysis assumes that cooperation and coordination of policies is feasible, it has been argued that identifying regimes shows that macropolitics is not an ➤anarchy. The working assumption that the creation and maintenance of regimes necessitates behaviour patterns that are norm-governed is incompatible with dogmatic realist assumptions about anarchy. It should be noted that some scholars have seen an explanatory link between the three facets outlined above and ➤hegemonic stability theory. In this version, the ➤hegemon is seen to play a crucial role in the creation and maintenance of regimes. Collapse or removal of the hegemon, conversely, is a necessary condition for regime transformation or redundancy.

The idea of regime is a conceptualisation not a theory. As such it is a way of organizing the existential reality of world politics. Strange (1983) criticized the early work on regimes for its vagueness and lack of precision. More recent scholarship has tended to examine particular instances of regime formation: notably in the field of ►trade relations and the ►environment. In the former case, regime change has been effected via ►multilateral 'Rounds', in the latter case by ►conventions and ►protocols. In these instances another of Strange's criticisms – that regime analysis was too ►status quo – seems not proven. Without doubt the concept of regime has become an intellectual life-raft onto which a number of IR approaches have climbed. Both ►neorealists and ►neoliberals can be found on board.

**Region** This term is used in a number of contexts with a number of meanings in ►international relations. Sometimes these meanings overlap: sometimes they contradict one another. The primary, common sense usage connotes physical contiguity. Indeed proximity seems to be a necessary, although not sufficient, condition for confident stipulation of a region. Within state actors physical contiguity or proximity seems to be an important prerequisite for creating and maintaining a sense of unity. The example of the failure of the two halves of Pakistan to maintain a united ►state when separated by the territory of the state of India and its dismemberment into Pakistan and Bangladesh in 1971 is surely instructive here. What is called elsewhere centrifugal ►insurgency is clearly assisted by geographical isolation and remoteness.

Between state actors, contiguity as a variable in delineating regions produces mixed results. For example, there is a core area contained within the concept of 'Europe' which includes the founding six of the ►European Union. At the periphery things become more confused. Iceland and Ireland presumably mark the western fringes but where is the eastern fringe? The end of the ►Cold War has altered these parameters it seems. Similarly, with the region of the 'Middle East'. A core area can be identified but is Libya part of it, or North Africa? Is Turkey part of Europe or part of the Middle East? Michael Edwardes (1962) opens his work on Asia with a chapter on the theme 'Asia: Does it Exist? Clearly, more is needed than proximity to confidently stipulate the meaning of region.

Between state actors, indeed, it is possible to arrive at groupings based upon homogeneity. Social homogeneity may be defined as involving socio-cultural factors such as race, religion, language and history. Factors which, within the state, can contribute to a sense of ►nationalism, between states can contribute to a sense of ►regionalism. Economic homogeneity may be defined as involving factors such as level of economic development, evidence of ►trade blocs and ►common markets and possibilities of economic ►integration. Political homogeneity relies upon one predominant variable: type of political system and its degree of stability. External homogeneity may be defined as the extent to which states in their foreign ►policy-making seek to cooperate, coordinate and harmonize their goals and the degree to which this leads to institution building, ➤bloc politics and the formation of regional organizations. In this respect homogeneity or similarity, as defined above, may reinforce or revise ideas about region based upon proximity.

The variable of social homogeneity is very evident in the Middle Eastern region where ➤Islam and Arabic are powerful factors in the regionalism. At the same time this criterion perforce excludes Israel and makes Turkey and Iran peripheral actors. South America is closer than Europe to the Middle East on these dimensions. In Europe on the other hand these cultural factors are divisive, particularly on language and ➤religion, and Europe scores very high on economic homogeneity throughout the global system. Conversely, this same economic factor which is so unifying in Europe pulls Japan out of its geographical context. Through the ➤OECD and the ➤IMF Japan is economically part of the West.

Political homogeneity is also high in Europe. Taking a historical perspective this is not surprising: the strong centralizing tendencies that produced the state and the ➤state–system first occurred in that region. Later, following the French and US revolutions, the expansion of political participation followed the ➤modernization of political structures on both sides of the Atlantic. Thus it is possible to identify a European/North Atlantic region of political homogeneity. No other region matches this one on the criteria of politics. In the past South America has evinced a strong tendency towards ➤militarism as a distinctive regional characteristic but this is now weakening.

Studies of voting behaviour in the ➤General Assembly of the ➤UN show the extent to which external homogeneity is reflected in the phenomena of the voting bloc. Further evidence for the growth of this variable throughout the global system is produced by the increase in regional organizations since 1945. This growth can be correlated with the idea of regionalism. Europe would seem to head the field although in the ➤issue area of military–security policies in the region is linked via ➤NATO with the United States. Proposals for a European Defence Community failed to gain sufficient support when moved in the 1950s and the West European Union has only very limited military significance without NATO.

On the basis of the criteria of proximity and homogeneity discussed here it seems to be valid to conclude that some regions are more 'regional' than others. In all instances, though, it also seems valid to distinguish what have been called 'core areas' within the region from peripheral areas. It should be noted that the idea of periphery is not wholly or essentially geographic. Thus the United Kingdom's peripheral role *vis-à-vis* Europe was more the result of a lack of external homogeneity than anything else. This attitude persisted in the United Kingdom throughout the 1950s and only changed slowly and somewhat hesitantly thereafter. ➤Sub-system

**Regionalism** Regionalism is to ➤region what ➤nationalism is to ➤nation. A complex of attitudes, loyalties and ideas which concentrates the individual and collective minds of people(s) upon what they perceive as 'their' region. Regionalism exists both within ►states and between states. Within states it can be one manifestation of ►ethnic nationalism and the political goal of separatism and ►independence. On the other hand, regionalism may simply reflect an organizational desire to increase efficiencies and make administration more accountable to the ►population. Regionalism within states is thus a very broad-based set of ideas and aspirations which may see much or little conflict between the concept of ►region and the concept of centre.

Between states regionalism is positively correlated with the idea of region. It has to be said that, in the conduct of their ►foreign policy, leaders of states frequently approach their external environment wearing 'regional' lenses. This ►definition of the situation is widely reflected among mass publics as well; the mass media will reinforce this tendency in reporting and covering foreign news. On the ►issue areas of military-security policies and wealth/welfare policies, problem solving is often perceived in terms of regional solutions. Thus regional arrangements such as ►alliances, ►*ententes*, ►common markets, and ►free trade areas are typical institutional responses.

The attempt in the twentieth century to establish global international institutions such as the ►League of Nations and the ►United Nations was seen, by some, to be a task that was inhibited by regionalism. This came to a head when the framers of the UN ►charter found that the primacy of the ►Security Council in matters involving ►peace and security might be challenged by regional pacts and arrangements. Chapter VIII of the Charter entitled 'Regional Arrangements' represents a compromise formula between universalism and regionalism. In retrospect this *modus vivendi* was almost certainly prudent. The UN has failed to substantiate the ►collective security provisions of the Charter and the post-1945 system saw a renewal of regionalism.

The same tendency has been apparent in global economic relations. Regional cooperation and ►integration via the wealth/welfare dimension has been one of the most distinctive features of ►macropolitics, and the UN system has been permissive. The General Agreement on Tariffs and Trade (GATT) has made specific provisions for these trading arrangements to be effected. Western Europe has long gone as far as any region in building economic regionalism into a complex of institutions. The ►European Union is now a powerful economic ►actor in its own right and it has certainly functioned as a systemic modifier accordingly. It seems plausible to suppose that these trends will continue into the immediate future and that other actors will seek to improve the prospects for regionalism.

**Religion** Despite its neglect by contemporary scholars religion has had, and continues to have, an enormous effect on ►international relations both in the structural sense and as part of its process. The neglect has not been total; there have been a number of studies of the influence of belief systems and ➤ideologies, for example, but the apparent secularization of twentieth-century politics has tended to marginalize its overall significance. Where it has been considered in, for example, explanations of the Iranian ➤revolution of 1979 and its subsequent ➤foreign policy, it has usually been seen as an atavistic aberration which has temporarily distorted more orthodox explanations of state behaviour. Realists in particular have tended to subsume religion under the all-embracing concept of ideology which in any case only conceals the true nature of foreign policy (ie Morgenthau's (1948) 'interest defined in terms of power'). Where it has been given serious consideration, usually by sociologists, it has been defined largely in terms of its social functions as a set of ideas or beliefs which bind people into distinct social groups and in this way has been extended to include ideas such as ➤nationalism and ➤communism.

In fact, religion and the notions of law and ➤justice it generated had a significant influence on the development of the classical ➤state-systems of Europe, Islam, India and China. The idea of ➤*res publica christiana*, to take one example, underpinned the ➤Westphalian codification of an association of states. Christianity became the dominant religion in Roman Europe in the fourth century. Subsequently, with the disappearance of the empire, the single most important binding force (the word religion comes from Latin *religare* – to bind) was Christianity. Although in the later conflicts between Church and State the temporal power was almost universally successful, the ideas that had been generated, especially concerning ➤sovereignty, law and ➤morality persisted. The state was the victor, but the state itself was premised on religious ideas. Despite the distinction drawn in the New Testament between God's domain and Caesar's, religion provided the justification for claims to state ➤sovereignty, whether this was divine rights for kings, or later for peoples. Apart from its role in state-building and system building it also had an incalculable effect on the development of modern ➤international law. From the Romans onwards, Christian teachings and precepts were used to codify rules for mutual relationships and dealings. The ➤Grotian concept of ➤international society is in essence a Christian one. The ideas of religious ➤internationalism, which is the tendency to organize a multinational society around identical legal and moral principles, is integral to the development of modern ➤international organizations. In sum, the structural effects of religion on world politics is by no means marginal.

On a more empirical level, its effect on the process of world politics is no less important. At the beginning of the 1980s, according to UN data, the world contained more than one thousand million Christians, around six hundred million Muslims, four hundred and fifty million Hindus, two hundred and fifty million Buddhists, one hundred and seventy million Confucians, and nearly seventeen million Jews. The notion of religious freedom was recognized internationally for the first time in the Oliva Peace Treaty of 1660, and was subsequently endorsed in Roosevelt's Four Freedoms in 1941 and by the UN

Commission on the Rights of Man (1955–60). Despite this, the sheer weight of numbers and the diversity of beliefs is bound to affect the stability of the contemporary ➤international order. No theory of state behaviour can afford to ignore it, or to relegate it to the outer edges of the discipline. ➤➤Clash of civilizations; Islam; liberation theology; Vatican city state

**Renewalism** This rejoinder to ➤declinism first appeared in the form of a point by point refutation in Huntington's *Foreign Affairs* article (Huntington 1988/89). Arguing that the ability to renew itself is the litmus test of a great power, Huntington saw the United States as a society possessing three sources of self-renewal: competition, mobility and immigration. Moreover because American power is multidimensional, the United States is enhanced by its structural position within world politics. In the last analysis, Huntington argues, predicting American decline will galvanize the nation to seek its renewal to confound the pessimists!

Renewalism is essentially a series of arguments based upon two axioms: the Declinists misunderstand the nature of power in international relations and because of this they misperceive the essence of American power in particular. These themes are developed in Nye's (1990) volume *Bound to Lead*. Arguing for an expansion of the concept of power to include 'soft power', Nye asserts that in cultural and ideological terms America has more power than any of its putative rivals. Moreover echoing Huntington, he views power in structural as well as relational terms. In the book Nye concedes that power in international relations has changed. In particular military power is not fungible and complex interdependence has enhanced other types of capability. Arguing in effect that everyone's power has declined, Nye suggests that in terms of power relativities America is at least *primus inter pares* if no longer the hegemon. Nye explicitly rejects the kinds of historical comparisons used in the Kennedy (1988) declinist tract. For America in the next century the problem is less one of confronting new challengers but rather of confronting new challenges including the changing nature of power.

As Cooper, Higgott and Nossal have noted (1991), the renewalist side in the 'debate' received a significant fillip from the ➤Persian Gulf War here indeed was America 'leading' in the manner predicted in the Nye title. Cooper et al. argue that in reality closer analysis of 'followership' suggests that if America is bound to lead the majority of the coalition were not bound to follow. Indeed in their analysis only one state evinces classic 'followership' behaviour patterns – the United Kingdom. Most states went along with the coalition for their own foreign policy goals rather than because they accepted American leadership per se. The Persian Gulf War far from confirming American leadership might actually proximate closer to the declinist paradigm because American 'leadership' was not the cement that held together its coalition partners.

**Reneversement des alliances** Diplomatic term meaning 'reversal of alliances'. It refers to the practice of abandoning an ally and entering a new ➤alliance with a recent enemy. The Nazi–Soviet pact of 1939 is sometimes regarded, not altogether correctly, as *renversement des alliances*. The practice was much more common in the non-ideological or classical period of ➤balance of power in the eighteenth and nineteenth centuries. Indeed, in the realist view of ➤international politics, flexibility of alignments is a fundamental requirement of successful power management. This practice was specifically endorsed in the Washington Doctrine of Unstable Alliances promulgated by President Jefferson in his inaugural speech to Congress on 7 January 1801. Following George Washington's strictures against entangling alliances, Jefferson argued that the United States should regard their ➤war alliances as temporary and change or reverse them as soon as interest dictated. Sometimes, of course, *renversement* can occur not as a result of the general configuration of power and interest, but as a consequence of a ➤revolution or a change of ➤regime. In these cases, *renversement* is an ideological policy by-product rather than a more or less continuously available diplomatic tactic, which is closer to its original meaning.

**Reparations** Reparations are compensation claims made of and effected upon vanquished by the victors following the cessation of hostilities. Reparations may involve financial payments and/or physical requisition of goods. By exercising reparations the victor(s) may be seeking to indemnify itself/themselves for losses incurred during the ➤war. Additionally, reparations may be seen as an instrument that will reduce the ability of the vanquished to wage war or otherwise pose a ➤security threat in the future. Reparations – in both forms – were exacted from Germany after the First World War; the French, in particular, demanding large amounts to cover war damage and individual claims for loss. The Allied reparations policy was heavily criticized by the economist J. M. Keynes and the political scientist E. H. Carr as a major contributory factor in the collapse of the German economy and its aggrieved and unbending ➤foreign policy posture. After the Second World War, both the Soviet Union and Israel claimed the right to exact reparations from Germany. Following the end of the ➤Vietnam War, the Vietnamese sought reparations from the United States of America.

**Repatriation** Policy of returning people to their country of origin or legal home. Repatriation can be voluntary or involuntary; in the case of the former some form of 'inducement' is often resorted to, although where this does not succeed mandatory deportation usually follows. Inducement was mooted, though not undertaken, by sections of the UK Conservative Party in relation to immigrants from the Caribbean during the late 1950s and early 1960s. In relation to the ➤Vietnamese 'boat people' the United Kingdom, in 1989, pursued policies both of inducement and enforcement. It often involves ➤bilateral or ➤multilateral international agreements as was the case in the aftermath of the two World Wars when thousands of eastern and central Europeans were sent back to their countries of origin, often against their express wishes and even under cover of some form of subterfuge. The cases of the forcible repatriation of Cossacks to the Soviet Union and of the Vietnamese seeking refuge in Hong Kong demonstrate that this policy is invariably a risky one which flirts dangerously near to infringements of ►human rights. This was clearly the case with President Amin's expulsion in 1972–3 of 50,000 Ugandan Asians to various ►Commonwealth countries. In attempting to minimize domestic and international criticism of such policies, the UK government, in particular, has tended to distinguish between 'genuine' ►refugees and what it terms 'economic migrants'. The issue of the rights of illegal immigrants will continue to bedevil ►international relations since there is no universally agreed solution to the problem. ►►Orbiters; prisoners of war

**Reprisal** A form of retaliation falling short of ►war, in which ►states engage to punish a wrongdoer or to obtain redress for some injurious act. Fear of reprisals is an important sanction underlying the effectiveness of international norms of behaviour. Reprisals include any measure which does not actually constitute an act of war, ►boycotts, seizure of assets or property, peaceful ►blockades or simply 'showing the ►flag' as a threatening gesture. Although not overtly an ►aggressive act, it is often seen as such by target states. Reprisal must be distinguished from ►retortion since reprisals are technically illegal. They must also be preceded by a demand that the offender make amends and the act of reprisal itself must not be excessive – the punishment must fit the crime. Reprisals involving the use of armed ►force must comply with the ►self-defence and ►collective security provisions of the ►charter of the UN. Reprisals can also be used in wartime, usually to force the enemy to comply with the laws of warfare. ►►Self-help

**Res publica Christiana** Term used mainly by diplomatic historians to delineate what is now more commonly called 'Western Christendom'. Before the establishment of the ►Westphalian system in the seventeenth century, which affirmed that Europe consisted of a largely secular multiplicity of states, post-Roman Europeans continued to regard themselves as part of a distinctive whole. Even as the rival ►imperial and papal claims to the government of Europe were being undermined in the fourteenth and fifteenth centuries, the emerging monarchical states interpreted their mutual relations not in terms of relations between totally separate and isolated units, but rather in terms of politically distinct parts of what was once a unified whole. As M Keens-Soper (1978) puts it 'the implications of political fragmentation did not call in question the continued spiritual and legal unity of Christendom'. The net result of the process was that the modern European ►states-system which was supposedly created at Westphalia in 1648 was not particularly new and was in any case superimposed on an established sense of unity and common purpose. This enabled 'Christian' or 'European' states (the terms became interchangeable) to distinguish between relations among themselves, where certain conventions and rules were to be followed, and relations with outsiders where no such constraints operated. Thus, outsiders such as the Turks, the Aztecs or the Indians were deemed incapable of belonging to the Christian ➤Commonwealth of states. They were therefore legitimate targets for ➤imperialism conquest, subjection and subversion.

This sense of Europe as a self-conscious association of states, politically fragmented but culturally ➤interdependent, had profound consequences for the development of a truly global states-system in the twentieth century. In particular, the persistence of its peculiar institutions (➤diplomacy, the law of nations, the rules of ➤war, ➤balance of power and ➤international organizations) can be directly attributed to this conception of belonging to a common civilization. And although the last public occasion where the term was officially used was in the preamble to the Treaty of Utrecht in 1714, there can be little doubt that the practice of shared assumptions and common rules of conduct that it signifies persists to this day. Despite secularization and a widening of its geographical limits, the important ground rules of modern ➤international relations are rooted in the notion of *res publica Christiana*. ➤➤Clash of civilizations

**Research Institutes** ➤think tanks

**Resource wars** Since 'resources' can be defined as anything which is the object of desire or need all ➤wars are in an important sense, resource wars. However, in the post-➤Cold War period, this term has come to refer to national ➤security issues arising from ➤environmental stresses of one kind or another. The uneven distribution of ➤natural resources coupled with the problems of ➤pollution and environmental degradation could lead to national rivalries over the availability or distribution of scarce goods. Thus, the contemporary concept of resource war involves four possible scenarios where ➤issue areas that were previously regarded as ➤low politics could be elevated into the ➤high political realm of ➤peace and security.

1  water wars: Disputes over access to water supplies could erupt either through global warming or through the activities of upstream states in rivers which cross international ➤boundaries. The Nile, for example, is sometimes referred to as 'one river; nine states.' The problems of sharing this resource are therefore potentially vast. The same holds true of other volatile ➤regions, notably the Middle East.

2  poverty wars: The central thesis here is that economic stagnation and the inability to meet economic expectations could trigger off violent responses, particularly in authoritarian/➤revolutionary states. The theory that poverty leads to ➤aggression has, however, been challenged by, amongst others, the noted military strategist Bernard Brodie who observed that 'The predisposing factors to military aggression are full bellies, not empty ones' (see D. Deudney, 1996). (This homily though, can be countered by ex-President de Klerk's argument for power-sharing in South Africa: 'If they don't eat, we don't sleep.')

3 power wars: This is a variant of the realist argument that changes in relative wealth and power caused by environmental degradation could lead to military conflict. Examples cited in this scenario, are the newly independent republics of the former Soviet Union where 'dissatisfied' nuclear states exist side-by-side with relatively 'satisfied' non-nuclear states.

4 pollution wars: The fourth scenario envisages a situation in which one ➤actor pollutes another either through deliberate policies of external dumping or through the emissions of unregulated toxic fumes. Also, this type of resource war could result from attempts to preserve the global commons (under the doctrine of the ➤Collective Heritage of Mankind) from despoilers or 'free riders'. The problem here is that any state sufficiently industrialized to cause these problems is unlikely to be a good target for coercion. It was inconceivable for example, that states in Western Europe would seek to coerce the USSR for the Chernobyl nuclear disaster in 1986.

All of the above, refer to the possibility of inter-state conflict. However, a much more likely situation might well be ➤communal conflict caused by resource scarcity. Competition over ➤water and ➤food, could easily exacerbate if not cause, inter-ethnic violence in ➤failed states or those whose authoritative structures are weak. Demographic pressures on space and resources coupled with ethnic cleansing and hatreds are indeed well recognized as a cause of inter-societal conflict. ➤➤Quasi-status

**Retortion** A legal measure designed to punish an unfriendly act. For example, denial of economic ➤aid after acts of ➤nationalization would be retortion. In US ➤foreign policy, the 'Hickenlooper Amendment' required the President to forgo economic assistance to ➤states which have expropriated US property without compensation. Thus, retortion was invoked against Ceylon in 1963 – 5 and was only withdrawn when a new government decided to pay compensation. This has now been repealed by the American Foreign Assistance Act of 1973. ➤➤Helms–Burton

**Revisionism** Most often used to denote challenges to the ➤status quo. The term is especially associated with realists who view ➤international politics in terms of a more-or-less permanent structural tension between defenders of the prevailing order and opponents of it. Thus, 'satisfied/dissatisfied', 'satiated/unsatiated', '➤have/have not' and 'status quo/revisionist', are dichotomies commonly employed by theorists to describe this process. 'Revisionist' is especially associated with E H Carr's (1946) *Twenty Years' Crisis 1919–1939* and refers to types of ➤foreign policies practised by certain states (Germany, Italy and Japan) in the inter-➤war period whereby they attempted to alter the existing international ➤power and territorial distribution to their own advantage. Instead of accepting the inferior position accorded to them by the prevailing order (in this case the ➤Versailles system), revisionist states attempt, by means of

➤diplomatic pressure, threats, ➤force, disregard for ➤international law and existing ➤treaty obligations, to alter the situation in their favour. It is bound up with the power model and as such encourages the formation of ➤alliances, coalitions and ➤blocs in accordance with the principles of balance. Conflicts that result from this process are usually ➤zero-sum. H. J. Morgenthau (1948), the doyen of the post-war school of US realists, substituted the term ➤imperialist to indicate similar challenges, but this was less helpful since it carried moral and/or ➤ideological overtones: the status quo then appears positive, normal and proper, the imperialist negative, abnormal and improper. Indeed, the idea of revisionism has suffered in the West because it has so often been linked with the policies of Hitler and Stalin, and the tendency of historiography to label pro-Soviet, anti-US analyses of the ➤Cold War revisionist reinforces this prejudice.

Barry Buzan (1983), attempting to obliterate this ➤ethnocentric distortion and to clarify the term, identifies a three-tier classification of revisionist objectives – 'orthodox', ➤revolutionary and 'radical'. Orthodox challenges operate within the prevailing framework of ideas and relations and are geared towards giving the challenger a better pecking order position within the hierarchical system (e.g. Imperial Germany and Imperial Japan prior to the First World War). Revolutionary revisionism involves a challenge to the organizing principles of the system itself (France after 1789, the Soviet Union after 1917 and perhaps Libya and Iran today). Radical revisionists fall between the other two groupings; they aim both for self-advantage and reform of the system. The Group of 7 and the quest for a ➤New International Economic Order (➤NIEO) typifies this approach. Buzan's classification, while in general confirming the insights of the realist model, indicates a much more complex pattern and variety of challenges than the simple, zero-sum ➤high politics model presented earlier. Revisionism is now seen to be multifaceted and is applicable to ➤great, ➤middle and ➤small power politics and need not be tied to a particular ideological stance.

Other senses in which the term is used are as a description of reinterpretations of ➤Marxist/Leninist dogma, where it usually implies a deviation from the orthodox view (eg peaceful coexistence), or to indicate a fundamental reappraisal of the causes of the Cold War, especially in US historiography.

**Revolution** In ➤international relations this is usually used in the following senses: (a) referring to a radical and sudden change in a system of government, often accompanied by violence; (b) referring to *any* fundamental change or transition in the institutions and values of a society, ➤state or system. The first sense is clearly restrictive since it does not distinguish between changes of government which are not accompanied by radical social change (e.g. ➤*coups d'état* or 'palace revolutions') and those which are. The second sense is restrictive in the opposite way, since it allows the term to be used in any context which has undergone radical transformation, to the extent that we can speak of an 'industrial revolution', a 'strategic' revolution, an 'intellectual' revolution and so on. For the ➤Marxist/Leninists who have dominated modern discussions of the phenomena, revolutions properly so-called involve not just a change of political regime; they also involve a fundamental change in the social and economic organization of society. Using this criterion, genuine revolutions in world politics, although enormously influential in terms of its structure and process, are comparatively rare. The French Revolution of 1789, the Bolshevik Revolution of 1917, the Chinese Revolution of 1949 and the Cuban Revolution of 1959 all clearly qualify, whereas the English 'Glorious Revolution' of 1688 and the American Revolution of 1776 equally clearly do not.

Apart from disagreements about its nature and cause and despite a general consensus about its overall importance in setting the agenda of modern world politics, most non-Marxist and non-sociological commentators have tended to ignore or marginalize the phenomena. Political ➤realists, for example, given the ➤state-centric bias of the approach, have considered revolutions primarily in the context of nonconformity with the prevailing system, rather than *sui generis*. Thus, for example, it is a common generalization that after the initial heat and light of the revolutionary period, the affected state soon settles into, or is socialized by, the constraints imposed by the ➤state-system itself. Even realists who have devoted considerable time and energy investigating revolutions, eg E. H. Carr (1946) and Martin Wight (1978), have tended to assume that revolutions lead to instability and therefore are not conducive to the maintenance of order in ➤international politics. The ➤foreign policies of revolutionary states are thus classified as 'revisionist' or 'dissatisfied' and must be responded to either through the process of ➤accommodation (often called ➤appeasement) or through counter-revolutionary methods involving direct or indirect ➤intervention. Behaviouralists (who often regard themselves as 'revolutionaries' within the discipline) are also prone to treat revolutions as just a variant of violent group behaviour. J. N. Rosenau (1964), for example, preferred the term 'internal ➤war' to revolution implying that it is a particular form of a general social phenomenon.

Reasons for this apparent neglect are not difficult to find. For most analysts of international affairs, the 'domestic' variables are held constant. Revolutions therefore, when they have been considered at all, have been viewed primarily in terms of the effect that they have had on foreign policy style or behaviour. Despite Martin Wight's assertion that between 1492 and 1960 ➤international relations has been more 'revolutionary' than 'unrevolutionary' (1978, p. 92), there is a prevailing assumption that it is somehow 'abnormal' or an 'aberration'. Outside ➤communist literature, where the distinction between domestic and international politics is unknown and where the concepts of permanent revolution and ➤wars of national liberation are central, very little theoretical attention has been given to it as a formative influence on the development of world politics. The relationship between revolution and war is usually subsumed under studies of the general conditions of permissible intervention or else on the role and methods of the 'revolutionary liberator state'. In ►international law consideration of the concept is marginal. The presumption in favour of ►sovereignty and ►domestic jurisdiction means that apart from such metalegal ideas as ►legitimacy or ►recognition and rules relating to compensation, revolution is treated as a temporary deviation from the norm. The assumption of the UN ►charter, especially Article 2, paragraph 7 (►non-intervention) is that internal upheavals are essentially domestic matters and as such are beyond the range and ►scope of the international legal regime. All this is in spite of the fact that twentieth century international politics in the ►First, Second and ►Third Worlds has largely been about the realization of, or responses to, revolutions. ►Insurgency, j-curve, nineteen eighty nine

**Revolution in Military Affairs (RMA)** This refers to the impact of new technologies on organised armed conflict. The term was especially associated with the early period of the ►Cold War when Soviet strategists in particular sought to integrate the acquisition of ►nuclear weapons into conventional strategic analysis. The advent of weapons of mass destruction was deemed 'revolutionary' in the sense that it represented a transformatory moment in thinking about the conduct of ►war and ►diplomacy. The revolutionary effect was that they made total war between possessing powers inherently irrational (►deterrence, MAD). In the 1990s the new RMA refers to 'the strategic consequences of the marriage of systems that collect, process and communicate information with those that apply military force' (Freidman, 1997). The effects of this coupling were dramatically demonstrated during the 1991 ►Persian Gulf War, the abiding memory of which to many Western observers was the battlefield devastation and more or less discriminate lethality of 'smart weapons' hitting their targets with extraordinary precision and ►accuracy. This conflict demonstrated the new possibilities involved in harnessing information technology to an ►actor's war-fighting ►capability. The collecting, processing and transmitting of information is thus the crux of the contemporary RMA; the overriding objective being to achieve information dominance and to use it. Sometimes referred to as 'information war' this post-modernist concept seems to imply that large, territorially based ground forces confronting an enemy position may no longer be a pre-requisite of future warfare. The ability to strike with precision over great distances obviously has important, if unclear, implications for land, sea and ►air power as traditionally conceived. Whether this has rendered armed forces obsolete as some proponents allege, is of course quite another matter.

**Rush—Bagot treaty** An agreement between Britain and the United States concluded in 1818 to demilitarize the US-Canadian border and to prevent the Great Lakes becoming a zone of naval competition. It is still in force and can therefore be described as the longest lasting and most successful ►disarmament

➤treaty in international history. In addition to fostering good neighbourliness between the United States and Canada and making ➤war unthinkable, it has also been an important factor in the ➤special relationship between the United States and the United Kingdom. This treaty was part of the general settlement of the war of 1812 and since then all disagreements between these two states have been settled without resort to the use of ➤force.

# S

**Saddle point** A term used in ➤game theory. A saddle point is that point on the matrix in a zero-sum game which is the smallest in its row and the largest in its column. The saddle point represents a stable solution to the ➤zero-sum game. Stability in game terms means that neither player can improve his position by moving independently away from the saddle point. This reasoning assumes that both players will act rationally throughout the exercise.

**SALT** An acronym for the Strategic Arms Limitation Talks. These were ➤bilateral ➤arms control ➤negotiations held between the United States and the Soviet Union between 1967 and 1979. Two conventions were produced: SALT I ran as an Interim Agreement for five years after 1972. SALT II was never ratified. Subsequently the SALT process was replaced by the more radical START I and II agreements. SALT I and its accompanying ➤ABM Treaty (there was no time limit on the latter) sought to substitute mutual restraint for self-restraint in controlling the ➤arms race. In fact the failure to address the issue of multiple warheads in SALT I was seen *ex ante* as a major omission. SALT II sought to rectify this with a further interim convention up to 1985. By this time the relations between the two ➤superpowers were deteriorating as their ➤*détente* relationship was unravelling. The Soviet ➤intervention in ➤Afghanistan meant that the draft treaty was withdrawn from the US Senate without forcing the issue to a vote. In the end it was not possible to isolate the SALT process from the general drift in superpower relations. In particular in the United States SALT ran up against domestic interests which wanted to use SALT as a stick with which to beat particular Administrations in the White House. Viewed from the situation following the end of the ➤Cold War with an expanding ➤security ➤regime evident in the arms control ➤issue area, SALT looks modest and almost innocuous. It needs to be remembered that at the time it was the jewel in the crown of the ➤Nixon Doctrine's *détente* strategy with the former Soviet Union.

***Salus populi suprema lex*** The supreme law is the health/security of the people. A classic metalegal doctrine of necessity associated with ➤*raison d'état* and the right of self-preservation. Its essential character is that it gives virtually unrestricted freedom to a state to take any action it deems necessary to protect its own self-defined interests. ➤International law has attempted to restrict the sway of the doctrine but in the final analysis states can, and do, appeal to 'necessity' as a legitimate ground for action.

**Scenario** An imagined, hypothetical future state of affairs. The term is particularly popular within the ➤strategic studies tradition where '➤war gaming' has been used for decades by senior military officers both for training purposes and for actual contingency planning before hostilities. The advent of civilian strategists as the dominant intellectual influence after 1945 led to the scenario replacing the war game as the primary vehicle for such speculation. Whereas war games were rather narrowly confined to what were perceived to be purely military matters, constructing scenarios required the author(s) to have regard to a much greater range of variables, including economic, legal and ➤diplomatic.

The late Herman Kahn (1960) probably represents the best individual example of how thinking through the possibilities on ➤nuclear war or escalation can produce a series of colourful – or disturbing – scenarios. Probably his most famous instance was that of the so-called Doomsday Machine. It is no accident that Kahn moved on to ➤futurology in later life, because in the process of thinking through the next decades/centuries, use must necessarily be made of scenarios. If reference is made to Malthus (1826) and the theory of population growth, such speculation is – like war gaming – not new. Malthus established an early inclination towards pessimism in scenario building about the future and this tradition has been continued into the present context by groups such as the Club of Rome.

Trend analysis is a well-established methodology and in general terms ➤policymakers and their advisers often have to take account of future trends and tendencies in making policy in the present context. In this sense scenario construction is simply prudential and it should not be condemned as a fad or a fetish of a particular individual, school or approach. ➤WOMP

**Scope** An ➤actor's scope is a measure of the ➤issue areas on which it can effectively ➤influence world politics. The concept is used in the analysis of ➤power relations and is usually used in conjunction with the concept of ➤domain. As intervening variables in the explanation of how power – as a possession – is converted into power – as a relationship – the two ideas are crucial.

**SDI** An acronym for the Strategic Defence Initiative. This was a United States ballistic missile defence (➤BMD) research programme initiated during the Presidency of Ronald Reagan. In March 1983, during an address to the American people, the President challenged the US scientific and strategic community to develop means of intercepting and destroying ballistic missiles before they reached the territory of the United States. This 'Star Wars' speech, as it became known, was the proximate initiator for increased funding over a five-year period (commencing in 1985) to investigate whether new ➤technologies could be harnessed to this role.

America had always been interested in anti–ballistic missile (➤ABM) technology from the 1950s. Although the SDI was at least in part driven by technological innovation, it also reflected a growing unease about the stability of the ➤Cold War nuclear deterrence relationship with the Soviet Union. SDI seemed to offer the possibility of reducing American vulnerabilities to a Soviet ➤pre-emptive strike, and there was always the possibility that if America did engage in denying itself the option the Soviet Union might not. Although SDI was supported by interest groups such as the so-called 'High Frontier' and by some strategists, it proved to be controversial. Scientific opinion was divided about its practicalities whilst ➤peace movements expressed unease about its potential to induce a new ➤arms race. In the late spring of 1993 Defence Secretary Aspin announced the demise of SDI. The Initiative fell victim to the ending of the Cold War, the collapse of ➤communism and the implosion of the Soviet Union. Although the United States continues to show interest in the possibility of ABM technologies, these concerns are now directed at states perceived to be ➤pariahs/rogues. Defending itself or its allies against these contingencies is more specific and less exotic than SDI.

**Secession** Defined by Mayall (1990) as the ➤mirror image of ➤irredentism, the term refers to the political expression of separation by the inhabitants of a ➤region from some pre-existing ➤state structure. Secessionist sentiments may therefore be seen as indicative of the rejection of some of the most basic ground rules of the ➤state-system in favour of ➤nationalism that owes more to ideas about kinship and ethnicity. Modern examples of secessionist movements that challenged existing state structures are Biafra and Bangladesh, while at the time of writing secessionism has produced the complete demise of the state of ➤Yugoslavia. As all three instances quoted above show, secession is rarely attempted or achieved through peaceful change. A more typical outcome is ➤civil war. The association of secessionist politics with violence and ➤communal conflict can be anticipated from the previous discussion. Since secession represents such a powerful centrifugal challenge to ➤state-centrism, seccessionist tendencies and factions will be resisted by political authorities at the centre.

**Second Gulf War** ➤Persian Gulf War

**Second Strike** A term used in strategic analysis. It refers to the ➤capability of an ➤actor to retaliate violently against an adversary having sustained in the meantime a ➤first strike. Second-strike capabilities are therefore those residual forces available for use against an opponent after her/his initial move has been made. As defined here, the idea of second strike is highly relative and contingent. These contingencies will depend upon two crucial variables: the state of ➤technology at any given moment and the capabilities and intentions of the adversary.

The development of ➤strategic studies as an area of ➤international relations during the ➤Cold War era was responsible for a new emphasis upon the importance of second-strike capabilities in the new age of ➤nuclear ➤deterrence.

Informed discussion of these ideas and issues began in the United States during the closing years of the Eisenhower Presidency. In particular in a seminal article in *Foreign Affairs* (1959) Wohlstetter argued for the centrality of the notion of second strike to a full understanding of deterrence or the 'delicate balance of terror'. Wohlstetter argued quite deliberately that effective deterrence meant a 'capability to strike second.' These arguments coincided neatly with the development – firstly in the United States – of missiles that could be based upon submarines. Once again the symbiotic relationship between technology and strategic thinking was there for all to observe.

**Secretary-General** The establishment of the first modern international governmental organizations (►IGOs) in the nineteenth-century led to the consequential development of international secretariats, and with them the office of Secretary-General. The first proposal for a neutral body of international civil servants was made in 1694 by William Penn in his *Essay towards the Present and Future Peace of Europe*. The nineteenth century secretariats, however, were composed mainly of 'national' civil servants or politicians whose primary loyalty was to their own member governments. The breakthrough in the development of a genuine international secretariat and Secretary-General, whose primary loyalty and responsibility was to the organization itself rather than to individual governments, came with the establishment of the ►League of Nations and ►specialized agencies after 1919. It has been argued since that in the careers of Sir Eric Drummond, the first Secretary-General of the League, and Albert Thomas, the first Secretary-General of the International Labour Organization (ILO) are the paradigm examples of the two modern traditions: the administrator/civil servant and the ►diplomat/politician.

The starting point for the analysis of the role and function of any Secretary-General is an examination of the constitutional position of that office as stated in the documentation establishing the organization. This documentation will seek to address itself to the issue of whether the office of Secretary-General is to be primarily that of an administrator or that of a diplomat – or some combination of both roles. The administrator is seen as faithfully implementing the decisions and directives of the member ►states, as conveyed through their national delegations. The diplomat/politician tends to have a much greater degree of ►autonomy to initiate policies, at least for discussion, among member states. Indeed in this latter tradition the Secretary-General might pursue an independent line in public by making speeches, giving lectures and interviews and writing articles on questions actually or potentially within the remit of their organization. Recent instances of Secretaries-General taking this approach to their office might include Dag Hammarskjöld (UN), Raul Prebisch, United Nations Conference on Trade and Development (UNCTAD), and Diallo Telli, Organization of African Unity (OAU).

When the ►UN was established in 1945 the duality of the role of Secretary-

General was recognized. Thus in Article 99 of its charter, the incumbent is given certain powers of initiative: 'the Secretary-General may bring to the attention of the Security Council any matter which in his opinion may threaten the maintenance of international peace and security'. If this can be seen as creating greater ►scope for the incumbent to act independently in voicing his views and concerns, the actual nominating procedure gives ►authority to member states to refrain from supporting a contender for office, or an incumbent for a further term, if they are unhappy with his performance. In the instance of the UN, the Secretary-General is nominated by the ►Security Council and confirmed by the Assembly for a five-year period of office. Incumbents such as Lie (UN) and Telli (OAU) were denied further terms in office because they fell foul of important states in their respective organizations.

The Secretary-General of any organization will be expected to fulfil the role of head of the secretariat in the appropriate organization. An important constraint upon any Secretary-General will be the extent to which he has a free hand to choose those who staff the secretariat. Normally member states will expect allocations to reflect various ideas about 'balance' between geographic areas and political divisions. This can result in ►geopolitical differences being imported into the secretariat with divisive results. 'Promotion by favour' rather than 'promotion by merit' is the likely outcome from these intrusions.

Personality, skill and reputation, although difficult to stipulate objectively, must be included as factors in any assessment of the role and relevance of the office of Secretary-General in any organization. Two career patterns appear to be particularly productive of putative Secretaries-General: the world of politics and diplomacy is one, and the world of the academic and the public administrator is the other. Appropriately Albert Thomas and Eric Drummond represent these two backgrounds, while Hammarskjöld is perhaps the nearest to a synthesis of the two. His background was in the Drummond role but he saw the need to develop the office into directions more akin to Thomas-typologies. Hammarskjöld was fortunate that his period of office coincided with fundamental changes in the character and composition of the UN as the log-jam on membership was broken and the organization moved towards universality. He was thus able to build a consensus of support amongst the emerging majority of non-aligned states from 1955 onwards until the Congo crisis of 1960 and the subsequent power struggle in that state led to the Soviet attack upon the man and the office of Secretary-General. The Soviet proposal that the office should become a troika of three Secretaries-General, representing the ►First, Second and ►Third worlds was the result of this attack. Although this troika proposal failed to win enough support, it was based upon plausible analysis, whatever the motivations of the Soviet Union for proposing it. The troika recognized that the UN was polarized into a number of factions. When this occurs in an intergovernmental organization (IGO) the Secretary-General is faced with two equally damaging choices, either to be impartial – and ineffective

– or committed – and controversial. The paradigm instance of such organizational polarization is surely UNCTAD, which has had this characteristic
since its inception. The various Secretaries-General of this IGO have tended
to opt for the committed/controversial role.

The office of Secretary-General of any IGO is one of the most varied and
vexatious positions available to international diplomats. It seems to be the case
that once states have gone beyond a certain point in their relations they perceive
the need to establish permanent institutions, including a Secretariat and a
Secretary-General, the ➤Commonwealth being a case in point. At the same
time the role and function of the Secretary-General will depend upon the three
variables discussed above: (a) what stipulations the constitution of the IGO
makes for the office; (b) the personality, training and background of the
incumbent; and (c) the kind of a global or regional system the IGO is envisaged
as operating in. The systemic factor will provide constraints or opportunities
working for or against take expansion in this regard.

**Security** A term which denotes the absence of threats to scarce values. In
principle security can be absolute, that is to say freedom from all threat is the
equivalent of complete security. Conversely in a totally threatening system
of relations, a system of implacable hostility verges into systemic paranoia.
Empirically security is a relative term and in ➤international relations scholarship
it has been established custom to analyse the concept in terms of more or less
rather than all or none (Wolfers 1962, Baldwin 1997). Historically security has
been seen as a core value and ultimate ➤goal of ➤state behaviour. This position
was often latent and assumed rather than manifest and stated. Recently ➤neoreal-
ism has raised the profile of the idea of security to that of a central – if contested
– concept. Waltz states that, 'in ➤anarchy security is the highest goal (p. 126).
Baldwin in his recently stipulative analysis of the concept (redolent of American
➤social science literature on relational ➤power) rejects this 'prime value
approach' to security analysis. Using instead 'marginal value approaches' Baldwin restates the relativist approach referred to above in terms of marginal utility.
'How much security is enough?' becomes a relevant question. Since absolute
security is not available outcome within any rational cost calculation, there is
no point in going for it as a goal. Baldwin suggests a 7-point checklist to break
down the analysis of security and to avoid Waltz-type 'simplifications'.

Traditionally analyses of security in a ➤foreign policy context concentrated
on the military dimension. Here threats implicit in ➤war and near violent
➤conflict situations raised acute national security questions for political ➤leader-
ships. Strategies of 'balancing' or 'band-waggoning', of ➤ally-seeking and
coalition-building, of ➤arms racing and ➤defence spending were the common
currency of classical security policy making. The end of the ➤Cold War has
allowed for a burgeoning of the security agenda to include ideas about economic
and ecological/environmental ➤security to set alongside the more familiar

military. Economic security concerns are implicit in ➤mercantilism. Economic security is essentially a 'supply-side' problem in IR, which is why mercantilism sets so much store by ➤self-sufficiency. If the control of the supply of goods and services falls into hostile hands or if the price for the supply of the same is set by a hostile actor with monopoly control then the economic security of the recipient is potentially under threat. The growth of ➤interdependence and ➤globalization in economic relations enhances the problem in one sense but offers a solution in another if all parties redefine their security in cooperative rather than conflictual terms. ➤Multilateralism is an escape route but the consequence will be the abandonment of mercantilism/➤neo-mercantilism.

There are similarities to note with the conclusion above in respect of ecological or environmental security. As noted elsewhere the environment as an issue area is structurally compatible with a ➤mixed actor view of things. The ➤nuclear winter thesis is an example of how environmental security concerns are truly ➤transnational. Strategies based upon narrow ➤state-centric views are ultimately self-defeating in environmental policy making. Writers like Buzan (1991) recognize the dilemma and in his case modify the concept of anarchy by talking of a 'mature anarchy'. If assumptions can be made about common security as an alternative to state-centric versions of security then it might be possible to go even further and see the security concept becoming part of the agenda for ➤global governance to consider.

**Security community** This concept was developed by Karl Deutsch in the 1950s after extensive empirical study of the North Atlantic area. Deutsch (Rosenau, 1961) maintained that the security community idea – and there were two versions of it – was a form of international cooperation which, under certain circumstances, could lead to ➤integration. Deutsch argued that a security community was formed amongst participating ➤actors when their peoples, and particularly their political ➤elites, held stable expectations of ➤peace between themselves in the present and for the future. Thus for Deutsch the United Kingdom and Eire, Norway and Sweden, the United States and Canada are all instances of security communities. The idea of what he called the 'no ➤war community' would spill over into the absence of significant organized preparations for war or large scale violence. Deutsch argued that empirical evidence of this lack of preparation would tend to validate the 'no war' idea. The corollary of the idea that a security community is distinguished in this way was that when conflicts did occur between the participants, ➤conflict management and ➤conflict resolution would be attempted.

Deutsch actually distinguishes two types of security community: the pluralistic from the amalgamated. The difference is the presence – or absence – of institutions. Thus in the amalgamated version the constituent members actually create a political community between themselves by institution-building. For Deutsch (1968) 'any reasonably well-integrated nation state' is an example of an 'amalgamated security community'. The examples cited above are, therefore, of pluralistic security communities. These are easier to establish and maintain. They require three antecedent conditions: compatibility of values, responsiveness to each other's needs and predictability of policy goals by political elites.

The argument that a number of states now conduct their relationships according to the 'no war' principle is an important insight. If validated it would certainly suggest that in at least those instances the traditional ➤state-centric idea that war was the final arbiter between states needs to be dropped. It also leads to the conclusion that traditionally conceived conceptions of ➤high politics are not the defining characteristics of these relationships. As such Deutsch's work represents an important break with previous perspectives on ➤macropolitics. Along with other academics he points towards a greater emphasis in teaching and research upon a viewpoint that favours ➤complex interdependence as a growing characteristic of the study.

**Security complex**  A term used by Buzan (1991) to facilitate ➤security analysis facing particular ➤regions. Geography and history means that most ➤states conduct their security relations in a regional rather than global context; proximity and familiarity breed fear in this respect. Thus the amity/enmity check-list will be one indicator of a security complex whilst the ➤power relationships will be the other. Thus for Buzan a security complex is a 'group of states whose primary security concerns link together sufficiently closely that their national securities cannot be realistically considered apart from one another' (p. 190).

The security complex idea recognizes the fact of life that in terms of ➤foreign policy-making most states define their security relations in regional rather than global terms and that when they confront global issues there is a tendency to see these determined by the regional context. In effect the region dominates the ➤perception of security. The role of outside ➤actors and ➤great powers in the security complex dynamic may well be crucial. Thus in Europe the effect of the Second World War was to produce what Buzan calls a 'higher-level' security complex with the emergence of the United States of America and the Soviet Union as ➤bloc leaders. Not surprisingly the shifts in the tectonic plates of the European security complex with the end of the ➤Cold War and the demise of ➤communism have alerted ➤diplomats and scholars to the likelihood that these changes will require a new definition of the complex. The reduction in what Buzan calls 'overlay' will allow local security considerations to come to the surface as the movement for ➤NATO expansion into Central and Eastern Europe demonstrates.

The security complex idea is essentially a plea to consider the regional level of analysis operating in terms of security issues. In some ways it is an attempt to raise questions rather than to supply answers and it is replete with difficulties when empirical application is sought. Buzan's struggle even to stipulate the boundaries of extant security complexes bears testimony to these queries.

**Security Council** The Security Council is that organ of the ➤United Nations system given primary responsibility (see Article 24 of the Charter) for the maintenance of international peace and security. In one respect the establishment of the Council as the centrepiece of this arrangement was an intentional step predicated upon the perception that the ➤League of Nations had lacked 'bite' and that its successor should be better equipped to take decisive action. Thus whereas the Council of the League had been hidebound and hamstrung by the ➤unanimity principle, no such blocking mechanisms were built into the Security Council – with one exception. The five permanent members of the Council: the United States, Russia, the United Kingdom, China and France, through the exercise of the ➤veto, retain the unanimity rule. In other respects, through, it is possible for the Council to override any other ➤state members and still make binding decisions. Moreover by allowing permanent members to abstain on a resolution without regarding such a move as an exercise of the veto, the Council has expanded its competence to make decisions on the key issue area of peace and security.

Analytically the Council was seen as the hub of the ➤collective security system of the UN Charter. By stipulating that five of the most significant states in the ➤hierarchy should concur with all Council decisions (other than procedural ones), the founders of the UN sought to ensure that whenever the Council decided to act the preponderance of available ➤power and ➤influence in the system would be committed in support of the decision. Under Chapter VII of the Charter the Council is given binding ➤decision-making authority and in support of such commitments the same Chapter made a wide range of ➤diplomatic, economic and military sanctions available for use against the recalcitrant state(s). In this way it is possible to see the veto provisions of the charter as an essentially realistic and judicious recognition of the power configurations in ➤international relations in 1945.

The outbreak of the ➤Cold War seriously damaged the ability of the Security Council to work as envisaged by the Charter. Article 43 on the establishment of a permanent UN force became inoperable. The veto became a means of paralysing decision-making and neutralizing the Council as an effective deliberating body. The veto was even used to restrict the entry of new members into the Organization, until the log-jam was broken in 1955. Cold War antagonisms prevented the People's Republic of China from occupying that seat designated for China on the Council until 1971. When the Security Council did work as intended in these early years – as in the case of the ➤Korean War – it was a fluke made possible by the absence of the Soviet Union from the Council. The low point in the post-war decline was reached in 1955 when the Council held only twenty-two meetings. Many of the key issue areas of the early post-1945 period were simply not brought before the Council.

The influx of new members from the ➤Third World did much to revive the fortunes of the UN in general and the Council in particular. The second

➤Secretary-General Dag Hammarskjold was responsible for developing the concept of ➤peacekeeping or preventative diplomacy after 1956. The council played a major decision-making role in these developments in particular during the Congo and Cyprus operations of the early 1960s. In December 1963 the assembly agreed to expand the size of the Council from eleven to fifteen member states in order to increase Third World representation. In resolving upon this expansion it was decided that half the non-permanent seats should go to Afro-Asian states (the remaining five are divided on a regional basis between Latin America, 2; Eastern Europe, 1; and Western Europe, and other states, 2:). A major proposal for ➤reform of the UN involves allocating permanent membership to select representative states of the Third World. The candidates most often suggested are Brazil, India and South Africa.

The Council played a central role in the Rhodesian ➤economic sanctions issue, instructing all member states to implement mandatory measures against the illegal regime in December 1966. These selective sanctions were followed by comprehensive ones in May 1968. Although the sanctions policy was deliberately evaded by key multinational corporations (➤MNCs) and governments friendly towards the illegal regime in Rhodesia, the willingness of the Council to resort to such measures was indicative of its resuscitation.

The development of the peacekeeping competence of the Council following the intrusion of Cold War considerations in the early years must be seen as the major development in the issue area of peace and security since 1945. Of course, the collective security provisions of the Charter remain available for use in any future contingency. Moreover the possibility appears to be emerging that Russia intends to take a higher diplomatic profile in the UN in the future. Such changes could encourage the permanent members to work closer in the future than they have sometimes in the past. The General Assembly has become increasingly unwieldy as its membership has expanded and this development alone might encourage the permanent members to keep issues within the Council. In ➤crisis situations it will be the Council rather than the Assembly that member states, and the world in general, will look towards for a position on an issue. This was confirmed by the importance attached to the Security Council resolutions before, during and after the ➤Persian Gulf War. Its representative character could be further improved by increasing the number of permanent members to include perhaps India, South Africa and Brazil. France and the United Kingdom might collapse their representation if the ➤European Union becomes a ➤confederal actor or this could be shared with a united Germany. ➤➤P5

**Security dilemma** A central tenet of ➤realism and the realist ➤paradigm, the ➤security dilemma arises for the situation of ➤anarchy that ➤states find themselves in. By striving to increase their on security – by following policies that enhance their military ➤capabilities – states inadvertently make others feel less secure. As a result of this behaviour a vicious circle or spiral of security-insecurity arises to which there is no permanent and lasting solution. John H. Herz. (1950) was among the first to develop these ideas. Herz rested the dilemma not on any innate anti-social attributes of man *per se* but rather upon the social nexus – and the idea of anarchy – within which men, and groups, operate. The security dilemma may therefore be regarded as a structural attribute rather than a psychological one. It is to nurture, rather than nature, that one should look for explanations of why the dilemma occurs.

Herz returned to the subject in Chapter 10 of his 1959 book. The 'power and security dilemma', as it had now become, is still seen as immutable. Herz argued that the emerging ➤bipolar configuration of the ➤Cold War period had exacerbated the dilemma. Comparing the bipolar system unfavourably with the ➤balance of power, Herz concluded that 'bipolarity has given the security dilemma its utmost poignancy' (p. 241). Buzan (1983) seems to reflect similar views; again in his seventh chapter referring to the power-security dilemma, Buzan argues for what he terms a 'mature anarchy' (p. 208) as the most stable outcome of the constant ➤action-reaction pattern.

The most original contribution to the security dilemma idea since its inception has come from Robert Jervis in his book on ➤perception and ➤misperception (1976) and then in his *World Politics* article (1978). In both publications Jervis analyses the dilemma in terms of ➤game theory, and particularly the variable sum Prisoner's Dilemma – which balances its players between ➤conflict and cooperation strategies. Jervis argues that if ➤war is costly and cooperation beneficial there will be strong incentives to overcome the dilemma by following policies that ameliorate rather than exacerbate relations between putative adversaries. If military ➤technology favours the ➤defence, and if the opportunity costs of defence policy are high, incentives to manage the dilemma will correspondingly be high. Moreover if defensive postures can be easily distinguished form offensive postures – so that the risks of misperception are reduced – the dilemma will be reduced. Like Herz and Buzan, Jervis believes that a ➤status quo orientation by the leading players in the system helps the management process.

There is no antidote to the dilemma within realism, of course. Realists are committed to its principles. ➤Regime analysis offers a possible way out analytically. Philosophically the ➤idealists believed that systems such as their ➤collective security idea offered more permanent solutions, but this requires the importation of assumptions which realism cannot tolerate.

**Security regime** Attempts to identify and stipulate the ground rules for ➤security arrangements that produce a ➤regime have not formed the main thrust of the study of ➤international regimes. In Krasner's (1993) edition Robert Jervis attempted this exercise. The attempt to apply regime analysis to what other writers would term a ➤security complex is fraught with difficulties because it implies a meeting of minds between the ➤neorealist concept of ➤anarchy and the ➤pluralist concept of regime. Security can however be saved in this analysis by defining it in terms of common security rather than ➤state security.

Jervis sees the following conditions as being necessary to the formation and continuation of a security regime: the ➤great powers must support the scheme, the states must be willing to forgo what Wolfers (1962) calls self-extension in favour of mutual security, the opportunity costs of not establishing a security regime outweigh the benefit of continuation with anarchy. It might be possible to view the security regime as a step along the way towards a ➤security community defined as the absence of the threat of war and therefore a low probability of its occurrence amongst states.

It seems plausible to suggest that the ➤Gorbachev Doctrine was working towards the establishment of a security regime between the former Soviet Union and the United States of America at the time of his demise and the subsequent collapse of the Soviet state. As Jervis himself unwittingly anticipated in 1983, the need for a security regime between the US and the SU was occasioned by the fact that previous national security policies were leading to disaster. ➤➤Concert system

**Security studies** A sub-field of ➤international relations which is concerned with the elucidation of the concept of ➤security its ➤implementation in ➤foreign policy making and its consequential effect upon structures and processes in world politics. During the ➤Cold War era security studies was narrowly defined in terms of military-security ➤issue areas. It was heavily policy-orientated and there was a large overlap with ➤strategic studies. The post-Cold War system has changed all of these assumptions and the issue area of political economy and the ➤environment have broadened the agenda of security studies from what traditionalists would have referred to as '➤high politics' to embrace so-called '➤low politics' of economics and the environment. The distinction has lost much validity in fact because issue of economic or environmental security can be defined in terms which conform to most common-sense ideas of high politics. As a result security studies is one of the most buoyant areas of IR scholarship currently. In shape and substance it is coming to resemble ➤international political economy (IPE) in the sense that it is highly eclectic and shows little signs of reaching a consensus about it operating principles or ➤ideology. Although ➤realist and ➤neorealist scholars have traditionally dominated the field, the opening up of the new economic/environmental agendas is challenging this dominance. In particular the growth of critical security studies (Camnbell 1992) and the idea of common security confirm that various perspectives are evident under the security studies umbrella. In a recent review essay David Baldwin (1995) tentatively argued for a 'reintegration' of security studies into mainstream IR. This is unlikely to happen if only because too many academic careers would be at stake in the demise of the sub-field.

**Self-defence** A legal sub-species of the more general political right of ➤self-help. The evolution of the right of self-defence in customary and contemporary international law is a legal acknowledgement of political reality. As such, the dilemmas of politics are clearly reflected in the ambiguities of international law. Consequently, the right is fraught with uncertainties. International law is by no means clear as to what the 'self' refers to. Does it refer only to the use of ➤force for the protection of a ➤state's territorial integrity or can it be broadened to include other interests that states deem essential to their security? Is it limited to the employment of force in response to a prior attack or is there a right of anticipatory or pre-emptive self-defence? How are the requirements of immediacy, necessity and proportionality defined? Is it possible to distinguish operationally between matters of 'security' and matters of 'survival'? The traditional metalegal doctrine of ➤*salus populi suprema lex* cuts across these difficulties and asserts that the state has a right to interpret the notion of self-defence expansively; that is, that it is permissible to undertake any action it considers necessary to protect itself against any actual or threatened injury to its self-defined interests. However, contemporary international law attempts to restrict the use of force to circumstances of prior use of force. But this does not resolve the issue of the nature of 'self' or whether it is legitimate to use force against acts that may not involve force but are nevertheless considered to imperil the interests of state.

Article 2, paragraph 4 and Article 51 of the ➤UN Charter are ambiguous on this and may indeed be contradictory. As with other quasi-legal rights asserted by states the matter of limits and ➤scope will always be compromised by the claims of ➤sovereignty and the overriding duty of self preservation from which these rights derive (see Osgood and Tucker, 1967).

**Self-determination** The right or aspiration of a group, which considers itself to have a separate and distinct identity, to govern itself and to determine the political and legal status of the territory it occupies. Thus, in the political sense it refers both to a process and to an idea. Closely identified with ➤nationalism and ➤liberalism it is probably best understood as a theory of the relationship between ➤nation and ➤state which finds its fullest expression in the concept of the democratic ➤nation-state. However, there is nothing in the term itself that indicates preference for a particular form of political organization and it can mean the right of an established state to determine its own form of government free from external interference. In a general sense, then, political self-determination refers to the right of peoples to determine their own destiny in their own way.

The concept was implicit in the US Declaration of Independence of 1776 ('the consent of the governed') and in the French revolutionary Declaration of the Rights of Man in 1789 ('the divine right of the people'). Its influence was especially felt in the nineteenth-century European ➤states-system and apart from France, it played an important part in the unification of Germany and of

Italy and the independence of Belgium and Greece. Outside Europe it was the prime mover in the process of the liberation of South America from colonial rule. But it was not until the First World War that, under the impact of President Wilson's ➤fourteen points, the idea of national ➤independence came to be known as national self-determination. Thereafter it has become one of the 'absolutes' of contemporary international thought and it featured prominently in the Covenant of the ➤League of Nations and in the ➤United Nations Charter.

Despite its ubiquity the concept has never carried a clear legal connotation. The problem of determining which groups of people may legitimately claim this right had bedevilled its application in the twentieth-century world. This is further complicated by the legal restrictions against ➤intervention in another state's internal affairs. Consequently, in practice the emphasis has been placed on the notion of 'self' rather than on any external application of a known rule. Even so, the United Nations has attempted on a number of occasions to link the concept to the process of ➤decolonization and thereby make it a positive duty and a legal right rather than an aspiration. The Declaration on the Granting of Independence of Colonial Countries and Peoples in 1960, for example, stated that 'all people have the right to self-determination; by virtue of that right they freely determine their political status and freely pursue their economic, social and cultural development'. The right of self-determination was again reaffirmed in the 1970 Declaration of Principles of ➤international law which further emphasized that all states were under a positive duty to promote it. This all-embracing linkage with anti-colonialism, equal rights, economic, social and cultural development has in effect robbed the term of any practical meaning. Questions of definition remain. Who are the 'peoples' to whom it applies? Does it justify rebellion, ➤revolution or ➤secession? Must it result in full independence or can it be partial or fulfilled by means of ➤association? Answers to these questions are by no means clear-cut and the international community, both inside and outside the ➤General Assembly, has tended to react to them in an *ad hoc*, interest-based fashion rather than in accordance with the guidelines of the 1970 Declaration, which in any case are much too vague for the practical application.

**Self-fulfilling prophecy** Originally developed by the sociologist R. K. Merton in 1949, this theory refers to the way in which social behaviour is conditioned by the expectations that individuals and groups have of each other. Its basic premise is that these expectations will produce an erroneous ➤definition of the situation which will then feed back into a pattern of behaviour that will seem to confirm the initial position. For instance, ➤state A perceives State B as having aggressive intentions towards it and, accordingly, in a ➤show of force moves its troops to the border. State B responds with some equally determined move and State A feels that its original position has been vindicated. This clearly oversimplified example nonetheless shows the principle of the theory.

The self-fulfilling prophecy has been widely applied by educational sociologists to such issues as the way tutors grade students and then seek confirmation of this grading subsequently. Economists are agreed that it is a contributory factor in 'panic buying' and banking and stock market crashes. Application to politics has been more popular among psychologists than sociologists, with Stagner probably the most influential.

**Self-help** For the ➤realist the notion of self-help is a logical consequence of the anarchical structure of international ➤states-system. For the ➤idealist it is the cause of it. Either way, self-help is endemic in ➤international relations. Given that ➤states are ➤independent political units that are primarily concerned with their own survival and advancement but are not subordinate to a central ➤authority, the idea of self-reliance is a compelling one. The search for ➤security in a system of politics without government means that self-help is a necessary function of self-preservation. It is a natural response to the ➤security dilemma as traditionally conceived. However, the right to self-help is not an absolute one. States might not be expected to surrender the general right of self-help but the ➤international system does not attempt to restrict its ➤scope. Both ➤international law and the ➤United Nations Charter are founded on the premise that there is no unrestricted right of self-help. Indeed, in this context the primary purpose of law and of ➤supranational institutions is to map out areas of consensus on permissible limits of the private use of force by ➤sovereign states. Thus, ➤self-defence is regarded as the most basic manifestation and requirement of the institution of self-help. Other characteristic forms of it are ➤retortion and ➤reprisals. Historically, states have been reluctant to allow encroachments on the rights of self-preservation but the nineteenth and twentieth centuries in particular have witnessed considerable, though frequently ambiguous, inroads into this entrenched doctrine. To date, there have been no viable or effective replacements, ➤balance of power and ➤collective security are variants of it, not alternatives. Accordingly, to some the persistence of the notion is an impediment to progress towards the establishment of a centralized executive world authority possessing a monopoly of the legitimate use of force. But since self-help is a consequence of political independence, so long as the world is organized on a decentralized multi-state basis, it is unlikely to be replaced. Clearly, the absence of self-help as a fundamental behavioural principle would mean a radical transformation of the system. This eventuality is, at present, extremely unlikely.

**Self-sufficiency** A form of economic ➤foreign policy which seeks to reduce the dependence of a state ➤actor for external goods and services to a minimum. Since the ➤trade system is based upon ➤reciprocity – one actor's ➤imports are another's ➤exports – widespread pursuit of self-sufficiency as a long term goal will have deleterious effects upon the whole system. Self-sufficiency may also be pursued as a short-term expedient during times of acute ➤crisis and violence

– such as ➤war. In this instance the aim is to conduct a kind of 'siege economy' system. Instruments such as rationing and substitution will be used to reduce dependence, but in the final analysis abstinence and denial may be necessary.

Self-sufficiency was rejected by classical economic theory and has always been attacked by ➤economic liberalism. It does have its advocates in ➤mercantilism, however. The welfare implications of self-sufficiency in the twentieth century are dire and few political ➤leaderships could sustain such an arrangement over a long period without the robust use of instruments of social control. If ➤interdependence is regarded as a defining characteristic of ➤macropolitics then self-sufficiency is bound to have a bad press.

**Show of force**  The deliberate use of an ➤actor's military ➤capability to coerce an opponent by implication. The show of force is thus a diplomatic gesture, but one carrying coercive and punitive connotations. The coercion may be aimed directly at the opposition, or indirectly at a third party whose ties with the putative opponent are sufficiently strong and unequivocal for the true intention of the imposer to be understood. Whatever target is chosen, the essence of the show of force is its ambiguity. While this can leave the party making such a move with considerable flexibility, without more precision being introduced into the relationship – such as precise verbal statement of intent, i.e. an ➤ultimatum – the political leadership in the target actor may be unclear about what is required of them if they wish to seek redemption in the eyes of the imposer. The most intimidatory show of force is that which implies that the imposer's forces are being prepared for military action. Putting one's forces on an alert status, dispersing existing forces to more secure positions and calling up reserves all come in this category. ➤➤Gunboat diplomacy

**Single market**  A shorthand term for the European economic system anticipated in the original ➤treaties of the 1950s which established the ➤European community and currently being realized with the 'relaunching' of ➤integration in the 1980s and 1990s. Whilst much of the decision-making on the single market has been aimed at liberalisation and removal of barriers, in respect of Economic and Monetary Union (EMU) positive steps towards a single currency zone are currently being ➤implemented towards a 1999 target. The term 'internal market' is sometimes used in the literature instead of single market but either way '➤common market' is now no longer used. The integrative process in Europe has now proceeded further than any comparable instance in the ➤international system. The single market is testimony to the fact that – as far as the rest of the world is concerned – Europe is now a viable economic system in holistic terms.

**SIPRI**  ➤Think tanks

**Small powers/Small states**  Some scholars allege that all ➤states that are not ➤great powers are small powers. The distinction is usually made on the basis of a state's ability to provide for its own ►security needs. Thus, small powers are those states that have to rely on external assistance for their security needs. Clearly this definition is too general to be useful and most commentators and practitioners, while acknowledging the difficulties of precise categorization, assert that small powers are those which fall between ►middle powers and ►microstates. In this way most states are small or 'minor' powers. Speigel (1972) identifies three groups of states in this class. The largest class consists of states which seek to play an important regional role (e.g. Zimbabwe). The second group he terms 'the mavericks' – those states which seek ►influence within it (e.g. Libya). The third group consists of states which are similar to middle powers in terms of ►foreign policy style, material resources and development, but they usually have smaller populations, lower GNPs and tend to allocate less expenditure on armed forces and ►defence (e.g. Denmark, Norway, New Zealand). These are also termed 'miniature middle powers'. The question 'how small is small?' is thus a problematical one. Acknowledging the dangers of generalization, and bearing in mind the distinction between the older small ►developed states (mainly Western European) and the newer small developing states (mainly African, Asian and Latin American), the following appear to be characteristic behaviour patterns: limited involvement in world affairs, strong attachment to intergovernmental organizations (►IGOs), support for ►international law, avoidance of the use of ►force and a limited geographical and functional range of foreign policy activities. The acquisition of ►nuclear weapons by small states is one of the most important considerations in the debate about ►nuclear proliferation. The fear of the great powers is that this kind of ►horizontal proliferation will destabilize regional and/or international systems since it would increase the likelihood of ►accidental nuclear war or indeed deliberate recourse to war in a last-ditch gamble.

**Social science approach** The term 'social science' is here taken to refer to those studies such as sociology, psychology, anthropology and political science. Distinctive in terms of such factors as their ►level of analysis, they are similar in terms of their most fundamental methodological assumptions. Thus the social science approach to ►international relations involves applying the same methods, concepts, models and theories from any one or group of the above disciplines to the subject matter at hand. ►decision-making, game theory and ►systems analysis are but three examples of the inter-disciplinary borrowing. The social science approach is therefore consistently and intentionally eclectic.

Historically, this approach to the subject matter has been US-inspired and wholly post-1945 in its development. The ascendancy of the United States as a ►superpower in the system meant that the intellectual challenges presented by a global ►foreign policy had a spillover effect upon the colleges and research institutes of the United States. In short, US ►perception of its new role in ►macropolitics encouraged a new interest in the subject. In the years after 1945, moreover, funds for basic research were available in the United States. The US Government played an important, if controversial, role in some of this funding but private foundations like Ford, Carnegie and Rockefeller were also important.

Political science had already developed some significance before 1945 in the United States. Probably the most famous faculty was that located at the University of Chicago under the leadership of Charles Merriam. After 1945 political scientists such as Lasswell (1948) and Almond, nurtured in the Chicago tradition of social science, began to move into ►international relations, a field traditionally reserved for historians, lawyers philosophers and strategists: the so-called 'classical' tradition. Publication of the influential journal, *World Politics*, by Princeton Center for International Studies began in 1948. Thereafter there was a mushrooming of talented scholarship as various campuses in the United States developed an interest in the new field. Publications soon followed. Rosenau's 1961 *Reader* stands as an exemplification of the contributions made in the previous decade. By the beginning of the 1960s indeed the social science approach was well represented in US colleges and institutes and was beginning to have an impact across the Atlantic. In Europe the classical tradition was more entrenched and less willing to welcome these changes, preferring to see them as challenges instead. Hedley Bull's (1966b) article was typical of the unfavourable reaction from many European-based scholars. Accordingly the impact of the growth of a social science of world politics was delayed and somewhat diffused in Europe. Earlier, Dahl (1961b) labelled 'behaviouralism' as a protest movement. ►Traditional analysis simply left a vacuum which was filled by borrowing the concepts theories and techniques of the mainstream social sciences identified above.

Seemingly no sooner was one chapter closed than another opened. In 1969, David Easton, a leading exponent of the deductive mode of systems analysis, proclaimed a 'new revolution' in political science and characterized the epoch as 'post-behavioural'. Attacking what he called the 'empirical conservatism' (p. 1052) of the behavioural approach, Easton called for a new emphasis upon the study of values and, conversely, for the abandonment of the value-free approach. In calling for more value-orientated, politically relevant research at the end of the turbulent 1960s, Easton anticipated certain trends that have been evident in the study of IR since. There has been a definite proliferation of broad based perspectives and ►paradigms of late. Indeed the term 'paradigm proliferation' has been coined to characterize the unruly flock of activities currently ongoing in IR. There seems to have been a conscious shift away from epistemology towards ontology as the substance of inquiry and speculation. Walker's (1993) collection of essays being a case in point. Groom and Light's (1994) trend survey shows neatly the directions in which IR is currently going. Indeed the attempt implicit in the social science approach to locate the study within that broad tradition has been challenged by developments in the last quarter of the century. Many would now concur with Hedley Bull's wistful suggestion that

IR's place is forever in the philosophical toolshed and that accordingly IR's genealogy includes philosophy and political theory in the blood line.

**South** A collective noun used in the context of ➤international political economy to identify a group of ➤state ➤actors. The first ➤Brandt Report referred to the 'South' as broadly synonymous with 'developing' and 'poor' (Brandt, 1980, p. 31). The burden of the Brandt case was that the term was a kind of dialectic antithesis to ➤north and that the 'divide' could and should be bridged by Northern policies of self-interested cooperation. Gill and Law (1988) criticize 'South' as a contestable label but then proceed to use it, thereby selling the pass of conceptual clarity for the sake of convenience. Unlike the term ➤Third World 'South' is not derived from a particular ➤ideological persuasion but it is rather a stipulative term for a typology of state action as the Brandt usage demonstrates.

The case against using the term at all in the analysis of ➤international relations (IR) is that there is so much differentiation within the classification as to render it useless. At the top end of the range are the ➤NICs as the archetype middle income growth-orientated economies. At the bottom end are located the 'famine belt' states of the ➤fourth world. The end of the ➤Cold War era in world politics and the collapse of ➤communism has left the South with an absence of alternatives to the Northern model of market economics. In many parts of the South economic inefficiencies are compounded by political corruption and failure of ➤leadership. Defections from Southern ranks will continue as individual states break out of the vicious cycle of low income-growing population-low growth. This will lead to an increasing fragmentation of Southern solidarity. The nightmare scenario for the rump of the South may be Northern indifference more than anything else. ➤➤North-south; quasi-states

**Southern Cone** Geopolitical term referring to a sub-division of South America. It includes Chile, Argentina, Brazil, Bolivia, Paraguay and Uruguay. Of the various sub-division of South America – Southern Cone, Andean Region, Amazon Basin, River Plate Basin – this includes the largest number of key actors and is regarded as a loose but important international/➤regional sub-system. The most significant actor, Brazil is not exclusively 'southern' but is included because of the importance of its domestic centre – south political and economic orientation and for its traditional rivalry with Argentina. The Southern Cone region has been the setting for a number of ➤boundary disputes and resource conflicts, the main protagonists being Chile-Argentina and Argentina-Brazil. In the 1990s cooperation rather than conflict has been the dominant characteristic of regional relations, and there have been integrative developments in the economic sphere, the most significant being ➤Mercosur. The Southern Cone region is likely to play an increasing role in world politics in the 1990s, particularly since Brazil is now an upwardly mobile ➤middle power anxious to redefine its traditionally subordinate relationship with the 'Colossus to the North' – The USA. This region is also important in that it contains 49 per cent of the population of ➤Latin America, 56 per cent of its economic production and is the wealthiest part of the Western Hemisphere outside of North America. In addition, Brazil is now actively pursuing, under the leadership of former academic President Henrique Cardoso, permanent membership status on the UN's ➤Security Council. (See *Latin American Nations in World Politics*, ed. H. Muñoz and J. S. Tulchin, Westview Press, 1984.)

**Sovereignty** Often regarded as the enabling concept of ➤international relations whereby ➤states assert not only ultimate ➤authority within a distinct territorial entity but also assert membership of the international community. The doctrine of sovereignty implies a double claim: ➤autonomy in ➤foreign policy and exclusive competence in internal affairs. Internal sovereignty thus refers to a supreme ➤decision-making and enforcement authority with regard to a particular territory and population. External sovereignty on the other hand refers to its antithesis: the absence of a supreme international authority and hence the independence of sovereign states. Paradoxically, therefore, the doctrine of state sovereignty necessarily leads to the concept of ➤international ➤anarchy: the idea of a supreme authority within the state logically leads to a denial of the existence of a supra-sovereign above the state.

Historically, in the development of the European ➤states-system, it is usually associated with the works of Bodin (1576) and Hobbes (1651) where it appeared to be synonymous with the right to exercise unrestricted power. Thus, the ➤Hobbesian system of International Relations was characterized as a near-permanent state of war where sovereign authorities are not restrained by a common power. On this view, ➤international law, because its provenance must be doubtful, cannot circumscribe or set limits on state behaviour. Sovereign states are judges in their own cause, have an absolute right to go to war to pursue their conceived interests and can treat those who fall within their ➤domestic jurisdiction in their own way. However, in practice the denial of a supra-sovereign authority beyond the state has never meant that sovereign states are free to do as they please. The history of the modern states system (which is to say the history of state sovereignty) from the seventeenth century onwards has been a conscious attempt to move away from the apparent rigidity of the early formulation of the doctrine while retaining its more useful characteristics, especially the idea of formal ➤equality which it implies. The notion of absolute unlimited sovereignty, while being a useful and indeed an indispensable instrument to employ against the claims of a pope or emperor, was never more than a convenient fiction in the development of the modern ➤state-system. Increasing ➤interdependence, the reciprocal nature of international law and membership of ➤international organizations have thus led to the acceptance of the doctrine of 'divided sovereignty' where supremacy is qualified either through consent or auto-limitation. The ➤UN Charter, for example, is an implicit ➤recognition of this (Article 2 para. 1 recognizes the 'sovereign equality' of member states yet exhorts them to settle their disputes by 'peaceful means').

Many scholars today regard the doctrine of sovereignty not only as inimical to the development of international law, but as inherently misleading since few if any states are impermeable, or as impenetrable as it implies. All states are to a greater or lesser extent ►penetrated. They argue that integrative developments such as the ►EC/►EU and the whole process associated with ►complex interdependence have rendered the practice of sovereignty (if not the idea) anachronistic. Sovereignty has been eroded on all fronts, especially with the development of ►human rights and ►humanitarian intervention norms. Indeed for some writers, the end of the ►Westphalia system and the beginning of the post-Westphalian or post-modernist age is bound up with the demise of the sovereignty idea. As a legal absolute and a unitary idea, sovereignty has always been suspect; recognizing this one writer has postulated a distinction between 'positive' and 'negative' sovereignty (►quasi-states). However the continued relevance of the idea of sovereignty in international affairs is testified by the fact that at the political level it remains the primary organizing principle of world politics. Since sovereignty implies constitutional independence from other states a decentralized international system will always have recourse to some such ideas. Even the case of the most ambitious challenge to the sovereign idea is ambiguous. The EC/EU may not generate a real alternative to sovereignty. Many on both sides of the 'Euro-debate' recognize that the EC/EU by creating a new form of political authority would essentially be creating a European super-state. This entity will not transcend sovereignty it will merely enlarge or reinforce it.

**Special Drawing Rights (SDR)** A reserve asset created by the ►IMF. The facility was formally approved by the Board of Directors of the Fund in September 1967 and the requisite amendments to the Articles of the ►IMF were made by March 1968. By July 1969 sufficient member ►states had ratified these arrangements for them to come into force. The Managing Director of the Fund proposed the creation of 9.5 billion dollars of SDRs over the following three years and the first allocation was made in January 1970. The SDR is now the principal reserve asset of the IMF.

The creation of this new facility in the period 1967–9 was a significant, if belated, recognition by the membership of the IMF and the Group of Ten that a reserve asset, in addition to the traditional ►gold exchange standard, was needed. The SDR is a fiduciary issue, not backed by gold or indeed any national currency. Instead the value of the SDR is calculated against a basket of some sixteen currencies. Since it is both a store of value and a means of settling indebtedness it does have many of the characteristics of money. SDRs are, moreover, interest bearing assets, states in credit earning small interest while states in deficit on their allocation are charged interest.

The creation of the SDR coincided with the demise of the dollar as the basis of the post-1945 system. Had the politicians and bankers acted sooner when the first intimation of the dilemma inherent in the ➤Bretton Woods system was being pointed out at the end of the 1950s, events twenty years later might have been different. As it was, the fact that the SDR was not a national currency was its strength. It meant that the total reserve figure of SDRs could be expanded without a country running a balance of payments deficit. In the past this had been the only way whereby a leading state actor, such as the United States, could pump-prime the system. The creation of the SDR made such dollar deficit financing unnecessary.

A major issue that arose from the creation of the SDR was how this new reserve asset should be distributed. ➤Third World interests and economic liberals seek in the SDR the opportunity to expand the reserve position of developing states on the basis of need rather than the ability to pay. Various proposals have been made for a so-called 'link' to be made between the creation and distribution of SDRs and other activities, notably international and transnational economic assistance – or aid. The difficulty with all these initiatives is that they imply introducing new, and probably controversial, criteria into the SDR mechanism and ultimately into the IMF. If implemented these proposals would take the Fund further away from the original intentions of its founders and closer to the activities of other intergovernmental organizations (➤IGOs), notably the ➤World Bank group.

**Special relationship** Term commonly used to describe the relations between the United Kingdom and the United States since 1940. The phrase has become part of the rhetoric of the UK ➤foreign policy in particular, and every Prime Minister from Churchill onwards has alluded to it in one form or another, to the extent that in popular mythology the 'Special Relationship' with the United States is regarded as a permanent, almost structural feature of contemporary ➤world politics. A shared language, an overlapping culture, a similar commitment to the values of capitalism, representative democracy and the common law system have combined to produce, in the public mind at least, feelings of mutual affinity between the two ➤states. However, this relationship has rarely, except for relatively brief periods during and after the Second World War and again sporadically in the 1950s and 1960s, been quite as affectionate or intimate as the phrase suggests. In fact, some commentators suggest that the idea of the singularity of the relationship was a deliberate ploy of Winston Churchill who not only had family connections with the United States but also pressing strategic and economic reasons for propagating the uniqueness of the United Kingdom's relations with the United States. Both his short-term goals (defeating Hitler's Germany) and his long-term goals (➤encircling the Soviet Union and preserving the Empire) needed the active assistance of the US colossus. Churchill had a world view (the 'three circles' idea) in which the United Kingdom and the United States in equal measure would form an impenetrable axis which could dominate and stifle the growth of international ►communism and at the same time prolong the active life of the British Empire. The practical symbols of this bonding of 'the English-speaking peoples' were ►lend-lease, Marshall Aid and ►NATO.

The myth of the special relationship was, on this view, created to paper over gaping ►credibility gaps in the belief that the United Kingdom still had a major role to play in the post-war world. The US ►nuclear umbrella and dollar support for sterling appeared, temporarily, to do the trick. For its part, the United States, after initial ►isolationist and almost virginal reluctance to get involved, came to embrace the idea realizing that military and economic support for the United Kingdom and Western Europe was essential to contain the spread of communist influence. The American policy-making elite had read Marx and understood that the economic and social devastation in Europe after the war had created a very fertile soil for the growth of socialist ideas. It was therefore in their own interests to encourage a compliant, receptive, pro-market capitalist system in Western Europe to stave off the classic ►revolutionary symptoms that had begun to appear. The United Kingdom, in their eyes, was valuable both as Trojan Horse and Airstrip One in the coming battle with the Soviet Union.

Clearly interest, not emotion, both created and sustained the special relationship. Above all, the fear of Soviet expansionism did much to shape its course, and without this common ►Cold War ►perception Anglo-American relations may well have taken a different turn. Most commentators agree that as the perception of the Soviet threat diminished, so too did the sense of common purpose and affinity between the United States and the United Kingdom. That the myth lingers may be due more to personality factors than objective assessments of strategic or economic realities. Looking at post-war relationships between the respective national leaders it emerges that it was 'special' when there were mutual personal friendships both at the highest level and at the level of officials concerned with formulating and implementing policy. Thus the administrations of Churchill-Roosevelt, Atlee-Truman, Macmillan-Kennedy, Callaghan-Carter, Thatcher-Reagan and Major-Bush all had at different levels, and for different reasons, unusual degrees of sentimental attachment to one another. At these times, the level of mutual trust and respect was high, and at least from the UK point of view, benefits accrued: Churchill secured lend-lease, Atlee Marshall Aid and NATO, Macmillan Polaris, Callaghan economic support for an ailing economy and Thatcher vital US backing in the ►Falklands. When personal relations were non-existent or frosty, the relationship was anything but special and at times spilled over into tacit if not active hostility. Eisenhower scuppered Eden's career over Suez, Wilson refused Johnson's request for UK assistance in ►Vietnam, and Heath made it clear that the United Kingdom's future lay in Europe and not across the Atlantic. All these issues were more than mere domestic tiffs within a basically happy union and clearly when interests diverged, as they began to in the 1970s and 1980s, sentiment took a back seat. What is clear is that the special relationship between the two states is an unusual phenomenon in world politics. The Blair-Clinton version may improve the relationship and extend it into the new millenium. Other special relationships, not necessarily expressed in ➤alliance formation, have existed in international affairs (e.g. between Germany and Austria or Russia and France in the nineteenth century, or between South Africa and Rhodesia in the 1970s) but none of these have had quite the force or vitality as that between the United Kingdom and the United States in the years following the Second World War. Indeed, the term, especially expressed in capitals, is reserved almost exclusively for this.

**Specialized agency** Associated with the UN framework but not strictly a part of it, these are autonomous functional organizations dealing on an international level with economic, social, cultural, educational medical, agricultural and other diverse fields. Each has its own headquarters, staff and budget. Membership is independent of UN membership but since the aim is universality, there is considerable overlap. Each agency was established by multilateral ➤treaty and maintains a special and close relationship with the UN through the coordinating role adopted by its Economic and Social Council (ECOSOC). Their organizational structures are broadly similar: (a) an assembly or conference which is the basic ➤policy-making organ; (b) a council which is the executive agency; (c) a secretariat and director-general which provides the overall administration. There exist to date seventeen specialized agencies. These are as follows: International Labour Organization (ILO), Food and Agriculture Organization (FAO), United Nations Education, Scientific and Cultural Organizations (UNESCO), ➤World Health Organization (WHO), International Bank for Reconstruction and Development (➤World Bank or ➤IBRD), International Finance Corporation (IFC), International Development Association (IDA), ➤International Monetary Fund (IMF), International Civil Aviation Organization (ICAO), Universal Postal Union (UPU), International Telecommunication Union (ITU), World Meteorological Organization (WMO), Intergovernmental Maritime Consultative Organization (IMCO), World Intellectual Property Organization (WIPO), International Fund for Agricultural Development (IFAD), United Nations Industrial Development Organization (UNIDO) and ➤World Trade Organization (WTO).

These specialized agencies can be seen as part of the ➤functionalist approach to world peace which views the solving of common social and economic problems as a necessary step in the direction of the creation of an orderly and stable ➤international society. However, the present structure for controlling these operations and their budgets is often a matter of bitter dispute. In addition, ➤north-south issues have led to fundamental divisions among member ➤states, so much so that the future of some of these agencies often seems in doubt. ➤UN reform

**Sphere of influence** Refers to a territory or ►region over which an outside ►state claims control, influence or preferential status. The preferred state does not claim ►sovereignty but does claim military, political or economic exclusiveness and in so doing not only restricts the rights of other foreign powers but imposes limitations on the ►independence and ►autonomy of the targeted area. These claims may or may not be enshrined in ►treaty form but in either case have usually been conceded on a *quid pro quo* basis with third parties. The legal status of a sphere of influence is thus ambiguous. The first international agreement specifically to employ this term was the agreement between Germany and the United Kingdom in 1885 regarding their respective claims to territories on the Gulf of Guinea. Under the terms of this agreement both sides recognized each others' paramountcy in the specified areas and contracted not to interfere therein with the other's pursuit of its ►national interest. This agreement set the pattern for others and in the two decades spanning the end of the nineteenth century and the beginning of the twentieth similar ones were concluded by the major ►imperial powers. The most notable (and indeed, notorious) example was in relation to China, which between 1896−8 was subjected to various forms of monopolistic servitude by the United Kingdom, France, Germany, Japan and Tsarist Russia and which incidentally, prompted the US ►open door notes of 1899. Other agreements related to North Africa (1904, France and the United Kingdom), Persia (1907, the Tsarist Russia and the United Kingdom). In relation to Latin America the ►unilateral declaration by the United States of the ►Monroe Doctrine in 1823 had the effect of establishing, with the tacit connivance of the United Kingdom, unrivalled US dominance in the Western Hemisphere. Since World War Two the term has carried a somewhat looser connotation and refers generally to hemispheric regions dominated by the ►great powers: the former Soviet Union in Eastern Europe, China in Southeast Asia and the United States in the Western Hemisphere. However, the difference between 'spheres of influence' and 'spheres of control' is not always easy to delineate as territories or states may be so overwhelmed by the hegemonic power as to be little more than protectorates or satellite states. In diplomatic terms the polar opposite of the sphere of influence is the American idea of the open door.

**Spillover** A term used in the ►neo-functionalist approach to ►integration. Spillover is a dynamic process which occurs during sector integration. By integrating a particular activity certain goals are set but once integration has occurred the participants see that goal-attainment can only be guaranteed by further integration. Conceptually spillover is linked to ideas about ►feedback because both positive and negative feedback can create spillover tendencies. If things are going well, the participants will be encouraged to move towards further task expansion. If things are going badly, the participants may need to remove distortions or impediments in other sectors to give their original purpose the chance of success. Haas (1964), the leading exponent of the neo-functionalist logic in the 1950s, modified his ideas about spillover to include an important distinction between manifest and latent functions of integration. According to this later gloss on the process, spillover occurs as much because of the unantici-pated consequences of integration as the anticipated.

The main laboratory for the validation of these ideas has been the integration process that commenced in Western Europe with the Schuman Plan. Through-out the 1950s progress seemed to confirm these ideas but the advent of ➤Gaullism provided a severe check. In the light of this experience it is clear that spillover cannot proceed without confronting issues of ➤high politics. This confrontation may not be settled at all or, if settled, it may not be in favour of extending integration. ➤➤Confederalism

**Spratly Islands** A group of over one hundred islets, coral reefs, atolls, shoals, sandbars and sea mounts dispersed over 600 miles (965 k) in the South China Seas. Although the total land area is negligible and they are uninhabited the islands are strategically located near several primary shipping lanes in the central South China Sea, in particular the sea passage from Japan to Singapore. In addition, the Spratlys possess (as yet undermined) oil and natural gas potential. The islands are the subject of an increasingly bitter international ➤sovereignty dispute between China (the 'Nansha' islands), Vietnam (the 'Truong Sa'), the Philippines ('Kalayaan'), Taiwan, Malaysia and Brunei. The islands were occupied and annexed by Japan in 1939 but following defeat in World War II, Japan renounced its claim in the San Francisco peace treaty of 1951. However, this peace treaty did not re-assign ownership. Since 1951, China, Taiwan, Vietnam and the Philippines have each affirmed territorial claims and established military garrisons on the islands. The dispute is a major factor in diplomatic tensions between China and Vietnam and forms an integral part of the on-going China/Taiwan dispute. After the transfer of Hong Kong to China in June 1997. the question of ownership of the Spratlys is likely to precipitate an international ➤crisis since China shows every indication of wishing to establish a military grip on the navigation lanes of the South China Sea. This is bound to lead to a deterioration in Sino-US relations. At present, the contending parties have not agreed to refer the case to the ➤International Court of Justice (ICJ) and given China's persistence over the Taiwan issue, this is unlikely to happen. The Spratlys therefore, represent a dangerous confrontation waiting to happen in the post Cold-War period.

**Sputnik** The world's first artificial satellite was launched from the Soviet Union in October 1957 and promptly dubbed 'Sputnik'. Weighing approxi-mately 180 lbs, its signals to earth (which were easily picked up in the West) symbolized the apparent primacy of Soviet space ➤technology. When, six weeks later, Sputnik II was launched, carrying a dog and weighing approximately half a ton, the demise of the United States seemed complete. Eventually in

February 1958 the United States succeeded in placing an Explorer satellite in orbit. Although much smaller than Sputnik, it carried more instruments and thus provided much more scientific data than its Soviet rival. The fact remains that few outside the scientific community remember Explorer, while Sputnik has passed into the folklore of the period.

The advent of Sputnik in the autumn of 1957 caused consternation in the United States. It was clear that the Soviets possessed very powerful and reliable rockets which could perform these tasks and the implication that they might have a more than passing likeness to intercontinental ballistic missiles (ICBMs) was accepted as part of the US ➤definition of the situation. At the same time the informed public in the United States was becoming used to thinking in terms of an adverse ➤missile gap with the Soviet Union, and these events served to increase that ➤perception.

**Stalemate** A term borrowed from the game of chess and used to describe and identify a situation of deadlock or impasse. Its usage is particularly prevalent in ➤diplomacy and ➤negotiation where parties have taken positions which are mutually exclusive or incompatible. Failing ➤unilateral measures, a stalemate may only be resolved by third party ➤intervention.

**START I** Acronym for the Strategic Arms Reduction Talks which commenced in June 1982 and were concluded with a draft ➤treaty in July 1991. Seen originally as both a successor to and an improvement upon the SALT process of the 1960s and 1970s, START began to show significant progress following the assumption of power in the former Soviet Union by ex-President Gorbachev. Like the earlier SALT talks, START was ➤bilateral throughout – so that the British and French nuclear systems are not included in the final package. Like SALT, START works by establishing a variety of limits and sub-limits within the classes of weapon systems. In summary the main limits are as follows:

1 Each side is limited to 1,600 strategic nuclear delivery vehicles (that is to say, ICBMs, SLBMs and heavy bombers).
2 Each side is limited to 6,000 total accountable warheads. (This represents a reduction of 40 per cent + for both parties).
3 Each side is limited to 4,900 accountable warheads on ICBMs or SLBMs.
4 The former Soviet Union agreed to limits on so-called 'heavy' missiles of not more than 1,540 accountable warheads deployed on 154 'heavies'.

In general terms the agreement discriminates against land-based and sea-launched ballistic missiles and in favour of bombers and ➤cruise missiles, but seeks to maintain ➤parity between the parties throughout.

As with the earlier ➤INF Treaty, START seeks to establish an elaborate ➤verification regime based upon both national technical means (i.e. intelligence monitoring of the adversary's movements) and ➤inspection facilities. Unlike the INF, however, START verification is intrinsically more difficult because of the problem of verifying limits as opposed to verifying bans.

**START II** The dramatic changes in world politics caused by ►nineteen eighty-nine and the events thereafter have put a rather different complexion on the nuclear ►arms race and policy initiatives such as the ►START I process. During the ►Cold War era indeed ►nuclear weapons were seen as part of the solution to the vexed questions of both national and international ►security. With the end of the Cold War, the collapse of ►communism and the implosion of the Soviet Union, these same weapons systems became part of the problem instead. As a result START II has been able to effect much more radical cuts in nuclear weapons and delivery systems. Perceived by both sides as the successor state to the USSR in nuclear weapons terms, Russia and the United States formally signed the START II ►treaty in January 1993. This agreement envisages further deep cuts in nuclear warheads so that by January 1 2003 each side will be limited to 3,500 total accountable warheads. All land-based missiles with 'mirved' warheads (multiple independently targeted re-entry vehicles) will be completely eliminated. Submarine-launched ballistic missiles (SLBM) will be capped at 1,750. Substantial cuts have also been agreed for manned bombers under START II.

In pure quantitative terms START II gets the two leading nuclear ►states somewhere back to the position occupied by the US and the SU at the end of the 1960s. Whether this qualifies within the definition of a ►minimum deterrent remains a moot point. Certainly the 'downloading' of the multiple warheads and their elimination on land can be counted as a significant achievements. The ►feedback in the ►issue area of ►nuclear proliferation can only be positive. Both the United States and the Russian Federation are now committed to 'denuclearization' and ►non-proliferation as a result of START II.

**State** Sometimes called the ►nation-state, this is the main ►actor in ►international relations. It has a legal personality and as such in ►international law possesses certain rights and duties. According to the Montevideo Convention on Rights and Duties of States (1933), which is widely regarded as the classic legal definition, states must possess the following qualifications: a permanent population, a defined territory and a government capable of maintaining effective control over its territory and of conducting international relations with other states. In respect of the last qualification the role of ►recognition by other states can often be crucial since it implies acceptance into the international community. These qualifications are not absolute and permit variations. For example there is no necessity in international law for settled ►boundaries or ►frontiers. Many international conflicts take the form of boundary disputes, but their existence does not rob the disputants of legal personality. Israel, for example, is generally accepted as a state even though the precise demarcation of its boundaries has never been settled. Although there is a general requirement that a state has some form of government or means of exercising control, a state does not cease to exist when this control is in dispute or when it is 'temporarily' deprived of effective control as in wartime, ►civil wars, or ►revolutions. Indeed, the attribute of ►sovereignty itself, which is widely regarded as the defining characteristic of statehood, is by no means absolute. Some states, such as those in post-war Eastern Europe, were regarded as 'penetrated' or 'satellite' states, since the control they exercise over their internal and external environments was circumscribed by a powerful neighbour or ►hegemon. In the real world, as opposed to the world of political or legal theory, sovereignty can differ in degree and intensity among states without deprivation of international personality status. In general the capacity to enter into international relations with others is a necessary requirement but not a sufficient one. Non-state actors, for example the African National Congress (►ANC), may have had diplomatic relations with some states, but because they did not possess the other defining qualifications could not be considered states. Regarding ►secessionary movements or national liberation organization, ►recognition is generally withheld until victory over the mother state (or occupying power) is secured. Yet even in these cases, recognition as a gesture of support can be given though the legal status may be in abeyance or dispute. Thus, in 1968 some states recognized Biafra even though Nigeria continued to exercise effective control. As with other rights, the right to ►self-determination depends to a great degree on ►self-help. In sum, although the state has legal personality and essential defining characteristics, these are not static or absolute.

Not only is the state the main agent in international law, politically too it is dominant and has been for over four hundred years. With the exception of ►Antarctica no significant territorial area is exempt from state control (terra nullis). Recognition of 'new' states therefore is likely to be at the expense of existing ones (Bangladesh in 1971 for example, at the expense of Pakistan, or Namibia in 1990 at the expense of South Africa). To date, there are nearly two hundred states in the international system, an increasing number of them being categorized as ►microstates. Despite their number and despite the fact that many liberation movements are still actively seeking statehood, some commentators have argued that the state is declining as the primary actor in world politics. Not only is it functionally obsolete (because of its military and economic penetrability) but it is no longer capable of adequately handling global problems. The challenge of ►interdependence and the proliferation of non-state actors have questioned the traditional assumptions concerning the dynamics of world politics. Yet, on the evidence presented so far, it is difficult to escape the conclusion that reports of its death have been greatly exaggerated. ►Failed states; quasi-states

**State-centrism** The state-centred or state-centric approach to IR is the traditional view that the most valid perspective that can be taken of the subject matter is based upon the ►state as dominant ►actor. This perspective is associated with the ►realist paradigm which sees world politics in terms of ►independent states engaged in an endless competitive existence to preserve their ►security and well being. State-centrism often depicts world politics in terms of the metaphor of the billiard table. In this view states are impermeable, self-contained units which can influence each other by external pressure, as a billiard ball is moved by external and surface contact with other balls on the table. The contact was restricted to this external dimension by the concept of ►sovereignty. Accordingly there was no authority higher than the state and state-centrism concluded that state interaction was conducted under a system of ►anarchy.

If the first rule of state-centrism was that states must be regarded as cohesive ►autonomous actors, then the second rule was the territorial basis of the state. Planet Earth is parcelled out among the state units of the system, accordingly. The concept of territorial jurisdiction asserted that rights to control territory and rights to control peoples settled on those territories was a fundamental precept of state-centrism. This approach therefore lays great stress upon the spatial identity of the state and the belief that loyalty to the state and identity with it could be provided through the concept of ►nationalism. While it was understood that individuals would have other claims on their loyalties – for example to their tribe – it was assumed that in the last analysis any conflict of loyalties would be resolved in favour of the state.

In the actual conduct of ►foreign policy, the state-centred view assumed that ►high politics of military-security issues would prevail over ►low politics. In the last analysis a state's most vital interests were those derived from conceptions of security and these questions would always predominate. The ►security dilemma dictated that states must assume responsibility for their own existence. If they could not resolve the dilemma themselves they attempted to do so by forming ►alliances. However, ally-seeking can be provocative and force others to seek allies in return. The ►balance of power which emerges from these collective efforts to achieve security represents one of the most persistent features of world politics.

State-centrism sees ►power as a possession or attribute as the single most important characteristic of world politics. Recognition of this trait in the system leads state-centrism towards the idea of a power ►hierarchy headed up by ►great powers or ►superpowers. Unfortunately the idea of power hierarchy weakens the ►billiard ball metaphor because the conclusion is inescapable that the balls on the table are not equal. State-centrism thus had to distinguish between formal legal sovereignty and actual political sovereignty. The one is prescriptive, the other empirical. Clearly a stable hierarchy is not anarchic, in any common sense use of that term. So state-centrism modified the idea of ►anarchy towards the idea of an 'anarchical society'.

**Statelessness** Usually refers to individuals (though it can encompass other entities, such as ships) who do not possess ➤nationality of any ➤state. This condition was defined by the UN Conference on the Status of Stateless Persons in 1954 as 'a person who is not considered as a national by any state under the operation of its law'. This can come about as a consequence of ➤war or ➤revolution where people can lose the nationality of one state and are not able to acquire the nationality of another. It is also possible to be born without nationality; in this case neither the enabling principles of *jus sanguinis* or of *jus soli* (or a combination of the two) are deemed to apply and the individual is placed in a legal limbo. Expatriation can also result in statelessness if the individual cannot acquire another nationality. This status is clearly disadvantageous since without a passport or visa, no ➤diplomatic protection can be enjoyed, civil liberties may be denied and ➤deportation is a constant threat.

This problem, along with that of ➤refugees, has been a growing one in the upheavals of twentieth-century world politics, and both the ➤League of Nations and the ➤United Nations have attempted to address it. The principle that everyone has a right to nationality was first formulated in Article 15 of the 1948 Universal Declaration of ➤human rights, and thereafter a number of UN-sponsored conferences have considered ways of resolving the issue, so far without conspicuous success. In 1961 the Convention on the Elimination or Reduction of Statelessness adopted a resolution recommending ➤*de jure* ➤recognition of ➤*de facto* stateless persons to enable them to apply for national status, but this has not been universally adopted or ratified. Since ➤international law recognizes the primacy of the state regarding the acquisition of nationality, and since states are notoriously parsimonious in this regard, the problem is likely to persist. ➤➤Orbiters

**State-system** A term used to describe the relationships that were developed after the ➤state became the significant, and then dominant, ➤actor in ➤macropolitics. The emergence of states as first order political actors followed the gradual withering away of the political and social nexus that was known in Western Europe as feudalism. Strong, centralizing monarchies emerged in England (the Tudors), in Sweden (the Vasas), in Spain (the Hapsburgs) and in France (the Bourbons) to challenge such ➤transnational institutions as the Catholic Church and the Holy Roman Empire. Absolute monarchy – as this system was termed – had become the predominant form of government by the beginning of the sixteenth century and these developments were supported by the new bourgeoisie, in opposition to the feudal nobility. This new class saw the monarchs as natural allies and accordingly they supported the growth of strong central government. The Treaty of ➤Westphalia of 1648 confirmed and consolidated these developments.

Interstate politics, as an activity, was a reserved area on the agenda for these monarchs, their personal advisers and ➤ambassadors. The most important activity was associated with the conduct of warfare: the making of ➤alliances, the fighting of campaigns, and the conclusion of settlements and ➤peace ➤treaties. Alliances were typically secret and often offensive in character and spirit, in contrast to twentieth century ideas. Apart from the conduct of ➤war, the main activities of the absolute monarchs were the courtly politics associated with arranged marriages and the fostering of economic growth via trading policies which broadly reflected state interests and have come to be known as ➤mercantilism.

The state-system underwent a fundamental, once-and-for-all change with the rise of ➤nationalism following the French and US ➤revolutions. The typical unit of the system was now thought to be the ➤nation-state, although multinational states such as the Austro–Hungarian Empire under the Habsburgs continued until 1919. The concept of ➤sovereignty, which was a key characteristic of the state-system from its inception, was carried over from the absolutist state to the nation-state. However, the locus of sovereignty ceased to be the person of the monarch but was instead held to reside in more representative institutions such as assemblies and parliaments. Between themselves, the absolutist monarchs had recognized no superior – at least no earthly superior – so the idea of equality had been included in the concept of sovereignty. In substance, therefore, the claim to sovereign ➤equality remained the same between the absolutist state and the nation-state. This inalienable principle of the state-system is reflected in the ➤United Nations Charter, which states in Article 2: 1 that 'The Organization is based upon the principle of the sovereign equality of all its members.'

The structural implications of the principle of sovereign equality were profound. In ➤international law all states are formally equal. In the ➤general assembly of the UN all states have formal equality – one vote. The ➤unanimity rule in international institutions is derived from the same idea. The ➤international system took on a fundamentally decentralized characteristic as a result of these developments. ➤Power and ➤influence in the system was dispersed among the constituent state units rather than being centralized in some sort of superordinate structure. International law, therefore, was similarly decentralized. States are traditionally the enforcers of international law as well as the makers. If one party is deemed to have broken the law, then under traditional conceptions, other states may take ➤reprisal action. Law enforcement, in the state-system, was horizontally effected.

Any system of relations, even one as decentralized as the state-system, still requires some means of regulation. For long periods, until the rise of ➤international organizations in the twentieth century, the principal means of regulation was the ➤balance of power. This was a very informal arrangement and for a brief period after the Napoleonic Wars an attempt at a ➤security regime was made under the ➤Concert of Europe. The Concert began to weaken in the 1820s because the principal states managing the security regime could not agree about whether to intervene to prevent the emergence of ➤liberal nationalist systems in Greece and Spain.

In retrospect the period 1815–1914 looks to have been the peak of the state-system. Although there has been a massive growth in state numbers in the twentieth century – particularly following ►decolonization after 1945 – at the same time the state is under siege. ►Technology and economics have increased the permeability of the state from within, while the rise in mixed ►actors from without has complicated the structural simplicity of the classic period. There is now a lively debate between realist ►state-centrism and ►pluralism as to how far these trends and tendencies have gone.

It should be noted that the rise of the state-system led to the growth of an intellectual tradition of speculation and scholarship about interstate relations. This intellectual analysis, which might be called the 'classical' tradition, stems from four mainsprings: international lawyers contributed ideas about sovereignty, ►domestic jurisdiction and non-►intervention; political philosophers added ideas about international ►anarchy; practitioners and diplomats, with ideas about ►*raison d'état* and the ►national interest and strategists who stressed the importance of ►war completed the quartet.

**Status quo** It means 'the existing state of affairs' and refers to the prevailing pattern of relations in ►international relations. Essentially a conservative notion it implies that change is likely to be destructive of social order and therefore often tends to be imbued with connotations of sanctity, which the term itself does not necessarily warrant. Defenders of the status quo regard stability and order as key values and ►international law, treaties and orthodox diplomatic procedures are portrayed as legitimizing or codifying the system. A disturbance of the status quo is often met with the demand that a precondition of settlement would be a return to the status quo ante – the previous state of affairs.

It is linked with the ►realist model and is most often juxtaposed with ►revisionism. Morgenthau (1948) identifies three basic policy types in relation to the power struggle: to preserve the status quo, to achieve imperialistic expansion, to gain prestige. Status quo policies are likely to be adopted by those states with most to gain from a preservation of the existing territorial, ideological and power distribution. Although change is generally inimical, not all international change is opposed. The ►Monroe Doctrine of 1823 is cited as a case in point: on one hand it was designed to preserve and promote US hemispheric superiority and on the other it was meant to encourage anti-imperialist drives within Latin America. Status quo states are also likely to have domestic values and structures which support and in turn are reinforced by the prevailing ►international order.

Since the Second World War, the United States has been the dominant status quo ►power and it defined its security (and hence the stability of the system) in terms of ►containment of ►revisionism. As the ►hegemon it collected a number of sympathetic states (more than forty) around it, all of whom to a greater or lesser degree define their diplomatic existence in relation to the preservation of the existing order. ►Coalitions, military alliances and ►blocs are thus characteristic behaviour patterns although in general status quo powers tend to react to revisionists rather than initiate action themselves. In this sense, it appears to have a static rather than a dynamic quality, but as the history of the Monroe doctrine illustrates, this lack of dynamism must not be overstressed.

Given that the realist model is addicted to hierarchies of power, status quo states can be differentiated according to position. Buzan (1983) has identified three categories besides the hegemon itself: an 'associate state', a 'client' state and a 'vassal' state. In the contemporary world the Western European states and Japan would claim associate status, South Korea and Egypt would be clients and South Vietnam (before 1973) and Cuba (before Castro) would be vassals. It must be emphasized, however, that the broad identity of interest in system maintenance does not preclude ►conflict between and among those in the status quo camp. Japan and states in Western Europe have had a number of public disagreements with the United States, for example. What it does ensure is that conflicts of interest tend not to become conflicts of ►force. In the case of Britain and Argentina in 1982, while both are broadly status quo states (one 'associate' the other 'client'), in relation to the specific issue of the ►Falklands/Malvinas one is overtly status quo and the other is revisionist. A similar dichotomy exists regarding the positions of the UK and Spain over the issue of Gibraltar

**Strategic studies** Strategic studies is that branch of the field of inquiry that is concerned to examine the ways in which ►actors use their military ►capability to achieve political ►goals, in particular, with the way in which the threat and the use of ►force has served these ends. It is sometimes referred to as the ►Clauswitzian tradition after the nineteenth-century Prussian strategist who did so much to advance the symbiosis between ►war and state policy. Judged by its historical pedigree, therefore, strategic studies must be regarded as a ►state-centric perspective. Until recently this characterization was perfectly legitimate. More recently studies of ►guerrilla warfare and its fusion with ►revolutionary ►insurgency have shown how essentially ►mixed actor activity can still conform to all the essentials of the Clausewitzian approach.

Strategic studies has been primarily concerned with ►military ►power as the key attribute which has to be converted into usable instruments. As a result this branch of inquiry is generically part of the ►realist ►paradigm. The values relevant to the realist are the same as those understood to operate with strategy. War is the inevitable result of actors pursuing mutually exclusive or incompatible goals in a system that lacks superordinate ►authority structures and can accordingly be termed ►anarchy. Because of its realists background, strategic studies has a strong ►traditional or 'classical' bias, particularly outside the United States. The growth of the ►social science approach has accordingly made fewer inroads in ►international relations than elsewhere.

Strategic studies according to its own lights has always been a 'policy science'. As a result, the ending of the ►Cold War era has profoundly affected this branch of the discipline. In retrospect historians of ideas will unequivocally see the Cold War years as the oft-quoted 'Golden Age' of strategic thinking. The introduction of ►nuclear weapons into world politics after 1945 created an intellectual gap which was filled by academic thinkers who responded to the contingent possibilities of ►deterrence and war with their own ideas. Beginning with the ►Gorbachev doctrine the realization has now taken hold that the key characteristic of a new 'policy science' should be the concept of ►security. As a result a transmogrofication into ►security studies is underway. Strategic studies will remain as the traditionally-conceived 'war studies' in this brave new world. It is plausible that letting in the idea of security studies will broaden the field and the participants, possibly well beyond the realist/state-centric origins referred to above.

**Structural power** An alternative to the ►pluralist analysis of ►power – which stresses relationships – structural power stresses choices and therefore ability to influence outcomes. It has been developed of late particularly within ►International Political Economy (IPE) and is often seen as having implications for the ►renewalist side of the debate with ►declinism. Many would see Strange's text *States and Markets* (1994) as a leading example of this type of analysis of the power concept. Strange defines structural power as: 'the power to decide how things shall be done, the power to shape frameworks within which states relate to each other. relate to people or relate to corporate enterprises' (p. 25). Strange is anxious to point out further that in her view there are four primary power structures: ►security, knowledge, production and finance. Later she suggests that there is another layer of secondary structures (including a ►trade structure). More than a quarter of a century ago, Dahl, working on a community power in New Haven, noted that different ►issue areas seemed to exhibit different structures – that the same people were not powerful or omnipresent in all instances. The same point can be made about Strange's four structures. Namely that a priori there would be no reason to suppose that the same structural top dogs and underdogs will occur across power structures. However it is clear from Strange's analysis that she certainly wished to assert the contrary. As far as a state-centric analysis of structural power proceeds, the United States is still the predominant actor. It is this kind of argument that has placed Strange within the renewalist camp accordingly. In fact closer analysis of her 1994 work and her 1996 volume *The Retreat of the State* shows that only in the security structure are states still the dominant actors. In essence therefore structural power is an attack upon state centrism not a relief column sent to its assistance.

In broad analytical terms structural power and ►structuralism are out of the same stable. Both views see more need for analysis to recognize the importance of ►hierarchy than does ►neorealism. Again as already noted above, both reject state-centrism. The idea of causality can be the conjunction between relational and structural power. In both uses of the term 'power' the idea of 'cause' is implicit. Possessing power enables the possessor to cause things to occur that would not otherwise do so. Whether the power is exercised in relationships or inheres in social structures is the point of departure.

**Structuralism** A perspective on ➤international relations which lays great stress upon the importance of social structures as the loci for explanations of the field. Structuralism is not a theory but, as suggested above, a perspective on the subject matter which contains a number of theoretical assumptions. It should not be confused with structural realism in any way. It has affinities with ➤Marxism/Leninism in the sense that it rejects ➤state-centrism in favour of a class-based or interest-based view of world politics. Structuralism thus shares with ➤pluralism an inclination to devalue the ➤state as the basic building block of theories. Unlike the pluralists, structuralists tend to emphasize ➤conflict as a systemic process rather than cooperation, although unlike the structural realists it is conflict between classes and groups that is crucial.

Historically structuralism can be positively correlated with the rise of the ➤Third World within world politics. In this sense it may be said to represent an underdog view of reality. For structuralists ➤hierarchy is more important than ➤anarchy as a key characteristic. The key to this inequality is the unequal division of power within the system – which structuralists usually refer to as a 'world' system rather than an 'international' one. Structuralism, obviously, emphasizes ➤structural power rather than relational power and moreover locates the key ➤capabilities in the economic system. Structuralists see that a particular division of labour has occurred historically in the world system as a result of the growth of ➤capitalism as the dominant form of production. In the structuralist schema production is more important than trade as a determinant of the pecking order in the system. Essentially structuralism is about ➤haves and have-nots and the two main streams within this tradition are ➤dependency theory and ➤world systems theory. Crucial to both streams is the dichotomy/trichotomy between centre and periphery and/or core, periphery and semi-periphery. The centre/ core is located in the ➤AICs of the West and these interests work to manipulate the periphery to sustain their domination over the system. The family resemblance with ➤imperialism is evident.

**Subsidiarity** A concept particularly associated with ➤supranational organizations and with the theory and practice of ➤federalism. Subsidiarity means that policy-making should be engaged at the lowest level commensurate with effective decision-taking and ➤implementation. The term has been of increasing significance in the context of the ➤integration process in Europe and in particular in the long history of proposals for a ➤European Union. Thus the ➤European Commission's reaction to the Tindemans Report of 1975 is probably the first occasion that the European bureaucracy recognized the 'principe de subsidiarité'. In this usage the Commission accepted that subsidiarity placed limits on the competence of the supranational union which would – it was hoped – succeed the ➤European Community as then constituted. In the late 1980s the Conservative government in the UK used the subsidiarity principle to reinforce its claims for national ➤sovereignty over the ➤perceived encroachments of the putative union. The concept has subsequently been enacted into ➤treaty law with the ➤Maastricht Treaty of 1992.

The term itself originated in nineteenth-century Catholic opposition to greater ➤state ➤intervention where it referred to the rights of individuals, groups and communities to 'sovereignty in their own spheres'. The Bill of Rights of the USA (the first ten amendments to the constitution) includes in the 10th amendment recognition that powers not explicitly reserved to the Federal government of the USA are reserved by the constituent states or the people. Thus the idea of subsidiarity can be used to buttress the claims of ➤self-determination at a number of levels, including that of the ➤nation and the state. Hence its significance in the context of the ➤scope and ➤domain of the EU.

**Sub-system** A sub-system or subordinate system is a term used in ➤systems analysis. Applied to IR it is virtually coterminous with the idea of ➤region. Binder (1958) and Brecher (1963) are generally credited with early promotion of this approach. In 1969 the International Studies Association advanced the concept further with a special issue of their Quarterly. The more traditional term 'region' and the systemic 'sub-system' are sometimes run together as in 'regional sub-system'.

As the term implies a sub-system is a means of categorizing a whole (or system) into discrete parts. Systems analysis would expect the sub-system to evince the same characteristics as the system, though at a different level. Thus the basic and essential search for characteristic *structures* and *processes* would proceed in sub-system analysis in the same way, although not necessarily with the same results. For example, whereas the structure of a ➤world system may be loose ➤bipolar, the structure of a sub-system might be ➤tripolar. Whereas ➤integration might be a peripheral trend in a world system, it might be a dominant trend in a sub-system. Ideas about ➤hierarchy, which have frequently been applied to the ➤macropolitical system of world politics, can with equal validity be applied to sub-systems analysis. In this way a state ➤actor that is only fairly modestly ranked at one level may be a significant actor at another. India is a case in point. Lastly, the two crucial systemic processes of ➤conflict and cooperation can, when manifest at the sub-system level, spill over into the macrosystem. Thus the ➤Arab-Israeli conflict, one of the most chronic conflicts within the Middle Eastern subordinate system, has spilled into the world political system drawing in the ➤superpowers and the UN.

**Summit diplomacy** Sometimes referred to as 'personal diplomacy' these are meetings of heads of governments of the major powers to resolve outstanding issues. As such, they bypass, or are superimposed upon, ➤diplomacy at the ➤ambassadorial or ministerial level. The term is often used loosely to denote any meeting between principals, whereas in fact the following conditions apply: they consist of bipartite or multipartite gatherings, heads of government must take part, the leading ➤states must be involved and there must be an effort to reach agreement. It is often assumed that summits are a twentieth-century diplomatic innovation but this is not so. The term may be a new one (from an election speech by Winston Churchill in 1950, 'to parley at the summit'), but the phenomenon is ancient. International history is replete with examples of personal diplomacy, especially during the period of absolute monarchies when the identification of the state with the ruler in person was near total. The practice fell out of favour in the seventeenth century when permanent diplomatic missions assumed responsibility for inter-state ➤negotiations and until the twentieth century the only major international conference to involve heads of government was the Congress of Vienna in 1815. The practice was revived by President Woodrow Wilson at the Paris Peace Conference in 1919 and was inspired by a profound distrust of professional diplomats and the 'secret diplomacy' they were alleged to indulge in. Since then in times of ➤peace and ➤war, summits have been a major feature of the international diplomatic landscape. During the ➤Cold War, especially after the ice-breaking Geneva Conference of 1955, it was widely believed that ➤superpower summits were indispensable for maintaining world peace. In fact, these conferences have rarely resolved matters of substance, and when they have (e.g. the ➤arms control agreement at Moscow in 1972) it has been as a result of protracted negotiations at professional levels conducted long before the actual event. Generally, the achievements are minimal; their value lies in the realm of psychology rather than diplomacy. They are useful devices for establishing goodwill or reopening communication but unless the groundwork has been professionally prepared, and unless the issue at stake is negotiable, summits are inherently risky. Given that heads of government are always aware of their domestic constituencies, the pressure for a 'successful' outcome within a narrow time-limit could prove disastrous. Henry Kissinger (1974), an experienced practitioner, referred to the process as 'a parody of diplomacy' and argued that the proper place of summit meetings in diplomacy was 'to put the finishing touches on agreements reached previously'. Without doubt, the drawbacks of summitry are now well known and well guarded against but by virtue of the domestic impact as well as the stature they confer on national leaders, these meetings will continue to feature prominently in world affairs. Their symbolic and ceremonial value alone will ensure this. ➤G7

**Superpower** A term first used extensively by Fox (1944) in his book of the same name (Fox hyphenated 'super' and 'power' to show the etymology). On page twenty-one he defined the superpower as 'great power plus great mobility of power' and identified three states, the United States, the Soviet Union and the United Kingdom, in this new category. Fox recognized that the Second World War had propelled the first two to the rank and status of world powers, while the United Kingdom was a residual member. The defeat of the ➤axis coalition was a demonstration of their great military ➤capability, while their wartime ➤conference diplomacy presaged the world role that they were to assume after 1945. Two developments occurred to alter Fox's ➤tripolarity thereafter: the United Kingdom rapidly dropped out of the ranking to take up a more modest position of regional rather than global significance, while the ➤Cold War confrontation between the two remaining 'supers' led to a new ➤perception of their world role. In particular, the United States' assumption of a ➤hegemonial position in the Western military-security and economic welfare systems after 1945 would not have been so pressing or significant without the added ➤issue area of the Cold War.

The development of ➤nuclear weapons by the superpowers after 1945 should be seen as an effect as much as a cause of these structural changes. The fission and fusion programmes confirmed a status that was already well established by the events referred to above. It would certainly be an unwarranted simplification to equate the superpower attribute to this development solely or exclusively. In any event nuclear weapons lack ➤fungibility as a capability.

In terms of the wealth/welfare area of political economy, the Soviet Union was never really a superpower. In its attempt to attain and then maintain ➤parity with the United States in the military-security field great opportunity costs were incurred by the Soviet economy and a highly distorted developmental pattern resulted. US hegemony in the political economy issue area began to wane in the 1960s as rival economic power centres in Japan and the ➤European Community emerged. The United States' ➤Vietnam ➤intervention created significant short-term economic problems and assisted in the demise of the dollar as the principal international currency.

The implosion of the Soviet Union after ➤nineteen eighty-nine seemingly left the United States as the only unambiguous superpower. This ➤unipolar moment was confirmed for some by the events of the ➤Persian Gulf War. However it is salutary to remember that both relational and ➤structural power require intent and motivation as well as capability and there is more than a hint that political ➤leaderships in the United States lack the will to exercise power in quite the way their predecessors did. The end of the Cold War has in any event removed the clear and present danger that was such a defining reality for that generation.

Superpower is an analytical distinction based upon structural power considerations. It assumes a ➤hierarchy of actors with the superpower at the top. In comparison with earlier periods, therefore, the superpower category may be seen as a replacement for the more traditional ➤great power category. Both stipulations share one characteristic: removal of the superpower/great power from the system would fundamentally change the overall structure of ➤world politics/international politics. Conversely, additions to that category would equally change systemic structures. Thus a tripolar system becomes ➤bipolar if a superpower/great power drops out, or becomes multipolar if additions occur. Because the idea of superpower is based upon structural rather than causal conceptions of power it is difficult to reconcile the concept with empirical instances. The student of ➤international relations would do well to resist being too dazzled by the putative power of the 'supers' and to concentrate instead upon a policy orientated approach. It may be concluded that the superpower has great ➤veto power to stop undesirable things happening in world politics but considerably less behaviour control over other actors needed to achieve more positive outcomes.

**Supranational** Refers to laws or institutions that are above the ➤state. The ➤power and ➤authority they exercise is not confined to one but to many. Thus, supranationalism refers to ➤decision-making bodies which supersede or override the ➤sovereign authority of individual states who are constituent members of the organization involved. Usually this transfer of authority from the state is voluntarily limited and specific (e.g. to issues of ➤trade, commerce or ➤defence). The clearest example of a supranational institution is the ➤European Union which has a common political structure authorized to make decisions by majority voting within prescribed areas for member states. The UN is not strictly speaking a supranational institution although under Article 25 of the ➤United Nations Charter the ➤Security Council is empowered to exercise executive powers in relation to ➤peace and ➤security matters. Until the ➤Persian Gulf War, this authority to compel all member states to act had only been used once, in relation to the imposition of ➤economic sanctions on Rhodesia in 1966. (The action undertaken by the Council in respect of Korea in 1950 was, contrary to the popular view, a ➤recommendation to member states, not an enforcement decision under Article 25.) Supranationalism is thus part of the general integrative process of ➤international relations whereby ➤interdependence is given institutional recognition. The process of whittling away at the traditional bastion of state sovereignty which supranationalism represents is likely to continue. ➤➤World government

**Surrender** Literally means handing over ➤power or control to another party. It generally refers to military units in the field or to governments themselves. All cases of surrender, even ➤unconditional surrender, involve the imposition of some obligations on the victor. Unlike Greek and Roman custom, modern practice does not permit annihilation as a consequence of surrender. The ➤Hague Conferences and subsequent rulings in ➤international law have underlined the obligation of the victors to at least spare the lives of the vanquished. Unless specifically unconditional, most surrenders are conditional and will be accompanied by articles of capitulation – terms or concessions agreed between the parties before the final act. These of course vary but are often conditioned by the remaining strength, or latent power, of the defeated side.

**Systems analysis** Systems analysis is a holistic perspective on a defined field of study. Thus if the field happens to be that of ➤international relations, the systems analyst would look for definable and regular patterns of interaction between the constituent ➤actors, in particular to see what structural characteristics and persistent and regular processes could be identified. Systems analysis is derived from General Systems Theory, which Young (1967) called 'a movement aimed at the unification of science and scientific analysis' (p. 14). General Systems Theory (GST) thus seeks to unify discrete scientific subjects by employing a common language of analysis and conceptualization. Ludwig von Bertalanffy, generally regarded as the inspiration of GST, sought thereby to integrate all the sciences, natural and social. The basis of von Bertalanffy's approach was towards what is called 'open' systems analysis, an open system being a set or field that interacts with an environment. If a system is seen as open in this way it will monitor its behaviour in relation to its environment via the process of ➤feedback. The end result of this adaptive behaviour should be ➤homeostasis or a steady state.

As stated above, systems analysis is a perspective or ➤paradigm. It is thus open to application at any or all of the ➤levels of analysis that can be stipulated for the study of world politics. Young states that the notion of system can be 'applied freely to virtually any set of related behaviour patterns . . .' (p. 20). Provided that the object of study can be recognized as what Young calls a 'complete functioning entity' (p. 23) the systems analysis can be relevant.

The impact of systems analysis upon ➤foreign policy analysis studies has been significant. According to this view foreign policy-making becomes a boundary activity between the national system and the international. The balance between internal and external attributes must eventually be answered by empirical research but the technique is broadly derived from the systems approach. Foreign policy analysts tend to use the term 'environment' extensively to identify these internal/external factors. Thus a ➤penetrated state is an actor for which the external environment or international system has come to totally dominate and determine mainsprings of political, economic and social life. Conversely a superpower actor can conduct a globally defined foreign policy on the basis of a secure and significant internal environment.

The most telling contribution of systems analysis has been at the macropolitical level. Systems analysts were in the vanguard of the social science approach of the 1950s/1960s and the main thrust of their interest has been upon the international system. A basic division is popularly made between the system *per se* and regionally based subsystems. Thereafter the basic structures and processes can be described and identified. Kaplan's 1957 work is widely regarded as an early example of an attempt at systemic understanding of macropolitics.

This work is highly deductive and in 1963 Rosecrance attempted to redress the balance in favour of a more inductive approach. Debate and dissension has raged on the basic structural question between those favouring a bipolar view and those a multipolar. Nogee (1975) pinpointed some of the ambiguities in this dispute. Conflict and cooperation are widely seen as fundamental processes by systems analysts. In 1979 Waltz in a seminal contribution to the field sought to apply systems analysis to the ➤realist tradition coming up with a theory that has been appropriately dubbed ➤neorealism. Using ideas about system and unit levels of explanation, Waltz sought to locate the realist perspective in systemic structures rather than in inherent instincts of man. As Buzan (1993) has noted, neorealist theory is now firmly rooted in systems analysis. ➤➤International system.

# T

**Tactical nuclear weapons** A broad classification that uses technical and functional criteria to distinguish these weapons from the strategic type. Technically, tactical nuclear weapons have a shorter range and a lower yield. Functionally, their envisaged purpose is to destroy specific targets, usually military or political command centres outside the territory of the major adversary. Since ►nuclear weapons have not been used in combat circumstances since 1945, the distinction is hypothetical and somewhat controversial. In the last analysis a nuclear weapon is a nuclear weapon and a single shot, however 'tactical' the intention, might be perceived as crossing a significant and symbolic threshold. In addition, the victims of the blast and radiation could be forgiven for regarding the distinction as invalid, at least as far as it applies to them.

In the immediate aftermath of ►Hiroshima it was thought that nuclear weapons would be used in future ►wars in a strategic context. This view prevailed for a number of years thereafter. In the early 1950s opinions changed and the possibility of a tactical weapon became technically feasible and functionally plausible. In the light of its ►NATO alliance commitments the United States saw the possibility for tactical weapons in the European theatre, particularly as an antidote to the perceived superiority of the ►Warsaw Pact in ►conventional warfare terms. Stockpiles of these weapons were established accordingly. NATO's declaratory policy sought to officially recognize the tactical/strategic distinction in 1967 with the adoption of the policy known as ►flexible response. Developments since have blurred rather than enhanced the dichotomy. Technically the range and yield of tactical weapons has expanded into what are grey areas of systems that are not envisaged for the battlefield but do not pose a threat to the homeland of the adversaries deploying them. Such a weapon would be the ►cruise missile. The development of the neutron bomb as a particular type of tactical weapon was also contentious.

Because of their size, tactical nuclear weapons have made ►verification of ►arms control agreements more difficult. They can be readily concealed and hidden. They have also placed more destructive capacity into the hands of subordinate military officers than ever before in the history of warfare. Whatever the merits of this in terms of ►deterrence requirements, it has undoubtedly increased the risks that nuclear violence might occur against the wishes of statesman and political leaders.

**Tariff** A tariff is a tax upon ►imports. Historically tariffs have been a favoured way of raising revenue. As such they can be extremely lucrative and viable, particularly if the goods and services subject to such charges are demand inelastic. More recently tariffs have been used as a means of ►protectionism by the authorities of ►states. Historically the United States was among the first industrialized countries to eschew ►free trade for tariff protection. In the post-1945 system of economic relations tariffs have been an important instrument in the formation of ►common markets and ►free trade areas. A common external tariff (cet) is the principal means whereby the participating states can shelter behind a 'tariff wall' thereby instituting protectionism upon a regional basis. Tariffs may be used as a foreign policy instrument, usually by a dominant state, either as a punitive retaliatory measure or to establish an economic ►sphere of influence. In the latter context, the institution of preferential arrangements is the usual method of creating such a sphere. The dominant state usually exchanges tariff preferences upon a ►bilateral basis with a number of target participants. The latter may exchange preferences with each other but that is not a requirement of the preferential system. The best known of these arrangements was the Imperial Preference system instituted in 1932 at Ottawa with the United Kingdom as the 'hub' of the scheme.

The existence of the General Agreement on Tariffs and Trade (►GATT) after 1947 concentrated minds upon the commitment of all the contracting parties to freer world trade and the ►implementation of the ►most favoured nation (MFN) principle. The general Agreement established parameters for a series of ►multilateral tariff reduction negotiations – popularly known as 'tariff disarmament' – in the years that followed. The replacement of the GATT by the more powerful ►World Trade Organization (WTO) marks a change of direction away from the tariff cutting as the main agenda item towards discussions on tariff cutting as the main agenda item towards discussions on ►non-tariff barriers, quotas and subsidies as the new concerns. In retrospect it is clear that the ►Kennedy and ►Tokyo Rounds conducted under the aegis of erstwhile GATT were the final acts of the early tariff centred system.

**Technology** Technology is the application of knowledge to practical problem-solving. Historically, such applications have been a continuous and persistent feature of all social systems, no matter how 'primitive' they may superficially appear to be. As a result a continual process of change may be identified as occurring via technology. Other factors being equal, therefore, the faster technology changes, the faster the ►feedback into the recipient systems. In passing, it should be noted that 'change' should not be confused with 'improvement', although many apologists for unrestrained technological change might like to argue otherwise.

In a series of changes made in the conduct of manufacturing industries during the late eighteenth and much of the nineteenth centuries available technology revolutionized economic activity and, via the feedback process, the societies in which it took place. This industrial ►revolution initiated a process that has continued ever since. It is now accepted as an axiom of economic development that significant and lasting inputs of technology will be required to achieve and sustain economic growth. Since available technology is differentially distributed among actors the issue of ►technology transfer raises difficult questions about the terms and conditions wherein this exchange should take place.

In the context of ►international relations, technology has had the most significant impact upon issues of a military security nature. Violence and threats of violence between actors have been constrained by the technologies available for them. What one author has called the 'war potential' of actors is a function of the technology available. Very often the technology that has been applied to military-security issue is itself derived from civilian contexts. Thus, the development of heavier than air flight at the beginning of the twentieth century was soon applied to the battlefield and, thereafter, to other theatres. The relationship between civilian and military technologies is, indeed, a complex feedback loop, the development of ►nuclear weapons in the Second World War having civilian applications in the post-1945 period. One of the factors that makes the stopping or controlling of ►nuclear proliferation so difficult to effect is this interconnectedness of civilian and military technologies.

There is an increasing conjecture, intellectually, about the balance sheet of technology. The unanticipated and unplanned effects of technology are the major contentious issues in this regard. The critique of unrestrained technological change is increasingly informed by empirical evidence that points to some of the more deleterious outcomes. Thus continued application of nuclear technology to energy production raises acute questions about the safety of plants from breakdown and malfunction and the toxicity of waste products from the generation process. The work of ►futurologists and ►green movements has stimulated this critical climate. The inexorable onrush of technology is unlikely to be deflected or denied by the heightened awareness of its mixed blessings, however. Research and development (often referred to simply as R&D) will continue and, for as long as it does, there will be good grounds perceived by vested interests for moving from that stage to application whenever and wherever possible. ►►Revolution in military affairs

**Technology transfer** This refers to the relationship between producers and consumers of ►technology as it can be identified to operate across ►state boundaries and to involve various international ►actors. Since the original industrial ►Revolution demonstrated the importance of technological inputs, the issue of the terms and conditions under which such knowledge should be made available to others has become crucial. In contemporary ►international relations the issue is exacerbated by the fact that the producers of technology are the advanced industrial companies (►AICs) and the consumers are the least developed countries (►LDCs). Moreover, the conduit for a considerable amount of this knowledge transfer is the multinational corporation (➤MNC). Technology transfer has thus become caught up in the ➤polarization of political economy issues between the rich states of the ➤north and the developing states of the ➤south.

Technology transfer can occur in a number of ways: by education and training programmes, by exchanges of consultants and experts, by licensing agreements to make patented instruments available, by consulting published sources and by copying products and techniques, with or without permission. Since technological innovation is occurring simultaneously with transfer, the latter process is likely to be continuous for the future as well. Since research and development is also differentially distributed in favour of the AICs, the perpetuation of this situation of technological dependence is very probable.

**Terms of trade** This is a means of expressing the ratio of ➤exports to imports for a particular ➤actor. Thus, if the terms of trade deteriorate, it will be because ➤imports (expressed in monetary values such as prices) have risen faster than exports (expressed in the same way) or because export prices have fallen faster than import prices. Both sets of circumstances will be detrimental. If an actor is a sole, or significant, supplier of goods and services, or if a number of suppliers can form a cartel such as OPEC then it/they may be able to manipulate the terms of trade to its/their advantage. Failing this, adverse shifts in the terms of trade can be highly damaging and, in the long term, even disastrous. It will lead to the slowing of growth of real income, or worse, to actual decline.

Since 1945 the terms of trade have, with some exceptions, moved against the ➤Third World ➤states and this factor has enhanced other structural difficulties they already have in achieving self-sustained growth. Following the establishment of the United Nations Conference on Trade and Development (UNCTAD) on a permanent basis after 1964 demands for intervention on behalf of the least developed countries (LDCs) were increasingly made. The New International Economic Order (NIEO) Programme and Charter of 1974 concentrated upon this as one of the key issue areas in global economic relations.

**Terrorism** The use or threatened use of violence on a systematic basis to achieve political objectives. While there is no agreed comprehensive definition as to its character, motive or mode of operation, (for example, Schmid, 1984, lists over one hundred different definitions of the term), most analysts agree that the element of fear-inducement both horizontally and vertically is crucial. In addition ruthlessness, a disregard for established humanitarian values and an unquenchable thirst for publicity are characteristic traits. By no means a recent phenomenon (it can be dated at least as far back as the seventh-century AD Muslim world of the 'assassins') it is in the post-war era of rapid ➤technological development and heightened media-awareness that terrorism has achieved its greatest global impact. Methods commonly used include hijacking, hostage-taking, bombings, indiscriminate shootings, assassinations and mass murders.

It is usual to distinguish between 'state' and 'political' or 'factional' terrorism. The former has been the more lethal due mainly to the monopolistic nature of the coercive agencies at the ➤state's disposal combined with ➤ideologies that rest on ends/means rationalizations. The latter is carried out by non-state ➤actors and its focus is usually internal. However, as a sustained campaign of terror requires financial support, a steady weapon supply and a place of sanctuary, most groups have an international dimension. Indeed, many commentators have identified significant recent developments not merely in state-sponsored terrorism (internal factional groups with outside governmental support) but also with regard to ➤transnational and even intercontinental terrorist infrastructures and mutual support groups. Terrorism is not a species of ➤guerrilla warfare although it is often confused with it. Nor is it an ➤ideology or a political movement. It is a strategy or a method that is common to groups of widely different political, philosophical and ➤religious beliefs. It is used by nationalists (the single most successful grouping), religious extremists, revolutionary ➤Marxists, racists and ➤fascists – the common denominator being the creation and spread of fear, unrest and instability in the targeted area. Yet despite its ubiquity as an instrument of ➤destabilization, its overall record of success is so far, a modest one. The collapse of the French and British colonial rule in Aden, Algeria, Cyprus and Palestine are the most notable examples, though even in these instances factors other than terrorism may have been decisive.

To date, the international community has not responded in any concerted way to the growth of modern terrorism. There have been regional initiatives (e.g. within the ➤European Union and ➤NATO) but generally the phenomenon has been addressed on a state-to-state basis. Apart from a few highly publicized events (e.g. the US bombing raid on Libya in 1986 or the Israeli raid on Entebbe airport ten years earlier) most states have responded to terrorism privately as a minor irritant and have been content to deal with it through 'quiet' ➤diplomacy and various forms of ➤appeasement. This can only serve to encourage more emphasis on this high-value, low risk strategy. W. Laqueur and P. Wilkinson among others have warned that notwithstanding the possible use by those groups of ➤weapons of mass destruction, terrorism is likely to outgrow its nuisance stage and without international cooperation at the highest level will inevitably become a major threat to international ➤peace and stability (see especially: Wilkinson, 1986).

**Think tank** A think tank is an independently financed research institute concerned with the study of ➤international relations and ➤foreign policy issue areas. With some important exceptions the 'independence' of the think tank is more likely to be prompted by the need to enjoy tax concessions (as a charity) than any desire for impartiality and objectivity. The 'research' is often heavily policy orientated and – as will be suggested – think tanks have on occasion produced seminal pieces of work which have influenced the conduct of policy and the climate within which it is discussed. Radical critics of the think tank have been ready to assert – particularly during the ➤Cold War era – that these institutes share the broad ideological assumptions of the political ➤leaderships in their societies. In this sense their independence is compromised and there is a trade-off between detachment and relevance in the work and publications of these bodies.

Think tanks can be classified as ➤INGOs and like other non-governmental ➤actors in ➤world politics their rise or demise is crucially correlated with developments in their environment. Causally the most important determinant was the Cold War which developed in the second half of the twentieth century between the ➤superpowers and their ➤blocs. Indeed the term itself 'think tank' comes from this era. The ➤paradigm instance of this genre is the ➤Rand Corporation. Rand began life as 'Project Rand' during the winter of 1945–46, Rand being an acronym for Research and Development. Funded from 1948 by the Ford Foundation and working on ➤defence contracts, Rand was the most significant think tank in the field of ➤strategic studies thereafter. Some of the most innovative studies of ➤nuclear deterrence were produced in the years that followed and the roll-call of scholars included many of the leading thinkers during the 'Golden Age' of strategic studies. There is no doubt that during the Cold War years Rand did symbolize what the radical critics always insisted upon, namely that the successful think tank must imbibe the values of the policy centre.

Groups like the Royal Institute for International Affairs (RIIA) in the UK and the Council on Foreign Relations (CFR) in the United States predate the Second World War and the symbiotic relationship between the Cold War and Rand-type institutes. Both the RIIA and the CFR emerged in the wake of the ➤Versailles treaty. The Council in particular sought to argue against the ➤isolationism of sections of the Leadership and ➤attentive public in America at the time. Earlier still were the Carnegie Endowment for International Peace and the Brookings Institution, both American and both founded before America's entry into the First World War. The Anglo-American tradition in think tanks has sought to promulgate its ideas through regular publications of books, papers and journals. Particularly influential have been the CFR's *Foreign Affairs* quarterly. The publication of the ➤X article in 1947 in the journal has been widely seen as providing the intellectual rationale behind the policy of ➤containment, although the author – George Kennan – parted company with the Truman Administration over its subsequent ➤implementation. The Stockholm International Peace Research Institute (SIPRI) has, following in this tradition, published a *Yearbook* which is arguably the most authoritative source of information about contemporary developments in ➤security studies and ➤peace research. Unlike some other think tanks SIPRI works entirely with published data and source materials and thus it is not constrained by the need for confidentiality in its publications.

Think tanks engage in what has been termed 'research brokerage' in International Relations. They are thus effective bellwethers of new intellectual trends and tendencies. Currently in the post Cold War era particular growth areas seem to be ➤environmental issues and ➤globalization – especially in relation to ➤international political economy.

**Third World** A portmanteau term for those ➤states in Central and South America, Africa, the Middle East, Asia (excepting Japan) and the Pacific islands (excepting Australia and New Zealand) which have experienced ➤decolonization over the last two centuries. The term 'Third World' is an anglicized rendition of the French 'Tiers-Monde' popularized in the 1950s by writers such as Georges Balandier and Alfred Sauvy. The Third World originally stood in contradistinction to the ➤First World (of capitalist liberal democracy) and the Second World (of command economic planning), but with the collapse of ➤communism the trichotomy has lost much of its significance. The retention of the term 'Third World', although difficult to justify in logic perhaps, is testimony to the custom and usage of thirty years and the enduring significance of the ➤Cold War ideological debates. China was always marginalized by the idea of Third World. Possessing many of the attributes of the typical Third World state, ideology ruled China out of all identification. Also at the margin were Israel and South Africa, geographically and historically within the meaning of the term but nevertheless regarded as near ➤pariahs on ideological grounds.

Although the Third World has shaken off the formal political control of ➤colonialism, legacies of the past remain. Thus the actual territorial dimensions of many Third World states, notably in Africa, are the results of colonialist cartographers and political geographers. As a consequence of this arbitrary demarcation, many states in the Third World are ethically heterogeneous. ➤ethnic nationalism, as a centrifugal tendency working against the centripetal state nationalism, is a divisive factor in these states as a result.

➤Marxist-inclined analyses of ➤international relations deny that the formal granting of ➤independence made any substantial difference to the relative ➤power positions of the Third World *vis-à-vis* the First World – wherein, according to Marxists, ➤imperialism arose. In particular the considerable economic power of the AICs of the First World is a determining factor in these relations. Assisting First World domination are the multinational corporations (MNCs), which function as conduits for this influence. Many of the examples that inform this view are taken from Latin American experience, and it would appear that a comprador middle class has developed in the ➤region to provide a ➤linkage with the dominant economic interests in the First World. Latin America may not be typical, however, and in other parts of the Third World, notably in Asia, a more nationalist bourgeoisie has developed. In the most dynamic NICs, indeed, countervailing corporative growth can counterbalance the economic domination of First World interests.

As far as intergovernmental relations are concerned, the Third World has responded to this domination through organizations such as OPEC and UNCTAD by making a number of demands under the ➤new international economic order initiative. The Third World states have also used their majority membership of organizations like the ➤United Nations to call for closer control and supervision to be exercised of MNCs. Again they have campaigned through UNCTAD for the abandonment of the ➤Bretton Woods system of non-discrimination in favour of ➤trade preferences aimed at assisting their development goals.

In the military-security ➤issue area the Third World states have often faced significant problems in managing their national security. The centrifugal ethnic tendencies referred to above have in extreme cases produced the disintegration of states (for example Pakistan) or significant and damaging civil strife. Additionally, with such notable exceptions as India affords, many Third World states lacked the habits of the heart to ensure effective governance of their states. The term ➤quasi-state has been coined to identify this problem. The cold war environment into which these states had to conduct their ➤foreign policies probably exacerbated these problems. From the ➤Truman Doctrine onwards all that Third World ➤leaderships had to show to engage United States in military AID arrangements was the presence of an internal/external threat that could plausibly be ➤perceived as communist.

Interventionist policies have not been the prerogative of the First or Second Worlds of course. States within the Third World have been prompted to intervene in a variety of military-security issue areas. Thus Vietnam, India, Libya, Tanzania, Cuba and Nigeria have shown a willingness towards intervention in regional conflict situations. The ➤Persian Gulf War's proximate cause was Iraqi intervention and ➤annexation of neighbouring Kuwait, whilst Syrian intervention in the Lebanon altered the communal balance significantly.

The end of the Cold War era in world politics has affected both the position and the policies of the Third World states. Indeed it has substantially altered the ideological assumptions that might be called 'Third Worldism. The self-destruction of the Second World has at one and the same time removed a viable alternative 'model' for national economic development and substantially reduced the intrinsic importance of the Third World in First World considerations. Market orientated approaches underpinned by a belief in ➤economic liberalism can now be given full scope and significance.

**Thucydides** Thucydides' *History of the Peloponnesian War* is widely regarded as one of the very few classic studies of international affairs and of the anatomy of ➤war. The *History*, which recounts the fifth century BC struggle between Athens and Sparta for mastery of the Hellenic world, is the first recorded political and ethical analysis of interstate ➤conflict which is not a mere chronical of events. As Thucydides put it: '. . . I have written not for immediate applause but for posterity, and I shall be content if the future student of these events, or of other similar events which are likely in human nature to occur in after ages, finds my narrative of them useful'.

Although the study does not, as it is sometimes alleged, display any developed theory of ►balance of power, most commentators regard it as the first to show glimmerings of an equilibrium theory as well as being the first sustained ►realist attempt to explain the origins of international conflict. His emphasis on the structure and process of Hellenic status-system as a causal factor in individual state behaviour was an important conceptual leap in thinking about external affairs (see Fliess, 1966). The enduring quality of the work, apart from its literary merit, is that it penetrates beneath the superficial causes of a particular war and offers an analysis of the dynamics of ►power politics which is timeless with regard to the insights it offers. In many ways, Thucydides can be regarded as the starting point of modern doctrines and practices in ►international relations.

In this study of ►great power rivalry most of the now familiar concepts appear in embryonic form, including ►power, diplomacy, alliances, neutralism, imperialism. ►Total war, ideology, hegemony and the perennial conflict between expediency and ethics in state policy (►Melian dialogue). In addition, it analyses domestic influences on ►foreign policy formulation, siege warfare, the strategic requirements of land- and sea-based power, the economic costs of prolonged warfare as well as ►treaty formulation and ►arbitration. In sum, it is the earliest and one of the best accounts of the systematic use of ►force to achieve political ends and the consequences of this for the stability of the system as a whole.

**Tokyo Round**  The Tokyo Round of Multilateral Trade Negotiations (often abbreviated to MTN) was conducted under the aegis of the General Agreement on Tariffs and Trade (►GATT) between September 1973 and April 1979. This round constituted the seventh of such negotiations since the inception of GATT. It was the first of these sessions to specifically and explicitly confront the issue of ►non-tariff barriers (NTBS) to ►trade as well as the traditional fields of ►tariffs and their reduction.

Significant and disturbing shifts occurred in the international economic system during the five-and-a-half years that Tokyo was under discussion. The era of cheap oil prices ended abruptly within weeks of the original Tokyo declaration, while in January 1976 the articles of agreement of the IMF were revised to allow for the new system of floating exchange rates. Trends towards the resurgence of ►protectionism were being detected and the whole philosophical assumptions of the ►Bretton Woods system appeared to be under critical scrutiny. Additionally, large sections of the system – often subsumed under the term ►Third World – were explicitly calling for changes in the ground rules of this system.

Tokyo may therefore be seen as either the last post for the old system or the reveille for the new. By addressing, once again, the problem of manufacturing tariffs and obtaining agreement to further reductions phased in over eight years, the negotiations were a continuation of standard GATT procedures. By seeking to stipulate codes of conduct for the NTBs, Tokyo was breaking new ground. By re-establishing the principle that disputes about the trade ➤regime should be settled within the GATT structure, Tokyo maintained an important role for ➤multilateralism within the system.

**Total war** Strategists and historians of warfare are agreed that over the last two hundred years the character of ➤war has changed. Some have sought to encapsulate this trend by referring to 'absolute' or 'total' war. Perhaps the best aphorism that can be quoted to summarize these changes is the statement that '➤nations not armies fight wars'. Certainly this points to one of the most persistent and pertinent causal factors in the development of total war – the growth of ➤nationalism. Other causes include the impact of demographic and ➤technological change, generation of national wealth through economic development, growth of ➤ideological factors (other than nationalism), growth in the size of the military as a class or interest group and the growth of totalitarian political systems and leaderships.

Nationalism is important to the concept of total war because it enables appeals to be made to individuals to fight, not for gain or financial reward but to defend or advance the interests of the national group. This enables the ➤leadership within the nation to mobilize large numbers of people both for active military service and for ancillary and support functions. When nationalism becomes coterminous with the ➤state, so that one might identify ➤nation-states as ➤actors, then the dynamic impact of national mobilization is more profound. If nationalism is combined with demographic growth then, in principle, large numbers of able-bodied citizens can be recruited into the war effort.

Technological change has placed in the hands of warring actors the means to conduct such violent relations on a more destructive basis than before; in particular, those changes generically referred to as the industrial ➤revolution, increased the war potential of state actors. The ➤feedback loop between technological change and economic growth is evident in the total war concept. Technology creates the opportunities for growth and income generation which then provide the investment capital for technological research and development. Recently this symbiosis has continued beyond warfare and a ➤military-industrial complex has been identified in some states with an alleged interest in extending the total war economy into peacetime.

The growth of ideologies, particularly those that present violence and warfare as natural and desirable, have also contributed to the idea that war should be total. Often these ideologies are associated with demands for revolutionary change. Such belief systems show a tendency to look for external enemies even after they have gained political ➤power. The mobilization of particular classes, and the creation thereafter of political demands, can provide the rationale for the initiation and continuation of total warfare.

**Trade** Trade, that is the exchange of goods and services between ➤actors is probably the most prolific relationship within ➤international relations at the present time. Since the series of innovations known as the Industrial ➤revolution first occurred in Western Europe at the end of the eighteenth century, the rationale for such exchange relationships has been apparent. Indeed intellectual justification for the expansion of trade was provided by economists such as Smith (1776) and Ricardo (1817) at the time. Ricardo, in particular, using concepts about comparative advantage, demonstrated how a trading system could function to the benefit of all parties. The impact of these views upon ➤policy-makers and intellectuals has been immense. The principle of ➤free trade as a policy goal, as well as an end state, has had its advocates ever since.

As trade is about exchange, there is an implied or putative element of ➤power in such relationships. Further, the more an actor gains from trade, the more dependent that actor becomes upon the trading relationship. It is thus possible for one actor, in a ➤bilateral relationship, or for a number of actors in a ➤multilateral relationship, to manipulate the situation to achieve political goals. In this way trading relationships have been used to increase cooperation and even ➤integration among actors on one hand, or to increase ➤coercion and ➤conflict on the other. In short, trading relationships may serve positive or negative ends. Since economic power is differentially distributed the ability to use trade relationships in this way will vary. ➤➤Trade bloc; trade system

**Trade bloc** A grouping of ➤actors with a common interest in better trade relations, possibly seen as leading to closer cooperation and even ➤integration in the long term. The simplest form of trade ➤bloc is the *preferential area*. In this arrangement all members extend ➤tariff preferences to each other over certain stipulated goods that are, or will be, the subject of mutual trade. The significance of the preferential area depends upon its ➤scope and ➤domain, scope begin defined as the number of goods covered and domain being the number of actors included in the area. Such arrangements can be quite discriminatory if the members of the area maintain differentially high tariffs with third parties outside the arrangement. Probably the most famous example in the twentieth century of such a system was that created from the British Dominion and Imperial interests known as Imperial Preference.

The ➤free trade area is an elaboration of the preferential system. Herein the members abolish tariffs over a specified range of goods traded between themselves. The variables of scope and domain are indicators of the significance of the system. Similarly, the higher the differential between tariff policy within the area and with the rest of the world, the more discriminatory the arrangement will be.

A ➤customs union is the most complex trade bloc. Here the members have a common external tariff (cet) *vis-à-vis* the rest of the system. Within this cet the members will progressively reduce tariffs until a complete system of free trade obtains. Such arrangements as these involve a good deal of coordination of ➤decision-making and a complex administration, both in order to secure the establishment of the union and to supervise it thereafter. Customs unions are often taken to be indicators that the member ➤states intend to pursue a policy of integration rather than mere cooperation. The logic of ➤functionalism argues that beyond a certain point integration becomes difficult to halt.

It is a moot point as to how far trade blocs create trade and how far they diversify existing trade into new patterns. Under the General Agreement on Tariffs and Trade (GATT) rules trade blocs were not prohibited *per se*. This was perhaps surprising given the commitment to MFN principles in GATT. In the event GATT presided over a system which saw the growth of trade blocs after 1945, the most powerful and significant of these being the ➤European Union. ➤➤NAFTA

**Trade-off** A term used in negotiations between international ➤actors. Its use signifies that an exchange of preferences has taken place between the parties. This exchange may take place as part of an overall agreement or as part of the process leading towards agreement. The exchange may be made about similar things or different things. Thus, parties may trade off landing rights for their civil aircraft with each other or the may trade off landing rights, on one hand, for fishing rights on the other. A trade-off may be seen as a form of concession, but clearly the concessions are made on both sides. Trade-offs are particularly appropriate to those negotiating situations where the positions of the parties can be quantified – for instance in ➤trade negotiations – because herein it is much easier to enumerate the preferences. ➤➤Reciprocity

**Trade system** The activity of engaging in ➤trade between international ➤actors has created a trade system. The contemporary system is the outgrowth of the nineteenth century. In the period after the end of the European wars against revolutionary France international trade grew by, on average, 4 per cent per year until 1914. The generating force for this was the rapid industrialization that took place, initially in Western Europe and then in the Americas and in Asia. The primary result of this was an increase in wealth in these ➤states so that as foreign trade increased so did national income, sometimes faster. As a result the phenomenon known as 'export-led growth' became recognized by political economists and sought after by political leaders.

Under the monetary system known as the ➤gold standard what would now be called a highly ➤interdependent set of relationships developed. Scholars such as Professor K. Waltz (1979) have argued that the nineteenth-century trade and payments system was the height of ➤interdependence, at least in terms of wealth/welfare ➤issue areas. Because the system was so interdependent, individual actors were highly vulnerable to adverse and unanticipated changes.

This system was irreparably damaged by the First World War and the economic depression thereafter. World trade did not begin to grow significantly after 1914 until the decade of the 1950s when a new but less open system was created under the aegis of the United States as the ➤hegemonial actor. Trade growth was spectacular during the years that followed, but very uneven in its impact. Unlike the nineteenth century, the post-1950s trade system has seen the benefits from this expansion going mainly to a small group of advanced industrial countries (AICs) and an even smaller group of newly industrialized countries (NICs) in the ➤Third World. This is quite different from the preceding century when many of the 'new' states in the Americas and Asia were fully and successfully integrated into the system. The duality of the trading system since the 1950s has led some observers to speak of a ➤polarization between the ➤north and the ➤south as a result of these differential benefits.

The trade system since 1945 is also substantially more institutionalized than in the previous one hundred years. In the wake of the ➤Bretton Woods agreements it was anticipated that a trading ➤regime committed to the principle of non-discrimination would be established. The failure to ratify the International Trade Organization (ITO) left the General Agreement on Tariffs and Trade (GATT) by default as the principle organizational expression of this philosophy. In practice the non-discriminatory principle was not applied with sufficient determination and, in particular, when the United States positively encouraged the establishment of a major ➤trading bloc among Western European states in the 1950s a potentially fatal flaw was generated.

The establishment of the OECD and the United Nations Conference on Trade and Development (UNCTAD) in the 1960s when the growth of trade was fastest indicate the extent to which the unevenness of this growth was to be institutionalized. The principle of non-discrimination is now firmly rejected by the majority membership of UNCTAD which has pressed for a return to preferential tariffs rather than reciprocal ➤most favoured nation (MFN) treatment as the functional expression of their approach to the trade system. ➤World Trade Organization (WTO)

**Trade wars** In his standard work on the subject Conybeare (1987) defines a trade war as 'a category of intense international conflict where states interact, bargain and retaliate primarily over economic objectives directly related to the traded goods or service sectors of their economies, and where the means used are restrictions on the free flow of goods or services' (p. 4). Trade wars are thus a subset of ➤economic statecraft. As in other reaches of IPE, trade wars are also political but in this instance the outward and visible manifestation is wholly economic. Trade wars must be distinguished throughout any analysis from the more generalized use of trade ➤sanctions in ➤international relations. As Conybeare makes clear trade as an instrument of policy during a ➤conflict situation and trade as the ➤goal or objective of the conflict can be treated separately for analytical purposes. Commonly trade wars occur because a party is ➤perceived to have infringed the letter or spirit of some economic relationship. Thus ➤dumping can provoke a trade war if other parties react by retaliatory measures of their own whilst specifically citing the original cause to have been the dumping policy. Trade wars are implicit in all competitive economic activities and in this sense they may be held up as examples of how parties can slip into a more adversarial mode. In particular once retaliatory behaviour is evident and is linked to specific economic goals and outcomes then it may be possible to stipulate with confidence that a trade war is ongoing. Large economic powers can push the costs of economic adjustment onto others. The difficulty arises when they try to do this to each other because the result is likely to be trade disputes and trade wars. Trade wars between large economies are more likely to end in ➤stalemate because the parties are more willing to absorb the costs and continue the conflict rather than submit. Trade wars have a significant domestic content in the sense that particular economic interests, lobby groups and so on will have a greater vested interest in the outcome than the ➤mass public. This can contribute to the longevity of the conflict but it also means that trade wars are rarely seen as ➤high politics within the standard definition of that term.

During the ➤Cold War era in world politics, trade wars figured regularly in relations between the United States of America and the ➤European Community/European Union, and to a lesser extent between the former and Japan. The explanation for this is implicit in the analysis offered earlier. As the dominant economies in the ➤trade system of that period, these actors were potentially likely to find themselves in conflict over policy and outcomes and equally they had the economic ➤power to retaliate. Again particularly in the case of the US/EU relationship both parties have strong, identifiable and highly articulate lobby groups with well established access points to decision centres. (This overlap makes trade wars a form of ➤intermestic policy-making, it should be noted). In their highly adversarial relationship with the former Soviet Union on the other hand the United States used trade as a strategic weapon in its confrontation and so the idea of trade war does not apply.

In the light of the above analysis it is possible to see that trade wars neatly balance cooperative and confrontational behaviour patterns between parties. The high costs of the war can push the parties towards diffusing the conflict but at the same time these cost calculations make it imperative that diffusion is mutual and balanced. Trade wars have many of the characteristics of that branch of ➤game theory which concerns itself with 'mixed-motive' games, that is to say games which offer both cooperative and confrontational strategies. By definition almost, a trade war should never end in a fight to the finish because ➤rationally such an outcome would be too damaging for all the parties.

**Traditionalism** Sometimes called the 'classical' or 'non-scientific' approach, this term was popularized by Kaplan (1966) to describe the methodological position adopted by opponents of the behavioural ➤revolution in the study of ➤international relations. According to this characterization, traditionalists rely overmuch on idiosyncratic, highly personalized insights from history, philosophy, political theory and law and consequently tend to employ intuitive, subjective judgements unsupported by empirical evidence to explain international phenomena. For their part, the traditionalists argue that scientific methods involving strict standards of proof and verification, quantification, measurement and the construction of hypothetical models are wholly inappropriate when dealing with a subject matter that involves human purpose (see Hedley Bull, 1966b). This 'debate' which raged throughout the 1960s and early 1970s, was thus essentially about methodology. In this sense, it was not an off-shoot of the earlier ➤realist-idealist controversy. It is generally agreed now that although at the time it generated much heat in academic circles, the argument about methods and approaches is somewhat sterile. Since the substantive issue of subject matter was never in dispute both 'tradition' and 'science' can, and do, coexist as complementary modes within the field (see Knorr and Rosenau, 1969). ➤➤Neoliberalism; neorealism; critical theory and postmodernism.

**Transgovernmental relations** This term is used to refer to what might be termed the 'unofficial ➤foreign policy' that is frequently conducted between government departments of one ➤state and those of another. To be able and willing to behave in this way, the departments have to operate in a system that is relatively autonomous from the constitutionally defined ➤decision-makers. Again, such behaviour is incompatible with the idea that states are unitary actors. Recognition that state-to-state relations are transgovernmental as well as intergovernmental thus represents a shift in the ➤paradigm away from traditional ➤state-centric ideas.

The developments in contemporary ➤international relations would appear to have influenced the growth of these relations. First, increasing ➤interdependence among all actors has increased both the sensitivity and the vulnerability of state actors. Implementing and coordinating policy, particularly in ➤issue areas that are highly complex and specialized, means that bureaucracies take over from cabinets. Second, the growth of ➤intergovernmental organizations (IGOs) means that the institutional framework for such interaction is already in place. As a result, ➤policy-making is more complex and more in need of continual adjustment. Formal office holders are unable to cope and transgovernmental relations become prevalent.

**Transnational** Literally implying 'across nations', the term is now widely used in ➤international relations both with regard to relationships or transactions and with regard to organizations. In both instances the usage connotes activities that cross ➤state, rather than national, ➤boundaries. Transnational relations are dependent upon three kinds of movements: (a) the movement of physical objects, including human populations; (b) the movement of information and ideas; and (c) the movement of money and credit. Such transactions are certainly not novel or peculiar to the contemporary system. Thus the ➤gold standard, the movement of European peoples to the United States and the contagious spread of ideas about ➤nationalism are all nineteenth-century instances of what would now be called transnationalism. Notwithstanding this historical background, the growth of such transnational linkages has been a feature of world politics in the contemporary period. Two ➤macropolitical conditions seem to have been particularly important here: the growth of the ➤technologies of communication and transportation and the growth of ➤interdependence between ➤actors. The twentieth-century communications revolution has enabled transnational actors to control their activities, while the growth of interdependence has created a permissive climate for transnationalism to expand.

Huntington (1973), in a seminal article in *World Politics*, defined a transnational organization according to three criteria: that they are complex organizations internally, that they are functionally specific and that they operate, intentionally, across state frontiers. Huntington notes that since 1945, these organizations have proliferated both in ➤domain and ➤scope. The best example of contemporary transnational organization is the multinational corporation (MNC). Incorporated in one state (the 'home'), with subsidiaries in others (the 'hosts'), these corporate actors are involved in all three types of transnational movements identified earlier. Other contemporary instances of transnational organizations would be the PLO and the Roman Catholic Church. Within a particular ➤issue area, such as civilian air transport, it is possible to identify a whole complex ➤regime including states, intergovernmental organizations (NGOs) and transnational organization – in this instance large civilian airline companies. It should be noted that international non-governmental organisations (IGOs) are, by definition, transnational organizations, although their scope and domain is relatively insignificant in comparison with some of the other examples cited earlier.

The growth of transnational relations and transnational organizations has been identified with approaches favouring a ➤mixed actor view of macropolitics. The more traditional, ➤state-centric approaches can no longer suffice to provide a relevant isomorphism. There is, accordingly, the need for greater ➤pluralism if these changes are to be accommodated. Governments cannot control the contacts across state boundaries that are the essence of transnationalism and recognition of this empirical reality has led to a further loss of confidence in traditional models. All in all, the empirical evidence adduced to support the growth of transnationalism is matched by the analytical shift in the paradigm of macropolitics away from state-centred thinking. ➤➤Globalization

**Treaty** A written contract or agreement between two or more parties which is considered binding in ►international law. Parties to treaties may be ►states, heads of states, governments or ►international organizations. They are normally negotiated by plenipotentiaries on behalf of governments and are usually subject to ►ratification which is an executive act. Oral agreements are not treaties though verbal undertakings are sometimes claimed to have the same validity. The term is an elastic one but generally its use is confined to more formal agreements concerning fundamental relations. Other terms denoting agreement which bear a family resemblance to 'treaty' are ►protocol, agreement, arrangement, accord, act, general act, declaration, compromise and charter (see Myers, 1957, p. 576). Treaty is the most formal and highest instrument of agreement on this list. It is a moot point whether 'exchanges of notes', a common ►diplomatic practice, actually constitutes a treaty (the ►Rush–Bagot agreement of 1817 is often referred to as a treaty whereas it began life as an exchange of notes between the United Kingdom and the United States). Treaties can be ►multilateral or ►bilateral, can involve a definite transaction or seek to establish general rules of conduct. Usually they are binding only on signatories but there are exceptions to this rule. Sometimes treaties establish ►regimes which are considered objectively valid (*erga omnes*) for non-signatory third parties. For example, multilateral agreements made under the auspices of the UN and its agencies dealing with matters of common interest such as ►diplomatic immunity or the ►law of the sea create obligations and duties for non-members like Switzerland. In cases of this kind, the notion of 'consent' is implied thus safeguarding the rights of ►sovereignty upon which the ►international system is built. Besides multilateral and bilateral treaties (which are sometimes called 'treaty contracts' to distinguish them from the more general kind), treaties can be political (e.g. ►peace or ►disarmament), commercial (e.g. ►tariffs or fisheries), constitutional or administrative (e.g. ►UN Charter and agencies) or legal (e.g. ►extradition, laws of war). They are usually constructed to a set pattern involving a preamble, specific articles, a time-scale, ratification procedure, signatures and added articles (Kant wrote *Perpetual Peace* in treaty form – even adding a 'secret article' according to normal eighteenth century diplomatic practice).

Treaties are considered binding (►*pacta sunt servanda*) but may lapse naturally, through ►war or by denunciation. Some international lawyers argue that all treaties are subject to the principle of ►*rebus sic stantibus*; that is, that the treaty ceases to be binding when a fundamental change of circumstance has occurred. The doctrine of changed circumstance leading to termination, though is not generally applied to fundamental treaties of communal application such as the UN Charter, the ►Geneva Convention or the Vienna Conventions. A further point of legal dispute is whether the treaty itself constitutes the agreement or whether it is merely the instrument that records it. The latter appears more sensible and is in fact the common view. Treaties are an important and recognized source of ►international law, the others being custom, general principles of law recognized by civilized nations and judicial decisions and teachings (see Article 38, para. 1 of the *Statute of the International Court of Justice*).

**Treaty Port** A term used to describe ports in Asia, mainly China and Japan, which were forcibly opened up for ►foreign trade and residence in the nineteenth century by the United Kingdom, France, Germany and the United States. Treaty ports first occurred in China in 1842 following defeat in the Chinese – United Kingdom ►trade war (the Opium Wars, 1839–42). The system was introduced to Japan in 1854 when Commodore Matthew C. Perry forced the Japanese to open the door to US commerce. They were abolished in Japan in 1899 when Japanese industrial and military strength began to assert itself. They continued in China, which by 1911 had over fifty such ports, until after the Second World War. In these treaty ports, Western subjects enjoyed the rights of ►extraterritoriality and were granted quasi-►diplomatic privileges. Usually, the ports developed their own (i.e. the ►imperial states) legal, judicial, police and taxation systems, and in this sense can be considered to be a form of ►annexation.

**Trilateralism** An analysis of ►international relations which sees ►tripolarity as the most significant structural characteristic. Trilateralism is thus a from of applied ►systems analysis. Its influence can be dated from the early years of the 1970s and was particularly influential among US scholars, ►diplomats and politicians. Applying an essentially economic concept of ►power, the trilateralists saw the possibilities of ►hegemonial cooperation between the 'poles' of the United States, Japan and the ►European Community. Given their emphasis upon ►interdependence as a systemic characteristic trilateralists, almost by definition, were committed to a cooperative rather than ►conflict model of world politics. Trilateralism was not exclusively ►state-centric because the important role of non-state ►actors such as the ►transnational corporations was recognized and included in their assumptions and prescriptions.

**Tripolarity** A variation of the ►multipolar system structure which identifies three 'poles' or polar ►actors. The actors that dominate a tripolar system need not be ►states; blocs or ►coalitions may qualify. On the vexed issue of stability – often held to be one of the key benchmarks in this type of ►systems analysis – tripolar systems tend to be unstable. Thus, if any two actors combine against the third, the system will become ►bipolar. If any one of the three slips out of the dominant category, the system will again become bipolar. If further dominant actors emerge, the system will become ►multipolar. In short tripolarity has the tendency to revert to a less ambiguous bipolarity, or to develop into a more complex multipolarity.

Central to the tripolar configuration is the concept of polarity. Having identified the determinants of ►polarity, it is possible to see what relevance tripolarity has for contemporary ►international relations. Herein, a favoured ►issue area is that of political economy. Many would see the United States,

Japan and the ►European Union as the tripolar actors. In the military-security issue area, tripolarity is less discernible. At the ideational level, tripolarity configurations have clearly influenced those who saw a ►Third World as separate from the ►First and Second, during the ►Cold War era.

**Trip-wire** A term used in strategic analysis. A trip-wire is a small token force which has a ►deterrent function, out of all proportion to its size because it symbolizes the commitment of the ►actor(s) concerned to escalate their military response rapidly and significantly should the token force be attacked. In this way the token force 'trips' the escalatory response. Trip-wire forces are invariably part of a situation of ►extended deterrence where an ►intervening third party adopts one side as a protégé and seeks to deter others by stationing trip-wire forces on or near the territory of the protégé. The term was popular in NATO circles during the ►Cold War era when American forces stationed in Europe – particularly in forward position such as ►Berlin – were regarded as trip-wires for full-blown United States military intervention.

**Truce** A contemporary cessation of physical violence between ►actors. It may be used to alleviate some immediate and pressing situation, such as the removal of sick and wounded, or the provision of essential food and medical services. Alternatively, or additionally, a truce may be seen as the preliminary stage in the ►implementation of a permanent settlement to the ►conflict situation.

Negotiating a truce may not be easy. For example, in the ►Korean War (1950–53) negotiations for a truce between the parties proved costly and contentious. While the truce talks were being conducted the hostilities continued and significant casualties resulted, both among the combatants and the civilian population of Korea. Indeed the United States lost more men during the period of the truce ►negotiations than in the initial period of the ►war, when both sides were seeking forcible reunification of the divided peninsula.

Parties seeking a truce will often turn to an appropriate third party for mediation purposes and to assist in implementation once an agreement has been reached. ►intergovernmental organizations (IGOs) such as the ►United Nations have often been used both for mediation and implementation purposes. The ►Arab-Israeli conflict would be an appropriate example in this regard.

**Truman Doctrine** An all-embracing ►foreign policy statement proclaimed by President Truman which provided the framework of US ►Cold War strategy for more than twenty years. It began with a speech to a joint session of Congress on 12 March 1947 in which Truman, while requesting 400 million dollars aid to Greece and Turkey, declared that 'it must be the policy of the United States to support free peoples who are resisting subjection by armed minorities or outside pressures'. Truman asked for, and got, the largest American ►bilateral government aid programme in peacetime history. In addition, provision was made for the dispatch of military personnel to Europe, the United States thus assuming chief responsibility for the active peacetime defence of the Eastern Mediterranean. This dramatic speech and policy implications it contained amounted to a ➤revolution in US peacetime policy. It marked a clear break with the long-standing ➤isolationist tradition and it established a precedent for US economic and military aid programmes throughout the world. Although the Soviet Union was not specifically mentioned it was widely and correctly assumed the 'free peoples' and 'anti-communist' were synonymous. Under the doctrine, the United States was committed on a global scale to oppose the spread of ➤communism and to intervene, by force of arms if necessary, in any 'threatened area'. Although Truman specifically mentioned Greece and Turkey, it soon became clear that the doctrine itself knew no general geographical limits. The economic dimension of this strategy of world-wide ➤containment of communism was provided by the ➤Marshall Plan, both of which in Truman's words constituted 'two halves of the same walnut'. Critics have argued that the sweeping ideological generalizations the doctrine contained, especially the simplistic division of the world into 'good' and 'evil' states, prevented US ➤policy-makers for at least a generation from identifying genuine mass-based ➤nationalist movements and resulted in US aid to regimes with appalling records on ➤human rights merely because they publicly opposed communism. The tragedy of ➤Vietnam was thus directly attributable to the Truman doctrine. Domestically, the doctrine represents the first post-war assertion of the 'Imperial Presidency'; Congress was informed of the new policy direction, not consulted. As a result of this precedent, Congress became virtually a passive participant in the making of US ➤foreign policy until, in the wake of the Vietnam debacle, it reasserted its authority with the War Powers Act of 1973. For a quarter of a century the philosophical and ideological premises upon which US policy rested were not publicly or seriously questioned by the legislature. The doctrinal statements made by Truman became articles of faith which were almost universally accepted as authoritative and unquestioned. In the words of one commentator it amounted to 'the American Declaration of the ➤Cold War' and in this respect it may have been a ➤self-fulfilling prophecy. ➤➤X

**Trusteeship** The notion of international supervision of ➤colonial territories was introduced by President Woodrow Wilson in Paris in 1919. The purpose was to prevent ➤annexation of territories previously controlled by the defeated ➤states. The system operated by the ➤League of Nations was known as the ➤mandate system. The trusteeship system is thus the newer version of the original, and has the same general purpose; former colonies of defeated states were to be administered by a 'trust' power under overall international supervision until such time as the inhabitants were able to determine their own future either as self-governing units or as independent states. However, it differs from the earlier system in that the supervisory body, the UN Trusteeship Council, has wider powers of overview than the more limited Mandates

Commission. Chapters 12 and 13 of the ➤United Nations Charter established an institution that is broader and more objective than its predecessor. The council is one of the six principal organs of the UN yet is subject to ➤General Assembly authority and review. Its role is to provide supervision of those non-self-governing territories that are designated as trust territories. Articles 87 and 88 set out the main methods for exercising this supervisory role. These are: (a) the preparation of detailed questionnaires on the political, economic, social and educational progress of the inhabitants of the territory; (b) the provision of an annual report by the administering authority; (c) an oral examination of agents of the administering authority; (d) the receipt and examination of petitions from individuals or groups within the trust territory; (e) periodic visits to each trust territory by delegates of the Trusteeship Council. These devices were meant to give more effective supervision of conditions within these territories. By 1950, eleven territories had been put under trusteeship and seven states acted as trustees. All, except for Somalia which was under Italian trusteeship, had been former mandates within the League. (South Africa continually refused to place its mandated territory, South West Africa/Namibia, under the trust system and until recently this remained the one unresolved legacy of the First World War. However, in 1989 in return for the supervised withdrawal of Cuban forces from Angola, South Africa agreed to set in motion the process of ➤self-determination.) Of the eleven territories, only one (the US-held Trust Territory of the Pacific Islands) has not achieved independence though some measures of self-government have been granted. This latter territory was designated a 'strategic territory' in order to accommodate the military-security interests of the United States in the Pacific. In this case supervisory powers are exercised by the Security Council, thus giving to the United States a potential ➤veto over any action considered prejudicial to its security interests.

# U

**UDI** Unilateral Declaration of Independence. In November 1965, in defiance of the ➤colonial power of the United Kingdom and of the international community at large, Rhodesia's White settler government declared itself ➤independent. This amounted to a complete reversal of the post-war anti-colonial process in British Africa. The United Kingdom from the start was reluctant to use force to ensure compliance and settled for policies of ➤negotiation and ➤economic sanctions. In 1966 the ➤Security Council called for mandatory sanctions to be imposed by all member ➤states. France and the Soviet Union abstained, while Portugal and South Africa refused to impose an embargo. In 1970 Rhodesia unilaterally declared itself a republic. The issue is significant in ➤international relations in that the period 1965–80 (the date of the creation of Zimbabwe) demonstrates the general ineffectiveness of economic sanctions as a means of ensuring compliance. Despite hardships the white ➤regime was able to survive due mainly to overt assistance from South Africa and covert sanctions-breaking from, among others, the United Kingdom, the United States and France. The regime eventually collapsed as a direct consequence of the armed struggle waged by the Zimbabwean liberation armies.

**Ultimatum** Used in two senses in ➤diplomacy. The first and most common use is with reference to a formal communication (a note or memorandum) from one government to another requiring compliance on some issue – failure to do so carrying the threat of a penalty. Used in this way it takes the form of a final demand and signals the beginning of the end of the negotiating process. It involves a time-scale both for presentation and response. Thus, it is a critical instrument of diplomacy and its use is generally confined to conditions of extreme international crisis, involving as it does an implicit or explicit threat to use means other than normal diplomatic bargaining to achieve objectives. The second sense is more general and does not involve threats of compliance. Here it refers simply to the 'ultimate' or maximum amount of concessions one side is prepared to concede in ➤negotiations in order to reach a settlement.

**Unanimity** The unanimity principle or rule is a fundamental tenet of the traditional ➤state-centred approach to ➤world politics. It derives its significance from the legal concept of state ➤sovereignty, and in particular on the derivation known as sovereign ➤equality. Given the principle that at least in law, if not in terms of political realities, all ➤states are equal, it follows that whenever states are gathered together in ➤diplomatic meetings and conferences, each participating state should have equality of treatment. Voting procedures should reflect this equality, and therefore, each state will have the same vote – as opposed to the system known as 'weighted voting' – and, moreover, no state can be committed to a course of action against its consent. Voting, therefore, is also an expression of consent in these circumstances. It can now be seen that following the strict application of these prescriptions every participating state has to vote in favour of a proposed course of action and/or statement of principles for that resolution to be carried by the meeting.

The unanimity rule was written into the Covenant of the ➤League of Nations in the fifth Article, which specifically stipulated that voting in both the main organs of the League would be on the unanimity rule. The ➤United Nations, on the other hand, has gone a long way towards modifying these norms in its Charter. The major exception to this is exemplified in the ➤veto provisions concerning voting in the Security Council. Article 27 of the ➤UN Charter states that the concurrence of the five permanent members will be required on all questions other than those on procedural matters.

The effect of the unanimity requirement upon interstate organizations is to restrict ➤decision-making to the lowest common denominator of agreement and to stifle and stultify the efforts of those parties who might wish to expand and enhance the role of the institution. As such it is quite appropriate to regard the unanimity principle as a bastion of traditional state-centrism. Strict adherence to its letter and spirit considerably weakens the impact that these organization can have on world politics.

**Unconditional surrender**  The termination of armed ➤conflict without prior stipulation of conditions. In such a surrender, the victorious side may legally impose whatever terms seem appropriate. The defeated are entirely under the discretionary authority of the victors. As a consequence, ➤annexation, division, occupation, ➤reparations, war crimes trials, as well as enforced changes in economic, social and political institutions are all possible policy implications. The doctrine of unconditional surrender, while by no means unknown before the twentieth century, is particularly associated with the concept of ➤total war and as such is alien and inimical to the idea of ➤limited war which for the most part dominated nineteenth-century ➤international relations. Unconditional surrender was demanded in both World Wars and at the Casablanca Conference in 1943 President Roosevelt justified it in this way: its aim was 'not the destruction of the populace but the destruction of a philosophy which is based on conquest and subjugation of other people'. In this sense, it is more likely to be an instrument of ➤idealism rather than of ➤realism. The policy was criticized on the grounds that it prolonged the ➤war, it led to the use of ➤nuclear weapons, it postponed serious discussion on the nature of post-war settlement and it prevented the re-entry of the defeated ➤states into the full play of post-war world politics.

**Unification** ➤integration

**Unilateralism** A policy of reliance on one's own resources in the pursuit of ➤foreign policy objectives. An important consequence of the ➤Westphalia system it was once the most sought-after ideal in ➤international relations since it maximized a ➤state's freedom to manoeuvre and did not involve the compromises implicit in ➤alliance politics. A commitment to unilateralism was expressed in a number of ways, the most common forms being ➤isolationism, neutralism and ➤non-alignment, all of which involve some degree of non-participation in world politics. Traditionally, island states (e.g. the United Kingdom, Japan), or states logistically remote from the main arenas of diplomatic activity (e.g. the United States, China) have been the main beneficiaries but ➤technological developments in the nineteenth and twentieth centuries have now rendered unilateralism difficult, if not impossible for any state to achieve. Most states, willingly or unwillingly, now define their military-security issues in terms of ➤bilateral or ➤multilateral regional alliance systems. The term is most often used in contemporary literature in connection with ➤disarmament particularly with regard to the possession of ➤nuclear weapons. In 1992–93 South Africa adopted this posture. The idea does have a measure of popular appeal and is high on the agenda of activists within the ➤peace movement. The arguments advanced by its proponents have both ethical and political components. Renunciation of nuclear weapons by a single state would set a moral example to the rest of the system and encourage others to follow suit. In addition, since many states are hosts to foreign nuclear bases and arsenals, the act of expulsion would reestablish their ➤independence and ➤sovereignty. These beliefs, particularly varieties of the latter, have had an effect on ➤defence issues in Western Europe, and further afield have led the New Zealand government to refuse to allow US nuclear warships landing rights on their territory. While NATO and ➤ANZUS appear to have been affected by unilateral impulses within the alliances, these have not structurally altered the ability of the alliances to survive.

**Unipolarity** A type of system structure with one 'pole' or a polar ➤actor being identified as predominant. In a unipolar system the dominant actor need not be a ➤state and indeed historically where unipolar systems have existed they have usually been multinational empires. Hypothetically, the limiting case of a unipolar system would be a ➤world government where, by definition, the ➤sub-systems are subordinate to the overall system structure. Unipolar systems are more likely to show stability if the dominant actor can establish ground rules which are widely accepted throughout the system. Even ➤imperial systems cannot live by coercion alone in this respect. In setting and maintaining the ground rules, the dominant actor may have to bear considerable direct and opportunity costs. The dynamics of unipolar ➤leadership in this context have been well analysed by ➤hegemonial stability theorists.

The ending of the ►Cold War era in world politics has produced some speculation that the United States is now the only ►superpower and that this primacy implies a 'unipolar moment' for America. Such thinking begs a host of questions about the ►declinist and ►renewalist debate and arguments about the ending of ►pax americana. If the system is unipolar, it is in the realm of ideas that this exists. ►economic liberalism and, to a lesser extent, participatory democracy now hold centre stage. However these ideas can equally underpin ►multilateralism as they might unipolarity.

**Unit veto** A hypothetical international system discussed in the second chapter of Kaplan's book (1957). The defining characteristic of this system is held to be the 'possession by all actors of weapons of such a character that any actor is capable of destroying any other actor that attacks it even though it cannot prevent its own destruction' (p. 50). Although seemingly highly deductive, the unit veto capability bears a family resemblance to ►weapons of mass destruction. In contemporary IR, the unit veto system is sometimes referred to as 'the equalizer' for this reason.

**United Nations Charter** The Charter is in effect the written constitution of the UN. It is also a ►multilateral treaty which in respect of the agreements, rights and duties it confers on its signatories and members is an important source of ►international law. It was signed in San Francisco on 26 June 1945, was subsequently ratified by fifty-one states and came into being on 24 October 1945 (United Nations Day). The Charter, which runs to 111 articles, provides the UN's organizational structure, principles, functions and powers. It designates six agencies as principal organs:

1 The ►General Assembly.
2 The ►Security Council.
3 The Economic and Social Council.
4 The ►Trusteeship Council.
5 The Secretariat.
6 The ►International Court of Justice.

The primary objectives stated in the Charter are the following: (a) to maintain international ►peace and ►security through peaceful settlement of disputes and ►collective security; (b) to promote international economic and social cooperation; (c) to promote respect for ►human rights for all. The fact that the Charter has survived and grown over the last forty years or so is testimony not just to the general and vague nature of the principles initially agreed upon but also to the flexibility and adaptability of the original document. In addition, although the Covenant of the ►League of Nations was its intellectual forerunner, the Charter itself displays a much more realistic grasp of the mechanics of world affairs. For example, the allocation of ►veto powers to the five permanent members of the Security Council may on occasion have stultified the organization, but without it in all likelihood the UN would have fared no better than its predecessor. That it survived intact the austere political climate of the ➤Cold War is ample evidence of the sagacity of its original framers.

**United Nations Organization** The UNO is the world's second attempt at creating an intergovernmental organization (IGO) to ensure world ➤peace, and to establish the economic, social and political foundations through which this can be realized. The organization developed directly from discussions among the Allies during the Second World War (in fact the term 'United Nations' was originally used to denote those ➤states which were allied against the ➤axis powers), and subsequently at ➤Dumbarton Oaks and San Francisco between 1944–5. Indeed the San Francisco conference (April–June, 1945) was the first major international conference in the history of the ➤states-system which was not dominated by European states. (Of fifty-one signatories only nine were European.) The UN therefore marks the formal end of the European states-system and its replacement by a genuinely global one. Although it relied heavily on the experience of the ➤League of Nations the founders of the UN were anxious from the outset to create a new international organization and not merely a revised, patched-up version of the League. To this end, stronger executive powers were assigned to the ➤security council, member states were required to make armed forces available as ➤peacekeepers and a range of ➤specialized agencies was envisaged to foster and sustain a global economic and social order. However, the fundamental premises of the old organization remained virtually intact in the new; state ➤sovereignty persisted alongside the notion of voluntary ➤collective security as the twin basic tenets of the ➤UN Charter. Like the League, members' obligations are limited, the organization has no means of enforcing its decisions and determination of obligations is left to members themselves.

Structurally, the UN has six main organs. The Security Council is the most important executive agency and sits in permanent session. It has fifteen members, five of which, Britain, China, France, United States and Russia, have permanent membership and enjoy the privileges of the ➤veto. The ➤General Assembly, in which every member state has a vote, is central to the organization and is in effect a world forum. It also exercises supervisory and coordinating functions for all other agencies associated with the UN. The ➤trusteeship Council succeeded the ➤Mandates Commission of the League, the ➤International Court of Justice (ICJ) succeeded the ➤Permanent Court of International Justice and the Economic and Social Council succeeded the Economic Consultative Committee. All these organs are served by a Secretariat and ➤Secretary-General who is chief officer.

The UN has been continuously active in ➤international relations since 1945 and has been especially innovative in preventative ➤diplomacy, peacekeeping and fact-finding missions. However, on military-security issues the UN has, at best, a mixed record. After the ➤Korean War (1950–3) the collective security principle upon which the organization was founded gave way under the pressure of ►superpower rivalry to the watered-down security concept of peacekeeping. The end of the ►Cold War era in world politics seemed to come to open new possibilities for organizational task employment more akin to the hopes of the founders. The UN's role in the ►Persian Gulf War apparently confirmed this optimism. Instead since 1991 the Organization has foundered rather than flourished. The challenge of ►communal conflict situations and the appropriate role for the UN remains to be successfully addressed. The real achievement of the UN lies elsewhere. Paradoxically, whatever success the UN may claim to date appears to lie in its non-political, non-security aspects, in particular in the extensive welfare network that is associated with the ►specialized agencies. Commonly described as 'the UN development system' the services presided over by the General Assembly and the Economic and Social Council have brought far-reaching changes to the ►international system. The ►functionalist view that cooperation in non-political matters will create an international constituency where parochial interests are minimal (and which incidentally would make the UN obsolete) may be idealistic but few doubt that it is in this area that the UN system has had most impact. Even so, questions are continually being asked, especially in the developed West, whether the 'politicization' of the welfare agencies (e.g. UNESCO) has undermined their original humanitarian functions. In addition to the relative success of the practical social service aspects of the organization, the dominant position of ►human rights, environmental and ►north-south issues on the agenda of contemporary world politics owes much to the expansive interpretation of its powers by the General Assembly, especially during periods when the exercise of the ►veto has paralysed the Security Council. In sum, the UN system has proved more effective in dealing with low-profile functional issues than with the larger question of the preservation of peace which was its original rationale. ►►UN reform

**United Nations reform** There is widespread agreement on the need to reform aspects of the UN system. This is hardly surprising considering that the organization is now over 50 years old, and confronts a vastly different set of international ►issue areas from those which characterized the immediate post-World War Two period. While the ►Cold War provided a convenient alibi for some of the UN's shortcomings, its demise coupled with the euphoria generated by the UN's role in the ►Persian Gulf War of 1991 generated a hope that a reformed UN could become the central supporting structure in the architecture of the ►New World Order. This optimism proved short-lived. Not only has there been a reluctance to confront the issue of reform, but during the 1991−95 period the UN was overwhelmed by active involvement in seemingly intractable intra-state ►conflicts, rather than the inter-state variety it was designed to deal with. ►Communal conflicts in Angola, Cambodia, El Salvador, Haiti, Rwanda, Burundi, Liberia, Palestine, Mozambique, as well as the republics of the former Soviet Union and ex-Yugoslavia extended the Organization to the limits of its competence. In particular the debacle in Bosnia (where UN troops were taken hostage) and Somalia (where the UN withdrew ignominiously after US troops suffered casualties) raised the questions about the need to confront anew the principles and purposes that the UN should stand for.

There are three general categories of reform proposals: structural/contitutional, finance and funding, and operational. Structurally the aim is to make the UN more ►democratic, more responsive and more authoritative. This involves reforming the ►General Assembly, the ►Security Council – including the P5 – and the ►secretariat. Other proposals in this category involve a rationalization of the functions of the Economic and Social Council, particularly the ►specialized agencies. On the financial front the aim is to make the UN solvent and less reliant on a handful of ►First World states, particularly the United States. Operationally the objective is to redefine its role in communal conflicts, to expand its competence in ►complex emergencies, global governance, humanitarian intervention and the global protection of ►human rights and the ►environment. All of these issue areas were addressed by ►Secretary-General Boutros-Ghali's 'Agenda for Peace' (1992) but characteristically for a near universal organization of this kind, agreement on specifics is difficult to obtain, and if obtained, to sustain.

**Uruguay Round** Initiated in September 1986 at a GATT ministerial meeting at Punta del Este, Uruguay, ►negotiations for what was to become the eighth in the sequence of multilateral trade negotiations (►MTNs) began in 1987. Following the precedent of the ►tokyo round, Uruguay sought to address new ►issue areas in the political economy of the world. In particular the parties sought to establish liberal trade rules with regard to service industries (i.e. economic activity which provides a service rather than producing a product – such as banking or insurance), the parties sought safeguards regarding intellectual property rights and investment decisions which appeared to discriminate in favour of local interests. In the actual negotiations it was not so-called 'new issues' which provoked the greatest conflict. Rather the perennial questions of agriculture, ►dumping and subsidies was resuscitated. The principal parties were the United States and the so-called 'Cairns Group' of agricultural exporters on one side and the EC/EU on the other. Essentially the argument was over the ►scope and significance of the kinds of reductions that the Round would be able to stipulate relating to subsidies. Eventual agreement was reached in Morocco in April 1994 to be ►implemented from January 1995 onwards. A ►compromise was reached on the question of agricultural subsidies. The Common Agricultural Policy (CAP) of the EC/EU remains the main stumbling block in any event. It is likely that continual external pressure from mainstream agricultural exporters will conspire with the internal demands to seek reform of the CAP in the future.

The main institutional innovation to emerge from the Uruguay Round was the establishment of a ►world trade organization (WTO). Technically a ►treaty has been replaced by an ►IGO with this move. The evident growth of economic ►regionalism in the system in the 1990s enhances the felt need for a more powerful means to supervise the trade agreements reached under the ►GATT aegis over many years.

**uti possidetis** A politico-legal principle associated with rights of ►sovereignty and in particular territorial claims made by successor states to former imperial possessions. Originally a Latin American concept used to define and delimit the boundaries of the old Spanish empire, it was explicitly adopted by the Organization of African Unity (OAU) at its second summit in Cairo in 1964. Essentially, it reaffirmed African colonial boundaries established at the Berlin Conference of 1885 and all member states pledged to respect the 'intangibility of frontiers inherited from colonisation.' This has subsequently become an important principle of African politics and 'uti possidetis' has been used to counter secessionist arguments throughout the continent. In particular, the acceptance of colonial boundaries by the newly independent states meant that Kwame Nkrumah's proposal for a 'United States of Africa' which would transcend the colonial legacy was defeated. Thereafter, the Pan-African ideal has expressed itself in terms of 'solidarity and cooperation' between states rather than in terms of political integration. Since 1964 Africa's boundaries have remained more or less stable despite disintegrative movements especially in the former Belgian Congo, Nigeria and Sudan. Two notable successful challenges to the principle of 'uti possidetis' were the creation of Eritrea in 1991 and the transfer of the port and harbour of Walvis Bay from South African to Namibian sovereignty in 1994. Despite this apparent boundary stability, the fragility of many African states as well as their cross-cutting ethnic loyalties indicates that this principle may not prove immutable in a post-►Cold War period characterized by increasing intra-state conflict. It may well prove to be the case, as Basil Davidson suggests, that the attempt to create a European-style states-system in Africa is the final curse left behind by the imperial powers.

**Utopianism** Refers to a tradition of thought in ►international relations which argues that perpetual ►peace, equality and the full satisfaction of wants is both desirable and possible in world politics. The term was popularized by Carr (1939), whose book itself was a devastating critique of this mode of thinking. Carr used the term in two distinct but related senses.

1 Utopianism is the first or 'primitive stage in the development of a science of ►international politics where the 'the element of wish or purpose is overwhelmingly strong'. This was the case, he believed, in the period immediately following the First World War when the inclination to analyse facts was weak or non-existent and when visionary projects (e.g. ►world

government, collective security) dominated thinking about the subject. This stage was followed by political ➤realism which is 'a stage of hard and ruthless analysis' of external reality. Only when international politics has passed through both these stages could it properly be called a science or discipline and even then, as a social science, elements of utopianism would remain.

2 Utopianism also refers to a specific school of thought whose proponents, arguing from the first principles, construct schemes for the elimination of ➤war and the establishment of eternal peace. In this sense the term is interchangeably with ➤idealism, liberalism and rationalism. Central to this school, according to Carr, is the *laissez faire* doctrine of ➤harmony of interests, whereby each ➤actor in pursuing his own rationally perceived good, also pursues the good of the international community as a whole. Politically, this doctrine of the identity of interests took the form of 'an assumption that every nation has an identical interest in peace, and that any nation which desires to disturb the peace is therefore both irrational and immoral' (p. 51). Principal twentieth-century proponents were Woodrow Wilson, Bertrand Russell, Norman Angell, A. E. ➤Zimmern, G. Lowes-Dickinson and Gilbert Murray, but the tradition also embraced philosophers such as the Abbé Saint-Pierre and Kant.

Carr's critique of utopianism in 1939 set the stage for the somewhat sterile realist/idealist debate which dominated Anglo-American academic international politics for at least the next two decades. ➤➤Neorealism

# V

**Vatican City State** Official name of the ➤independent state created in 1929 by the treaty of the Lateran Pacts. It is the smallest ➤state in the world occupying 108.7 acres and it forms an ➤enclave in the city of Rome. Outside this area there are other buildings and land belonging to the Holy See which have the status of permanent ➤extraterritorality; these include the papal palace at Castel Gandolfo and the transmitting centre of the Vatican radio station at Santa Maria di Galeria. Vatican City is a state in all the formal senses: it possesses territory, population and ➤sovereignty. It maintains four armed corps (two of which, the Noble Guard and the Palatine Guard of Honour, are ceremonial) and also the Swiss Guards (133 in all) and a Gendarmarie of 184 policemen. It does not maintain armed forces in the sense of the term. It is an accepted member of the international community and maintains permanent ➤diplomatic relations with about fifty states. According to the Lateran Treaty its territory is inviolable and its political status is one of permanent ➤neutrality. Thus it eschews ➤alliances, associations and overtly political unions and avoids full participation in international affairs unless specifically appealed to. However, the role of the Vatican in world affairs has not been without controversy, especially concerning its alleged silence concerning the Nazi treatment of the Jews, and its conservative position with regard to ➤liberation theology. It is not a member of the ➤United Nations but maintains official observer status. Vatican City and the Holy See are in theory distinct entities, and both are recognized as such by ➤international law. The former represents the temporal power and the latter the spiritual but both are united in the person of the Pope who is simultaneously head of the sovereign state and head of the Catholic Church.

This close union between the Catholic Church and this mini or minuscule state renders it politically as well as juridically unique in ➤international relations. The influence it wields is out of all proportion to its size. As the only religious institution recognized in international law as having full diplomatic status, the Holy See might be regarded as an historical anomaly, but given the origins of the European ➤state-system and the development of the institution of ➤diplomacy it is not difficult to see why. ➤➤Religion; *res publica Christiana*

**Ver** Voluntary Export Restraint. A ver is a ➤self-imposed quota. A deliberate decision by an ➤exporter to exercise quantitative restraint *vis-à-vis* a particular market. As such a ver is a system of ➤protectionism because market access, although available, is not fully exploited. It may be difficult to see why any trading ➤state would rationally agree to implement such a policy. Usually a ver decision is made because the exporter fears that otherwise the market will be closed altogether. In short a ver is an instance of the old adage that 'half a loaf is better than no bread'. In terms of ➤power analysis ver ➤implementation may be forced upon a trading ➤actor because the relative bargaining position favours the ➤importer. Thus the ➤European Union is able to exercise this kind of bargaining leverage to force trading actors wanting access to its substantial internal market to observe vers.

**Verification** This is the process whereby ➤actors seek to confirm that others are complying with agreements, conversions and understandings. Verification is particularly important where parties to an agreement see that it is to their advantage to act ➤unilaterally to break or infringe the understanding. In these circumstances, the successful defector gains at the expense of those who abide by the terms. Eventually all parties will lose confidence and mass defections will occur. Alternatively, the defector will be brought to account and attempts will be made to reconstitute and redefine the understanding.

Verification is the inverse of trust. In a system based upon mutual trust and understanding, verification of compliance would be both unnecessary and contrary to the spirit of the relationship. Indeed, in such circumstances requiring verification would be a contradiction in terms. Equally, in a system of total ➤conflict and suspicion agreement would be impossible and verification unnecessary. In such a ➤zero-sum relationship ➤worst-case analysis would be the prevailing perception. Verification is thus crucial in those relationships that ➤game theory calls mixed-motive. Verification that compliance is being observed strengthens trust, reduces suspicion and increases the incentives for cooperation.

➤Verification requires ➤implementation and actors can either attempt to verify each other's compliance unilaterally, using their own instruments, or ➤multilaterally, using ➤intergovernmental, transgovernmental or ➤transnational organizations. Since the verification agency may have to adjudicate competing claims, impartiality is an advantage. Since the verification agency requires the ➤capability to monitor what the parties are actually doing, as opposed to what they are saying, good ➤intelligence is an advantage. Since the verification agency may have to respond to non-compliance, a repertoire of sanctions is an advantage.

Monitoring activity by actors is a continuous and continuing process. Verification is only one aspect of this activity. It is perhaps the most overt and explicit. It is certainly crucial if collaboration and cooperation between actors in controversial areas such as ➤arms control and ➤disarmament are to be effectively implemented.

**Versailles Treaty (1919)** Signed on 28 June 1919 in the Hall of Mirrors at Versailles, this settlement formed part of the Paris Peace Conference (1919–

20) that formally ended the First World War. The bulk of the ►treaty concerned territorial transfers from Germany: Alsace Lorraine which was restored to France, Eupen-Malmedy to Belgium, the Saar which was placed under the control of the ►league of nations, the Rhineland was demilitarized and Poland was given a corridor of land affording access to the Baltic. Danzig was to be a 'free city' under a League of Nations commissioner. In addition Germany's union with Austria ('*anschluss*') was forbidden. It has been estimated that as a result of this treaty Germany lost 13.5 per cent of its territory, 13 per cent of its economic productive capacity and 10 per cent of its population. All ►colonies of the German empire became mandates of the League, the German army was limited to 100,000 men, conscription was forbidden and the navy and air force were seriously reduced in both capacity and ►capability. The most contentious of the 440 articles was Article 231 (the War Guilt Clause) which placed responsibility on Germany and it allies for all the loss and damaged caused by the war. Costs of ►reparation exceeded 6,000 million pounds but these were subsequently reduced in the Dawes (1924) and Young (1929) plans in response to a growing awareness in the United Kingdom and the United States that the terms were unrealistic and punitive. The Covenant of the League of Nations was, on Woodrow Wilson's insistence, made part of the treaty.

This settlement is one of the best examples of a ►peace treaty creating the preconditions for a future war and many ►realists accordingly regard the events of 1939−45 as the second instalment of the First World War. Not surprisingly most Germans resented this 'Diktat' of Versailles and the success of the Nazis in the later 1920s and 1930s depended in no small part on their manipulation of the real and imagined consequences of the settlement. Outside Germany, the economist J. M. Keynes (1919) denounced its socio-economic implications and the political and strategic aspects were condemned by Carr (1939). The accumulated feelings of guilt about an excessive and unreasonable settlement imposed on post-war Germany led directly in some circles to the promotion of policies of ►accommodation and ►appeasement during the inter-war years.

**Vertical proliferation** ►Nuclear proliferation

**Veto** A veto is an attribute of ►power. It is an ability to stop undesirable outcomes. Moreover, it is an ability which exists ►unilaterally, although ►actors may cooperate to exercise a combined veto. As an attribute of power, exercising a veto requires skill and motivation as well as the necessary ►capability. Veto power can become legitimized into international conventions or ►treaties, or it can inhere in ►structural power and be exercised arbitrarily. If such veto power is legitimized by international agreement and convention, it can be argued that the veto has thereby become an attribute of ►authority. Such authorization of veto power in organizations containing state actors is an exemplification of the ►unanimity rule which is itself derived from notions of ►sovereignty, equality and consent.

The best example of legitimate veto power is to be found in the ➤United Nations Charter although it should be noted that the word itself does not appear in the document. In Chapter V, Article 2 on the voting arrangements in the ➤Security Council, the five permanent members (China, France, Russia, the United Kingdom and the United States) are given veto powers over all substantive, as opposed to procedural, questions. Moreover, through the ➤double veto procedure they can decide whether a question is substantive or otherwise. Possession of veto power was regarded by the framers as a vital mechanism for maintaining international ➤peace, since without the cooperation or acquiescence of the more powerful states (which abstention from the use of the veto power implied) international disputes would be that much more difficult to resolve. The veto states in the UN can be regarded as a self-created oligarchy. The move to create an oligarchy was strenuously resisted by a number of states that attended the Charter conference in 1945 and is still a matter of some resentment today. There have been some attempts to moderate or eliminate it altogether but to date the privileged position of the five permanent members is entrenched. Voluntarily relinquishment of this power is extremely unlikely. It is certainly arguable that the window of opportunity that 1945 presented to the veto powers would have been closed to them decades later when the composition of the UN had began its quantum shift towards the ➤Third World states. By stipulating that the veto power should apply to revisions of the Charter as well, the veto powers ensured that their oligarchy should be self-perpetuating. ➤diplomatic practice since 1945 has clarified the status of abstentions and absences from the Council. Neither of these situations is regarded as a legitimate instance of the veto power being activated.

As suggested above, veto power is inherent in power structures. The United States has substantial veto power in such ➤issue areas as ➤arms control and the ➤environment at present. States wishing to conclude ➤multilateral agreements in these areas may be forestalled or ➤implementation may be weakened by US exercise of its veto powers. Some would see this as the unacceptable face of American ➤leadership or primacy. ➤➤P5; UN reform

**Vietnam** Vietnam, a South East Asian state of approximately 330 thousand square kilometres with a population of some 55 million people (making it about the equivalent in physical and demographic size to Italy) has been the arena for two twentieth-century ➤wars. The first was conducted by the Vietminh (a ➤nationalist/communist revolutionary movement) against French ➤colonial control of the territory. Beginning at the end of 1946, the war ended with the withdrawal of France in 1954 and ➤independence but division of Vietnam in the aftermath. The second war was fought to reunite the partitioned ➤state. This goal was eventually achieved in 1975 after a long and bitter struggle into which the United States became increasingly drawn under Presidents Kennedy and Johnson. This second Vietnamese War is arguably one of the most traumatic and divisive violent conflicts of the twentieth century. It is certainly one of the best known and most keenly debated.

The background to US involvement in Vietnam after 1950 was the policy of ➤containment and the ➤Truman Doctrine. Following the ➤perception that China had been 'lost' in 1949 after the Maoist forces' victory, the decision to assist France in Vietnam was taken at the same time as the decision to intervene in Korea. Both moves were conditioned by a perception of Asian communism which tended to see the United States' relation with communism (itself viewed at the time as a monolith) in ➤bipolar terms. As a result the issues to be found in Vietnam were perceived as being much greater than a mere colonial war. In rejecting its own historical tradition of anti-colonialism, the United States embarked upon a course of action that produced in the years that followed a broad commitment to the prevention of a united, Communist-led state of Vietnam.

Militarily, French defeat in Vietnam was partial rather than total. The collapse of French resistance was more a matter of will and loss of political confidence in Paris than total defeat on the battleground. This is not to gainsay the significance of the engagement at Dien Bien Phu in 1954 in any way. The Vietminh abandoned their guerrilla tactics for a set-piece battle using artillery and trench warfare to lay siege to the French garrison. The latter's request for direct US intervention was rejected by a divided Eisenhower Administration.

The Geneva Conference of 1954 which addressed the issue of what were legally speaking the three Associated States of Indo-China produced an interim settlement which realized some goals and frustrated or ignored others. The conference reached a series of agreements which effectively ended French control over all of Indo-China. The Geneva accords did not provide for the immediate unification of Vietnam, however. Under considerable pressure from China, the Vietminh agreed at Geneva to the partition of Vietnam at the 17th parallel with the understanding that elections would be held after two years on a nation-wide basis which would lead to the eventual reunification of Vietnam. A cease-fire agreement was also concluded at Geneva between the French and the Vietminh. In fact, in South Vietnam a government was established under Ngo Dinh Diem, a Catholic and staunch anti-Communist, which refused to recognize and implement those parts of the Geneva Accords regarding elections and reunification. In the United States, the Eisenhower Administration which came into office in January 1953 was equally committed to the policy of containment. Indeed it was President Eisenhower himself who did much to popularize the image of the 'falling dominoes' which, it was alleged, would be the fate of South Vietnam under the ➤domino theory. In September 1954 the United States obtained approval for a ➤protocol to the ➤SEATO ➤treaty which included the territory of South Vietnam in its ➤scope. During 1955 the United States assumed responsibility for large-scale economic and military assistance to the Diem government.

Between the Geneva cease-fire of 1954 and the formation of the National Liberation Front by Southerners opposed to Diem, South Vietnam became in effect a US ➤dependency. Consequently, when it became clear to the incoming Kennedy Administration in 1961 that Diem faced an insurgency which threatened the continuation of this rule, the decision was taken, in the words of the Pentagon Papers, to convert the 'limited-risk gamble' under Eisenhower to the 'broad commitment' under Kennedy.

In summary, therefore, the years between the inauguration of Kennedy in 1961 and the 'abdication' speech of Lyndon Johnson on 31 March 1968 saw the rise and demise of US intervention in South Vietnam. Johnson's address to the American people wherein he announced that he was no longer a candidate for the 1968 Presidential election marks the turning from escalation to de-escalation. The Tet offensive of January 1968 and the request for substantially more US troops to restore the initiative thereafter was the precipitant cause. Only by placing the United States on a semi-war footing could these demands be met. Instead, in what was to be the out-going Democratic Administration, the decision was taken to begin to scale down the war, to reduce US involvement in proportion to South Vietnamese (a policy known as 'vietnamization') and to look for a negotiated withdrawal.

Under Kennedy and his successor, the United States had first attempted to address the Second Vietnamese War as an example of counterinsurgency and, when that failed, had sought to 'conventionalize' the violence into a mode that was closer to the tradition of two World Wars and the ➤Korean War. The war of attrition which the United States conducted between 1965 and 1968 resulted in an unsatisfactory ➤stalemate which was manifested sharply by the events of the Tet surprise attacks. Diplomatically the conventionalization of the war under Johnson meant that the United States was a combatant and that, accordingly, any cease-fire or ➤truce would involve the United States as a party. The principal demands of the National Liberation Front and the Democratic Republic of Vietnam (DRV) were for a phased withdrawal of US forces and the cessation of US bombing of Vietnamese targets – particularly strategic bombing of the DRV. Politically the main goal was recognition of the objective of reunification of the two halves and, implicitly, the establishment of a communist regime. Although the war was dragged out for a further period until 1972 under Richard Nixon, the agreement of January 1973 ending the war effectively met all the above demands. With the withdrawal of US support the Southern Republic of Vietnam (RVN) rapidly collapsed into chaos. The final denouement came in the spring of 1975.

In the history of twentieth-century conflicts the Vietnam Wars remain the most prolonged and traumatic instances of violent ➤decolonization. In pursuing this goal the Vietnamese political ➤leadership was probably pushed further into the arms of China and the former Soviet Union than it cared to go. Since 1975 relations with China have deteriorated to the point of war, whilst events following ➤nineteen eighty-nine impacted upon Vietnam adversely. The implosion of the Soviet Union removed Vietnam's principal patron, whilst the collapse of ➤communism left Vietnam ideologically bereft. It seems probable that Vietnam's future as a regional actor will depend upon its ties with the ➤ASEAN states and its old adversary, the United States.

For America the Vietnam intervention was a searing experience. It produced a period of introversion and resentment which is often referred to as the ➤Vietnam syndrome. It was a contributory factor in the ➤declinist assessment of the end of ➤Pax Americana. It even led to a questioning of the institutions of government in the United States and an attempt to redress the institutional balance in ➤policy-making between the Executive and the Legislative branches. Analytically, the American defeat demonstrated a number of paradoxes about the concept of ➤power as writers sought to explain how a big state could lose what began as a small war.

**Vietnam syndrome** As the use of the term 'syndrome' implies, this refers to a complex of attitudes and reactions to the trauma of American ➤intervention in the post-war politics of ➤Vietnam. Ole Holsti and James Rosenau (1984) have argued that the manner of American intervention and the conduct of American policy thereafter led to a collapse in the ➤Cold War consensus in America which had created a permissive climate among both ➤attentive and ➤mass publics for ➤globalism and its corollary of a 'world policeman' role for the United States. Post-1975 analyses of the Vietnam debacle argued that the lessons were more thorough-going than poor policy ➤implementation. Vietnam seemed to cast doubts on the whole Cold War policy of knee-jerk interventionism.

Public opinion polls during the 1970s seemed to confirm that received opinion at all levels now saw Vietnam as a 'mistake'. President Reagan's policy of ➤destabilization of the Nicaraguan government via the so-called 'Contras' seemed to evoke nasty memories of the 'salami tactics' under President Kennedy which produced an exponential rise in American 'advisers' in South Vietnam after 1961. In a desire to nip the possibility of intervention by stealth in the bud and at the same time to avoid the syndrome, Congress effected the Boland amendments during Reagan's first term.

In 1984 the Secretary of Defense Casper Weinberger sought to lay down ground rules for the future use of American force, implicitly recognizing in the process that the syndrome was now setting more explicit limits than before. Weinberger's suggestions included: the provision that American forces should only be committed if vital interests were at stake and thereafter the commitment should be sufficiently comprehensive to ensure victory, that a clear set of political goals must inform the use of force and that such actions should be seen as a last result. All of this might seem nothing more than prudent pre-requisites but Weinberger's stipulation that reasonable assurances of support from the

American people via their Congress was needed indicates a more significant obeisance to the syndrome.

Since Vietnam, America has certainly circled around the kinds of open-ended commitments that were such a feature of its Cold War ➤diplomacy. If anything the Weinberger ground rules have been tightened up since 1984. Thus time limits (which are in any case a feature of the War Powers Act of 1973) and exit strategies are pre-requisites even before force commitments are made. The ➤Persian Gulf War was held by some to have cured the Vietnam syndrome. This conclusion, though understandable, seems premature. Rather the syndrome was avoided by consulting Congress in January 1991 and fighting a '100-hours' war. It should not be thought that the syndrome has placed absolute constraints on the use of force by America. Short-term commitments involving minimal casualties (at least for America) seem to be the ➤paradigm for the future.

**Vulnerability**  Vulnerability is a condition where an ➤actor, or group of actors, is/are exposed to events and circumstances which are difficult to control, even in the long term. These moreover will contain threats to scarce values and will raise issues about ➤security both for ➤states and non-state actors. Vulnerability tends to be seen therefore as an unacceptable condition, certainly in the long term. ➤Neorealists would certainly argue that in a system of ➤anarchy, vulnerability is a persistent condition and that strategies which seek to escape from it will simply create a sense of vulnerability for someone else. The idea of the ➤security dilemma exemplifies this paradox. For ➤pluralists vulnerability is a function of ➤interdependence as Keohane and Nye (1977) argue with their concept of 'vulnerability interdependence'. Recognizing the mutuality of vulnerability leads to ➤multilateralism and ➤regime building. Accepting that in some senses we are all vulnerable to someone or something is an escape route towards a more cooperative set of relationships according to this view.

Traditionally by pursuing strategies of ➤autarky states and their ➤leaderships have sought to escape from or substantially reduce their vulnerabilities by reducing their dependence upon others. The demise of the territorial state identified by Hertz (1957) shows how chimerical such approaches are. Rose-crance's idea of the 'Trading State' (1986) makes a virtue out of vulnerability by arguing that territorialism is neither necessary nor desirable. Vulnerability culminates in the modern ➤city-state like Singapore which is the ultimate 'trader'.

# W

**War** War is direct, somatic violence between state ➤actors. Wars occur when states in a situation of social ➤conflict and opposition find that the pursuit of incompatible or exclusive goals cannot be confined to non-violent modes. As a form of direct violence, war occurs in different forms within social systems. Thus gang war, range war, class war, civil or internal war are distinguishable typologies. Analytically separate, these levels can interact and produce complex ➤feedback loops. Civil war can become internationalized through ➤intervention into inter-state war. The various levels at which violence occurs can influence the occurrence of violence at other levels.

The idea of levels intrudes into the study of war in a second way. Within academic disciplines it is possible to discern differences in the manner in which violence is explained and discussed. This is made clear in a work such as that of Waltz (1959). Waltz examines the phenomenon from the levels of individual theories, societal theories and structural theories. Academically, therefore, a psychologist might be interested in war as a function of ➤perception, an anthropologist in why certain cultures seem to foster ➤aggression. Sociology has drawn attention to the positive functions that violence can play within and between systems. Economists have, for instance, applied ➤game theory concepts to the analysis of conflict, while political scientists have sought through policy analysis and ➤systems analysis to examine both the micro and macro aspects of war.

Taking up the point attributed above to sociology, war should not necessarily be regarded as dysfunctional. War in the ➤international system is not necessarily like disease in the biological system. Conflict and the fear of war have often been used to integrate ➤states. In such circumstances the search for enemies assists in maintaining or increasing group solidarity. The threat of war can be used by groups within states to extend their control over the political and economic life of the state. Violence can even be used to create states. In the nineteenth century German ➤unification was achieved via the defeat of such neighbouring states as Denmark, Austria and France. Marxist theories of the twentieth century regard ➤wars of national liberation as serving specific functional purposes.

The idea that violence and war are intrinsic parts of the ➤international system is the distinctive hallmark of ➤realism. The forms of violence may change – under the influence of ➤technology, for instance. The scope of violence may differ as the actors in the system change. Notwithstanding these parameters, violence and war remain fundamental. Recognition by realism that war was a systemic variable of some persistence led to the search for some amelioration. Realism has usually found this in the ➤balance of power mechanism. As Claude (1962) pointed out the balance of power was not fundamentally a means of war prevention but rather a means of structural maintenance which, in certain circumstances, might involve the use of ➤force. The implausibility of war serving this function in the era of ➤nuclear weapons forced realists to modify their structural models in keeping with ideas about ➤polarization and ➤bipolar/ multipolar configurations. Bipolarity or multipolarity were now favoured because violence would be reduced under one or the other.

If violence and war have long been recognized as regular occurrences in the ➤world system, it is still the case that their intensity has increased. Thus the two World Wars (1914–18 and 1939–45) killed over sixty million persons among the major participants. More than eight million soldiers and one million civilians were killed in the first instance, while almost seventeen million soldiers and thirty-five million civilians were killed in the second. Significant advances in medical ➤technology notwithstanding, it would seem that the intensity of violence is considerable.

While intensity has increased, frequency of inter-state war has decreased – at least in Europe where the ➤state-system originated. European evidence seems to show that wars are more concentrated and destructive but less frequent. In his 1964 study on the subject of war, Wright noted that there had been a decline in frequency in Europe from the sixteenth and seventeenth centuries to the nineteenth and twentieth. Whereas in the earlier period European states were more often at war than not, by the twentieth they spent less than one-fifth of their time at war.

The characteristic of systemic violence within the state-system has affected other processes. Violence among states has given rise to the ➤international laws of war. Traditional international law did little to outlaw war, but rather to reduce its worst excesses and, as far as possible limit the disruption and damage to third parties. Although the ➤United Nations system has introduced some further restrictions upon the use of ➤force, it is still permitted under the doctrine of ➤self-defence. Under Article 51 of the ➤UN Charter, states can effect self-defence measures unless and until the ➤Security Council can agree upon a collective response to any breach of the ➤peace.

➤Alliance formation among states appears to be related generally to recognition of the intrinsically violent nature of the system. The First World War was preceded by the formation of rival alliances in the Triple Alliance of 1882 and the Triple ➤entente of 1907. The outbreak of hostilities further expanded these alliances with Turkey and Bulgaria joining one side and Italy the other. Following the establishment of the ➤League of Nations, the alliances disintegrated but during the 1930s a new ➤axis emerged between Germany, Italy and Japan. After the Second World War alliance formation resumed, with NATO and the ➤Warsaw Pact being leading instances. During the nineteenth century states formed an alliance about every other year. In the twentieth the rate increased more than four-fold to more than two new alliances per year.

➤Arms races have followed the same pattern as alliances, since the dynamic for the arms race is at least initially ➤perception of external threat and general instability in the system. States arm themselves to provide a margin of equivalent or superior ➤capability *vis-à-vis* an adversary, according to worst case thinking. While it would be invalid to suggest that arms races cause violence to occur, there is a strong correlation between the activity of arms racing and ally-seeking by states and increases in international tension and hostility.

War, violence, ally-seeking and arms racing increase the level of military expenditures within states. Within societies the military mobilizes enormous resources and organizes such complex tasks as research, development, production and maintenance of the military capability of the state. The existence of what some have identified as ➤military-industrial complexes implies a strong vested interest in the continuation of a perceived level of hostility and tension between states. More generally there is a tendency for societies frequently threatened with violent conflict to become militarized. The military may eventually take over political leadership roles from civilians if this militarization persists.

Any attempt at ameliorating violence, ➤conflict management and/or ➤resolution must first identify who the parties are and what the issues dividing them consist of. This preliminary inquiry will precede any type of third party intervention in the violence. There is often a tendency within ➤diplomacy to seek short-term palliatives through management techniques and instruments. Thus UN ➤peacekeeping has sometimes been held up as an example of this concentration on the short-term need to end direct violence without always addressing the underlying issues in conflict between the parties. It is well to remember that, as stated at the outset, war is the most fundamental manifestation of conflict as a systemic process in ➤international relations. ➤➤Cold War

**War Crimes trials** The right of a victor to put to trial individual members of enemy forces for violations of the ➤international laws of war has long been a customary one in international affairs but the twentieth century has seen some refinements and developments. The ➤Treaty of Versailles made provision for the trial of the German Emperor and individual members of the German armed forces, although this was not carried out. After the Second World War, though, the Nuremberg and Tokyo trials set a precedent by trying German and Japanese leaders not only for 'war crimes' but also for 'crimes against peace' and 'crimes against humanity' – the last two being regarded in some quarters as retrospective legislation. Crimes against ➤peace were defined by the Nuremberg Tribunal as '. . . planning, preparation, initiation or waging of a war of aggression, or a war in violation of international treaties'. In this respect only leaders of a ➤state are liable. Crimes against humanity were defined as follows: '. . . murder, extermination, enslavement, deportation and other inhumane acts committed against any civilian population before or during the war, or persecutions on political, racial or religious grounds in execution of or in connection with any crime within the jurisdiction of the Tribunal, whether or not in violation of the domestic law of the country where perpetrated'. Thus, crimes against humanity are wider than war crimes; they can be committed on one's own population and they are not confined to wartime. These precedents set at Tokyo and Nuremberg were subsequently approved by the ►General Assembly of the UN and by the International Law Commission. They are now seen as part of international law and must therefore be regarded as a further nail in the coffin of the traditional rule that a state may treat its own nationals as it pleases. A War Crimes Court has been set up in the Hague to deal with alleged perpetrators of ►ethnic cleansing and ►genocide in the former ►Yugoslavia and Rwanda.

**Wars of national liberation** A doctrine developed by ►Marxist/Leninists calling for armed uprisings against the established orders in the developing world. Primarily directed at ►colonial territories the concept argues that these ►wars are ►just wars since their purpose is to liberate the masses from ►alien rule and establish the right to ►self-determination. Both Marx and Lenin advocated proletarian ►revolution to establish a just social order but the anti-Western, anti-colonial and anti-imperial elements of the doctrine were first elaborated by Khrushchev in 1961. In this case ►intervention by external forces on behalf of the insurgents is justified and may also be a moral duty.

The idea of liberation wars became an important practical instrument of international ►communism, especially in post-war Asia, Africa and Latin America. The official Soviet position was that Western capitalism either directly or by proxy had deliberately exploited and oppressed both its own and independent populations. Wars which seek to break this chain of ►dependence and liberate the masses are therefore entirely justified. Since the Western capitalists are constantly engaged in exporting 'counter-revolution', ►aid must be given to those engaged in the process of liberation. The form that this aid took could involve external intervention but as a matter of practical policy, the Soviet Union, and to a lesser extent China, avoided direct physical intervention and instead concentrated on supplying military advisers, arms and other forms of economic assistance. While Western states regarded wars of national liberation as civil wars communist states viewed them as international wars, and this had important consequences in ►international law. Since civil wars are not covered entirely by the laws of war (although the ►Geneva conventions of 1949 tried to remedy this), international wars are. The First ►Protocol to the 1949 Conventions, signed in 1977, asserted that 'armed conflicts in which peoples are fighting against colonial domination and alien occupation and against racist regimes in the exercise of their right of 'self-determination' are to be considered 'international' wars for the purpose of applying the laws of war generally. Out of a total 163 signatories to the 1949 Convention, only 59 accepted this definition, reflecting the deep divisions in the international community over its exact status. If wars of national liberation are classified as international and not civil wars, then under an extended version of ➤self-defence, external intervention may be justified. As a general rule external intervention is forbidden in civil wars so that there is clear disagreement between Western states and others as to the legality of active interference in wars of national liberation. As a rule the ➤General Assembly has adopted a permissive stance in these matters and has consistently opposed the Western view.

**Warsaw Pact** Founded in May 1955 when the Soviet Union signed a ➤multilateral treaty with Albania, Bulgaria, Czechoslovakia, Hungary, Poland and Romania. The pact was a direct response to the expansion of NATO with the inclusion of the Federal Republic of Germany. Its military significance at its inception was slight since the Soviet Union already had ➤bilateral treaties in existence with all the ➤states concerned. The Pact was a political statement of ➤bloc solidarity rather than a system of ➤collective defence.

The cohesion of the new group was soon challenged in 1956 when the Hungarian government attempted to leave. The subsequent ➤intervention of Soviet military forces in Hungary established the principle that loyalty to the Pact was regarded by the ➤hegemonial state as a touchstone of commitment to 'socialist solidarity'. These tendencies within the Soviet ➤leadership were again confirmed within the so-called ➤Brezhnev doctrine in 1968.

The Soviet Union had a complete monopoly within the Pact as a supplier of military equipment. This gave the Pact forces a high degree of inter-operability but it meant that competitive procurement was denied to members. It legitimized the stationing of Soviet troops on the territories of Pact members and thereby contributed to ➤worst-case analysis of the Pact's intentions by Western ➤defence analysts and military establishments throughout the ➤cold war period. The ending of that particular confrontation following the events of ➤nineteen eighty-nine led to the demise of the Pact and its dissolution in 1991. The ➤security architecture of Europe has changed totally since that denouement. NATO is now perceived as an inclusive ➤security regime rather than an exclusive ➤alliance as previously thought.

**Water** Possession of or access to water has always been a major feature of international relations. Historically, the seas have performed two major functions: first as a means of communication and second as a repository of living and non-living resources. Over the centuries, a comprehensive, if untidy, legal regime has evolved to moderate inter-state competition regarding the sea (➤law of the sea). However, agreement over freshwater resources is in its infancy, and competition over this life-giving and life sustaining element is an increasingly important aspect of contemporary world politics. At the Earth Summit II in New York in 1997 it was estimated that over 20 per cent of the world ➤population did not have access to safe drinking water and 50 per cent lacked water for proper sanitation. Furthermore, up to 800 rivers, including the Amazon, Euphrates and Danube, were likely subjects of inter-state disputes as countries along their lengths extract increasing amounts of water to irrigate crops and supply growing populations. Failure to regulate this could lead to ➤resource-wars as the quality and quantity of water for downstream states is diminished. According to the summit's report, *A Comprehensive Assessment of Freshwater Resources of the World*, the capacity of the hydrological cycle to supply water is being outstripped by the volume of human demands, pollution of water resources and poor management. It estimates that by 2025, two-thirds of low-income states in Africa, Asia and Latin America will suffer 'moderate to severe water stress.'

Tackling this freshwater crisis is now an urgent international task. However, as with other ➤environmental issues, the financial, technological and political ability or will to do this is not universally shared. Since water-rich states have a different ➤perception of the urgency of the crisis than that held by water-poor states, the absence of a comprehensive, regionally based freshwater regime will inevitably increase the intensity of the conflict and the consequent likelihood of resource wars. In 1966 the International Law Asociation laid down the 'Helsinki Rules' for shared watercourses. These guidelines are used by states, though they do not, as yet, have the status of law. Generally, the resolution of water disputes is via ➤treaties.

**Weapons of mass destruction** A collective term which is now increasingly used for three classes of weapons systems: ➤nuclear weapons, Biological and Chemical weapons. The colloquial acronym ABC – from atomic, biological and chemical – is sometimes also found. WMD systems can thus be distinguished from ➤conventional weapons in terms of their ➤collateral damage potential most objectively but also in terms of their ➤deterrent potential. WMD weapons pose qualitatively different challenges for both sides in a deterrent relationship in comparison with the conventional variety. WMD weapons also pose near insuperable challenges of an ➤environmental kind which again places them in a different class from conventional weapons. The ➤Persian Gulf War brought many of the issues of WMD weapons to the attention of ➤elites and mass publics throughout the ➤international system. ➤Regimes have been established to cover all three categories within the WMD class – the ➤biological and ➤chemical weapons conventions and the NPT. The end of the ➤Cold War era has placed America in a ➤leadership position on this ➤issue area and American ➤perceptions are particularly focused on the ➤pariah/rogue state ➤actors and ➤regional security complexes such as Asia-➤pacific.

**Weinberger doctrine** ➤Vietnam syndrome

**Western European Union (WEU)** The WEU is an ►IGO based, as its title states, in the regional context of Europe. Its concern is the ►issue area of military ►security. Although the term 'Western European Union' first appeared in the ►protocol in 1954, the idea of a specific European initiative on ►defence originated in the Brussels Pact of 17 March 1948 signed by the foreign ministers of ►Benelux, France and the UK. Ostensibly aimed at deterring German revanchism, the Pact should more plausibly be seen as contributing towards the ►polarization of Europe into ►Cold War confrontation zones. As such it was a forerunner to NATO, formed the following year. By taking the initiative in this way the European states were signalling to the US ►superpower their ►perception that European security questions would be central to the post-1945 system. The formation of the Brussels ►alliance seemed to be validated with the onset of the first ►Berlin crisis later in 1948.

With the formation of NATO the need for a separate Brussels Treaty organization ended, and on 10 December 1950 the Consultative Council of the Brussels Treaty states agreed that the organization's defence functions should be subsumed into NATO. This situation obtained until interest in a specific European initiative on defence was revived as a result of the so-called 'sector approach' to ►integration. Following the collapse of proposals for what was termed the European Defence Community (EDC), the Brussels Treaty powers invited the Italian and Federal German governments to join them by signing a protocol to the 1948 Treaty and establishing the WEU as a result. *Inter alia* the British Government pledged to station four divisions and a tactical air force on continental Europe. Some have seen this British decision as a concession to ►supranationalism, since the withdrawal of these forces could be sanctioned only by a majority vote on the Council of Ministers of the WEU.

The pattern established in 1948 and confirmed in 1954 meant that actor autonomy for the WEU crucially depended upon the member states taking specifically European perceptions of their defence needs. When these were absent or minimized Atlanticist attitudes would predominate and the WEU would function as an amplification of or adjunct to NATO. It is now clear that for more than a quarter of a century these latter views dominated and the WEU was seen as the European pillar of NATO (particularly by the British ►elite). The French decision of 1966 to withdraw from the integrated NATO command structure meant that until the French re-integration began under President Mitterrand, the WEU functioned as a bridge organization which enabled France to collaborate on defence issues with Nato's European members.

Developments within the European region and within world politics in the last two decades of the twentieth century have profoundly altered the environment within which the WEU operates. In Europe the most profound changes have been occasioned by the end of the Cold War and the chain reaction of events and consequences generated thereby. The collapse of the Soviet Union and of ►Yugoslavia, the coming together of the two Germanies, and the bifurcation of Czechoslovakia have rearranged the security politics of the continent along with its frontiers. At the same time moves towards Western Europe ➤integration have flagged up a new role for the WEU as the security wing of the EU. This in turn has resuscitated French interest in – and no doubt putative ➤leadership of – a distinctly European-orientated WEU. Membership of the WEU now can be categorized as: full members, including now Portugal and Spain, associate/observers including the Nordic states and ➤neutrals such as Austria and Ireland, and associate partners from the old ➤Warsaw Pact. These complexities mirror the strategic environment in Europe following the ending of cold war ➤bipolarity.

The future for the WEU is highly contingent. There are a number of variables which can be adduced to enhance both the desirability and the feasibility of closer European cooperation on defence and security matters. Within the EU a role as the institutional expression of European security was clearly implied by the 1992 Treaty on European union (signed at Maastricht in December 1991) and in the subsequent Petersberg Declaration of June 1992. Outside the Union, the two imponderables remain: the direction of Russian foreign policy and the commitment of the United States to European security into the twenty-first century. Like any IGO, task expansion by the WEU cannot proceed without an appropriate configuration of its operational environment.

**Westphalia, peace of (1648)** A series of treaties (principally Münster and Osnabrück) which collectively ended hositilities in the Thirty Years War (1618–48). It is commonly said to mark the beginning of the modern system of➤international relations. In relation to seventeenth-century Europe, it marked the culmination of the anti-➤hegemonic struggle against the Habsburg aspirations for a ➤supranational empire. It signalled the collapse of Spanish power, the fragmentation of Germany (thus delaying German unity for over two hundred years) and the rise of France as the major European power. A number of important principles, which were subsequently to form the legal and political framework of modern inter-state relations, were established at Westphalia. It explicitly recognized a society of ➤states based on the principle of territorial ➤sovereignty, it established the ➤independence of states and emphasized that each had jural rights which all others were bound to respect. It recognized the legitimacy of all forms of government and established the notion of religious freedom and toleration (*cuius regio, eius religio*). In sum, it established a secular concept of international relations replacing for ever the medieval idea of a universal religious authority acting as final arbiter of Christendom. By destroying the notion of universalism, the 'Westphalia system' gave impetus to the notions of ➤reason of state and ➤balance of power as key concepts in ➤foreign policy conduct and formulation. From 1648 onwards, the particularist interests of states became paramount both politically and legally. It should be noted, though, that the ➤state-system established at Westphalia was primarily Christian and European. The codification of rules concerning non-➤intervention did not apply to ➤Islam or to the rest of the world. This double standard persisted in European ➤diplomacy into the nineteenth and twentieth centuries when the Westphalia system gradually and often reluctantly became a global one.

It is conventional wisdom in IR that the misnamed 'treaty' of Westphalia was an epoch-making single historic event that 'created' the modern system of sovereign states, each claiming exclusive control over a given territory. Recent scholarship has cast doubt on this cosy view. According to Krasner (1993), the Westphalia settlement was in fact a very conservative arrangement which could be seen as a legitimization of the old Holy Roman imperial order rather than the precursor of the modern one. Sovereignty existed in practice long before the mid-seventeenth century and medieval practices continued long after. The term 'the Westphalian system' is thus a convenient shorthand for systemic changes which took place over a lengthy period of time. ➤➤*res publica christiana*

**Wilson doctrine** Refers to ➤interventionist policies initiated by President Woodrow Wilson in relation to Central and Latin America in 1913. In his declaration Wilson states 'We do not sympathize with those who establish their government authority in order to satisfy their personal interests and ambitions. . . . We must teach the Latin Americans to select the right man.' In accordance with this doctrine, on 21 April 1914 Wilson ordered military intervention in Mexico and American Marines occupied the port of Veracruz. This doctrine was a logical consequence of the Roosevelt corollary to the ➤Monroe Doctrine, which asserted that 'chronic wrongdoing, or an impotence which results in a general loosening of the ties of civil society' would result in US intervention in the form of a ➤unilateral 'exercise of an international police power'. As with most US presidential 'doctrines' this was directed specifically at developments in ➤Third World ➤states and characteristically used high moral pretext to disguise basic ➤national interests.

**Wilsonianism** ➤fourteen points

**WOMP** World Order Models Project. This project was initiated by a group of radical international lawyers and political scientists in 1967 under the auspices of the Institute for World Order. The scholar most closely associated with it is the Princeton professor of ➤international law, Richard A. Falk. The initial impetus came from international lawyers who were anxious to effect a transition, or paradigm shift, in the subject's focus from a ➤status quo orientated 'law of coexistence' to a more radical 'law of cooperation.' The central idea was that international law should concern itself more with ➤normative issues rather than the given set of rules relating to inter-state behaviour within a more-or-less fixed ➤anarchic framework. In Falk's *A Study of Future Worlds* (1975) these normative concerns cover four distinct, but related areas: the minimalization of large scale collective violence, the maximisation of social and economic well being, the realization of fundamental ➤human rights and the conditions of political justice and the maintenance and rehabilitation of ecological quality. Thus, the WOMP anticipated the new agenda of IR that began to emerge in the 1980s, especially in respect of its dismissive critique of traditional anarchy-based problem solving, its quest for 'a central guiding mechanism' in world politics and its encouragement of 'World order activism' and consciousness-raising. An important component of the approach, shared later by many ➤critical theorists and ➤postmodernists, is that the rationalist notion of scholarly detachment all too often leads to actual indifference. To counter this, the WOMP approach to the 'endangered planet' (Falk, 1971) is overtly prescriptive, subjective and salvationist.(➤►Alternative world futures)

**World Bank group** This collectivity consists of three intergovernmental organizations (IGOs): the International Bank for Reconstruction and Development (IBRD), the International Development Association (IDA) and the International Finance Corporation. The first named, the IBRD, is popularly known as the ➤World Bank. As the title implies the twin purposes of setting up the World Bank, as part of the ➤Bretton Woods system of international economic institutions, was to facilitate the rebuilding of those essentially developed economies which had been shattered by ➤war and to assist in the more basic task of economic development of the less developed countries (LDCS). The Bank is the twin organization of the IMF and indeed membership of the Bank is restricted to ➤states which are also members of the Fund. Like the Fund, the Bank has a system of weighted voting which gives ➤power to effect outcomes to those states which make the greatest contributions. These contributions are, in fact, expressed as subscriptions to the Bank and these member state subscriptions are one of the main sources of Bank funds. In addition the Bank goes into the private capital markets to raise funds and these borrowings now constitute the largest source of Bank liquidity. Being heavily infused with commercial banking principles it comes as no surprise that the Bank's lending policy follows fairly strict commercial criteria.

The need for an institution that would provide 'soft' loans led to the establishment of the IDA in 1960. Like the Bank the IDA makes loans rather than grants and, again as with the IBRD, the would-be recipients are vetted beforehand. Loans are made to recipients to encourage the development of their infrastructure. Unlike the Bank, the IDA is totally dependent upon member states' contributions for its source of funds.

The International Finance Corporation was established in 1956 to encourage the growth of private enterprise and entrepreneurial skills in the ➤LDCs. It limits its participation in projects to a minority share-holding and has particularly concentrated on secondary or manufacturing sectors.

The conservative orthodoxy of the Bank and the extent of the depressed situation in the world economy (outside of North America) after 1947 meant that the Bank was something of a bystander. The United States took steps through measures like the ➤Marshall Plan, through its ➤defence spending and through other aid measures to pump-prime the economies of the ➤AICs by running dollar deficits. As the ➤Cold War became the clear and present danger for American ➤leaders from Truman onwards so the foreign assistance programme was seen as too crucial to military-➤security interests to be left to ➤multilateralism as represented by the Bank.

The collapse of the Bretton Woods system and the ➤oil shocks of the 1970s did nothing to reduce the marginalization of the Bank in the context of aid flows. The Bank did play some role in the recycling of petrodollars through the Western system after the oil shocks. It was rather two developments in the 1980s which served to resuscitate the fortunes of the Bank. The demise of collectivist economic strategies in favour of privatization and free-market reforms meant that the principles of ➤economic liberalism which is the dominant ➤ideology of the Bank now found a more receptive environment – both intellectually and politically. Second, the ➤debt crisis and the various proposals mooted to deal with it such as the Baker and Brady Plans have brought the Bank in from the cold as a key player in administering their ➤implementation.

**World government** The centralization of ➤authority in a unitary ➤supra-national body which would possess legislative and executive powers as well as monopoly of the use of ➤force. The ➤sovereignty of ➤states would be surrendered and disputes would be settled by ➤adjudication under a single system of ➤world law. The concentration of powers and the creation of a singular world authority would normally involve the ➤disarmament of states and its primary purpose and rationale would be the maintenance of international ➤peace and order. Most advocates envisage a ➤federal system whereby the central authority is vested with specific functions (establishing the rule of law and maintaining order) while the constituent units (previously states) are non-sovereign members of the global community holding residual powers of local administration. Such schemes have generally been advanced as solutions to the problems of ➤anarchy and power-management in ➤international relations. Indeed, it could be argued that world government is the only theoretically correct solution to these problems since the traditional alternatives, ➤balance of power and ➤collective security, are at best only partial solutions and at worst mere institutional disguises for the unbridled exercise of national self-interest (see Claude, 1962). It is not surprising, therefore, that the idea of a single world state has been a seductive and a pervasive one in the history of international thought. On a more practical level, its actualization is envisaged in two ways. It could be achieved either through military conquest in the form of a single world imperium or through consent and cooperation on the lines of the ➤domestic analogy. The Roman Empire is cited as the clearest historical example of the former while the ➤League of Nations and the ➤United Nations are often presented as early prototypes of the latter. Critics of such schemes, whatever their genesis, argue that world government might lead to world tyranny; that wars, in the sense of interstate violence, would merely be replaced by ➤civil wars or ➤regional insurrections; that constitutions do not create ➤integration but are themselves products of it and that the practical question of simultaneously obtaining a consensus on relinquishing sovereignty among more than one hundred and ninety states has never been properly addressed. For these and other reasons, advocates of world government have generally been side-lined as well-intentioned but misguided ➤idealists and ➤utopians.

While most of the older approaches to the idea of supranational governance have been preoccupied with the creation of formal political organizations much of the recent literature in this vein has come from the world governance perspective and is structural, systemic and functional in character rather than simply ➤actor and/or institution orientated. Although not advocating world government in the above sense, this school shares a family resemblance in that it seeks alternatives to the present ➤state-system and seeks an erosion of sovereignty. The approach represents a shift from the traditional near-exclusive focus on war prevention to a more dynamic framework for future order which includes economic well-being, social ➤justice and ➤ecological balance as well as ➤peace among its priorities. ➤➤Good governance; WOMP

**World Health Organization (WHO)** Health problems, especially ➤transnational diseases, have been a matter for practical international concern since at least medieval times but rarely do they figure in academic considerations of world politics. The dominance of the ➤state-centric approach and its consequent concern with the diplomatic-strategic milieu has relegated most issues of social welfare, including health, to the level of Any Other Business on the agenda of ➤international relations. However, since the establishment of WHO as a ➤specialized agency of the ➤United Nations in 1948 the issue of global health, like that of ➤ecology, has become a high profile one both for practitioners anxious to control and eradicate disease and for theorists concerned to move beyond the state and develop a wider understanding of the scope of international activity.

In 1851 a series of international conferences met to discuss quarantine regulations; this resulted eventually in the adoption of the International Sanitary Convention in 1903 and the establishment of the International Office of Public Hygiene in Paris in 1909. The ➤League of Nations established a Health Organization in 1920 to work in conjunction with the Paris office and both of these were absorbed by the WHO in 1948. Since then it has become the largest of the specialized agencies, its general purpose being 'the attainment by all peoples of the highest possible level of health'. Its headquarters is in Geneva and its operations are decentralized into six regional committees and offices. It has a Director-General, a Secretariat and an Executive Board and it convenes an annual World Health Assembly as well as various international health conventions. Membership is open to all ►states; members of the UN join automatically and other states become members when the World Health Assembly approves their application by a simple majority vote. Territories which are not responsible for the conduct of their ►foreign policy may become associate members.

The general record of WHO is impressive not just in the control or eradication of epidemic diseases such as smallpox or malaria but also in the areas of promoting primary health care and assisting developing states in the creation of health services and training facilities. It maintains an Epidemiological Intelligence Network which can rapidly and efficiently collate and disseminate information about the intensity and likely spread of life-threatening diseases including cholera, typhoid, plague, smallpox, yellow fever and AIDS. In 1967 the WHO began a global campaign to eradicate smallpox within ten years. That year 131,418 cases were reported in 43 countries. By 1984, according to WHO, the smallpox plague had been totally eradicated. In addition to combating disease, WHO functions effectively in the area of prevention and has initiated numerous projects on air ►pollution, water supply, sewage disposal and the use of insecticides. The organization is at the forefront of global campaigns to popularize and highlight the importance of transnational cooperation in health care matters. In 1978 for example, it convened the Alma-Ata Conference on primary health care which formulated the campaign for 'Health for All' by the year 2000. Whether or not these goals will be achieved in the face of entrenched beliefs about the primacy of economic growth (most commentators think not) none can doubt that the WHO is one of the most successful of the UN's specialized agencies. ►►AIDS

**World law** Term popularized by Corbett (1956) and others to indicate an apparent post-war shift away from traditional ►state-centric international law towards a much wider based 'law of the world community'. It is especially associated with the ►world governance perspective and is designed to promote a conception of law which reflects the dynamism of contemporary social values rather than one which is locked in to the predominantly Eurocentric assumptions of the ►Westphalia system. They assert that the transition from 'international' to 'world' law is revealed in four broad areas: subjects of law are increasingly individuals and groups rather than just ►states; the scope of law has moved from an almost exclusive concern with political and strategic matters to economic, social, environmental and communication matters; the sources of law are now regarded as being community based rather than narrowly national and the role of the international lawyer has changed from exposition and interpretation of existing rules to a more dynamic 'policy orientated jurisprudence'. According to the adherents of this school (mainly, though not exclusively,

US) this transition not only reflects reality, it also represents progress. However, many ➤traditionalists regard this optimism as both premature and misplaced. They contend that the persistence of the older view of consent-based law defining basic principles of coexistence within a society of states should not be underestimated (Bull, 1977).

The term is also used loosely to describe the legal system envisaged in the event of the establishment of ➤world government.

**World politics** Unlike ➤international politics or ➤international relations this term does not stress the primacy of intergovernmental relations and transactions. Instead its use indicates reference to a much wider range of ➤actors and activities than the ➤war/peace/security/order scenarios involved in the classical ➤state-centred paradigms The 'world politics perspective' is closely identified with the work of Keohane and Nye (especially *Transantional Relations and World Politics*, 1972) who argued that the state-centric view and its obsession with the interstate system provides an inadequate analytical framework for comprehending the contemporary world. This was not merely a question of semantics (the word ➤international has long been thought of as unsatisfactory); it denoted a profound change in the structure, procedure and substance of the subject in the 1960s and 1970s. As the authors point out, given that many business enterprises have annual turnovers larger than the GNP of many voting members of the UN, and given that large private financial corporations can frustrate the financial policies of even powerful sovereign states, substantial modifications are needed to the original state-orientated model of international politics if those developments are to be grasped. The term 'world politics' is thus intended to expand the boundaries of the subject of inquiry, away from the narrow confines of interstate relations towards a recognition of global developments which are in effect beyond the range of the traditional approach. In this way it is closely allied to the world order and ➤world society approaches in that it seeks to draw attention to the increasingly complicated network of relationships that now exist between non-governmental actors. Whereas international politics is concerned primarily with relationships between governments that involve conflicts of interest, world politics is characterized by a multiplicity of actor types and issue areas. ➤➤Macropolitics; mixed actor model; pluralism

**World public opinion** Refers to the supposed existence of a global consensus as to what constitutes legitimate moral, legal or social behaviour in ➤international relations. Apart from obvious cases such as ➤genocide or the unrestricted use of ➤chemical or ➤biological warfare, it is difficult to establish a core of widely shared patterns of values, norms and beliefs in an ➤international system characterized more by diversity than unity. ➤International law does provide a rudimentary framework for the expression of international social norms but this does not, as such, represent the embodiment of world public opinion. General international norms exist (e.g. about ➤human rights, self-determination or

➤aggression) but formulations of them are hedged about with ambiguities and inconsistencies. The incompleteness of the international political system, which is to say its ➤state-centric character, is a severe limitation on the development of anything other than a vague humanitarianism which is difficult to translate into practical ➤policy-making. However, difficult as it may be to codify, most governments are sensitive to outside opinion about their policies, although they are not equally sensitive to all sources of opinion. Gauging the likely response of the international community to a proposed action is part of the ➤decision-maker's function but if achieving or defending their declared objectives is regarded as vital, global opinion, however vociferously expressed, is likely to be ignored. 'World public opinion', then, is at best an elusive concept and should be approached with caution in ➤foreign policy analysis.

**World society** A challenging, if controversial, body of literature has emerged over the last twenty years under the rubric of the World Society Perspective. The perspective is derived from the writings of the Australian diplomat/scholar John W. Burton. In a series of books and articles of which *Systems, States, Diplomacy and Rules* (1968) and *World Society* (1972) are the most important, Burton has sought to advance his ideas about ➤international relations and his criticism of more traditionally conceived approaches. Probably the best single-volume treatment of this perspective is the collection of essays dedicated to Burton, *Conflict in World Society* (Banks, 1984).

With remarkable prescience, Burton arrived at a set of conclusions about the redundancy of the state-centred or ➤state-centric approach at approximately the same time as US ➤pluralists were beginning to emphasize the significance of ➤transnational and ➤transgovernmental ➤actors and processes. Burton labelled the traditional paradigm the ➤billiard ball model and he contrasted it with a three-dimensional cobweb model which he argued should replace it. By using the analogy of the billiard table Burton emphasized the way in which concepts such as ➤sovereignty seemed to suggest a hard and fast division between domestic politics on the one hand and world politics on the other. The billiard ball also emphasized the idea of territoriality as an attribute of state-centred approaches. Emphasizing the importance of transactions amongst a complex of actors, Burton suggested that traditional 'maps' were irrelevant and that the three-dimensional cobweb idea was more isomorphic with an increasingly complex world politics. These ideas owed a great deal to the pioneering work of Karl Deutsch, although unlike Deutsch, Burton did not immediately seek rigorous empirical testing of his ideas.

In earlier works Burton had sought to repudiate the concept of ➤power as a central organizing idea in IR. He subsequently linked the billiard ball model and power together in these later works by suggesting that the latter is an attribute of the former. Moreover, in the view of Burton and many of those who have followed him, over-emphasis upon power leads to what are termed 'self-defeating' strategies based upon such coercive instruments as ➤deterrence and ideas about power 'balances'. Burton has for this reason become associated with non-coercive, cooperative approaches to problems of ➤conflict and this has led some of his critics to dub him an ➤idealist or 'neo-idealist'. Certainly, by repudiating power so totally Burton and his followers have denied themselves access to a rich vein of modern scholarship which has attempted a new and better understanding of one of the most contested, but important, concepts in IR.

The world society literature remains a fascinating, if flawed, field of analysis. Burton is without question one of the most challenging social theorists writing in the field. His refusal to be bound by the conventional canons of academic scholarship has left him free to mix analysis and prescription, fact and value, theory and practice in a way that few others would have the inclination or imagination to attempt.

**World Trade Organization (WTO)** This new IGO was established as a result of the ➤Uruguay Round of ➤trade negotiations conducted under the aegis of the GATT process. In effect the establishment of the WTO realises the intentions of the ➤Bretton Woods system that an International Trade Organization would be set up to match the other Bretton Woods institutions – the IMF and the ➤World Bank. The WTO is more than simply a 'tidying up operation'. It does represent the collection under one rubric of all the GATT agreements reached at the various 'rounds' since 1947. Additionally, WTO has enhanced the bureaucracy available to monitor adherence to the principles of ➤multilateralism inherent in the GATT philosophy. WTO also has greater powers for identifying non-compliance with agreements and for the resolutions of disputes between parties. It is reasonable to assume that future trade negotiations will be conducted upon a more regular and routine basis than hitherto.

The establishment of the WTO does not mean that all road blocks to a more liberal trade regime have been removed. In particular the ➤issue area of the ➤environment has not been addressed until recently. ➤Free traders and ➤protectionists both tend to hijack the arguments on the environment to support their point of view. It is likely that the WTO will be far more cognizant of the environmental aspects of trade agreements than GATT was. The continued subsidization of agriculture is another issue area which the WTO will have to address. This is mainly a ➤First World dispute at present with the United States ranged on the one side in favour of proceeding faster and further, while the ➤European Union and Japan are more cautious. Finally it is salutary to remember that over 30 per cent of world trade is conducted between MNCs and that the ➤state-centrism of the WTO will need to change if it is to become truly an institution for the management of trade, rather than simply for trade between states.

**Worst-case analysis** Sometimes rendered as worst-case assumptions, worst-case forecasting or worst-case thinking. Worst-case analysis is a ➤definition of the situation that is applied in military-➤security policy-making and, in particular in ➤defence planning. It rests upon a ➤scenario that takes the most pessimistic assumptions and estimates, both of ➤capabilities and intentions, of a putative adversary. Having taken such a pessimistic view the ➤analysis proceeds to stipulate a series of responses that are perceived to meet the initial position. To this extent worst-case analysis can lead to the ➤self-fulfilling prophecy dynamic. In the sixth chapter of his 1979 study of ➤ethnocentrism, Ken Booth argues that what he calls the 'operating principle' of worst-case analysis is: 'when in doubt, think the worst' (p. 126). For Booth the perceptual framework for the worst-case analyst is the 'inherently bad faith model'. Less critically perhaps, worst-case analysis can be seen as the development of the desire to insure prudentially for an uncertain future. As a result it stimulates the tendency to allow a margin of error or safety in estimating adversaries' intentions and capabilities. Gwyn Prins (1983) argues that worst-case analysts become preoccupied with capabilities rather than intentions in this regard. Capability analysis certainly produces what can be seen as 'hard data' about the adversary, whereas intention analysis is much more prone to conjecture and speculation.

It should not be thought that worst-case analysis is only stimulated by the kind of psychological mind set discussed above. Politicians, strategists and senior military figures may use worst case analysis to manipulate public and ➤elite support for greater and greater amounts of defence spending by constantly bidding up the size and magnitude of the adversaries' threat.

# X

**X** *Nom de plume* of George F. Kennan, American diplomat credited with formulating the doctrine of ➤containment. Kennan had been a high ranking envoy in the US embassy in Moscow and in his famous 'long telegram' had warned Washington of the fanaticism of Soviet ➤ideology and of its unswerving commitment to world ➤revolution. In 1947, as head of the State Department's policy-planning staff he enlarged on this and published, under the pseudonym 'X', 'The Sources of Soviet Conduct', in the influential journal *Foreign Affairs* (pp. 566–82). The article contained an ominous appraisal of Soviet intentions written from a ➤realist perspective and was clearly designed to alert US ➤decision-makers to the dangers posed by the Soviet doctrine of the inevitability of ➤conflict with capitalist powers and the expansive nature of Soviet ➤foreign policy. He concluded that 'In these circumstances it is clear that the main element of any United States policy toward the Soviet Union must be that of long-term, patient but firm and vigilant application of ➤counterforce at a series of constantly shifting geographical and political points, corresponding to the shifts and manoeuvres of Soviet Policy'. This assessment crystallized into the main intellectual foundation of post-war US policy towards the Soviet Union and was specifically incorporated into the ➤Truman Doctrine and the policy of containment.

Kennan (1984, p. 16) subsequently disavowed the policies which his article inspired and claimed that his advice was misinterpreted and taken out of context:

> . . . I did not believe . . . that there was the slightest danger of a Soviet military attack against the major western powers or Japan. This was, in other words, a political danger, not a military one. And the historical record bears out that conclusion. But for reasons I have never fully understood, by 1949 a great many people in Washington – in the Pentagon, the White House and even the Department of State – seemed to have come to the conclusion that there was a real danger of the Soviets unleashing, in the fairly near future, what would have been World War Three.

Nevertheless, the doctrine of containment and 'X' 's role in it, has remained a controversial one in contemporary reviews of US ➤Cold War policies. It seems clear in retrospect that the 'X' article served to capture the public imagination by providing an explanation for a policy already adopted. In this sense 'X' 's long telegram may have been the real genesis of containment.

**Xenophobia** Fear, dislike, distrust or intolerance of foreigners either as individuals or groups. It is closely associated with extreme forms of ➤nationalism and ➤ethnocentrism and often manifests itself in expressions of hostility towards outsiders. This can take the form of condemning whole groups (anti-Semitism), ➤nations (anti-English) or even continents (anti-American, anti-European). It is often linked with ➤isolationism and in this sense xenophobia was the underlying emotion which spawned the policies of China and Japan (with good reason; ➤treaty ports) towards Europeans prior to the twentieth century. To a certain extent all states are tinged with xenophobia but the degree to which it intrudes into ➤policy-making varies. During wartime it is deliberately encouraged and fostered by governments anxious to maintain social cohesion and direct all attention towards the war effort. In peacetime, xenophobic tendencies can be manipulated to provide scapegoats for policy failures, both internally and externally. In this connection the UNHC Round Table on Refugees, Victims of Xenophobia held in Geneva in 1984 warned that this was a growing, rather than a diminishing problem in world politics, especially in the advanced industrial countries (AICs) '. . . the phenomenon of xenophobia is on the upsurge, more visible in Western industrialized societies where xenophobic tendencies contrast with previously tolerant attitudes to foreigners and where liberal admission policies in the past have permitted the growth of sizeable populations'. This tendency has been especially noticeable in the EC/EU countries which collectively employ over 15 million *Gastarbeiter* (guest workers) mainly in agriculture, services and industry. Apart from legal disputes between employers and employees, immigrant workers often face hostility and abuse from indigenous inhabitants anxious to protect their own livelihoods and cultural values.

In its most extreme form, xenophobia often reflects a paranoid view of the outside world. Hitler and Stalin were both xenophobic, and this was clearly reflected in their policies. One of the most blatant recent examples of state directed paranoiac xenophobia was General Amin's expulsion of 50,000 Ugandan Asians in 1972 to the obvious detriment of his domestic economy and his international standing. ➤➤Ethnic cleansing; genocide

# Y

**Yalta conference** An agreement reached in the Crimea in February 1945 between Roosevelt, Stalin and Churchill concerning the future conduct of the ►war and the shape of the post-war ►international order. In relation to the war it was agreed that Germany should ►surrender unconditionally, ►reparations should be extracted, ►war crimes should be punished and that the Soviet Union would join the war against Japan within three months of Germany's defeat. Regarding the post-war order, the Polish and Soviet borders would move westwards to the Oder-Neisse and Curzon lines at the territorial expense of Germany, Germany itself was to be divided into four zones of occupation and an Inter-Allied Control Council was established for Berlin. In addition there was an agreement that the liberated ►states of Eastern Europe should hold free democratic elections. The Conference also made important decisions regarding the proposed ►United Nations organization, in particular that the ►great powers would be given the power of ►veto in the ►Security Council, and that the Soviet Union would receive three memberships (the Soviet Union, Byelorussia and Ukraine).

Since no formal peace ►treaty was signed at the end of the Second World War, the Yalta agreements formed the basis of the post-war European settlement, and ever after have been the subject of considerable dispute. It has been alleged that Roosevelt, in his anxiety to appease the Soviet Union, in effect sold out most of Eastern Europe to ►communist domination; that Yalta gave Stalin a position of dominance which otherwise he may not have achieved. On the other hand, it could be said that the West conceded very little since the Soviet armies were already firmly emplaced and that the most that could be achieved was some form of ►multilateral agreement concerning how this ►power should be exercised. The Yalta agreement, especially provisions relating to the post-war frontiers in Europe, became a matter of bitter dispute during the early years of the ►Cold War and continued to beset German politics up to and beyond ►ostpolitik. The absence of a specific ►peace treaty in Europe in 1945 has led to a complex and somewhat ambiguous legal position with regard to the status of Germany. In effect, three Germanies were recognized in ►international law: the Federal Republic (West Germany), the Democratic Republic (East Germany) and the Germany that existed in 1937. At the Potsdam conference, six months after Yalta, the German/Polish frontier along the rivers Oder and Neisse was referred to as 'provisional' since 'the final delimitation of the western frontier of Poland should await the peace settlement'. The Yalta system was effectively ended by the events of ➤nineteen eighty-nine, German reunification and the ➤Gorbachev doctrine.

## Yaoundé Convention ➤ACP

**Yen power** A phrase indicating Japan's remarkable rise to the status of an economic ➤superpower, putative rival in the ➤Pacific Basin to the USA, and ➤tripolar 'pole' in the world's global political economy. Some prefer the term 'Pax Nipponica', but this can be rejected on the grounds that – except in strictly regional terms – Japan does not dominate the system. Moreover, unlike Britain in the nineteenth century and America in the twentieth, Japan is not a first-order military power. Under its constitution, imposed by the United States after the Second World War, Japan is bound over to keep the ➤peace by renouncing ➤war as an instrument of ➤state policy (Article 9). This position was confirmed under the so-called Yoshida doctrine, which set Japan upon its post-war path of maintaining only self-defence forces, keeping its defence expenditure tied to 1 per cent of GNP (Gross National Product) and relying upon an ➤alliance with the USA for external ➤security. Indeed a virtue was gleaned from this necessity because under these stipulations Japan has been able to devote more of its national wealth to economic growth than some of its main ➤trade competitors – including the USA!

Japan's ➤influence in world politics is based solely upon its economic ➤capability. Johnson (1982) has dubbed Japan the 'developmental state', meaning that economic growth has become a core value of Japanese society and a continual goal of the policy ➤elite. Japan since 1950 is indeed the best example of ➤neo-mercantilism as a set of operating national principles in world politics. Politically the country has been governed for over four decades by the same party – the Liberal Democratic Party – and bureaucratically it has been administered by a large civil service which recruits the brightest and the best into its higher echelons. Indeed a close symbiotic relationship exists between the Liberal Democrats, the senior bureaucrats and the leaders of industry, a tradition – like that of public service – which goes back before 1945. The Japanese population is ethnically homogenous, well educated, highly cooperative, intensely loyal to national and corporate goals and consensus-minded. As a result of these cultural factors the Japanese economy has since 1950 shown the following consistent characteristics: high growth, few strikes, low inflation, great technological innovation and an ongoing trade and payments surplus with the rest of the world. This is despite the fact that Japan is highly dependent upon many imported raw materials and – as the ➤oil shocks demonstrated – vulnerable to cut-offs and interruptions.

Japan's influence in world politics was dramatically demonstrated at the funeral of Emperor Hirohito in February 1989 where a record 163 countries were represented. In 1989 it was estimated that Japan will overtake the USA as the world's largest donor of overseas financial ➤aid. In a five-year aid plan

Japan intends to give nearly £28 billion to developmental projects on a global scale. Thus, during a period of financial retrenchment in the West, Tokyo seemed poised to become the financial centre and a major instigator of global economic development. In 1988 the Japanese announced an International Cooperation Initiative which was specifically designed to heighten Japan's global profile through increased financial support for ➤United Nations peace projects, through more extensive cultural exchanges and through a general hike in overseas aid programmes. The overall financial dominance of Japan is viewed as a mixed blessing by the West. In the USA, for example, Japan is seen to be its strongest ally and trading partner as well as its greatest creditor and its most feared economic competitor. The ➤European Union too is wary of increased Japanese economic penetration and is designing strategies to counter it. In the ➤Third World, on the other hand, especially in Africa and South America, the new donor role of Japan is generally welcomed. Clearly, if the twenty-first century is to be the Pacific century then Japan, well placed as it is on its ➤geopolitical rim, is destined to be one of its most powerful, albeit non-military components. While the decline in the Japanese economy in the mid-1990s might render some of these predictions suspect, most commentators argue that Japan's position within the globalization nexus will ensure its continued prominence into the millenium and beyond. ➤➤East Asia crisis

**Yugoslavia** Yugoslavia ('the Kingdom of the Southern Slavs') was created in 1919 as a result of the ➤Versailles settlement. Before its dissolution in 1991 it consisted of six federal republics, it had three official languages, two alphabets and a number of distinct ethnic groups. Historically this part of the Balkans has been the confluence of a number of ➤imperial systems and ➤spheres of influence, including at various times: Roman, Byzantine, Ottoman, Austrian, French and Russian. In particular what Huntington (1993) calls a 'Fault Line' between civilizations – European/Central Asian/Middle Eastern/Mediterranean – runs through the heart of this part of the Balkans. During the nineteenth century the area was recognized by European ➤diplomacy to be a source of great instability with its ethnic complexities, overlapping political jurisdictions and ➤nationalist aspirations. These stirrings of demands for ➤autonomy and ➤independence were particularly evident in Serbia and Croatia. Early in the twentieth century, Austrian plans for territorial aggrandizement at the expense of Bosnia provoked a major European ➤crisis which was only settled after Russia and Serbia were forced to make concessions. One of the proximate causes of the First World War was ➤revolutionary activity amongst Serbian secret societies. These Serbian plots were directed against Austria and they culminated in the assassination of the Austrian Archduke Ferdinand in Sarajevo, Bosnia on 28 June 1914. The failure of ➤crisis management on this occasion produced ➤war amongst all the European powers by the end of that summer.

The settlement at the end of the First World War recognized the demands from Serbs, Croats and Slovenes for a united Yugoslavia. Creating a Yugoslavia in 1919 did not create a sense of a Yugoslav nation and tensions – particularly between Croats and Serbs – were a feature of the inter-war period. The German invasion of the country during the Second World War exacerbated these tensions and led to claims and counter-claims between the ethnic groups which are still part of the 'history' of the conflict. In particular Croat collaboration with Fascism clashed violently with Serbian opposition to the German occupation. Germany partitioned Yugoslavia during its occupation following a deliberate policy of divide-and-rule, which in its ➤implementation was highly successful. There is no doubt that as a ➤communal conflict the ethnic tensions generated between the Serbs and Croats during these years remain significant latent grievances today.

The partisan leader Josip Broz Tito emerged at the end as the undisputed Nationalist/Communist leader of Yugoslavia. In the years until his death in 1980 Tito sought to balance the conflicting ethnic forces in the country whilst pursuing a highly individual path to socialism and a highly original ➤foreign policy. During the ➤Cold War years indeed Yugoslavia was widely studied and much admired for its decentralized political economy and its ➤non-aligned orientation.

From 1980 onwards the fragile unity that the federation had enjoyed began to break down. The collapse of ➤communism throughout Eastern Europe in 1989–90 and the nationalist policies of the ➤leaderships in the republics led to a constitutional crisis in 1991 when the Croatian and Slovene parliaments passed independence resolutions in June. Between 1991 and 1995 large scale violent communal conflict took place between the various ethnic groupings, in particular Serbs, Croats and Muslims. It is estimated that during this period over 150,000 people were killed, three million became ➤refugees and thousands were subjected to the horrors of ➤ethnic cleansing and ➤genocide. The ➤United Nations dispatched a ➤peacekeeping force to the region in 1992. The UN mission failed both at the political and the military levels. The situation in Bosnia was the epicentre of the violence. Various 'Peace Plans' were proposed for the republic including the Vance-Owen Plan of 1993 and the European Union Plan of 1994. Both recognized the ethnic complexities of Bosnia and sought to address them through various forms of partition.

In 1994–95 NATO succeeded the UN as peacemaker with a more robust mandate to bring the warring parties together. This has only been partially successful. The Dayton (Ohio) Agreement of 1995 stopped the war but no party is satisfied with the outcome. In particular the Bosnian Serbs have unsettled ➤irredentist territorial claims. It is likely that the former Yugoslavia will remain highly unstable despite the efforts of the OSCE, the UN and NATO to settle the dispute. The continued unrest in Bosnia, in particular the desire of the newly established Republika Srpska to unite with Serbia, the reluctance to extradite individuals to the ➤war crimes tribunal at the Hague, and the unwillingness of Serbs, Croats and Muslims to return to the ►status quo *ante*, makes it extremely unlikely that the problems of the region will be settled in the near future. The failure of the Dayton Agreement of 1995 to address the problem of Kosovo, which until 1989 was an autonomous province within Yugoslavia, meant that despite the settlement in Bosnia, the Balkan Question would remain high on the post-Cold War international agenda. In 1998 unrest in the province, with its large Albanian population, resulted in a demand for independence from nationalists led by the Kosovo Liberation Army (KLA). Violence once again broke out and massive human rights violations, including ethnic cleansing, shelling of civilians and wholesale destruction of villages, followed the familiar pattern set in Bosnia. Early in 1999 the departure of 800 international 'peace verifiers' and the subsequent Serbian refusal to countenance the presence of 28,000 NATO-led peacekeepers in Kosovo persuaded the NATO allies to take direct action. On 24 March NATO aircraft began a bombing campaign against military targets, initially within Kosovo but later extending to Serbia itself. After a devastating and highly controversial campaign in June 1999 the Federal Republic of Yugoslavia (i.e. Serbia) agreed to retract its forces and permit the entry of NATO peacekeepers into Kosovo to begin the massive task of reconstruction of the devastated province. Kosovo is now *de facto* a NATO/UN protectorate, but its constitutional/legal status has yet to be resolved. NATO's aerial intervention was opposed throughout by Russia and China on the grounds that it was a serious violation of international law and an infringement of Yugoslavia's territorial sovereignty under Article 2 of the UN Charter. NATO defended its action by reference to the doctrine of humanitarian intervention and the just war thesis.

The tension between the claims of sovereignty, self-determination and humanitarianism will continue to dog policy-makers and analysts well into the new millennium. Western vascillation concerning Russian actions in Chechnya in late 1999 illustrate the continued difficulty of seeking to persuade or coerce a determined great power that the traditional permissive rights associated with state sovereignty must now bow down to post-Westphalian imperatives of humanitarianism and solidarist/cosmopolitan ethics. The failure of NATO to resolve the Kosovo issue and to formulate a consistent and coherent policy on Chechnya illustrates the legal and moral conundrums that occupy the nexus between the old and the new world orders; i.e. between the old privileges of sovereign inviolability and an emerging body of customary international law which obliges states to act where human rights are clearly being violated. Thus the empirical and conceptual fall-out from the political disintegration of the old Yugoslavia will continue to be felt well into the twenty-first century, not just in the Balkans but in many other multi-ethnic and multi-cultural states including Russia, China and Indonesia, to name but a few.➤➤**Balkanization**

# Z

**Zero-sum** A term derived from ➤game theory. It refers to the fact that the numerical value of the 'pay-offs' add up to zero. It is therefore held to represent in mathematical terms a situation of pure ➤conflict where a gain to one party is a loss to the other.

The term is also used outside the strict confines of game theory. Students of ➤conflict analysis will often use it to characterize a particular ➤perception held by participants of the nature of their conflict. ➤Conflict resolution may be made more difficult if this type of perception appears to be influential and deeply held.

**Zimmern, A. E.** First holder of the first chair of ➤international politics in the world, the Woodrow Wilson chair at the University of Wales, Aberystwyth in 1919. As with other contemporaries who share the distinction of founding the academic study of ➤international relations (notably Gilbert Murray and G. Lowes Dickinson) Zimmern was a classicist who steadfastly believed in the latent ➤harmony of interests of ➤states and in the inevitability of progress. Best known for his belief in the application of the 'rule of law' to world politics through the principle of the 'hue and cry'. A fervent supporter of the ➤League of Nations and a founder member of the Royal Institute Of International Affairs, Zimmern's ➤idealism was brilliantly savaged by one of his successors at the University of Wales (Carr, 1946). Zimmern's importance in the study owes less to the enduring value of his ideas (which at this distance seem simplistic and hopelessly optimistic) than to his lifelong concern to establish a secure academic base for inquiry into international politics (as distinct from diplomatic history) into the undergraduate curriculum. He also succeeded in popularizing the study in London, Geneva and in the United States, which he regarded as the world's first 'free' ➤great power and which he hoped fervently would pave the way to ➤internationalism and the collective abolition of ➤war as an instrument of state policy.

**Zionism** The ideology of Jewish ➤nationalism. Zionism became a powerful ➤transnational movement particularly amongst Eastern European Jews in the last decades of the nineteenth century and the first decades of the twentieth. Zionism confronted the problems inherent in the Jewish Diaspora by arguing that the only solution was auto-emancipation via the establishment of a Jewish homeland where Jews could escape from their permanent minority status by becoming a majority people attached to a recognized territorial base. In this respect Zionism is typical of the kinds of nationalist fervour that was a feature of the European ➤region throughout the nineteenth and twentieth centuries. Following the publication of Herzl's book *Der Judenstaat* in 1896 political activity picked up and Jews began returning (in small numbers) to the territory of Palestine which was then under the Ottoman Turkish control. During the First World War Zionist lobbying concentrated its efforts in the UK and in the United States and this pressure culminated in the proclamation of the so-called 'Balfour Declaration' by the British government in 1917. This indicated that the British and their allies and associates would look with favour on the establishment of a homeland for the Jews in Palestine in the post-war settlement. Britain and France were at the same time covertly agreeing between themselves to establish ➤spheres of influence in the Middle East, and Britain, in particular, was encouraging Arab opinion to believe that after the end of the hostilities, their majoritarian interests in Palestine and elsewhere would not be ignored. This circle of contradictory understandings was never satisfactorily squared and it became clear after 1919 when an American fact-finding commission known as the King-Crane Commission was sent to the area of Palestine that large scale, politically motivated Jewish immigration would not be welcomed by the Arab communities in the area.

Jewish immigration into Palestine after 1920 (when the ➤League of Nations Mandate was granted to Britain) was wholly different from the age-old return of religious zealots. Secular and socialist, Zionism was a movement with a mission statement which could not but create communal tensions amongst the Arab majority. Britain presided over a growing ➤communal conflict during the first half of the twentieth century, eventually proposing partition in 1937 in a Royal Commission report. Ten years later the United Kingdom government handed the ➤issue area back to the ➤United Nations by which time the ➤Arab–Israeli dispute was taking on its present structure.

With the foundation of the State of Israel in 1948 the main target of Zionist pressure politics had switched from the United Kingdom to the United States. The 'Jewish lobby' remains the best example of an Ethnic Interest Group operating in the American ➤foreign policy system. Well organized under the umbrella AIPAC (American-Israel Public Affairs Committee) the Jewish lobby is a ➤paradigm instance of how the 'boundary' can effectively be crossed from domestic to foreign and back again. It should be recognized that during the ➤Cold War era the United States might have had strong ➤security motives for supporting Israel even if the Jewish lobby had not existed. Notwithstanding this reservation the Jewish lobby shows how the Zionist movement's commitment to pressure politics culminated in the crucial linkage between the United States and the state of Israel.

**Zones of peace/Zones of turmoil** Post-➤cold war concepts relating to the division of the world into two not necessarily hostile, but certainly highly differentiated, camps. First mooted by Singer and Wildavsky (1993), zones of peace are ➤regions that embrace democratic governance, capitalist modes of production and distribution and have an overall level of prosperity and affluence that precludes structural instability. This zone includes much of North America, Western Europe, Japan, part of SE Asia and Australasia. It is therefore virtually coterminous with the Cold War term 'the West.' In all cases the defining criterion is ➤peace. These are regions in which military conflict between or amongst component parts is unthinkable. These zones are generally regarded as conclusive empirical evidence of the validity of the Kantian/➤liberal thesis that 'democracies don't fight each other'. By contrast, zones of turmoil are those areas where inter- and intra-state ➤war is endemic. The prevalence of insecurity in these regions mitigates against ➤good governance and economic prosperity. In policy terms, the interests of inhabitants of zones of peace lie in preventing conflict ➤spillover from zones of turmoil. Two dominant and competing policy perspectives flow from this: 'protectionist' or 'Fortress' policies designed to insulate or exclude, and 'emancipatory' or 'interventionist' policies aimed at pacification and development. The latter are usually premised on considerations of enlightened self-interest ('If they don't eat, we don't sleep'). Whereas EU and US policies *vis-à-vis* Central and Eastern Europe and Russia illustrate these general policy tendencies (NATO expansion and 'Partnership for peace' programmes), attitudes to sub-Saharan Africa, arguably the biggest single zone of turmoil, are ambivalent. This suggests that the key determinant of policy is strategic/pragmatic rather than ideological/humanitarian. Following from this, a third, but generally unstated policy orientation may be identified: that of indifference or benign neglect.

# BIBLIOGRAPHY

The purpose of this section is to acknowledge sources used in writing the entries and to enable the reader to explore and expand on the explanations given.

Abercrombie, N., Hill, S. and Turner, B. S. (1984), *Dictionary of Sociology* (Penguin, Harmondsworth).

Akehurst, M. (1984), *A Modern Introduction to International Law*, sixth edition (George Allen & Unwin, London).

Allison, G., Carnesale, A. and Nye, J. Jnr. (eds) (1985), *Hawks, Doves and Owls* (W. W. Norton, New York).

Allison, G. and Treverton, G. F. (eds) (1992), *Rethinking America's Security: Beyond Cold War to New World Order* (W. W. Norton, New York).

Allison, G. T. (1971), *Essence of Decision: Explaining the Cuban Missile Crisis* (Little, Brown, Boston).

Almond, G. A. (1966), *The American People and Foreign Policy* (Secker & Warburg, London).

Alperovitz, G. (1985), *Atomic Diplomacy: Hiroshima and Potsdam* (Penguin, New York).

Ambrose, S. (1993), *Rise to Globalism*, seventh revised edition (Penguin, New York).

Andrew, C. and Dilks, D. (eds) (1984), *The Missing Dimension: Governments and Intelligence Communities in the Twentieth Century* (Macmillan, London).

Angell, N. (1910), *The Great Illusion* (Heinemann, London).

Archer, C. (1983), *International Organizations* (Allen & Unwin, London).

Armitage, M. J. and Mason, R. A. (1985), *Air Power in the Nuclear Age, 1945–84: Theory and Practice* (Macmillan, London).

Arms Project of Human Rights Watch and Physicians for Human Rights (1993), *Land Mines: A Deadly Legacy*

Aron, R. (1975), *The Imperial Republic: The United States and the World, 1945–73*, tr. F. Jellinek (Weidenfeld & Nicolson, London).

Aron, R. (1966), *Peace and War: A Theory of International Relations* (Weidenfeld & Nicolson, London).

Art, R. J. (1973), 'Bureaucratic Politics and American Foreign Policy: A Critique' in Ikenberry, J. G. (ed) (1989), *American Foreign Policy: Theoretical Essays* (Scott, Foresman, Boston).

Aryubi, N. M. (1991), *Political Islam: Religion and Politics in the Arab World* (Routledge, London).

Ashley, R. K. (1984), 'The Poverty of Neorealism', *International Organization*, **38** (2) pp. 225–86.

Ashley, R. K. and Walker, R. B. J. (eds) (1990), 'Speaking the Language of Exile: Dissidence in International Studies', Special Issue: *International Studies Quarterly*, **34** pp. 259–417.

Austin, J. (1954), *The Province Of Jurisprudence Determined* (Weidenfeld & Nicolson, London, first published 1832).

Axelrod, R. (1984), *The Evolution of Cooperation* (Basic Books, New York).

Axelrod, R. and Keohane, R. O. (1985), 'Achieving Cooperation under Anarchy: Strategies and Institutions', *World Politics*, **38** (October) pp. 226–54.

Azar, E. (1990), *The Management of Protracted Social Conflict* (Dartmouth, Aldershot).

Bailey, S. D. (1987), *War and Conscience in the Nuclear Age* (Macmillan, London).

Bainbridge, T. and Teasdale, A. (1996), *The Penguin Companion to European Union* (Penguin, Harmondsworth).

Baldwin, D. A. (1971), 'Money and Power', *Journal of Politics*, **33** no. 3 (August) pp. 578–614.

Baldwin, D. A. (1979), 'Power Analysis and World Politics: New Trends versus Old Tendencies', *World Politics*, **31** (January) pp. 161–95.

Baldwin, D. A. (1985), *Economic Statecraft* (Princeton University, Princeton).

Baldwin, D. A. (1989), *Paradoxes of Power* (Basic Books, New York).

Baldwin, D. A. (ed.) (1993), *Neorealism and Neoliberalism: the Contemporary Debate* (Columbia University Press, New York).

Banks, M. (ed) (1984), *Conflict in World Society* (Harvester Wheatsheaf, Hemel Hempstead).

Barber, J. (1979), 'Economic Sanctions as a Policy Instrument', *International Affairs*, **55** (3) pp. 367–84.

Barber, J. (1985), *The Presidential Character*, third edition (Prentice Hall, Englewood Cliffs).

Barber, J. and Smith, M. (eds) (1974), *The Nature of Foreign Policy: A Reader* (Open University Press, Milton Keynes).

Barkin, J. S. and Cronin, B. (1994), 'The State and the Nation: Changing Norms and Rules of Sovereignty in International Relations', *International Organisation*, **48** (1) pp. 107–30.

Barnet, R. J. and Cavanagh, J. (1994), *Global Dreams: Imperial Corporations and the New World Order* (Simon and Schuster, New York).

Barnet, R. J. and Muller, R. E. (1974), *Global Reach: The Power of the Multinational Corporations* (Simon and Schuster, New York).

Barry, Brian and Hardin, Russell (eds) (1982), *Rational Man and Irrational Society* (Sage Publications, Beverly Hills).

Barston, R. P. (1988), *Modern Diplomacy* (Longman, London).

Bartlett, C. J. (1972), *The Long Retreat: A Short History of British Defence Policy, 1945–70* (Macmillan, London).

Baylis, J. and Rengger, N. (1992), *Dilemmas of World Politics: International Issues in a Changing World* (Clarendon Press, Oxford).

Beales, A. C. F. (1931), *The History of Peace: A Short Account of the Organized Movements for International Peace* (Bell, London).

Beard, C. A. and Smith, G. H. E. (1934), *The Idea of the National Interest: An Analytical Study in American Foreign Policy* (Macmillan, New York).

Beaufre, A. (1965), *Deterrence and Strategy* (Faber, London).

Beitz, C. R. (1979), *Political Theory and International Relations* (Princeton University, Princeton).

Bell, C. (1971), *The Conventions of a Crisis: A Study of Diplomatic Management* (RIIA, London).

Beloff, M. (1977), *Foreign Policy and the Democratic Process* (Greenwood Press, Westport, Conn.).

Bendor, J. and Hammond, T. H. (1992), 'Rethinking Allinson's Models', *American Political Science Review*, vol. 86, no. 2, pp. 301–22.

Bennett, A. Leroy (1988), *International Organizations: Principles and Issues*, fourth edition (Prentice Hall, Englewood Cliffs).

Bentham, J. (1970), *Introduction to the Principles of Morals and Legislation*, J. H. Burns and H. L. A. Hart (eds) (Oxford University Press, London, first published 1780).

Berdal, M. R. (1993), *Whither UN Peacekeeping*, Aldelphi Paper 281 (IISS, London).

Berki, R. N. (1971), 'On Marxian thought and the problem of International Relations', *World Politics*, **24** (1) (October) pp. 80–105.

Berridge, G. R. (1987), *International Politics: States, Power and Conflict Since 1945* (Harvester Wheatsheaf, Hemel Hempstead).

Berridge, G. R. (1992), *International Politics: States, Power and Conflict since 1945*, second edition, (Harvester Wheatsheaf, New York).

Berridge, G. R. (1995), *Diplomacy: Theory and Practice* (Harvester Wheatsheaf, London).

Bertalanffy, L. von (1967), 'General System Theory', in N. J. Demereth and R. A. Peterson (eds), *System, Change and Conflict* (Free Press, New York, pp. 115–29).

Best, G. (1980), *Humanity in Warfare: The Modern History of the International Law of Armed Conflicts* (Weidenfeld & Nicolson, London).

Best, G. (1994), *War and Law Since 1945* (Clarendon Press, Oxford).

Best, G. (1995), 'Justice, International Relations and Human Rights', *International Affairs*, **71** (4).

Betts, R. (1982), *Surprise Attack* (Brookings Institution, Washington D.C.).

Betts, R. (1987), *Nuclear Blackmail and Nuclear Balance* (Brookings Institution, Washington D.C.).

Binder, L. (1958), 'The Middle East as a Subordinate International System', *World Politics* **10** (3), 408–29.

Blake, D. H. and Walters, R. S. (1991), *The Politics of Global Economic Relations* (Prentice Hall, London).

Bobbitt, P., Freedman, L. and Treverton, G. (1989), *U.S. Nuclear Strategy: A Reader* (Macmillan, Basingstoke).

Bodin, J. (1955), *Six Books of the Commonwealth*, M. J. Tooley (abridged and tr) (Blackwell, Oxford).

Booth, K. (1979), *Strategy and Ethnocentrism* (Croom Helm, London).

Booth, K. (1985), *Law, Force and Diplomacy at Sea* (Allen & Unwin, London).

Booth, K. (1991), *New Thinking about Security and International Relations* (Harper-Collins, London).

Booth, K. and Smith, S. (1995), *International Relations Theory Today*, (Oxford University Press, Oxford).

Booth, K. and Vale, P. (1995), 'Security in Southern Africa: after apartheid, beyond realism', *Internationl Affairs*, vol. 71, no. 2, April.

Boulding, K. E. (1956), *The Image: Knowledge in Life and Society* (University of Michigan Press, Ann Arbor).

Boulding, K. (1962), *Conflict and Defense: A General Theory* (Harper & Row, New York).

Boulding, K. (1975), 'National Images and International Systems', in W. D. Copely and C. W. Kegley Jr (eds), *Analyzing International Relations* (Praeger, New York).

Boutros-Ghali, B. (1992), *An Agenda for Peace* (United Nations, New York).

Bowen, W. Q. and Dunn, D. H. (1996), *American Security Policy in the 1990s: Beyond Containment* (Dartmouth, Aldershot).

Bowers, P. (1997), *The Commonwealth*. Research Paper, 97/47, 29 April 1997, House of Commons Library.

Boyd, A. (1971), *Fifteen Men on a Powder Keg: A History of the UN Security Council* (Methuen, London).

Bozeman, A. B. (1994), *Politics and Culture in International History* (Transaction, New Brunswick).

Braybrooke, D. and Lindblom, C. E. (1963), *A Strategy of Decision* (Free Press, New York).

Brecher, M. (1963), 'International Relations and Asian Studies: The Subordinate State System of Southern Asia', *World Politics*, **15** (2) pp. 213–35.

Brecher, M. (1972), *The Foreign Policy System of Israel* (Oxford University Press, London).

Brecher, M. (1993), *Crises in World Politics: Theory and Reality* (Pergamon Press, Oxford).

Brenton, T. (1994), *The Greening of Machiavelli: The Evolution of International Environmental Politics* (Earthscan/RIIA, London).

Brewer, A. (1990), *Marxist Theories of Imperialism: A Critical Survey* (Routledge, London).

Brierly, J. L. (1958), *The Basis of Obligation in International Law and Other Papers*, H. Lauterpacht and C. H. M. Waldcock (eds) (Clarendon Press, Oxford).

Brierly, J. L. (1963), *The Law of Nations: An Introduction to the International Law of Peace* (Clarendon Press, Oxford).

Brodie, B. (1965), *Strategy in the Missile Age* (Princeton University Press, Princeton).

Bronfenbrenner, U. (1961), 'The Mirror-Image in Soviet–American Relations: A Psychologist's Report', *Journal of Social Issues*, **XVII** (3) pp. 45–57.

Brown, Chris (1992), *International Relations Theory: New Normative Approaches* (Harvester Wheatsheaf, Hemel Hempstead).

Brown, Chris (1994), 'Critical theory and postmodernism in International Relations' in *Contemporary International Relations: A Guide to Theory*, A. J. R. Groom & M. Light (eds) pp. 56–9 (Pinter, London).

Brown, C. (1997), *Understanding International Relations* (Macmillan, Basingstoke).

Brown, L. *et al.* (1989), *State of the World 1989* (W. W. Norton, New York).

Brown, L. R. (1990), *State of the World* (Allen & Unwin, London).

Brown, S. (1996), *International Relations in a Changing Global System* (Westview, Boulder).

Brownlie, I. (1963), *International Law and the Use of Force by States* (Oxford University Press, London).

Brownlie, I. (1967), *Basic Documents in International Law* (Clarendon Press, London).

Brownlie, I. (1973), *Principles of Public International Law* (Clarendon Press, London).

Brownlie, I. (ed) (1981), *Basic Documents on Human Rights* (Clarendon Press, London).

Buchan, A. (1966), *War in Modern Society* (Watts, London).

Bull, H. (1961), *The Control of the Arms Race: Disarmament and Arms Control in the Missile Age* (Weidenfeld & Nicolson, London).

Bull, H. (1966a), 'Grotian Conceptions of International Society', in Butterfield, H. and Wight, M. (eds) *Diplomatic Investigations* (Allen & Unwin, London).

Bull, H. (1966b), 'International Theory: The Case for a Classical Approach', *World Politics*, **18**, pp. 361–77.

Bull, H. (1977), *The Anarchical Society: A Study of Order in World Politics* (Macmillan, London).

Bull, H. (1979a), 'Recapturing the Just War for Political Theory', *World Politics*, **31** (4) (July) pp. 588–99.

Bull, H. (1979b), 'Natural Law and International Relations', *British Journal of International Studies*, **5** (2) (July) pp. 171–81.

Bull, H. (1984), *Intervention in World Politics* (Oxford University Press, London).

Bull, H. and Watson, A. (eds) (1984), *The Expansion of International Society* (Clarendon Press, London).

Bundy, McGeorge *et al.* (1984), 'Nuclear Weapons and the Atlantic Alliance', in F. Blackaby *et al.* (eds), *No-First-Use* (Taylor and Francis, London).

Burchill, S. and Linklater, A. (eds) (1996), *Theories of International Relations* (Macmillan, London).

Burton, J. W. (1965), *International Relations: A General Theory* (Cambridge University Press, Cambridge).

Burton, J. W. (1968), *Systems, States, Diplomacy and Rules* (Cambridge University Press, Cambridge).

Burton, J. W. (1969), *Conflict and Communication* (Macmillan, London).

Burton, J. W. (1972), *World Society* (Cambridge University Press, Cambridge).

Burton, J. W. (1990), *Conflict: Resolution and Prevention* (Macmillan, Basingstoke).

Butterfield, H. (1953), *Christianity, Diplomacy and War* (Epworth Press, London).

Butterfield, H. and Wight, M. (eds) (1966), *Diplomatic Investigations: Essays in the Theory of International Politics* (Allen & Unwin, London).

Buzan, B. (1987), *An Introduction to Strategic Studies: Military Technology and International Relations* (Macmillan Press for the International Institute for Strategic Studies, London).

Buzan, B. (1990), *People, States and Fear: The National Security Problem in International Relations* (Harvester Wheatsheaf, Hemel Hempstead).

Buzan, B., Jones, C. and Little, R. (1993), *The Logic of Anarchy: Neorealism to Structural Realism* (Columbia University Press, New York).

Calvert, P. (1984), *Revolution and International Politics* (Frances Pinter, London).

Calvert, P. (1986), *The Foreign Policy of New States* (St Martin's Press, New York).

Calvocoressi, P. (1997), *World Politics Since 1945*, seventh edition (Longman, London).

Calvocoressi, P. and Wint, G. (1974), *Total War* (Penguin, Harmondsworth).

Camilleri, J. A. and Falk, J. (1992), *The End of Sovereignty? The Politics of a Shrinking and Fragmenting World* (Edward Elgar, Aldershot).

Cardoso, F. and Faletto, E. (1979), *Dependency and Development in Latin America* (University of California Press, Berkeley).

Carpenter, T. G. (1992), *A Search for Enemies: America's Alliances after the Cold War* (Cato Institute, Washington D.C.).

Carr, E. H. (1946), *The Twenty Years' Crisis, 1919–1939* (Macmillan, London), originally published 1939.

Carrol, B. (1972), 'Peace Research: The Cult of Power, *Journal of Conflict Resolution*, **16** pp. 585–616.

Cavanagh, J., Wysham, D. and Arruda, M. (1994), *Beyond Bretton Woods: Alternatives to the Global Economic Order* (Pluto Press, London).

Charny, Israel W. (1988), *Genocide: A Critical Bibliographic Review* (Mansell, London).

Chase, R. S., Hill, E. B. and Kennedy, Paul (1996), 'Pivotal States and US Strategy', *Foreign Affairs*, **75** (1) pp. 33–52.

Childers, E. and Urquhart, B. (1994), 'Renewing the United Nations System', *Development Dialogue*, vol. 1 (Hammarskjöld Foundation, Uppsala).

Choucri, N. and North, R. (1975), *Nations in Conflict* (W. H. Freeman & Co., San Francisco).

Choudhury, G. W. (1993), *Islam and the Modern Muslim World* (Scorpion Publishing, Essex).

Clark, G. and Sohn, L. B. (1960), *World Peace Through World Law* (Harvard University Press, Cambridge MA).

Clark, I. (1980), *Reform and Resistance in the International Order* (Cambridge University Press, Cambridge).

Clark, I. (1988), 'Making Sense of Sovereignty', *Review of International Studies*, **14** (4) (October) pp. 303–8.

Clark, I. (1997), *Globalization and Fragmentation: International Relations in the Twentieth Century* (Oxford University Press, Oxford).

Claude, I. L. (1962), *Power and International Relations* (Random House, New York).

Claude, I. L. (1971), *Swords into Ploughshares: The Problems and Prospects of International Organization*, fourth edition (Random House, New York).

Claude, I. L. (1986a), *American Approaches to World Affairs* (University Press of America, Charlottesville).

Claude, I. L. (1986b), 'Myths About the State', *Review of International Studies* **12** (1) (January). pp. 1–12.

Clausewitz, C. M. von (1968), *On War*. A. Rapoport (ed) (Penguin Classics, Harmondsworth).

Cobban, A. (1969), *The Nation State and Self-Determination* (Collins, London).

Cohen, R. (1981), *International Politics: The Rules of the Game* (Longman, London).

Conybeare, J. A. (1987), *Trade Wars* (Columbia University Press, New York).

Cooper, A. F., Higgott, R. A. and Nossal, K. R. (1991), 'Bound to Follow? Leadership and Followership in the Gulf Conflict', *Political Science Quarterly*, vol. 106, no. 3, pp. 392–410.

Corbett, P. E. (1956), *Morals, Law and Power in International Relations* (J. R. and D. Hayes Foundation, Los Angeles).

Council on Environmental Quality and the U.S. Department of State (1982), *The Global 2000 Report to the President: Entering the Twenty-First Century* (Penguin, Harmondsworth).

Cox, R. (1979), 'Ideologies of the New International Economic Order: Reflections on Some Recent Literature', *International Organization*, **33** (2) pp. 257–302.

Cox, R. (1981), 'Social Forces, States and World Orders: Beyond International Relations Theory', *Millennium*, **10** pp. 126–55.

Cox, R. (1987), *Production, Power and World Order: Social Forces in the Making of History* (Columbia University Press, New York).

Cox, R. (1992), 'Towards a post-hegemonic conceptualization of world order' in J. N. Rosenau and E. O. Czempial (eds) *Governance without Government: Order and Change in World Politics* (Cambridge).

Crabb, C. V. (1965), *The Elephants and the Grass, A Study of Nonalignment* (Praeger, New York).

Czempial, E. O. and Rosenau, J. N. (eds) (1973), *Global Changes and Theoretical Challenges* (Lexington Books, Lexington).

Dahl, R. (1961a), *Who Governs?* (Yale University Press, New Haven).

Dahl, R. (1961b), 'The Behavioural Approach in Political Science: Epitaph for a Monument to a Successful Protest', *American Political Science Review*, **55** (4) (December) pp. 763–72.

Dahl, R. (1984), *Modern Political Analysis*, fourth edition (Prentice Hall, Englewood Cliffs).

Danchev, A. (ed) (1995), *Fin de Siècle: The Meaning of the Twentieth Century* (I. B. Tauris, London).

Davidson, B. (1992), *The Black Man's Burden* (Random House, New York).

Davies, James C. (1969), 'The J curve of rising and declining satisfactions as a cause of some great revolutions and contained rebellion' in H. D. Graham and T. R. Gurr (eds), *The History of Violence in America* (New York).

Day, A. J. (ed) (1987), *Border and Territorial Boundaries*, second edition (Longman, Harlow).

De Conde, A. (ed) (1978), *Encyclopedia of American Foreign Policy: Studies of Principal Movements and Ideas* (Scribner, New York).

Dehio, L. (1965), *The Precarious Balance* (Knopf, New York).

Del Rosso Jr., S. J. (1995), 'The Insecure State: Reflections on "the State" and "Security", in a Changing World', *Daedalus*, **124** (2) pp. 175–208.

Der Derian, J. (1987), *On Diplomacy: A Genealogy of Western Estrangement* (Basil Blackwell, Oxford).

Der Derian, J. and Shapiro, M. (eds) (1989), *International/Intertextual Relations: Postmodern Readings in World Politics* (Lexington Books, Lexington).

Der Derian, J. (1992), *Antidiplomacy: Spies, Terror, Speed and War* (Blackwell, Oxford).

Deudney, D. (1990), 'The Case Against Linking Environmental Degradation and National Security', *Millennium*, **19** (3) pp. 461–76.

Deudney, D. (1995), 'Environment and Security: Muddled Thinking' in *The Global Agenda: Issues and Perspectives* in C. W. Kegley, Jr and E. R. Wittkopf (eds) (McGraw Hill, New York).

Deutsch, K. (1953), *Nationalism and Social Communications* (MIT Press, Cambridge).

Deutsch, K. (1963), *The Nerves of Government* (Free Press, New York).

Deutsch, K. W. (1968), *The Analysis of International Relations* (Prentice Hall, Englewood Cliffs).

Deutsch, K. and Singer, J. D. (1964), 'Multipolar Systems and International Stability', *World Politics*, **16** (April) pp. 390–406.

Devetak, R. (1996), 'Postmodernism' in *Theories of International Relations*, S. Burchill and A. Linklater (eds) (Macmillan, Basingstoke).

Dickinson, G. L. (1916), *The European Anarchy* (Allen & Unwin, London).

Dickinson, G. L. (1926), *The International Anarchy* (Allen & Unwin, London).

Donelan, M. (ed) (1978), *The Reason of States: A Study in International Political Theory* (George Allen & Unwin, London).

Donnelly, J. (1993), *International Human Rights* (Westview Press, Boulder).

Dougherty, J. E. and Pfaltzgraff, R. L. (1981), *Contending Theories of International Relations* (Harper and Row, New York).

Doxey, M. (1971), *Economic Sanctions and International Enforcement* (Oxford University Press, London).

Doyle, M. (1986), 'Liberalism and World Politics', *American Political Science Review*, **80** pp. 1151–70.

Dunant, H. (1947), *A Memory of Solferino* (Cassell, London).

Dunn, D. (1995), 'Articulating an alternative: the contribution of John Burton', *Review of Internationl Studies*, vol. 21, no. 2 (April), pp. 197–208.

Dunn, L. A. (1991), *Containing Nuclear Proliferation*, Adelphi Paper 263 (Brassey's, London).

Easton, D. (1969), 'The New Revolution in Political Science', *American Political Science Review*, **58** (4) (December) pp. 1051–61.

Edwardes, M. (1962), *Asia in the Balance* (Penguin, Harmondsworth).

Ekins, P. (1992), *A New World Order: Grassroots Movements for Global Change* (Routledge, London).

Elshtain, J. B. (1987), *Women and War* (Harvester Wheatsheaf, Brighton).

Elshtain, J. B. (ed) (1981), *Public Man, Private Woman* (Martin Robertson, Oxford).

Encloe, C. (1989), *Bananas, Beaches and Bases* (Pandora Books, London).

Encloe, C. (1993), *The Morning After: Sexual Politics at the End of the Cold War* (University of California Press, Berkeley).

Esposito, J. L. (1995), *The Islamic Threat: Myth or Reality?* (Open University Press, New York).

Evans, G. (1981), 'All States are Equal, but. . .', *Review of International Studies* **7** pp. 59–66.

Evans, G. (1994), 'The International Community and the Transition to a New South Africa', *The Round Table* **330** pp. 175–87.

Evans, G. (1996), 'South Africa in Remission: the Foreign Policy of an Altered State', *The Journal of Modern African Studies* **34** (2) pp. 249–71.

Evans, G. (1997), 'The Vision Thing: in search of the Clinton Doctrine' *World Today* **53** (8–9) (August/September) pp. 213–16.

Eysenck, H. J. (1954), *The Psychology of Politics* (RKP, London).

Faber, M. (1984), 'Island Microstates: Problems of Viability', *The Round Table*, **292** (October) pp. 372–76.

Falk, R. A. (1970), *The Status of Law in International Society* (Princeton University Press, Princeton).

Falk, R. A. (1971), *This Endangered Planet* (Random House, New York).

Falk, R. A. (1975), *A Study of Future Worlds* (Free Press, New York).

Falk, R. A. (1995), *On Human Governance: Toward a New Global Politics* (Polity Press, Cambridge).

Farrell, R. B. (1966), *Approaches to Comparative and International Politics* (Northwestern University Press, Evanston).

Fawcett, L. and Hurrell, A. (eds) (1995), *Regionalism in World Politics: Regional Organisation and International Order* (Oxford University Press, Oxford).

Fink, C. F. and Boulding, E. (eds) (1972), 'Peace Research in Transition: A Symposium', *Journal of Conflict Resolution*, Special Issue, **xvi** (4) pp. 461–616.

Fisas, V. (1995), *Blue Geopolitics. The United Nations Reform and the Future of the Blue Helmets* (Pluto Press, London).

Fisher, R. and Brown, S. (1988), *Getting Together: Building a Relationship That Leads to YES* (Houghton Mifflin, Boston).

Fisher, R., Ury, W. and Patton, B. (1981), *Getting to YES: Negotiating Agreement without Giving In* (Houghton Mifflin, Boston).

Fleiss, P. J. (1966), *Thucydides and the Politics of Bipolarity* (Louisiana State University Press, Baton Rouge).

Forsythe, D. P. (1977), *Humanitarian Politics: The International Committee of the Red Cross* (Johns Hopkins University Press, Baltimore).

Forsyth, M. G., Keens-Soper, M. and Savigear, P. (eds) (1970), *The Theory of International Relations: The State of War* (Allen & Unwin, London).

Forsyth, M. (1979), 'Thomas Hobbes and the External Relations of States', *British Journal of International Studies* **5** (3) (October) pp. 196–209.

Forsyth, M. (1989), *Federalism and Nationalism* (Leicester University Press, Leicester and London).

Fox, W. T. R. (1944), *The Super-Powers: The United States, Britain and the Soviet Union – their Responsibility for the Peace* (Harcourt, Brace, New York).

Frank, A. G. (1971), *Capitalism and Underdevelopment in Latin America* (Penguin, Harmondsworth).

Frank, A. G. and Gills, B. (eds) (1993), *The World System: Five Hundred Years or Five Thousand Years* (Routledge, London).

Frankel, J. (1963), *The Making of Foreign Policy: An Analysis of Decision Making* (Oxford University Press, London).

Frankel, J. (1970), *The National Interest* (Pall Mall and Macmillan, London).

Freedman, L. (1981), *The Evolution of Nuclear Strategy* (Macmillan, London).

Freedman, L. (1988), *Britain and the Falklands War* (Blackwell, London).

Freedman, L. (ed.) (1994), *War* (Oxford University Press, Oxford).

Freedman, L. (1997), 'War Designed for One', *World Today* 53 (8–9) (August/ September) pp. 217–22.

Freedman, L. *et al.* (1986), *Terrorism and International Order* (Routledge, London).

Frieden, J. A. and Lake, D. A. (eds) (1995), *International Political Economy: Perspectives on Global Wealth and Power* (Routledge, London).

Frost, M. (1996), *Ethics in International Relations* (Cambridge University Press, Cambridge).

Fukuyama, F. (1992), *The End of History and the Last Man* (Hamish Hamilton, London).

Gaddis, J. L. (1983), 'Containment: Its Past and Future', in C. W. Kegley, Jr and E. R. Wittkopf (eds), *Perspectives on American Foreign Policy*, (St Martins Press, New York).

Gaddis, J. L. (1986), 'The Long Peace: Elements of Stability in the Postwar International System', *International Security*, 10 (4).

Gallie, W. B. (1978), *Philosophers of Peace and War: Kant, Clausewitz, Marx, Engels and Tolstoy* (Cambridge University Press, Cambridge).

Gamble, A. and Payne, T. (eds) (1996), *Regionalism and World Order* (Macmillan, London).

Gardner, R. N. (1980), *Sterling–Dollar Diplomacy in Current Perspective: The Origins and Prospects of our International Economic Order* (Columbia University Press, New York).

Garnett, J. C. (1984), *Commonsense and the Theory of International Politics* (Macmillan, London).

Garthoff, R. (1994a), *The Great Transition: American–Soviet Relations and the End of the Cold War* (Brookings Institute, Washington).

Garthoff, R. (1994b) *Detente and Confrontation* (Brookings Institute, Washington).

GATT (1979), *The Tokyo Round of Multilateral Trade Negotiations* (Gatt, Geneva).

Geldenhuys, D. (1984), *The Diplomacy of Isolation: South African Foreign Policy Making* (Macmillan, Johannesburg).

Gellner, E. (1983), *Nations and Nationalism* (Blackwell, Oxford).

George, A. and George, J. (1964), *Woodrow Wilson & Colonial House: a Personality Study* (Dover, New York).

George, A. L. (1971), *The Limits of Coercive Diplomacy* (Little Brown, Boston).

George, J. (1994), *Discourses of Global Politics: A Critical (Re)Introduction to International Relations* (Lynne Reinner, Boulder).

Giddens, A. (1985), *The Nation-State and Violence* (Polity Press, Cambridge, USA).

Gill, S. (ed) (1993), *Gramsci, Historical Materialism and International Relations* (Cambridge University Press, Cambridge).

Gill, S. and Law, D. (1988), *The Global Political Economy* (Harvester Wheatsheaf, Hemel Hempstead).

Gilpin, R. (1975), *U.S. Power and Multinational Corporation* (Basic Books, New York).

Gilpin, R. (1981), *War and Change in World Politics* (Cambridge University Press, Cambridge).

Gilpin, R. (1985), 'The Politics of Transnational Economic Relations', in R. Maghroori and B. Ramberg (eds), *Globalism Versus Realism: International Relations' Third Debate* (Westview Press, Boulder, Colorado).

Gilpin, R. (1986), 'The Richness of the Tradition of Political Realism' in R. O. Keohane (ed), *Neorealism and Its Critics* (Columbia University Press, New York).

Gilpin, R. (1987), *The Political Economy of International Relations* (Princeton University Press, Princeton).

Gordenker, L. (1987), *Refugees in International Politics* (Columbia University Press, New York).

Gowa, J. (1983), *Closing the Gold Window: Domestic Politics and the End of Bretton Woods* (Cornell University Press, Ithaca).

Grant, R. and Newland, K. (eds) (1991), *Gender and International Relations* (Bloomingtons, University of Indiana Press).

Greenwood, C. (1993), 'Is there a right of humanitarian intervention?' *The World Today, 49.*

Griffiths, M. (1992), *Realism, Idealism and International Politics: A Reinterpretation* (Routledge, London).

Groom, A. J. R. and Light, M. (1994), *Contemporary International Relations: A Guide to Theory* (Pinter, London).

Groom, A. J. R. and Taylor, P. (eds) (1975), *Functionalism: Theory and Practice in World Politics* (University of London Press, London).

Grossner, A. (1980), *The Western Alliance: European–American Relations Since 1945* (foreword by Stanley Hoffman) (Macmillan, London).

Grotius, H. (1949), *The Law and Peace (De Jure Belli ac Pacis)* tr. L. R. Loomis, introduction P. E. Corbett (Walter J. Black, New York).

Grubb, M. *et al.* (1993), *The Earth Summit Agreements: A Guide and Assessment* (Earthscan/RIIA, London).

Guicciardini, F. (1567), *Storia d'Italia (1573)* (Torretino, Florence).

Gulick, E. V. (1967), *Europe's Classical Balance of Power* (Norton, New York, first published 1955).

Gurr, T. R. (1993), *Minorities at Risk: A Global View of Ethnopolitical Conflict,* (United States Institute of Peace, Washington).

Gurr, T. R. and Harff, B. (1994), *Ethnic Conflict in World Politics* (Westview Press, Boulder).

Haas, E. B. (1953), 'The Balance of Power: Prescription, Concept or Propaganda', *World Politics* **5** (July) pp. 442–77.

Haas, E. B. (1958), *The Uniting of Europe* (Stevens, London; Stanford University Press, Stanford).

Haas, E. B. (1964), *Beyond the Nation State: Functionalism and International Organization* (Stanford University Press, Stanford).

Haas, P. M. (1989), 'Do Regimes Matter: Epistemic Communities and Mediterranean Pollution Control', *International Organisation*, **43** pp. 377–403.

Haas, P. M. (1990), *Saving the Mediterranean: The Politics of Environmental Cooperation* (Columbia University Press, New York).

Haas, P. M. (ed) (1992), 'Knowledge, Power and International Policy Coordination', *International Organisation* (special issue) **46** (1).

Haas, P. M., Keohane, R. O. and Levy, M. (eds) (1994), *Institutions for the Earth: Sources of Effective Environmental Protection* (MA. MIT Press, Cambridge).

Halliday, F. (1995), *Islam and the Myth of Confrontation: Religion and Politics in the Middle East* (I. B. Tauris, London).

Halperin, M. (1963), *Limited War in the Nuclear Age* (John Wiley, New York).

Halperin, M. H. (1974), *Bureaucratic Politics and Foreign Policy* (The Brookings Institution, Washington DC).

Hansen, R. D. (1979), *Beyond the North–South Stalemate* (McGraw Hill, New York).

Hardin, G. (1977), 'The Tragedy of the Commons', in G. Hardin and J. Baden (eds), *Managing the Commons* (Freeman, San Francisco).

Harris, N. (1986), *The End of the Third World* (Penguin, Harmondsworth).

Hayter, T. (1971), *Aid as Imperialism* (Penguin, Baltimore).

Held, D. (1995), *Democracy and the Global Order* (Polity Press, Cambridge, USA).

Hermann, C. F. (1969), 'International Crisis as a Situational Variable', in J. N. Rosenau (ed), *International Politics and Foreign Policy* (Free Press, New York), pp. 409–21.

Hermann, C. F. (ed) (1972), *International Crisis: Insights from Behavioural Research* (Free Press, New York).

Herz, J. H. (1950), 'Idealist Internationalism and the Security Dilemma', *World Politics*, **2** (2) (January) pp. 157–80.

Herz, J. H. (1951), *Political Realism and Political Idealism* (Chicago University Press, Chicago).

Herz, J. H. (1957), 'Rise and Demise of the Territorial State', *World Politics* **9** pp. 473–93.

Herz, J. H. (1959), *International Politics in the Atomic Age* (Columbia University Press, New York).

Higgins, R. (1978), 'Conceptual Thinking about the Individual in International Law', *British Journal of International Studies*, **3** (1) (April).

Hinsley, F. H. (1963), *Power and the Pursuit of Peace: Theory and Practice in the History of Relations between States* (Cambridge University Press, Cambridge).

Hinsley, F. H. (1973), *Nationalism and the International System* (Hodder & Stoughton, London).

Hinsley, F. H. (1982), 'The Rise and Fall of the Modern International System', *Review of International Studies*, **8** (1) (January) pp. 1–8.

Hinsley, F. H. (1986), *Sovereignty* (Cambridge University Press, Cambridge).

Hipper, J. and Luege, A. (1995), *The Next Threat: Western Perceptions of Islam* (Pluto Press, London).

Hobbes, T. (1965), *Leviathan* (introduction A. D. Lindsay) (Everyman edition, Dent, London).

Hobson, J. A. (1938), *Imperialism: A Study*, third edition (Allen & Unwin, London, first published 1902).

Hocking, B. and Smith, M. (1995), *World Politics. An Introduction to International Relations*, second edition (Prentice Hall/Harvester Wheatsheaf, Hemel Hempstead).

Hoffman, M. (1987), 'Critical Theory and the Inter-Paradigm Debate', *Millennium* **16** (2) pp. 231–49.

Hoffman, M. (1994), 'Normative International Theory: Approaches and Issues' in *Contemporary International Relations: A Guide to Theory*, A. J. R. Groom and M. Light (eds) (Pinter, London).

Hoffman, S. (1965), *The State of War* (Pall Mall, London).

Hoffman, S. (1968), *Gulliver's Troubles or the Setting of American Foreign Policy* (McGraw Hill, New York).

Hoffman, S. (1978), *Primacy or World Order: American Foreign Policy Since the Cold War* (McGraw Hill, New York).

Hoffman, S. 'In Defence of Mother Teresa: Morality in Foreign Policy', *Foreign Affairs* **75** (2) pp. 172–5.

Hogan, M. (ed) (1992), *The End of the Cold War* (Cambridge University Press, Cambridge).

Holbraad, C. (1970), *The Concert of Europe: A Study in German and British International Thought, 1815–1914* (Longman, Harlow).

Holbraad, C. (ed) (1971), *Superpowers and World Order* (Australian National University Press, Canberra).

Holbraad, C. (1984), *Middle Powers in International Politics* (Macmillan, London).

Hollis, M. and Smith, S. (1991), 'Beware of gurus: structure and action in international relations', *Review of International Studies* **17** (4) pp. 393–410.

Hollis, M. (1995), and Smith, S. (1991), *Explaining and Understanding International Relations* (Clarendon Press, Oxford).

Holloway, D. (1988/89), 'Gorbachev's New Thinking', *Foreign Affairs*, **68** (1) pp. 66–81.

Holsti, D. (1992), *International Politics: A Framework for Analysis*, sixth edition (Prentice Hall, Englewood Cliffs).

Holsti, K. J. (1985), *The Dividing Discipline: Hegemony and Diversity in International Theory* (Allen & Unwin, Boston).

Holsti, O. R. and Rosenau, J. N. (1984), *American Leadership in World Affairs: Vietnam and the Breakdown of Consensus* (Allen & Unwin, Boston).

Hopkins, R. F. and Mansbach, R. W. (1973), *Structures and Process in International Theory* (Harper and Row, New York).

Horowitz, D. (1969), *Imperialism and Revolution* (Allen Lane, London).

Howard, M. (1978), 'The Strategic Approach to International Relations', *British Journal of International Studies*, **2** (1) (April) pp. 67–75.

Howard, M. (1978), *War and the Liberal Conscience* (Temple Smith, London).

Howard, M. (1984), *The Causes of War* (Unwin, London).

Hsü, I. C. Y. (1960), *China's Entrance into the Family of Nations* (Harvard University Press, Cambridge, MA).

Hunt, P. and Thompson, G. (1996), *Globalization in Question* (Polity Press, Cambridge, USA).

Huntington, S. P. (1973), 'Transnational Organisation in World Politics', *World Politics*, **25** (3) (August). pp. 333–68.

Huntington, S. P. (1993), 'The Clash of Civilizations', *Foreign Affairs* **72** (3) (summer) pp. 22–49.

Hurrell, A. (1995), 'Explaining the Resurgence of Regionalism in World Politics', *Review of International Studies*, **21** (4).

Hurrell, A. and Kingsbury, B. (eds) (1992), *The International Politics of the Environment* (Oxford University Press, Oxford).

Huth, P. K. (1988), *Extended Deterrence and the Prevention of War* (Yale University Press, New Haven).

Iklé, F. C. (1964), *How Nations Negotiate* (Harper and Row, New York).

Jackson, R. H. (1986), 'Negative Sovereignty in sub-Saharan Africa', *Review of International Studies*, **12** (4) (October) pp. 247–64.

Jackson, R. H. (1990), *Quasi-States: Sovereignty, International Relations and the Third World.* (Cambridge University Press, Cambridge).

James, A. (1964), 'Power Politics', *Political Studies*, **12** (3) (October) pp. 307–26.

James, A. (1969), *The Politics of Peace-Keeping* (Chatto and Windus, London).

James, A. (1973), *The Bases of International Order: Essays in Honour of C. A. W. Manning* (Oxford University Press, London).

James, A. (1978), 'International Society', *British Journal of International Studies*, **4** (2) (July) pp. 91–106.

James, A. (1984), 'Sovereignty: Ground Rule or Gibberish?', *Review of International Studies*, **10** pp. 1–18.

James, A. (1986), *Sovereign Statehood: The Basis of International Society* (Allen & Unwin, London).

James, A. (1990), *Peacekeeping in International Politics* (IISS/Macmillan, Basingstoke).

Janis, I. (1972), *Victims of Groupthink* (Houghton Mifflin, Boston).

Jervis, R. (1976), *Perception and Misperception in International Politics* (Princeton University Press, Princeton).

Jervis, R. (1978), 'Co-operation Under the Security Dilemma', *World Politics*, **30** (2) (January) pp. 167–214.

Jervis, R. (1984), *The Illogic of American Nuclear Strategy* (Cornell University Press, Ithaca).

Jervis, R. (1985), 'From Balance to Concert: A Study of International Security Co-operation', *World Politics*, **38** (1) (October) pp 58–79.

Johnson, C. (1982), *MITI and the Japanese Miracle* (Stanford University Press, Stanford).

Jones, R. E. (1981), 'The English School of International Relations: A Case for Closure', *Review of International Studies* **7** (1) (January) pp. 1–14.

Kahn, H. (1960), *On Thermonuclear War* (Princeton University Press, Princeton).

Kaiser, K. (1968), *German Foreign Policy in Transition: Bonn between East and West* (Oxford University Press, London).

Kant, I. (1948), 'On Eternal Peace', tr. in Carl J. Friedrich, *Inevitable Peace* (Harvard University Press, Cambridge MA).

Kaplan, L. S. (1984), *The United States and NATO: The Formative Years* (Kentucky University Press, Lexington).

Kaplan, M. A. (1957), *System and Process in International Politics* (Wiley, New York).

Kaplan, M. A. and Katzenbach, N. de B. (1961), *The Political Foundations of International Law* (Wiley, New York).

Kaplan, M. A. (1966), 'The New Great Debate: Traditionalism vs. Science in International Relations', *World Politics*, **19** (1) (October) pp. 1–20.

Kaplan, R. D. (1994), 'The Coming Anarchy', *Atlantic Monthly*, February.

Kaufmann, W. (1989), 'The Requirements of Deterrence', in P. Bobbit *et al.*, *US Nuclear Strategy* (Macmillan, London), pp. 168–90.

Keens-Soper, M. (1978), 'The Practice of a States System', in *The Reason of States*, M. Donelan (ed) (Allen & Unwin, London), pp. 25–44.

Kegley, C. W. (1995), *Controversies in International Relations Theory* (St Martin's Press, New York).

Kegley, C. W. and Wittkopf, E. R. (1995), *World Politics: Trend and Transformation*, fifth edition (St Martin's Press, New York).

Kegley, C. W. and Wittkopf, E. R. (1996) fifth edition, *American Foreign Policy: Pattern and Process* (St Martin's Press, New York).

Kegley, C. W. and Wittkopf, E. R. (1995), *The Global Agenda* (McGraw-Hill, New York).

Kellas, J. G. (1991), *The Politics of Nationalism and Ethnicity* (Macmillan, London).

Kelsen, H. (1967), *Principles of International Law* (revised and edited R. W. Tucker) (Rhinehart and Winston, New York).

Kennan, G. F. (1954a), *Realities of American Foreign Policy* (Princeton University Press, Princeton).

Kennan, G. F. (1954b), *American Diplomacy, 1900–1950* (New American Library, New York).

Kennan, G. F. (1984), *American Diplomacy*, expanded edition (University of Chicago Press, Chicago).

Kennedy, P. (1988), *The Rise and Fall of the Great Powers* (Random House, New York).

Kennedy, P. (1994), *Preparing for the Twenty-First Century* (Fontana, London).

Keohane, R. O. (1984), *After Hegemony* (Princeton University Press, Princeton).

Keohane, R. O. (1985), 'Achieving Cooperation under Anarchy: Strategies and Institutions', *World Politics* **38** (October) pp. 226–54

Keohane, R. O. (ed.) (1986), *Neorealism and Its Critics* (Columbia University Press, New York).

Keohane, R. O. and Nye, J. S. (eds) (1972), *Transnational Relations and World Politics* (Harvard University Press, Cambridge MA).

Keohane, R. O. and Nye, J. S. (1977), *Power and Interdependence: World Politics in Transition* (Little, Brown, Boston).

Keohane, R. O. and Nye, J. E. (1981), 'Realism and Complex Interdependence', in Smith, M., Little, R. and Shackelton, M. (eds), *Perspectives on World Politics* (Croom Helm, London), pp. 120–131.

Keohane, R. O. and Nye J. S. (1987), 'Power and Interdependence Revisited', *International Organization*, **41** (4) pp. 725–53.

Keylor, W. R. (1984), *The Twentieth-Century World* (Oxford University Press, London).

Keynes, J. M. (1919), *The Economic Consequences of Peace* (Macmillan, London).

Kindleberger, C. P. (1973), *The World in Depression 1929–1939* (University of California Press, Berkeley).

Kissinger, H. A. (1957), *A World Restored: The Politics of Conservatism in a Revolutionary Era* (Houghton Mifflin, Boston).

Kissinger, H. A. (1960), *The Necessity for Choice: Prospects of American Foreign Policy* (Chatto & Windus, London).

Kissinger, H. A. (1969), *Nuclear Weapons and Foreign Policy* (Norton, New York).

Kissinger, H. A. (1974), *American Foreign Policy* (Norton, New York).

Kissinger, H. A. (1979), *The White House Years* (Little, Brown, Boston).

Kissinger, H. A. (1994), *Diplomacy* (Simon and Schuster, London).

Kitson, F. (1971), *Low Intensity Operations* (Faber & Faber, London).

Knorr, K. (1956), *The War Potential of Nations* (Princeton University Press, New Jersey).

Knorr, K. (1973), *Power and Wealth: The Political Economy of International Power* (Basic Books, New York).

Knorr, K. (1975), *The Power of Nations: The Political Economy of International Relations* (Basic Books, New York).

Knorr, K. and Rosenau, J. N. (eds) (1969), *Contending Approaches to International Politics* (Princeton University Press, Princeton).

Knorr, K. and Verba, S. (eds) (1961), *The International System* (Princeton University Press, Princeton).

Krasner, S. D. (1976), 'State power and the structure of international trade', *World Politics*, **28** (3) (April) pp. 317–43.

Krasner, S. D. (1983), *International Regimes* (Cornell University Press, Ithaca, New York).

Krasner, S. D. (1985), *Structural Conflict: The Third World against Global Liberalism* (University of California Press, Berkeley).

Krasner, S. D. (1993), 'Westphalia and All That', in *Ideas and Foreign Policy: Beliefs, Institutions and Political Change*, J. Goldstein and R.O. Keohane (eds) (Cornell University Press, New York).

Kratchowil, F. (1989), *Rules, Norms and Decisions* (Cambridge University Press, Cambridge).

Kratchowil, F. and Mansfield, E. (eds) (1994), *International Organisation: A Reader* (HarperCollins, New York).

Krepinevich, A. F. (1989), *The Army and Vietnam* (Free Press, New York).

Kubalkova, V. and Cruickshank, A. A. (1980), *Marxism-Leninism and Theory of International Relations* (Routledge & Kegan Paul, London).

Kubalkova, V. and Cruickshank, A. A. (1986), *Marxism and International Relations* (Oxford University Press, Oxford).

Kuhn, T. (1962), *The Structure of Scientific Revolutions* (University of Chicago Press, Chicago).

Lacqueur, W. (1977), *Terrorism* (Weidenfeld & Nicolson, London).

Lacqueur, W. (1986), 'Reflections on Terrorism', *Foreign Affairs*, **65** (Fall) pp. 86–100.

Lakatos, I. and Musgrave A. (eds) (1970), *Criticism and the Growth of Knowledge* (Cambridge University Press, Cambridge).

Langhorne, R. (1986), 'The Significance of the Congress of Vienna', *Review of International Studies*, **12** (4) (October) pp. 313–24.

Lapid, Y. (1989), 'The Third Debate: On the Prospects of International Theory in a Post-Positivist Era', *International Studies Quarterly*, **33** (3).

Lapping, B. (1987), *Apartheid: A History* (Paladin, London).

Lasswell, H. D. (1948), *The Analysis of Political Behaviour: An Empirical Approach* (Routledge and Kegan Paul, London).

Lasswell, H. D. and Kaplan, A. (1950), *Power and Society: A Framework for Political Enquiry* (Yale University Press, New Haven).

Lauterpacht, H. (1933), *The Function of Law in the International Community* (Clarendon Press, Oxford).

Lauterpacht, H. (1950), *International Law and Human Rights* (Stevens, London).

Lawrence, T. E. (1935), *Seven Pillars of Wisdom: A Triumph* (Cape, London).

Layne, C. (1994), 'Kant or Cant: the Myth of Democratic Peace', *International Security* **19** (2) pp. 5–50.

Lebow, R. N. (1981), *Between Peace and War* (Johns Hopkins University Press, Baltimore).

Lebow, R. N. and Risse-Kappen T. (eds) (1995), *International Relations Theory and the End of the Cold War* (Columbia University Press, New York).

Lebow, R. N. and Stein, J. G. (1994), *We All Lost the Cold War* (Princeton University Press, New Jersey.).

Leffler, M. (1992), *A Preponderance of Power* (Stanford University Press, California).

Leffler, M. and Painter, D. (eds) (1994), *Origins of the Cold War: An International History* (Routledge, New York).

Lemkin, R. (1944), *Axis Rule in Occupied Europe* (Carnegie Endowment for World Peace, Washington DC).

Lenin, V. I. (1970), *Imperialism: The Highest Stage of Capitalism (1916)* (Foreign Languages Press, Peking).

Levy, J. (1983), 'Misperception and the Causes of War', *World Politics*, **36** (October) pp. 76–99.

Lichtheim, G. (1971), *Imperialism* (Praeger, New York).

Lindblom, C. E. (1965), *The Intelligence of Democracy* (Free Press, New York).

Lindblom, C. E. (1977), *Politics and Markets* (Basic Books, New York).

Linklater, A. (1986), 'Realism, Marxism and Critical International Theory', *Review of International Studies*, **12** (4) (October) pp. 301–12.

Linklater, A. (1990), *Beyond Realism and Marxism* (Macmillan, London).

Linklater, A. (1990), *Men and Citizens in International Theory* (Macmillan, London).

Liska, G. (1967), *Imperial America: The International Politics of Primacy* (Johns Hopkins Press, Baltimore).

Little, R. (1975), *Intervention: External Involvement in Civil Wars* (Robertson, London).

Little, R. (1987), 'Revisiting Intervention: A Survey of Recent Developments', *Review of International Studies*, **13** (1) (January) pp. 49–60.

Little, R. and Smith, M. (eds) (1991), *Perspectives on World Politics: A Reader* (Routledge, London).

Lorenz, K. (1963), *On Aggression* (Harcourt, Brace and World, New York).

Louis, W. R. and Bull, H. (eds) (1986), *The Special Relationship: Anglo-American Relations Since 1945* (Clarendon Press, Oxford).

Luard, E. (1982), *A History of the United Nations* (Macmillan, London).

Luard, E. (1990), *The Globalization of Politics* (Macmillan, London).

Lynne-Jones, S. M. and Miller, S. (eds) (1995), *Global Dangers: Changing Dimensions of International Security* (MA: MIT Press, Cambridge).

Lyon, P. (1963), *Neutralism* (Leicester University Press, Leicester).

Lyons, G. M. and Mastanduno, M. (1995), *Beyond Westphalia? State Sovereignty and International Intervention* (Johns Hopkins, Baltimore/London).

Machiavelli, N. (1950), *The Prince and the Discourses*, introduction Max Lerner (Modern Library edition, Random House, New York).

Mack, A. J. R. (1975), 'Why Big Nations Lose Small Wars: The Politics of Asymmetric Conflict', *World Politics*, **27** (2) pp. 175–201.

Mackinder, H. J. (1904), 'The Geographical Pivot of History', *Geographical Journal*, **23**.

Mackinder, H. J. (1919), *Democratic Ideals and Reality: A Study in the Politics of Reconstruction* (Constable, London).

Mahan, A. T. (1890), *The Influence of Sea Power upon History: 1660–1783* (Boston).

Malthus, T. R. (1826), *An Essay in the Principles of Population, or a view of its past and present effects on human happiness, with an enquiry into our prospecting the future removal or mitigation of the evils which it occasions*, 6th edition (Ward Lock, London).

Mandelbaum, M. (1988), *The Fate of Nations: The Search for National Security in the Nineteenth and Twentieth Centuries* (Cambridge University Press, Cambridge).

Mandelbaum, M. (1996), 'Foreign Policy as Social Work', *Foreign Affairs* **75** (1).

Manning, C. A. W. (1962), *The Nature of International Society* (Bell, London).

Mao Tse-Tung (1971), *Selected Readings* (Foreign Languages Press, Peking).

March, J. G. and Simon, H. A. (1958), *Organizations* (Wiley, New York).

Markwell, D. J. (1986), 'Sir Alfred Zimmern revisited: 50 years on', *Review of International Studies* **12** (4) (October) pp. 279–392.

Marx, K. and Engels, F. (1968), *Selected Works* (Lawrence and Wishart, London).

Mattingly, G. (1955), *Renaissance Diplomacy* (Cape, London).

Mayall, J. (ed) (1982), *The Community of States: A Study in International Political Theory* (Allen & Unwin, London).

Mayall, J. (1990), *Nationalism and International Society* (Cambridge University Press, Cambridge).

Mayall, J. (ed) (1996), *The New Interventionism: 1991–94* (Cambridge University Press, Cambridge).

Mayer, P. (ed) (1966), *The Pacifist Conscience: An Anthology of Pacifist Writings* (Hart-Davies, London).

Mazrui, A. (1977), *Africa's International Relations: The Diplomacy of Dependency and Change* (Heinemann, London).

McClelland, C. (1966), *Theory and the International System* (Macmillan, New York).

McGrew, A. (ed) (1994), *Empire* (Hodder and Stoughton for the Open University, London).

McGrew, A. *et al.* (1992), *Global Politics: Globalisation and the Nation State* (Open University Press, Milton Keynes).

McKinlay, R. D. and Little, R. (1986), *Global Problems and World Order* (Pinter, London).

Meadows, D. H. *et al.* (1992), *Beyond the Limits: Global Collapse or a Sustainable Future?* (Earthscan, London).

Meadows, D. H., Meadows, D. L., Randers, J. and Behrens, W. III (1974), *The Limits to Growth* (Pan, London).

Mearsheimer, J. (1990), 'Back to the Future: Instability in Europe after the Cold War', *International Security* **19** pp. 5–56.

Medvedev, Z. (1986), *Gorbachev* (Blackwell, London).

Meinecke, F. (1957), *Machiavellism: The Doctrine of Raison d'Etat and Its Place in Modern History* (tr. D. Scott) (New Haven, Conn).

Melanson, R. A. (1983), *Writing History and Making Policy: The Cold War, Vietnam, and Revisionism* (Press of America, Lanham).

Melman, S. (1985), *The Permanent War Economy* (Simon & Schuster, New York).

Merle, M. (1987), *The Sociology of International Relations* (tr. D. Parkin) (Berg, Leamington Spa).

Merton, R. K. (1949), 'The Self-Fulfilling Prophecy', in *Social Theory and Social Structure* (Free Press, New York, 1957).

Midlarsky, M. I. (ed) (1992), *The Internationalisation of Communal Strife* (Routledge, London).

Miller, J. D. B. (1981), *The World of States* (Croom Helm, London).

Miller, J. D. B. (1986), 'Sovereignty as a Source of Vitality for the State', *Review of International Studies*, **12** (2) (April) pp. 79–90.

Miller, L. H. (1994), *Global Order, Values and Power In International Politics* (Westview Press, Boulder).

Mills, C. W. (1956), *The Power Elite* (Oxford University Press, New York).

Mitchell, C. (1981), *The Structure of International Conflict* (Macmillan, London).

Mitrany, D. (1943), *A Working Peace System* (RIIA, London).

Mitrany, D. (1975), *The Functional Theory of Politics* (Robertson, London).

Modelski, G. (1972), *Principles of World Politics* (Collier, Macmillan, New York).

Modelski, G. (ed) (1972), *Multinational Corporations and World Order* (Sage Publications, Beverly Hills).

Moore, B. (1967), *Social Origins of Dictatorship and Democracy* (Allen Lane, London).

Morgan, P. M. (1983), *Deterrence: A Conceptual Analysis* (Sage Publications, Beverly Hills).

Morgenthau, H. J. (1948), *Politics Among Nations: The Struggle for Power and Peace* (Knopf, New York).

Morgenthau, H. J. (1951), *In Defence of the National Interest* (Knopf, New York).

Morgenthau, H. J. and Thompson, K. W. (eds) (1950), *Principles and Problems of International Politics* (Knopf, New York).

Moynihan, D. P. (1993), *Pandaemonium: Ethnicity in International Politics* (Oxford University Press, Oxford).

Murphy, C. N. (1996), 'Gender in International Relations', *International Organisation* **50** (3) pp. 513–38.

Myers, D. P. (1957), 'The Names and Scope of Treaties', *American Journal of International Law*, **51**.

Nag, K. (n.d.), 'The Diplomatic Theories of Ancient India and the Arthastra', *Journal of Indian History*, **V** pp. 331–58.

Nardin, T. (1983), *Law, Morality and the Relations of Nations* (Princeton University Press, Princeton).

Nardin, T. (ed) (1996), *The Ethics of War and Peace* (Princeton University Press, Princeton).

Nardin, T. and Mapel, D. (eds) (1992), *Traditions of International Ethics* (Cambridge University Press, Cambridge).

Navari, C. (1978), 'Knowledge, the State and the State of Nature', in *The Reason of States*, M. Donelan (ed.).

Neufeld, M. (1995), *The Restructuring of International Relations Theory* (Cambridge University Press, Cambridge).

Nicholson, M. (1996), *Causes and Consequences in International Relations: A Conceptual Survey* (Pinter Publishers, London).

Nicolson, H. (1950), *Diplomacy* (Oxford University Press, London).

Nicolson, H. (1954), *The Evolution of Diplomatic Method* (Constable, London).

Niebuhr, R. (1936), *Moral Man and Immoral Society* (Scribners, New York).

Niebuhr, R. (1953), *Christian Realism and Political Problems* (Scribners, New York).

Niebuhr, R. (1959), *Nations and Empires* (Faber & Faber, London).

Nixon, R. (1976), 'Asia after Vietnam', *Foreign Affairs*, **46** (1) pp. 111–25.

Nkrumah, K. (1965), *Neocolonialism: The Last Stage of Capitalism* (Heinemann, London).

Nogee, J. L. (1975), 'Polarity: An Ambiguous Concept', ORBIS, **18** (4) (Winter) pp. 1193–225.

Northedge, F. S. (1976), *The International Political System* (Faber & Faber, London).

Northedge, F. S. (1976), 'Transnationalism: The American Illusion', *Millennium*, **5** (1) (Spring) pp. 21–7.

Northedge, F. S. (1986), *The League of Nations: Its Life and Times, 1920–46* (Leicester University Press, Leicester).

Nussbaum, A. (1961), *A Concise History of the Law of Nations* (Macmillan, New York).

Nye, J. S. (1986), *Nuclear Ethics* (Collier Macmillan, London).

Nye, J. S. Jr. (1990), *Bound to Lead* (Basic Books, New York).

Nye, J. S. Jr. (1996), 'Conflicts After the Cold War', *The Washington Quarterly*, **19** (1), pp. 5–24.

O'Connell, D. P. (1970), *International Law* (2 volumes), second edition (Stevens, London).

O'Connell, D. P. (1975), 'The Law of the Sea: Some Reflections on Caracas', *British Journal of International Studies*, **1** (1) (April) pp. 20–26.

Onuf, N. (1989), *A World of Our Making: Rules and Risk in Social Theory and International Relations* (Cambridge University Press, Cambridge).

Osgood, C. (1962), *An Alternative to War or Surrender* (University of Illinois Press, Urbana).

Osgood, R. E. (1953), *Ideals and Self-Interest in America's Foreign Relations* (Chicago University Press, Chicago).

Osgood, R. E. and Tucker, R. W. (1967), *Force, Order and Justice* (Johns Hopkins Press, Baltimore).

Osmanczyk, E. J. (1985), *The Encyclopedia of the United Nations and International Agreements* (Taylor and Francis, Philadelphia).

Owen, J. M. (1994), 'How Liberalism Produces Democratic Peace', *International Security* **19** (2) pp. 87–125.

Paige, G. (1968), *The Korean Decision* (Free Press, New York).

Paige, G. (1977), *The Scientific Study of Political Leadership* (Free Press, New York).

Paret, P. (ed) (1986), *Makers of Modern Strategy from Machiavelli to the Nuclear Age* (Princeton University Press, Princeton).

Parkinson, F. (1977), *The Philosophy of International Relations* (Sage Publications, Beverly Hills).

Penn, W. (1694), *An Essay Toward the Present and Future Peace of Europe* (American Peace Society, Washington DC, 1912).

Penrose, E. (1976), 'Oil and International Relations', *British Journal of International Studies* **2** (1) (April) pp. 41–50.

Pentland, C. (1973), *International Theory and European Integration* (Faber & Faber, London).

Pepper, D. and Jenkins, A. (1985), *The Geography of Peace and War* (Blackwell, Oxford).

Perkins, D. (1955), *A History of the Monroe Doctrine* (Boston, Toronto).

Pettman, R. (1979), *State and Class: A Sociology of International Affairs* (Croom Helm, London).

Pettman, R. (ed) (1979), *Moral Claims in World Affairs* (Croom Helm, London).

Plano, J. C. and Olton, R. (1982), *The International Relations Dictionary* (third edition) (ABC-Clio, Santa Barbara).

Plischke, E. (1977), *Microstates in World Affairs: Policy Problems and Options* (AEI, Washington DC).

Polanyi, K. (1975), *The Great Transformation* (Beacon Books, Boston).

Porter, G. and Welsh Brown, J. (1991), *Global Environmental Politics* (Westview Press, Boulder).

Poznanski, K. Z. (1984), 'Technology Transfer: West-South Perspective', *World Politics*, **37** (1) (October) pp. 134–52.

Prebisch, R. (1964), *Towards a New Trade Policy for Development*. Report by the Secretary-General of UNCTAD (UN, New York).

Prestowitz, C. V. Jr., Morse, R. A. and Tonelson, A. (eds) (1991) *Powernomics: Economics and Strategy after the Cold War* (Madison Books, Maryland).

Princen, M. and Finger, M. (eds) (1994) *Environmental NGOs in World Politics: Linking the Local and the Global* (Routledge, London).

Prins, G. (ed) (1983), *Defended to Death* (Penguin Books, London).

Pruitt, D. G. (1966), 'Definition of the Situation as a Determinant of International Action', in H. C. Kelman (ed), *International Behaviour* (Holt, Rinehart Winston, New York).

Puchala, D. (1972), 'Of Blind Men, Elephants and International Integration', *Journal of Common Market Studies*, **10:3** pp. 267–84.

Pugh, M. (ed) (1997) *The UN, Peace and Force* (Frank Cass, London).

Purnell, R. (1973), *The Society of States: An Introduction to International Politics* (Weidenfeld & Nicolson, London).

Purnell, R. (1976), 'The Relevance of Ancient History to the Contemporary Study of International Politics', *British Journal of International Studies* **2** (1) (April) pp. 27–40.

Putman, R. and Bayne, N. (1987), *Hanging Together* (Sage Publications, London).

Rapoport, A. (1960), *Fights, Games and Debates* (Michigan University Press, Michigan).

Rapoport, A. (1964), *Strategy and Conscience* (Harper and Row, New York).

Rapoport, A. (1974), *Conflict in Man Made Environment* (Penguin, Harmondsworth).

Reynolds, C. (1973), *Theory and Explanation in International Politics* (Robertson, London).

Reynolds, C. (1981), *Modes of Imperialism* (Robertson, London).

Reynolds, P. A. (1971), *An Introduction to International Relations* (Longman, Harlow).

Reynolds, P. A. (1975), 'The Balance of Power. New Wine in an Old Bottle', *Political Studies*, **xxiii** (2) and (3) (June/September) pp. 352–64.

Ricardo, D. (1817), *Principles of Political Economy and Taxation*, reprinted in *The Works & Correspondence of David Ricardo*, Volume 1, P. Sraffa (ed) (Cambridge University Press, Cambridge, 1970).

Risse-Kappen, T. (ed) (1995), *Bringing Transnational Relations Back In: Non-State Actors, Domestic Structures and International Relations* (Cambridge University Press, Cambridge).

Roberts, A. (1976), *Nations in Arms: The Theory and the Practice of Territorial Defence* (Chatto & Windus, London).

Roberts, A. (1991), 'A New Age in International Relations', *International Affairs* **67** (3) pp. 509–26.

Roberts, A. and Guelff, R. (eds) (1982), *Documents on the Laws of War* (Clarendon Press, London).

Roberts, A. and Kingsbury, B. (eds) (1984), *United Nations, Divided World: The UN's Role in International Relations*, second edition (Clarendon, Oxford).

Robinson, D. (1985), *Dictionary of Politics* (Penguin, Harmondsworth).

Rosecrance, R. N. (1963), *Action and Reaction in World Politics* (Little, Brown, Boston).

Rosecrance, R. N. (1973), *International Relations: Peace or War?* (McGraw Hill, New York).

Rosecrance, R. N. (ed) (1976), *America as an Ordinary Country* (Cornell University Press, Ithaca, New York, and London).

Rosenau, J. N. (1961), *International Politics and Foreign Policy: A Reader in Research and Theory* (The Free Press, New York).

Rosenau, J. N. (1961a), *Public Opinion and Foreign Policy* (Random House, New York).

Rosenau, J. N. (ed) (1964), *International Aspects of Civil Strife* (Princeton University Press, Princeton).

Rosenau, J. N. (1966), 'Pre-theories and Theories of Foreign Policy', in *Approaches to Comparative and International Politics*, R. Barry Farrell, (ed) (Northwestern University Press, Evanston).

Rosenau, J. N. (1967a), 'Foreign Policy as an Issue Area', in *Domestic Sources of Foreign Policy*, Rosenau, J.N. (ed) (The Free Press, New York).

Rosenau, J. N. (1968), 'The Concept of Intervention', *Journal of International Affairs*, **22** (2), pp. 165–77.

Rosenau, J. N. (ed) (1969), *International Politics and Foreign Policy* (The Free Press, New York).

Rosenau, J. N. (1969a), 'Intervention as a scientific concept', *Journal of Conflict Resolution*, **13** (2) pp. 149–71.

Rosenau, J. N. (1969b), *Linkage Politics* (The Free Press, New York).

Rosenau, J. N. (1971), *A Scientific Study of Foreign Policy* (The Free Press, New York).

Rosenau, J. N. (1980), *The Study of Global Interdependence* (Frances Pinter, London).

Rosenau, J. N. and Czempial E. O. (eds) (1992), *Governance without Government: Order and Change in World Politics* (Cambridge University Press, Cambridge).

Rothstein, R. L. (1972), 'On the Costs of Realism', *Political Science Quarterly*, **87** (September) pp. 347–62.

Roy, O. (1994), *The Failure of Political Islam* (I. B. Tauris, London).

Ruggie, J. G. (ed) (1993), *Multilateralism Matters* (Columbia University Press, New York).

Rummel, R. J. (1972), *The Dimensions of Nations* (Sage, Beverly Hills).

Russell, F. M. (1936), *Theories of International Relations* (Appleton Century Crofts, New York).

Russett, B. (1993), *Grasping the Democratic Peace: Principles for a Post-Cold War World* (Princeton University Press, Princeton).

Ryan, S. (1995), *Ethnic Conflict and International Relations* (Dartmouth, Aldershot).

Sachs, W. (ed) (1993), *Global Ecology: A New Arena of Political Conflict* (Zed Books, London).

Sagan, S. D. and Waltz, K. (1995), *The Spread of Nuclear Weapons* (W. W. Norton, New York).

Said, A. A. and Simmons, L. R. (eds) (1975), *The New Sovereigns* (Prentice Hall, Englewood Cliffs, NJ).

Satow, E. (1957), *A Guide to Diplomatic Practice* (Longman, London).

Schelling, T. C. (1960), *The Strategy of Conflict* (Harvard University Press, Cambridge).

Schelling, T. C. (1966), *Arms and Influence* (Yale University Press, New Haven).

Schelling, T. C. and Halperin, M. H. (1985), *Strategy and Arms Control* (Pergamon-Brassey Classic Reprint, Washington).

Schlesinger, A. (1967), *A Thousand Days: John F. Kennedy in the White House* (Mayflower Dell, London).

Schlesinger, A. (1991), *The Cycles of American History* (Houghton Mifflin, Boston).

Schlesinger, A. (1995), 'Back to the Womb? Isolationism's Renewed Threat', *Foreign Affairs*, vol. 74, no. 4 July/August, pp. 2–8.

Schmid, A. P. (1983), *Political Terrorism: A Research Guide to Concepts, Theories, Data Bases and Literature* (North Holland Publishing Company, Amsterdam).

Schumacher, E. F. (1973), *Small is Beautiful: Economics as if People Mattered* (Harper & Row, New York).

Schuman, F. L. (1933), *International Politics: Anarchy and Order in World Society* (McGraw Hill, New York, 1969 edition).

Schumpeter, J. A. (1951), 'Imperialism and Capitalism', in Sweezy, P. M. (ed), *Imperialism and Social Classes* (Blackwell, Oxford).

Schwarzenberger, G. (1941), *Power Politics* (Stevens, London).

Scott, A. (1965), *The Revolution in Statecraft* (Random House, New York).

Scruton, R. (1982), *A Dictionary of Political Thought* (Macmillan, London).

Seabury, P. (1963), *Power, Freedom and Diplomacy* (Random House, New York).

Segal, G. (1988), *Guide to the World Today* (Simon & Schuster, London).

Segal, G. (1990), *Rethinking the Pacific* (Oxford University Press, London).

Shaw, M. N. (1977), *International Law* (Hodder & Stoughton, London).

Shaw, M. N. (1991), *International Law*, 3rd Edition (Grotius Publications, Cambridge).

Sheffer, G. (ed) (1986), *Modern Diasporas in International Politics* (Croom Helm, London).

Sills, D. (ed) (1960), *International Encyclopedia of the Social Sciences* (Macmillan and Free Press, New York).

Simon, H. A. (1965), *Administrative Behaviour* (Free Press, New York).

Singer, J. D. (1969), 'The Level of Analysis Problem in International Relations', in J. N. Rosenau (ed), *International Politics and Foreign Policy* (Free Press, New York), pp. 20–29.

Singer, M. and Wildavsky, A. (1993), *The Real World Order: Zones of Turmoil* (Chatham House Publishers, New Jersey).

SIPRI (annual) *Yearbook of World Armaments and Disarmament* (Almqvist & Wiksell, Stockholm).

Skocpol, T. (1979), *States and Revolutions: A Comparative Analysis of France, Russia and China* (Cambridge University Press, Cambridge).

Small, M. and Singer, J. D. (1966), 'The Composition and Status Ordering of the International System 1815–1940' *World Politics* **18** (January) pp. 236–82.

Smith, A. (1776), *An Enquiry into the Nature and Causes of the Wealth of Nations* (Dent, London, Everyman edition, 1977).

Smith, B. L. R. (1966), *The Rand Corporation* (Harvard University Press, Cambridge, MA).

Smith, M., Little, R. and Shackleton, M. (1981), *Perspectives on World Politics: A Reader* (Croom Helm, London).

Smith, M. J. (1986), *Realist Thought from Weber to Kissinger* (Louisiana State University Press, Baton Rouge).

Smith, S. (1992), 'The Forty Years Detour: The Resurgence of Normative Theory in International Relations', *Millennium: Journal of International Studies* **21** (3) pp. 489–509.

Snyder, G. H. (1961), *Deterrence and Defence* (Princeton University Press, Princeton, NJ).

Snyder, G. H. (1984), 'The Security Dilemma in Alliance Politics'. *World Politics*, **36** (4) (July) pp 461–95.

Snyder, G. H. and Diesing, P. (1977), *Conflict Among Nations: Bargaining, Decision Making and System Structure in International Crises* (Princeton University Press, Princeton).

Snyder, R. C., Bruck, H. W. and Sapin, B. (eds) (1962), *Foreign Policy Decision-Making: An Approach to the Study of International Politics* (Free Press, New York).

Speigel, S. L. (1972), *Dominance and Diversity: The International Hierarchy* (Little, Brown, Boston).

Spence, J. E. (1988), *The Soviet Union, The Third World and Southern Africa*, South African Institute of International Affairs, Bradlow Series, No. 5 (November).

Spero, J. E. (1985), *The Politics of International Economic Relations* (third edition) (St Martin's Press, New York).

Spero, J. E. and Hart, J. (1997), *The Politics of International Economic Relations* (St Martin's/Routledge, New York and London).

Sprout, H. (1963), 'Geopolitical Hypotheses in Technological Perspective', *World Politics*, **15**.

Sprout, H. and Sprout, M. (1957), *Man–Milieu Relationship in the Context of International Politics* (Princeton University Press, Princeton, NJ).

Sprout, H. and Sprout, M. (1957), 'Environmental Factors in the Study of International Politics', *Journal of Conflict Resolution*, **1** pp. 309–28.

Sprout, H. and Sprout, M. (1965), *The Ecological Perspective on Human Affairs: with special reference to International Politics* (Princeton University Press, Princeton, NJ).

Sprout, H. and Sprout, M. (1968), 'The Dilemma of Rising Demands and Insufficient Resources', *World Politics*, **20**, pp. 660–93.

Sprout, H. and Sprout, M. (1971), *Towards a Politics of the Planet Earth* (Van Nostrand, New York).

Sprout, H. and Sprout, M. (1972), *The Politics of Planet Earth* (Van Nostrand, New York).

Spykman, N. J. (1938), 'Geography and Foreign Policy', *American Political Science Review*, **32** pp. 28–50.

Spykman, N. J. (1942), *America's Strategy in World Politics* (Harcourt Brace, New York).

Stagner, R. (1965), 'The psychology of human conflict', in E. McNeil (ed), *The Nature of Human Conflict* (Prentice Hall, Englewood Cliffs, NJ).

Sterling, R. W. (1958), *Ethics in World Power: The Political Ideas of Friedrich Meinecke* (Princeton University Press, Princeton, NJ).

Stockholm International Peace Research Institute (SIPRI) (1991), *SIPRI Yearbook* (Oxford University Press, Oxford).

Stoessinger, J. G. (1985), *Crusaders and Pragmatists of Modern American Foreign Policy* (Norton, New York).

Strange, S. (1976), 'The Study of Transnational Relations', *International Affairs*, **52** (3) (July) pp. 333–45.

Strange, S. (1994), *States and Markets*, second edition (Frances Pinter, London).

Strange, S. (1996), *The Retreat of the State* (Cambridge University Press, Cambridge).

Stumpf, W. (1995–6), 'South Africa's Nuclear Weapons Program: From Deterrence to Dismantlement', *Arms Control Today* **25** (10) (December/January) pp. 3–8.

Suganami, H. (1978), 'A Note on the Origin of the Word "International"', *British Journal of International Studies*, **4** (3) (October) pp. 226–32.

Suganami, H. (1986), 'Reflections on the Domestic Analogy: The Case of Bull, Beitz and Linklater', *Review of International Studies*, **12** (2) (April) pp. 145–58.

Suganami, H. (1989), *The Domestic Analogy and World Order Proposals* (Cambridge University Press, Cambridge).

Suganami, H. (1996), *On the Causes of War* (Clarendon Press, Oxford).

Sylvester, C. (1994), *Feminist Theory and International Relations in a Post Modern Era* (Cambridge University Press, Cambridge).

Tanter, R. and Stein, J. (1980), *Rational Decision Making* (Ohio State University Press, Columbia).

Tanter, R. and Ullman, R. (eds) (1972), *Theory and Policy in International Relations* (Princeton University Press, New Jersey).

Taylor, A. J. P. (1979), *How Wars Begin* (Hamilton, London).

Taylor, P. (1993), *International Organization in the Modern World* (Pinter, London).

Taylor, P. and Groom, A. J. R. (eds) (1978), *International Organisation: A Conceptual Approach* (Pinter, London).

Taylor, P. J. (1985), *Political Geography: World-Economy, Nation-State and Locality* (Longman, London).

Taylor, T. (ed) (1978), *Approaches and Theory in International Relations* (Longman, London).

Thee, M. (ed) (1986), *Arms and Disarmament: SIPRI Findings* (Oxford University Press, Oxford). *Third World Guide (1991/1992)* (Instituto del Tercer Mundo, Montevideo).

Thomas, C. (1987), *In Serarch of Security: The Third World in International Relations* (Harvester Wheatsheaf, Brighton).

Thomas, C. (1992), *The Environment in International Relations* (RIIA, London).

Thomas, W. I. and Znanieki, F. (1958), *The Polish Peasant in Europe and America*, Vol. I (Dover Publications, New York).

Thompson, K. W. (1960), *Political Realism and the Crisis of World Politics* (Princeton University Press, Princeton).

Thompson, K. W. (1977), 'Idealism and Realism: Beyond the Great Debate', *British Journal of International Studies*, **3** (2) (July) pp. 199–209.

Thucydides (1959), *The Peloponnesian War* (tr. R. Warner) (Penguin, Harmondsworth).

Tickner, J. A. (1992), *Gender in International Relations* (Columbia University Press, New York).

Timmerman, K. R. (1991), *The Death Lobby: How the West Armed Iraq* (Houghton Mifflin, Boston).

Tocqueville, A. de (1955), *Democracy in America* (tr. H. Reeve) (Oxford University Press, New York).

Toffler, A. and Toffler, H. (1993), *War and Anti-War: Survival at the Dawn of the 21st Century* (Little, Brown and Company, Boston).

Tucker, R. W. (1977), *The Inequality of Nations* (Robertson, London).

Tucker, R. W. (1988/89), 'Reagan's Foreign Policy', *Foreign Affairs*, **68** (1) pp. 1–27.

Tucker, R. W. and Hendrickson, D. C. (1992), *The Imperial Temptation: The New World Order and America's Purpose* (Council on Foreign Relations, New York).

Valenta, J. and Potter, W. (eds) (1984), *Soviet Decisionmaking for National Security* (George Allen & Unwin, London).

Vasquez, J. A. (1983), *The Power of Power Politics: A Critique* (Pinter, London).

Vattel, E. de (1758), *The Law of Nations* (Carnegie Institute, Washington, 1916).

Vincent, R. J. (1974), *Nonintervention and International Order* (Princeton University Press, Princeton).

Vincent, R. J. (1978), 'Western Conceptions of a Universal Moral Order', *British Journal of International Studies*, 4 (1) (April) pp. 20–46.

Vincent, R. J. (1986), *Human Rights and International Relations* (Cambridge University Press, Cambridge).

Viotti, P. and Kauppi, M. (1993), *International Relations Theory* (Macmillan, New York).

Vital, D. (1967), *The Inequality of States: A Study of the Small Power in International Relations* (Clarendon Press, Oxford).

Vogler, J. (1995), *The Global Commons: A Regime Analysis* (Wiley, Chichester).

Vogler, J. and Imber, M. (eds) (1996), *The Environment in International Relations* (Routledge, London).

Waever, O. *et al.* (1993), *Migration, Identity and the New European Security Order* (Pinter, London).

Walker, R. B. J. (1993), *Inside/Outside: International Relations as Political Theory* (Cambridge University Press, Cambridge).

Wallace, W. (1971), *Foreign Policy and the Political Process* (Macmillan, London).

Wallace, W. (1990), *The Transformation of Western Europe* (Pinter/RIIA, London).

Wallerstein, I. (1974), *The Modern World System. Capitalist Agriculture and the Origins of the European World-Economy in the Sixteenth Century* (Academic Press, New York).

Wallerstein, I. (1979), *The Capitalist World Economy* (Cambridge University Press, Cambridge).

Walt, S. (1987), *The Origins of Alliances* (Cornell University Press, Ithaca).

Waltz, K. N. (1959), *Man, The State and War* (Columbia University Press, New York).

Waltz, K. N. (1964), 'The Stability of a Bipolar World', *Daedelus* (Summer). pp. 881–909.

Waltz, K. N. (1979), *Theory of International Politics* (Addison-Wesley, Reading, MA).

Waltz, K. N. (1990), 'Realist Thought and Realist Theory', *Journal of International Affairs*, 44 (1).

Waltz, K. (1981), *The Spread of Nuclear Weapons: More May be Better*. Adelphi Paper No. 171 (International Institute for Strategic Studies, London).

Walzer, M. (1978), *Just and Unjust Wars* (Allen Lane, London).

Warren, B. (1980), *Imperialism: Pioneer of Capitalism* (New Left Books, London).

Waste, R. (ed) (1986), *Community Power* (Sage, Beverly Hills).

Watson, A. (1982), *Diplomacy: The Dialogue Between States* (Methuen, London).

Watson, A. (1992), *The Evolution of International Society: A Comparative Historical Analysis* (Routledge, London).

Weber, M. (1947), *The Theory of Social and Economic Organisation*, tr. A. M. Henderson and Talcott Parsons (Oxford University Press, New York).

Wendt, A. (1987), 'The Agent/Structure Problem in International Relations Theory', *International Organisation* **41** pp. 335–70

Wendt, A. (1992), 'Anarchy is What States Make of It: The Social Construction of Power Politics', *International Organisation* **46** pp. 391–426.

Whaley, B. (1973), *Codeword Barbarossa* (MIT, Cambridge, MA).

White, B., Little, R. and Smith, M. (eds) (1997), *Issues in World Politics* (Macmillan, London).

Widgren, J. (1990), 'International Migration and Regional Stability', *International Affairs*, **66** (4).

Wight, M. (1966), 'Western Values in International Relations', in H. Butterfield and M. Wight (eds) *Diplomatic Investigations: Essays in the Theory of International Politics* (Allen & Unwin, London).

Wight, M. (1977), *Systems of States*, Hedley Bull (ed) (Leicester University Press, Leicester).

Wight, M. (1978), *Power Politics*, Hedley Bull and Carsten Holbraad (eds) (Leicester University Press, Leicester).

Wilkinson, P. (1974), *Political Terrorism* (Macmillan, London).

Wilkinson, P. (1986), *Terrorism and the Liberal State* (second edition) (Macmillan, London).

Willets, P. (1979), *The Non-Aligned Movement* (Nichols, New York).

Williams, P. (1976), *Crisis Management: Confrontation and Diplomacy in the Nuclear Age* (Wiley, New York).

Windsor, P. (1971), *Germany and the Management of Detente* (Chatto & Windus, London).

Wohlstetter, R. (1962), *Pearl Harbor: Warning and Decision* (Stanford University Press, Stanford).

Wolf, E. (1971), *Peasant Wars of the Twentieth Century* (Faber, London).

Wolfers, A. (1949), 'Statesmanship and Moral Choice', *World Politics*, **1** pp. 175–95.

Wolfers, A. (1962), *Discord and Collaboration* (Johns Hopkins University Press, Baltimore).

Wolfers, A. and Martin, L. (1956), *The Anglo-American Tradition in Foreign Affairs* (Yale, New Haven).

Worsley, P. (1964), *The Third World* (Weidenfeld & Nicolson, London).

Wright, Q. (1955), *The Study of International Relations* (Appleton Century Crofts, New York).

Wright, Q. (1964), *A Study of War* (Chicago University Press, Chicago).

'X' (Kennan, G.F.) (1947), 'The Sources of Soviet Conduct', *Foreign Affairs*, **25** (July).

Yalem, R. J. (1972), 'Tripolarity and the International System', *Orbis*, **15** (Winter) pp. 1051–63.

Yergin, D. (1980), *Shattered Peace: The Origins of the Cold War and the National Security State* (Penguin, Harmondsworth).

Young, O. R. (1967), *Systems of Political Science* (Prentice Hall, Englewood Cliffs).

Young, O. R. (1972), 'The actors in world politics' in J. N. Rosenau, V. Davis and M. East (eds), *The Analysis of International Politics* (Free Press, New York), pp. 125–44.

Young, O. R. (1986), 'International Regimes: Toward a New Theory of Institutions', *World Politics*, **39** (1) (October) pp. 104–22.

Zalewski, M. and Enloe, C. (1995), 'Questions of identity in IR' in Booth, K. and Smith, S. (eds) *International Relations Theory Today* (Oxford University Pres, Oxford).

Zartman, W. I. (1989), *Ripe for Resolution* (Oxford University Press, New York/Oxford).

Zartman, W. I. (1995), *Collapsed States* (Lynne Renner, Boulder, Colorado).

Zimmern, A. (1939), *The Prospects of Civilization* (Oxford University Press, London).

Zimmern, A. (1945), *The League of Nations and the Rule of Law, 1918–1935* (Macmillan, London).

# PENGUIN ONLINE

News, reviews and previews of forthcoming books

read about your favourite authors

•

investigate over 12,000 titles

•

browse our online magazine

•

enter one of our literary quizzes

•

win some fantastic prizes in our competitions

•

e-mail us with your comments and book reviews

•

instantly order any Penguin book

'To be recommended without reservation ... a rich and rewarding online experience' *Internet Magazine*

# www.penguin.com

# READ MORE IN PENGUIN

In every corner of the world, on every subject under the sun, Penguin represents quality and variety – the very best in publishing today.

For complete information about books available from Penguin – including Puffins, Penguin Classics and Arkana – and how to order them, write to us at the appropriate address below. Please note that for copyright reasons the selection of books varies from country to country.

**In the United Kingdom**: Please write to *Dept. EP, Penguin Books Ltd, Bath Road, Harmondsworth, West Drayton, Middlesex UB7 ODA*

**In the United States**: Please write to *Consumer Sales, Penguin Putnam Inc., P.O. Box 12289 Dept. B, Newark, New Jersey 07101-5289*. VISA and MasterCard holders call 1-800-788-6262 to order Penguin titles

**In Canada**: Please write to *Penguin Books Canada Ltd, 10 Alcorn Avenue, Suite 300, Toronto, Ontario M4V 3B2*

**In Australia**: Please write to *Penguin Books Australia Ltd, P.O. Box 257, Ringwood, Victoria 3134*

**In New Zealand**: Please write to *Penguin Books (NZ) Ltd, Private Bag 102902, North Shore Mail Centre, Auckland 10*

**In India**: Please write to *Penguin Books India Pvt Ltd, 11 Community Centre, Panchsheel Park, New Delhi 110017*

**In the Netherlands**: Please write to *Penguin Books Netherlands bv, Postbus 3507, NL-1001 AH Amsterdam*

**In Germany**: Please write to *Penguin Books Deutschland GmbH, Metzlerstrasse 26, 60594 Frankfurt am Main*

**In Spain**: Please write to *Penguin Books S. A., Bravo Murillo 19, 1° B, 28015 Madrid*

**In Italy**: Please write to *Penguin Italia s.r.l., Via Benedetto Croce 2, 20094 Corsico, Milano*

**In France**: Please write to *Penguin France, Le Carré Wilson, 62 rue Benjamin Baillaud, 31500 Toulouse*

**In Japan**: Please write to *Penguin Books Japan Ltd, Kaneko Building, 2-3-25 Koraku, Bunkyo-Ku, Tokyo 112*

**In South Africa**: Please write to *Penguin Books South Africa (Pty) Ltd, Private Bag X14, Parkview, 2122 Johannesburg*

# READ MORE IN PENGUIN

## REFERENCE

### The Penguin Dictionary of the Third Reich
James Taylor and Warren Shaw

This dictionary provides a full background to the rise of Nazism and the role of Germany in the Second World War. Among the areas covered are the major figures from Nazi politics, arts and industry, the German Resistance, the politics of race and the Nuremberg trials.

### The Penguin Biographical Dictionary of Women

This stimulating, informative and entirely new Penguin dictionary of women from all over the world, through the ages, contains over 1,600 clear and concise biographies on major figures from politicians, saints and scientists to poets, film stars and writers.

### Roget's Thesaurus of English Words and Phrases
Edited by Betty Kirkpatrick

This new edition of Roget's classic work, now brought up to date for the nineties, will increase anyone's command of the English language. Fully cross-referenced, it includes synonyms of every kind (formal or colloquial, idiomatic and figurative) for almost 900 headings. It is a must for writers and utterly fascinating for any English speaker.

### The Penguin Dictionary of International Relations
Graham Evans and Jeffrey Newnham

International relations have undergone a revolution since the end of the Cold War. This new world disorder is fully reflected in this new Penguin dictionary, which is extensively cross-referenced with a select bibliography to aid further study.

### The Penguin Guide to Synonyms and Related Words
S. I. Hayakawa

'More helpful than a thesaurus, more humane than a dictionary, the *Guide to Synonyms and Related Words* maps linguistic boundaries with precision, sensitivity to nuance and, on occasion, dry wit' *The Times Literary Supplement*

# READ MORE IN PENGUIN

## REFERENCE

### The Penguin Dictionary of Troublesome Words  Bill Bryson

Why should you avoid discussing the *weather conditions*? Can a married woman be celibate? Why is it eccentric to talk about the aroma of a cowshed? A straightforward guide to the pitfalls and hotly disputed issues in standard written English.

### Swearing  Geoffrey Hughes

'A deliciously filthy trawl among taboo words across the ages and the globe' Valentine Cunningham, *Observer*, Books of the Year. 'Erudite and entertaining' Penelope Lively, *Daily Telegraph*, Books of the Year.

### Medicines: A Guide for Everybody  Peter Parish

Now in its seventh edition and completely revised and updated, this bestselling guide is written in ordinary language for the ordinary reader yet will prove indispensable to anyone involved in health care: nurses, pharmacists, opticians, social workers and doctors.

### Media Law  Geoffrey Robertson QC and Andrew Nichol

Crisp and authoritative surveys explain the up-to-date position on defamation, obscenity, official secrecy, copyright and confidentiality, contempt of court, the protection of privacy and much more.

### The Penguin Careers Guide
Anna Alston and Anne Daniel; Consultant Editor: Ruth Miller

As the concept of a 'job for life' wanes, this guide encourages you to think broadly about occupational areas as well as describing day-to-day work and detailing the latest developments and qualifications such as NVQs. Special features include possibilities for working part-time and job-sharing, returning to work after a break and an assessment of the current position of women.

# READ MORE IN PENGUIN

## DICTIONARIES

Abbreviations
Ancient History
Archaeology
Architecture
Art and Artists
Astronomy
Biographical Dictionary of
 Women
Biology
Botany
Building
Business
Challenging Words
Chemistry
Civil Engineering
Classical Mythology
Computers
Contemporary American History
Curious and Interesting Geometry
Curious and Interesting Numbers
Curious and Interesting Words
Design and Designers
Economics
Eighteenth-Century History
Electronics
English and European History
English Idioms
Foreign Terms and Phrases
French
Geography
Geology
German
Historical Slang
Human Geography
Information Technology

International Finance
International Relations
Literary Terms and Literary
 Theory
Mathematics
Modern History 1789–1945
Modern Quotations
Music
Musical Performers
Nineteenth-Century World
 History
Philosophy
Physical Geography
Physics
Politics
Proverbs
Psychology
Quotations
Quotations from Shakespeare
Religions
Rhyming Dictionary
Russian
Saints
Science
Sociology
Spanish
Surnames
Symbols
Synonyms and Antonyms
Telecommunications
Theatre
The Third Reich
Third World Terms
Troublesome Words
Twentieth-Century History
Twentieth-Century Quotations